GABRIEL GARC

NEWS OF A KIDNAPPING

TRANSLATED FROM THE SPANISH
BY EDITH GROSSMAN

PENGUIN BOOKS

PENGUIN BOOKS

Published by the Penguin Group
Penguin Books Ltd, 80 Strand, London WC2R ORL, England
Penguin Group (USA) Inc., 375 Hudson Street, New York, New York 10014, USA
Penguin Group (Canada), 90 Eglinton Avenue East, Suite 700, Toronto, Ontario, Canada M4P 2Y3
(a division of Pearson Penguin Canada Inc.)
Penguin Ireland, 25 St Stephen's Green, Dublin 2, Ireland (a division of Penguin Books Ltd)
Penguin Group (Australia), 250 Camberwell Road, Camberwell, Victoria 3124, Australia
(a division of Pearson Australia Group Pty Ltd)
Penguin Books India Pvt Ltd, 11 Community Centre, Panchsheel Park, New Delhi – 110 017, India
Penguin Group (NZ), 67 Apollo Drive, Rosedale, North Shore 0632, New Zealand
(a division of Pearson New Zealand Ltd)
Penguin Books (South Africa) (Pty) Ltd, 24 Sturdee Avenue,
Rosebank, Johannesburg 2196, South Africa

Penguin Books Ltd, Registered Offices: 80 Strand, London WC2R ORL, England

www.penguin.com

First published in Spanish as *Noticia de un Secuestro* by Mondadori
(Grijalbo Commercial, S. A.) 1996
This English translation first published in Great Britain by Random House 1996
Published in Penguin Books 1998
This edition published 2007

004

Copyright © Gabriel García Márquez, 1996
Copyright © Mondadori (Grijalbo Commercial, S. A.), 1996
All rights reserved

The moral right of the author and translator has been asserted

Printed in England by Clays Ltd, St Ives plc

ISBN: 978-0-141-03250-4

www.greenpenguin.co.uk

MIX
Paper from
responsible sources
FSC™ C018179

Penguin Books is committed to a sustainable
future for our business, our readers and our planet.
This book is made from Forest Stewardship
Council™ certified paper.

ALWAYS LEARNING   **PEARSON**

ACKNOWLEDGMENTS

IN OCTOBER 1993, Maruja Pachón and her husband, Alberto Villamizar, suggested I write a book about her abduction and six-month captivity, and his persistent efforts to obtain her release. I was already well into the first draft when we realized it was impossible to separate her kidnapping from nine other abductions that occurred at the same time in Colombia. They were not, in fact, ten distinct abductions—as it had seemed at first—but a single collective abduction of ten carefully chosen individuals, which had been carried out by the same group and for only one purpose.

This belated realization obliged us to begin again with a different structure and spirit so that all the protagonists would have their well-defined identities, their own realities. It was a technical solution to a labyrinthine narrative that in its original form would have been confused and interminable. But this meant that what had been foreseen as a year's work extended into almost three, even with the constant, meticulous assistance and collaboration of Maruja and Alberto, whose personal stories are the central axis, the unifying thread, of this book.

I interviewed all the protagonists I could, and in each of them

ACKNOWLEDGMENTS

I found the same generous willingness to root through their memories and reopen wounds they perhaps preferred to forget. Their pain, their patience, and their rage gave me the courage to persist in this autumnal task, the saddest and most difficult of my life. My only frustration is knowing that none of them will find on paper more than a faded reflection of the horror they endured in their real lives—above all, the families of Marina Montoya and Diàna Turbay, the two hostages who were killed, and in particular Diana Turbay's mother, doña Nydia Quintero de Balcázar, whose interviews were a heartrending, unforgettable human experience for me.

I share this sense of inadequacy with the two people who suffered along with me through the intimate hammering out of the book: the journalist Luzángela Arteaga, who tracked down and captured innumerable impossible facts with the tenacity and absolute discretion of a crafty hunter, and Margarita Márquez Caballero, my first cousin and private secretary, who took care of the transcription, verification, and confidentiality of the intricate raw material that we often thought would overwhelm us.

To all the protagonists and all my collaborators, I offer my eternal gratitude for not allowing this gruesome drama to sink into oblivion. Sadly, it is only one episode in the biblical holocaust that has been consuming Colombia for more than twenty years. I dedicate this book to them, and to all Colombians—innocent and guilty—with the hope that the story it tells will never befall us again.

G. G. M.

Cartagena de Indias, May 1996

NEWS OF A KIDNAPPING

1

SHE LOOKED OVER her shoulder before getting into the car to be sure no one was following her. It was 7:05 in the evening in Bogotá. It had been dark for an hour, the Parque Nacional was not well lit, and the silhouettes of leafless trees against a sad, overcast sky seemed ghostly, but nothing appeared to be threatening. Despite her position, Maruja sat behind the driver because she always thought it was the most comfortable seat. Beatriz climbed in through the other door and sat to her right. They were almost an hour behind in their daily schedule, and both women looked tired after a soporific afternoon of three executive meetings—Maruja in particular, who had given a party the night before and had slept for only three hours. She stretched out her tired legs, closed her eyes as she leaned her head against the back of the seat, and gave the usual order:

"Please take us home."

As they did every day, they sometimes took one route, sometimes another, as much for reasons of security as because of traffic jams. The Renault 21 was new and comfortable, and the chauffeur drove with caution and skill. The best alternative that night was

Avenida Circunvalar heading north. They had three green lights, and evening traffic was lighter than usual. Even on the worst days it took only half an hour to drive from the office to Maruja's house, at No. 84A-42 Transversal Tercera, and then the driver would take Beatriz to her house, some seven blocks away.

Maruja came from a family of well-known intellectuals that included several generations of reporters. She herself was an award-winning journalist. For the past two months she had been the director of FOCINE, the state-run enterprise for the promotion of the film industry. Beatriz, Maruja's sister-in-law and personal assistant, had been a physical therapist for many years but had decided on a change of pace for a while. Her major responsibility at FOCINE was attending to everything related to the press. Neither woman had any specific reason to be afraid, but since August, when the drug traffickers began an unpredictable series of abductions of journalists, Maruja had acquired the almost unconscious habit of looking over her shoulder.

Her suspicion was on target. Though the Parque Nacional had seemed deserted when she looked behind her before getting into the car, eight men were following her. One was at the wheel of a dark blue Mercedes 190 that had phony Bogotá plates and was parked across the street. Another was in the driver's seat of a stolen yellow cab. Four of them were wearing jeans, sneakers, and leather jackets and strolling in the shadows of the park. The seventh, tall and well-dressed in a light-weight suit, carried a briefcase, which completed the picture of a young executive. From a small corner café half a block away, the eighth man, the one responsible for the operation, observed the first real performance of an action whose intensive, meticulous rehearsals had begun twenty-one days earlier.

The cab and the Mercedes followed Maruja's automobile, keeping a close distance just as they had been doing since the previous Monday to determine her usual routes. After about twenty minutes the three cars turned right onto Calle 82, less than two hundred meters from the unfaced brick building where Maruja lived with her husband and one of her children. They had just begun to drive up the steep slope of the street, when the yellow cab passed Maruja's car, hemmed it in along the left-hand curb, and forced the driver to slam on the brakes to avoid a collision. At almost the same time, the Mercedes stopped behind the Renault, making it impossible to back up.

Three men got out of the cab and with resolute strides approached Maruja's car. The tall, well-dressed one carried a strange weapon that looked to Maruja like a sawed-off shotgun with a barrel as long and thick as a telescope. It was, in fact, a 9mm Mini-Uzi equipped with a silencer and capable of firing either single shots or fifteen rounds per second. The other two were armed with submachine guns and pistols. What Maruja and Beatriz could not see were the three men getting out of the Mercedes that had pulled in behind them.

They acted with so much coordination and speed that Maruja and Beatriz could remember only isolated fragments of the scant two minutes of the assault. With professional skill, five men surrounded the car and at the same time dealt with its three occupants. The sixth watched the street, holding his submachine gun at the ready. Maruja's fears had been realized.

"Drive, Angel," she shouted to the driver. "Go up on the sidewalk, whatever, but drive."

Angel was paralyzed, though with the cab in front of him and the Mercedes behind, he had no room to get away in any case. Fearing the men would begin shooting, Maruja clutched at her handbag as if it were a life preserver, crouched down behind the driver's seat, and shouted to Beatriz:

"Get down on the floor!"

"The hell with that," Beatriz whispered. "On the floor they'll kill us."

She was trembling but determined. Certain it was only a holdup, she pulled the two rings off her right hand and tossed them out the window, thinking: "Let them earn it." But she did not have time to take off the two on her left hand. Maruja, curled into a ball behind the seat, did not even remember that she was wearing a diamond and emerald ring and a pair of matching earrings.

Two men opened Maruja's door and another two opened Beatriz's. The fifth shot the driver in the head through the glass, and the silencer made it sound no louder than a sigh. Then he opened the door, pulled him out, and shot him three more times as he lay on the ground. It was another man's destiny: Angel María Roa had been Maruja's driver for only three days, and for the first time he was displaying his new dignity with the dark suit, starched shirt, and black tie worn by the chauffeurs who drove government ministers. His predecessor, who had retired the week before, had been FOCINE's regular driver for ten years.

Maruja did not learn of the assault on the chauffeur until much later. From her hiding place she heard only the sudden noise of breaking glass and then a peremptory shout just above her head: "You're the one we want, Señora. Get out!" An iron hand grasped her arm and dragged her out of the car. She resisted as much as she could, fell, scraped her leg, but the two men picked her up and carried her bodily to the car behind the Renault. They did not notice that Maruja was still clutching her handbag.

Beatriz, who had long, hard nails and good military training, confronted the boy who tried to pull her from the car. "Don't touch me!" she screamed. He gave a start, and Beatriz realized he was just as nervous as she, and capable of anything. She changed her tone.

"I'll get out by myself," she said. "Just tell me what to do."

The boy pointed to the cab.

"Into that car and down on the floor," he said. "Move!" The doors were open, the motor running, the driver motionless in his seat. Beatriz lay down in the back. Her kidnapper covered her with his jacket and sat down, resting his feet on her. Two more men got in: one next to the driver, the other in back. The driver waited for the simultaneous thud of both doors, then sped away, heading north on Avenida Circunvalar. That was when Beatriz realized she had left her bag on the seat of the Renault, but it was too late. More than fear and discomfort, what she found intolerable was the ammonia stink of the jacket.

They had put Maruja into the Mercedes, which had driven off a minute earlier, following a different route. They had her sit in the middle of the back seat, with a man on either side. The one on the left forced Maruja's head against his knees, in a position so uncomfortable she had difficulty breathing. The man beside the driver communicated with the other car by means of an antiquated two-way radio. Maruja's consternation was heightened because she could not tell which vehicle she was in—she had not seen the Mercedes stop behind her car—but she did know it was comfortable and new, and perhaps bulletproof, since the street noises sounded muted, like the whisper of rain. She could not breathe, her heart pounded, and she began to feel as if she were suffocating. The man next to the driver, who seemed to be in charge, became aware of her agitation and tried to reassure her.

"Take it easy," he said, over his shoulder. "We only want you to deliver a message. You'll be home in a couple of hours. But if you move there'll be trouble, so just take it easy."

The one who held her head on his knees also tried to reassure her. Maruja took a deep breath, exhaled very slowly through her mouth, and began to regain her composure. After a few blocks the situation changed because the car ran into a traffic jam on a steep incline. The man on the two-way radio started to shout impossible orders that the driver of the other car could not carry out. Several ambulances were caught in traffic somewhere along the highway, and the din of sirens and earsplitting horns was maddening even for someone with steady nerves. And for the moment, at least, that did not describe the kidnappers. The driver was so agitated as he tried to make his way through traffic that he hit a taxi.

It was no more than a tap, but the cab driver shouted something that made them even more nervous. The man with the two-way radio ordered him to move no matter what, and the car drove over sidewalks and through empty lots.

When they were free of traffic, they were still going uphill. Maruja had the impression they were heading toward La Calera, a hill that tended to be very crowded at that hour. Then she remembered some cardamom seeds, a natural tranquilizer, in her jacket pocket, and asked her captors to let her chew a few. The man on her right helped her look for them, and this was when he noticed she was still holding her handbag. They took it away but gave her the cardamom. Maruja tried to get a good look at the kidnappers, but the light was too dim. She dared to ask a question: "Who are you people?" The man with the two-way radio answered in a quiet voice:

"We're from the M-19."

A nonsensical reply: The M-19, a former guerrilla group, was legal now and campaigning for seats in the Constituent Assembly.

"Seriously," said Maruja. "Are you dealers or guerrillas?"

"Guerrillas," said the man in front. "But don't worry, we just want you to take back a message. Seriously."

He stopped talking and told the others to push Maruja down on the floor because they were about to pass a police checkpoint. "Now if you move or say anything, we'll kill you." She felt the barrel of a revolver pressing against her ribs, and the man beside her completed the thought:

"That's a gun pointing at you."

The next ten minutes were eternal. Maruja focused her energy, chewing the cardamom seeds that helped to revive her, but her position did not let her see or hear what was said at the checkpoint, if in fact anything was said. Maruja had the impression that they went through with no questions asked. The suspicion that they were going to La Calera became a certainty, and the knowledge brought her some relief. She did not try to sit up because she felt more comfortable on the floor than with her head on the man's knees. The car drove along a dirt road for about five minutes, then stopped. The man with the two-way radio said:

"This is it."

No lights were visible. They covered Maruja's head with a jacket and made her look down when she got out, so that all she saw was her own feet walking, first across a courtyard and then through what may have been a kitchen with a tile floor. When they uncovered her head she found herself in a small room, about two by three meters, with a mattress on the floor and a bare red light-bulb hanging from the ceiling. A moment later two men came in, their faces concealed by a kind of balaclava that was in fact the leg of a pair of sweatpants with three holes cut for the eyes and mouth. From then on, during her entire captivity, she did not see her captors' faces again.

She knew that these two were not the same men who had abducted her. Their clothes were shabby and soiled, they were shorter than Maruja, who is five feet, six inches tall, and they had the voices and bodies of boys. One of them ordered Maruja to hand over her jewelry. "For security reasons," he said. "It'll be safe here." She gave him the emerald ring with the tiny diamonds, but not the earrings.

In the other car, Beatriz could draw no conclusion regarding their route. She lay on the floor the entire time and did not recall driving up any hill as steep as La Calera, or passing any check-points, though the cab might have had a special permit that allowed it through without being stopped. The atmosphere in the car was very tense because of the heavy traffic. The man at the wheel shouted into the two-way radio that he couldn't drive over the other cars and kept asking what to do, which made the men in the lead car so nervous they gave him different, and contradictory, instructions.

Beatriz was very uncomfortable, with one leg bent under her and the stink of the jacket making her dizzy. She tried to find a less painful position. Her guard thought she was struggling and attempted to reassure her: "Take it easy, sweetheart, nothing's going to happen to you. You just have to deliver a message." When he realized at last that the problem was her leg, he helped her straighten it and was less brusque with her. More than anything else, Beatriz could not bear the "sweetheart," a liberty that offended her almost more than the stench of the jacket. But the more he tried to reassure her, the more convinced she became that they were going to kill her. She estimated the trip as taking no more than forty minutes, so it must have been about a quarter to eight when they reached the house.

Her arrival was identical to Maruja's. Her head was covered by the foul-smelling jacket, and they led her by the hand, warning her not to look anywhere but down. She saw what Maruja had seen: the courtyard, the tile floor, and two steps. They told her to move left, and then they removed the jacket. There was Maruja, sitting on a stool, looking pale in the red glow of the only light in the room.

"Beatriz!" said Maruja. "You're here too?"

She did not know what had happened to Beatriz, but thought they had let her go because she was not really involved in anything. When she saw her she felt great joy at not being alone, and at the same time immense sadness because she had been kidnapped too. They embraced as if they had not seen each other for a long time.

It was inconceivable that the two of them could survive in that squalid room, sleeping on a single mattress on the floor, with two masked guards who did not take their eyes off them for an instant. Then another man in a mask—elegant, well built, at least five feet, ten inches tall—whom the others called "Doctor," the title used for any professional, took charge with the air of someone who had great authority. The rings were removed from Beatriz's left hand, but they did not notice that she was wearing a gold chain with a medal of the Virgin.

"This is a military operation, and nothing's going to happen to you," he said, and repeated: "We've only brought you here so that you can deliver a communiqué to the government."

"Who's holding us?" Maruja asked.

He shrugged. "That doesn't matter now," he said. He raised the machine gun so they had a clear view of it, and went on: "But I want to tell you one thing. This machine gun has a silencer, nobody knows where you are, or who you're with. The minute you scream or do anything else, we'll get rid of you and nobody will ever see you again." They held their breath, expecting the worst. But when he had finished his threats, the boss turned to Beatriz.

"Now we're separating you, we're going to let you go," he said. "We took you along by mistake."

Beatriz's response was immediate.

"Oh, no," she said without any hesitation. "I'm staying with Maruja."

Her decision was so brave and generous that even her abductor exclaimed in amazement, without a shred of irony: "What a loyal friend you have, doña Maruja!" And she, grateful despite her consternation, agreed and thanked Beatriz. Then the "Doctor" asked if they wanted anything to eat. They refused but asked for water since their mouths were bone dry. Maruja, who always has a cigarette lit and keeps the pack and lighter in easy reach, had not smoked during the trip. She asked for her bag, where she kept her cigarettes, and he gave her one of his.

Both women asked to use the bathroom. Beatriz went first, her head covered by a torn, dirty cloth. "Keep your eyes on the floor," someone ordered. She was led by the hand along a narrow hall to a tiny, filthy lavatory with a sorry little window looking out on the night. The door had no inside lock, but it did close, and so Beatriz climbed up on the toilet and looked out the window. In the light of a streetlamp all she could see was a small adobe house with red roof tiles and a patch of grass in front, the kind of house seen all along the roads through the savanna.

When she returned to the room, she found a drastic change in circumstances. "We know who you are now, and we can use you, too," the "Doctor" said. "You'll stay with us." They had found out on the radio, which had just announced the kidnapping.

Eduardo Carrillo, who reported on legal issues for the National Radio Network (RCN), had been discussing another matter with one of his sources in the military when the officer received a report of the abduction on his two-way radio. The news was announced without delay, or further details. That was how the kidnappers learned Beatriz's identity.

The radio also said that the cab driver could remember two numbers on the license plate, and had given a general description of the car that had bumped into his taxi. The police had determined their escape route. The house had become dangerous for everyone, and they had to leave right away. Even worse: They were going to use a different car, and the two women would have to be put in the trunk.

They protested but to no avail because their kidnappers seemed as frightened as they were, and made no effort to conceal it. Maruja asked for a little rubbing alcohol, terrified at the thought they would suffocate in the trunk.

"We don't have any alcohol," said the "Doctor" in a harsh voice. "You'll ride in the trunk and that's all there is to it. Hurry up."

They were obliged to take off their shoes and carry them as they were led through the house to the garage. There their heads were uncovered, and they were put into the trunk of the car in a fetal position. No force was used. The space was big enough, and it was well ventilated because the rubber seals had been removed. Before he closed the trunk, the "Doctor" filled them with dread. "We're carrying ten kilos of dynamite," he said. "At the first shout, cough, cry, whatever, we'll get out of the car and blow it up."

To their relief and surprise, a breeze as cold and pure as air-conditioning came in the sides of the trunk. The desperate anguish disappeared, leaving only uncertainty. Maruja turned inward, an attitude that could have been confused with complete withdrawal but was in fact her magic formula for dealing with anxiety. Beatriz, on the other hand, driven by an insatiable curiosity, looked through the illuminated opening of the poorly sealed trunk. She could see the passengers through the back window: two men in the back seat, and next to the driver a woman with long hair, holding a baby about two years old. To her right she saw the yellow lights of the huge sign for a well-known shopping center. There could be no doubt: They were on the highway heading north. It was well lit for a long time, then they were in total darkness on an unpaved road, and the car slowed down. After about fifteen minutes, it stopped.

It must have been another checkpoint. Beatriz heard indistinct voices, the sound of other cars, music, but it was too dark to see anything. Maruja roused herself and became alert, hoping it was an inspection station where the men would be obliged to show what they were carrying in the trunk. After about five minutes the car pulled away and drove up a steep incline, but this time they could not determine the route. Some ten minutes later the automobile stopped, and the trunk was opened. Again their heads were covered, and their captors helped them out into darkness.

Together this time, Maruja and Beatriz walked as they had in the other house, looking down, and were led by their kidnappers along a hall, through a small living room where other people were speaking in whispers, until they came to a room. Before they went in, the "Doctor" prepared them:

"Now you're going to see a friend of yours," he said.

The light in the room was so dim it took a moment for their eyes to adjust. It was a space no larger than the other room, with one boarded-up window. Two men, sitting on a single mattress on the floor and wearing hoods like the ones in the first house, were absorbed in watching television. Everything was dismal and oppressive. In the corner, to the left of the door, on a narrow bed with iron posts, sat a spectral woman with limp white hair, dazed eyes, and skin that adhered to her bones. She gave no sign of having heard them come in: not a glance, not a breath, nothing. A corpse could not have seemed so dead. Maruja had to control her shock.

"Marina!" she whispered.

Marina Montoya, kidnapped three months earlier, was thought to be dead. Her brother, don Germán Montoya, had been secretary general to the presidency and a powerful figure in the Virgilio Barco government. His son, Alvaro Diego, the director of an important insurance company, had been abducted by the narco-traffickers to put pressure on their negotiations with the government. The accepted story, which was never confirmed, was that he had been released following a secret agreement that the government had not lived up to. The kidnapping of his aunt Marina nine months later could only be interpreted as a brutal reprisal because by then she no longer had exchange value. The Virgilio Barco government was out of office, Germán Montoya was Colombia's ambassador to Canada, and the thought in everyone's mind was that Marina had been kidnapped for the sole purpose of killing her.

After the initial outcry over her abduction, which had mobilized both national and international opinion, Marina's name had disappeared from the papers. Maruja and Beatriz knew her well, but it was difficult for them to recognize her. As far as they were concerned, the fact that they had been brought to the same room could only mean that they were in the cell for prisoners condemned to death. Marina did not move a muscle. Maruja squeezed her hand, then shuddered. Marina's hand was neither cold nor warm; it conveyed nothing.

The theme music for the television newscast brought them out of their stupor. It was nine-thirty on the night of November 7, 1990. Half an hour earlier, Hernán Estupiñán, a reporter for the program "National News," had been informed of the kidnapping by a friend at FOCINE and had hurried to the site of the abduction. He had not yet returned with complete details, but Javier Ayala, the director and announcer, began the program by reading an emergency bulletin before the credits came on: "The director of FOCINE, doña Maruja Pachón de Villamizar, wife of the well-known politician Alberto Villamizar, and his sister, Beatriz Villamizar de Guerrero, were kidnapped at seven-thirty this evening." The purpose seemed clear: Maruja was the sister of Gloria Pachón, the widow of Luis Carlos Galán, the young journalist who, in 1979, had founded the New Liberalism in an effort to revitalize and modernize the corrupt Liberal Party; the New Liberalism was the most serious and energetic force that opposed drug trafficking and supported the extradition of Colombian nationals.

2

THE FIRST FAMILY member to learn about the abduction was Dr. Pedro Guerrero, Beatriz's husband. He was at the Clinic for Psychotherapy and Human Sexuality—about ten blocks away—preparing a lecture on the evolution of animal species from the elementary functions of single-celled organisms to human emotions and affections. He was interrupted by a phone call from a police officer who asked in a cold, professional way if he was acquainted with Beatriz Villamizar. "Of course," Dr. Guerrero replied, "she's my wife." The officer was silent for a moment and then, in a more human tone, said, "All right, try to stay calm." Dr. Guerrero did not need to be a distinguished psychiatrist to understand that those words were the preamble to something very serious.

"What's happened?" he asked.

"A driver was murdered at the corner of Carrera Quinta and Calle 85," said the officer. "The car's a Renault 21, light gray, Bogotá license plate PS-2034. Do you know the number?"

"I have no idea," said Dr. Guerrero in an impatient voice. "Just tell me what happened to Beatriz."

"The only thing we can tell you now is that she's missing," the officer said. "We found her handbag on the seat, and a notebook where it said to call you in case of emergency."

There could be no doubt. Dr. Guerrero was the one who had advised his wife to put an emergency number in her datebook. Although he did not know the license number, the description matched Maruja's car. The corner where the crime occurred was just a few steps from Maruja's house, their first stop before Beatriz was driven home. Dr. Guerrero canceled his lecture with a hurried explanation. His friend, the urologist Alonso Acuña, drove him to the crime scene, through the heavy seven o'clock traffic, in fifteen minutes.

Alberto Villamizar, Maruja Pachón's husband and Beatriz's brother, was only two hundred meters from the corner where the abduction took place, but heard about it when the doorman called him on the house phone. He had come home at four, after spending the afternoon at the offices of the newspaper *El Tiempo*, working on the campaign for the Constituent Assembly whose members were to be elected in December, and he had fallen asleep fully dressed, exhausted by the previous night's party. His son Andrés came in a little before seven, accompanied by Beatriz's son Gabriel, who had been his best friend since childhood. Andrés looked for his mother in the bedroom and woke Alberto, who was surprised to see that it was already dark. Still half asleep, he turned on the light and checked the time. It was almost seven, and Maruja was not back yet.

The delay was unusual. She and Beatriz were always home earlier than this, regardless of traffic, or called if they were detained for some reason. And Maruja and he had both arranged to be at home by five. Alberto was worried and asked Andrés to call FOCINE. The watchman said that Maruja and Beatriz had left a little later than normal and would be there any minute. Villamizar had gone to the kitchen for a glass of water when the telephone rang. Andrés answered. Just by the sound of his son's voice, Alberto could tell it was an alarming call. He was right. Something had happened on the corner, and the car seemed to be Maruja's. The doorman's account was confused.

Alberto asked Andrés to stay home in case anyone called, then raced out. Gabriel ran after him. They were too impatient to wait for the elevator, and they dashed down the stairs. The doorman shouted after them:

"I think somebody was killed."

The street looked as if a celebration were in progress. The neighbors were at the windows of the residential buildings, and the horns of cars stalled on the Circunvalar were blaring. At the corner a squad car attempted to keep a curious crowd away from the abandoned automobile. It surprised Villamizar to see Dr. Guerrero there before him.

It was, in fact, Maruja's car. At least half an hour had gone by since the kidnapping, and all that was left were the remains: bullet-shattered glass on the driver's side, blood and broken glass on the seat, and the dark wet stain on the asphalt where the driver had been lying. He had just been taken away, still alive. Everything else was clean and in order.

An efficient, well-mannered policeman gave Villamizar the details provided by the few witnesses. They were fragmentary, imprecise, sometimes contradictory, but left no doubt that it had been an abduction, and that the driver was the only one wounded. Alberto wanted to know if he had said anything, given any clues. But that had been impossible: The driver was in a coma, and no one had said where he had been taken.

Dr. Guerrero, on the other hand, seemed anesthetized by shock, incapable of assessing the gravity of the situation. When he arrived he had identified Beatriz's bag, her cosmetic case, her datebook, a leather cardcase that held her identity card, her wallet containing twelve thousand pesos and a credit card, and concluded that only his wife had been abducted.

"See, Maruja's bag isn't here," he said to his brother-in-law. "She probably wasn't even in the car."

Perhaps this was a kind of professional delicacy intended to distract him while they both caught their breath. But Alberto was beyond that. What interested him now was to find out if the only blood in and around the car was the driver's, to be certain neither woman had been wounded. Everything else seemed clear to him, and what his feeling most resembled was guilt at never having foreseen that this kidnapping might happen. He had the absolute conviction that it was a personal act directed at him, and he knew who had done it, and why.

He had just left the house when radio programs were interrupted by the announcement that Maruja's driver had died in the private car that was taking him to the Clínica del Country. A short while later Guillermo Franco, the crime reporter for Caracol Radio, came on the scene, alerted by the report of a shooting, but all he found was the abandoned car. He picked up glass fragments and a blood-stained cigarette paper from the driver's seat and placed them in a small, transparent box that was numbered and dated. That same night the box joined the extensive collection of artifacts in the chronicle of crime created by Franco during his long years in the profession. The police officer accompanied Villamizar back to his house, asking a series of informal questions that might prove helpful to his investigation, but Alberto responded without thinking of anything but the long, difficult days that lay ahead of him. The first thing was to tell Andrés about the decision he had made. He asked him to see to the people who were beginning to come to the house, while he made some urgent phone calls and put his ideas in order. He went to the bedroom, closed the door, and called the presidential palace.

He had a very good political and personal relationship with President César Gaviria, and Gaviria knew Alberto as an impulsive but cordial man capable of maintaining his sangfroid under the most stressful circumstances. He was struck, therefore, by the abrupt vehemence with which Villamizar informed him that his wife and sister had been abducted, concluding with a brusque:

"I'm holding you responsible for their lives."

César Gaviria can be the harshest of men when he believes he should be, and this was one of those times.

"You listen to me, Alberto." His tone was curt. "Everything will be done that can be done."

And then, with the same coldness, he said he would immediately instruct his adviser on security, Rafael Pardo Rueda, to take charge of the matter and keep him up-to-date regarding the situation. Subsequent events would prove that his decision was the correct one.

The media arrived en masse. Villamizar knew that other kidnapping victims had been allowed to listen to the radio and television, and he improvised a message in which he demanded that Maruja and Beatriz be treated with the respect they deserved as honorable women who had nothing to do with the war, and announced that from this moment on he would devote all his time and energy to obtaining their release.

One of the first to come to the house was General Miguel Maza Márquez, head of the Administrative Department for Security (DAS), whose responsibility it was to investigate the abduction. The general had held this position for seven years, since the days of the Belisario Betancur government; he had continued in office under President Virgilio Barco, and had just been confirmed by César Gaviria—unprecedented longevity in a post from which it is almost impossible to emerge unscathed, above all during the most difficult days in the war against the drug traffickers. Compact and hard, as if forged in steel, with the bull neck typical of the warlike people from La Guajira, the general is a man of long, gloomy silences, and at the same time capable of openhearted intimacy with friends: He is pure Guajiran. But in his work there were no nuances. To his mind, the war against the drug dealers was a personal struggle to the death with Pablo Escobar. And the feeling was more than mutual. Escobar had used 2,600 kilos of dynamite in two successive attempts against his life: the highest distinction Escobar had ever granted to an enemy. Maza Márquez escaped unharmed on both occasions, attributing this to the protection of the Holy Infant—the same saint, of course, to whom Escobar attributed the miracle of his not being killed by Maza Márquez.

President Gaviria had made it a matter of policy that no armed force was to attempt a rescue without the prior agreement of the kidnap victim's family. But the political rumor mill produced a good deal of talk regarding procedural differences between the president and General Maza. Villamizar was taking no chances.

"I want you to know that I'm opposed to an armed rescue," he told General Maza. "I want to be sure it won't happen, and that I'm consulted before any decision is reached."

Maza Márquez agreed. At the end of their long, informative talk, he ordered a tap on Villamizar's telephone in the event the kidnappers attempted to communicate with him at night.

That same evening Villamizar had his first conversation with Rafael Pardo, who informed him that the president had appointed him mediator between the government and the family, and that he, Pardo, was the only one authorized to make official statements regarding the case. It was clear to both men that Maruja's abduction was a move by the drug dealers to exert pressure on the government through her sister, Gloria Pachón, and they decided to proceed on that assumption without hypothesizing any further.

Colombia had not been aware of her own importance in the international drug trade until the traffickers invaded the country's highest political echelons through the back door, first with their increasing ability to corrupt and suborn, and then with their own ambitions. In 1982 Pablo Escobar had tried to find a place in the New Liberalism movement headed by Luis Carlos Galán, but Galán removed his name from the rolls and exposed him before a crowd of five thousand people in Medellín. A short while later Escobar was in the Chamber of Deputies as a representative of a marginal wing of the official Liberal Party, but he had not forgotten the insult and unleashed an all-out war against the state, in particular against the New Liberalism. Rodrigo Lara Bonilla, who represented the New Liberalism as justice minister in the Belisario Betancur government, was murdered in a drive-by shooting on the streets of Bogotá. His successor, Enrique Parejo, was pursued all the way to Budapest by a hired assassin who shot him in the face with a pistol but did not kill him. On August 18, 1989, Luis Carlos Galán, who was protected by eighteen well-armed bodyguards, was machine-gunned on the main square in the municipality of Soacha, some ten kilometers from the presidential palace.

The main reason for the war was the drug traffickers' fear of extradition to the United States, where they could be tried for crimes committed there and receive extraordinarily harsh sentences, like the one given Carlos Lehder, a Colombian drug dealer who had been extradited to the United States in 1987 and sentenced to life imprisonment plus 130 years. This was possible because a treaty signed during the presidency of Julio César Turbay allowed the extradition of Colombian nationals for the first time. After the murder of Lara Bonilla, President Belisario Betancur applied its provisions with a series of summary extraditions. The traffickers—terrified by the long, worldwide reach of the United States—realized that the safest place for them was Colombia, and they went underground, fugitives inside their own country. The great irony was that their only alternative was to place themselves under the protection of the state to save their own skins. And so they attempted—by persuasion and by force—to obtain that protection by engaging in indiscriminate, merciless terrorism and, at the same time, by offering to surrender to the authorities and bring home and invest their capital in Colombia, on the sole condition that they not be extradited. Theirs was an authentic shadow power with a brand name—the Extraditables—and a slogan typical of Escobar: "We prefer a grave in Colombia to a cell in the United States."

President Betancur kept up the war. His successor, Virgilio

Barco, intensified it. This was the situation in 1989 when César Gaviria emerged as a presidential candidate following the assassination of Luis Carlos Galán, whose campaign he had directed. In his own campaign, he defended extradition as an indispensable tool for strengthening the penal system, and announced an unprecedented strategy against the drug traffickers. It was a simple idea: Those who surrendered to the judges and confessed to some or all of their crimes could obtain non-extradition in return. But this idea, as formulated in the original decree, was not enough for the Extraditables. Through his lawyers, Escobar demanded that non-extradition be made unconditional, that confession and indictment not be obligatory, that the prison be invulnerable to attack, and that their families and followers be guaranteed protection. Holding terrorism in one hand and negotiation in the other, he began abducting journalists in order to twist the government's arm and achieve his demands. In two months, eight had been kidnapped. The abduction of Maruja and Beatriz seemed to be one more in that ominous series.

Villamizar thought this was the case as soon as he saw the bullet-riddled car. Later, in the crowd that invaded his house, he was struck by the absolute certainty that the lives of his wife and sister depended on what he could do to save them. Because this time, as never before, the war was being waged as an unavoidable personal challenge.

Villamizar, in fact, was already a survivor. When he was a representative in the Chamber, he had achieved passage of the National Narcotics Statute in 1985, a time when there was no ordinary legislation against drug trafficking but only the scattershot decrees of a state of siege. Later, Luis Carlos Galán had told him to stop passage of a bill introduced in the Chamber by parliamentarians friendly to Escobar, which would have removed legislative support for the extradition treaty then in effect. It was nearly his death sentence. On October 22, 1986, two assassins in sweatsuits who pretended to be working out across from his house fired submachine guns at him as he was getting into his car. His escape was miraculous. One assailant was killed by the police, and his accomplices arrested, then released a few years later. No one took responsibility for the attempt, but no one had any doubt as to who had ordered it.

Persuaded by Galán himself to leave Colombia for a while, Villamizar was named ambassador to Indonesia. After he had been there for a year, the U.S. security forces in Singapore captured a Colombian assassin traveling to Jakarta. It was never proved that he had been sent to kill Villamizar, but it was established that in the United States a fake death certificate had declared him dead.

On the night that Maruja and Beatriz were abducted, Villamizar's house was filled to overflowing. There were people in politics and the government, and the families of the two victims. Aseneth Velásquez, an art dealer and close friend of the Villamizars, who lived in the apartment above them, had assumed the duties of hostess, and all that was missing was music to make the evening seem like any other Friday night. It can't be helped: In Colombia, any gathering of more than six people, regardless of class or the hour, is doomed to turn into a dance.

By this time the entire family, scattered all over the world, had been informed. Alexandra, Maruja's daughter by her first marriage, had just finished supper in a restaurant in Maicao, on the remote Guajira peninsula, when Javier Ayala gave her the news. The director of "Enfoque," a popular Wednesday television program, she had gone to Guajira the day before to do a series of interviews. She ran to the hotel to call her family, but all the telephones at home were busy. By a lucky coincidence, on the previous Wednesday she had interviewed a psychiatrist who specialized in treating cases of clinical depression brought on by imprisonment in high-security institutions. When she heard the news in Maicao, she realized that the same therapy might be useful for kidnapping victims as well, and she returned to Bogotá to start to apply it, beginning with the next program.

Gloria Pachón, Maruja's sister, who was then Colombia's representative to UNESCO, was awakened at two in the morning by Villamizar's words: "I have something awful to tell you." Maruja's daughter Juana, who was vacationing in Paris, learned the news a moment later in the adjoining bedroom. Maruja's son Nicolás, a twenty-seven-year-old musician and composer, was in New York when he was awakened by a phone call.

At two o'clock that morning, Dr. Guerrero and his son Gabriel went to see the parliamentarian Diego Montaña Cuéllar, president of the Patriotic Union—a movement linked to the Communist Party—and a member of the Notables, a group formed in December 1989 to mediate between the government and the kidnappers of Alvaro Diego Montoya. They found him not only awake but very dejected. He had heard about the abduction on the news that night and thought it a demoralizing symptom. The only thing Guerrero wanted to ask was if he would act as mediator with Pablo Escobar and persuade him to hold Guerrero hostage in exchange for Beatriz. Montaña Cuéllar's answer was typical of his character.

"Don't be an ass, Pedro," he said. "In this country there's nothing you can do."

Dr. Guerrero returned home at dawn but did not even try to sleep. His nerves were on edge. A little before seven he received a call from Yami Amat, the news director at Caracol, and in the worst state of mind responded with a rash challenge to the kidnappers.

At six-thirty, without any sleep, Villamizar showered and dressed for his appointment with Jaime Giraldo Angel, the justice minister, who brought him up-to-date on the war against narcoterrorism. Villamizar left the meeting convinced that his struggle would be long and difficult, but grateful for the two hours he had spent finding out about recent developments, since for some time he had paid little attention to the issue of drug trafficking.

He did not eat breakfast or lunch. By late afternoon, after various frustrating errands, he too visited Diego Montaña Cuéllar, who surprised him once again with his frankness. "Don't forget that this is for the long haul," he said, "at least until next June, after the Constituent Assembly, because Maruja and Beatriz will be Escobar's defense against extradition." Many of his friends were annoyed with Montaña Cuéllar for not disguising his pessimism in the press, even though he belonged to the Notables.

"Anyway, I'm resigning from this bullshit," he told Villamizar in his florid language. "We don't do anything but stand around like assholes."

Villamizar felt drained and alone when he returned home after a fruitless day. The two neat whiskeys he drank one after the other left him exhausted. At six in the evening his son, Andrés, who from then on would be his only companion, persuaded him to have breakfast. They were eating when the president telephoned.

"All right, Alberto," he said in his best manner. "Come over and we'll talk."

President Gaviria received him at seven in the library of the private wing in the presidential palace, where he had lived for the past three months with his wife, Ana Milena Muñoz, and his two children, eleven-year-old Simón, and María Paz, who was eight. A small but comfortable refuge next to a greenhouse filled with brilliant flowers, it had wooden bookshelves crowded with official publications and family photos, a compact sound system, and his favorite records: the Beatles, Jethro Tull, Juan Luis Guerra, Beethoven, Bach. After long days of official duties, this was where the president held informal meetings or relaxed with friends at nightfall with a glass of whiskey.

Gaviria greeted Villamizar with affection and spoke with solidarity and understanding, and with his rather abrupt frankness as well. But Villamizar was calmer now that he had recovered from the initial shock, and he had enough information to know there was very little the president could do for him. Both men were sure the abduction of Maruja and Beatriz had political motivations, and they did not need to be fortune-tellers to realize that Pablo Escobar was behind it. But the essential thing, Gaviria said, was not knowing it but getting Escobar to acknowledge it as a first important step in guaranteeing the safety of the two women.

It was clear to Villamizar from the start that the president would not go beyond the Constitution or the law to help him, nor stop the military units that were searching for the kidnappers, but it was also clear he would not attempt any rescue operations without the authorization of the families.

"That," said the president, "is our policy."

There was nothing else to say. When Villamizar left the presidential palace, twenty-four hours had passed since the kidnapping, and he felt like a blind man facing the future, but he knew he could count on the government's cooperation to undertake private negotiations to help his wife and sister, and he had Rafael Pardo, the president's security adviser, ready to assist him. But what seemed to deserve his deepest belief was Diego Montaña Cuéllar's crude realism.

THE FIRST IN that unprecedented series of abductions—on August 30, 1990, a bare three weeks after President César Gaviria took office—was the kidnapping of Diana Turbay, the director of the television news program "Criptón" and of the Bogotá magazine *Hoy x Hoy*, and the daughter of the former president and leader of the Liberal Party, Julio César Turbay. Four members of her news team were kidnapped along with her—the editor Azucena Liévano, the writer Juan Vitta, the cameramen Richard Becerra and Orlando Acevedo—as well as the German journalist Hero Buss, who was stationed in Colombia. Six in all.

The trick used by the kidnappers was a supposed interview with Manuel Pérez, the priest who was supreme commander of the guerrilla group called the Army of National Liberation (ELN). Few people knew about the invitation, and none thought Diana should accept it. Among them were the defense minister, General Oscar Botero, and Rafael Pardo, who had been informed of the danger by the president so that he could communicate his concerns to the Turbay family. But anyone who thought Diana would cancel the trip did not know her. In fact, the press interview with Father Manuel Pérez probably did not interest her as much as the possibility of a dialogue on peace. Years earlier, in absolute secret, she had traveled on muleback to talk to armed self-defense groups in their own territory, in a solitary attempt to understand the guerrilla movements from a political and journalistic point of view. The news had no relevance at the time, and the results were not made public. Later, despite her long-standing opposition to the M-19, she became friends with Commander Carlos Pizarro, whom she visited in his camp to search for peaceful solutions. It is clear that the person who planned the deception in order to abduct her must have known her history. At that time, no matter what the reason, no matter what the obstacle, nothing in this world could have stopped Diana from talking to Father Pérez, who held another of the keys to peace.

A variety of last-minute problems had postponed the appointment the year before, but on August 30, at five-thirty in the afternoon, and without informing anyone, Diana and her team set out in a battered van with two young men and a girl who passed themselves off as representatives of the ELN leadership. The drive from Bogotá was a faithful parody of the kind of trip real guerrillas would have organized. Their traveling companions must have been members of an armed group, or had been once, or had learned their lessons very well, because they did not make a single mistake, in speech or behavior, that would have betrayed the subterfuge.

On the first day they had reached Honda, 146 kilometers to the west of Bogotá, where other men were waiting for them in two vehicles that were more comfortable. They had supper in a roadside tavern, then continued along a dark, hazardous road under a heavy downpour, and dawn found them waiting for a landslide to be cleared. At last, weary from lack of sleep, at eleven in the morning they reached a spot where a patrol was waiting for them with five horses. Diana and Azucena rode for four hours, while their companions traveled by foot, first through dense mountain forest and then through an idyllic valley with peaceful houses among the coffee groves. People came out to watch them go by, some recognized Diana and called out greetings from their terraces. Juan Vitta estimated that no fewer than five hundred people had seen them along the route. In the evening they dismounted at a deserted ranch where a young man who looked like a student identified himself as being from the ELN but said nothing about their destination. They were all confused. No more than half a kilometer away was a stretch of highway, and beyond that a city that had to be Medellín. In other words: This was not ELN territory. Unless—it occurred to Hero Buss—this was a masterful move by Father Pérez to meet them in an area where no one expected to find him.

About two hours later they came to Copacabana, a municipality that had been devoured by the urban sprawl of Medellín. They dismounted at a little house with white walls and moss-covered roof tiles that seemed imbedded in a steep, overgrown slope. It had a living room, with a small room on either side. In one of them there were three double beds, which were taken by the guides. The other, with a double bed and a bunk bed, was for the men on the crew. Diana and Azucena had the best room, which was in the rear and showed signs of having been occupied before by women. The light was on in the middle of the day because all the windows were boarded over.

After waiting for about three hours, a man in a mask came in, welcomed them on behalf of the high command, and announced that Father Pérez was expecting them but for reasons of security the women should go first. This was the first time that Diana showed signs of uneasiness. Hero Buss took her aside and said that under no circumstances should she agree to break up their group. Because she could not prevent that from happening, Diana slipped him her identity card. She did not have time to explain why, but he understood it to be a piece of evidence in the event she disappeared.

Before daybreak they took away the women and Juan Vitta. Hero Buss, Richard Becerra, and Orlando Acevedo stayed in the room with the double bed and the bunk bed, and five guards. The suspicion that they had fallen into a trap grew as the hours passed. That night, while they were playing cards, Hero Buss noticed that one of the guards was wearing an expensive watch. "So now the ELN can afford Rolexes," he joked. But the man ignored him. Another thing that perplexed Hero Buss was that their guns were not typical guerrilla weapons but the kind used for urban operations. Orlando, who spoke little and thought of himself as the poor relation on this expedition, did not need as many clues to discover the truth, for he had an unbearable feeling that something very serious was going on.

The first change of house occurred in the middle of the night on September 10, when the guards burst in shouting: "It's the cops!" After two hours of a forced march through the underbrush, in a terrible storm, they reached the house where Diana, Azucena, and Juan Vitta were being held. It was roomy and well furnished, with a large-screen television set and nothing that could arouse any suspicions. What none of them imagined was how close they all were to being rescued that night through sheer coincidence. The stop there of a few hours allowed them to exchange ideas, experiences, plans for the future. Diana unburdened herself to Hero Buss. She spoke of how depressed she was because she had led them into the trap, and confessed that she was trying to push away the thought of her family—husband, children, parents—which did not give her a moment's peace, but her efforts always had the opposite result.

The following night, as Diana, Azucena, and Juan Vitta were walked to a third house, along a very rough path and under a steady rain, she realized that nothing they had been told was true. And that same night a new guard erased any final doubts she might have had.

"You're not with the ELN; you're being held by the Extraditables," he said. "But don't worry, because you're going to see something you won't forget."

The disappearance of Diana Turbay's team was still a mystery nineteen days later, when Marina Montoya was abducted. She had been dragged away by three well-dressed men carrying 9mm pistols and Mini-Uzis equipped with silencers, just as she was closing her restaurant, Donde las Tías, in the northern section of Bogotá. Her sister Lucrecia, who worked with her, was lucky enough to have her foot in a cast because of a sprained ankle, which kept her from going to the restaurant. Marina had already locked the doors but opened them again because she recognized two of the three men who were knocking. They had come in for lunch several times during the past week and impressed the staff with their amiability and Medellinese humor and the 30 percent tips they left the waiters. That night, however, they were different. As soon as Marina opened the door, they immobilized her with an armlock and forced her out of the restaurant. She managed to clutch at a lamppost and began to scream. One of them kneed her in the spine with so much force she could not catch her breath. She was unconscious when they put her into the trunk of a blue Mercedes 190, which had been prepared to allow her to breathe.

Luis Guillermo Pérez Montoya, one of Marina's seven children, was a forty-eight-year-old executive with the Kodak Company in Colombia. His interpretation of events was the same as everyone else's: His mother had been abducted in retaliation for the government's failure to comply with the agreements reached by her brother Germán Montoya and the Extraditables. Distrustful by nature of everything having to do with officialdom, he set himself the task of freeing his mother through direct negotiation with Pablo Escobar.

Without orientation, without prior contact with anyone, without even knowing what he would do when he got there, he left two days later for Medellín. At the airport he took a cab but had no address to give the driver and told him simply to take him into the city. Reality came out to meet him when he saw the body of a girl about fifteen years old lying by the side of the road, wearing an expensive party dress and very heavy makeup. There was a bullet hole and a trickle of dried blood on her forehead. Luis Guillermo, who could not believe his eyes, pointed at the corpse.

"There's a dead girl over there."

"Yes," said the driver without looking. "One of the dolls who party with don Pablo's friends."

This broke the ice. Luis Guillermo told the driver the reason for his visit, and he in turn told him how to meet with a girl who was supposed to be the daughter of one of Pablo Escobar's first cousins.

"Tonight at eight o'clock go to the church behind the market. A girl named Rosalía will be there."

And in fact she was there, waiting for him, sitting on a bench in the square. She was almost a child, but her demeanor and the assurance of her words were those of a mature woman who had been instructed with care. To begin negotiations, she said, he would need half a million pesos in cash. She told him the hotel where he should register the following Thursday and wait for a call at either seven in the morning or seven in the evening on Friday.

"The woman who'll call you is named Pita."

He waited in vain for two days and part of a third. At last he realized it was all a joke and was thankful Pita had not called to ask for the money. He behaved with so much discretion that not even his wife knew about these trips or their deplorable results until four years later, when he spoke about them for the first time for this report.

FOUR HOURS AFTER the kidnapping of Marina Montoya, on a side street in the Las Ferias district to the west of Bogotá, a Jeep and a Renault 18 hemmed in the car of Francisco Santos, nicknamed Pacho, the editor in chief at *El Tiempo*. His vehicle looked like an ordinary red Jeep, but it had been bulletproofed at the factory, and the four assailants who surrounded it were not only carrying 9mm pistols and Mini-Uzi submachine guns equipped with silencers, but one also held a special mallet for breaking glass. None of that was necessary. Pacho, an incorrigible talker, opened the door to speak to the men. "I preferred to die rather than not know what was going on," he has said. One of his abductors immobilized him with a pistol to the forehead and forced him to get out of the car with his head lowered. Another opened the front door and fired three shots: One hit the windshield, and two shattered the skull of Oromansio Ibáñez, the thirty-eight-year-old driver. Pacho was not aware of what had happened. Days later, as he was thinking about the attack, he recalled hearing the whine of three bullets muffled by the silencer.

The operation was so rapid that it attracted no attention in the middle of the busy Tuesday traffic. A police officer discovered the blood-soaked body in the front seat of the abandoned vehicle; he picked up the two-way radio and immediately heard on the other end a voice half-lost among distant galaxies.

"Hello."

"Who is this?" asked the officer.

"El Tiempo."

The news was on the air in ten minutes. In reality, preparations for his abduction had been going on for close to four months but almost failed because Pacho Santos's movements were so unpredictable and irregular. Fifteen years earlier the same reasons had stopped the M-19 from kidnapping his father, Hernando Santos.

This time the smallest details had been taken into account. The kidnappers' automobiles, caught in a traffic jam on Avenida Boyacá at Calle 80, drove on the sidewalks to make their escape and disappeared down the winding streets of a working-class neighborhood. Pacho Santos sat between two of the kidnappers, his eyes covered by glasses that had been painted over with nail polish, but in his mind he followed all the car's turns until it screeched to a stop in a garage. By the route and the length of time they had been driving, he formed a tentative idea of the neighborhood they were in.

One kidnapper led him by the arm—he was still wearing the painted glasses—to the end of a hall. They climbed to the second floor, turned left, walked about five paces, and went into a place that was icy cold. This is where they removed the glasses. Then he saw that he was in a dismal bedroom with boarded-up windows and a single bulb in the ceiling. The only furnishings were a double bed, whose sheets had seen too much use, and a table with a portable radio and a television set.

Pacho realized that his abductors had been in a hurry not only for reasons of security but in order to get back in time for the soccer game between Santafé and Caldas. To keep everybody happy, they gave him a bottle of *aguardiente*, left him alone with the radio, and went downstairs to watch the game. He drank half the bottle in ten minutes and felt no effects, though it did put him in the mood to listen to the game on the radio. A devoted Santafé fan since his childhood, the tie—the score was 2–2—made him so angry he could not enjoy the liquor. When it was over, he saw himself on the nine-thirty news on file footage, wearing a dinner jacket and surrounded by beauty queens. That was when he learned his driver was dead.

At the end of the newscast, a guard wearing a heavy flannel

mask came in and had him remove his clothes and put on a gray sweatsuit, which seemed a requirement in the prisons of the Extraditables. He also tried to take the inhaler for asthma that was in his jacket pocket, but Pacho convinced him that keeping it was a matter of life and death. The guard explained the rules of his captivity: He could use the bathroom in the hall, listen to the radio, and watch television with no restrictions, but at normal volume. When he was finished, he made Pacho lie down, then used a heavy rope to tie him to the bed by his ankle.

The guard laid a mattress on the floor beside the bed, and a few moments later began to snore with an intermittent whistle. The night thickened. In the dark, Pacho became aware that this was the first night of an uncertain future in which anything could happen. He thought about María Victoria—her friends called her Mariavé—his pretty, intelligent, and strong-willed wife, and about their two sons, twenty-month-old Benjamín and seven-month-old Gabriel. A rooster crowed nearby, and Pacho was surprised at its mistaken timing. "A rooster that crows at ten at night must be crazy," he thought. He is an emotional, impulsive man, easily moved to tears: the image of his father. Andrés Escabi, his sister Juanita's husband, had died in a plane that had been blown up in midair by the Extraditables. In the midst of the family upheaval, Pacho said something that made all of them shudder: "One of us will not be alive in December." He did not think, however, that the night of his abduction would be his last. For the first time his nerves were calm, and he felt sure he would survive. Pacho knew the guard lying on the floor was awake by the rhythm of his breathing. He asked him:

"Who's holding me?"

"Who do you want to be held by," asked the guard, "the guerrillas or the drug dealers?"

"I think I'm being held by Pablo Escobar," Pacho replied.

"That's right," said the guard, and made an immediate correction, "the Extraditables."

The news was in the air. The switchboard operators at *El Tiempo* had notified his closest relatives, who had notified others, who called others, until everybody knew. Through a series of peculiar circumstances, one of the last in the family to find out was Pacho's wife. A few minutes after the abduction she had received a call from his friend Juan Gabriel Uribe, who still was not sure what had happened and could only ask if Pacho was home yet. She said no, and Juan Gabriel did not have the heart to tell her what was still an unconfirmed report. A few minutes after that she had a call from Enrique Santos Calderón, her husband's double first cousin and the assistant manager at *El Tiempo*.

"Have you heard about Pacho?" he asked.

María Victoria thought he was referring to another matter having to do with her husband, which she already knew about.

"Of course," she said.

Enrique said a quick goodbye so he could call other family members. (Years later, commenting on the mistake, María Victoria said: "That happened to me because I wanted to pass myself off as a genius.") Then Juan Gabriel called back and told her the whole story: They had killed the driver and taken Pacho.

PRESIDENT GAVIRIA and his closest advisers were reviewing television ads to promote the election campaign for the Constituent Assembly when his press adviser, Mauricio Vargas, whispered in his ear: "They've kidnapped Pachito Santos." The viewing was not interrupted. The president, who needs glasses to watch movies, took them off and looked at Vargas.

"Keep me informed," he told him.

He put on his glasses again and continued to watch the ads. His close friend Alberto Casas Santamaría, the communications minister, was sitting beside him and heard the news, and it was whispered from ear to ear along the row of presidential advisers. A shudder passed through the room. But the president did not blink, following a norm in his life that he expresses in a schoolboy's rule: "I have to finish this assignment." When the tape had ended, he took off his glasses again, put them in his breast pocket, and told Mauricio Vargas:

"Phone Rafael Pardo and tell him to call a meeting of the Council on Security right away."

Then he began the planned discussion of the ads. Only when a decision had been reached did he reveal the impact that the news of the abduction had on him. Half an hour later he walked into the room where most of the members of the Council on Security sat waiting for him. They had just started the meeting when Mauricio Vargas tiptoed in and whispered in his ear:

"They've kidnapped Marina Montoya."

It had, in reality, occurred at four o'clock, before Pacho's kidnapping, but the news did not reach the president until four hours later.

TEN THOUSAND kilometers away, in a hotel in Florence, Pacho's father, Hernando Santos Castillo, had been asleep for three hours. His daughter Juanita was in an adjoining room, and his daughter Adriana and her husband were in another. They had been informed by telephone and had decided not to disturb their father. But his nephew Luis Fernando called him direct from Bogotá, using the most cautious opening he could think of for waking his uncle, who was seventy-eight years old and had undergone five bypasses.

"I have some very bad news for you," he said.

Hernando, of course, imagined the worst, but he put on a good front.

"What happened?"

"They kidnapped Pacho."

News of a kidnapping, no matter how painful, is not as irremediable as news of a murder, and Hernando breathed a sigh of relief. "Thank God," he said, and then changed his tone:

"Okay. Don't worry. We'll see what we have to do."

An hour later, in the middle of a fragrant Tuscan autumn night, they began the long trip home to Colombia.

THE TURBAY FAMILY, distraught at having heard nothing from Diana in the week since her departure, requested the government to make official inquiries through the principal guerrilla organizations. A week after the date on which Diana was due back, her husband, Miguel Uribe, and Alvaro Leyva, a member of parliament, traveled in secret to Casa Verde, the general headquarters of the Revolutionary Armed Forces of Colombia (FARC) in the eastern mountains. There they were able to contact all the armed groups in an effort to determine if Diana was with any of them. Seven denied it in a joint communiqué.

Not knowing what to expect, the presidency alerted the public to a proliferation of false communiqués and asked the people not to put more faith in them than in announcements from the government. But the grave and bitter truth was that the public had implicit trust in the Extraditables' communiqués, which meant that on October 30—sixty-one days after the abduction of Diana Turbay, forty-two days after the kidnapping of Francisco Santos—everyone gave a sigh of relief when the last remaining doubts were dispelled by a single sentence from the Extraditables: "We acknowledge publicly that we are holding the missing journalists." Eight days later, Maruja Pachón and Beatriz Villamizar were abducted. There were plenty of reasons for assuming that this escalation had even broader implications.

On the day following the disappearance of Diana and her crew, when there was still no suspicion in anyone's mind that they had been kidnapped, Yami Amat, the distinguished news director at

Caracol Radio, was intercepted on a street in downtown Bogotá by a group of thugs who had been following him for several days. Amat slipped out of their hands with an athletic maneuver that caught them off guard, and somehow survived a bullet in the back. Just a few hours later, María Clara, the daughter of former president Belisario Betancur, and her twelve-year-old daughter Natalia, managed to escape in her car when another armed gang blocked her way in a residential neighborhood in Bogotá. The only explanation for these two failures is that the kidnappers must have had strict orders not to kill their victims.

THE FIRST PEOPLE to have definite knowledge of who was holding Maruja Pachón and Beatriz Villamizar were Hernando Santos and former president Julio César Turbay, because forty-eight hours after their abduction, Escobar himself informed them in writing through one of his lawyers: "You can tell them that the group is holding Pachón." On November 12, there was another oblique confirmation in a letter written on the Extraditables' stationery to Juan Gómez Martínez, director of the Medellín newspaper *El Colombiano*, who had mediated on several occasions with Escobar on behalf of the Notables. "The detention of the journalist Maruja Pachón," said the letter from the Extraditables, "is our response to the recent tortures and abductions perpetrated in the city of Medellín by the same state security forces mentioned so often in our previous communiqués." And once again they expressed their determination not to free any of the hostages as long as that situation continued.

Dr. Pedro Guerrero, Beatriz's husband, overwhelmed by his utter powerlessness in the face of these crushing events, decided to close his psychiatric practice. "How could I see patients when I was in worse shape than they were," he has said. He suffered attacks of anxiety that he did not want to impart to his children. He did not have a moment's peace, at nightfall he consoled himself with whiskey, and his insomnia was spent listening to tearful boleros of lost love on "Radio Recuerdo." "My love," someone sang, "if you're listening, answer me."

Alberto Villamizar, who had always known that the abduction of his wife and sister was one more link in a sinister chain, closed ranks with the families of the other victims. But his first visit to Hernando Santos was disheartening. He was accompanied by Gloria Pachón de Galán, his sister-in-law, and they found Hernando sprawled on a sofa in a state of total demoralization. "What I'm doing is getting ready to suffer as little as possible when they kill Francisco," he said when they came in. Villamizar attempted to outline a plan to negotiate with the kidnappers, but Hernando cut him off with irreparable despair.

"Don't be naive, my boy," he said, "you have no idea what those men are like. There's nothing we can do."

Former president Turbay was no more encouraging. He knew from a variety of sources that his daughter was in the hands of the Extraditables, but he had decided not to acknowledge this in public until he knew for certain what they were after. A group of journalists had asked the question the week before, and he had eluded them with a daring swirl of the cape.

"My heart tells me," he said, "that Diana and her colleagues have been delayed because of their work as reporters, but that it isn't a question of their being detained."

Their disillusionment was understandable after three months of fruitless efforts. This was Villamizar's interpretation, and instead of being infected by their pessimism, he brought a new spirit to their common struggle.

During this time a friend was asked what kind of man Villamizar was, and he defined him in a single stroke: "He's a great drinking companion." Villamizar had acknowledged this with good humor as an enviable and uncommon virtue. But on the day his wife was abducted, he realized it was also dangerous in his situation, and decided not to have another drink in public until she and his sister were free. Like any good social drinker, he knew that alcohol lowers your guard, loosens your tongue, and somehow alters your sense of reality. It is a hazard for someone who has to measure his actions and words in millimeters. And so the strict rule he imposed on himself was not a penitential act but a security measure. He attended no more gatherings, he said goodbye to his light-hearted bohemianism, his jovial drinking sessions with other politicians. On the nights when his emotional tension was at its height, Andrés listened as he vented his feelings, holding a glass of mineral water while his father found comfort in drinking alone.

In his meetings with Rafael Pardo, they studied alternative courses of action but always ran up against the government policy that left open the threat of extradition. They both knew this was the most powerful tool for pressuring the Extraditables into surrendering, and that the president used it with as much conviction as the Extraditables when they used it as a reason for not surrendering.

Villamizar had no military training, but he had grown up near military installations. For years his father, Dr. Alberto Villamizar Flórez, had been physician to the Presidential Guard and was very close to the lives of its officers. His grandfather, General Joaquín Villamizar, had been minister of war. One of his uncles, Jorge Villamizar Flórez, had been the general in command of the Armed Forces. From them Alberto had inherited his dual nature as a native of Santander and a soldier: He was cordial and domineering at the same time, a serious person who loved to drink, a man who never misses when he takes aim, who always says what he has to say in the most direct way, and who has never used the intimate *tú* with anyone in his life. The image of his father prevailed, however, and he completed his medical studies at Javieriana University but never graduated, swept away by the irresistible winds of politics. Not as a military man but as a Santanderean pure and simple, he always carries a Smith & Wesson .38 that he has never tried to use. In any case, armed or unarmed, his two greatest virtues are determination and patience. At first glance they may seem contradictory, but life has taught him they are not. With this kind of heritage, Villamizar had all the daring necessary to attempt an armed solution, but rejected it unless the situation became a matter of life or death.

Which meant that the only solution he could find in late November was to confront Escobar and negotiate, Santanderean to Antioquian, in a hard and equal contest. One night, tired of all the wheel-spinning, he presented his idea to Rafael Pardo. Pardo understood his anguish, but his reply was unhesitating.

"Listen to me, Alberto," he said in his solemn, direct way. "Take whatever steps you like, try anything you can, but if you want our cooperation to continue, you must know you can't overstep the bounds of the capitulation policy. Not one step, Alberto. That's all there is to it."

No other virtues could have served Villamizar as well as his determination and patience in sorting through the internal contradictions present in these conditions. In other words, he could do as he wished in his own way, using all his imagination, but he had to do it with his hands tied.

3

MARUJA OPENED HER eyes and thought of an old Spanish proverb: "God doesn't send anything we can't bear." It had been ten days since their abduction, and both she and Beatriz were growing accustomed to a routine that had seemed unthinkable on the first night. The kidnappers had repeated over and over again that this was a military operation, but the rules of their captivity were harsher than those of a prison. They could speak only if the matter was urgent, and never above a whisper. They could not get off the mattress that was their common bed, and they had to ask the two guards—who watched them all the time, even when they were sleeping—for everything they needed: permission to sit, to stretch their legs, to speak to Marina, to smoke. Maruja had to cover her mouth with a pillow to muffle the sound of her cough.

Marina had the only bed, lit day and night by a perpetual candle. On the floor beside the bed lay the mattress where Maruja and Beatriz slept, their heads facing opposite directions like the fish in the zodiac, with only one blanket for the two of them. The guards sat on the floor to watch them, leaning against the wall. The space was so narrow that if they straightened their legs, their feet were on the prisoners' mattress. They lived in semi-darkness because the one window was boarded over. Before they went to sleep, the cracks around the only door were stuffed with rags so that the light from Marina's candle would not be seen in the rest of the house. The only other light came from the television set, because Maruja had them turn off the blue lightbulb in the ceiling that gave them all a terrifying pallor. The closed, unventilated room was heavy with foul-smelling heat. The worst time was between six and nine in the morning, when the prisoners were awake, with no air, with nothing to drink or eat, waiting for the rags to be pulled away from the door so they could begin to breathe. The only consolation for Maruja and Marina was that they were given coffee and cigarettes whenever they asked for them. For Beatriz, a respiratory therapist, the smoke hanging in the little room was a calamity. She suffered it in silence, however, since it made the other two so happy. Marina, with her cigarette and her cup of coffee, once exclaimed: "How nice it will be when the three of us are in my house, smoking and drinking our coffee and laughing about this awful time." Instead of suffering, on that day Beatriz regretted not smoking.

The fact that the three women were in the same prison may have been an emergency measure: Their captors must have decided that the house where they had been taken first could not be used after the cab driver indicated the route they had taken. This was the only way to explain the last-minute change, the wretched fact that there was only one narrow bed, a single mattress for two people, and less than six square meters for the three hostages and the two guards on duty. Marina had also been brought there from another house—or another farm, as she called it—because the drinking and disorderliness of the guards at her first prison had endangered the entire organization. In any case, it was inconceivable that one of the largest transnational enterprises in the world did not have enough compassion to provide humane conditions for its kidnappers and their victims.

They had no idea where they were. They knew from the sound that they were very close to a highway with heavy truck traffic. There also seemed to be a sidewalk café with drinking and music that stayed open very late. Sometimes they heard a loudspeaker announcing either political or religious meetings, or broadcasting deafening concerts. On several occasions they heard campaign slogans for the Constituent Assembly that was to convene soon. More often they heard the whine of small planes taking off and landing just a short distance away, which led them to suppose they were somewhere near Guaymaral, a landing field for small aircraft about twenty kilometers to the north of Bogotá. Maruja, who had known savanna weather from the time she was a girl, felt that the cold in their room was not the chill of the countryside but of the city. And their captors' excessive precautions made sense only if they were in an urban center.

Most surprising of all was the occasional roar of a helicopter so close it seemed to be on the roof. Marina Montoya said it meant the arrival of an army officer who was responsible for the abductions. As the days passed, they would become accustomed to the sound, for during their captivity the helicopter landed at least once a month, and the hostages were sure it had something to do with them.

It was impossible to distinguish the line between truth and Marina's contagious fantasies. She said that Pacho Santos and Diana Turbay were in other rooms of the house, so that the officer in the helicopter could take care of all three cases during each visit. Once they heard alarming noises in the courtyard. The majordomo, the man who managed the house, was insulting his wife as he gave hurried orders to move it that way, bring it over here, a little higher, as if they were trying to force a corpse into a place that was too small. Marina, in her gloomy delirium, thought that perhaps they had cut up Francisco Santos and were burying the pieces under the tiles in the kitchen. "When the killings begin, they don't stop," she kept saying. "We're next." It was a terrifying night until they learned by chance that they had been moving an old wash tub that was too heavy for four men to carry.

At night the silence was total, interrupted only by a demented rooster with no sense of time who crowed whenever he felt like it. Barking dogs could be heard in the distance, and one very close by sounded to them like a trained guard dog. Maruja got off to a bad start. She curled up on the mattress, closed her eyes, and for several days did not open them again except when she had to, trying to think with more clarity. She was not sleeping for eight hours at a time but would doze off for half an hour and wake to find the same agony always lying in wait for her. She felt permanent dread: the constant physical sensation in her stomach of a hard knot about to explode into panic. Maruja ran the complete film of her life in an effort to hold on to good memories, but disagreeable ones always intervened. On one of three trips she had made to Colombia from Jakarta, Luis Carlos Galán had asked her, during a private lunch, to help him in his next presidential campaign. She had been his media adviser during an earlier campaign, traveling all over the country with her sister Gloria, celebrating victories, suffering defeats, averting mishaps, and so the offer was logical. Maruja felt appreciated and flattered. But when lunch was over, she noticed a vague look in Galán, a supernatural light: the instantaneous and certain vision that he would be killed. The revelation was so strong that she persuaded her husband to return to Colombia even though General Maza Márquez had warned him, with no further explanation, that they were risking death. A week before they left Jakarta, they heard the news that Galán had been murdered.

The experience left her with a depressive propensity that intensified during her captivity. She could find nothing to hold on to, no way to escape the thought that she too was pursued by mortal danger. She refused to speak or eat. She was irritated by Beatriz's indolence and the masked guards' brutishness, and she could not endure Marina's submissiveness or the way she identified with the regime of her kidnappers. She seemed like another jailer who admonished her if she snored or coughed in her sleep or moved more than she had to. Maruja would set down a glass, and Marina with a frightened "Careful!" would put it somewhere else. Maruja would respond with immense contempt. "Don't worry about it," she would say. "You're not the one in charge here." To make matters even worse, the guards were always uneasy because Beatriz spent the day writing down details of her imprisonment so she could tell her husband and children about them when she was set free. She had also made a long list of everything she hated in the room, and had to stop when she discovered there was nothing she did not hate. The guards had heard on the radio that Beatriz was a physical therapist, confused this with a psychotherapist, and would not allow her to write anymore because they were afraid she was developing a scientific method to make them lose their minds.

Marina's deterioration was understandable. After almost two months in the antechamber of death, the arrival of the other two hostages must have been an intolerable dislocation for her in a world she had made hers, and hers alone. Her relationship to the guards, which had become very close, changed on account of them, and in less than two weeks she was suffering again from the same terrible pain and intense solitude she had managed to overcome.

And yet, no night seemed as ghastly to Maruja as the first one. It was interminable and freezing cold. At one in the morning the temperature in Bogotá—according to the Meteorology Institute—had been between 55 and 59 degrees, and it had rained downtown and in the area around the airport. Maruja was overcome by exhaustion. She began to snore as soon as she fell asleep, but her persistent, uncontrollable smoker's cough, aggravated by the damp walls that released an icy moisture at dawn, kept waking her. Each time she coughed or snored, the guards would kick her in the head with their heels. Marina's fear was uncontrollable, and she backed them up, warning Maruja that they were going to tie her to the mattress so she wouldn't move around so much, or gag her to stop her from snoring.

Marina had Beatriz listen to the early morning news. It was a mistake. In his first interview with Yami Amat of Caracol Radio, Dr. Pedro Guerrero attacked the abductors with a string of defiant insults. He challenged them to behave like men and show their faces. Beatriz was prostrate with terror, certain that she and the others would be the ones to pay for his abuse.

Two days later, one of the bosses, his well-dressed bulk packed into six feet, two inches, kicked the door open and stormed into the room. His impeccable tropical wool suit, Italian loafers, and yellow silk tie were at variance with his churlish behavior. He cursed the guards with two or three obscenities, and raged at the most timid one, whom the others called Spots. "They tell me you're very nervous," he said. "Well let me warn you that around here nervous people get killed." And then he turned to Maruja and said in a rude, impatient voice:

"I heard you caused a lot of trouble last night, making noise and coughing."

Maruja replied with an exemplary calm that could have been mistaken for contempt.

"I snore when I'm asleep, and don't know I'm doing it," she said. "I can't control the cough because the room is freezing and the walls drip water in the middle of the night."

The man was in no mood for complaints.

"Do you think you can do whatever you want?" he shouted. "Let me tell you: If you snore again or cough at night, we can blow your head off."

Then he turned to Beatriz.

"And if not you, then your children and husbands. We know all of them, and we know exactly where they are."

"Do what you want," said Maruja. "There's nothing I can do to stop snoring. Kill me if you want to."

She was sincere, and in time would realize she had said the right thing. Harsh treatment beginning the first day is a method used by kidnappers to demoralize their captives. Beatriz, on the other hand, still shaken by her husband's rage on the radio, was less haughty.

"Why do you have to bring our children into it? What do they have to do with any of this?" she said, on the verge of tears. "Don't you have children?"

Perhaps he softened; he said he did. But Beatriz had lost the battle; her tears did not allow her to continue. Maruja had regained her composure and said that if they really wanted to settle things they should talk to her husband.

She thought the hooded man had followed her advice because on Sunday, when he came back, his manner had changed. He brought the day's papers with statements by Alberto Villamizar, which attempted to come to some agreement with the kidnappers. And they, it seems, began to change their behavior in response to that. The boss, at least, was so conciliatory that he asked the hostages to make a list of things they needed: soap, toothbrushes, toothpaste, cigarettes, skin cream, and books. Some of the things on the list arrived that same day, but they did not get certain books until four months later. As time passed they accumulated all kinds of pictures and mementos of the Holy Infant and Our Lady of Perpetual Help, which the various guards gave to them as gifts or souvenirs when they left or came back from their time off. After ten days a domestic routine had already been established. Their shoes were kept under the bed, and the room was so damp they had to be taken out to the courtyard from time to time to let them dry. The prisoners could walk around only in heavy wool men's socks, in a variety of colors, which had been given to them on the first day, and they had to put on two pairs at a time so that no one would hear their footsteps. The clothes they had been wearing on the night of the abduction had been confiscated, and they were given sweatsuits—one gray set and one pink for each of them—

which they lived and slept in, and two sets of underwear that they washed in the shower. At first they slept in their clothes. Later, when they had nightgowns, they wore them over their sweatsuits on very cold nights. They were also given bags to hold their few possessions: the spare sweatsuit and a clean pair of socks, their change of underwear, sanitary napkins, medicines, their grooming articles.

There was one bathroom for three prisoners and four guards. The women could close the bathroom door but not lock it, and were permitted no more than ten minutes in the shower even when they had to wash their clothes. They were allowed to smoke as much as they wanted, which for Maruja was over a pack a day, and even more for Marina. The room had a television set and a portable radio, so the captives could hear the news and the guards could listen to music. The morning news programs were played at very low volume, as if in secret, while the guards played their raucous music at a volume dictated only by their mood.

The television was turned on at nine, and they watched educational programs, then the soap operas and two or three other shows until the midday newscast. It played the longest from four in the afternoon until eleven at night. The television stayed on, as if it were in a child's room, but no one watched it. Yet the hostages scrutinized the newscasts with microscopic care, trying to discover coded messages from their families. They never knew, of course, how many they missed or how many innocent phrases were mistaken for messages of hope.

Alberto Villamizar appeared on various news shows eight times in the first two days, certain that the victims would hear his voice on at least one of them. And almost all of Maruja's children worked in the media. Some had regularly scheduled television programs and used them to maintain communication that they assumed was unilateral, and perhaps useless, but they persisted.

The first one the prisoners saw, on the following Wednesday, was the program aired by Alexandra on her return from La Guajira. Jaime Gaviria, a psychiatrist, a colleague of Beatriz's husband, and an old friend of the family, broadcast a series of instructions for maintaining one's spirit in confined spaces. Maruja and Beatriz knew Dr. Gaviria, understood the purpose of the program, and took careful note of his instructions.

This was the first in an eight-program series produced by Alexandra and based on a long conversation with Dr. Gaviria on the psychology of hostages. Her primary consideration was to se-lect topics that Maruja and Beatriz would find interesting and to conceal personal messages that only they would understand. Then Alexandra decided that each week she would have a guest who was prepared to answer preselected questions that would stimulate im-mediate associations in the captives. The surprise was that many viewers who knew nothing about her plan could at least tell that something else was hidden behind the apparent innocence of the questions.

NOT FAR AWAY—in the same city—Francisco Santos lived in his captive's room under conditions as miserable as Maruja's and Bea-triz's, but not as harsh. One explanation is that in addition to the political usefulness of their abduction, there may also have been a desire for revenge as far as the women were concerned. And it is almost certain that their guards and Pacho's belonged to two dif-ferent crews. Though it may have been only for reasons of secu-rity, the crews acted on their own and did not communicate with each other. But even so, there were incomprehensible differences. Pacho's guards were more informal, more autonomous and ac-commodating, and less concerned with hiding their identities. The worst difficulty for Pacho was having to sleep shackled to the bars of the bed with a metal chain that was wrapped to prevent skin abrasions. The worst for Maruja and Beatriz was not even having a bed to be chained to.

From the very beginning of his captivity, Pacho was given

newspapers every day. In general, the press reports on his kidnapping were so inaccurate and fanciful they made his captors double over with laughter. His schedule had already been established when Maruja and Beatriz were abducted. He would stay awake all night and go to sleep at about eleven in the morning. He watched television, alone or with his guards, or chatted with them about the news of the day, soccer games in particular. He read until he got bored, yet still had enough nervous energy to play cards or chess. His bed was comfortable, and he slept well from the first night until he developed a painful rash and a burning in his eyes, which cleared up when the cotton blankets were washed and the room given a thorough cleaning. They never worried about anyone seeing the light from the outside because the windows were boarded over.

In October an unexpected hope presented itself: Pacho was ordered to send proof to his family that he was alive. He had to make a supreme effort to maintain his self-control. He asked for black coffee and two packs of cigarettes, and began to compose a message straight from the heart, not changing a comma. He recorded it onto a minicassette, which couriers preferred over full-size tapes because they were easier to conceal. Pacho spoke as slowly as he could and tried to keep his voice calm and to adopt an attitude that would not reveal the dark shadows in his spirit. He concluded by reading aloud the headlines in that day's *El Tiempo* as proof of the date on which he taped the message. He felt satisfied, above all with the first sentence: "Everyone who knows me knows how difficult this message is for me." Yet when the heat of the moment had passed and he read it in published form, Pacho had the impression that with the last sentence he had put the noose around his own neck: He asked the president to do everything he could to free the journalists. "But," he warned, "what matters is not to ignore the laws and precepts of the Constitution, for these benefit not only the nation but the freedom of the press, which is now being held hostage." His depression deepened a few days later when Maruja and Beatriz were abducted, because he interpreted their kidnapping as a sign that matters would be drawn out and complicated. This was the moment of conception for an escape plan that would become his irresistible obsession.

CONDITIONS FOR DIANA and her crew—five hundred kilometers north of Bogotá, and three months after their capture—were different from those of the other hostages, since holding two women and four men at the same time presented complex logistical and security problems. In Maruja's and Beatriz's prison, the surprising element was the total absence of leniency. In the case of Pacho Santos, it was the informal, easy behavior of the guards, who were all his age. In Diana's group, an improvisatory atmosphere kept captives and captors alike in a state of alarmed uncertainty; the instability infected everything and grated on everyone's nerves.

Diana's captivity was notable too for its migratory nature. During their long imprisonment the hostages were moved, with no explanation, at least twenty times, in Medellín and near it, to houses of differing styles and quality, and varying conditions. Perhaps this mobility was possible because their abductors, unlike those in Bogotá, were in their natural environment, over which they had complete control, and maintained direct contact with their superiors.

The hostages were not all together in the same house except on two occasions, and for only a few hours. At first they were divided into two groups: Richard, Orlando, and Hero Buss in one house, Diana, Azucena, and Juan Vitta in another not far away. Some of the moves came without warning—sudden, unplanned, no time to gather up their possessions because a police raid was imminent, almost always on foot down steep hillsides, slogging through mud in endless downpours. Diana was a strong, resilient woman, but those merciless, humiliating flights, in the physical and moral conditions of captivity, undermined her endurance. Other moves were heartstopping escapes through the streets of Medellín, in ordinary cabs, eluding checkpoints and street patrols. The hardest thing for all of them during the first few weeks was that they were prisoners and no one knew it. They watched television, listened to the radio, read the papers, but there was no report of their disappearance until September 14, when the news program "Criptón" announced, without citing sources, that they were not on assignment with the guerrillas but had been kidnapped by the Extraditables. And several more weeks had to go by before the Extraditables issued a formal acknowledgment of their abduction.

The person in charge of Diana's crew was an intelligent, easygoing Medellinese whom they all called don Pacho, with no last name or any other clue to his identity. He was about thirty but had the settled look of someone older. His mere presence had the immediate effect of solving the problems of daily living and sowing hope for the future. He brought the hostages gifts, books, candy, music cassettes, and kept them up-to-date on the war and other national news.

His appearances were infrequent, however, and he did not delegate authority well. The guards and couriers tended to be undisciplined, they were never masked and used nicknames taken from comic strips, and they carried oral or written messages—from one house to the other—that at least brought the hostages some comfort. During the first week the guards bought them the regulation sweatsuits, as well as toilet articles and local newspapers. Diana and Azucena played Parcheesi with them and often helped to prepare shopping lists. One of the guards made a remark that a stunned Azucena recorded in her notes: "Don't worry about money, that's one thing there's plenty of." At first the guards lived a chaotic life, playing music at top volume, not eating at regular hours, wandering through the house in their underwear. But Diana assumed a certain authority and imposed order. She obliged them to wear decent clothes, to lower the volume of the music that kept them awake, and even made one of them leave the room when he tried to sleep on a mattress next to her bed.

Azucena, at the age of twenty-eight, was a serene romantic who could not live without her husband after spending four years learning to live with him. She suffered attacks of imaginary jealousy and wrote him love letters knowing he would never receive them. During the first week of captivity she began to take daily notes that were very bold and quite useful in writing her book. She had worked on Diana's newscast for some years, and their relationship had never been more than professional, but they identified with each other in their misfortune. They read the papers together, talked all night, and tried to sleep until it was time for lunch. Diana was a compulsive conversationalist, and from her Azucena learned lessons about life that never would have been taught in school.

The members of her crew recall Diana as an intelligent, cheerful, animated companion, and an astute political analyst. When she felt discouraged, she confessed her sense of guilt for having involved them in this unforeseen adventure. "I don't care what happens to me," she said, "but if anything happens to you, I'll never have a moment's peace again." She was uneasy about Juan Vitta's health. An old friend, he had opposed the trip with great vehemence and even better arguments, and yet he had gone with her soon after his stay in the hospital because of a serious heart ailment. Diana could never forget it. On the first Sunday of their captivity, she came into his room in tears and asked if he didn't hate her for not having listened to him. Juan Vitta replied with absolute honesty. Yes, he had hated her with all his soul when they were told they were in the hands of the Extraditables, but he had come to accept captivity as a fate that could not be avoided. His initial rancor had also turned into guilt over his inability to talk her out of it.

For the moment, Hero Buss, Richard Becerra, and Orlando

Acevedo, who were in a nearby house, had fewer reasons for alarm. In the closets they had found an astonishing quantity of men's clothing still in the original packaging, with leading European designers' labels. The guards said that Pablo Escobar kept emergency wardrobes in various safe houses. "Go on, guys, ask for anything you want," they joked. "Transportation takes a little while, but in twelve hours we can satisfy any request." At first the amount of food and drink carried in by mule seemed the work of madmen. Hero Buss told them that no German could live without beer, and on the next trip they brought him three cases. "It was a carefree atmosphere," Hero Buss has said in his perfect Spanish. It was during this time that he persuaded a guard to take a picture of the three hostages peeling potatoes for lunch. Later, when photographs were forbidden in another house, he managed to hide an automatic camera on top of a closet and took a nice series of color slides of himself and Juan Vitta.

The guards played cards, dominoes, chess, but the hostages were no match for their irrational bets and sleight-of-hand cheating. They were all young. The youngest might have been fifteen and was proud of having won grand prize in a contest for the most police killed—two million pesos apiece. They were so contemptuous of money that Richard Becerra sold them sunglasses and his cameraman's jackets for a sum that would have purchased five new ones.

Sometimes, on cold nights, the guards smoked marijuana and played with their weapons. Twice they fired off shots by accident. One bullet went through the bathroom door and wounded a guard in the knee. When they heard on the radio that Pope John Paul II had called for the release of the hostages, one of the guards shouted:

"What the hell is that son of a bitch sticking his nose in for?"

Another guard jumped to his feet, offended by the insult, and the hostages had to intervene to keep them from pulling out their guns and shooting each other. Except for that incident, Hero Buss and Richard took everything as a joke to avoid bad feelings. Orlando, for his part, thought he was odd man out, that his name headed the list of those who would be executed.

At this time the captives had been divided into three groups in three different houses: Richard and Orlando in one, Hero Buss and Juan Vitta in another, and Diana and Azucena in a third. The first two groups were transported by taxi in plain view through snarled midtown traffic, while every security agency in Medellín was hunting for them. They were put in a house that was still under construction, into one two-by-two-meter room that was more like a cell, with a filthy unlit bathroom, and four men guarding them. They slept on two mattresses on the floor. In an adjoining room that was always locked, there was another hostage for whom—the guards said—they were demanding millions of pesos in ransom. A stout mulatto with a heavy gold chain around his neck, he was kept handcuffed and in total isolation.

The large, comfortable house where Diana and Azucena were taken and held for most of their captivity seemed to be the private residence of a high-ranking boss. They ate at the family table, took part in private conversations, listened to the latest CDs, Rocío Durcal and Juan Manuel Serrat among them, according to Azucena's notes. This was the house where Diana saw a television program filmed in her own apartment in Bogotá, which reminded her that she had hidden the keys to the armoire but could not recall if they were behind the cassettes or the television in the bedroom. She also realized she had forgotten to lock the safe in the rush to leave on her calamitous trip. "I hope nobody's rummaging around in there," she wrote in a letter to her mother. A few days later, on what seemed an ordinary television program, she received a reassuring reply.

Life in the house did not seem affected by the presence of the hostages. There were visits from women they did not know who treated them as if they were family and gave them medals and pictures of miracle-working saints in the hope they would help them go free. There were visits from entire families with their children and dogs who scampered through all the rooms. The worst thing was the bad weather. The few times the sun shone they could not go outside to enjoy it because there were always men working. Or, perhaps, they were guards dressed as bricklayers. Diana and Azucena took pictures of each other in bed, and there was no sign yet of any physical changes. In another taken of Diana three months later, she looked very thin and much older.

On September 19, when she learned of the abductions of Marina Montoya and Francisco Santos, Diana understood—with no access to information from the outside—that her kidnapping was not an isolated act, as she thought at first, but a long-term political operation to force the terms for Escobar's surrender. Don Pacho confirmed this: There was a select list of journalists and celebrities who would be abducted as necessary to further the interests of the abductors. It was then she decided to keep a diary, not so much to narrate her days as to record her states of mind and interpretations of events. She wrote down everything: anecdotes of her captivity, political analyses, human observations, one-sided dialogues with her family or with God, the Virgin, the Holy Infant. Several times she transcribed entire prayers—including the Our Father and Hail Mary—as an original, perhaps more profound way of saying prayers in writing.

It is obvious that Diana was not thinking about a text for publication but of a political and personal journal that the dynamic of events transformed into a poignant conversation with herself. She wrote in her large, rounded hand, clear-looking but difficult to decipher, that completely filled the spaces between the lines in her copybook. At first she wrote in secret, in the middle of the night, but when the guards discovered what she was doing they gave her enough paper and pencils to keep her busy while they slept.

She made the first entry on September 27, a week after the kidnapping of Marina and Pacho, and it read: "Since Wednesday the 19th, when the man in charge of this operation came here, so many things have happened that I can hardly catch my breath." She asked herself why their abduction had not been acknowledged by those responsible, and her reply to herself was so that perhaps they could kill them with no public outcry in the event the hostages did not serve their ends. "That's my understanding of it and it fills me with horror," she wrote. She was more concerned with her companions' condition than with her own, and was interested in news from any source that would allow her to draw conclusions about their situation. She had always been a practicing Catholic, like the rest of her family, her mother in particular, and as time passed her devotion would become more intense and profound until it reached mystical states. She prayed to God and the Virgin for everyone who had anything to do with her life, even Pablo Escobar. "He may have more need of your help," she wrote to God in her diary. "May it be your will that he see the good and avoid more grief, and I ask you to help him understand our situation."

THERE IS NO DOUBT that the most difficult thing for everyone was learning to live with the guards. The four assigned to Maruja and Beatriz were young, uneducated, brutal, and volatile boys who worked in twos for twelve-hour shifts, sitting on the floor, their submachine guns at the ready. All in T-shirts with advertisements printed on them, sneakers, and shorts they had cut themselves with shears. When the shift came in at six in the morning, one could sleep until nine while the other stood guard, but both would almost always fall asleep at the same time. Maruja and Beatriz thought that if a police assault team raided the house early in the morning, the guards would not have time to wake up.

The boys' common condition was absolute fatalism. They knew they were going to die young, they accepted it, and cared only about living for the moment. They made excuses to themselves for their reprehensible work: It meant helping the family, buying nice clothes, having motorcycles, and ensuring the happiness of their mothers, whom they adored above all else in the world and for whose sakes they were willing to die. They venerated the same Holy Infant and Lady of Mercy worshipped by their captives, and prayed to them every day with perverse devotion, for they implored their protection and forgiveness and made vows and sacrifices so that their crimes would be successful. Second only to the saints, they worshipped Rohypnol, a tranquilizer that allowed them to commit movie exploits in real life. "You mix it with beer and get high right away," explained one guard. "Then somebody lends you a good knife and you steal a car and go for a ride. The fun is how scared they look when they hand you the keys." They despised everything else: politicians, the government, the state, the law, the police, all of society. Life, they said, was shit.

At first it was impossible to tell them apart because the only thing the women could see was their masks, and all the guards looked the same. In other words, like only one guard. In time they learned that masks can hide faces but not character. This was how they individualized them. Each mask had a different identity, its own personality, an unmistakable voice. Even more: It had a heart. Without wanting to, they came to share the loneliness of confinement with them. They played cards and dominoes and helped each other solve crosswords and puzzles in old magazines.

Marina was submissive to her jailers' rules, but she was not impartial. She was fond of some and despised others, gossiped to them about the others as if she were their mother, and sooner or later provoked internal discord that threatened peace in the room. But she obliged them to pray the rosary, and they all did.

Among the guards on duty during the first month, there was one who suffered from sudden and recurrent fits of rage. They called him Barrabás. He adored Marina and caressed and flirted with her. But from the first day he was Maruja's bitter enemy. With no warning he would go wild, kicking the television and banging his head against the wall.

The strangest guard was somber, silent, very thin, and almost six and a half feet tall. He wore a second dark-blue sweatshirt hood on top of his mask, like a demented monk. And that's what they called him: Monk. For long periods he would crouch down in a kind of trance. He must have been there a long time because Marina knew him very well and singled him out for special favors. He would bring her gifts when he came back from his time off, including a plastic crucifix that Marina hung around her neck on the ordinary string it had when she received it. She was the only hostage who had seen his face: Before Maruja and Beatriz arrived, none of the guards wore a mask or did anything to hide his identity. Marina had interpreted this as a sign she would not leave her prison alive. She said he was a good-looking teenager with the most beautiful eyes she had ever seen, and Beatriz believed it because his lashes were so long and curly they protruded from the holes in his mask. He was capable of the best and worst actions. It was he who discovered that Beatriz wore a chain with a medal of the Virgin of Miracles.

"No chains are allowed here," he said. "You have to give that to me."

Beatriz protested, distraught.

"You can't take it away," she said. "That would be a really bad omen, something awful will happen to me."

Her distress was contagious and affected him. He said medals were not allowed because they might have long-distance electronic trackers inside. But he found the solution:

"Here's what we can do," he proposed. "You keep the chain but give me the medal. I'm sorry, but those are my orders."

Spots, on the other hand, suffered panic attacks and was obsessed by the idea that he would be killed. He heard imaginary noises, and he pretended to have a huge scar on his face, perhaps to confuse anyone trying to identify him. He cleaned everything he touched with alcohol so he would leave no fingerprints. Marina made fun of him, but he could not control his manias. He would wake with a start in the middle of the night. "Listen!" he whispered in terror. "It's the cops!" One night he put out the candle and Maruja walked into the bathroom door, hitting her head so hard she almost passed out. To make matters worse, Spots shouted at her for not knowing how to walk in the dark.

"Cut it out," she stood up to him. "This isn't a gangster movie."

The guards seemed like hostages too. They were not allowed in the rest of the house, and when they were not on duty they slept in another room that was padlocked so they could not escape. They were all from the Antioquian countryside, they did not know Bogotá, and one said that when they had time off, every three or four weeks, they were blindfolded or put in the trunk of the car so they would not know where they were. Another was afraid he would be killed when he was no longer needed, a guarantee he would take his secrets to the grave. Bosses in hoods and better clothes would put in irregular appearances to receive reports and give instructions. Their decisions were unpredictable, and both the hostages and the guards were at their mercy.

The captives' breakfast—coffee and a corncake with sausage on top—would arrive at any hour. For lunch they had beans or lentils in grayish water, bits of meat in puddles of grease, a spoonful of rice, and a soda. They had to eat sitting on the mattress because there was no chair in the room, and they had to use only a spoon because knives and forks were not allowed for reasons of security. At supper they made do with reheated beans and other leftovers from lunch.

The guards said that the owner of the house, whom they called the majordomo, kept most of their allotment of money. He was a robust man in his forties, of medium height, whose satyr's face could be guessed at from his nasal voice and the tired, bloodshot eyes visible through the holes in his hood. He lived with a short, shrill woman who wore shabby clothes and had rotting teeth. Her name was Damaris, and she sang salsa, *vallenatos*, and *bambucos* all day at the top of her lungs and with the ear of an artilleryman but with so much enthusiasm it was impossible not to imagine her dancing alone to her own music in every room of the house.

The plates, glasses, and sheets were used over and over again without being washed until the hostages protested. The toilet could be flushed only four times a day, and the bathroom was locked on Sundays when the family went out so the neighbors would not hear the sound of running water. The guards urinated in the sink or the shower drain. Damaris attempted to conceal her negligence only when she heard the bosses' helicopter, and then she moved like lightning, using a fireman's technique to wash down floors and walls with a hose. She watched soap operas every morning until one, the hour when she tossed the food for lunch into a pressure cooker—meat, vegetables, potatoes, beans all mixed together—and heated it until the whistle blew.

Her frequent arguments with her husband displayed a capacity for rage and an originality in creating curses that sometimes reached inspired heights. She had two daughters, aged nine and seven, who attended a nearby school and on occasion invited other children to watch television or play in the courtyard. Their teacher dropped in from time to time on Saturdays, and other noisier friends came by any day of the week and had impromptu parties with music. Then the door of the room was padlocked and those inside had to turn off the radio, watch television without the sound, and not use the bathroom even in an emergency.

TOWARD THE END of October, Diana Turbay observed that Azucena was distracted and melancholy. She had not spoken the whole day, and was in no frame of mind to talk about anything. This was not unusual: Her powers of concentration were extraordinary, above all when she was reading, in particular if the book was the Bible. But this time her silence coincided with her alarming mood and exceptional pallor. After some urging, she revealed to Diana that for the past two weeks she had been afraid she was pregnant. Her calculations were exact. She had been a hostage for more than fifty days, and had missed two periods in a row. Diana was overjoyed at the good news—a typical reaction for her—but took responsibility for Azucena's distress.

On one of his early visits, don Pacho had promised them that they would be released on the first Thursday in October. They believed him because major changes occurred: better treatment, better food, greater freedom of movement. And yet there was always some pretext for shifting the date. After the Thursday had passed, they were told they would be freed on December 9 to celebrate the election of the Constituent Assembly. And so it continued—Christmas, New Year's Day, Epiphany, somebody's birthday—in a string of delays that seemed like little spoonfuls of consolation.

Don Pacho continued to visit them in November. He brought new books, current newspapers, back issues of magazines, and boxes of chocolates. He spoke about the other hostages. When Diana learned she was not the prisoner of Father Pérez, she was determined to have an interview with Pablo Escobar, not so much to publish it—if in fact it was true—as for the chance to discuss with him the terms of his surrender. At the end of October, don Pacho said her request had been approved. But the newscasts of November 7 struck the first mortal blow to her illusions: The broadcast of the soccer game between Medellín and El Nacional was interrupted by the announcement that Maruja Pachón and Beatriz Villamizar had been abducted.

Juan Vitta and Hero Buss heard the announcement in their prison and thought it the worst news possible. They too had reached the conclusion that they were no more than extras in a horror film. "Just filler," as Juan Vitta said. "Disposable," as the guards said. One of them, during a heated argument, had shouted at Hero Buss:

"You shut up! Nobody invited you here!"

Juan Vitta sank into a depression, stopped eating, slept badly, felt lost, and opted for the merciful solution of dying just once instead of a thousand times a day. He looked pale, one arm was numb, he found it difficult to breathe, his dreams were terrifying. His only conversations were with his dead relatives whom he saw standing around his bed. An alarmed Hero Buss created a Germanic uproar. "If Juan dies here, you're responsible," he told the guards. They heeded the warning.

The physician they brought in was Dr. Conrado Prisco Lopera, the brother of David Ricardo and Armando Alberto Prisco Lopera—of the famous Prisco gang—who had worked with Pablo Escobar since his early days as a trafficker, and were known as the creators of the crew of adolescent killers from the northeastern slums of Medellín. They were said to be the leaders of a gang of teenage assassins who took on the dirtiest jobs, among them guarding hostages. On the other hand, Conrado was deemed an honorable professional by the medical community, and the only mark against him was being, or having been, Pablo Escobar's principal physician. He wore no mask when he came in and surprised Hero Buss by greeting him in fluent German:

"Hallo Hero, wie geht's uns."

It was a providential visit for Juan Vitta, not because of the diagnosis—severe stress—but for the good it did him as a passionate reader. The only treatment the doctor prescribed was a dose of decent reading—just the opposite of the political news Dr. Prisco Lopera was in the habit of bringing, which for the captives was like a potion capable of killing the healthiest man.

Diana's malaise grew worse in November—severe headaches, attacks of colitis, intense depression—but there are no indications in her diary that the doctor visited her. She thought the depression might have been caused by the paralysis in her situation, which grew more uncertain as the year drew to a close. "Time passes here in a way we're not used to dealing with," she wrote. "There's no enthusiasm about anything." A note from this period spoke of the pessimism that was crushing her: "I've reexamined my life up to this point: so many love affairs, so much immaturity in making important decisions, so much time wasted on worthless things!" Her profession occupied a special place in this drastic stocktaking: "Though my convictions grow stronger about what the practice of journalism is and what it should be, I don't see it with any clarity or breadth." Her doubts did not spare even her own magazine, "which I see as so poor, not only financially but editorially." And she judged without flinching: "It lacks profundity and analysis."

The days of all the hostages, despite their separation, were spent waiting for don Pacho; his visits were always announced, rarely took place, and were their measure of time. They heard small planes and helicopters flying over the house and had the impression they were routine surveillance flights. But each one mobilized the guards, who assumed combat positions, weapons at the ready. The hostages knew, because it had been repeated so often, that in the event of an armed attack, the guards would begin by killing them.

In spite of everything, November ended with a certain amount of hope. Azucena Liévano's doubts melted away: Her symptoms were a false pregnancy, perhaps brought on by nervous tension. But she did not celebrate. On the contrary: After her initial fear, the idea of having a baby had become a desire, and she promised herself she would satisfy it as soon as she was released. Diana also saw signs of hope in statements by the Notables regarding the possibility of an agreement.

THE REST OF NOVEMBER had been a time of accommodation for Maruja and Beatriz. Each in her own way devised a survival strategy. Beatriz, who is brave and strong willed, took refuge in the consolation of minimizing reality. She dealt very well with the first ten days, but soon realized that the situation was more complex and hazardous than she had thought, and she faced adversity by looking away from it. Maruja, who is a coldly analytic woman despite her almost irrational optimism, had known from the start that she was facing an alien reality, and that her captivity would be long and difficult. She hid inside herself like a snail in its shell, hoarded her energy, and reflected deeply until she grew used to the inescapable idea that she might die. "We're not getting out of here alive," she thought, and was astonished that this fatalistic revelation had a contrary effect. From then on she felt in control of herself, able to endure everything and everybody, and, through persuasion, to make the discipline less rigid. By the third week of captivity, television had become unbearable; they had used up the crossword puzzles and the few readable articles in the entertainment magazines they had found in the room, the remains, perhaps, of some previous abduction. But even at her worst times, and as she always did in her real life, Maruja set aside two hours each day for absolute solitude.

In spite of everything, the news early in December indicated that there were reasons for them to be hopeful. As soon as Marina made her terrible predictions, Maruja began to invent optimistic games. Marina caught on right away: One of the guards had raised his thumb in a gesture of approval, and that meant things were going well. Once Damaris did not go to market, and this was interpreted as a sign she did not have to because they would be released soon. They played at visualizing how they would be freed, and they set the date and the method that would be used. Since they lived in gloom, they imagined they would be released on a sunny day and have a party on the terrace of Maruja's apartment. "What do you want to eat?" Beatriz asked. Marina, who was a skilled cook, recited a menu fit for a queen. They began it as a game, and it ended as a truth: They dressed to go out, they made each other up. On December 9, one of the dates that had been mentioned for their release because of the elections to the Constituent Assembly, they were ready, even for the press conference: They had prepared every answer. The day passed in nervous anticipation but ended without bitterness, because Maruja was certain, beyond the shadow of a doubt, that sooner or later her husband would free them.

4

THE ABDUCTION of the journalists was, in effect, a response to the idea that had preoccupied President César Gaviria since the time he was a minister in Virgilio Barco's government: how to create a judicial alternative to the war against terrorism. It had been a central theme in his campaign for the presidency. He had emphasized it in his acceptance speech, making the important distinction that terrorism by the drug traffickers was a national problem and might have a national solution, while the drug traffic was international and could only have international solutions. His first priority was narcoterrorism, for after the first bombs, public opinion demanded prison for the terrorists, after the next few bombings the demand was for extradition, but as the bombs continued to explode public opinion began to demand amnesty. For this reason, extradition had to be considered an emergency measure that would pressure the criminals into surrendering, and Gaviria was prepared to apply that pressure without hesitation.

In the first days after he took office, Gaviria barely had time to talk to anyone; he was exhausted by the job of organizing his government and convening a Constituent Assembly that would undertake the first major reform of the state in over a hundred years. Rafael Pardo had shared his concern with terrorism ever since the assassination of Luis Carlos Galán. But he too was caught up in endless organizational duties. He was in a peculiar position. His appointment as adviser on security and public order had been one of the first in a government palace shaken by the renovative drive of one of this century's youngest presidents, a Beatles fan and an avid reader of poetry, who had given his ideas for drastic changes a modest name: "The Shake-up," the *Revolcón*. Pardo walked through this windstorm carrying the briefcase he always had with him, working wherever he could find space. His daughter Laura thought he had lost his job because he did not leave for work or come home at regular hours. The truth is that the informality imposed by circumstances was well suited to Rafael Pardo, whose nature was more that of a lyric poet than a governmental bureaucrat. He was thirty-eight years old, with a solid academic background: a diploma from the Gimnasio Moderno in Bogotá, a degree in economics from the University of the Andes, where for nine years he had been a teacher and researcher in that same field, and a graduate degree in planning from the Institute for Social Sciences in The Hague. He was also a voracious reader of every book he could lay his hands on, in particular those dealing with two dissimilar subjects: poetry and security. He owned four ties, which he had received for Christmas over the past four years; he never chose to put them on but carried one in his pocket for emergencies. He never noticed if his trousers and jackets matched, was so absentminded that his socks were often different colors, and whenever possible he was in shirtsleeves because he made no distinction between heat and cold. His greatest excesses were poker games with his daughter Laura until two in the morning, played in absolute silence and using beans instead of money. Claudia, his beautiful and patient wife, would become irritated because he wandered the house like a sleepwalker, not knowing where the water glasses were kept or how to close a door or take ice cubes from the freezer, and he had an almost magical faculty for ignoring the things he despised. And yet his most uncommon traits were a statue's impassivity that did not give the slightest clue as to what he was thinking, and a merciless talent for ending a conversation with two or three words, or a heated discussion with a single polished monosyllable.

His office and university colleagues, however, could not understand his lack of standing at home, for they knew him as an intelligent, organized worker who possessed an almost terrifying serenity, and whose befuddled air was no doubt intended to befuddle others. He became irritated with simple problems, displayed great patience with lost causes, and had a strong will tempered by an imperturbable, sardonic sense of humor. President Virgilio Barco must have recognized how useful his hermeticism and fondness for mysteries could be, for he put him in charge of negotiations with the guerrillas, and the rehabilitation programs in war zones, and in that capacity he achieved the peace accords with the M-19. President Gaviria, who was his equal in secretiveness and unfathomable silences, appointed him head of security and public order in one of the least secure and most disordered countries in the world. Pardo assumed the post carrying his entire office in his briefcase, and for two weeks had to ask permission to use the bathroom or the telephone in other people's offices. But the president often consulted with him on a variety of subjects, and listened with premonitory attention when he spoke at difficult meetings. One afternoon, when they were alone in the president's office, Gaviria asked him a question:

"Tell me something, Rafael, aren't you worried that one of these guys will suddenly turn himself in and we won't have any charge to arrest him with?"

It was the essence of the problem: The terrorists hunted by the police would not surrender because they had no guarantees for their own safety or the safety of their families. And the state had no evidence that would convict them if they were captured. The idea was to find a judicial formula by which they would confess their crimes in exchange for the state's guarantee of protection for them and their families. Rafael Pardo had worked on the problem for the previous government, and when Gaviria asked the question, he still had his notes among all the other papers in his briefcase. They were, in effect, the beginning of a solution: Whoever surrendered would have his sentence reduced if he confessed to a crime that would allow the government to prosecute, and a further sentence reduction if he turned goods and money over to the state. That was all, but the president could envision the entire plan because it was consonant with his own idea of a strategy focused not on war or peace but on law, one that would be responsive to the terrorists' arguments but not renounce the compelling threat of extradition.

President Gaviria proposed it to Jaime Giraldo Angel, his justice minister, who understood the concept immediately; he too had been thinking for some time about ways to move the problem of drug trafficking into a judicial framework. And both men favored the extradition of Colombian nationals as a means of forcing surrender.

Giraldo Angel, with his air of a distracted savant, his verbal precision, and his genius for organization, completed the formula, adding some of his own ideas combined with others already established in the penal code. Between Saturday and Sunday he composed a first draft on a laptop computer, and first thing Monday morning showed the president a copy that still had his handwritten deletions and corrections. The title, written in ink across the top of the first page, was a seed of historic importance: "Capitulation to the Law."

Gaviria is meticulous about his projects and would not present them to his Council of Ministers until he was certain they would be approved. He therefore reviewed the draft in detail with Giraldo Angel and with Rafael Pardo, who is not a lawyer but whose sparing comments tend to be accurate. Then he sent a revised version to the Council on Security, where Giraldo Angel found support from General Oscar Botero, the defense minister, and the head of Criminal Investigation, Carlos Eduardo Mejía Escobar, a young, effective jurist who would be responsible for implementing the decree in the real world. General Maza Márquez did not oppose the plan, though he believed that in the struggle against the Medellín cartel, any formula other than war would be useless. "This country won't be put right," he would say, "as long as Escobar is alive." For he was certain Escobar would only surrender in order to continue trafficking from prison under the government's protection.

The project was presented to the Council of Ministers with the specification that the plan did not propose negotiations with terrorism in order to conjure away a human tragedy for which the consuming nations bore primary responsibility. On the contrary: The aim was to make extradition a more useful judicial weapon in the fight against narcotraffic by making non-extradition the grand prize in a package of incentives and guarantees for those who surrendered to the law.

One of the crucial discussions concerned the time limits for the crimes that judges would have to consider. This meant that no crime committed after the issuing date of the decree would be protected. The secretary general of the presidency, Fabio Villegas, who was the most lucid opponent of time limits, based his position on a cogent argument: When the period of pardonable offenses ended, the government would have no policy. The majority, however, agreed with the president that for the moment they should not extend the time limits because of the certain risk that this would become a license for lawbreakers to continue breaking the law until they decided to turn themselves in.

To protect the government from any suspicion of illegal or unethical negotiations, Gaviria and Giraldo Angel agreed not to meet with any direct emissary from the Extraditables while the trials were in progress, and not to negotiate any question of law with them or with anyone else. In other words, they would not discuss principles but only procedural matters. The national head of Criminal Investigation—who is not dependent on or appointed by the chief executive—would be the official in charge of communicating with the Extraditables or their legal representatives. All exchanges would be written and, therefore, on record.

The proposed decree was discussed with an intensity and secrecy that are in no way usual in Colombia, and was approved on September 5, 1990. This was Decree 2047 under Martial Law: Those who surrendered and confessed to their crimes could receive the right not to be extradited; those who confessed and also cooperated with the authorities would have their sentences reduced, up to a third for surrender and confession, up to a sixth for providing information—in short, up to half of the sentence imposed for one or all the crimes for which extradition had been requested. It was law in its simplest, purest form: the gallows and the club. The same Council of Ministers that signed the decree rejected three extradition requests and approved three others, a kind of public announcement that the new government would view non-extradition only as a privilege granted under the decree.

In reality, rather than an isolated decree, this was part of a well-defined presidential policy for fighting terrorism in general, not only narcoterrorism but common criminal acts as well. General Maza Márquez did not express to the Council on Security what he really thought of the decree, but some years later, in his campaign for the presidency, he censured it without mercy as "a fallacy of the times." "With it the majesty of the law is demeaned," he wrote, "and traditional respect for the penal code is undermined."

The road was long and complex. The Extraditables—which everyone knew was a trade name for Pablo Escobar—rejected the decree out-of-hand while leaving doors open so they could continue to fight for much more. Their principal argument was that it did not state in an incontrovertible way that they would not be extradited. They also wanted to be considered as political offenders and therefore receive the same treatment as the M-19 guerrillas, who had been pardoned and recognized as a political party. One of the M-19's members was the minister of health, and all of them were participating in the campaign for the Constituent Assembly. Another concern of the Extraditables was the question of a secure prison where they would be safe from their enemies, and guarantees of protection for their families and followers.

It was said that the government had issued the decree as a concession to the traffickers under the pressure of the abductions. In fact, it had been in the planning stage before Diana's kidnapping, and had already been issued when the Extraditables tightened the vise with the almost simultaneous abductions of Francisco Santos and Marina Montoya. Later, when eight hostages were not enough to get them what they wanted, they took Maruja Pachón and Beatriz Villamizar. That was the magic number: nine journalists. Plus one—already condemned to death—who was the sister of a politician hunted by Escobar's private police force. In this sense, before the decree could prove its efficacy, President Gaviria began to be the victim of his own creation.

LIKE HER FATHER, Diana Turbay Quintero had an intense, passionate feeling for power, a capacity for leadership that shaped her life. She grew up surrounded by the great names in politics, and it was to be expected that she would have a political perspective on the world. "Diana was a stateswoman," a friend who understood and loved her has said. "And the central concern of her life was a stubborn desire to serve her country." But power—like love—is a double-edged sword: One wields it and is wounded by it. It generates a state of pure exaltation and, at the same time, its opposite: the search for an irresistible, fugitive joy, comparable only to the search for an idealized love that one longs for but fears, pursues but never attains. Diana experienced an insatiable hunger to know everything, be involved in everything, discover the why and how of things, the reason for her life. Some of those who were close to her perceived this in the uncertainties of her heart, and believed she was not happy very often.

It is impossible to know—without asking her the question directly—which of the two edges of power inflicted the more serious wounds. She must have felt them in her own flesh when she was her father's private secretary and right hand at the age of twenty-eight, and found herself trapped in the crosswinds of power. Her friends—and she had many—have said she was one of the most intelligent people they had ever known, with an unsuspected store of knowledge, an astonishing capacity for analysis, and a supernatural gift for sensing another person's most hidden agenda. Her enemies say straight out that she was a disruptive influence behind the throne. But others think she disregarded her own well-being in a single-minded desire to defend her father against everything and everybody, and could therefore be used by hypocrites and flatterers.

She was born on March 8, 1950, under the inclement sign of Pisces, at a time when her father was already in line for the presidency. She was an innate leader wherever she happened to be: the Colegio Andino in Bogotá, the Academy of the Sacred Heart in New York, or Saint Thomas Aquinas University of Bogotá, where she completed her law studies but did not wait to receive her degree.

Her belated career in journalism—which is, fortunately, power without the throne—must have been a reencounter with the best in herself. She founded the magazine *Hoy x Hoy* and the television news journal "Criptón" as a more direct way to work for peace. "I'm not ready to fight anymore, or give anybody any arguments," she said at the time. "I've become totally conciliatory." To the point where she sat down to talk about peace with Carlos Pizarro, the commander of the M-19, who had fired the rocket that just missed the room where President Turbay had been sitting. The friend who told this story says, with a laugh: "Diana understood that in this business she had to be a chess player, not a boxer punching at the world."

And therefore it was only natural that her abduction—above and beyond its emotional impact—would have a political weight that was difficult to control. Former President Turbay said, in public and in private, that he had heard nothing from the Extraditables, because this seemed the most prudent course until it was known what they wanted, but in fact he had received a message from them soon after the kidnapping of Francisco Santos. He had told Hernando Santos about it as soon as Santos returned from Italy, when Turbay invited him to his house to devise a common strategy. Santos found Turbay in the semi-darkness of his immense library, devastated by the certainty that Diana and Francisco would be executed. What struck him—and everyone else who saw Turbay during this time—was the dignity with which he bore his misfortune.

The letter addressed to both men consisted of three handwritten pages printed in block letters, with no signature, and an unexpected salutation: "A respectful greeting from the Extraditables." What did not permit any doubt regarding its authenticity was the concise, direct, unequivocal style typical of Pablo Escobar. It began by taking responsibility for the abduction of the two journalists who, the letter said, were "in good health and in good conditions of captivity that can be considered normal in such cases." The rest was a brief against abuses committed by the police. Then it stated three nonnegotiable conditions for the release of the hostages: total suspension of military operations against them in Medellín and Bogotá; withdrawal of the Elite Corps, the special police unit dedicated to the fight against drug trafficking; dismissal of its commander and twenty other officers accused of responsibility for the torture and murder of some four hundred young men from the northeastern slums of Medellín. If these conditions were not met, the Extraditables would undertake a war of extermination, including bombings in major cities and the assassinations of judges, politicians, and journalists. The conclusion was simple: "If there is a coup, then welcome to it. We don't have much to lose."

Their written response, with no preliminary discussions, was to be delivered within three days to the Hotel Intercontinental in Medellín, where a room would be reserved in Hernando Santos's name. The Extraditables would choose the intermediaries for any further communications. Santos agreed with Turbay's decision not to say anything about this message, or any that might follow, until they had more substantive information. "We cannot allow ourselves to be anybody's messengers to the president," Turbay concluded, "or to behave in an improper way."

Turbay suggested to Santos that each of them write a separate response, which they would then combine into a single letter. This was done. The result, in essence, was a formal statement to the effect that they had no power to interfere in governmental matters but were prepared to make public any violation of the law or of human rights for which the Extraditables had conclusive evidence. As for the police raids, they reminded the Extraditables that they had no means to stop them, could not seek to have the twenty accused men removed from office without proof, or write editorials against a situation they knew nothing about.

Aldo Buenaventura, a public notary and solicitor, a fervent aficionado of the bullfights since his student days at the Liceo Nacional in Zipaquirá, and an old and trusted friend of Hernando Santos's, agreed to carry the letter. No sooner had he walked into room 308 at the Hotel Intercontinental, than the phone rang.

"Are you Señor Santos?"

"No," Aldo replied, "but I am here as his representative."

"Did you bring the package?"

The voice sounded so proprietary that Aldo wondered if it was Pablo Escobar himself, and he said he had. Two young men who dressed and behaved like executives came to the room. Aldo gave them the letter. They shook his hand with well-bred bows and left.

In less than a week, Turbay and Santos were visited by Guido Parra Montoya, an Antioquian lawyer, who had another letter from the Extraditables. Parra was not unknown to political circles in Bogotá, but he always seemed to live in the shadows. He was forty-eight years old, had served twice in the Chamber of Deputies as a replacement for two Liberal representatives, and once as a principal for the National Popular Alliance (ANAPO), which gave rise to the M-19. He had been an adviser to the judicial office of the presidency in the government of Carlos Lleras Restrepo. In Medellín, where he had practiced law since his youth, he was arrested on May 10, 1990, on suspicion of abetting terrorism, and released two weeks later because the case lacked merit. Despite these and other lapses, he was considered an expert lawyer and a good negotiator.

However, as a confidential representative of the Extraditables, it was hard to imagine anyone less likely to be self-effacing. He was one of those men who take ceremony seriously. He wore silver-gray suits, which were the executive uniform of the time, with bright-colored shirts and youthful ties with wide Italian-style knots. His manners were punctilious, his rhetoric high-flown, and he was more obsequious than affable—suicidal circumstances if one wishes to serve two masters at the same time. In the presence of a former Liberal president and the publisher of the most important newspaper in the country, his eloquence knew no bounds. "My illustrious Dr. Turbay, my distinguished Dr. Santos, I am completely at your service," he said, and then made the kind of slip that can cost a man his life:

"I am Pablo Escobar's attorney."

Hernando caught the error in midflight.

"Then the letter you've brought is from him?"

"No," Guido Parra corrected the mistake without batting an eye, "it is from the Extraditables, but you should direct your response to Escobar because he will be able to influence the negotiation."

The distinction was important, because Escobar left no clues for the police. Compromising letters, such as those dealing with the abductions, were printed in block letters and signed by the Extraditables or a simple first name: Manuel, Gabriel, Antonio. When he played the part of accuser, however, he wrote in his own, rather childish hand, and not only signed the letters with his name and rubric but drove the point home with his thumbprint. At the time the journalists were abducted, it would have been reasonable to doubt his very existence. The Extraditables may have been no more than his pseudonym, but the opposite was also possible: Perhaps Pablo Escobar's identity was nothing more than a front for the Extraditables.

Guido Parra always seemed prepared to go beyond what the Extraditables stated in writing. But everything had to be examined with a magnifying glass. What he really wanted for his clients was the kind of political treatment the guerrillas had received. He brought up the question of internationalizing the narcotics problem by proposing the participation of the United Nations. Yet in the face of Santos's and Turbay's categorical refusal, he was ready with a variety of alternative suggestions. This was the beginning of a long, fruitless process that would go in circles until it reached a dead end.

After the second letter, Santos and Turbay communicated in person with the president. Gaviria saw them at eight-thirty in the evening in the small room off his private library. He was calmer than usual, and anxious to have news about the hostages. Turbay and Santos brought him up-to-date regarding the two exchanges of letters and the mediation of Guido Parra.

"A bad emissary," said the president. "Very smart, a good lawyer, but extremely dangerous. Of course, he does have Escobar's complete backing."

He read the letters with the power of concentration that always impressed everyone: as if he had become invisible. His complete comments were ready when he finished, and his conjectures on the subject were laconic. He said that none of the intelligence agencies had the slightest idea where the hostages were being held. The important news for the president was confirmation that they were in the hands of Pablo Escobar.

That night Gaviria demonstrated his skill at questioning everything before reaching a final decision. He thought it possible that the letters were not genuine, that Guido Parra was working for somebody else, even that it was all a clever ploy by someone who had nothing to do with Escobar. Santos and Turbay left more discouraged than when they came in, for the president seemed to view the case as a serious problem of state that left very little room for his own feelings.

A major obstacle to an agreement was that Escobar continued to change the terms as his own situation evolved, delaying the release of the hostages in order to obtain additional, unforeseen advantages while waiting for the Constituent Assembly to pass judgment on extradition, and perhaps on a pardon. This was never made clear in the astute correspondence that Escobar maintained with the families of the hostages. But it was very clear in the secret correspondence he maintained with Guido Parra to instruct him in strategy and the long-term view of the negotiation. "It's a good idea for you to convey all concerns to Santos so we don't get further entangled in this," he said in one letter. "Because it must be in writing, in a decree, that under no circumstances will we be extradited, not for any crime, not to any country." He also asked for specific details regarding the confession required for surrender. Two other essential points were security at the special prison, and protection for families and followers.

HERNANDO SANTOS's friendship with former President Turbay, which had always had its foundation in politics, now became personal and very close. They could spend hours sitting across from each other in absolute silence. Not a day went by that they did not speak on the phone, exchanging their intimate thoughts, secret assumptions, new information. They even devised a code for handling confidential matters.

It could not have been easy. Hernando Santos is a man with extraordinary responsibilities: With a single word he could save or destroy a life. He is emotional and raw-nerved, and has a tribal sense of family that weighs heavily in his decisions. Those who accompanied him during his son's captivity were afraid he would not survive the blow. He did not eat, or sleep through the night, he always kept a telephone within reach and grabbed at it on the first ring. During those months of grief, he socialized very little, received psychiatric counseling to help him endure his son's death, which he viewed as inevitable, and lived in seclusion, in his office or rooms, looking at his brilliant collection of stamps, and letters scorched in airplane accidents. Elena Calderón, his wife and the mother of his seven children, had died seven years earlier, and he was truly alone. His heart and vision problems grew worse, and he made no effort to hold back his tears. His exemplary virtue in these dramatic circumstances was keeping the newspaper separate from his personal tragedy.

One of his essential supports in that bitter period was the strength of his daughter-in-law María Victoria. Her memory of the days following the abduction was of her house invaded by relatives and her husband's friends who stretched out on the carpets and drank whiskey and coffee until the small hours of the morning. They always said the same thing, while the impact of the abduction, the very image of the victim, grew fainter. When Hernando came back from Italy, he went straight to María Victoria's house and greeted her with so much emotion that she broke down, but when he had anything confidential to say about the kidnapping, he asked her to leave him alone with the men. María Victoria, who has a strong character and mature intelligence, realized she had always been a marginal figure in a male-dominated family. She cried for an entire day, but in the end she was fortified by the determination to have her own identity and place in her own house. Hernando not only understood her reasoning but reproached himself for his own thoughtlessness, and he found in her the greatest support in his sorrow. From then on they maintained an invincible intimacy, whether face-to-face, or on the telephone, or in writing, or through an intermediary, and even by telepathy: In the most intricate family meetings they only needed to exchange glances to know what the other was thinking, and what they should say. She had some very good ideas, among them to publish editorial notes in the paper—making no effort to conceal their purpose—to let Pacho know about events in the life of the family.

THE LEAST-REMEMBERED victims were Liliana Rojas Arias, the wife of the cameraman Orlando Acevedo, and Martha Lupe Rojas, Richard Becerra's mother. Though they were not close friends, or relatives—despite their last names—the abduction made them inseparable. "Not so much because of our pain," Liliana has said, "but to keep each other company."

Liliana was nursing Erick Yesid, her eighteen-month-old son, when "Criptón" called to tell her that Diana Turbay's entire crew had been abducted. She was twenty-four years old, had been married for three, and lived on the second floor of her in-laws' house in the San Andrés district in southern Bogotá. "She's such a happy girl," a friend has said, "she didn't deserve such ugly news." And imaginative as well as happy, because when she recovered from the initial blow she sat the child in front of the television set during the news programs so that he could see his daddy, and continued to do this without fail until his release.

Both she and Martha Lupe were informed by the people at the news program that they would continue to provide them with money, and when Liliana's son became sick, they took care of the expenses. Nydia Quintero, Diana's mother, also called the two women to try to imbue them with a serenity she herself never had.

She promised that all the efforts she made with the government would be not only for her daughter but also for the entire crew, and that she would pass on any information she received about the hostages. And she did.

Martha Lupe lived with her two daughters, who were then fourteen and eleven years old, and was supported by Richard. When he left with Diana's team, he said it would be a three-day trip, so that after the first week she began to feel uneasy. She does not believe it was a premonition, she has said, but the fact is that she called the news program over and over again until they told her that something strange had happened. A little while later it was announced that the crew had been abducted. From then on she played the radio all day, waiting for them to be returned, and called the show whenever her heart told her to. She was troubled by the thought that her son was the most vulnerable of the hostages. "But all I could do was cry and pray," she says. Nydia Quintero convinced her there were many other things she could do for their release. She invited her to civic and religious meetings and filled her with her own fighting spirit. Liliana had a similar feeling about Orlando, and this caught her in a dilemma: He might be the last one executed because he was the least valuable, or the first because his death would provoke the same public out-cry but with fewer serious consequences for the kidnappers. This idea made her burst into uncontrollable weeping, and continued to do so throughout his entire captivity. "Every night after I put the baby to bed, I would sit on the terrace and cry, watching the door so I would see him come in," she has said. "And that is what I did, night after night, until I saw him again."

IN MID-OCTOBER Dr. Turbay called Hernando Santos with a message worded in their personal code. "I have some very good newspapers if you're interested in bullfighting. I'll send them to you if you like." Hernando understood this to mean an important development concerning the hostages. In fact, it was a cassette sent to Dr. Turbay's house and postmarked Montería, the evidence that Diana and her companions were still alive, which the family had asked for over and over again during the past few weeks. The voice was unmistakable: "Daddy, it's difficult to send you a message under these conditions, but after our many requests they've allowed us to do it." Only one sentence gave any clues to possible future actions: "We watch and listen to the news constantly."

Dr. Turbay decided to show the message to the president, and find out at the same time if there were new developments. Gaviria received Turbay and Santos as his workday was ending, as always in his private library, and he was relaxed and more talkative than usual. He closed the door, poured the whiskey, and allowed himself a few political confidences. The capitulation process seemed to have run aground because of the Extraditables' obstinacy, and the president was prepared to get it back in the water by appending certain legal clarifications to the original decree. He had worked on this all afternoon and was confident it would be resolved that same night. Tomorrow, he promised, he would have good news for them.

They returned the next day, as arranged, and found him transformed into a wary, morose man whose first words set the tone for a conversation without hope. "This is a very difficult moment," Gaviria said. "I've wanted to help you, and I have been helping within the limits of the possible, but pretty soon I won't be able to do anything at all." It was obvious that something fundamental in his spirit had changed. Turbay sensed it right away, and before ten minutes had passed he rose from his chair with solemn composure. "Mr. President," he said without a trace of resentment, "you are proceeding as you must, and we must act as the fathers of our children. I understand, and ask you not do anything that might create a problem for you as head of state." As he concluded he pointed at the presidential chair.

"If I were sitting there, I would do the same."

Gaviria stood, pale as death, and walked with them to the elevator. An aide rode down with them and opened the door of the car waiting for them in the courtyard of the private residence. Neither of them spoke until they had driven out into the melancholy rain of an October evening. The noisy traffic on the avenue sounded muffled through bulletproof windows.

"We shouldn't expect anything else from him," Turbay said with a sigh after a long, thoughtful silence. "Something happened between last night and today, and he can't say what it is."

This dramatic meeting with the president was the reason doña Nydia Quintero moved to the foreground. She had been married to former president Turbay Ayala, her uncle, and the father of her four children, the eldest of whom was Diana. Seven years before the abduction, her marriage to Turbay had been annulled by the Holy See; her second husband was Gustavo Balcázar Monzón, a Liberal parliamentarian. She had been first lady and knew the limits protocol placed on a former president, above all in his dealings with a successor. "The only thing he could have done," Nydia had said, "was try to make President Gaviria see his obligation and his responsibilities." And that was what she attempted, though she had few illusions.

Her public activity, even before the official announcement of the abduction, reached staggering proportions. She had planned the appearance of groups of children on radio and television newscasts all over the country to read a plea for the release of the hostages. On October 19, the "Day of National Reconciliation," she had arranged for simultaneous noon masses in various cities and towns to pray for goodwill among Colombians. In Bogotá, while crowds waving white handkerchiefs gathered in many neighborhoods to demonstrate for peace, the ceremony took place on the Plaza de Bolívar, where a torch was lit, the flame to burn until the safe return of the captives. Through her efforts, television newscasts began each program with photographs of all the hostages, kept a tally of the days they had been held captive, and removed the corresponding picture as each prisoner was freed. It was also on her initiative that soccer matches throughout the country opened with a call for the release of the hostages. Maribel Gutiérrez, Colombia's beauty queen for 1990, began her acceptance speech with a plea for their freedom.

Nydia attended the meetings held by the families of the other hostages, listened to the lawyers, made efforts in secret through the Colombian Solidarity Foundation, which she has presided over for twenty years, and almost always felt as if she were running in circles around nothing. It was too much for her resolute, impassioned nature, her almost clairvoyant sensitivity. She waited for results of other people's efforts until she realized they had reached an impasse. Not even men as influential as Turbay and Hernando Santos could pressure the president into negotiating with the kidnappers. This certainty seemed absolute when Dr. Turbay told her about the failure of his last meeting with the president. Then Nydia decided to act on her own and opened a freewheeling second front to try to obtain her daughter's freedom by the most straightforward route.

It was during this time that the Colombian Solidarity Foundation received an anonymous phone call in its Medellín offices from someone who said he had firsthand information about Diana. He stated that an old friend of his on a farm near Medellín had slipped a note into his basket of vegetables, claiming that Diana was there, that the guards watched soccer games and swilled beer until they passed out, and that there was no chance they could react to a rescue attempt. To make a raid even more secure, he offered to send a sketch of the farm. The message was so convincing that Nydia traveled to Medellín to give him her answer. "I asked the informant," she has said, "not to discuss his information with anybody, and I made him see the danger to my daughter, and even to her guards, if anyone attempted a rescue."

The news that Diana was in Medellín suggested the idea of paying a visit to Martha Nieves and Angelita Ochoa, the sisters of

Jorge Luis, Fabio, and Juan David Ochoa, who had been accused of drug trafficking and racketeering and were known to be personal friends of Pablo Escobar. "I went with a fervent hope that they would help me contact Escobar," Nydia reported years later, recalling those bitter days. The Ochoa sisters told her of the abuse their families had suffered at the hands of the police, listened to her with interest, expressed sympathy for her situation, but also said there was nothing they could do as far as Pablo Escobar was concerned.

Martha Nieves knew what an abduction meant. In 1981 she had been kidnapped by the M-19, who demanded an exorbitant ransom from her family. Escobar responded by creating a brutal gang called the MAS, or Death to Kidnappers, which obtained her release after three months of bloody war with the M-19. Her sister Angelita also considered herself a victim of police violence, and both women recounted devastating stories of police abuses, raids on their homes, and countless violations of human rights.

Nydia did not lose heart. If nothing else, she wanted them to deliver a letter for her to Escobar. She had sent one earlier through Guido Parra but had received no reply. The Ochoa sisters refused to deliver another for fear Escobar would accuse them later of creating problems for him. By the end of the visit, however, they were more responsive to Nydia's fervent pleas, and she returned to Bogotá certain that a door had been opened that could lead in two different directions: one toward the release of her daughter, the other toward the peaceful surrender of the three Ochoa brothers. This made it seem appropriate to tell the president in person about her visit.

He saw her without delay. Nydia came right to the point, recounting the Ochoa sisters' complaints about the actions of the police. The president let her speak, asking only a few pertinent questions. His obvious intention was to give less weight to the accusations than she did. As for her own situation, Nydia wanted three things: the release of the hostages, the assertion of presidential authority to prevent a rescue attempt that could have calamitous results, and the extension of the time limit for the surrender of the Extraditables. The only assurance the president gave her was that no rescue of Diana or any other hostage would be attempted without authorization from their families.

"That's our policy," he said.

Even so, Nydia wondered if the president had taken sufficient precautions against someone making the attempt without authorization.

In less than a month, Nydia returned for more talks with the Ochoa sisters at the home of a mutual friend. She also visited one of Pablo Escobar's sisters-in-law, who spoke to her at length of the brutality she and her family had suffered at the hands of the police. Nydia brought her a letter for Escobar: two and a half full-size sheets covered almost completely by her ornate hand and written with an expressive precision achieved after many drafts. Her purpose was to touch Escobar's heart. She began by saying that she was not writing to the fighter capable of doing anything to achieve his ends, but to Pablo the man, "a feeling man who loves his mother and would give his life for her, who has a wife and young, innocent, defenseless children whom he wishes to protect." She understood that Escobar had abducted the journalists as a means of calling public attention to his cause, but in her opinion he had already succeeded. And so—the letter concluded—"show the world the human being you are, and in a great, humanitarian act that everyone will understand, return the hostages to us."

Escobar's sister-in-law seemed truly moved as she read it. "You can be absolutely sure this letter will touch him," she said as if to herself. "Everything you're doing touches him, and that can only work in your daughter's favor." Then she refolded the letter, put it in the envelope, and sealed it herself.

"Don't worry," she told Nydia with evident sincerity. "Pablo will have the letter today."

Nydia returned to Bogotá that night, hopeful about the effect the letter would have and determined to ask the president for what Dr. Turbay had not dared to request: a halt in police operations while the release of the hostages was being negotiated. She did so, and Gaviria told her straight out he could not give that order. "It was one thing for us to offer an alternative judicial policy," he said later. "But suspending operations would not have meant freedom for the hostages but only that we had stopped hunting down Escobar."

Nydia felt she was in the presence of a man of stone who cared nothing for her daughter's life. She had to control her rage as the president explained that law enforcement was not a negotiable subject, that the police did not have to ask permission to act, that he could not order them not to act within the limits of the law. The visit was a disaster.

After their failed efforts with the president, Turbay and Santos decided to try other avenues, and they could think of none better than the Notables. The group was composed of two former presidents, Alfonso López Michelsen and Misael Pastrana; the parliamentarian Diego Montaña Cuéllar; and Cardinal Mario Revollo Bravo, archbishop of Bogotá. In October the families of the hostages met with them at the home of Hernando Santos. They began by recounting their conversations with President Gaviria. The only part that interested López Michelsen was the possibility of amending the decree with judicial specifications, which might create new openings for the capitulation policy. "We have to get a foot in the door," he said. Pastrana favored formulas that would pressure the drug dealers into surrender. But using what weapons? Hernando Santos reminded Montaña Cuéllar that he could mobilize the guerrilla forces.

After a long, informed discussion, López Michelsen reached the first conclusion. "Let's play the Extraditables' game," he said. And he proposed writing a public letter announcing that the Notables were now spokesmen for the families of the hostages.

The unanimous decision was that López Michelsen would write the letter.

Two days later the first draft was read to a second gathering attended by Guido Parra and another of Escobar's lawyers. This document articulated for the first time the thesis that drug trafficking could be considered a collective, sui generis crime, which meant that the negotiation could move in unprecedented directions. Guido Parra was startled.

"A sui generis crime," he exclaimed in astonishment. "That's brilliant!"

With that as a starting point, Guido Parra elaborated the concept in his own way, as a God-given right on the murky border between ordinary and political crimes, making possible the dream that the Extraditables, like the guerrillas, would be treated as political offenders. Each man spoke. Then, one of Escobar's lawyers asked the Notables to obtain a letter from Gaviria that would guarantee Escobar's life in an explicit, unequivocal way.

"I'm very sorry," said Hernando Santos, shocked at the request, "but I won't get involved in that."

"And I certainly won't," said Turbay.

López Michelsen's refusal was vehement. Then the lawyer asked them to arrange a meeting between him and the president so that Gaviria could give him an oral guarantee for Escobar. "We won't deal with that subject here," López Michelsen replied.

Before the Notables met to revise the draft of their statement, Pablo Escobar had already been informed of their most confidential intentions. This is the only way to explain his extraordinary instructions in an urgent letter to Guido Parra. "You are free to find some way to have the Notables invite you to their discussion," he wrote. And then he listed a series of decisions the Extraditables had already made in anticipation of any fresh initiative.

The Notables' letter was ready in twenty-four hours, and contained an important departure with regard to their previous efforts: "Our good offices have acquired a new dimension, not limited to an occasional rescue but concerned with how to achieve peace for all Colombians." It was a new definition of their function that could only increase hope. President Gaviria approved but thought it prudent to establish a certain distance to avoid any mis-interpretation of the official attitude, and he instructed the justice minister to issue a statement affirming that the capitulation policy was the government's sole position with respect to the surrender of the terrorists.

Escobar did not like a word of the Notables' letter. As soon as he read it in the papers on October 11, he sent Guido Parra a fu-rious response, which he wanted him to circulate in the salons of Bogotá. "The letter from the Notables is almost cynical," it said. "We are supposed to release the hostages quickly because the gov-ernment is dragging its feet as it studies our situation. Can they really believe we will let ourselves be deceived again?" The posi-tion of the Extraditables, it continued, was the same one indicated in their first letter. "There was no reason to change it, since we have not received positive replies to the requests made in our first communication. This is a negotiation, not a game to find out who is clever and who is stupid."

The truth was that by this time Escobar had traveled light-years ahead of the Notables. His aim was for the government to give him his own secure territory—a prison camp, as he called it—like the one granted the M-19 while the terms of their surrender were being negotiated. More than a week earlier he had sent Guido Parra a detailed letter regarding the special prison he wanted for himself. The perfect location, he said, twelve kilome-ters outside Medellín, was a property he owned, though an agent of his was listed as owner, which the municipality of Envigado could lease and convert into a prison. "Since this requires money, the Extraditables would assume the costs," the letter continued. It ended with an astounding disclosure: "I'm telling you all this be-cause I want you to talk to the mayor of Envigado and tell him you represent me and explain the idea to him. But the reason I want you to talk to him is to get him to write a public letter to the justice minister saying he thinks the Extraditables have not accepted Decree 2047 because they fear for their safety, and that the municipality of Envigado, as its contribution to peace for the Colombian people, is prepared to build a special prison that will offer protection and security to those who surrender. Talk to him in a direct, clear way so he'll talk to Gaviria and propose the camp." The stated goal was to force a public response from the justice minister. "I know that will have the impact of a bomb," said Escobar's letter. And it ended with stunning arrogance: "This way we'll have them where we want them."

The minister, however, turned down the terms of the offer as presented to him, and Escobar found himself obliged to soften his tone with another letter in which, for the first time, he offered more than he demanded. In exchange for the prison camp, he promised to resolve the conflicts among the various cartels, crews, and gangs, to guarantee the surrender of more than a hundred repentant traffickers, and to at last open an avenue to peace. "We are not asking for amnesty, or dialogue, or any of the things they say they cannot give," he said. This was a simple offer to surrender, "while everybody in this country is calling for dialogue and for treating us as politicals." He even downplayed what he held most dear: "I have no problem with extradition, since I know that if they take me alive they'll kill me, like they've done with everybody else."

His strategy at this time was to demand huge favors in exchange for mail from the hostages. "Tell Señor Santos," he said in another letter, "that if he wants proof that Francisco is alive, he should first publish the report from Americas Watch, an interview with Juan Méndez, its director, and a report on the massacres, tortures, and disappearances in Medellín." But by this time Hernando Santos had learned how to cope with the situation. He knew that the constant flow back and forth of proposals and counterproposals was a strain not only on him but on his adversaries as well. Guido Parra, for one, was in a state of nervous exhaustion by the end of October. Santos's reply to Escobar was that he would not publish a line of anything or see his emissary again until he had conclusive proof that his son was alive. Alfonso López Michelsen backed him up by threatening to withdraw from the Notables.

It worked. In two weeks Guido Parra called Hernando Santos from a truck stop. "I'm in the car with my wife, and I'll be at your house by eleven," he said. "I'm bringing you the most delicious dessert, and you can't imagine how much I've enjoyed it, and how much you're going to enjoy it." Hernando was elated, thinking he was bringing Francisco home. But it was only his voice recorded on a minicassette. They could not listen to it for over two hours because they did not have the right equipment, and then someone discovered they could play it on the answering machine.

Pacho Santos could have been successful in many professions, but not as a diction teacher. He tries to speak at the speed of his thoughts, and his ideas come in a simultaneous rush. The surprise that night was his slow speech, modulated voice, and perfectly constructed sentences. In reality there were two messages—one for his family and the other for the president—which he had recorded the week before.

The guards' idea that Pacho should read the day's headlines to prove the date of the recording was a mistake that Escobar probably never forgave them for. It did, however, give Luis Cañón, the legal editor of *El Tiempo*, the opportunity to display a piece of brilliant journalism.

"They're holding him in Bogotá," he said.

The paper Pacho had read from had a late headline that appeared only in the local edition, whose circulation is limited to the northern part of the city. This fact was worth its weight in gold and would have been decisive if Hernando Santos had not been opposed to an armed rescue attempt.

The moment restored him, above all because the content of the message convinced him that his captive son approved of how he was handling matters. Besides, the family had always thought of Pacho as the most vulnerable of the children because of his impulsive temperament and volatile spirit, and no one could have imagined that he would be so rational and self-possessed after sixty days of captivity.

Hernando called the entire family to his house, and they listened to the message till dawn. Only Guido Parra gave in to his emotions. He wept. Hernando came over to comfort him, and in the perspiration that soaked his shirt he recognized the smell of panic.

"Remember, I won't be killed by the police," Guido Parra said through his tears. "I'll be killed by Pablo Escobar because I know too much."

María Victoria was not moved. She thought Parra was toying with Hernando's feelings, exploiting his weakness, giving a little so he could get back more. At some point during the evening, Guido Parra must have sensed this because he said to Hernando: "That woman's an iceberg."

Matters had reached this stage on November 7, when Maruja and Beatriz were abducted. The Notables had no firm ground to stand on. On November 22—following his prior announcement—Diego Montaña Cuéllar made the formal proposal to his fellow members that the group disband, and they, in a solemn meeting, presented the president with their conclusions regarding the Extraditables' principal demands.

If President Gaviria was hoping that the capitulation decree would elicit an immediate mass surrender by the drug traffickers, he must have been disappointed. It did not. Reactions in the press, in political circles, among distinguished jurists, and even some of the valid objections raised by the Extraditables' lawyers, made it clear that Decree 2047 had to be revised. To begin with, it left the possibility wide open for any judge to interpret the extradition process in his own way. Another weakness was that although conclusive evidence against the drug dealers lay outside the country, the entire question of cooperation with the United States had reached a critical stage, and the time limits for obtaining evidence were too short. The solution—not contained in the decree—was to extend the time limits and transfer to the presidency the responsibility for negotiating the return of evidence to Colombia.

Alberto Villamizar had also not found in the decree the decisive support he was hoping for. Until now his exchanges with Santos and Turbay, and his initial meetings with Pablo Escobar's lawyers, had allowed him to form a broad view of the situation. His first impression was that the capitulation decree, a flawed move in the right direction, left him very little maneuvering room to obtain the release of his wife and sister. In the meanwhile, time was passing without any news of them, without the slightest proof they were still alive. His only opportunity to communicate with them had been a letter sent through Guido Parra, in which he gave them his optimistic assurance that he would do nothing else but work for their release. "I know your situation is terrible but stay calm," he wrote to Maruja.

The truth was that Villamizar had no idea what to do. He had exhausted every avenue, and the only thing he could hold on to during that long November was Rafael Pardo's assurance that the president was considering another decree to complement and clarify 2047. "It's just about ready," he said. Rafael Pardo stopped by his house almost every evening and kept him up-to-date on his efforts, but not even he was very certain how to proceed. Villamizar concluded from his long, slow conversations with Santos and Turbay that negotiations had reached an impasse. He had no faith in Guido Parra. He had known him since the days when he stalked the halls of congress, and he thought him an opportunist and a crook. But for better or worse, Parra was the only card, and Villamizar decided to gamble everything on him. He had no other choice, and time was pressing.

At his request, former president Turbay and Hernando Santos made an appointment to see Guido Parra, on the condition that

Dr. Santiago Uribe, another of Escobar's attorneys, with a good reputation as a serious man, also be present. Guido Parra began the conversation with his usual high-flown rhetoric, but Villamizar brought him back down to earth with the brutal directness of a man from Santander.

"Don't fuck with me," he said. "Let's get to the point. You've stalled everything because your demands are moronic, and there's only one damn thing at issue here: Your boys have to turn themselves in and confess to some crime that they can serve a twelve-year sentence for. That's what the law says, period. And in exchange for that, they'll get a reduced sentence and a guarantee of protection. All the rest is bullshit."

Guido Parra had no choice but to change his tone.

"Look, Doctor," he said, "the thing is that the government says they won't be extradited, everybody says so, but where does the decree say it specifically?"

Villamizar agreed. If the government was saying there would be no extraditions, since that was the sense of the law, then their job was to persuade the government to eliminate the ambiguities. All the rest—clever interpretations of a sui generis crime, or refusing to confess, or the immorality of implicating others—amounted to nothing more than Guido Parra's rhetorical distractions. It was obvious that for the Extraditables—as their very name indicated—the only real and urgent requirement was not to be extradited. And it did not seem impossible to have this spelled out in the decree. But first Villamizar demanded from Guido Parra the same frankness and determination demanded by the Extraditables. First, he wanted to know how far Parra was authorized to negotiate, and second, how soon after the decree was amended would the hostages be released. Guido Parra was solemn.

"They'll be free in twenty-four hours," he said.

"All of them, of course," said Villamizar.

"All of them."

5

A MONTH AFTER the abduction of Maruja and Beatriz, the absurd rules of their captivity had been relaxed. They no longer had to ask permission to stand, and they could pour their own coffee or change television channels. Inside the room they still spoke in whispers, but their movements had become more spontaneous. Maruja did not have to bury her face in the pillow when she coughed, though she did take minimal precautions not to be heard outside the room. Lunch and dinner were still the same, the same beans, the same lentils, the same bits of dry meat and ordinary packaged soup.

The guards talked a good deal among themselves, taking no precaution except to speak in whispers. They exchanged blood-soaked news about how much they had earned hunting down the police at night in Medellín, about their sexual prowess and their melodramatic love affairs. Maruja had succeeded in convincing them that in the case of an armed rescue attempt, it would be more realistic to protect the captives so that they at least would be sure of receiving decent treatment and a compassionate trial. At first they seemed indifferent, for they were absolute fatalists, but her strategy of mollification meant they no longer pointed their guns at the prisoners while they slept, and their weapons, wrapped in cloths, were kept out of sight behind the television. Little by little, their mutual dependence and shared suffering brought a thin veneer of humanity to their relations.

It was in Maruja's nature not to keep bitter feelings to herself. She gave vent to her emotions with the guards, who were always ready for violence, and faced them down with a chilling determination: "Go on, kill me." Sometimes she turned on Marina, whose eagerness to please the guards infuriated her, and whose apocalyptic fantasies drove her to distraction. Sometimes, for no apparent reason, Marina would look up and make a disheartening remark or sinister prophecy.

"On the other side of that courtyard is a repair shop for the killers' cars," she once said. "They're all there, day and night, armed with rifles, ready to come and shoot us."

Their most serious quarrel, however, occurred one afternoon when Marina began her habitual cursing of journalists because her name had not been mentioned on a television program about the hostages.

"They're all sons of bitches," she said.

Maruja confronted her.

"You're out of line," she replied in a rage. "You can show a little respect."

Marina did not answer and later, in a calmer moment, apologized. In reality, she lived in a world apart. She was sixty-four years old and had been a famous beauty, with wonderful large black eyes and silver hair that still gleamed even in misfortune. She had become nothing but skin and bones. When Beatriz and Maruja arrived, she had spent almost two months with no one to talk to but her guards, and time and effort were needed for her to assimilate their presence. Fear had wreaked havoc on her: She had lost forty-five pounds, and her morale was very low. She was a phantom.

When she was very young, she had married a chiropractor who

was well respected in the athletic world, a stout, good-hearted man who loved her without reservation and with whom she had four daughters and three sons. She managed everything, in her own house and in several others, for she felt obliged to solve the problems of her large family in Antioquia. Marina was like a second mother to them all, as much for her authority as her solicitude, but she also concerned herself with any outsider who touched her heart.

Because of her indomitable independence rather than any financial need, she sold cars and life insurance, and seemed able to sell anything simply because she wanted to spend her own money. But those closest to her lamented the fact that a woman with so many natural talents was also hounded by misfortune. For almost twenty years her husband had been incapacitated by mental illness, two brothers had been killed in a terrible car accident, one died of a heart attack, another was crushed by a traffic light in a freak mishap, and still another, who loved to wander, had disappeared forever.

Her situation as a hostage had no solution. Even she accepted the widespread idea that she had been abducted only because her captors wanted a significant hostage whom they could kill without thwarting the negotiations for their surrender. But the fact that she had spent sixty days in prison may have allowed her to think that they saw a chance to obtain some advantage in exchange for her life.

It was noteworthy that even at her worst moments she spent long hours absorbed in the meticulous care of her fingernails and toenails. She filed and buffed them, and brightened them with natural polish, so that they looked like the nails of a younger woman. She devoted the same attention to tweezing her eyebrows and shaving her legs. Once they were past their initial problems, Maruja and Beatriz helped her. They learned to deal with her. She held interminable conversations with Beatriz about people she loved and people she hated, speaking in an endless whisper that irritated even the guards. Maruja tried to comfort her. Both felt distress at being the only people, apart from her jailers, who knew she was alive, yet could not let anyone else know.

One of the few diversions during this time was the unexpected return of the masked boss who had visited them on the first day. Cheerful and optimistic, he brought the news that they might be released before December 9, the date of the election for the Constituent Assembly. This had special significance for Maruja because December 9 was her birthday, and the thought of spending it with her family filled her with anticipatory joy. But it was an ephemeral hope: A week later, the same boss said that not only would they not be released on December 9, but their captivity would be a long one and they would not be free by Christmas or the New Year. It was a harsh blow. Maruja suffered the onset of phlebitis that caused severe pains in her legs. Beatriz had an attack of asphyxia, and her gastric ulcer began to bleed. One night, maddened by pain, she pleaded with Spots to make an exception to the prison rules and let her have an unscheduled visit to the bathroom. He agreed, after thinking it over for a long time, and told her he was taking a great risk. But it did not help. Beatriz continued to whimper in pain like a wounded dog, and thought she was dying until Spots took pity on her and got some Buscapina from the majordomo.

In spite of their efforts, the hostages had no reliable clues as to where they were. The guards' fear that neighbors might hear them, and the sounds and voices coming from outside, led them to think they were in the city. A confirmation seemed to be the deranged rooster that crowed at any hour of the day or night, since roosters kept on high floors tend to lose their sense of time. Nearby they often heard different voices calling the same name: Rafael. Small, low-flying planes passed overhead, and when the helicopter arrived it sounded as if it were right on top of the house. Marina insisted on the unproven theory that a high-ranking army officer was supervising their imprisonment. For Maruja and Beatriz it was just another fantasy, but whenever they heard the helicopter, strict military rules were reimposed: the house as orderly as a barracks, the door latched on the inside and padlocked on the outside, conversation in whispers, weapons always at the ready, and a slight improvement in the vile food.

The four guards who had been with them since the first day were replaced by another four early in December. One was distinctive and strange and looked like a character in a horror movie. They called him Gorilla, and in fact he resembled one: enormous and strong as a gladiator, with dark black skin covered in thick, curly hair. His voice was so loud he had difficulty whispering, and no one dared to ask him to lower his voice. The sense of inferiority felt by the other guards was obvious. Instead of the cutoffs worn by everyone else, he wore gymnast's shorts, a ski mask, and a tight undershirt that displayed his perfect torso. He had a Holy Infant medal around his neck, handsome arms, and a Brazilian wristband that he wore for good luck. His hands were enormous, and the fate lines seemed etched into his pale palms. He barely fit into the room, and every time he moved he left chaos in his wake. For the hostages, who had learned how to deal with the previous guards, this was a disturbing turn of events—above all for Beatriz, whom he hated on sight.

The condition shared by both guards and hostages was absolute boredom. As a prelude to their celebration of Christmas, the owners of the house held a novena with a priest of their acquaintance, perhaps innocent, perhaps not. They prayed, sang carols, gave candy to the children, and toasted one another with the apple wine that was the family's official drink. At the end the house was exorcised with sprinklings of holy water. They needed so much that it was brought in gallon oil cans. When the priest left, Damaris came into the room and sprinkled the television, the mattresses, the walls. The three captives, taken by surprise, did not know what to do. "It's holy water," she said as she sprinkled everything with her hand. "It'll help to make sure nothing happens to us." The guards crossed themselves, fell to their knees, and received the purifying shower with angelic devotion.

That love of parties and prayer, so typical of Antioquians, did not let up for a moment during the month of December. Maruja, in fact, had been careful not to let her captors know that December 9 was her fifty-third birthday. Beatriz agreed to keep the secret, but the guards found out while they were watching a special television program that Maruja's children dedicated to her on the evening of December 8.

The guards could not hide their emotion at feeling themselves somehow involved in the intimacy of the program. "Doña Maruja," said one, "how young Dr. Villamizar looks, how nice he looks, how he loves you." They hoped Maruja would introduce them to her daughters so they could take them out. In any case, watching that program in captivity was like being dead and watching life from the next world without taking part, and without the living knowing you were there. At eleven the next morning, the majordomo and his wife burst into the room with a bottle of local champagne, enough glasses for everyone, and a cake that looked as if it were covered in toothpaste. They congratulated Maruja with great displays of affection, and they and the guards sang "Happy Birthday." They all ate and drank, and left Maruja struggling with contrary emotions.

JUAN VITTA WOKE on November 26 to learn that he was being released because of ill health. He froze in terror, for in recent days he had been feeling better than ever, and he thought the announcement was simply a subterfuge that would give the public its first corpse. As a consequence, when the guard told him a few hours later to get ready for his release, he had an attack of panic. "I would have preferred to die on my own," he has said, "but if this was my fate, I had to accept it." He was told to shave and put on clean clothes, and he did, certain he was dressing for his own funeral. He was given instructions on what he must do once he was free, and above all, on what he must say during press interviews to avoid giving clues the police might use in a rescue operation. A little after twelve, they drove him through some labyrinthine districts in Medellín and then, without ceremony, dropped him off on a street corner.

After Vitta's release they moved Hero Buss again, this time to a good neighborhood, across the street from an aerobics school for women. The owner of the house was a free-spending, high-living mulatto. His wife, about thirty-five years old and in her seventh month of pregnancy, spent the day from breakfast on covering herself in expensive jewelry that was far too noticeable. They had a young son who was staying in another house with his grandmother, and it was his room, filled with every kind of mechanical toy, that was occupied by Hero Buss. And he, considering how they made him part of the family, prepared himself for a long captivity.

The owners must have enjoyed this German like the ones in Marlene Dietrich's movies: more than six feet tall and a yard wide, a fifty-year-old adolescent with a sense of humor that protected him from creditors, and who spoke a Spanish spiced with the Caribbean slang of his wife, Carmen Santiago. He had faced real dangers as a correspondent for German newspapers and radio in Latin America, including the night he had spent, under the military regime in Chile, expecting to be shot at dawn. So he already had a tough hide, and could enjoy the folkloric aspects of his captivity.

And it was just as well in a house where a courier made regular visits bringing bags full of money for expenses, and still there was never enough. The owners would spend it as soon as they could on parties and trinkets, and in a few days they had nothing left for food. On weekends they gave parties and huge dinners for their brothers and sisters, cousins and close friends. Children took over the house. On the first day they were overwhelmed with emotion when they recognized the German giant, whom they treated as if he were a soap opera star because they had seen him so often on television. No fewer than thirty people who had nothing to do with the abduction asked to take his picture, requested autographs, ate with him, and even danced with him, all without masks in that madhouse where he lived until his captivity ended.

Their accumulated debts drove the owners to distraction, and they had to pawn the television, the VCR, the stereo, whatever, to feed the hostage. The wife's jewelry began to disappear from her throat, wrists, and ears, until there was nothing left. Once, in the middle of the night, the owner woke Hero Buss to ask for a loan because his wife had gone into labor and he did not have a penny to pay the hospital. Hero Buss lent him his last fifty thousand pesos.

They freed him on December 11, two weeks after Juan Vitta. For the occasion they bought him a pair of shoes that he could not use because he wore size 46 and the largest they could find, after much searching, was a 44. They bought him a shirt and trousers two sizes smaller because he had lost thirty-five pounds. They returned his camera equipment and the bag with his notebooks hidden in the lining, and they paid him back the fifty thousand pesos for the birth and another fifteen thousand he had lent them earlier to replace money that had been stolen from them at the market. They offered him a great deal more, but the only thing he asked them for was an interview with Pablo Escobar. They never replied.

The crew that had been with him in recent days drove him away in a private car. After taking a circuitous route through the best neighborhoods in Medellín, they dropped him half a block from the newspaper *El Colombiano*, with his bags on his back and a message from the Extraditables; it recognized his struggle in defense of human rights in Colombia and other Latin American countries, and reiterated the determination of the Extraditables to accept the capitulation policy with no conditions other than judicial guarantees of safety for themselves and their families. A journalist to the end, Hero Buss handed his camera to the first passerby and asked him to take a picture of his release.

DIANA AND AZUCENA heard the news on the radio, and their guards said they would be next. But they had been told the same thing so often, they did not believe it. In the event only one was freed, each woman wrote a letter for the other to give to her family. And then nothing happened, nothing else was said, until two days later—at dawn on December 13—when Diana was awakened by whispers and unusual movements in the house. The feeling that they would be released made her jump out of bed. She alerted Azucena, and before anyone announced anything to them they began to pack.

Both Diana and Azucena recounted that dramatic moment in their journals. Diana was in the shower when one of the guards, without any ceremony, told Azucena to get ready to go. Only Azucena. In the book she would publish a short while later, she narrated this with admirable simplicity:

> I went to the room and put on the clothes I had laid out on the chair while doña Diana was still in the bathroom. When she came out and saw me she stopped, looked at me, and said:
>
> "Are we going, Azu?"
>
> Her eyes shone, waiting for the answer she longed to hear. And I could not tell her anything. I lowered my head, took a deep breath, and said:
>
> "No. I'm going alone."
>
> "I'm so happy for you," Diana said. "I knew it would be this way."

In her diary, Diana wrote: "I felt as if I had been stabbed in the heart, but I said I was happy for her, and not to worry." She gave

Azucena the letter to Nydia she had written earlier, in the event she was not released. In the letter she asked Nydia to celebrate Christmas with Diana's children. Azucena was crying, and Diana put her arms around her to comfort her. Then she walked with Azucena to the car, and they embraced again. Azucena turned to watch her through the car window, and Diana waved goodbye.

An hour later, in the car that was taking her to the Medellín airport where she would catch a plane to Bogotá, Azucena heard a reporter on the radio asking her husband what he had been doing when he heard the news of her release. He replied with the truth:

"I was writing a poem for Azucena."

And so their wish was granted, and they were together on December 16 to celebrate their fourth wedding anniversary.

RICARDO AND ORLANDO, tired of sleeping on the floor of their foul-smelling cell, persuaded the guards to put them in another room. They moved the hostages to the bedroom where they had seen the handcuffed mulatto, whom they never saw again. To their horror, they discovered that the mattress on the bed had large, recent bloodstains that might have come either from slow tortures or sudden slashes with a knife.

They had learned of the release of other hostages on television and radio. Their guards had said they would be next. Very early on December 17 a boss they knew as the Old Man—and who in fact was the same don Pacho in charge of Diana—walked into Orlando's room without knocking.

"Put on some clothes because you're leaving now," he said.

He barely had time to shave and dress, and no time to tell Richard, who was in the same house. They gave him a communiqué for the press, put a pair of strong glasses over his eyes, and the Old Man, on his own, drove him with the ritual twists and turns through various neighborhoods in Medellín, gave him five thousand pesos for a cab, and left him at a traffic circle he could not identify because he does not know the city. It was nine in the morning on a cool, clear Monday. Orlando could not believe it: Until that moment, while he signaled in vain for cabs that were all occupied, he had been sure it would be cheaper for his captors to kill him than run the risk of freeing him while he was alive. He called his wife from the first telephone he saw.

Liliana was bathing the baby, and ran to answer the phone with soapy hands. She heard a stranger's calm voice:

"Slim, it's me."

She thought it was a joke and was about to hang up when she recognized his voice. "Oh my God," she cried. Orlando was in such a hurry he only managed to tell her he was still in Medellín and would be in Bogotá that afternoon. Liliana was tormented the rest of the day because she had not recognized her husband's voice. Juan Vitta had told her when he was released that Orlando had changed so much in captivity that it was hard to recognize him, but she never thought the change would affect even his voice. That afternoon at the airport it was even worse when she made her way through the crowd of reporters and did not recognize the man who kissed her. But it was Orlando after four months of captivity, fat and pale, with a dark, rough mustache. Each of them had decided on their own to have a second child as soon as they were together again. "But there were so many people around we couldn't that night," Liliana has said, weak with laughter. "Or the next day either, because of the shock." But at last they made up for lost time: Nine months after the third day they had another boy, and twins the following year.

THE SERIES OF RELEASES—a breath of hope for the other captives and their families—were a convincing sign to Pacho Santos that no reasonable progress had been made in his favor. He thought Pablo Escobar had simply gotten rid of the low cards to increase the pressure for amnesty and non-extradition in the Constituent Assembly, and was holding on to his three aces: the daughter of a former president, the son of the publisher of the most important paper in the country, and the sister-in-law of Luis Carlos Galán. Beatriz and Marina, on the other hand, felt renewed hope, though Maruja preferred not to deceive herself with overly optimistic interpretations. Her spirits were low, and the approach of Christmas was devastating. She despised obligatory holidays. She never put up crèches or Christmas trees, did not send cards or give gifts, and found nothing more depressing than dreary Christmas Eve celebrations when people sing because they're sad or cry because they're happy. The majordomo and his wife prepared a ghastly dinner. Beatriz and Marina made an effort to join in, but Maruja took two strong sleeping pills and woke with no regrets.

On the following Wednesday, Alexandra's weekly program was devoted to Christmas night at Nydia's house with the entire Turbay family around the former president, along with the families of Beatriz, and of Maruja and Alberto Villamizar. The children were in the foreground: Diana's two boys, and Maruja's grandson—Alexandra's son. Maruja wept with emotion: The last time she had seen him he barely babbled a few words, and now he could talk. At the end, Villamizar spoke, slowly and in great detail, about the progress of his efforts. Maruja summed up the program with absolute precision: "It was very nice, and really awful."

Villamizar's message raised Marina Montoya's spirits. She became human again and revealed the greatness of her heart. With a political acumen they had not known she possessed, she began to show interest in listening to the news and interpreting its significance. Her analysis of the decrees led her to conclude that their chances for freedom were greater than ever. Her health improved so much that she ignored the rules and spoke in her natural voice, which was beautiful and well modulated.

December 31 was their big night. When Damaris brought breakfast she said they would celebrate with a real party, complete with champagne and a pork roast. Maruja thought it would be the saddest night of her life, the first New Year's Eve away from her family, and she sank into depression. Beatriz was in a state of total collapse. The last thing they wanted was a party. Marina, however, was overjoyed by the news and used all her persuasive powers to cheer them up, even the guards.

"We have to be fair," she told Maruja and Beatriz. "They're away from their families too, and our job is to make their New Year's Eve as pleasant as it can be."

She had been given three nightgowns on the night of her abduction, but she had used only one and kept the other two in her bag. Later, when Maruja and Beatriz were captured, the three women used sweatsuits as their prison uniform, washing them every two weeks.

No one thought about the nightgowns again until the afternoon of December 31, when Marina carried her enthusiasm one step further. "I have an idea," she said. "I have three nightgowns here, and we'll wear them for good luck in the new year." And she asked Maruja:

"All right, darling, which color do you want?"

Maruja said it was all the same to her. Marina decided that green suited her best. She gave the pink gown to Beatriz, and kept the white one for herself. Then she took a cosmetics case out of her bag, and suggested they make each other up. "So we'll look pretty tonight," she said. Maruja, who'd had all she could bear with the idea of dressing up in nightgowns, turned her down with sour humor.

"I'll go so far as to put on the nightgown," she said. "But paint myself up like a madwoman, under these circumstances? No, Marina, that's something I won't do."

Marina shrugged.

"Well, I will."

Because they had no mirror, she handed the case to Beatriz and sat down on the bed to be made up. Beatriz did a complete and tasteful job in the light of the bedside candle, some blush to hide the deathly pallor of her skin, bright lipstick, eye shadow. They were both surprised at how attractive this woman, who had been famous for her grace and beauty, could still look. Beatriz settled for her ponytail and schoolgirl appearance.

That night Marina displayed all her irresistible Antioquian charm. The guards followed suit, and they all said what they had to say in their God-given voices, except the majordomo, who even on the high seas of intoxication still spoke in whispers. Spots, emboldened by drink, found the courage to give Beatriz a bottle of aftershave: "So you can all smell nice when you get a million hugs on the day you're released," he said to the women. The boorish majordomo could not let it pass and said it was the gift of a secret admirer. A new terror was added to the many that plagued Beatriz.

The party consisted of the hostages, the majordomo and his wife, and the four guards. Beatriz had an unbearable lump in her throat. Maruja felt nostalgic and embarrassed, but even so she could not hide her admiration for Marina who looked splendid, rejuvenated by makeup, with her white gown and snowy hair, her delicious voice. It was inconceivable that Marina could be happy, but she made everyone think she was.

She joked with the guards who lifted their masks to drink. Sometimes, when the heat got to be too much for them, they asked the hostages to turn their backs so they could take a free breath. At midnight, when the fire engine sirens wailed and the church bells rang, they were all crowded into the room, sitting on the bed, on the mattress, sweating in the infernal heat. The national anthem began to play on television. Then Maruja stood and told them all to get to their feet and sing with her. When it was over she raised her glass of apple wine and made a toast to peace in Colombia. The party ended half an hour later when the bottles were empty and nothing was left on the platter but bones and the remains of some potato salad.

The hostages greeted the replacement crew of guards with a

sigh of relief, for they were the same ones who had been waiting for them on the night of the abduction and the prisoners knew how to deal with them. Maruja in particular felt a sense of deliverance, for her poor health had kept her in low spirits. At first her terror had taken the form of erratic pains all over her body, which forced her into uncomfortable postures. But then the pain became concrete as a result of the inhuman regime imposed by the guards. Early in December, to punish her rebelliousness, they would not allow her to use the bathroom for an entire day, and when at last they gave permission, nothing happened. This was the beginning of a chronic cystitis, and then bleeding, which lasted until the end of her captivity.

Marina, who had learned sports massage from her husband, committed her meager strength to healing her. She still had high spirits left over from New Year's Eve. She remained optimistic, told stories: She was alive. The inclusion of her name and photograph in a television campaign in support of the hostages restored her sense of hope and joy. She was her old self again: She existed again, she was there. Her picture was always shown in the first segment of the campaign, and then one day, with no explanation, it did not appear. Maruja and Beatriz did not have the heart to tell her that perhaps she had been removed from the list because no one thought she was still alive.

December 31 was important to Beatriz because that was the latest date she had fixed for her release. She was so devastated by disappointment that her cellmates did not know what to do for her. At one point Maruja could not look at her because when she did, Beatriz broke down and burst into tears, and they began to ignore each other in a space not much larger than a bathroom. The situation became untenable.

The most reliable distraction for the three hostages, in the endless hours following their bathroom privileges, was to massage their legs with the moisturizing cream their jailers supplied in sufficient quantities to keep them from going mad. One day Beatriz realized it was running out.

"What are we going to do when there's no more cream?" she asked Maruja.

"Well, we can always ask for more," Maruja replied in a caustic tone. And she added with an emphasis that was even more caustic: "Or else we'll just have to make a decision when the time comes. Okay?"

"Don't you dare talk to me like that!" Beatriz shouted in a sudden explosion of rage. "Not when it's your damn fault I'm here!"

The explosion was inevitable. In an instant she said everything she had kept to herself during so many days of repressed tensions, so many nights of horror. The surprise was that it had not happened earlier or been more rancorous. Beatriz had kept to the sidelines, holding back, swallowing her rancor whole without tasting it. The inconsequential effect, of course, was that sooner or later a simple, thoughtless phrase would release the fury that terror had suppressed. But the guard on duty did not think that way, and fearing a major blowup, threatened to lock Beatriz and Maruja into separate rooms.

They were dismayed. The dread of sexual assault was still very much alive. Certain that being together made it difficult for the guards to attempt a rape, they were alarmed by the thought of being separated. On the other hand, the guards, who were always in pairs, did not get along and seemed to keep a cautious eye on one another as a way of maintaining internal discipline and avoiding serious incidents with the hostages.

But the repression of the guards created an unhealthy atmosphere in the room. Those on duty in December had brought in a VCR and watched violent films with strong erotic elements, and some pornographic movies. At times the room became saturated with unbearable tension. Furthermore, when the prisoners went to the bathroom, they had to leave the door partially opened, and on more than one occasion they had caught a guard watching them. One of the guards, who insisted on holding the door with his hand so it would not close all the way while the women were using the bathroom, almost lost his fingers when Beatriz slammed it shut. Another unsettling sight was a pair of homosexual guards who worked the second shift and kept each other in a perpetual state of arousal with all kinds of perverse games. Spots's excessive vigilance at Beatriz's slightest gesture, his gift of aftershave, and the majordomo's insolent remark were all unsettling. The stories the guards told each other about their rapes of strangers, their erotic perversions, their sadistic pleasures, rarefied the atmosphere even further.

At the request of Maruja and Marina, the majordomo had a doctor come to see Beatriz on January 12, sometime before midnight. He was a young, well-dressed man with beautiful manners, wearing a yellow silk mask that complemented his outfit. It is difficult to believe in the seriousness of a hooded physician, but this one demonstrated his skill as soon as he came in. His self-assurance was comforting. He carried a fine leather bag as big as a suitcase, with a phonendoscope, a tensiometer, a battery-operated electrocardiograph, a laboratory kit for home-analysis, and other emergency equipment. He gave each hostage a thorough examination, and analyzed their blood and urine in the portable laboratory.

As he was examining Maruja, the doctor whispered in her ear: "I am the most embarrassed person in the world at having to see you in this situation. I want to tell you that I am not here voluntarily. I was a great friend and supporter of Dr. Luis Carlos Galán, and I voted for him. You don't deserve to suffer like this, but try to endure. Serenity is good for your health." Maruja appreciated his explanations but could not overcome her astonishment at his moral flexibility. He made identical comments to Beatriz.

The diagnosis for both women was severe stress and incipient malnutrition, for which he ordered an enriched, more balanced diet. He discovered circulatory problems and a serious bladder infection in Maruja, and prescribed a course of treatment based on Vasotón, diuretics, and tranquilizers. He prescribed a sedative for Beatriz's gastric ulcer. As for Marina—whom he had seen before—he only advised that she take better care of her health but did not find her very receptive. He ordered all three to walk at a brisk pace for at least an hour every day.

After this, each woman was given a box with twenty tranquilizers. They were to take one pill in the morning, another at noon, and the third before they went to sleep. In an emergency they could exchange the tranquilizer for a powerful barbiturate that allowed them to escape many of the horrors of their captivity. Just a quarter of a pill was enough to make them lose consciousness before the count of four.

At one o'clock that morning, they began their walks in the dark courtyard with the nervous guards, who kept their submachine guns, safeties off, trained on them. The women felt dizzy their first time out, in particular Maruja, who had to lean against the walls to keep from falling. With the help of the guards, and sometimes Damaris, they grew accustomed to the exercise. At the end of two weeks, Maruja was able to circle the yard up to a thousand times—two kilometers—at a quick pace. Their spirits rose, and this in turn improved domestic tranquillity.

The courtyard was the only part of the house they saw except for their room. They took their walks in the dark, but on moonlit nights they could make out a large laundry area half in ruins, clothes hung out to dry on lines, and a great jumble of broken packing cases and worn-out household articles. Above the canopy over the laundry, there was a second story with a sealed window, its streaked panes curtained by sheets of newspaper. The hostages thought it must be where the guards slept when they were not on duty. There was a door to the kitchen, another to the room where the prisoners were kept, and a gate made of old boards that did not reach all the way to the ground. It was the gate out to the world.

Later they would learn that it led to a quiet pen where Easter lambs and a few hens were kept. It seemed very simple to open it and get away, but it was guarded by a German shepherd that looked incorruptible. Still, Maruja became his friend, and at a certain point he stopped barking when she came close to pet him.

AFTER AZUCENA'S RELEASE, Diana was alone. She watched television, listened to the radio, at times she read the papers with more interest than ever, but knowing the news and not having anyone to discuss it with was almost worse than not knowing anything at all. She thought the guards treated her with decency, and she recognized their efforts to accommodate her. "I don't want, and it isn't easy, to describe what I feel at each moment: the pain, the anguish, the terrifying days I've experienced," she wrote in her diary. She feared for her life, in fact, in particular because she dreaded an armed rescue attempt. The possibility of her release was reduced to a single, insidious phrase: "Pretty soon, now." She was terrified at the idea that this was a delaying tactic, a way of waiting for the Constituent Assembly to convene and reach concrete decisions on extradition and amnesty. Don Pacho, who used to spend long hours with her discussing various matters and keeping her well informed, grew more and more distant. With no explanation, they stopped bringing her the papers. The news, even the soap operas on television, acquired the slow pace of a country brought to a standstill by the New Year's holiday exodus.

For over a month they had distracted her with the promise that she would meet Pablo Escobar in person. She rehearsed her attitude, her arguments, her tone, sure she would be able to open a negotiation with him. But the eternal delay had brought her to inconceivable depths of pessimism.

In this horror, her tutelary image was that of her mother, from whom she inherited, perhaps, her passionate nature, unshakable faith, and elusive dream of happiness. They had a gift for communicating with each other that appeared, like a clairvoyant miracle, during the dark months of captivity. Each word uttered by Nydia on radio or television, each of her gestures, the most casual emphasis, conveyed volumes to Diana's imagination in the dark days of her confinement. "I have always felt she was my guardian angel," she wrote. She was sure that in the midst of so many frustrations the final victory would belong to her mother's devotion and strength. Encouraged by this certainty, she conceived the illusion of a Christmas night release.

That illusion kept her in a state of anticipation during the party that the owners of the house had for her on Christmas Eve, complete with barbecued meat, salsa records, liquor, fireworks, and colored lights. Diana interpreted this as a going-away party. Even more: she had her bag—prepared in November so as not to lose any time when they came for her—ready on the bed. The night was freezing and the wind howled through the trees like a pack of wolves, but she interpreted this as an omen of better times. While they gave gifts to the children, she thought about her own, and consoled herself with the hope that she would be with them the following night. The dream became less improbable when her jailers presented her with a lined leather jacket, chosen perhaps to keep her warm in this foul weather. She was certain her mother had supper waiting for her, as she did every year, and had hung the wreath of mistletoe on the door with a message for her: *Welcome*. Diana was so sure of her release that she waited until the final holiday lights were turned off in the distance, and another morning dawned, full of uncertainties.

The following Wednesday she was sitting alone in front of the television, changing channels, and all at once she saw Alexandra's little boy on the screen. It was a Christmas show put on by "Enfoque." Her surprise increased when she realized it was the Christmas Eve she had requested of her mother in the letter delivered by Azucena. Maruja's and Beatriz's family were there, and all of the Turbays: Diana's two children, her brothers and sisters, and her tall, morose father in the center. "We were in no frame of mind for celebrations," Nydia has said. "Still, I decided to give Diana her wish, and in one hour I set up the Christmas tree and the crèche by the fireplace." In spite of everyone's best intentions not to leave the hostages with a sad impression, it was more a mourning rite than a celebration. But Nydia was so sure Diana would be released that night that she hung the Christmas decoration on the door with the sign in gold letters: *Welcome.* "I confess my sorrow at not being there, not sharing the day with all of them," Diana wrote in her journal. "But it cheered me so, I felt very close to everyone, it made me happy to see them all together." She was delighted by how María Carolina had grown, concerned about Miguelito's shyness, and recalled with alarm that he was not yet baptized; her father's sadness made her sad, and she was moved by her mother, who had put a gift for her in the crèche and hung a welcome on the door.

Instead of feeling demoralized by the disillusionment of Christmas, Diana's reaction was to turn against the government. At one time she had shown a certain enthusiasm for Decree 2047, the basis for the illusions of November. She was encouraged by the efforts of Guido Parra, the diligence of the Notables, the expectations for the Constituent Assembly, the possibilities for amendments to the capitulation policy. But her frustration at Christmas overflowed the dikes of her understanding. She was appalled when she asked herself why the government could not even conceive of a dialogue that was not determined by the absurd pressure of the abductions. She made it clear that she was well aware of how difficult it was to act under threat of blackmail. "I'm pure Turbay as far as that's concerned," she wrote, "but I believe that as time has passed, things have moved backwards." She could not understand the government's passivity in the face of what she considered deception by the abductors. She could not understand why the government was not more energetic in pursuing their surrender if it had established a policy and satisfied some of their reasonable requests. "As long as that is not demanded of them," she wrote in her journal, "they will feel more comfortable about taking their time, knowing they have in their power the most important weapon for exerting pressure on the government." It seemed to her that good offices and mediation had turned into a chess game in which the players moved their men around until somebody declared a checkmate. "But which piece am I?" she asked herself. And answered the question without any evasions: "I can't help thinking we're all dispensable." As for the Notables—now extinct—she gave the group her coup de grâce: "They started out with an eminently humanitarian mission and ended up doing a favor for the Extraditables."

ONE OF THE GUARDS finishing his tour of duty in January burst into Pacho Santos's room.

"It's all fucked up," he said. "They're going to kill hostages."

According to him, this was in retaliation for the death of the Priscos, Escobar's close associates. The communiqué was ready and would be released in the next few hours. First they would kill Marina Montoya, and then one hostage every three days in this order: Richard Becerra, Beatriz, Maruja, and Diana.

"You'll be the last," the guard concluded by way of consolation. "But don't worry, this government can't stomach more than two dead bodies."

Pacho made his terrified calculations based on the guard's information: He had eighteen more days to live. Then he decided to write to his wife and children, and with no rough draft he composed a letter that filled six full-size sheets of notebook paper, printing the words in lowercase letters as he always did, but these were more legible than usual, and his hand was steady though he knew this was not only a letter of farewell, but also his will and testament.

"My only wish is for this drama to end as soon as possible, regardless of the outcome, so that we may all have some peace at last," it began. He was profoundly grateful, he said, to María Victoria, with whom he had grown as a man, as a citizen, and as a father, and his only regret was having given greater importance to his work as a journalist than to his life at home. "I take this remorse with me to the grave," he wrote. As for his children, who were still babies, he was reassured by the certainty that he was leaving them in the best hands. "Tell them about me when they can understand what happened and accept with some equanimity the needless pain of my death." He thanked his father for all that he had done for him in his life, and asked him only "to take care of everything before you come to join me so my children can receive their inheritance without major difficulties." In this way he led into a subject that he considered "boring but fundamental" for the future: financial security for his children and family unity within *El Tiempo*. The first depended in large part on the life insurance the paper had purchased for his wife and children. "I ask you to demand what they promised," he said, "because it would not be fair if my sacrifices for the paper proved to be completely useless." As for the professional, commercial, or political future of the paper, his only concerns were its internal rivalries and disagreements, though he knew that in great families discord is never trivial. "It would be very sad, after this sacrifice, if *El Tiempo* were broken up or sold to outsiders." The letter closed with final words of gratitude to Mariavé for the memory of the good times they had shared.

The guard was moved when Pacho handed it to him.

"Don't you worry, man," he said, "I'll make sure it gets there."

The truth was that Pacho Santos did not have the eighteen days he had calculated but just a few hours. He was first on the list, and the killing had been ordered the day before. Fortunately, Martha Nieves Ochoa happened to hear about it—from third parties—at the eleventh hour and sent Escobar a plea for a reprieve, convinced that this killing would leave the country in ruins. She never knew if he received it, but the fact was that the order to kill Pacho Santos was not carried out, and in its place a second, irrevocable order was issued against Marina Montoya.

Marina seemed to have foreseen this early in January. For reasons she never explained, she decided to take her exercise in the company of her old friend the Monk, who had returned with the year's first change of guard. They would walk for an hour after the television programs went off the air, and then Maruja and Beatriz would go out with their guards. One night Marina came in very frightened because she had seen a man dressed in black, wearing a black mask, watching her in the dark from the laundry area. Maruja and Beatriz thought it had to be another of her recurrent hallucinations, and they paid no attention to it. Their impression was confirmed that same night, because there was not enough light to see a man in black standing in the darkness of the laundry. And if by some chance it were true, he had to be someone well known in the house because the German shepherd did not raise the alarm, and the dog barked at its own shadow. The Monk said it must have been a ghost that only she could see.

Two or three nights later, however, she came back from her walk in a real state of panic. The man had returned, still dressed all in black, and with frightening attention had watched her for a long time, not caring that she was looking at him too. On this night, in contrast to the previous occasions, there was a full moon illuminating the courtyard with an eerie green light. Marina told her story in front of the Monk, and he denied it, but with such tangled reasoning that Maruja and Beatriz did not know what to believe. Marina stopped going out for walks. The doubts regarding her fantasies and reality made so strong an impression that Maruja experienced a real hallucination when she opened her eyes one night and saw the Monk in the light of the bedside candle, squatting as always, his mask turned into a skull. The effect on Maruja was even greater because she connected the vision to the anniversary of her mother's death on January 23.

Marina spent the weekend in bed, suffering from an old back pain that she thought had been cured long ago. Her dark mood returned. Because she could do nothing for herself, Maruja and Beatriz did everything for her. They almost had to carry her to the bathroom. They fed her and held the glass for her, and arranged a pillow behind her back so she could watch television from bed. They pampered her, and felt real affection for her, but never had they felt so despised.

"Look how sick I am and you two won't even help me," Marina would say. "And I've done so much for you."

Often she only succeeded in deepening the sense of abandonment that tormented her. Marina's only real solace during that final crisis were the furious prayers she murmured without letup for hours on end, and the care of her nails. After several days, weary of everything, she lay prostrate on her bed and whispered with a sigh:

"All right, it's in God's hands now."

On the afternoon of January 22, they were visited by the "Doctor" who had been there during the first few days of captivity. He spoke in secret to the guards and listened with great attention to Maruja's and Beatriz's comments on Marina's health. At last he sat down on the edge of the bed to talk to her. The topic must have been serious and confidential because their whispers were so faint no one could make out a word. The "Doctor" left the room in a better humor than when he came in, and promised to return soon.

Marina remained in bed in a state of utter dejection. She cried from time to time. Maruja attempted to comfort her, and Marina thanked her with gestures so as not to interrupt her prayers, and almost always responded with affection, squeezing Maruja's hand with her stiff, ice-cold one. She treated Beatriz, with whom she had a warmer relationship, with the same affection. The only habit that kept her alive was filing her nails.

At ten-thirty on the night of Wednesday, January 23, they began to watch "Enfoque," eager for any unusual word, familiar joke, casual gesture, or subtle changes in the lyrics of a song that might contain a coded message. But there was no time. Just as the theme music began, the door opened at this unusual hour and the Monk came in, though he was not on duty that night.

"We came to take Granny to another house," he said.

He said it as if it were a Sunday outing. In her bed, Marina looked like a marble carving, with her hair disheveled and a pallor so intense that even her lips were white. Then the Monk spoke to her in the affectionate tones of a grandson.

"Get your things together, Granny," he said. "You have five minutes."

He tried to help her up. Marina opened her mouth to say something, but no sound came out. She stood without help, picked up the bag that held her personal effects, and went to the bathroom with the light step of a sleepwalker who does not seem to touch the ground. Maruja confronted the Monk, her voice steady.

"Are you going to kill her?"

The Monk bristled.

"You can't ask a thing like that!" he said. But he regained his composure right away and said: "I told you she's going to a better house. I swear."

Maruja tried everything to stop them from taking her away. Because no boss was there, which was very unusual in so important a decision, she told them to call one for her so that they could discuss it. But the dispute was interrupted when another guard came in to take away the radio and television. He disconnected them with no further explanation, and the last traces of the New Year's Eve party vanished from the room. Maruja asked them to at least let them see the end of the program. Beatriz's response was even more aggressive, but it did no good. They took the radio and television and said they would be back for Marina in five minutes. Maruja and Beatriz, alone in the room, did not know what to believe, or whom, or to what extent this inscrutable decision played a part in their own destinies.

Marina spent much more than five minutes in the bathroom. She came back wearing the pink sweatsuit, the maroon men's socks, and the shoes she had worn on the day of her abduction. The sweatsuit was clean and freshly ironed. The shoes were mildewed and seemed too big, because her feet had shrunk two sizes in four months of suffering. Marina looked ashen and gleaming with icy perspiration, but she still held on to a shred of hope.

"Who knows, maybe they're going to release me!" she said.

Without arranging it ahead of time, Maruja and Beatriz each decided that, regardless of Marina's fate, the most Christian thing was to deceive her.

"Of course they are," said Beatriz.

"That's right," said Maruja with her first radiant smile. "How wonderful!"

Marina's reaction was surprising. In a half-joking, half-serious way she asked what messages they wanted to send to their families. They did their best to improvise something. Marina, laughing at herself a little, asked Beatriz to lend her some of the aftershave that Spots had given her on New Year's Eve. Beatriz did, and Marina dabbed it behind her ears with innate elegance, arranged her beautiful snow-white hair without a mirror, touching it lightly with her fingertips, and when she was finished seemed ready to be free and happy.

In reality she was on the verge of fainting. She asked Maruja for a cigarette and sat on the bed to smoke it until they came for her. She smoked slowly, in great, anguished mouthfuls, while she looked over every millimeter of that hole where she had not found a moment's pity, and where at the end they did not even grant her the dignity of dying in her bed.

Beatriz, to keep from crying, repeated with absolute gravity the message for her family: "If you have a chance to see my husband and children, tell them I'm well and love them very much." But Marina was no longer of this world.

"Don't ask me to do that," she replied, not even looking at her. "I know I'll never have the chance."

Maruja brought her a glass of water with two of the barbiturates that could have put her to sleep for three days. She had to hold the glass for her while she drank because Marina's hands were trembling so much she could not raise it to her lips. That was when Maruja looked deep into her brilliant eyes and realized that Marina was deceiving no one, not even herself. She knew very well who she was, how much she was worth to her captors, and where they were taking her, and if she had followed the lead of the last friends left to her in life, it had been out of compassion.

They brought her a new hood of pink wool that matched her sweatsuit. Before they put it over her head, she said goodbye to Maruja with a hug and a kiss. Maruja blessed her and said, "Don't worry." She said goodbye to Beatriz with another hug and kiss and said: "God bless you." Beatriz, true to herself to the end, kept up the illusion.

"How marvelous, you'll be seeing your family," she said.

Marina turned to the guards without a tear. They turned the hood around, with the openings for the eyes and mouth at the back of her head so she could not see anything. The Monk took both her hands and led her out of the house, walking backward. Marina followed with unfaltering steps. The other guard locked the door from the outside.

Maruja and Beatriz stood motionless in front of the closed door, not knowing how to take up their lives again, until they heard the engines in the garage and then the sound fading away in the distance. Only then did they realize that the television and radio had been taken away to keep them from knowing how the night would end.

6

AT DAWN THE NEXT DAY, Thursday, January 24, the body of Marina Montoya was found in an empty lot north of Bogotá. Almost sitting upright in grass still damp from an early rain, she was leaning against the barbed-wire fence, her arms extended. Criminal Investigation magistrate 78, who examined the body, described her as a woman of about sixty with abundant white hair, dressed in a pink sweatsuit and a pair of maroon men's socks. Beneath the sweatsuit she wore a scapular with a plastic cross. Someone who had arrived on the scene before the police had stolen her shoes.

The head of the corpse was covered by a hood, stiff with dried blood, that had been put on with the openings for the mouth and eyes at the back of the head, and it was almost in tatters because of the entrance and exit holes of six bullets fired from a distance of more than fifty centimeters, since they had left no powder burns on the cloth and skin. The bullet holes were distributed over the skull and the left side of the face, and there was one very clean hole, like a coup de grâce, in the forehead. However, only five 9mm shells were found near the body soaked by wet grasses, and the technical unit of the investigative police had already taken five sets of fingerprints.

Some students from the San Carlos secondary school across the street from the lot had gathered there with other curious on-lookers. Among those who watched the examination of the body was a flower-seller at the Northern Cemetery who had gotten up early to enroll her daughter in a nearby school. The body made a strong impression on her because of the fine quality of the dead woman's underwear, her beautiful, well-tended hands, and her obvious distinction despite her bullet-riddled face. That after-noon, the wholesaler who supplied the flower-seller at her stand in the Northern Cemetery—some five kilometers away—found her suffering from a severe headache and in an alarming state of depression.

"You can't imagine how sad it was to see that poor lady just thrown onto the grass," the flower-seller told her. "You should have seen her underwear, she looked like a great lady with her white hair, her fine hands, her beautiful nails."

The wholesaler was concerned about her and gave her an anal-gesic for her headache, advised her not to think sad thoughts, and above all not to take other people's problems to heart. Neither of them realized until a week later that they had been involved in an unbelievable event: The wholesaler was Marta de Pérez, the wife of Marina's son, Luis Guillermo Pérez.

The Institute of Forensic Medicine received the corpse at five-thirty on Thursday afternoon and left it in storage until the next day because bodies with more than one bullet hole are not autop-sied at night. Two other corpses, males picked up on the streets that morning, were also awaiting identification and a postmortem. During the night two more adult males, also discovered outdoors, were brought in, as well as the body of a five-year-old boy.

Dr. Patricia Alvarez, who began the autopsy of Marina Mon-toya at seven-thirty Friday morning, found the remains of recog-nizable food in her stomach and concluded that death had occurred very late Thursday night. She too was impressed by the quality of the underwear and the buffed and polished nails. She called to her supervisor, Dr. Pedro Morales, who was performing another autopsy two tables away, and he helped her find other unequivocal signs of the dead woman's social position. They took a dental impression, photographs, X rays, and three more sets of fingerprints. Finally they did an atomic absorption test and discovered no trace of psychopharmacologicals despite the two barbiturates that Maruja Pachón had given Marina a few hours before her death.

When they had completed the essential procedures, they sent the body to the Southern Cemetery, where three weeks earlier a mass grave had been dug for two hundred corpses. She was buried there along with the four unidentified males and the boy.

IT WAS EVIDENT during that savage January that Colombia had reached the worst circumstances imaginable. Since 1984, when Minister Rodrigo Lara Bonilla had been assassinated, we had experienced all kinds of abominable acts, but it was not over yet, and the worst was not behind us. All the elements of violence had been unleashed and exacerbated.

Among the many atrocities that had convulsed the country, narcoterrorism stood out as the most virulent and cruel. Four presidential candidates had been assassinated before the 1990 campaign. Carlos Pizarro, the M-19 candidate, was killed by a lone assassin on a commercial plane, even though his flight reservations had been changed four times, in absolute secrecy and with every kind of misleading subterfuge. Ernesto Samper, a precandidate, survived eleven bullets and reached the presidency five years later with four of them still in his body; they set off airport security alarms. A car bomb made with 350 kilos of dynamite exploded in the path of General Maza Márquez, and he had escaped from his lightly armored automobile, pulling out one of his wounded bodyguards. "All at once I felt as if I had been tossed into the air by the surf," the general commented. The upheaval was so great that he needed psychiatric help to regain his emotional equilibrium. He was still in treatment seven months later, when a truck carrying two tons of dynamite destroyed the huge Administrative Department for Security building in an apocalyptic explosion that left 70 dead, 620 wounded, and incalculable physical destruction. The terrorists had waited for the precise moment when the general walked into his office, but in the midst of the cataclysm he was not even scratched. That same year, a bomb exploded aboard a passenger plane five minutes after takeoff, causing 107 deaths, among them Andrés Escabí—Pacho Santos's brother-in-law—and Gerardo Arellano, the Colombian tenor. The accepted version of events was that the intended victim had been the candidate César Gaviria—a sinister mistake, since Gaviria never intended to take that flight. His campaign security services had forbidden him to use commercial planes, and on one occasion when he made the attempt he had to stop because the other passengers panicked and tried to get off to avoid the danger of flying with him.

The truth was that the country was trapped in a vicious circle. On one hand, the Extraditables refused to surrender or temper the violence because the police gave them no quarter. Escobar had denounced in all the media the fact that the police would go into the Medellín slums at any hour of the day or night, pick up ten boys at random, ask no questions, and shoot them in basements or empty lots. Their blanket assumption was that most of the boys were working for Pablo Escobar, or supported him, or soon would do one or the other, either by choice or through coercion. On the other hand, the terrorists were relentless in their murder of ambushed police, their assaults and abductions. And for their part, the two oldest and strongest guerrilla movements, the Army of National Liberation (ELN) and the Revolutionary Armed Forces

(FARC), had just responded with all kinds of terrorist acts to the first peace proposal offered by the government of César Gaviria.

One of the groups most affected by the blind warfare were journalists, the victims of assassinations and abductions, and also of desertions because of threats and corruption. Between September 1983 and January 1991, twenty-six journalists working in various Colombian media were murdered by the drug cartels. Guillermo Cano, director of *El Espectador*, and the gentlest of men, was killed on December 17, 1986, by two gunmen who followed him to the door of his newspaper. He drove his own van, and although he was one of the most threatened men in the country because of his suicidal editorials attacking the drug trade, he refused to use a bulletproof car or travel with a bodyguard. His enemies even tried to go on killing him after his death. A bust erected in his memory was dynamited in Medellín. Months later, a truck carrying three hundred kilos of dynamite exploded, reducing the paper's presses to rubble.

Easy money, a narcotic more harmful than the ill-named "heroic drugs," was injected into the national culture. The idea prospered: The law is the greatest obstacle to happiness; it is a waste of time learning to read and write; you can live a better, more secure life as a criminal than as a law-abiding citizen—in short, this was the social breakdown typical of all undeclared wars.

Abduction was not a new element in recent Colombian history. None of the four preceding presidents had escaped the destabilizing trials of an abduction. And certainly, as far as anyone knows, none had given in to the demands of the kidnappers. In February 1976, during the government of Alfonso López Michelsen, the M-19 had kidnapped José Raquel Mercado, the president of the Federation of Colombian Workers. He was tried and condemned to death by his captors as a traitor to the working class, and executed with two bullets in the back of the head when the government refused to comply with a series of political demands.

Sixteen elite members of the same armed movement took over the embassy of the Dominican Republic in Bogotá as they were celebrating their national holiday on February 27, 1980, during the presidency of Julio César Turbay. For sixty-one days almost the entire accredited diplomatic corps in Colombia, including the ambassadors of the United States, Israel, and the Vatican, were held hostage. The M-19 demanded a fifty-million-dollar ransom and the release of 311 of their members who were in prison. President Turbay refused to negotiate, but the hostages were freed on April 28 with no expressed conditions, and their abductors left the country under the protection of the Cuban government, which had responded to a request by the Colombian government. The guerrillas stated in private that they had received a ransom of five million dollars in cash collected by the Jewish community in Colombia with the help of other Jews throughout the world.

On November 6, 1985, a commando unit of the M-19 took over the crowded Supreme Court building at the busiest time of day and demanded that the highest court in the nation put President Belisario Betancur on trial for not having kept his promise to establish peace. The president did not negotiate, and the army stormed the building and recaptured it after ten hours of bloody fighting that cost an unknown number of missing and ninety-five civilian deaths, including nine magistrates of the Supreme Court and its president, Alfonso Reyes Echandía.

President Virgilio Barco, who was almost at the end of his term, did not resolve the abduction of Alvaro Diego Montoya, the son of his secretary general. Seven months later, Pablo Escobar's rage blew up in the face of Barco's successor, César Gaviria, who began his presidency facing the grave crisis of ten well-known hostages.

In his first five months, however, Gaviria had created a less turbulent atmosphere for weathering the storm. He had achieved a political agreement to convene a Constituent Assembly, invested by the Supreme Court with unlimited power to decide any issue—including, of course, the hottest ones: the extradition of Colombian nationals, and amnesty. But the underlying problem, for the government as well as the drug traffickers and the guerrillas, was that as long as Colombia did not have an effective judicial system, it was almost impossible to articulate a policy for peace that would position the state on the side of good, and criminals of any stripe on the side of evil. But nothing was simple in those days, least of all obtaining objective information from any quarter, or teaching children the difference between good and evil.

The government's credibility was not at the high level of its notable political successes but at the abysmal level of its security forces, which were censured in the world press and by international human rights organizations. Pablo Escobar, however, had achieved a credibility that the guerrillas never enjoyed in their best times. People tended to believe the lies of the Extraditables more than the truths told by the government.

DECREE 3030 was issued on December 14, 1990, modifying 2047 and nullifying all previous decrees. Among other innovations, it introduced the judicial accumulation of sentences; that is, a person tried for several crimes, whether in the same trial or in subsequent ones, would not serve the total time of the various sentences, but only the longest one. It also established a series of procedures and time limits relating to the use of evidence from other countries in trials held in Colombia. But the two great obstacles to surrender were still firmly in place: the somewhat uncertain conditions for non-extradition, and the fixed time limit on pardonable crimes. In other words, capitulation and confession remained the indispensable requirements for non-extradition and reduced sentences, as long as the crimes had been committed before September 5, 1990. Pablo Escobar objected in an angry message. His reaction this time had another motivation he was careful not to reveal in public: the accelerated exchange of evidence with the United States that facilitated extradition hearings.

Alberto Villamizar was the most surprised of men. His daily contacts with Rafael Pardo had led him to expect a more lenient decree, but this one seemed harsher than the first. And he was not alone in his response. Criticism was so widespread that on the same day the second degree was issued, a third one began to be considered.

An easy conjecture as to the reasons for the greater severity of Decree 3030 was that the more radical sector of the government—in reaction to a campaign of conciliatory communiqués and the gratuitous release of four journalists—had convinced the president that Escobar was cornered. In fact, he had never been stronger than he was then, with the tremendous pressure of the abductions and the possibility that the Constituent Assembly would abolish extradition and proclaim an amnesty.

The three Ochoa brothers, on the other hand, took immediate refuge in the capitulation option. This was interpreted as a rupture at the top of the cartel. In reality, however, the process of their surrender had begun in September, at the time of the first decree, when a well-known senator from Antioquia asked Rafael Pardo to see a person he would not identify ahead of time. It was Martha Nieves Ochoa, who with this bold step initiated negotiations for the surrender of each of her three brothers, at one-month intervals. And that is how it happened. Fabio, the youngest, turned himself in on December 18; on January 15, when it seemed least feasible, Jorge Luis surrendered, as did Juan David on February 16. Five years later, a group of reporters from the United States put the question to Jorge Luis in prison, and his reply was categorical: "We surrendered to save our skins." He acknowledged that behind it lay irresistible pressure from the women in his family, who would not rest until their brothers were safe inside the fortified prison in Itagüí, an industrial suburb of Medellín. It was an act of familial confidence in the government, which at the time could still have extradited them to serve life sentences in the United States.

DOÑA NYDIA QUINTERO, always mindful of her premonitions, did not discount the importance of the Ochoas' surrender. Less than three days after Fabio turned himself in, she went to see him in prison, accompanied by her daughter María Victoria, and María Carolina, Diana's daughter. Faithful to the tribal protocol of Medellín, five members of the Ochoa family had come for her at the house where she was staying: the mother, Martha Nieves and one of her sisters, and two young men. They took her to Itagüí prison, a forbidding structure at the top of a narrow, hilly street decorated with colored-paper wreaths for Christmas.

Waiting for them in the prison cell, in addition to the younger Fabio, was the father, don Fabio Ochoa, a patriarch weighing 330 pounds with the face of a boy, who at the age of seventy bred fine-gaited Colombian horses and was the spiritual head of a vast family of intrepid men and powerful women. He liked to preside over family visits sitting in a thronelike chair and wearing his perpetual horseman's hat with a ceremonious air that suited his slow, determined speech and folk wisdom. Beside him was his son, who is lively and talkative but barely uttered a word that day while his father was speaking.

Don Fabio began by praising the courage with which Nydia had moved heaven and earth to rescue Diana. He formulated the possibility of his intervening with Pablo Escobar on her behalf with masterful rhetoric: He would, with the greatest pleasure, do whatever he could, but he did not believe he could do anything. At the end of the visit, the younger Fabio asked Nydia to please explain to the president the importance of extending the time limit for surrender in the capitulation decree. Nydia said she could not do it but they could, with a letter to the appropriate authorities. It was her way of not permitting them to use her as their messenger to the president. The younger Fabio understood this, and said goodbye with the comforting phrase: "Where there's life, there's hope."

When Nydia returned to Bogotá, Azucena gave her the letter in which Diana asked that she celebrate Christmas with her children, and Hero Buss telephoned, urging her to come to Cartagena so that they could talk in person. She found him in good physical and emotional condition after three months of captivity, and that helped to reassure Nydia somewhat about her daughter's health. Hero Buss had not seen Diana after the first week, but there had been a constant exchange of news among the guards and the people who ran the houses, which filtered down to the hostages, and he knew that Diana was well. The only serious and ongoing danger was an armed rescue. "You cannot imagine the constant threat that they'll kill you," said Hero Buss. "Not only because the law, as they call it, is there, but because they're always so edgy they think the tiniest noise is a rescue operation." His only advice to her was to prevent an armed rescue at any cost, and to persuade the government to change the time limit on surrender in the decree.

On the same day she returned to Bogotá, Nydia expressed her forebodings to the justice minister. She visited the defense minister, General Oscar Botero, accompanied by her son, the parliamentarian Julio César Turbay Quintero, and her anguished plea, on behalf of all the hostages, was that they use intelligence agencies rather than rescue teams. Her disquiet was accelerating, the premonition of tragedy becoming more and more acute. Her heart was breaking. She wept constantly. Nydia made a supreme effort to regain her self-control, but bad news gave her no peace. On the radio she heard a message from the Extraditables, threatening to dump the captives' bodies, in sacks, outside the presidential palace if the terms of the second decree were not modified. In mortal despair, Nydia called the president. He was at a meeting of the Council on Security, and she spoke to Rafael Pardo.

"I implore you to ask the president and the members of the Council on Security if they need to find bags of dead hostages at their door before they change the decree."

She was in the same agitated state hours later, when she asked the president in person to change the time limit in the decree. He had already heard that Nydia was complaining about his insensitivity to other people's grief, and he made an effort to be more patient and forthcoming. He said that Decree 3030 had just been issued, and the least they could do was give it enough time to work. But Nydia thought the president's arguments were no more than rationalizations for not doing what he should have done at the opportune moment.

"A change in the deadline is necessary not only to save the lives of the hostages," Nydia replied, tired of so much talk, "but it's the one thing that will make the terrorists surrender. Change it, and they'll let Diana go."

Gaviria did not yield. Convinced that the time limit was the greatest obstacle to the capitulation policy, he resisted changing it in order to keep the Extraditables from getting what they were after when they took the hostages. The Constituent Assembly, shrouded in uncertainties, would meet in the next few days, and he could not allow weakness on the part of the government to result in an amnesty for the drug traffickers. "Democracy was never endangered by the assassinations of four presidential candidates, or because of any abduction," Gaviria would later comment. "The real threat came at those moments when we faced the temptation, or risk, or even the rumor of a possibility of an amnesty"—in short, the unthinkable danger that the conscience of the Constituent Assembly would also be taken hostage. Gaviria already knew what he would do: If that happened, his calm, irrevocable decision was to dissolve the Assembly.

For some time Nydia had been thinking that Dr. Turbay should do something for the captives that would shake the entire country: a mass demonstration outside the presidential palace, a general strike, a formal protest to the United Nations. But Dr. Turbay tried to mollify her. "He was always that way, because he was responsible and moderate," Nydia has said. "But you knew that inside he was dying of grief." That certainty, rather than soothing her, only intensified her anguish. This was when she decided to write a private letter to the president "that would move him to take the action he knew was necessary."

Dr. Gustavo Balcázar, Nydia's husband, was worried about her, and on January 24 he persuaded his wife to spend a few days with him in their house in Tabio—an hour's drive from the city, on the Bogotá savanna—to try to alleviate her despair. She had not been there since her daughter had been abducted, and so she brought her statue of the Virgin, and two large fifteen-day candles, and everything she needed to stay connected to reality. In the icy solitude of the savanna, she spent an interminable night on her knees, praying to the Virgin to protect Diana with an invulnerable bell jar that would shield her from abuse and fear, and not let bullets touch her. At five in the morning, after a brief, troubled sleep, she sat at the dining-room table and began to write the letter from her soul to the president of the republic. Dawn found her scrawling random ideas, crying, tearing up drafts as she wept, making clean copies in a sea of tears.

In contrast to her own expectations, she was writing the most judicious and forceful letter of her life. "I don't pretend to be composing a public document," it began. "I want to communicate with the president of my country and, with all due respect, convey to him my most considered thoughts, and a justifiably anguished plea." Despite the president's repeated promise that no armed effort to rescue Diana would ever be attempted, Nydia left written evidence of a prescient appeal: "The country knows, and all of you know, that if they happen to find the kidnappers during one of those searches, a terrible tragedy might ensue." Convinced that the obstacles present in the second decree had interrupted the process of releasing hostages begun by the Extraditables before Christmas, Nydia alerted the president to a new, self-evident danger: If the government did not take some immediate action to remove those obstacles, the hostages risked having the issue left in the hands of the Constituent Assembly. "This would mean that the distress and anguish suffered not only by the families but by the entire nation would be prolonged for endless months," she wrote. Nydia ended with an elegant closing: "Because of my convictions, because of the respect I have for you as First Magistrate of the Nation, I would be incapable of suggesting any initiative of my own devising, but I do feel inclined to entreat you, for the sake of innocent lives, not to underestimate the danger that time represents." When it was finished and copied out in a fair hand, it came to two and a quarter full-size sheets. Nydia called the president's private secretary to find out exactly where it should be sent.

That same morning the storm broke with the news that the leaders of the Prisco gang had been killed: David Ricardo and Armando Alberto Prisco Lopera, the brothers accused of the seven assassinations of public figures during this time, and of being the brains behind the abductions, including the capture of Diana Turbay and her crew. One had died carrying false papers that identified him as Francisco Muñoz Serna, but when Azucena Liévano saw the photograph in the papers she recognized don Pacho, the man responsible for her and Diana in their captivity. His death and his brother's, at that turbulent moment, were an irreparable loss for Escobar, and he would not wait long to make that known by actions.

In a threatening communiqué, the Extraditables said that David Ricardo had not been killed in combat but cut down by the police in front of his young children and pregnant wife. As for his brother Armando, the communiqué insisted he had not been killed in a gunfight, as the police claimed, but murdered on a farm in Rionegro even though he was paralyzed as the result of an earlier attempt on his life. His wheelchair, the message said, could be seen clearly on the regional newscast.

This was the communiqué that had been mentioned to Pacho Santos. It was made public on January 25 with the announcement that two captives would be executed within a week's time, and that the first order had already been issued against Marina Montoya—a stunning piece of news, since it was assumed that Marina had been murdered at the time of her abduction in September.

"That's what I was referring to when I sent the president the message about the bodies in sacks," Nydia has said, recalling that ghastly day. "It's not that I was impulsive, or temperamental, or in need of psychiatric care. But they were going to kill my daughter because I might not be able to move the people who could stop it."

Alberto Villamizar was no less desperate. "That was the most horrible day of my life," he said at the time, convinced that the executions would not be long in coming. Who would be first: Diana, Pacho, Maruja, Beatriz, Richard? It was a deadly lottery he did not even want to imagine. He called President Gaviria in a rage.

"You have to stop these raids," he said.

"No, Alberto," Gaviria responded with his blood-chilling calm. "That isn't why I was elected."

Villamizar slammed down the phone, astonished at his own vehemence. "Now what do I do?" he asked himself. To begin with, he requested help from former presidents Alfonso López Michelsen and Misael Pastrana, and Monsignor Darío Castrillón, the bishop of Pereira. They all made public statements repudiating the methods used by the Extraditables and pleading for the lives of the captives. On the National Radio Network López Michelsen called for the government and Escobar to stop the war and search for a political solution.

AT THAT MOMENT the tragedy had already occurred. Minutes before dawn on January 21, Diana had written the last page of her diary. "It's close to five months, and only we know what this means," she wrote. "I don't want to lose the faith or the hope that I'll go home safe and sound."

She was no longer alone. Following the release of Azucena and Orlando, she had asked to be with Richard, and her request was granted after Christmas. It was good for both of them. They talked until they were exhausted, listened to the radio until dawn, and in this way acquired the habit of sleeping by day and living at night. They had learned about the death of the Priscos from the guards' conversation. One guard was crying. The other, certain this meant the end and no doubt referring to the hostages, asked: "And what do we do now with the merchandise?" The one who was crying did not have to give it a second thought.

"We'll get rid of it," he said.

Diana and Richard could not sleep after breakfast. Days earlier they had been told they would be changing houses. They had not paid much attention, since in the brief month they had been together they had been moved twice to nearby safe houses in anticipation of real or imaginary police raids. A little before eleven on the morning of January 25, they were in Diana's room discussing the guards' conversation in whispers, when they heard the sound of helicopters coming from Medellín.

In recent days police intelligence agencies had received numerous anonymous phone calls reporting the movement of armed people along the Sabaneta road—municipality of Copacabana—in particular around the farms of Alto de la Cruz, Villa del Rosario, and La Bola. Perhaps their captors planned to transfer Diana and Richard to Alto de la Cruz, the most secure of the properties because it was located at the top of a high, wooded hill and had a commanding view of the entire valley all the way to Medellín. As a result of the calls, and other leads of their own, the police were about to raid the house. It was a major military operation involving two captains, nine officers, seven noncommissioned officers, and ninety-nine agents, half of them traveling overland and half in four combat helicopters. The guards, however, no longer paid attention to helicopters because they flew over so often and nothing ever happened. Suddenly one of them was at the door and shouted at them in fright:

"The law's all over us!"

Diana and Richard took as long as they could because this was the right time for a police assault: The four guards on duty were not the toughest ones, and seemed too panicked to defend themselves. Diana brushed her teeth and put on a white shirt she had washed the day before; she put on her sneakers and the jeans she had been wearing the day she was kidnapped, too big for her now because she had lost weight. Richard changed his shirt and gathered up the camera equipment that had been returned to him in the past few days. The guards seemed crazed by the growing noise of the helicopters that flew over the house, went back toward the valley, and returned almost grazing the treetops. The guards shouted for them to hurry and pushed the hostages toward the outside door. They gave them white hats so they would look like campesinos from the air. They threw a black shawl over Diana, and Richard put on his leather jacket. The guards ordered them to run for the mountain, while they spread out and ran too, their weapons ready to fire when the helicopters were within range. Diana and Richard began to climb a narrow, rocky path. The slope was very steep, and the hot sun burned straight down from the middle of the sky. Diana was exhausted after only a few meters, when the helicopters were already in view. At the first burst of gunfire, Richard threw himself to the ground. "Don't move," Diana shouted. "Play dead." And then she fell facedown beside him.

"They killed me," she screamed. "I can't move my legs."

She could not, in fact, but she felt no pain either, and she asked

Richard to look at her back because before she dropped she had felt something like an electric shock at her waist. Richard raised her shirt and just above the left hip bone saw a clean tiny hole, with no blood.

The shooting continued, coming closer and closer, and a desperate Diana insisted that Richard leave her there and get away, but he stayed, hoping for help that would save her too. While they waited, he placed in her hand a Virgin that he always carried in his pocket, and he prayed with her. The gunfire came to an abrupt end, and two members of the Elite Corps appeared on the trail, their weapons at the ready.

Richard, who was kneeling beside Diana, raised his arms and said, "Don't shoot!" One of the agents stared at him with a look of astonishment and asked:

"Where's Pablo?"

"I don't know," Richard said. "I'm Richard Becerra, I'm a journalist. This is Diana Turbay, and she's wounded."

"Prove it," said an agent.

Richard showed him his identity card. With the help of some campesinos who emerged from the underbrush, they made an improvised litter from a sheet and carried her to the helicopter. The pain had become unbearable, but she was calm and lucid, and knew she was going to die.

HALF AN HOUR LATER, former president Turbay received a call from a military source informing him that his daughter Diana and Francisco Santos had been rescued in Medellín in an operation carried out by the Elite Corps. He immediately called Hernando Santos, who let out a victory whoop and ordered the telephone operators at his newspaper to relay the news to the entire family. Then he called Alberto Villamizar's apartment and repeated the news word for word. "How wonderful," shouted Villamizar. His joy was sincere, but he realized right away that with Pacho and Diana free, the only killable hostages still in Escobar's hands were Maruja and Beatriz.

As he made urgent phone calls, he turned on the radio and discovered that the news was not yet on the air. He was about to dial Rafael Pardo's number when the phone rang again. It was a disheartened Hernando Santos, calling to tell him that Turbay had amended his first information. It was not Francisco Santos who had been freed but the cameraman Richard Becerra, and Diana was seriously wounded. Hernando Santos, however, was not as disturbed by the error as he was by Turbay's consternation at having caused him a counterfeit happiness.

MARTHA LUPE ROJAS was not home when someone from the news program called to tell her that her son Richard was free. She had gone to her brother's house, and was so anxious for news that she carried a portable radio with her wherever she went, but that day, for the first time since the abduction, the radio was not working.

Someone told her that her son was safe, and in the cab on the way to the television station, she heard the familiar voice of the radio journalist Juan Gossaín bringing her back to reality: The reports from Medellín were still very confused. It had been confirmed that Diana Turbay was dead, but there was nothing definite about Richard Becerra. Martha Lupe began to pray in a quiet voice: "Dear God, send the bullets to the side, don't let them touch him." At that moment, Richard called his house from Medellín to tell her he was safe, and no one was home. But an emotional shout from Gossaín returned Martha Lupe's soul to her body:

"Extra! Extra! The cameraman Richard Becerra is alive!"

Martha Lupe burst into tears and could not stop crying until late that night, when she welcomed her son in the editorial offices of the newscast "Criptón." Today she recalls: "He was nothing but skin and bone, pale and bearded, but he was alive."

RAFAEL PARDO HAD received the news in his office just a few minutes earlier, when a reporter who was a friend of his called to confirm a version of the rescue. He telephoned General Maza Márquez and then the head of the National Police, General Gómez Padilla, and neither one knew anything about any rescue operations. A little while later, Gómez Padilla called to inform him that it had been a chance encounter with the Elite Corps during a search for Escobar. The units involved, Gómez Padilla said, had no prior information regarding hostages in that location.

Since receiving the report from Medellín, Dr. Turbay had been trying to reach Nydia at the house in Tabio, but her telephone was out of order. He sent his chief bodyguard in a van to tell her that Diana was safe and in a Medellín hospital for a routine examination. Nydia heard the news at two in the afternoon, but instead of shouting with joy, as the rest of the family had, she looked stunned by grief, and exclaimed:

"They've killed Diana!"

On the drive back to Bogotá, as they were listening to the news on the radio, her uncertainty intensified. "I was still crying," she would later say. "Not shrieking and moaning, as I had before, just shedding tears." She stopped at her house to change clothes before going on to the airport, where the presidential plane—a decrepit Fokker that flew only by the grace of God after almost thirty years of forced labor—was waiting for the family. The latest report said that Diana was in intensive care, but Nydia did not believe anyone or anything except her own instincts. She went straight to the telephone and asked to speak to the president.

"They killed Diana, Mr. President," she said. "And it's your doing, it's your fault, it's what comes of having a soul of stone."

The president was glad he could contradict her with a piece of good news.

"No, Señora," he said in his calmest voice. "It seems there was a raid, and nothing is confirmed yet. But Diana is alive."

"No," Nydia replied. "They killed her."

The president, who was in direct communication with Medellín, had no doubts.

"How do you know that?"

Nydia answered with absolute conviction:

"Because I'm her mother and my heart tells me so."

Her heart was correct. An hour later, María Emma Mejía, the presidential adviser for Medellín, came aboard the plane that was carrying the Turbay family and gave them the bad news. Diana had bled to death despite several hours of medical intervention, which would have been hopeless in any case. She had lost consciousness in the helicopter that transported her to Medellín, and had never regained it. Her spinal column had been shattered at the waist by a high-velocity, medium-caliber explosive bullet that splintered inside her body and caused a general paralysis from which she never would have recovered.

Nydia suffered a major shock when she saw her in the hospital, lying naked on the operating table under a blood-soaked sheet, her face without expression and her skin without color because of the loss of blood. There was an enormous incision in her chest where the doctors had inserted their hands to massage her heart.

As soon as she left the operating room, when she was beyond grief and despair, Nydia held a ferocious press conference right in the hospital. "This is the story of a death foretold," she began. Convinced that Diana had been the victim of an assault ordered from Bogotá—according to information she had received since her arrival in Medellín—she gave a detailed account of the appeals she and the family had made to the president that the police not attempt a rescue. She said that the stupidity and criminality of the Extraditables were responsible for her daughter's death, but the guilt was shared equally by the government and the president, above all by the president, "who with lack of feeling, almost with coldness and indifference, turned a deaf ear to the appeals that there be no rescues and that the lives of the hostages not be placed in danger."

This categorical statement, quoted verbatim in all the media, generated solidarity in public opinion, and indignation in the government. The president held a meeting with Fabio Villegas, his secretary general; Miguel Silva, his private secretary; Rafael Pardo, his security adviser; and Mauricio Vargas, his press adviser. The purpose was to devise a resounding denial of Nydia's statement. But more careful reflection led them to the conclusion that one cannot argue with a mother's grief. Gaviria understood this, rescinded the purpose of the meeting, and gave an order:

"We'll go to the funeral."

Not only he but the entire government.

Nydia's rancor gave her no peace. With someone whose name she could not remember, she had sent Gaviria Diana's letter—after she knew she was dead—perhaps so that he would always carry with him the burden of its premonition. "Obviously I didn't expect him to answer," she said.

At the end of the funeral mass in the cathedral—it had rarely been more crowded—the president rose from his seat and walked the empty central nave alone, followed by everyone's eyes, and photographers' flashbulbs and television cameras, and held out his hand to Nydia, certain she would leave him with his hand outstretched. Nydia took it with icy distaste. In reality, she felt relieved, for what she feared was that the president would embrace her. However, she appreciated the condolence kiss from his wife, Ana Milena.

It was not over yet. As soon as the obligations of mourning had eased somewhat, Nydia requested another meeting with the president to give him important information that he ought to know before delivering his speech that day on Diana's death. Silva conveyed the precise message he had received, and then the president gave the smile that Nydia would never see.

"She's coming to cut out my heart," he said. "But have her come, of course."

He greeted her as he always did. Nydia, however, dressed in black, walked into the office with a different air: simple, and grieving. She came straight to the point, which she revealed to the president with her opening words:

"I've come to do you a favor."

The surprise was that she began by begging his pardon for believing that he had ordered the raid in which Diana died. She knew now that he had not been aware of it. And she also wanted to tell him that at present he was being deceived again, because it was not true that the purpose of the mission had been to find Pablo Escobar, but to free the hostages, whose whereabouts had been revealed under torture by a gang member who had been captured by the police. And who, Nydia explained, had later shown up as one of those killed in the shooting.

She spoke with energy and precision, and with the hope of arousing the interest of the president, but she could not detect even the slightest sign of compassion. "He was like a block of ice," she would say later when recalling that day. Not knowing why, or at what point it happened, and unable to stop herself, she began to cry. Then the temperament she had kept under control rebelled, and her manner and the subject underwent a complete transformation. She berated the president for his indifference and coldness in not fulfilling his constitutional obligation to save the lives of the hostages.

"Just think about it," she concluded. "What if your daughter had been in this situation. What would you have done then?"

She looked straight into his eyes but was so agitated by this time that the president could not interrupt her. Later he would say: "She asked me questions but gave me no chance to answer them." Nydia, in fact, stopped him cold with another question: "Don't you think, Mr. President, that you were mistaken in your handling of this problem?" For the first time the president revealed a shred of doubt. "I've never suffered so much," he would say years later. But he only blinked and said in his natural voice:

"It's possible."

Nydia stood, extended her hand in silence, and left the office before he could open the door for her. Then Miguel Silva came into the office and found the president very affected by the story of the dead gunman. Gaviria lost no time in writing a personal letter to the prosecutor general telling him to investigate the case and bring it to trial.

MOST PEOPLE AGREED that the purpose of the raid had been to capture Escobar or one of the important capos, but that even with this rationale it was stupid and doomed to failure. According to the immediate police version, Diana had died in the course of a search mission carried out with the support of helicopters and ground personnel. Without intending to, they had encountered the armed unit guarding Diana Turbay and the cameraman Richard Becerra. As they were fleeing, one of the kidnappers shot Diana in the back and shattered her spine. The cameraman was not hurt. Diana was taken to the Medellín General Hospital in a police helicopter, and died there at 4:35 in the afternoon.

Pablo Escobar's version was quite different and agreed in its essential points with the story Nydia told to the president. According to him, the police had carried out the raid knowing that the hostages were in that location. They had obtained the information under torture from two of his men whom he identified with their real names and the numbers on their identity cards. His communiqué claimed they had been arrested and tortured by the police, and that one of them had guided the officers there from a helicopter. He said that Diana was killed by the police when she was running away from the fighting and had already been released by her captors. He concluded by stating that three innocent campesinos had also been killed in the skirmish, but the police described them to the press as criminals who had been shot during the fighting. This report must have given Escobar the satisfaction he had hoped for when he denounced police violations of human rights.

ON THE NIGHT of the tragedy, Richard Becerra, the only available witness, was besieged by reporters in a room at General Police Headquarters in Bogotá. He was still wearing the black leather jacket he had on when he had been kidnapped, and the straw hat his captors had given him so he would be mistaken for a campesino. He was not in any state of mind to provide illuminating details.

The impression he made on his more understanding colleagues was that the confusion of events had not allowed him to form an opinion about the incident. His statement that the bullet that killed Diana was fired intentionally by one of the kidnappers was not supported by any evidence. The widespread belief, over and above all the conjectures, was that Diana died by accident in the cross fire. But the definitive investigation would be handled by the prosecutor general, in accordance with the letter sent to him by President Gaviria following the revelations of Nydia Quintero.

The drama had not ended. In response to public uncertainty regarding the fate of Marina Montoya, the Extraditables issued another communiqué on January 30, acknowledging that they had given the order to execute her on January 23. But, "because we are in hiding and communications are poor, we have no information—at present—as to whether she was executed or released. If she was executed, we do not understand why the police have not yet reported finding her body. If she was released, it is now up to her family." Only then, seven days after the order to kill her was given, did the search for her body begin.

Pedro Morales, one of the pathologists who had performed the autopsy, read the bulletin in the paper and believed the corpse of the lady with the fine clothes and impeccable nails was in fact Marina Montoya. He was correct. As soon as her identity was established, however, someone claiming to be from the Justice Ministry called the Institute of Forensic Medicine, urging them not to reveal that the body was in a mass grave.

Luis Guillermo Pérez Montoya, Marina's son, was leaving for lunch when he heard the preliminary report on the radio. At the Institute, they showed him the photograph of the woman disfigured by bullets, and he had difficulty recognizing her. A special deployment of police was required at the Southern Cemetery, because the news had already been announced and they had to clear a path to the grave site for Luis Guillermo Pérez through a mass of curious onlookers.

According to regulations at the Institute, an anonymous corpse has to be buried with a serial number stamped on the torso, arms, and legs so that it can be identified even in case of dismemberment. It has to be enclosed in black plastic, the kind used for trash bags, and tied at the ankles and wrists with strong cord. The body of Marina Montoya—according to her son—was naked and covered in mud, and had been tossed into the common grave without the identifying tattoos required by law. Beside her was the body of the boy who had been buried at the same time, wrapped in the pink sweatsuit.

Back in the amphitheater, after she had been washed down with a high-pressure hose, her son examined her teeth and hesitated for a moment. He seemed to remember that Marina was missing her left premolar, and this corpse had all its teeth. But when he looked at the hands, and placed them over his own, all his doubts vanished: They were the same. Another suspicion would persist, perhaps forever: Luis Guillermo Pérez was convinced that his mother's corpse had been identified at the time of the on-site examination, and had been sent straight to the common grave to get rid of evidence that might upset the public or embarrass the government.

DIANA'S DEATH—even before the discovery of Marina's body— had a powerful impact on the country. When Gaviria had refused to modify the second decree, he had not given in to Villamizar's harshness or Nydia's entreaties. His argument, in brief, was that the decrees could not be judged in terms of the abductions but with a view to the public interest, since Escobar was not taking hostages to put pressure on the capitulation policy but to force non-extradition and obtain an amnesty. These thoughts led him to a final modification of the decree. It was difficult, after having resisted Nydia's pleas and the grief of so many other people, to change the date, but he resolved to do it.

Villamizar received the news through Rafael Pardo. The wait seemed infinite to him. He had not had a minute's peace. His life revolved around the radio and telephone, and his relief was immense when he heard no bad news. He called Pardo at all hours. "Any news?" he would ask. "How long can this go on?" Pardo calmed him down with doses of rationality. Every night he came home in the same state. "That decree has to be issued or they'll kill everybody in sight," he would say. Pardo calmed him down. At last, on January 28, it was Pardo who made the call to say that the final version of the decree was ready for the president's signature. The delay had been due to the fact that all the ministers had to sign it, and they had not been able to locate Alberto Casas Santamaría, the communications minister, until Rafael Pardo reached him by phone and threatened him, as amiable as an old friend.

"Mr. Minister," he told him. "Either you're here in half an hour to sign the decree, or you're not a minister anymore."

On January 29, Decree 303 was issued, clearing away all the obstacles that had interfered so far with the surrender of the drug traffickers. Just as many in the government expected, they were never able to dispel the widespread belief that the decree was an act of contrition for Diana's death. This, as usual, generated still other objections: those who thought it was a concession to the traffickers, the result of a stunned public opinion, and those who saw it as a step the president could not avoid taking, though it came too late for Diana Turbay. In any case, President Gaviria signed it out of conviction, knowing that the delay could be interpreted as proof of his hard heart, and the belated decision proclaimed as an act of weakness.

The next day, at seven in the morning, the president returned a call he had received from Villamizar the night before to thank him for the decree. Gaviria listened to his reasons in absolute silence, and shared with him his anguish of January 25.

"It was a terrible day for everyone," he said.

Then Villamizar called Guido Parra with a clear conscience. "You're not going to start all that shit now about how this decree is no good," he said. Guido Parra had already studied it with care.

"Right," he said, "no problem on this end. Just think how much grief it could have saved us if it had come out earlier."

Villamizar wanted to know what the next step would be.

"Nothing," said Guido Parra. "It's a matter of forty-eight hours."

The Extraditables immediately let it be known in a communiqué that they would cancel the announced executions in light of appeals from several well-known persons. They may have been referring to the radio messages addressed to them by former presidents López Michelsen and Pastrana, and Monsignor Castrillón. But in essence it could also be interpreted as their acceptance of the decree. "We will respect the lives of the remaining hostages," said the communiqué. As a special concession, they also announced that early that same day they would release a hostage. Villamizar, who was with Guido Parra, gave a start of surprise.

"What do they mean just one!" he shouted. "You said they'd let them all go!"

Guido Parra did not turn a hair.

"Take it easy, Alberto," he said. "It's a matter of a week."

7

MARUJA AND BEATRIZ had not heard about the deaths. With no television or radio, and the enemy their only source of information, it was impossible to guess the truth. The guards' contradictions undermined the story that they had taken Marina to a farm, and any other conjecture led to the same impasse: She was free, or she was dead. In other words, they had once been the only people who knew she was alive, and now they were the only people not to know she was dead.

Uncertainty about what they had done with Marina turned the empty bed into a phantom. The Monk had returned half an hour after she was taken away. He came in like a ghost and huddled in a corner. Beatriz asked him point-blank:

"What did you do with Marina?"

The Monk said that when he walked outside with her, two new bosses who had not come to the room were waiting for him in the garage. That he asked where they were taking her, and one of them answered in a rage: "You don't ask questions here, you son of a bitch." And that then they told him to get back in the house and leave Marina with Barrabás, the other guard on duty.

At first hearing the story seemed credible. It would not have been easy for the Monk to go away and come back so soon if he had taken part in the crime, or for him to have the heart to kill a ruin of a woman, whom he seemed to love as if she were his grandmother, and who doted on him as if he were her grandson. Barrabás, however, had a reputation as a heartless killer who even bragged about his crimes. The uncertainty became even more disquieting in the middle of the night, when Maruja and Beatriz were awakened by the moans of a wounded animal, and it was the Monk sobbing. He did not want breakfast, and they heard him sigh several times and say: "How sad that they took Granny away!" But he never said outright that she was dead. Even the majordomo's stubborn refusal to return the television and the radio increased their suspicion that she had been killed.

Damaris, after several days away from the house, returned in a frame of mind that only added to the confusion. During one of their night walks, Maruja asked her where she had gone, and Damaris answered in the same voice she would have used to tell the truth: "I'm taking care of doña Marina." And without giving Maruja time to think about it, she added: "She always thinks of you and sends you both her best." And then, in an even more casual tone, she said that Barrabás had not come back because he was in charge of her security. From then on, every time Damaris went out, she came back with news that grew less believable the more enthusiastic she became. She always ended with a ritual phrase: "Doña Marina is just marvelous."

Maruja had no reason to believe Damaris more than she believed the Monk or any of the other guards, but she also had no reason not to believe them in circumstances where everything seemed possible. If Marina really was alive, they had no motive for depriving the hostages of news and distractions, unless it was to hide the worst from them.

To Maruja's overheated imagination, nothing seemed absurd. So far she had hidden her worry from Beatriz, afraid she could not tolerate the truth. But Beatriz was safe from all infection. From the very first she had rejected any thought that Marina might be dead. Her dreams helped her. She dreamed that her brother Alberto, as real as he was in life, told her in detail about his efforts, about how well things were going, about how little time they had to wait to be free. She dreamed that her father reassured her with the news that the credit cards she had left in her bag were safe. The images were so vivid that when she recalled them later they were indistinguishable from reality.

At this time, a seventeen-year-old they called Jonás was finishing up his guard duty with Maruja and Beatriz. Beginning at seven in the morning, he would listen to music on a tinny cassette player. He played his favorite songs over and over, at a deafening volume, until they were sick of them. And in the meantime, as part of the chorus, he would shout: "What a fucking life, I don't know why I ever got into this!" In his calmer moments he would talk to Beatriz about his family. But this only brought him to the edge of the abyss, and with a measureless sigh he would say: "If you only knew who my father was!" He never told, but this and many other of the guards' enigmas made the atmosphere in the room even more rarefied.

The majordomo, caretaker of their domestic welfare, must have informed his bosses about the prevailing restiveness, because two showed up in a conciliatory mood. Again they refused to return the radio and television, but they did make an effort to improve the hostages' daily lives. They promised books but brought very few, and one was a novel by Corín Tellado. They gave them entertainment publications but no news magazines. A large light-bulb replaced the blue one, and orders were given to turn it on for an hour at seven in the morning, and an hour at seven in the evening, so they could read, but Beatriz and Maruja were so accustomed to semi-darkness they could not tolerate a bright light. Besides, the bulb heated the air in the room and made it unbreathable.

Maruja allowed herself to succumb to the inertia of the desperate. She spent days and nights lying on the mattress, pretending to be asleep, her face turned to the wall so she would not have to speak. She ate almost nothing. Beatriz occupied the empty bed and took refuge in the crossword puzzles and games in the magazines. The fact was brutal and painful, but it was the fact: There was more room with four people instead of five, fewer tensions, more air to breathe.

Jonás finished his tour of duty at the end of January and said goodbye to the hostages with a demonstration of his trust. "I'll tell you something if you promise not to say who told you." And then he revealed the news that had been gnawing at him inside:

"They killed doña Diana Turbay."

The blow woke them. For Maruja it was the most terrible moment of her captivity. Beatriz tried not to think about what seemed irremediable to her: "If they killed Diana, I'll be next." After all, since the first of January, when the old year had ended and they were still not free, she had been telling herself: "Either they let me go or I let myself die."

One day, when Maruja was playing a game of dominoes with another guard, the Gorilla touched various places on his chest with his index finger and said: "I feel something funny here. What do you think it is?" Maruja stopped playing, looked at him with all the contempt she could summon, and said: "It's either gas or a heart attack." He dropped his submachine gun to the floor, stood up in terror, spread his hand over his chest, and with a colossal shout he roared:

"My heart hurts, damn it!"

He collapsed onto the remains of breakfast and lay there, face-down. Beatriz, who knew he hated her, felt a professional impulse to help him, but just then the majordomo and his wife came in, frightened by the shouting and the noise of his fall. The other guard, who was small and thin, had tried to help him but his submachine gun got in the way, and he handed it to Beatriz.

"You're responsible for doña Maruja," he told her.

He, the majordomo, and Damaris together could not lift the Gorilla. They took hold of him and dragged him to the living room. Beatriz, weapon in hand, and a dumbfounded Maruja saw the submachine gun on the floor, and both were shaken by the same temptation. Maruja knew how to fire a revolver, and she had once been shown how to use a submachine gun, but a providential lucidity kept her from picking it up. For her part, Beatriz was familiar with military procedures. For five years she had trained with the reserves twice a week, and had been promoted from second lieutenant to lieutenant to the rank of captain as a civilian affiliated with the Military Hospital. She had taken a special artillery course. But she too realized that they had everything to lose. The two women consoled themselves with the thought that the Gorilla would never return. And, in fact, he never did.

WHEN PACHO SANTOS watched Diana's funeral and the exhumation of Marina Montoya on television, he knew his only alternative was escape. By this time he had a rough idea of where he was. From the guards' conversations and things they had let slip, and through other reporter's arts, Pacho had established that he was in a corner house in some sprawling, crowded neighborhood in western Bogotá. He was in the main room on the second floor, and the window faced the street but was boarded over. He knew the house was rented, perhaps without a lease, because the woman who owned it arrived at the beginning of each month to collect the rent. She was the only outsider who came in and went out, and before they opened the street door for her they would chain Pacho to the bed, warning him with threats to keep absolutely quiet, and turning off the radio and television.

He had established that the boarded window in his room overlooked the garden, and that there was a door to the outside at the end of the narrow hall where the bathroom was located. He could use it whenever he chose, with no one guarding him, just by walking across the hall, but first he had to ask to be unchained. The only ventilation in the bathroom was a window where he could see the sky. The window was very high and would not be easy to reach, but it was wide enough to get through. He had no idea where it led. In the adjoining room were the red metal bunk beds where the off-duty guards slept. There were four of them, and two-man teams worked six-hour shifts. In the ordinary course of events, they never displayed their weapons, though they always carried them. Only one slept on the floor next to the double bed.

He had established that they were close to a factory, whose whistle could be heard several times a day, and because of daily choral singing and the noise at recess, he knew he was near a school. On one occasion he had asked for a pizza, and it was still hot when they brought it back in less than five minutes, and so he knew it could have been made and sold on the same block. There was no doubt about their buying newspapers right across the street, in a shop large enough to carry *Time* and *Newsweek*. The smell of fresh-baked bread would wake him at night. With shrewd questions he managed to find out from the guards that within a hundred meters there was a pharmacy, an automobile mechanic, two bars, a restaurant, a shoemaker, and two bus stops. With these and many other scraps of information gathered piecemeal, he tried to solve the puzzle of his escape routes.

One of the guards had told him that in case the law came they had orders to go straight to his room and shoot him three times point-blank: one bullet in the head, another in the heart, the third in the liver. After he heard this, he managed to hide a liter soda bottle and kept it within reach to use as a club. It was the only weapon he had.

Chess—a guard taught him to play with outstanding skill—had given him a new way to measure time. Another guard on the October shift was an expert in television soap operas and introduced him to the vice of following them regardless of whether they were good or bad. The secret was not to worry too much about today's episode, and learn to imagine the surprises that tomorrow would bring. Together they watched Alexandra's programs, and listened to the news on radio and television.

Another guard had taken the twenty thousand pesos Pacho had in his pocket on the day of the kidnapping, but as compensation he promised to bring him anything he asked for, books in particular: several by Milan Kundera, *Crime and Punishment*, the biography of General Santander de Pilar Moreno de Angel. Pacho may have been the only Colombian of his generation who had heard of José María Vargas Vila, the world's most popular Colombian writer at the turn of the century, and he was moved to tears by his books. He read almost all of them, lifted for him by one of the guards from his grandfather's library. With the mother of another guard, he maintained a pleasant correspondence for several months until the men in charge of security made them stop. His reading ration was completed with the daily newspapers, which were given to him, still folded, in the afternoon. The guard whose job it was to bring them in had a visceral hatred for journalists. For a well-known television newscaster in particular, and when he appeared on the screen, the guard would aim his submachine gun at him.

"I'd do him for nothing," he would say.

Pacho never saw the bosses. He knew they visited from time to time, though they never came up to his bedroom, and held security meetings at a café in Chapinero. But with the guards he managed to establish a kind of emergency friendship. They had the power of life and death over him, but they always recognized his right to negotiate certain living conditions. Almost every day he would win some arguments and lose others. He always lost the one about sleeping with the chain, but he won their confidence playing *remis*, a childish, undemanding game that consists of making three- and four-card melds with ten cards. Every two weeks an invisible boss would send them a loan of 100,000 pesos that was divided among them so they could gamble. Pacho always lost. At the end of six months, they confessed that they had all cheated, and if they happened to let him win from time to time, it was only to keep him from losing his enthusiasm. They used sleight of hand with the mastery of professional magicians.

This had been his life until the New Year. From the first he had guessed it would be a long captivity, and his relationship with the guards had made him think he could get through it. But the deaths of Diana and Marina shattered his optimism. The same guards who used to cheer him up now came back to the house in low spirits. Everything seemed to be on hold until the Constituent Assembly made its decision on extradition and an amnesty. At this time he had no doubt that the escape option was possible. On one condition: He would attempt it only when he saw every other alternative closed to him.

FOR MARUJA AND BEATRIZ, prospects had also been dimmed after the hopes of December, but they began to brighten again toward the end of January with rumors that two hostages would be freed. They had no idea at the time how many were left or if there were any new ones. Maruja took it for granted that Beatriz would be the one released. On the night of February 2, during the walk in the courtyard, Damaris confirmed the rumors. She was so sure, she had purchased lipstick, blush, eyeshadow, and other cosmetics for the day they left. Beatriz shaved her legs on the assumption that there would be no time when the moment came.

But two bosses who visited them the next day gave no precise details about who would be released, or if in fact either one would go free. Their high rank was obvious. They were different from the others, and much more communicative. They confirmed that a communiqué from the Extraditables had announced the release of two hostages, but there might be some unforeseen obstacles. This reminded the captives of the earlier broken promise that they would be released on December 9.

The new bosses began creating an optimistic atmosphere. They came in at odd hours, jubilant for no reason. "Things are really moving along," they would say. They commented on the news with the enthusiasm of children, but refused to return the television and radio so that the hostages could hear it for themselves. One, through malice or stupidity, said goodbye one night with words whose double meaning almost scared them to death: "Don't worry, ladies, it'll be very quick."

The tension lasted for four days, while they were given discrete pieces of news, one item at a time. On the third day they said only one hostage would be released, and that it might be Beatriz because they were saving Francisco Santos and Maruja for higher things. What distressed the women most was not being able to compare this information with news from outside—above all, with news from Alberto, who may have known better than the bosses themselves the real cause for all the uncertainty.

At last, on February 7, the men arrived earlier than usual and laid their cards on the table: Beatriz was going. Maruja would have to wait another week. "Just a few minor details left to settle," said one of the men in hoods. Beatriz suffered an attack of loquacity that exhausted first the bosses, then the majordomo and his wife, and finally the guards. Maruja ignored her, for she was wounded by a wordless rancor toward her husband when it occurred to her that he had chosen to free his sister rather than his wife. She burned with festering rage the entire afternoon, and the embers remained warm for several days afterward.

She spent that night instructing Beatriz on what she should tell Alberto Villamizar about their captivity, how to handle the details to protect everyone's safety. Any mistake, no matter how innocent it might seem, could cost a life. So Beatriz had to provide her brother with a simple, truthful description of the situation without minimizing or exaggerating anything that would make him suffer less or worry more: just the bare truth. What she must not tell him was anything that could identify the house. Beatriz resented it.

"Don't you trust my brother?"

"More than anybody in this world," said Maruja, "but this is between you and me, and no one else. You have to promise me that nobody will find out."

Her fear was well founded. She knew her husband's impulsive nature, and for all their sakes she wanted to avoid an armed rescue attempt. She had another message for Alberto: Could he find out if the medicine she was taking for her circulation had any side effects? She spent the rest of the night devising a more efficient code for messages on radio and television, and for written correspondence in the event it was allowed in the future. Deep in her soul, however, she was dictating her will: what should be done with the children, with her antiques, with ordinary things that deserved special attention. She was so impassioned that one of the guards overheard her and said:

"Take it easy. Nothing's going to happen to you."

The next day they waited, even more uneasy, but nothing occurred. They talked through the afternoon. At last, at seven o'clock, the door burst open and the two bosses, and one they did not know, came in and walked over to Beatriz.

"We've come for you. Get ready."

Beatriz was terror-stricken at the dreadful repetition of the night they took away Marina: the same door opening, the same words that might mean either freedom or death, the same mystery regarding her fate. She did not understand why on both occasions they said: "We've come for you," instead of what she longed to hear: "We're letting you go." Trying to trick them into an answer, she asked:

"Are you going to release Marina too?"

The two bosses started.

"No questions!" one of them answered with a harsh growl. "How am I supposed to know that?"

Another, more conciliatory, ended the conversation:

"One thing has nothing to do with the other. This is political."

The word Beatriz longed to hear—freedom—was left unspoken. But the atmosphere was encouraging. The bosses were not in a hurry. Damaris, wearing a schoolgirl's miniskirt, brought in drinks and a cake for a farewell party. They discussed the big news of the day, news that the captives knew nothing about: In two separate operations the industrialists Lorenzo King Mazuera and Eduardo Puyana had been abducted in Bogotá, apparently by the Extraditables. But they also said that Pablo Escobar really wanted to turn himself in after living so long on the run. Even hiding in sewers, it was said. They promised to bring back the television and radio that same night so Maruja could see Beatriz with her family.

Maruja's analysis seemed reasonable. Until now she had suspected that Marina had been executed, but that night she had no doubts at all because of the difference in procedure. In Marina's case, bosses had not prepared them several days in advance. They had not come for her themselves but had sent two low-level killers with no authority and only five minutes to carry out their orders. The farewell cake and wine for Beatriz would have been a truly macabre celebration if they were going to murder her. In Marina's case the television and radio had been taken away so they would not find out about her execution, and now they were offering to give them back so that good news would soften the devastating effects of bad. This was when Maruja concluded, with no further hesitations, that Marina had been killed, and Beatriz was going free.

The bosses gave her ten minutes to get ready while they went to drink some coffee. Beatriz could not rid herself of the idea that she was reliving Marina's final night. She requested a mirror to put on her makeup, and Damaris brought her a large one with a gilt-leaf frame. Maruja and Beatriz, after three months without a mirror, rushed to look at themselves. It was one of the most shaking experiences of their captivity. Maruja had the impression she would not have recognized herself on the street. "I almost died of panic," she has said. "I looked skinny, unfamiliar, as if I had makeup on for a part in a play." Beatriz saw herself—ashen, weighing twenty-two pounds less, her hair long and limp—and exclaimed in horror: "That's not me!" She had often felt a half-serious embarrassment at the thought that one day she would be released and look awful, but she never dreamed the reality would be so bad. And then it became worse: One of the bosses turned on the overhead light, and the atmosphere in the room turned even more sinister.

One of the guards held the mirror for Beatriz while she combed her hair. She wanted to put on some makeup, but Maruja stopped her. "What's gotten into you?" she said in a shocked voice. "As pale as you are, you'll look awful if you put that on!" Beatriz listened. She dabbed on the aftershave that Spots had given her. Then, without water, she swallowed a tranquilizer.

The clothes she had been wearing on the night of her kidnapping were in the bag, along with her other things, but she preferred the least-worn pink sweatsuit. She hesitated about putting on her flat-heeled shoes, which had mildewed under the bed and did not really go with the sweatsuit. Damaris offered to give her a pair of sneakers she used when she exercised. They were her size but looked so shabby that Beatriz turned them down, saying they were too tight. And so she wore her own shoes, and used a rubber band to pull her hair back into a ponytail. In the end, making do with odds and ends, she looked like a schoolgirl.

They did not put a hood over her head, as they had with Marina, but tried to cover her eyes with adhesive tape so she would not see the route or their faces. She objected, knowing that when it was taken off it would tear away her eyebrows and lashes. "Wait," she told them, "I'll help you." Then, over each lid, she put a large ball of cotton that was taped in place.

Their goodbyes were brief and without tears. Beatriz was about to cry, but Maruja stopped her with a coldness intended to give her courage. "Tell Alberto not to worry, that I love him and the children very much," she said. They kissed. Both were suffering: Beatriz, because she was filled with terror that at the moment of truth it might be easier to kill her than to let her go; Maruja, because of the double terror that they would kill Beatriz, and that she would be alone with the four guards. The only thing she did not think of was that she might be executed once Beatriz was released.

The door closed, and Maruja did not move, did not know what to do next until she heard the engines start up in the garage and the sound of the cars growing fainter in the night. A feeling of immense abandonment overwhelmed her. Only then did she remember that they had not kept their promise to return the television and the radio so she would know how the night ended.

The majordomo had left with Beatriz, but his wife promised to make a call and have the radio and television brought back before the 9:30 news. They were not returned. Maruja begged the guards to let her watch the television in the house, but neither they nor the majordomo dared to break the rules in so serious a matter. Less than two hours later an excited Damaris came in to tell her that Beatriz was safe at home, and had been very careful in her statements, not saying anything that could do anyone any harm. The entire family, including Alberto, of course, was with her. The house was overflowing with people.

Maruja still suspected it was not true. She insisted that they lend her a radio. She lost control and confronted the guards with no regard for the consequences. These were not serious, because the guards had witnessed the treatment she had received from the bosses and preferred to calm her down with renewed efforts to obtain a radio. Later the majordomo came in and gave her his word that Beatriz was all right and in a safe place, and that the entire country had seen and heard her with her family. But what Maruja wanted was a radio so she could hear Beatriz's voice with her own ears. The majordomo promised to bring her one, but did not. At midnight, devastated by exhaustion and rage, Maruja took two of the powerful barbiturates and did not wake up until eight the next morning.

THE GUARDS' ACCOUNTS were true. Beatriz had been taken to the garage through the courtyard. They had her lie down on the floor of a vehicle that must have been a Jeep because they had to help her climb into it. At first they bounced over very rough roads. As soon as they began driving along a smooth, paved surface, one of the men riding with Beatriz began to make senseless threats. She could tell from his voice that he was in a nervous state his harshness could not hide, and that he was not one of the bosses who had been in the house.

"A mob of reporters will be waiting for you," the man said. "Well, you just be very careful. One wrong word can cost your sister-in-law her life. Remember: We never talked to you, you never saw us, and this drive took more than two hours."

Beatriz listened in silence to these threats and many others that he seemed to repeat only to calm his own fear. In a three-way conversation she realized she did not recognize any of the voices except the majordomo's, and he barely spoke. She began to tremble uncontrollably: The most sinister of her forebodings was still a possibility.

"I want to ask a favor," she said without thinking, her voice steady. "Maruja has circulatory problems, and we'd like to send her some medicine. Will you make sure she gets it?"

"Affirmative," the man said. "Don't worry."

"Thank you so much," said Beatriz. "I'll follow your instructions. I won't make trouble for you."

There was a long pause, and in the background she could hear fast-moving cars, heavy trucks, fragments of music, and loud voices. The men whispered among themselves. Then one spoke to Beatriz.

"There are a lot of checkpoints along here," he said. "If we're stopped, we'll say you're my wife; you're so pale we can tell them we're taking you to the hospital."

Beatriz, who was feeling calmer, could not resist the temptation to gamble:

"With these patches on my eyes?"

"They operated on your eyes," the man said. "You'll sit beside me, and I'll put my arm around you."

The kidnappers' concern was not unfounded. At that moment seven buses were burning in various neighborhoods in Bogotá, set on fire by incendiary bombs placed by urban guerrillas. At the same time, the FARC had dynamited the electric tower in the municipality of Cáqueza, on the outskirts of the capital, and had tried to take over the town. For this reason the police were carrying out some raids in Bogotá, but they went almost unnoticed. And so the traffic at seven was no different from any other Thursday evening: heavy and noisy, with long traffic lights, sudden maneuvers to avoid collisions, the most violent insults. The tension was noticeable even in the kidnappers' silence.

"We're going to drop you off at a certain place. You get out fast and count to thirty, nice and slow. Then take off the tape, walk away and don't turn around, and grab the first cab you see."

She felt a folded bill being placed in her hand. "For the taxi," said the man. "It's five thousand pesos." Beatriz put it in her pants pocket, where she happened to find another tranquilizer, which she swallowed. After half an hour the car stopped. Then the same voice pronounced a final warning:

"If you tell the press that you were with doña Marina Montoya, we'll kill doña Maruja."

They had arrived. The men were very clumsy as they tried to get Beatriz out of the car without taking off her blindfold, and so nervous they got in one another's way in a tangle of orders and curses. Beatriz felt solid ground under her feet.

"It's okay," she said. "I'm fine now."

She stood motionless on the sidewalk until they climbed back in the car and immediately drove away. Only then did she hear another car behind them, pulling away at the same time. Beatriz did not count as ordered but took two steps with arms outstretched and realized she must be in the middle of the street. She pulled off the blindfold and knew right away that she was in the Normandía district, because she used to visit a friend who lived there and sold jewelry from her house. Beatriz looked at the houses with lights in the windows, trying to choose one where they would let her in, since she felt too shabby to take a cab and wanted to call home and have them pick her up. She had not made her decision yet when a yellow cab in very good condition stopped beside her. The driver, who was young and well dressed, asked:

"Taxi?"

Beatriz agreed, and realized only when she was inside that so opportune a cab could be no accident. And yet, the very certainty that he was a final link in the chain of captors filled her with a strange sense of security. The driver asked the address, and she answered in a whisper. She could not understand why he did not hear her until he asked the address for the third time. Then she repeated it in her natural voice.

The night was cold and clear, with a few stars. The driver and Beatriz spoke no more than necessary, but he kept looking at her in the rearview mirror. As they drove toward her house, Beatriz had the feeling that the traffic lights were longer and more frequent. When they were two blocks away, she asked the driver to slow down in case they had to get around the reporters her captors had warned about. There were none. She saw her building and was surprised that it did not cause the intense emotion she had expected.

The meter read six hundred pesos. Since the driver did not

have change for five thousand, Beatriz went into the building for help, and the old porter gave a shout and threw his arms around her in a wild embrace. During the interminable days and fearful nights of her captivity, Beatriz had imagined that moment as a seismic upheaval that would expend all the strength of her body and her soul. It was just the opposite: a kind of stillwater in which she could barely feel the slow, regular beat of her heart, calmed by tranquilizers. Then she let the porter pay her fare, and she rang the bell of her apartment.

Gabriel, her younger son, opened the door. His shout could be heard throughout the house: "Mamaaaaá!" Catalina, her fifteen-year-old daughter, came running with a cry and threw her arms around her neck, then let go in consternation.

"But Mommy, why are you talking like that?"

It was the fortunate detail that broke through her state of shock. Beatriz would need several days, amid crowds of visitors, to lose the habit of talking in whispers.

They had been waiting for her since morning. Three anonymous phone calls—no doubt from the kidnappers—had announced her release. Countless reporters had called to find out if they knew the precise time. A few minutes after noon, it was confirmed by Alberto Villamizar, who had received a call from Guido Parra. The press was left in the dark. A journalist who called three minutes before Beatriz arrived told Gabriel in a firm, reassuring voice: "Don't worry, they'll let her go today." Gabriel had just put down the receiver when the doorbell rang.

Dr. Guerrero had waited for her in the Villamizars' apartment, assuming that Maruja would be released as well and both women would go there. He drank three whiskeys while he waited, until the seven o'clock news. Since they had not come, he thought it was just another of the false reports circulating at the time and went back to his house. He put on his pajamas, poured another whiskey, got into bed, and turned on "Radio Recuerdo," hoping the boleros would lull him to sleep. Since the beginning of his calvary, he had not been able to read. He was half-asleep when he heard Gabriel's shout.

He walked out of the bedroom with admirable self-control. Beatriz and he—married for twenty-five years—exchanged an unhurried embrace, not shedding a tear, as if she were back from a short trip. Both had thought so much about this moment that when the time came to live it, their reunion was like a scene in a play, rehearsed a thousand times, capable of moving everyone but the actors.

As soon as Beatriz walked into her house she thought of Maruja, alone and deprived of news in that miserable room. She telephoned Alberto Villamizar, and he answered at the first ring in a voice prepared for anything.

"Hello," she said. "It's Beatriz."

She knew her brother had recognized her voice even before she said her name. She heard a deep, rough sigh, like the growl of a cat, and then a question asked without the slightest alteration in his voice:

"Where are you?"

"At my house."

"Perfect," said Villamizar. "I'll be there in ten minutes. In the meantime, don't talk to anybody."

He was punctual. Beatriz had called just as he was about to fall asleep. Beyond the joy of seeing his sister and having the first and only direct news about his captive wife, he was moved by the pressing need to prepare Beatriz before the reporters and the police arrived. His son Andrés, who has an irresistible calling to be a race-car driver, got him there in record time.

Everyone was feeling calmer. Beatriz sat in the living room with her husband and children, her mother and two sisters, who listened with avid interest to her story. Alberto thought she looked pale after her long confinement, and younger than before, like a schoolgirl in her sweatsuit, ponytail, and flat shoes. She almost cried but he stopped her, eager to know about Maruja. "Believe me, she's all right," Beatriz told him. "Things there are difficult, but bearable, and Maruja is very brave." And then she attempted to answer the question that had tormented her for two weeks.

"Do you know Marina's telephone number?" she asked.

Villamizar thought the least brutal thing would be the truth.

"They killed her," he said.

The pain of the bad news threw Beatriz off balance with retroactive terror. If she had known two hours earlier, she might not have been able to endure the drive to her own freedom. She cried until she had no more tears. Meanwhile, Villamizar took precautions to make sure no one came in until they had decided on a public version of the abduction that would not put the other hostages at risk.

Details of her captivity could give an idea of the house where they had been imprisoned. To protect Maruja, Beatriz had to tell the press that the trip home was a three-hour drive from somewhere in the temperate zone, though the truth was just the opposite: The real distance, the hilly roads, the music on the loudspeakers that blared all night on weekends, the noise of airplanes, the weather, everything indicated a neighborhood in the city. And questioning four or five priests in the district would have been enough to find out which one exorcised the house.

Other even more careless oversights on the part of her captors provided enough clues for an armed rescue attempt with minimum risk. It ought to take place at six in the morning, after the change in shifts, because the guards who came on duty then did not sleep well at night and they sprawled on the floor, exhausted, not concerned with their weapons. Another important piece of information was the layout of the house, in particular the courtyard gate, where they saw only an occasional armed guard, and the dog was easier to bribe than his barking would lead one to believe. It was impossible to know in advance if there was also a security cordon around the place, though the lax disorder inside made it doubtful, and in any case that would be easy enough to find out once the house had been located. After the tragedy of Diana Turbay, Villamizar had less confidence than ever in the success of armed rescues, but he kept it in mind in the event that became the only alternative. This was, perhaps, the only secret he did not share with Rafael Pardo.

These pieces of information created a moral dilemma for Beatriz. She had promised Maruja not to reveal any clues that might lead to a raid on the house, but she made the grave decision to pass these facts on to her brother when she saw that he realized with as much clarity as Maruja and Beatriz herself how undesirable an armed solution would be, above all when her release proved that in spite of all the obstacles, the negotiation route was still open. And so the next day, fresh and rested after a good night's sleep, Beatriz held a press conference at her brother's house, where a forest of flowers made it almost impossible to walk. She gave the journalists and the public an accurate picture of the horror of her captivity, but not a single fact of use to those who might want to act on their own, and endanger Maruja's life.

The following Wednesday, positive that by now Maruja knew about the new decree, Alexandra decided to produce a program to celebrate it. In recent weeks, as negotiations progressed, Villamizar had made significant changes in his apartment, hoping his wife would find them to her liking when she was released. He had put in a library where she had wanted one, replaced some furniture, hung some new pictures, and found a prominent place for Maruja's prized possession, the Tang Dynasty horse she had brought home from Jakarta. At the last minute he remembered that she had complained about not having a decent rug in the bathroom, and one was bought without delay. The bright, transformed house was the backdrop for an unusual television program that allowed Maruja to know about the new decoration before she returned. It turned out very well, though they did not even know if Maruja saw it.

Beatriz soon took up her life again. In her captive's bag she kept the clothes she had worn when she was released, and it held the room's depressing odor that still woke her with a start in the middle of the night. She recovered her spiritual balance with her husband's help. The only ghost that still came to her from the past was the voice of the majordomo, who telephoned her twice. The first time it was the shout of a desperate man:

"The medicine! The medicine!"

Beatriz recognized his voice and her blood turned to ice in her veins, but she found enough breath to ask in the same tone:

"What medicine? What medicine?"

"The medicine for the señora!" shouted the majordomo.

Then it became clear that he wanted the name of the medicine Maruja took for her circulation.

"Vasotón," said Beatriz. And, having regained her composure, she asked: "How are things?"

"I'm fine, thanks," said the majordomo.

"Not you," Beatriz corrected him. "Her."

"Ah, don't worry," said the owner. "The señora is fine."

Beatriz hung up and burst into tears, overcome by the nausea of hideous memories: the wretched food, the dungheap of a bathroom, the days that were always the same, the horrific solitude of Maruja in the fetid room. In any case, a mysterious announcement appeared at the bottom of the screen during the sports segment of a television newscast: "Take Basotón." The spelling was changed to keep an uninformed laboratory from protesting the use of its product for mysterious purposes.

The second call from the majordomo, several weeks later, was very different. It took Beatriz a moment to identify the voice, distorted by some device. But the style was somewhat paternal.

"Remember what we talked about," he said. "You weren't with doña Marina. Or anybody."

"Don't worry," said Beatriz, and hung up.

Guido Parra, intoxicated by the first success after all his efforts, told Villamizar that Maruja's release was a matter of three days. Villamizar relayed this to Maruja in a press conference on radio and television. Moreover, Beatriz's accounts of the conditions of their captivity persuaded Alexandra that her messages were reaching their destination. And so she held a half-hour interview with Beatriz, who talked about everything Maruja wanted to know: how she had been freed, how the children were, and the house, and friends, and the hopes she should have for her release.

From that time on, Alexandra's program was based on trivia: the clothes they were wearing, the things they were buying, the people they were seeing. Someone would say, "Manuel cooked the pork roast," just so Maruja would know that the order she had left behind in her house was still intact. All of this, no matter how frivolous it might have seemed, had a reassuring significance for Maruja: Life was continuing.

The days passed, however, and no signs of her liberation could be seen. Guido Parra became entangled in vague explanations and puerile excuses; he stopped answering the phone; he dropped out of sight. Villamizar demanded an explanation. Parra wandered through long preambles. He said things had been complicated by an increase in the number of killings by the police in the Medellín slums. He asserted that until the government put an end to those barbaric methods, it would be very difficult for anybody to be released. Villamizar did not let him finish.

"This wasn't part of the agreement," he said. "Everything was based on the decree being explicit, and it is. This is a debt of honor, and nobody can play games with me."

"You don't know how fucked up it is being a lawyer for these guys," Parra said. "My problem isn't whether or not to charge them, my problem is that if things don't turn out right they'll kill me. What do you want me to do?"

"Let's talk straight, no more bullshit," said Villamizar. "What's going on?"

"If the police don't stop the killings and don't punish the ones responsible, there's no chance they'll let doña Maruja go. That's it in a nutshell."

Blind with rage, Villamizar cursed Escobar with a string of oaths and finished by saying:

"And you, you better get lost, because the man who's going to kill you is me."

Guido Parra vanished. Not only because of Villamizar's violent reaction but also because of Pablo Escobar's, who apparently did not forgive him for overstepping his authority as a negotiator. Hernando Santos could appreciate this when a terrified Guido Parra called to say that he had such an awful letter for him from Escobar that he did not even have the courage to read it to him.

"The man is crazy," he said. "Nobody can calm him down, and the only thing I can do is disappear from the face of the earth."

Hernando Santos, knowing this would cut off his only channel to Pablo Escobar, tried to convince him to stay on. He failed. The last favor Guido Parra asked was that he get him a visa for Venezuela and arrange for his son to finish his studies at the Gimnasio Moderno in Bogotá. Unconfirmed rumors say that he took refuge in a convent in Venezuela where one of his sisters was a nun. Nothing else was known about him until April 16, 1993, when he was found dead in Medellín, in the trunk of a car with no license plates, along with his son the secondary school graduate.

Villamizar needed time to recover from a terrible sense of defeat. He was crushed by remorse for having believed in Escobar's word. Everything seemed lost. During the negotiations he had kept Dr. Turbay and Hernando Santos informed, for they too had been left with no channels to Escobar. They saw one another almost every day, and little by little he stopped telling them about the setbacks and gave them only encouraging news. He spent long hours in the company of the former president, who endured the death of his daughter with heartrending stoicism; he retreated into himself and refused to make a statement of any kind: He became invisible. Hernando Santos, whose only hope of freeing his son had been based on Parra's mediation, slipped into a profound depression.

The murder of Marina, and in particular the brutal way it had been discovered and announced, gave rise to inevitable questions about what to do now. Every possibility for mediation of the kind provided by the Notables had been exhausted, yet no other intermediary seemed effective. Goodwill and indirect methods made no sense.

Villamizar was clearsighted about the situation, and he unburdened himself to Rafael Pardo. "Imagine how I feel," he said. "For all these years Escobar has been my family's cross, and mine. First he threatens me. Then he makes an attempt on my life, and it's a miracle I escape. He goes on threatening me. He assassinates Galán. He abducts my wife and my sister, and now he wants me to defend his rights." There was no consolation to be had, however, because his fate had been decided: The only certain road to freedom for the hostages led straight to the lion in his den. In plain language: The only thing left for him to do—and he was bound to do it—was fly to Medellín and find Pablo Escobar, wherever he might be, and discuss the situation face-to-face.

8

THE PROBLEM WAS how to find Pablo Escobar in a city martyrized by violence. In the first two months of 1991 there had been twelve hundred murders—twenty a day—and a massacre every four days. An agreement among almost all the armed groups had led to the bloodiest escalation of guerrilla violence in the history of the country, and Medellín was the center of urban terrorism. A total of 457 police had been killed in only a few months. The DAS had said that two thousand people in the slums were working for Escobar, many of them adolescents who earned their living hunting down police. For each dead officer they received five million pesos, for each agent a million and a half, and 800,000 for each one wounded. On February 16, 1991, three low-ranking officers and eight agents of the police were killed when a car was blown up with 150 kilos of dynamite outside the bullring in Medellín. Nine passersby were also killed and another 143, who had nothing to do with the war, were injured.

The Elite Corps, the frontline troops in the battle against drug trafficking, were branded by Pablo Escobar as the incarnation of all evil. The Corps had been created in 1989 by President Virgilio

Barco, when he was driven to despair by his inability to establish precise responsibility in entities as large as the army and the police. Its formation had been entrusted to the National Police in order to distance the military as much as possible from the deadly contagions of drug trafficking and paramilitarism. It began with only three hundred men, who had a special squadron of helicopters at their disposal and were trained by the Special Air Service (SAS) of the British government.

The new group had begun operations along the midsection of the Magdalena River, in the center of the country, at the time the paramilitary groups created by landowners to fight the guerrillas were most active. From there a group specializing in urban operations broke off and established itself in Medellín as a freewheeling body of legionnaires answerable only to the National Police Commission in Bogotá, without any intermediate jurisdictions, and, by its very nature, not overly meticulous regarding the limits of its authority. They sowed confusion among the criminals, and also among the local authorities, who were very reluctant to assimilate an autonomous force over which they had no control. The Extraditables fought them in a bloody war, and accused them of responsibility for every kind of human rights violation.

The people of Medellín knew that not all the Extraditables' denunciations of murder and abuse by the police were unfounded, because they witnessed them on the streets, though in most cases there was no official acknowledgment that they had occurred. National and international human rights organizations protested, and the government had no credible response. Months later it was decided that no raids could be made without the presence of a representative of the Prosecutor General's Office, leading to the inevitable bureaucratization of their operations.

There was little the judicial system could do. Judges and magistrates, whose low salaries were barely enough to live on, but not enough to pay for the education of their children, faced an insoluble dilemma: Either they sold themselves to the drug traffickers, or they were killed. The admirable and heartbreaking fact is that many chose death.

Perhaps the most Colombian aspect of the situation was the astonishing capacity of the people of Medellín to accustom themselves to everything, good and bad, with a resiliency that may be the cruelest form courage can take. Most did not seem aware that they were living in a city that had always been the most beautiful, the liveliest, the most hospitable in the country, and in recent years had become one of the most dangerous in the world. Until this time, urban terrorism had been a rare element in the centuries-old culture of Colombian violence. The same historical guerrilla groups who now practiced it had once condemned it, and with reason, as an illegitimate form of revolutionary struggle. People had learned to live with the fear of what had happened, but not with uncertainty about what might happen: an explosion that would blow up one's children at school, or disintegrate the plane in midair, or pulverize vegetables at the market. Random bombs that killed the innocent and anonymous threats on the telephone had surpassed all other causes of anguished anxiety in daily life. Yet the economy of Medellín was not affected in statistical terms.

Years earlier the drug traffickers had been popular because of their mythic aura. They enjoyed complete impunity and even a certain prestige because of their charitable works in the marginal neighborhoods where they had spent their impoverished childhoods. If anyone had wanted them arrested, he could have told the policeman on the corner where to find them. But a good part of Colombian society viewed them with a curiosity and interest that bore too close a resemblance to complacency. Politicians, industrialists, businesspeople, journalists, even ordinary freeloaders, came to the perpetual party at the Hacienda Nápoles, near Medellín, where Pablo Escobar kept a zoo with giraffes and hippos brought over from Africa, and where the entrance displayed, as if it were a national monument, the small plane used to export the first shipment of cocaine.

Luck and a clandestine life had left Escobar in charge of the henhouse, and he became a legend who controlled everything from the shadows. His communiqués, with their exemplary style and perfect cunning, began to look so much like the truth that one was mistaken for the other. At the height of his splendor, people put up altars with his picture and lit candles to him in the slums of Medellín. It was believed he could perform miracles. No Colombian in history ever possessed or exercised a talent like his for shaping public opinion. And none had a greater power to corrupt. The most unsettling and dangerous aspect of his personality was his total inability to distinguish between good and evil.

This was the invisible, improbable man Alberto Villamizar proposed to seek out in mid-February so that he could talk him into returning his wife. He would begin by making contact with the three Ochoa brothers in the high-security Itagüí prison. Rafael Pardo—with the president's approval—gave him the green light but reminded him of the limitations: This was not an official negotiation but an exploratory move. Pardo told him he could make no agreement in exchange for concessions from the government, but that the government was interested in the surrender of the Extraditables within the boundaries set by the capitulation policy. This new approach was the springboard for Villamizar's idea of also changing the thrust of his own efforts, centering them not on the release of the hostages—which had been the focus so far—but on the surrender of Pablo Escobar. One would be a simple consequence of the other.

And so began a second captivity for Maruja and a different kind of battle for Villamizar. Escobar probably intended to release her with Beatriz, but the Diana Turbay tragedy may have upset his plans. Aside from bearing responsibility for a death he had not ordered, the killing of Diana must have been a disaster for him, robbing him of an object of inestimable value and, in the end, complicating his life. Police activity flared up again with so much intensity that he was forced to submerge all the way to the bottom.

With Marina dead, he had been left with Diana, Pacho, Maruja, and Beatriz. If he had decided at that moment to execute one, perhaps it would have been Beatriz. With Beatriz free and Diana dead, he was left with two: Pacho and Maruja. Perhaps he would have preferred to keep Pacho for his exchange value, but Maruja had acquired an unforeseen and incalculable worth because of Villamizar's persistence in keeping contacts alive until the government decided to issue a more explicit decree. For Escobar too, the only lifesaver in the water was Villamizar's mediation, and the only thing that could guarantee it was holding on to Maruja. The two men were condemned to each other.

Villamizar began by visiting doña Nydia Quintero to learn the details of her experience. He found her generous, resolved, serene in her mourning. She recounted her conversations with the Ochoa sisters, with the old patriarch, with Fabio in prison. She gave the impression of having assimilated the awful death of her daughter, and she did not invoke it because of grief or for the sake of vengeance, but so that it might be useful in achieving peace. In that spirit she gave Villamizar a letter for Pablo Escobar in which she expressed her hope that Diana's death might help to prevent any other Colombian from ever feeling the sorrow she felt. She began by admitting that the government could not stop raids against criminals, but it could avoid attempts to rescue the hostages, for the families knew, the government knew, everyone knew that if they happened upon the captives during one of their raids, it could cause an irreparable tragedy, like the one that had befallen her daughter. "For this reason I come to you," the letter said, "my heart overflowing with pain, forgiveness, and goodwill, to implore you to free Maruja and Francisco." And she ended with a surprising request: "Give me your word that you did not want Diana to die." Months later, from prison, Escobar made public his astonishment at Nydia's having composed that letter free of recriminations or rancor. "How it grieves me," Escobar wrote, "that I did not have the courage to answer her."

Villamizar went to Itagüí to visit the three Ochoa brothers, carrying Nydia's letter and the government's unwritten authority. Two bodyguards from DAS accompanied him, and the Medellín police added six more. He found the Ochoas newly installed in the high-security prison, with three checkpoints that were slow, repetitive, and placed at regular intervals, and bare adobe walls that gave the impression of an unfinished church. The empty corridors, the narrow stairways with yellow pipe railings, the alarms in full view, ended at a cellblock on the third floor where the three Ochoa brothers whiled away the years of their sentences making fine leather goods: saddles and all kinds of equestrian trappings. The entire family was there: children, in-laws, sisters. Martha Nieves, the most active of them, and María Lía, Jorge Luis's wife, acted as hostesses with the exemplary hospitality of the Medellinese.

He arrived when it was time for lunch, which was served at the far end of the courtyard in a large open structure that had posters of movie stars on the walls, professional exercise equipment, and a dining table large enough to seat twelve. Under a security arrangement, the food was prepared at the nearby Hacienda La Loma, the family's official residence, and on that day it was a succulent display of local cuisine. While they were eating they followed the unbreakable Antioquian custom of discussing nothing but the food.

After the meal, with all the formality of a family council, the dialogue began. It was not as easy as the harmonious lunch might have led one to suppose. Villamizar started off in his slow, calculated, explanatory way that leaves little room for questions because everything seems to have been answered ahead of time. He gave a detailed account of his negotiations with Guido Parra and the abruptness with which they were broken off, and concluded with his conviction that only direct contact with Pablo Escobar could save Maruja.

"Let's try to stop this barbarism," he said. "Let's talk, instead of making more mistakes. First, let me assure you there is no possibility at all that we will attempt an armed rescue. I prefer to talk, to know what is going on and what people want."

Jorge Luis, the eldest brother, took the lead. He told about the losses suffered by the family in the turbulence of the dirty war, the reasons for their surrender and the difficulties surrounding it, and the unbearable fear that the Constituent Assembly would not prohibit extradition.

"This has been a very hard war for us," he said. "You can't imagine what we have suffered, what the family and our friends have suffered. Everything has happened to us."

He gave precise details: his sister, Martha Nieves, abducted; his brother-in-law, Alonso Cárdenas, abducted and murdered in 1986; his uncle, Jorge Iván Ochoa, abducted in 1983; and his cousins, Mario Ochoa and Guillermo León Ochoa, abducted and murdered.

Villamizar, in turn, tried to show that he was as victimized by the war as they, to make them understand they would all have to pay equally for anything that happened from then on. "It's been as hard for me as for you," he said. "The Extraditables tried to assassinate me in '86, I had to go to the ends of the earth and even there they pursued me, and now they've abducted my wife and my sister." He was not there to complain, however, but to put himself on an equal footing with them.

"It's an abuse," he concluded, "and the time has come for us to begin to understand one another."

Only the two men spoke. The rest of the family listened in the mournful silence of a funeral, while the women plied the visitor with attentions but did not take part in the conversation.

"We can't do anything," said Jorge Luis. "Doña Nydia was here. We understood her situation but we told her the same thing. We don't want any problems."

"As long as this war lasts, you are all in danger, even behind these fortified walls," Villamizar insisted. "But if it ends now, you'll have your father and mother, your entire family intact. And that won't happen until Escobar surrenders to the authorities and Maruja and Francisco return home safe and sound. But you can be sure that if they're killed, you'll pay too, your families, everyone will pay."

During the three long hours of their interview in the prison, each man demonstrated his courage at the very edge of the abyss. Villamizar appreciated the Medellinese realism in Ochoa. The Ochoas were impressed by the direct, frank manner in which their visitor analyzed all aspects of the subject. They had lived in Cúcuta—Villamizar's home region—knew many people there, and got along well with them. At last, the other two Ochoas spoke, and Martha Nieves lightened the atmosphere with her native grace. The men had seemed firm in their refusal to intervene in a war from which they now felt safe, but little by little they became more thoughtful.

"All right, then," Jorge Luis concluded. "We'll send the message to Pablo and tell him you were here. But my advice to you is to speak to my father. He's at La Loma, and he'll enjoy talking to you."

And so Villamizar went to the hacienda with the entire family, and with only the two bodyguards he had brought from Bogotá, since the full security team seemed too conspicuous to the Ochoas. They drove to the entrance and then continued on foot, walking about a kilometer to the house along a path lined with leafy, well-tended trees. Several men without visible weapons blocked the way of the bodyguards and asked them to take a different direction. It was an anxious moment, but the men from the house reassured the strangers with good manners and even better words.

"Walk around, have something to eat," they said. "The doctor has to talk with don Fabio."

The path ended in a small square, and on the other side stood the large, well-kept house. On the terrace overlooking fields that stretched to the horizon, the old patriarch was waiting for his visitor. With him was the rest of the family, all women, and almost all of them wearing mourning for their dead, casualties of the war. Although it was the siesta hour, they had prepared an assortment of food and drink.

They exchanged greetings, and Villamizar knew that don Fabio already had a complete report on the conversation held in the prison. That made the preliminaries shorter. Villamizar limited himself to repeating what he had said before: A flare-up in the war could cause much more harm to his large, prosperous family, who were not accused of either murder or terrorism. For the moment three of his sons were safe, but the future was unpredictable, which meant that no one ought to be more interested than they in achieving peace, and peace would not be possible until Escobar followed the example of don Fabio's sons.

Don Fabio listened with placid attention, approving with gentle nods when something seemed correct. Then, in sentences as brief and definitive as epitaphs, he said what he thought in five minutes. No matter what was done, he said, in the end they would find that the most important element was missing: talking to Escobar in person. "So the best thing is to start there," he said. He thought Villamizar was the right man to try it, because Escobar only trusted men whose word was as good as gold.

"And you are one of those men," don Fabio concluded. "The problem is proving it to him."

The visit had begun in the prison at ten in the morning and ended at six at La Loma. Its great achievement was breaking the ice between Villamizar and the Ochoas for the common goal—already agreed to by the government—of having Escobar turn himself in to the authorities. That certainty made Villamizar want to convey his impressions to the president. But when he reached Bogotá he was met with bad news: The president too had been wounded in his own flesh by an abduction.

This is what happened: Fortunato Gaviria Botero, his first cousin and dearest friend since childhood, had been taken at his country house in Pereira by four hooded men armed with rifles.

The president did not change his plans to attend a regional conference of governors on the island of San Andrés, and he left on Friday afternoon still not knowing if his cousin had been abducted by the Extraditables. On Saturday he woke at dawn to go diving, and when he came out of the water he was told that Fortunato's captors—who were not drug traffickers—had killed him and buried his body, without a coffin, in an open field. The autopsy showed earth in his lungs, and this was interpreted to mean that he had been buried alive.

The president's first reaction was to cancel the regional conference and return immediately to Bogotá, but he was stopped by physicians who told him he should not fly for twenty-four hours since he had spent more than an hour at a depth of sixty feet. Gaviria followed their recommendations, and the nation saw him on television presiding over the conference with his most mournful face. But at four that afternoon he ignored medical advice and returned to Bogotá to arrange the funeral. Some time later, recalling the day as one of the most difficult in his life, he said with acid humor:

"I was the only Colombian who didn't have a president to complain to."

As soon as his prison lunch with Villamizar had ended, Jorge Luis Ochoa sent Escobar a letter encouraging him to change his mind about surrender. He depicted Villamizar as a serious Santanderean who could be believed and trusted. Escobar's reply was immediate: "Tell that son of a bitch not to talk to me." Villamizar learned about it in a phone call from Martha Nieves and María Lía, who asked him to come back to Medellín anyway to continue to look for a solution. This time he went without an escort. He took a cab from the airport to the Hotel Intercontinental, and some fifteen minutes later he was picked up by an Ochoa driver. He was an amiable, bantering twenty-year-old from Medellín who observed him for some time in the rearview mirror. At last he asked:

"Are you scared?"

Villamizar smiled at him in the mirror.

"Don't worry, Doctor," the boy continued. And added, with a good deal of irony: "Nothing will happen to you while you're with us. How could you even think such a thing?"

The joke gave Villamizar a confidence and sense of security that remained with him during all of his subsequent trips. He never knew if he was followed, not even at a much more advanced stage, but he always felt sheltered by a supernatural power.

Escobar did not seem to feel he owed Villamizar anything for the decree that made his escape from extradition a certainty. As a hard-core gambler who kept track of every penny, he probably thought the favor had been paid for with the release of Beatriz, but that the old debt was still intact. The Ochoas, however, believed that Villamizar had to persevere.

And so he ignored the insults and decided to move ahead. The Ochoas supported him. He returned two or three times and together they devised a plan of action. Jorge Luis wrote Escobar another letter in which he stated that the guarantees for his surrender were in place, that his life would be protected, and that under no circumstances would he be extradited. But Escobar did not reply. Then they decided that Villamizar himself should write to Escobar explaining his situation and his offer.

The letter was written on March 4, in the Ochoas' cell, with the help of Jorge Luis, who told him what should be said and what might be out of place. Villamizar began by acknowledging that respect for human rights was fundamental to achieving peace. "There is a fact, however, that cannot be ignored: Those who violate human rights have no better excuse for continuing to do so than citing the same violations committed by others." This was an obstacle to action on both sides, and to whatever he had achieved in that regard during the months he had worked for his wife's release. The Villamizar family had been the target of a persistent violence for which it bore no responsibility: the attempt on his life, the murder of his sister-in-law's husband, Luis Carlos Galán, and the abduction of his wife and sister. "My sister-in-law, Gloria Pachón de Galán, and I," he added, "do not understand and cannot accept so many unjustified and inexplicable attacks." On the contrary: The release of Maruja and the other journalists was indispensable to finding the road to true peace in Colombia.

Escobar's reply two weeks later began with a bitter blow: "My dear Doctor, I regret that I cannot oblige you." He proceeded to call his attention to reports that certain members of the Constituent Assembly in the official sector, with the consent of the hostages' families, were proposing not to consider the subject of extradition if the captives were not freed. Escobar considered this inappropriate, for the abductions could not be thought of as a means of exerting pressure on members of the Constituent Assembly since the abductions predated the election. In any event, he allowed himself to issue a terrible warning: "Remember, Dr. Villamizar, extradition has taken many victims, and adding two more will not change the process or the continuing struggle very much."

The warning was a complete surprise, because Escobar had not referred again to extradition as a reason for war after the decree undermined that argument for anyone who surrendered, and had focused instead on human rights violations by the special forces that were fighting him. It was his grand strategy: to gain ground with partial victories, continue the war for other reasons that could go on multiplying forever, and not have to surrender.

In his letter, in fact, he claimed to understand that Villamizar's struggle was the same as his in the sense that both wanted to protect their families, but once again he insisted that the Elite Corps had killed some four hundred boys from the slums of Medellín and no one had been punished for it. Such actions, he said, justified the abduction of the journalists as a means of pressing for sanctions on the police who were guilty. He also expressed surprise that no public official had attempted to make direct contact with him concerning the hostages. In any event, he went on, calls and pleas for their freedom would be useless, since what was at stake were the lives of the Extraditables' families and associates. And he concluded: "If the government does not intervene and does not listen to our proposals, we will proceed to execute Maruja and Francisco, about that there can be no doubt."

The letter showed that Escobar was seeking contacts with public officials. Surrender had not been discarded, but it would come at a higher price than anyone had expected, and he was prepared to demand payment with no sentimental discounts. Villamizar understood this, and that same week he visited the president and brought him up-to-date. The president did no more than take careful notes.

At this time Villamizar also met with the prosecutor general, trying to find a different way to proceed in a new situation. The meeting was very productive. The prosecutor general told him that at the end of the week he would issue a report on the death of Diana Turbay holding the police responsible for acting without prudence or orders, and that he was filing charges against three officers of the Elite Corps. He also disclosed that he had investigated eleven agents whom Escobar had accused by name, and had filed charges against them as well.

He kept his word. On April 3 the president received an investigative study from the Prosecutor General's Office regarding the circumstances surrounding Diana Turbay's death. The operation—the study says—began to take shape on January 23, when the intelligence services of the Medellín police received a series of anonymous calls of a generic nature regarding the presence of armed men in the hilly areas of the municipality of Copacabana. Activity was centered—according to the phone calls—in the region of Sabaneta, in particular on the farm properties of Villa del Rosario, La Bola, and Alto de la Cruz. At least one of the calls suggested that this was where the journalists were being held hostage, and that the Doctor—that is, Pablo Escobar—might even be there as well. This piece of information was mentioned in the analysis that served as the basis for the next day's operations, but there was no mention of the probable presence of the abducted journalists. General Miguel Gómez Padilla, head of the National Police, stated that he had been informed on the afternoon of January 24 that on the following day a search-and-seizure verification operation would be carried out, "and the possible capture of Pablo Escobar and a group of drug traffickers." But, it seems, there was no mention at this time either of a possible encounter with the two hostages, Diana Turbay and Richard Becerra.

The operation began at eleven o'clock on the morning of January 25, when Captain Jairo Salcedo García left the Carlos Holguín Academy in Medellín with seven officers, five noncommissioned officers, and forty agents. An hour later, Captain Eduardo Martínez Solanilla was accompanied by two officers, two noncommissioned officers, and seventy-one agents. The report pointed out that in the relevant memorandum no record had been made of the departure of Captain Helmer Ezequiel Torres Vela, who was in charge of the raid on La Bola farm, where Diana and Richard were in fact being held. But in his subsequent statement to the Prosecutor General's Office, the same captain confirmed that he had set out at eleven in the morning with six officers, five noncommissioned officers, and forty agents. Four combat helicopters were assigned to the entire operation.

The raids on Villa del Rosario and Alto de la Cruz were carried out with no difficulty. At about one o'clock, the raid on La Bola began. Second Lieutenant Iván Díaz Alvarez stated that he was coming down from the mesa where the helicopter had left him when he heard shooting on the side of the mountain. Racing in that direction, he caught a glimpse of nine or ten men armed with rifles and submachine guns and running for their lives. "We stayed there a few minutes to see where the attack was coming from," the second lieutenant declared, "when much further down the slope we heard someone calling for help." The second lieutenant said he had hurried down and found a man who shouted: "Please help me." The second lieutenant shouted back: "Halt! Who are you?" The man replied that he was Richard, the journalist, and needed help because Diana Turbay had been wounded. The second lieutenant said that then, without knowing why, he asked the question: "Where's Pablo?" Richard answered: "I don't know, but help me, please." Then the soldier approached, taking all precautions, and then other men from his unit appeared. The second lieutenant concluded: "For us it was a surprise to find the journalists there because that wasn't our objective."

This account agrees almost point by point with the one given by Richard Becerra to the Attorney General's Office. Richard later amplified his statement, saying he had seen the man who shot at him and Diana, and that he had been standing to the left with both hands extended, at a distance of about fifteen meters. "By the time the shooting stopped," Richard concluded, "I had already dropped to the ground."

With regard to the single bullet that caused Diana's death, tests showed that it had entered the left iliac region and moved upward and to the right. The characteristics of the micrological damage indicated that it was a high-velocity bullet, traveling between two and three thousand feet per second, or some three times faster than the speed of sound. It could not be recovered because it shattered into three parts, which lessened its weight, altered its shape, and reduced it to an irregular fragment that continued its trajectory, causing damage of an essentially fatal nature. It was almost certainly a 5.56-caliber bullet, perhaps fired by a rifle similar, if not identical, to an Austrian AUG that had been found on the scene and was not a standard-issue police weapon. In a marginal note, the autopsy report indicated: "Diana had an estimated life expectancy of fifteen more years."

The most intriguing fact in the raid was the presence of a handcuffed civilian in the same helicopter that transported the wounded Diana to Medellín. Two police agents agreed he was a man who looked like a campesino, about thirty-five or forty years old, dark skin, short hair, rather robust, about five feet, seven inches tall, and wearing a cloth cap. They said he had been detained during the raid, and that they were trying to find out who he was when the shooting began, so they had to handcuff him and take him along to the helicopters. One of the agents added that they had left him with their second lieutenant, who questioned him in their presence and released him near the place where he had been picked up. "The gentleman had nothing to do with it," they said, "since the shots came from lower down and he was up there with us." These versions denied that the civilian had been on board the helicopter, but the crew of the aircraft contradicted this. Other statements were more specific. Corporal Luis Carlos Ríos Ramírez, the helicopter gunner, had no doubt that the man had been on board and was returned that same day to the zone of operations.

The mystery carried over to January 26 with the discovery of the body of one José Humberto Vázquez Muñoz, in the municipality of Girardota, near Medellín. He had been killed by three 9mm bullets in the thorax, and two in the head. In the files of the intelligence services, he was described as having a long criminal record as a member of the Medellín cartel. The investigators marked his photograph with the number 5, mixed it in with photographs of other known criminals, and showed them to those who had been held hostage with Diana Turbay. Hero Buss said: "I don't recognize any of them, but I think the person in number five looks a little like one of the thugs I saw a few days after the kidnapping." Azucena Liévano stated that the man in photograph number five, but without a mustache, resembled one of the guards on night duty at the house where she and Diana were held during the first few days of their captivity. Richard Becerra recognized number five as the handcuffed man in the helicopter, but he qualified this: "I think so, because of the shape of his face, but I'm not sure." Orlando Acevedo also recognized him.

Finally, Vázquez Muñoz's wife identified his body and said in a sworn statement that on January 25, 1991, at eight in the morning, her husband had left the house to find a taxi when he was seized by two men on motorcycles wearing police uniforms, and two men in civilian clothes, and put into a car. He managed to shout her name: "Ana Lucía." But they had already driven away. This statement, however, could not be admitted because there were no other witnesses to the abduction.

"In conclusion," said the report, "and on the basis of the evidence brought forward, it is reasonable to affirm that prior to the raid on the La Bola farm, certain members of the National Police in charge of the operation had learned from Mr. Vázquez Muñoz, a civilian in their custody, that some journalists were being held captive in the area, and that, subsequent to these events, he most surely was killed by their hand." Two other unexplained deaths at the site were also confirmed.

The Office of Special Investigations went on to conclude that there were no reasons to assume that General Gómez Padilla or any other high-ranking director of the National Police had been informed; that the weapon that caused Diana's wounds was not fired by any of the members of the special corps of the National Police in Medellín; that members of the unit that raided La Bola should be held accountable for the deaths of three persons whose bodies were found there; that a formal disciplinary investigation would be made into irregularities of a substantive and procedural nature on the part of magistrate 93 for Military Penal Investigation, Dr. Diego Rafael de Jesús Coley Nieto, and his secretary, as well as responsible parties of the DAS in Bogotá.

With the publication of this report, Villamizar felt he was on firmer ground for writing a second letter to Escobar. He sent it, as always, through the Ochoas, along with a letter to Maruja, and asked him to see that she got it. He took the opportunity to give Escobar a textbook explanation of the division of governmental powers into executive, legislative, and judicial, and to make him understand how difficult it was for the president, within these constitutional and legal mechanisms, to control entities as large and complex as the Armed Forces. However, he did acknowledge that Escobar was correct to denounce human rights violations by law enforcement agencies, and to insist on guarantees for himself, his family, and his people when they surrendered. "I share your opinion," he said, "that you and I are engaged in essentially the same struggle: to protect our families' lives and our own, and to achieve peace." On the basis of these two objectives, he proposed that they adopt a joint strategy.

Escobar, his pride wounded by the civics lesson, replied a few days later. "I know that the country is divided into President, Congress, Police, Army," he wrote. "But I also know that the president is in charge." The rest of the letter consisted of four pages that reiterated the actions of the police, adding new facts but no new arguments to what had been said earlier. He denied that the Extraditables had executed Diana Turbay or had any intention to do so, because if that were the case they would not have taken her out of the house where she was being held or dressed her in black so that she would look like a campesina from the helicopters. "A dead hostage has no value," he wrote. Then, without transitions or formulaic courtesies, he closed with these unexpected words: "Don't worry about [having made] statements to the press demanding my extradition. I know everything will work out, and that you will bear me no grudge, because your battle to defend your family has the same objectives as the one I am waging to defend mine." Villamizar related this statement to an earlier one of Escobar's in which he claimed to feel some embarrassment at holding Maruja prisoner when his quarrel was not with her but with her husband. Villamizar had said the same thing in a different way: "Why is it that if you and I are the ones doing battle, my wife is the one held prisoner?" and he proposed that Escobar take him in exchange for Maruja so they could negotiate in person. Escobar did not accept his offer.

By now Villamizar had been in the Ochoas' prison more than twenty times. He enjoyed the gems of local cuisine that the women from La Loma brought in, taking every possible security precaution. It was a reciprocal process of learning about one another and establishing mutual trust, and they devoted most of their time to dissecting every one of Escobar's sentences and actions to discover his hidden intentions. Villamizar would almost always take the last plane back to Bogotá. His son Andrés would meet him at the airport, and often had to drink mineral water while his father relieved his tension with slow, solitary whiskeys. He had kept his promise not to attend any public function, not to see friends: nothing. When the pressure grew intense, he would go out to the terrace and spend hours staring in the direction where he supposed Maruja was, sending her mental messages until he was overcome by exhaustion. At six in the morning he was on his feet, ready to start all over again. When they had an answer to a letter, or anything else of interest, Martha Nieves or María Lía would call and only have to say a single sentence:

"Doctor, tomorrow at ten."

When there were no calls, he spent his time and efforts on "Colombia Wants Them Back," the television campaign based on the information Beatriz had given them regarding conditions in captivity. The idea had originated with Nora Sanín, the head of the National Association of Media (ASOMEDIOS), and was produced by María del Rosario Ortiz—a close friend of Maruja's, and Hernando Santos's niece—in collaboration with her husband, who was a publicist, and with Gloria Pachón de Galán and other members of the family: Mónica, Alexandra, Juana, and their brothers.

The idea was for a daily succession of well-known personalities in film, the theater, television, soccer, science, or politics to deliver the same message, calling for the release of the hostages and respect for human rights. From the first it had provoked an overwhelming public response. Alexandra traveled from one end of the country to the other with a cameraman, chasing down celebrities. The campaign lasted three months, and some fifty people participated. But Escobar did not budge. When the harpsichordist Rafael Puyana said he was ready to get down on his knees to beg for the release of the hostages, Escobar responded: "Thirty million Colombians can come to me on their knees, and I still won't let them go." But in a letter to Villamizar he praised the program because it demanded not only freedom for the hostages but respect for human rights.

The ease with which Maruja's daughters and their guests trooped across television screens was disturbing to María Victoria, Pacho Santos's wife, because of her unconquerable stage fright. The unexpected microphones put in front of her, the indecency of the lights, the inquisitorial eye of the cameras, the same questions asked with the expectation of hearing the same answers, made her gorge rise with panic, and it was all she could do to swallow her nausea. Her birthday was observed on television; Hernando Santos spoke with professional ease, and then took her arm: "Say a few words." She often managed to escape, but sometimes she had to face it and not only thought she would die in the attempt, but felt awkward and stupid when she saw and heard herself on screen.

Then she reacted against this public servitude. She took a course in small business and another in journalism. By her own decision she became free, accepting invitations she had once despised, attending lectures and concerts, wearing cheerful clothing, staying out late, and at last destroying her image as a pitiful widow. Hernando and his closest friends understood and supported her, helped her to do as she chose. But before long she experienced social disapproval. She knew that many of those who praised her to her face were criticizing her behind her back. She began to receive bouquets of roses with no card, boxes of chocolates with no name, declarations of love with no signature. She enjoyed the illusion that they were from her husband, that perhaps he had managed to find a secret route to her from his prison. But the sender soon identified himself by phone: a madman. A woman also used the phone to tell her straight out: "I'm in love with you."

During those months of creative freedom, Mariavé happened to meet a clairvoyant she knew who had foretold Diana Turbay's tragic end. She was terrified by the mere thought that she too would hear some sinister prediction, but the psychic reassured her. Early in February Mariavé saw her again, and the clairvoyant murmured in her ear, without having been asked a question, and without waiting for a response: "Pacho's alive." She spoke with so much conviction that Mariavé believed it as if she had seen him with her own eyes.

THE TRUTH in February seemed to be that Escobar had no faith in decrees even when he said he did. Distrust was a vital state for him, and he often said he was still alive because of it. He delegated nothing essential. He was his own military commander, his own head of security, intelligence, and counterintelligence, an unpredictable strategist, and an unparalleled purveyor of disinformation. In extreme circumstances he changed his eight-man team of personal bodyguards every day. He was familiar with the latest technology in communications, wiretapping, and tracking devices. He had employees who spent the day engaging in lunatic conversations on his telephones so that the people monitoring his lines would become entangled in mangrove forests of non sequiturs and not be able to distinguish them from the real messages. When the police gave out two phone numbers for receiving information regarding his whereabouts, he hired whole schools of children to anticipate any callers and keep the lines busy twenty-four hours a day. His cunning in never leaving any clues was boundless. He consulted with no one, and provided strategies for his attorneys, whose only work was to outwit the judicial system.

His refusal to see Villamizar was based on his fear that he

might be carrying an electronic tracking device implanted under his skin. This was a tiny radio transmitter powered by a microscopic battery, whose signal could be picked up at great distances by a special receiver—a radiogonometer—that allows the approximate location of the signal to be established. Escobar had so much regard for the sophistication of this device that the idea of someone carrying a subcutaneous receiver did not seem fantastic to him. The gonometer can also be used to determine the coordinates of a radio transmission or a mobile or line telephone. This was why Escobar used phones as little as possible, and if he did, he preferred to be in moving vehicles. He employed couriers to deliver written notes. If he had to see someone, he went to the other person, they did not come to him. And when the meeting was over, he left in the most unpredictable ways. Or he went to the other extreme of technology and traveled in a public minibus that had false plates and markings and drove along established routes but made no stops because it always carried a full complement of passengers, who were his bodyguards. One of Escobar's diversions, in fact, was to act as driver from time to time.

In February, the possibility that the Constituent Assembly would decide in favor of non-extradition and an amnesty was becoming a probability. Escobar knew it and concentrated more energies in that direction than on the government. Gaviria must have turned out to be tougher than he had supposed. Everything relating to the capitulation decrees was kept current in the Office of Criminal Investigation, and the justice minister was prepared to deal with any judicial emergency. For his part, Villamizar acted not only on his own but at his own risk, though his close collaboration with Rafael Pardo kept open a direct channel to the government, which did not compromise him, and in fact allowed him to move forward without making concessions. At this time Escobar must have realized that Gaviria would never appoint an official representative to hold talks with him—which was his golden dream—and he clung to the hope that the Constituent Assembly would issue him a pardon, either as a repentant trafficker, or under the aegis of some armed group. It was not a foolish calculation. Before the swearing-in of the Constituent Assembly, the political parties had agreed on an agenda of closed subjects, and the government, using legal arguments, had succeeded in keeping extradition off the list because they needed it as a bargaining chip for their capitulation policy. But when the Supreme Court reached the spectacular decision that the Constituent Assembly could deal with any subject, without any restrictions whatsoever, the question of extradition reemerged from the ruins. Amnesty was not mentioned, but it was also possible: There was room for everything in the infinite.

PRESIDENT GAVIRIA was not one of those men who could leave a subject hanging and go on to another. In six months he had imposed on his colleagues a personal system of communicating by means of notes written on scraps of paper in cryptic sentences that summarized everything. Sometimes only the name of the individual he was writing to was on the note, which was handed to the closest person, and the addressee knew what he had to do. For his advisers, this method also had the terrifying virtue of making no distinction between work and leisure. Gaviria could not conceive of the difference, since he rested with the same discipline he applied to work, and continued sending his scraps of paper when he was at a cocktail party or as soon as he came up from diving. "A tennis game with him was like a meeting of the Council of Ministers," said one of his advisers. He could fall into a deep sleep for five or ten minutes, even sitting at his desk, and wake refreshed, while his colleagues collapsed with exhaustion. This method, however random it might appear, could trigger action with more urgency and energy than formal memos.

The system proved very useful when the president tried to parry the Supreme Court's blow against extradition with the argument that it was a question of law, not a constitutional issue. At first the government minister, Humberto de la Calle, succeeded in convincing the majority. But in the end, the things that interest individuals become more important than the things that interest governments, and people had been correct in identifying extradition as a contributing factor to social unrest, and in particular to the savagery of terrorism. And so, after much twisting and turning, it was at last included on the agenda of the Commission on Rights.

In the meantime, the Ochoas still feared that Escobar, pursued by his own demons, would decide to immolate himself in a catastrophe of apocalyptic proportions. Their fear was prophetic. Early in March, Villamizar received an urgent message from them: "Come immediately. Something very serious is going to happen." They had received a letter from Pablo Escobar threatening to set off fifty tons of dynamite in the historic district of Cartagena de Indias if there were no sanctions against the police who were devastating the slums of Medellín: 100 kilos for each boy killed outside of combat.

The Extraditables had considered Cartagena an untouchable sanctuary until September 28, 1989, when an explosion shook the foundations of the Hotel Hilton, blowing out windows and killing two physicians at a convention in session on another floor. From then on, it was clear that not even this historical treasure was safe from the war. The new threat did not permit a moment's hesitation.

Villamizar informed Gaviria a few days before the deadline. "Now we're not fighting for Maruja but to save Cartagena," he said, to provide the president with an argument. Gaviria's response was that he thanked him for the information, said the government would take steps to prevent the disaster, but under no circumstances would he give in to blackmail. And so Villamizar traveled to Medellín one more time, and with the help of the Ochoas succeeded in dissuading Escobar. It was not easy. Days before the deadline, Escobar guaranteed in a hurried note that for the moment nothing would happen to the captive journalists, and postponed the detonation of bombs in large cities. But he was also categorical: If police operations in Medellín continued past April, no stone would be left standing in the very ancient and noble city of Cartagena de Indias.

9

ALONE IN THE ROOM, Maruja knew she was in the hands of the same men who may have killed Marina and Beatriz, and were refusing to return the radio and television to keep her from finding that out. She moved from earnest pleading to enraged demands; she confronted her guards, shouting loud enough for the neighbors to hear; she refused to walk and threatened to stop eating. The majordomo and the guards, surprised by the unthinkable, did not know what to do. They conferred in whispers, went out to make phone calls, and came back even more indecisive. They tried to reassure Maruja with illusory promises, or intimidate her with threats, but they could not break her resolve not to eat.

She had never felt more self-possessed. It was clear that her guards had instructions not to mistreat her, and she gambled on their needing her alive at any cost. Her calculations were correct: Three days after Beatriz's release, the door opened very early in the morning and the majordomo came in carrying the radio and the television. "You'll learn something now," he said. And in an unemotional voice he announced:

"Doña Marina Montoya is dead."

In contrast to what she herself had expected, Maruja heard the news as if she had always known it. The astonishing thing for her would have been if Marina were alive. When the truth reached her heart, however, she realized how much she had loved her, how much she would have given to have it not be true.

"Murderers!" she screamed at the majordomo. "That's all you are: murderers!"

At that moment the "Doctor" appeared in the doorway and tried to calm Maruja with the news that Beatriz was safe at home, but she would not believe him until she saw it with her own eyes on television or heard it on the radio. Yet he seemed to have been sent to allow her to give vent to her feelings.

"You haven't been back," she said. "And I can understand that: You must be very ashamed of what you did to Marina."

He needed a moment to recover from his surprise.

"What happened?" Maruja provoked him. "Was she condemned to death?"

Then he said it had been a question of taking revenge for a double betrayal. "Your case is different," he said. And repeated what he had said earlier: "It's political." Maruja listened to him with the strange fascination that the idea of death holds for those who believe they are going to die.

"At least tell me how it happened," she said. "Did Marina know?"

"I swear to you she didn't," he said.

"How could that be?" Maruja insisted. "How could she not know?"

"They told her they were taking her to another house," he said with the urgency of someone who wants to be believed. "They told her to get out of the car, and she kept walking and they shot her in the back of the head. She couldn't have known anything."

The image of Marina with her hood on backward stumbling blindly toward an imaginary house would pursue Maruja through many sleepless nights. More than death itself, she feared the lucidity of the final moment. The only thing that gave her some consolation was the box of sleeping pills that she had saved as if they were precious pearls, and would swallow by the handful before allowing herself to be dragged off to the slaughter.

At last, on the midday news, she saw Beatriz surrounded by her family in a flower-filled apartment that she recognized in spite of all the changes: It was her own. But her joy at seeing it was ruined by her dislike for the new decoration. She thought the library was well done and just in the place she wanted it, but the colors of the walls and carpets were awful, and the Tang Dynasty horse was placed precisely where it would most be in the way. "How stupid they are!" she shouted. "It's just the opposite of what I said!" Her longing to be free was reduced for a moment to wanting to scold them for the poor job they had done.

In this whirlwind of contrary sensations and feelings, the days became intolerable, the nights interminable. Sleeping in Marina's bed unnerved her: Covered by her blanket, tormented by her odor, as she began to fall asleep she could hear in the darkness, beside her in the bed, the buzz of Marina's whispering. One night it was not a hallucination but miraculous and real. Marina grasped her arm with her warm, gentle, living hand, and breathed into her ear in her natural voice: "Maruja."

She did not consider it a hallucination because in Jakarta she had also had what seemed to be a fantastic experience. At an antiques fair she had bought the life-size sculpture of a beautiful youth who had one foot resting on the head of a conquered boy. Like the statues of Catholic saints, the figure had a halo, but this one was tin, and the style and material made it look like a shoddy afterthought. Only after keeping it for some time in the best spot in her house did she learn it was the God of Death.

One night Maruja dreamed she was trying to pull the halo off the statue because it seemed so ugly, but could not. It was soldered onto the bronze. She woke feeling troubled by the bad memory, hurried to look at the statue in the living room, and found the god uncrowned and the halo on the floor, as if this were the conclusion of her dream. Maruja—who is a rationalist and an agnostic—accepted the idea that she herself, in an episode of sleepwalking she could not recall, had torn the halo off the God of Death.

At the beginning of her captivity, she had been sustained by the rage she felt at Marina's submissiveness. Later it became compassion for her bitter fate and a desire to give her the will to live. She was sustained by having to pretend to a strength she did not have when Beatriz began to lose control, and the need to maintain her own equilibrium when adversity overwhelmed them. Someone had to take command to keep them from going under, and she had been the one to do it, in a grim, foul-smelling space that measured three meters by two and a half meters, where she slept on the floor, ate kitchen scraps, and never knew if she would live to see the next minute. But when no one else was left in the room, she no longer had any reason to pretend: She was alone with herself.

The certainty that Beatriz had told her family how to communicate with her on radio and television kept her alert. In fact, Villamizar appeared several times with his words of encouragement, and her children comforted her with their imagination and wit. Then, with no warning, that contact had been broken off for two weeks. This was when a sense of abandonment paralyzed her. She caved in. She stopped walking. She lay with her face to the wall, removed from everything, eating and drinking only enough to keep from dying. She experienced the same distress she had felt in December, the same cramps and shooting pains in her legs that had made the doctor's visit necessary. But this time she did not even complain.

The guards, involved in their personal conflicts and internecine quarrels, paid no attention to her. Her food grew cold on the plate, and both the majordomo and his wife seemed oblivious. The days became longer and emptier, so much so that she sometimes missed the worst moments of the early days. She lost interest in life. She cried. One morning she woke to discover in horror that her right arm had lifted by itself.

The change of guards in February was providential. As replacements for Barrabás's crew, they sent four new boys who were serious, well disciplined, and talkative. They had good manners and an ease of expression that were a relief to Maruja. As soon as they came in they invited her to play Nintendo and other video games. The games brought them together. From the start she knew they shared a common language, and that facilitated communication. They had, no doubt, been instructed to overcome her resistance and raise her morale with a different kind of treatment, for they tried to persuade her to follow the doctor's orders and walk in the courtyard, to think of her husband and children and not disappoint them when they were hoping to see her soon, and in good condition.

The atmosphere lent itself to confidences. Aware that they too were prisoners, and perhaps needed her as well, Maruja told them stories about her three sons, who had already gone through adolescence. She recounted the significant events in their lives as they were growing up and going to school, and talked about their habits and tastes. And the guards, feeling more confident, told her about themselves.

They had all finished secondary school, and one had completed at least a semester of college. In contrast to the previous guards, they said they were from middle-class families, but in one way or another had been marked by the culture of the Medellín slums. The oldest, a twenty-four-year-old whom they called Ant, was tall, good-looking, and rather reserved. His university studies had been interrupted when his parents died in a car accident, and his only recourse had been to join a gang of killers. Another, called Shark, recounted with amusement that he had passed half his courses in secondary school by threatening his teachers with a toy revolver. The most cheerful of this team, and of all the guards who had worked there, was called Top, and that, in effect, was what he resembled. He was very fat, with short, thin legs, and his love of dancing bordered on the maniacal. Once, after breakfast, he put a salsa tape in the cassette player and danced without a break, and with frenetic energy, until the end of his shift. The quietest one, whose mother was a schoolteacher, read books and newspapers and was well informed on current events. He had only one explanation for being in that life: "Because it's so cool."

Just as Maruja had first suspected, however, they were not insensible to human relationships. This, in turn, not only gave her back the will to live, but also the wit to gain advantages that the guards themselves may not have foreseen.

"Don't think I'm going to try anything stupid with you," she told them. "Believe me, I won't do any of the things I'm not allowed to, because I know this business will be over soon and turn out fine. So it doesn't make sense to put so many restrictions on me."

With an autonomy that none of the earlier guards—not even their bosses—had shown, the new guards dared to relax the rules much more than even Maruja had hoped. They let her move around the room, speak in a more natural voice, go to the bathroom without following a fixed schedule. The new regime gave her back the desire to take care of herself, which she attributed to her experience with the statue in Jakarta. She made good use of classes on Alexandra's program that had been prepared for her by a gymnastics teacher and were called, with her in mind, exercises in confined spaces. Her enthusiasm was so great that one of the guards asked with a suspicious look: "Is that program sending you some message?" Maruja had a hard time convincing him that it was not.

During this time she was also moved by the unexpected appearance of "Colombia Wants Them Back," which seemed not only well conceived and well produced, but also the best way to keep up the morale of the last two hostages. She felt more in touch with her family and friends. She thought about how she would have done the program, as a campaign, as a remedy, as a means of swaying public opinion, and began to make bets with the guards about who would appear on the screen the next day. Once she wagered it would be Vicky Hernández, the great actress and her close friend, and she won. The greater prize, in any case, was that just seeing Vicky and listening to her message produced one of the few happy moments of her captivity.

Her walks in the courtyard also began to bear fruit. The German shepherd, overjoyed at seeing her again, tried to squeeze under the gate to play with Maruja, but she calmed him down, petting and talking to him, afraid the guards would become suspicious. Marina had told her that the gate led to a quiet yard with sheep and chickens. Maruja confirmed this with a rapid glance in the moonlight. But she also saw a man with a rifle standing guard outside the enclosure. The hope of escaping with the complicity of the dog had been canceled.

On February 20, when life seemed to have reestablished its rhythm, the radio reported that the body of Dr. Conrado Prisco Lopera—a cousin of the gang's bosses, who had disappeared two days earlier—had been found in a field in Medellín. Another cousin, Edgar de Jesús Botero Prisco, was murdered four days later. Neither man had a criminal record. Dr. Prisco Lopera was the physician who had tended to Juan Vitta without concealing his name or his face, and Maruja wondered if he was the same masked doctor who had examined her earlier.

Like the death of the Prisco brothers in January, these killings had a serious effect on the guards and increased the anxiety of the majordomo and his family. The idea that the cartel would exact the life of a hostage as payment for their deaths, as it had with Marina Montoya, moved through the room like an ominous shadow. The majordomo came in the next day for no apparent reason, and at an unusual hour.

"I'm not trying to scare you," he told Maruja, "but something very serious has happened: A butterfly's been on the courtyard gate since last night."

Maruja, a skeptic regarding invisible forces, did not understand what he meant. The majordomo explained with calculated theatricality.

"You see, when they killed the other Priscos, the same thing happened," he said. "A black butterfly stayed on the bathroom door for three days."

Maruja recalled Marina's dark presentiments, but pretended not to understand.

"And what does that mean?" she asked.

"I don't know," replied the owner, "but it must be a very bad omen because that's when they killed doña Marina."

"The one now, is it black or tan?" Maruja asked.

"Tan," said the owner.

"Then it's a good omen," said Maruja. "It's the black ones that are unlucky."

His attempt to frighten her did not succeed. Maruja knew her husband, the way he thought and acted, and did not believe he would do anything rash enough to rob a butterfly of its sleep. She knew, above all, that neither he nor Beatriz would let slip any detail that could be of use in an armed rescue attempt. And yet, accustomed to interpreting changes in her inner state as reflections of the external world, she did not discount the fact that five deaths in the same family in one month might have terrible consequences for the last two hostages.

On the other hand, the rumor that the Constituent Assembly had certain doubts regarding extradition must have been some consolation to the Extraditables. On February 28, on an official visit to the United States, President Gaviria declared his firm commitment to maintaining it at all costs, but this caused no alarm: By now non-extradition had deep-rooted support throughout the country and required neither bribes nor intimidation to be enacted.

Maruja followed these events with close attention, in a routine that seemed to be the same day repeated over and over again. Then, without warning, while she was playing dominoes with the guards, the Top ended the game and picked up the tiles for the last time.

"We're leaving tomorrow," he said.

Maruja refused to believe him, but the schoolteacher's son confirmed the news.

"Really," he said. "Barrabás's crew is coming tomorrow."

This was the beginning of what Maruja would remember as her black March. Just as the guards who were leaving seemed to have been instructed to make her imprisonment a little easier, the ones who arrived had no doubt been told to make it unbearable again. They burst into the room like an earthquake: the Monk, tall, thin, more somber and introverted than last time; the others, the same ones, as if they had never left. Barrabás acted like a movie gangster, barking military orders at them to find the hiding place of something that did not exist, or pretending to search for it himself in order to terrorize his victim. They turned the room inside out with methodical brutality. They pulled the bed apart, emptied the mattress, and restuffed it so badly the lumps made it difficult to sleep on.

Daily life returned to the old style of keeping weapons at the ready if orders were not obeyed instantly. Barrabás never spoke to Maruja without aiming his submachine gun at her head. She, as always, responded by threatening to denounce him to his superiors.

"I'm not going to die just because you fire a bullet by mistake," she said. "You take it easy or I'll complain."

This time the strategy did not work. It seemed clear, however, that the disorder was not deliberate or meant to intimidate, but was the result of a system corroded from within by profound demoralization. Even the frequent, colorful arguments between the majordomo and Damaris became frightening. He would come home at all hours—if he came home at all—stupefied by drink, and have to confront his wife's obscene recriminations. Their screams and shouts, and the crying of their young daughters wakened from sleep, could be heard all over the house. The guards made fun of them with theatrical imitations that added to the noise. It seemed inconceivable that with all the uproar, no one was curious enough to come to the house.

The majordomo and his wife each came to Maruja for advice: Damaris, because of a plausible jealousy that gave her no peace, and he, to find some way to calm her down without giving up his escapades. But Maruja's good offices did not last beyond the majordomo's next fling.

During one of their many fights, Damaris clawed at her husband's face like a cat, and it was a long time before the marks disappeared. He hit her so hard she went through the window. It was a miracle he did not kill her, but she managed to hold on at the last minute and was left dangling from the balcony over the courtyard. It was the end. Damaris packed her bags and left with the girls for Medellín.

The house was now in the sole care of the majordomo, who sometimes stayed away until nightfall, when he showed up with yogurt and bags of potato chips. Every once in a while he would bring back a chicken. The guards, tired of waiting, would ransack the kitchen and come back to the room with stale crackers and some raw sausage for Maruja. Boredom made them touchy, and more dangerous. They railed against their parents, the police, society in general. They told about their gratuitous crimes and deliberate sacrileges to prove to one another that God did not exist, and went to insane lengths in recounting their sexual exploits. One of them described the aberrations he had inflicted on one of his girlfriends as revenge for her mocking and humiliating him. Resentful and out of control, they took to smoking marijuana and crack until the dense air in the room became unbreathable. They played the radio at ear-splitting volume, slammed the door when they went in or out, shouted, sang, danced, cavorted in the courtyard. One of them looked like a professional acrobat in a traveling circus. Maruja warned them that the noise would attract the attention of the police.

"Let them come and kill us," they shouted in chorus.

Maruja felt ready to snap, above all because of the crazed Barrabás, who liked to wake her by pressing the barrel of his machine gun against her temple. Her hair began to fall out. The pillow covered with strands of hair depressed her from the moment she opened her eyes at dawn.

She knew that each of the guards was different, but they all were susceptible to insecurity and mutual distrust. Maruja's fear exacerbated these feelings. "How can you live like this?" she would demand without warning. "What do you believe in? Do you have any idea of what friendship means?" Before they could respond she cornered them: "Does the word loyalty mean anything to you?" They did not reply, but the answers they gave themselves must have been disquieting, because instead of becoming defiant they deferred to Maruja. Only Barrabás stood up to her. "You rich motherfuckers!" he once shouted. "Did you really think you'd run things forever? Not anymore, damn it: It's all over!" Maruja, who had been so afraid of him, met the challenge with the same rage.

"You kill your friends, your friends kill you, you all end up killing each other," she screamed. "Who can understand you? Find me one person who can say what kind of animals you people are."

Driven, perhaps, to desperation because he could not kill her, Barrabás smashed his fist into the wall and damaged the bones in his wrist. He bellowed like a savage and burst into tears of fury. Maruja would not allow herself to be softened by compassion. The majordomo spent the entire afternoon trying to calm her down, and made an unsuccessful effort to improve supper.

Maruja asked herself how, with so much commotion, they could still believe it made sense to talk in whispers, confine her to the room, ration out the radio and television for reasons of security. Tired of all the madness, she rebelled against the meaningless rules of her captivity, spoke in her natural voice, went to the bathroom whenever she wanted. But her fear of sexual attack intensified, above all when the majordomo left her alone with the two guards on duty. It culminated one morning when a masked guard burst into the bathroom while she was in the shower. Maruja managed to cover herself with a towel, and her terrified scream must have been heard for miles around. He froze and stood like a statue, his heart in his mouth for fear of how the neighbors would react. But no one came, not a sound was heard. He backed out of the room on tiptoe, as if he had opened the bathroom door by mistake.

The majordomo showed up one day with another woman to run the house. But instead of controlling the disorder, they both helped to increase it. The woman joined him in his fierce bouts of drinking that tended to end in blows and smashed bottles. Meals were served at improbable hours. On Sundays they went out carousing and left Maruja and the guards with nothing to eat until the next day. One night, while Maruja was walking alone in the courtyard, the four guards went to raid the kitchen and left the machine guns in the room. An idea made her shudder. She relished it as she talked to the dog, petted him, whispered to him, and the overjoyed animal licked her hands with complicitous growls. A shout from Barrabás brought her back to reality.

It was the end of an illusion. They replaced the dog with a new one that had the face of a killer. They prohibited her walks, and Maruja was subjected to a regime of constant surveillance. What she feared most then was that they would shackle her to the bed with a plastic-wrapped chain that Barrabás moved back and forth in his hands like an iron rosary. Maruja tried to anticipate their next move.

"If I had wanted to leave, I would have done it a long time ago," she said. "I've been left alone lots of times, and if I didn't run away it's because I didn't want to."

Somebody must have complained, because one morning the majordomo appeared in the room, full of suspect humility and all kinds of excuses: that he could die of shame, that the boys would behave themselves from now on, that he had sent for his wife and she was coming back. And it was true: Damaris returned, the same as always, with her two girls, her Scottish bagpiper's miniskirts, and her endless lentils. Two bosses with masks and the same conciliatory attitude arrived the next day, shoved the four guards out, and imposed order. "They won't be back again," one of them said with hair-raising decisiveness. And it was over.

That same afternoon they sent the crew of high school graduates, and it was like a magical return to the peace of February: unhurried time, entertainment magazines, the music of Guns N' Roses, and Mel Gibson movies watched with hired gunmen well versed in unrestrained passions. Maruja was moved by the fact that the adolescent killers watched and listened with as much devotion as her children.

Toward the end of March, without any announcement, two strangers appeared, their faces hidden under hoods lent them by the guards. One, with barely a greeting, began to measure the floor with a tailor's metric tape, while the other tried to ingratiate himself with Maruja.

"I'm delighted to make your acquaintance, Señora," he said. "We're here to carpet the room."

"Carpet the room!" Maruja shouted in a blind fury. "You can go to hell! What I want is to get out of here! Right now!"

What troubled her was not the carpet but what it could mean: an indefinite postponement of her release. One of the guards would say later that Maruja's interpretation had been mistaken, since it could have meant she would be leaving soon and they were renovating the room for more important hostages. But at that moment Maruja was sure a carpet could only mean another year of her life.

PACHO SANTOS ALSO had to use all his wits to keep his guards occupied, because when they were bored with playing cards, seeing the same movie ten times in a row, and recounting their sexual exploits, they began to pace the room like caged lions. Through the holes in their hoods he could see their reddened eyes. The only thing they could do then was take a few days off—that is, stupefy themselves with alcohol and drugs during a week of nonstop parties, and come back worse than before. Drugs were prohibited and their use was punished with great severity, and not only during working hours, but the addicts always found a way around the vigilance of their superiors. The most common drug was marijuana, but their prescription for difficult times were Olympiads of crack that made him fear a calamity. One of the guards, after a night of carousing in the street, burst into the room and woke Pacho with a shout. He saw the devil's mask almost touching his face, the bloodshot eyes, the coarse hairs bristling from his ears, and smelled the sulfurous stink of hell. One of his guards wanted to finish up the party with Pacho. "You don't know how bad I am," he said while they drank a double *aguardiente* together at six in the morning. For the next two hours the guard, without being asked, told Pacho the story of his life, driven by the uncontrollable compulsion of his conscience. At last he passed out, and if Pacho did not escape then it was because he lost his courage at the last minute.

His most heartening reading in captivity were the personal notes that *El Tiempo*, on María Victoria's initiative, published for him, without concealment or reticence, on its editorial pages. One was accompanied by a recent photograph of his children, and in the heat of the moment he wrote them a letter filled with those thunderous truths that seem ridiculous to anyone who has not lived through them: "I'm sitting here in this room, chained to a bed, my eyes full of tears." From then on he wrote his wife and children a series of letters from the heart, which he could never send.

Pacho had lost all hope after the deaths of Marina and Diana, and then the possibility of escape came out to meet him without his looking for it. By now he was certain he was in one of the neighborhoods near Avenida Boyacá, to the west of the city. He knew these districts because he would make detours through them when traffic was very heavy on his way home from the newspaper, and he had been driving that route on the night he was abducted. Most of its structures were clusters of residences built in rows, the same house repeated many times over: a large door to the garage, a tiny garden, a second floor overlooking the street, and all the windows protected by wrought-iron gates painted white. And in one week he managed to find out the exact distance to the pizzeria, and learned that the factory was none other than the Bavaria Brewery. A disorienting detail was the demented rooster that at first crowed at any hour, and as the months passed crowed at the same hour in different places: sometimes far away at three in the afternoon, other times next to his window at two in the morning. It would have been even more disorienting if he had known that Maruja and Beatriz also heard it in a distant section of the city.

At the end of the hallway, to the right of his room, he could jump from a window that opened onto a small, enclosed courtyard, and then climb the vine-covered adobe wall next to a tree with sturdy branches. He did not know what lay on the other side of the wall, but since it was a corner house, it had to be a street. And almost certainly it was the street with the grocery store, the pharmacy, and an auto repair shop. This shop, however, could be a negative factor, since it might be a front for the kidnappers. In fact, Pacho once heard a conversation about soccer coming from that direction, and was sure the two voices belonged to his guards. In any case, climbing the wall would be easy, but the rest was unpredictable. The better alternative was the bathroom, which had the undeniable advantage of being the only place they let him go without the chain.

It seemed clear that his escape had to take place in the middle of the day, because he never went to the bathroom after getting into bed for the night—even if he stayed awake watching television or writing—and any deviation could betray him. Then too, the businesses closed early, the neighbors were in for the night after the seven o'clock news, and by ten there was not a soul on the streets. Even on Friday nights, which are very noisy in Bogotá, one heard only the slow wheeze of the brewery or the sudden wail of an ambulance speeding down Avenida Boyacá. And at night it would not be easy to find immediate refuge on the deserted streets, and the doors of businesses and houses would be locked and bolted against the dangers of the night.

However, the opportunity—stark and plain—presented itself on March 6, and it came at night. One of the guards had brought in a bottle of *aguardiente* and invited him to have a drink while they watched a program about Julio Iglesias on television. Pacho drank little and only to humor him. The guard, who had come on duty in the afternoon, had already been drinking and passed out before the bottle was emptied, and before he could put the chain on Pacho, who was collapsing with fatigue and did not see the chance that had fallen from the skies. Whenever he wanted to go to the bathroom at night, the guard on duty had to accompany him, but Pacho preferred not to disturb his blissful drunken stupor. He went out into the hallway in all innocence, just as he was, barefoot and in his underwear, and held his breath as he passed the room where the other guards were sleeping. One was snoring like a chainsaw. Pacho had not been aware until then that he was running away without realizing it, and that the most difficult part was over. A wave of nausea rose from his stomach, froze his tongue, and emptied out his heart. "It wasn't the fear of escaping but the fear of not daring to," he would say later. He went into the darkened bathroom and closed the door, his decision irrevocable. Another guard, still half-asleep, pushed the door open and shined a flashlight in his face. Both were astonished.

"What are you doing?" asked the guard.

Pacho responded in a firm voice:

"Taking a shit."

It was the only thing that occurred to him. The guard shook his head, not knowing what to think.

"Okay," he said at last. "Enjoy yourself."

He stayed at the door, shining the flashlight on him, not blinking, until Pacho pretended he had finished.

During that week, in the throes of depression at his failure, he resolved to escape in a radical and irremediable way. "I'll take the blade from the razor, cut my veins, and they'll find me dead in the morning," he told himself. The next day, Father Alfonso Llanos Escobar published his weekly column in *El Tiempo*, addressed it to Pacho Santos, and ordered him in the name of God not to even consider suicide. The article had been on Hernando Santos's desk for three weeks; without really knowing why, he had been unable to decide if he should publish it, and on the previous day—again without knowing why—he resolved at the last minute to use it. Each time he tells the story, Pacho again experiences the stupefaction he felt that day.

A LOW-RANKING BOSS who visited Maruja at the beginning of April promised to intercede to allow her to receive a letter from her husband, something she needed as if it were a medicine for her soul and her body. The response was astounding: "No problem." The man left around seven in the evening. At twelve-thirty, after her walk in the courtyard, the majordomo knocked with some urgency at the door, which was locked on the inside, and handed her the letter. It was not one of several sent by Villamizar with Guido Parra, but the one sent through Jorge Luis Ochoa, to which Gloria Pachón de Galán had added a consolatory postscript. On the back of the paper, Pablo Escobar had written a note in his own hand: "I know this has been terrible for you and your family, but my family and I have also suffered a great deal. But don't worry, I promise that nothing will happen to you, whatever else happens." And he concluded with a marginal confidence that Maruja found unbelievable: "Don't pay attention to my press communiqués, they're only to keep up the pressure."

Her husband's letter, however, disheartened her with its pessimism. He said that things were going well, but that she must be patient because the wait might be even longer. Certain that someone else would read it before it was delivered to her, Villamizar had concluded with words meant more for Escobar than Maruja: "Offer up your sacrifice for the peace of Colombia." She became furious. She had often intercepted the mental messages that Villamizar sent to her from their terrace, and she had responded with all her heart: "Get me out of here, I don't know who I am anymore after so many months of not seeing myself in a mirror."

The letter gave her one more reason for writing in her reply that what the hell did he mean by patience, damn it, she'd already shown more than enough and suffered more than enough during hideous nights when the icy fear of death would wake her with a start. She did not know it was an old letter, written between his failure with Guido Parra and his first interviews with the Ochoas, at a time when he saw no glimmer of hope. Not the kind of optimistic letter he would have written now, when the road to her freedom seemed clear and defined.

Fortunately, the misunderstanding allowed Maruja to realize that her anger was caused not so much by the letter as by an older, less conscious rancor toward her husband: Why had Alberto permitted them to release only Beatriz if he was the one handling the process? In the nineteen years of their life together, she had not had time, or reason, or courage to ask herself that kind of question, and her answer to herself made Maruja see the truth: She had been able to withstand captivity because of the absolute certainty that her husband was devoting every moment of his life to her release, and that he did this without rest and even without hope because of his absolute certainty that she knew what he was doing. It was—though neither of them realized it—a pact of love.

They had met nineteen years earlier at a business meeting

when they were both young publicists. "Alberto appealed to me right away," Maruja says. Why? She doesn't have to think twice: "Because he looks so helpless." It was the last answer one would expect. At first glance, Alberto seemed a typical nonconformist university student of the time, with hair down to his shoulders, a two-day growth of beard, and one shirt that was washed when it rained. "Sometimes I bathed," he says today, with a laugh. At second glance, he was a drinker and a womanizer, and had a short temper. But at third glance, Maruja saw a man who could lose his head over a beautiful woman, especially if she was intelligent and sensitive, and most especially if she had more than enough of the only thing lacking to turn the boy into a man: an iron hand and a tender heart.

Asked what he had liked about her, Villamizar answers with a growl. Perhaps because Maruja, apart from her visible charms, was not the best-qualified person to fall in love with. In the bloom of her early thirties, she had married in the Catholic Church at the age of nineteen, and had given her husband five children—three girls and two boys—born fifteen months apart. "I told Alberto everything right away," Maruja says, "so he'd know he was entering a mine field." He listened with another growl, and instead of asking her to lunch, he had a mutual friend ask them both. The next day he asked her to lunch, along with the same friend, on the third day he asked her alone, and on the fourth day they saw each other without having lunch. And so they continued to meet every day, with the best of intentions. When Villamizar is asked if he was in love or only wanted to take her to bed, he answers in pure Santanderese: "Don't screw around, it was serious." Perhaps not even he imagined just how serious it was.

Maruja had a marriage with no surprises, no arguments, a perfect marriage, but perhaps it was missing the gram of inspiration and risk she needed to feel alive. She made time for Villamizar by saying she was at the office. She invented more work than she had, even on Saturdays from noon until ten at night. On Sundays and holidays they improvised children's parties, lectures on art, midnight cinema clubs, anything, just so they could be together. He had no problems: He was single and available, came and went as he pleased, and had so many Saturday sweethearts it was as if he had none at all. He needed only to write his final thesis to be a surgeon like his father, but the times favored living one's life more than curing the sick. Love had escaped the confines of boleros, the perfumed love letters that had endured for four centuries were a thing of the past, as were tearful serenades, monogrammed handkerchiefs, the language of flowers, and empty movie theaters at three in the afternoon, and the whole world seemed protected from death by the inspired lunacy of the Beatles.

A year after they met they began to live together, with Maruja's children, in an apartment that measured a hundred square meters. "It was a disaster," says Maruja. And with reason: They lived amid free-for-all quarrels, the crash of breaking plates, jealousies and suspicions on the part of both children and adults. "Sometimes I hated him with all my heart," says Maruja. "I felt the same about her," says Villamizar. "But never for more than five minutes," Maruja laughs. In October 1971, they were married in Ureña, Venezuela, and it was as if they had added one more sin to their life, because divorce did not exist and very few believed in the legality of civil ceremonies. After four years Andrés was born, the only child they had together. The difficulties continued but caused them less grief: Life had taken on the task of teaching them that the joy of love was not meant to lull you to sleep, but to keep you struggling together.

Maruja was the daughter of Alvaro Pachón de la Torre, a star reporter of the 1940s who died with two well-known colleagues in a car crash of historic importance to the profession. Her mother was dead, and she and her sister Gloria had been on their own from the time they were very young. Maruja had been a draftsman and painter at the age of twenty, a precocious publicist, a director and scriptwriter for radio and television, the head of public relations or advertising for major companies, and always a journalist. Her artistic talent and impulsive nature attracted immediate attention, helped along by a gift for command that was concealed behind the quiet pools of her Gypsy eyes. Villamizar, for his part, forgot about medicine, cut his hair, threw out his one shirt, put on a tie, and became an expert in the mass marketing of anything they gave him to sell. But he did not change his nature. Maruja acknowledges that more than any of life's blows, it was he who cured her of the formalism and inhibitions of her social milieu.

They had separate, successful careers while the children were in school. Maruja came home every night at six to spend time with them. Smarting from her own strict, conventional upbringing, she wanted to be a different kind of mother who did not attend parents' meetings at school or help with homework. The girls complained: "We want a mommy like all the others." But Maruja pushed them in the opposite direction toward the independence and education to do whatever they wanted. The curious thing is that they all wanted to do precisely what she would have chosen for them. Mónica studied at the Academy of Fine Arts in Rome, and is a painter and graphic designer. Alexandra is a journalist and a television producer and director. Juana is a scriptwriter and director for television and films. Nicolás composes music for movies and television. Patricio is a psychologist. Andrés, a student of economics, was bitten by the scorpion of politics thanks to his father's bad example, and at the age of twenty-one was elected by popular vote to the alderman's seat on the town council of Chapinero, in northern Bogotá.

The complicity of Luis Carlos Galán and Gloria Pachón, dating back to the days before their marriage, proved decisive in the political career that Alberto and Maruja never expected. Galán, at the age of thirty-seven, ran for the presidential candidacy of the New Liberalism Party. His wife, Gloria, who was also a journalist, and Maruja, experienced in promotion and publicity, conceived and directed advertising strategies for six electoral campaigns. Villamizar's experience in mass marketing had given him a logistical knowledge of Bogotá that very few politicians possessed. As a team, the three of them created, in one frantic month, the first New Liberalism campaign in the capital, and swept away more seasoned candidates. In the 1982 elections, Villamizar was listed sixth in a slate that did not expect to elect more than five representatives to the Chamber, but in fact elected nine. Unfortunately, that victory was the prelude to a new life that would lead Alberto and Maruja—eight years later—to her abduction and its gruesome test of their love.

SOME TEN DAYS after the letter, the important boss they called the "Doctor"—acknowledged by now as the man in charge of her abduction and captivity—paid Maruja an unannounced visit. After seeing him in the house where she had been taken on the night of the kidnapping, he had come back about three times prior to Marina's death. He and Marina would have long whispered conversations together, as if they were old friends. His relationship to Maruja had always been strained. For any remark of hers, no matter how simple, he had a haughty, brutal reply: "You have nothing to say here." When the three hostages were still together, she tried to register a complaint with him about the wretched conditions in the room, to which she attributed her persistent cough and erratic pains.

"I've spent worse nights in places a thousand times worse than this," he answered in an angry tone. "Who do you people think you are?"

His visits were preludes to great events, good or bad, but always decisive. This time, however, encouraged by Escobar's letter, Maruja had the heart to confront him.

Their communication was immediate and surprisingly untroubled. She began by asking, with no resentment, what Escobar wanted, how the negotiations were going, what the chances were of his surrendering soon. He told her in a frank manner that nothing would be easy unless there were sufficient guarantees of safety for Pablo Escobar, his family, and his people. Maruja asked about Guido Parra, whose efforts had brought her hope and whose sudden disappearance intrigued her.

"Well, he didn't behave very well," he said in an unemotional way. "He's out of it now."

That could be interpreted in three ways: either he had lost his power, or he had really left the country—which was the public story—or he had been killed. The "Doctor" evaded the issue, saying that in fact he did not know.

In part to satisfy her irresistible curiosity, and in part to gain his confidence, Maruja also asked who had written a recent letter from the Extraditables to the ambassador of the United States regarding extradition and the drug trade. She had found it striking not only because of the strength of its arguments but because it was so well written. The "Doctor" was not certain, but he assured her that Escobar wrote his letters himself, rethinking and revising drafts until he said what he wanted to say without equivocations or contradictions. At the end of their conversation, which lasted almost two hours, the "Doctor" again raised the subject of surrender. Maruja realized he was more interested than he had first appeared to be, thinking not only about Escobar's future but about his own. She had a well-reasoned opinion about the controversies surrounding the decrees, knew the details of the capitulation policy, and was familiar with the tendencies of the Constituent Assembly regarding extradition and amnesty.

"If Escobar isn't willing to spend at least fourteen years in jail," she said, "I don't believe the government will accept his surrender."

He thought so much of her opinion that he had a startling idea: "Why don't you write a letter to the Chief?" And he repeated it when he saw how disconcerted Maruja became.

"I mean it, write to him," he said. "It could be very helpful."

And she did. He brought her paper and pencil, and waited without impatience, walking from one end of the room to the other. Maruja smoked half a pack of cigarettes from the start of the letter to the finish, sitting on the bed and writing on a board she held on her lap. In simple terms she thanked Escobar for the sense of security his words had given her. She said she had no desire for revenge against him or the people managing her captivity, and she thanked all of them for the respect with which she had been treated. She hoped Escobar could accept the government's decrees and provide a good future for himself and his children in their own country. She concluded with the formula that Villamizar had suggested in his letter, offering up her sacrifice for peace in Colombia.

The "Doctor" was hoping for something more concrete regarding the terms of the surrender, but Maruja convinced him that the effect would be the same without going into details that might seem impertinent or be misinterpreted. She was right: The letter was given to the press by Pablo Escobar, who had their ear just then because of the interest in his surrender.

Maruja also gave the "Doctor" a letter for Villamizar, one very different from the letter she had written under the effects of her rage, and as a result he appeared on television again after many weeks of silence. That night she took the powerful sedative and dreamed, in a futuristic version of a western movie, that Escobar was getting out of a helicopter and using her as a shield against a barrage of bullets.

At the end of his visit, the "Doctor" had instructed the people in the house to take greater pains in their treatment of Maruja. The majordomo and Damaris were so pleased with the new orders that they sometimes went overboard in complying with them. Before leaving, the "Doctor" had wanted to change the guards. Maruja asked him not to. The young high-school graduates on duty in April had been a relief after the excesses of March, and they continued to maintain peaceful relations with her. Maruja had gained their confidence. They told her what they heard from the majordomo and his wife, and kept her informed about the internal conflicts that had once been state secrets. They even promised—and Maruja believed them—that if anyone tried to do anything to her, they would be the first to stop him. They showed their affection with treats they stole from the kitchen, and they gave her a can of olive oil to help disguise the abominable taste of the lentils.

The only difficulty was the religious anxiety that troubled them and which she could not resolve because of her innate lack of belief and her ignorance in matters of faith. She often risked shattering the harmony in the room. "Let's see what this is all about," she would ask them. "If killing is a sin, why do you kill?" She would challenge them: "All those six o'clock rosaries, all those candles, all that business with the Holy Infant, and if I tried to escape you wouldn't think twice about shooting me." The debates became so virulent that one of them shouted in horror:

"You're an atheist!"

She shouted back that she was. She never thought it would cause such stupefaction. Knowing she might have to pay dearly for her idle iconoclasm, she invented a cosmic theory of life and the world that allowed them to talk without quarreling. And so the idea of replacing them with guards she did not know was not something she favored. But the "Doctor" explained:

"It'll take care of the machine guns."

Maruja understood what he meant when the new crew arrived. They were unarmed housekeepers who cleaned and mopped all day until they became more of a nuisance than the trash and dirt had been before. But Maruja's cough began to disappear, and the new order allowed her to watch television with a serenity and concentration that were beneficial to her health and stability.

Maruja the unbeliever did not pay the slightest attention to "God's Minute," a strange sixty-second program in which the eighty-two-year-old Eudist priest, Rafael García Herreros, would offer a reflection that was more social than religious, and often tended to be cryptic. Pacho Santos, however, who is a devout practicing Catholic, was very interested in his messages, so unlike those of professional politicians. Father García Herreros had been one of the best-known faces in the country since January 1955, when he began to air his program on Televisora Nacional's channel 7. Before that he had been a familiar voice on a Cartagena radio station since 1950, on a Cali station since January of 1952, in Medellín since September of 1954, and in Bogotá since December of the same year. He started on television at almost the same time that the system began operating. He was distinguished by his direct, sometimes brutal style, and as he spoke he fixed his falcon eyes on the viewer. Every year since 1961 he had organized the Banquet for a Million, attended by famous people—and those who aspired to fame—who paid a million pesos for a cup of consommé and a roll served by a beauty queen. The proceeds were used for the charity that had the same name as the program. The most controversial invitation was the one he sent in 1968 in a personal letter to Brigitte Bardot. Her immediate acceptance scandalized the local prudes, who threatened to sabotage the banquet. The priest stood firm. An opportune fire at the Boulogne studios in Paris, and the fantastic explanation that no seats were available on the planes, were the two excuses that saved the nation from utter embarrassment.

Pancho Santos's guards were faithful viewers of "God's Minute," but they were more interested in its religious content than in its social message. Like most families from the shantytowns of Antioquia, they had blind faith in the priest's saintliness. His tone was always abrupt, the content sometimes incomprehensible. But the April 18 program—directed beyond a doubt to Pablo Escobar, though his name was not mentioned—was indecipherable.

Looking straight into the camera, Father García Herreros said:

They have told me you want to surrender. They have told me you would like to talk to me. Oh sea! Oh sea of Coveñas at five in the evening when the sun is setting! What should I do? They tell me he is weary of his life and its turmoil, and I can tell no one my secret. But it suffocates me internally. Tell me, oh sea: Can I do it? Should I do it? You who know the history of Colombia, you who saw the Indians worshipping on this shore, you who heard the sound of history: Should I do it? Will I be rejected if I do it? Will I be rejected in Colombia? If I do it: Will there be shooting when I go with them? Will I fall with them in this adventure?

Maruja heard the program too, but it seemed less strange to her than to many Colombians because she always thought that the priest liked to wander until he lost his way among the galaxies. She viewed him as an inescapable prelude to the seven o'clock news. That night she paid attention because everything that concerned Pablo Escobar concerned her too. She was perplexed, intrigued, and very troubled by doubts about what lay behind that divine rigmarole. Pacho, however, was sure the priest would get him out of that purgatory, and he embraced his guard with joy.

10

FATHER GARCÍA HERREROS'S message created an opening in the impasse. It seemed a miracle to Alberto Villamizar, for at the time he had been going over the names of possible mediators whose image and background might inspire more trust in Escobar. Rafael Pardo heard about the program and was disturbed by the idea that there could be a leak in his office. In any case, both he and Villamizar thought Father García Herreros might be the right person to mediate Escobar's surrender.

By the end of March, in fact, the letters going back and forth had nothing left to say. Worse yet: It was evident that Escobar was using Villamizar as a means of sending messages to the government and not giving anything in return. His last letter was nothing more than a list of interminable complaints—that the truce had not been broken but he had given his people permission to defend themselves against the security forces, that these forces were on the list of people to be killed, that if solutions were not forthcoming then indiscriminate attacks against police and the civilian population would increase. He complained that the prosecutor had discharged only two officers, when twenty had been accused by the Extraditables.

When Villamizar reached a dead end he discussed it with Jorge Luis Ochoa, but for more delicate matters Jorge Luis would send him to his father's house for advice. The old man would pour him half a glass of his sacred whiskey. "Drink it all up," he would say. "I don't know how you stand so much tragedy." This was the situation at the beginning of April when Villamizar returned to La Loma and gave don Fabio a detailed accounting of his failures with Escobar. Don Fabio shared his disillusionment.

"We won't screw around anymore with letters," he decided. "At this rate it will take a hundred years. The best thing is for you to meet with Escobar and for the two of you to agree on whatever conditions you like."

Don Fabio himself sent the proposal. He let Escobar know that Villamizar was prepared to be taken to him, with all the risks this entailed, in the trunk of a car. But Escobar did not accept. "Maybe I'll talk to Villamizar, but not now," was his reply. Perhaps he was still wary of the electronic tracking device that could be hidden anywhere, even under the gold crown of a tooth.

In the meantime, he continued to insist on sanctions for the police and to repeat his accusations that General Maza Márquez had allied himself with the paramilitary forces and the Cali cartel to kill his people. This accusation, and his charge that the general had killed Luis Carlos Galán, were two of Escobar's fierce obsessions with Maza Márquez. The general's reply, in public or in private, always was that for the moment he was not waging war against the Cali cartel because his priority was terrorism by drug traffickers and not the drug traffic itself. Escobar, for his part, had written this aside in a letter to Villamizar: "Tell doña Gloria that Maza killed her husband, there can be no doubt about it." Maza's response to the repeated accusation was always the same: "Escobar knows better than anyone else that it isn't true."

In despair over this brutal, pointless war that vanquished all intelligent initiatives, Villamizar made one final effort to persuade the government to declare a truce in order to negotiate. It was impossible. Rafael Pardo told him that while the families of the hostages were opposing the government's decision not to make any concessions, the enemies of the capitulation policy were accusing the government of handing the country over to the traffickers.

Villamizar—accompanied on this occasion by his sister-in-law, doña Gloria Pachón de Galán—also visited General Gómez Padilla, director general of the National Police. She asked the general for a month's truce to allow them to attempt personal contact with Escobar.

"I cannot tell you how sorry we are, Señora," the general said, "but we cannot halt operations against this criminal. You are acting at your own risk, and all we can do is wish you luck."

This was all they accomplished with the police, whose hermeticism was meant to stop the inexplicable leaks that had allowed Escobar to escape the best-planned sieges. But doña Gloria did not leave empty-handed, for as they were saying goodbye an officer told her Maruja was being held somewhere in the department of Nariño, on the Ecuadoran border. She had learned from Beatriz that the house was in Bogotá, which meant that the police's misinformation lessened her fear of a rescue operation.

By this time speculation in the press regarding the terms of Escobar's surrender had reached the proportions of an international scandal. Denials from the police and explanations from all segments of the government, even from the president, had not convinced many people that there were no negotiations or secret agreements for his capitulation.

General Maza Márquez believed it to be true. What is more, he had always been certain—and said so to anyone who wanted to listen—that his removal would be one of Escobar's primary conditions for surrender. For a long time President Gaviria seemed angered by certain statements made by Maza Márquez to the press, and by unconfirmed rumors that the general was responsible for some of the sensitive leaks. But at this time—considering his many years in the position, his immense popularity because of the hard line he had taken against crime, and his ineffable devotion to the Holy Infant—it was not likely that the president would remove him without good reason. Maza had to be conscious of his power, but he also had to know that sooner or later the president would exercise his, and the only thing he had requested—through messages carried by mutual friends—was that he be told with sufficient warning to provide for his family's safety.

The only official authorized to maintain contacts with Pablo Escobar's attorneys—provided a written record was kept—was the director of Criminal Investigation, Carlos Eduardo Mejía. He was responsible by law for arranging the operative details of the surrender, and the security and living conditions in prison.

Minister Giraldo Angel personally reviewed the possible options. He had been interested in the high-security block at Itagüí ever since Fabio Ochoa's surrender the previous November, but Escobar's lawyers objected because it was an easy target for car bombs. He also found acceptable the idea of turning a convent in El Poblado—near the residential building where Escobar had escaped the explosion of two hundred kilos of dynamite, attributed to the Cali cartel—into a fortified prison, but the community of nuns who owned it did not wish to sell. He had proposed reinforcing the Medellín prison, but the Municipal Council opposed the plan in a plenary session. Alberto Villamizar, fearing that the surrender would be thwarted by lack of a prison, interceded with serious arguments in favor of the site proposed by Escobar in October: El Claret, the Municipal Rehabilitation Center for Drug Addicts, located twelve kilometers from Envigado's main park, on a property known as La Catedral del Valle, whose owner-of-record was one of Escobar's front men. The government studied the possibility of leasing the center and converting it into a prison, well aware that Escobar would not surrender if he could not resolve the problem of his own security. His lawyers demanded that the guards be Antioquian, and, fearing reprisals for the agents murdered in Medellín, that external security be in the hands of any armed force except the police.

The mayor of Envigado, who was responsible for completing the project, took note of the government's report and initiated the transfer of the prison, which had to be consigned to the Ministry of Justice according to the leasing contract both parties had signed. The basic construction displayed an elementary simplicity, with cement floors, tile roofs, and metal doors painted green. The administration area, in what had been the farmhouse, consisted of three small rooms, a kitchen, a paved courtyard, and a punishment cell. It had a dormitory measuring four hundred square meters, another large room to be used as a library and study, and six individual cells with private bathrooms. A common area in the center, measuring six hundred square meters, had four showers, a dressing room, and six toilets. The remodeling had begun in February, with seventy workers who slept in shifts at the site for a few hours a day. The rough topography, the awful condition of the access road, and the harsh winter obliged them to do without trucks and carriers, and to transport most of the furnishings by muleback. First among them were two fifty-liter water heaters, military cots, and some two dozen small tubular armchairs painted yellow. Twenty pots holding ornamental plants—araucarias, laurels, and areca palms—completed the interior decoration. Since the former rehabilitation center had no telephone lines, the prison's initial communications would be by radio. The final cost of the project was 120 million pesos, paid by the municipality of Envigado. Early estimates had calculated a period of eight months for the construction, but when Father García Herreros came on the scene, the pace of work was speeded up to a quick march.

Another obstacle to surrender had been the dismantling of Escobar's private army. He did not seem to consider prison a legal recourse but as protection from his enemies, and even from ordinary law enforcement agencies, but he could not persuade his troops to turn themselves in. He argued that he could not provide for the safety of himself and his family and leave his accomplices to the mercies of the Elite Corps. "I won't surrender alone," he said in a letter. But for many this was half a truth, since it is also likely that he wanted to have his entire team with him so he could continue to run his business from jail. In any case, the government preferred to imprison them along with Escobar. There were about a hundred crews that were not on permanent war footing but served as frontline reserve troops, easy to mobilize and arm in a few hours. It was a question of having Escobar disarm and bring to prison with him fifteen or twenty of his staunch captains.

In the few personal interviews that Villamizar had with the president, Gaviria's position was always to offer his personal efforts to free the hostages. Villamizar does not believe that the government held any negotiations other than the ones he was authorized to engage in, which were already foreseen in the capitulation policy. Former president Turbay and Hernando Santos—though they never expressed it, and were not unaware of the government's institutional difficulties—no doubt expected a minimum of flexibility from the president. His refusal to change the time limits established in the decrees, despite Nydia's insistence, entreaties, and protests, will continue to be a thorn in the hearts of the families who pleaded with him. And the fact that he did change them three days after Diana's death is something her family will never understand. Unfortunately—the president has said in private—by that time altering the date would not have stopped Diana's death or changed the way it happened.

Escobar never felt satisfied with only one avenue, and he never stopped trying to negotiate, with God and with the Devil, with every kind of legal or illegal weapon, not because he trusted one more than the other, but because he had no confidence in any of them. Even when he had secured what he wanted from Villamizar, he still embraced the dream of political amnesty, an idea that first surfaced in 1989 when the major dealers and many of their people obtained documents identifying them as members of the M-19 in order to find a place on the lists of pardoned guerrilla fighters. Commander Carlos Pizarro blocked their way with impossible demands. Two years later, Escobar tried it again through the Constituent Assembly, several of whose members were subjected to various kinds of pressure ranging from crude offers of money to the most serious intimidation.

But Escobar's enemies were also working at cross-purposes. This was the origin of a so-called narcovideo that caused an enormous, unproductive scandal. Presumably filmed in a hotel room with a hidden camera, it showed a member of the Constituent Assembly taking cash from an alleged lawyer for Escobar. The assembly member had been elected from the lists of the M-19 but in fact belonged to the paramilitary group that worked for the Cali cartel in its war against the Medellín cartel, and he did not have enough credibility to convince anyone. Months later, a leader of some private militias who turned in his weapons to the police said that his people had made that cheap soap opera in order to prove that Escobar was suborning members of the Assembly, and thereby invalidate amnesty or non-extradition.

One of the many new fronts that Escobar tried to open was his attempt to negotiate the release of Pacho Santos behind the back of Villamizar just as his efforts were beginning to bear fruit. In late April Escobar sent Hernando Santos a message through a priest he knew, asking that he meet with one of his attorneys in the church in Usaquén. It was—the message said—a matter of utmost importance regarding the release of Pacho. Hernando not only knew the priest but considered him a saint on earth, and so he went alone and arrived punctually at eight on the evening of the specified date. Inside the dim church the lawyer, almost invisible in the shadows, told him he had nothing to do with the cartels but that Pablo Escobar had paid for his education and he could not refuse

him a favor. His mission was only to hand him two texts: a report
from Amnesty International condemning the Medellín police, and
the original copy of an article that had all the airs of an editorial
attacking the abuses of the Elite Corps.

"I've come here with only your son's life in mind," said the
lawyer. "If these articles are published tomorrow, by the day after
tomorrow Francisco will be free."

Hernando read the manuscript with a political eye. It listed the
incidents denounced so often by Escobar, but with bloodcurdling
details that were impossible to prove. It was written with gravity
and subtle malice. The author, according to the lawyer, was
Escobar himself. In any case, the style seemed to be his.

The document from Amnesty International had already appeared in other newspapers, and Hernando Santos had no problem in publishing it again. The editorial, however, was too serious
to publish with no evidence. "If he sends me proof, we'll print it
right away even if they don't let Pacho go," said Hernando. There
was nothing more to discuss. The lawyer, aware that his mission
was over, took advantage of the opportunity to ask Hernando how
much Guido Parra had charged for his mediation.

"Not a cent," replied Hernando. "Money was never mentioned."

"Tell me the truth," said the lawyer, "because Escobar controls
the accounts, he controls everything, and he needs that information."

Hernando repeated his answer, and the meeting ended with
formal goodbyes.

PERHAPS THE ONLY person at this time who was convinced
that matters were close to resolution was the Colombian as-
trologer Mauricio Puerta—an attentive observer of national life by
means of the stars—who had reached some surprising conclusions
regarding Pablo Escobar's astrological chart.

Escobar had been born in Medellín on December 1, 1949, at 11:50 a.m. He was, therefore, a Sagittarius with Pisces in the ascendant, with one of the worst conjunctions: Mars and Saturn in Virgo. His tendencies were cruel authoritarianism, despotism, insatiable ambition, rebelliousness, turbulence, insubordination, anarchy, lack of discipline, attacks on authority. And an ineluctable outcome: sudden death.

Beginning on March 30, 1991, he had Saturn at five degrees for the next three years, and this meant that only three alternatives defined his future: the hospital, the cemetery, or prison. A fourth option—the monastery—did not seem applicable in his case. In any event, the period was more favorable for settling the terms of a negotiation than for closing a definitive deal. In other words: His best option was the conditional surrender proposed by the government.

"Escobar must be very worried if he's so interested in his chart," said one reporter. For as soon as he heard about Mauricio Puerta's reading, he wanted his analysis down to the smallest detail. But two messengers sent by Escobar never reached their destination, and one disappeared forever. Then Puerta arranged a well-publicized seminar in Medellín to make himself available to Escobar, but a series of strange difficulties made the meeting impossible. Puerta interpreted these as a defensive strategy by the stars to prevent anything from interfering with a destiny that was now inexorable.

Pacho Santos's wife also received supernatural revelations from a clairvoyant who had predicted Diana's death with amazing clarity, and had told her with equal certainty that Pacho was alive. In April they happened to meet again in a public place, and the clairvoyant murmured as she passed by:

"Congratulations. I can see his homecoming."

THESE WERE the only encouraging signs when Father García Herreros sent his cryptic message to Pablo Escobar. How he made that providential determination, and what the sea of Coveñas had to do with it, is something that still intrigues the nation. Yet how he happened to think of it is even more intriguing. On Friday, April 12, 1991, he visited Dr. Manuel Elkin Patarroyo—the inspired inventor of the malaria vaccine—to ask him to set up a clinic, in the area of the "God's Minute" charity, for the early detection of AIDS. In addition to a young priest from his community, he was accompanied by an old-style Antioquian, a great friend who advised him on earthly matters. By his own decision, this benefactor, who has asked that his name not be mentioned, not only had built and paid for Father García Herreros's private chapel, but also had made voluntary contributions to his social service projects. In the car that was taking them to Dr. Patarroyo's Institute of Immunology, he felt a kind of urgent inspiration.

"Listen, Father," he said. "Why don't you do something to move this thing along and help Pablo Escobar turn himself in?"

He said it with no preliminaries and no conscious motive. "It was a message from above," he would say later in the way he always refers to God, with the respect of a servant and the familiarity of a *compadre*. The father reacted as if an arrow had pierced his heart. He turned ashen. Dr. Patarroyo, who did not know him, was later struck by the energy shining from his eyes, and by his business sense, but to his Antioquian companion he seemed changed. "It was like Father was floating," he has said. "During the interview the only thing on his mind was what I had said, and when we left I thought he looked so excited that I began to worry." This is why he took the father away for the weekend to rest at a vacation house in Coveñas, a popular Caribbean resort that swarms with thousands of tourists and is the terminus of a pipeline bringing in 250,000 barrels of crude oil every day.

The father did not have a moment's peace. He hardly slept; he would leave the table in the middle of meals and take long walks along the beach at all hours of the day or night. "Oh sea of Coveñas," he shouted into the roar of the surf. "Can I do it? Should I do it? You who know everything: Will we not die in the attempt?" At the end of his tormented walks he would come into the house with absolute confidence, as if he had in reality received answers from the sea, and discuss every detail of the project with his host.

On Tuesday, when they returned to Bogotá, he could see the entire plan, and this gave him back his serenity. On Wednesday he returned to his routine: He got up at six, showered, put on his black cassock with the clerical collar, and over that his invariable white poncho, and brought his affairs up-to-date with the assistance of Paulina Garzón de Bermúdez, who had been his indispensable secretary for half her lifetime. The subject of his program that night had nothing to do with the obsession that drove him. On Thursday morning, just as he had promised, Dr. Patarroyo sent an affirmative reply to his request. The priest had no lunch. At ten to seven he reached the studios of Inravisión, where he broadcast his program, and in front of the cameras he improvised his direct message to Escobar. These were sixty seconds that changed the little life that still remained to him. When he came home he was greeted by a basket full of telephone messages from all over the country, and an avalanche of reporters who from that night on would not let him out of their sight until he had accomplished his goal of leading Pablo Escobar by the hand into prison.

The final process had begun but the outcome was uncertain because public opinion was divided between the masses of people who believed the good father was a saint, and the unbelievers who were convinced he was half-mad. The truth is that his life revealed him to be many things, but not that. He had turned eighty-two in January, would complete fifty-two years as a priest in August, and seemed to be the only well-known Colombian who had never dreamed of being president. His snowy head and the white poncho over his cassock complemented one of the most respected images in the country. He had written verses that he published in a book at the age of nineteen, and others, also composed in his youth, under the pen name Senescens. He was awarded a forgotten prize for a volume of stories, and forty-six decorations for his charitable projects. In good times and bad he always had his feet planted firmly on the ground, led the social life of a layman, told and listened to jokes of any color, and at the moment of truth revealed what he always had been under his cattleman's poncho: a dyed-in-the-wool Santanderean.

He lived in monastic austerity in the vicarage of San Juan Eudes Church, in a room riddled with leaks that he refused to repair. He slept on wooden planks without a mattress or pillow, and with a coverlet made of colored scraps of cloth cut in the shape of little houses that some charitable nuns had sewn for him. He refused a down pillow that someone once offered him because it seemed contrary to the will of God. He wore the same shoes until someone gave him a new pair, and did not replace his clothing and his eternal white poncho until someone provided him with new ones. He ate little, though he liked good food and appreciated fine wines, but would not accept invitations to expensive restaurants for fear people would think he was paying. In one restaurant he saw an elegant woman with a diamond the size of an almond on her finger.

"With a ring like that," he walked up to her and said, "I could build 120 houses for the poor."

She was too stunned to answer, but the next day she sent him the ring with a cordial note. It did not pay for 120 houses, of course, but the father built them anyway.

Paulina Garzón was a native of Chipatá, Santander del Sur, and had come to Bogotá with her mother in 1961, at the age of fifteen, with a letter of recommendation stating she was an expert typist. She was, in fact, though she did not know how to speak on the phone, and her shopping lists were indecipherable because of her calamitous spelling, but she learned both things well so that the priest would hire her. At twenty-five she married and had a son—Alfonso—and a daughter—María Constanza—who today are both systems engineers. Paulina arranged her life so that she could continue to work for Father García Herreros, who gave her more and more duties and responsibilities until she became so indispensable that she traveled with him in Colombia and abroad, but always accompanied by another priest. "To avoid gossip," Paulina explains. In the end she accompanied him everywhere, if only to put in and take out his contact lenses, something he never could do by himself.

In his final years the priest lost his hearing in his right ear, became irritable, and lost patience with the gaps in his memory. Little by little he had discarded classical prayers and improvised his own, which he said aloud and with a visionary's inspiration. His reputation as a lunatic grew along with the popular belief that he had a supernatural ability to talk with the waters and control their direction and movement. The understanding he showed toward Pablo Escobar recalled something he had said about the return of General Gustavo Rojas Pinilla, in August 1957, to be tried by Congress: "When a man turns himself over to the law, even if he is guilty, he deserves profound respect." Almost at the end of his life, at a Banquet for a Million that had been very difficult to organize, a friend asked what he would do now and he gave the answer of a nineteen-year-old: "I want to lie down in a meadow and look at the stars."

The day following his television message, Father García Herreros came to the Itagüí prison—unannounced and with no prior arrangements—to ask the Ochoa brothers how he could be useful in arranging Escobar's surrender. The Ochoas thought he was a saint, with only one problem that had to be taken into account: For more than forty years he had communicated with his audience through his daily sermon, and he could not conceive of any action that did not begin by telling the public about it. The decisive factor for the Ochoas, however, was that don Fabio thought he was a providential mediator—first, because with him Escobar would not feel the reluctance that kept him from seeing Villamizar, and second, because his image as a holy man could convince the entire Escobar crew to turn themselves in.

Two days later, at a press conference, Father García Herreros revealed that he was in contact with those responsible for the abduction of the journalists, and expressed his optimism that they would soon be free. Villamizar did not hesitate for a moment, and went to see him at "God's Minute." He accompanied him on his second visit to the Itagüí prison, and on the same day the costly, confidential process began that would culminate in the surrender. It began with a letter dictated by the priest in the Ochoas' cell and copied by María Lía on the typewriter. He improvised it as he stood in front of her, using the same manner, the same apostolic tone, the same Santanderean accent as in his one-minute homilies. He invited Escobar to join him in a search for the road that would bring peace to Colombia. He announced his hope that the government would name him as guarantor "that your rights, and those of your family and friends, will be respected." But he warned him not to ask for things the government could not grant. Before concluding with "affectionate greetings," he stated what was in reality the practical purpose of the letter: "If you believe we can meet in a place that is safe for both of us, let me know."

Escobar answered three days later, in his own hand. He agreed to surrender as a sacrifice for peace. He made it clear that he did not expect a pardon, was not asking for criminal prosecution but disciplinary action against the police wreaking havoc in the slums, and did not renounce his determination to respond with drastic reprisals. He was prepared to confess to any crime, though he knew with certainty that no judge, Colombian or foreign, had enough evidence to convict him, and he trusted that his adversaries would be subjected to the same strict procedures. However, despite the father's most fervent hope, he made no reference to his proposal to meet with him.

Father García Herreros had promised Villamizar that he would control his informative impulses, and at first he kept his word, but his almost boyish spirit of adventure was greater than his power to control them. The expectations created were so great, and there was so much coverage in the press, that from then on he could not make a move without a train of reporters and mobile television and radio crews following him right up to his front door.

AFTER FIVE MONTHS of working in absolute secret, under the almost sacramental silence imposed by Rafael Pardo, Villamizar thought that the easy talk of Father García Herreros put the entire operation at perpetual risk. This was when he requested and received help from the people closest to the father—beginning with Paulina—and was able to go forward with preparations for certain actions without having to inform the priest ahead of time.

On May 13 he received a message from Escobar in which he asked him to bring the father to La Loma and keep him there for as long as necessary. He said it might be three days or three months, because he had to review in person and in detail every stage of the operation. The possibility even existed that it could be canceled at the last minute if there were any doubts at all about security. Fortunately, the father was always available in a matter that had cost him so much sleep. At five o'clock on the morning of May 14, Villamizar knocked at his front door and found him working in his study as if it were the middle of the day.

"Come, Father," he said, "we're going to Medellín."

At La Loma the Ochoa sisters were prepared to entertain the father for as long as necessary. Don Fabio was not there, but the women in the house would take care of everything. It was not easy to distract him because the father knew that a trip as sudden and unplanned as this one could only be for something very serious.

The long breakfast was delicious, and the father ate well. At about ten, making an effort not to be too melodramatic, Martha Nieves told him that Escobar would be seeing him sometime soon. He gave a start, became very happy, but did not know what to do until Villamizar made the reality clear to him.

"It's better for you to know from the very beginning, Father," he said. "You may have to go alone with the driver, and nobody knows where he'll take you, or for how long."

The father turned pale. He could barely hold the rosary between his fingers as he paced back and forth, reciting his invented prayers aloud. Each time he passed the windows he looked toward the road, torn between terror that the car coming for him would appear, and fear that it would not come at all. He wanted to make a phone call but then realized the danger on his own. "Fortunately, there's no need for telephones when you talk to God," he said. He did not want to sit at the table during lunch, which was late and even more appetizing than breakfast. In the room that had been prepared for him, there was a bed with a passementerie canopy worthy of a bishop. The women tried to convince him to lie down for a while, and he seemed to agree. But he did not sleep. He was restive as he read Stephen Hawking's *A Brief History of Time*, a popular book that attempted to demonstrate with mathematical calculations that God does not exist. At about four he came to the room where Villamizar was dozing.

"Alberto," he said, "we'd better go back to Bogotá."

It was difficult to dissuade him, but the women succeeded with their charm and tact. At dusk he had another relapse, but by this time there was no escape. He knew the grave risks involved in traveling at night. When it was time to go to bed he asked for help in removing his contact lenses, since Paulina was the one who took them out and put them in for him, and he did not know how to do it alone. Villamizar did not sleep, because he accepted the possibility that Escobar might consider the dark of night as the safest time for their meeting.

The priest did not sleep at all. Breakfast at eight the next morning was more tempting than the day before, but he did not even sit at the table. He was in despair over his contact lenses, and no one had been able to help him until, after many tries, the woman who ran the farm managed to put them in. In contrast to the first day, he did not seem nervous or driven to pace back and forth, but sat with his eyes fixed on the road where the car would appear. He stayed there until impatience got the better of him and he jumped up from his chair.

"I'm leaving," he said, "this whole thing is as phony as a rooster laying eggs."

They persuaded him to wait until after lunch. The promise restored his good humor. He ate well, chatted, was as amusing as he had been in his best times, and at last said he would take a siesta.

"But I'm warning you," he said, his index finger wagging. "As soon as I wake up, I'm leaving."

Martha Nieves made a few phone calls, hoping to obtain some additional information that would help them to keep the priest there after his nap. It was impossible. A little before three they were all dozing in the living room when they were awakened by the sound of an engine. There was the car. Villamizar jumped up, gave a polite little knock, and pushed open the priest's door.

"Father," he said, "they've come for you."

The father was half-awake and struggled out of bed. Villamizar felt deeply moved, for he looked like a little bird without its feathers, his skin hanging from his bones and trembling with terror. But he recovered immediately, crossed himself, grew until he was resolute and enormous. "Kneel down, my boy," he ordered. "We'll pray together." When he stood he was a new man.

"Let's see what's going on with Pablo," he said.

Villamizar wanted to go with him but did not even try, since it had already been agreed that he would not, but he did speak in private to the driver.

"I'm holding you accountable for the father," he said. "He's too important a person. Be careful what you people do with him. Be aware of the responsibility you have."

The driver looked at Villamizar as if he were an idiot, and said:

"Do you think that if I get in a car with a saint anything can happen to us?"

He took out a baseball cap and told the priest to put it on so nobody would recognize his white hair. He did. Villamizar could not stop thinking about the fact that Medellín was a militarized zone. He was troubled by the idea that they might stop the father, that he would be hurt, or be caught in the cross fire between the killers and the police.

The father sat in front next to the driver. While everyone watched as the car drove away, he took off the cap and threw it out the window. "Don't worry about me, my boy," he shouted to Villamizar, "I control the waters." A clap of thunder rumbled across the vast countryside, and the skies opened in a biblical downpour.

THE ONLY KNOWN version of Father García Herreros's visit to Pablo Escobar was the one he recounted when he returned to La Loma. He said the house where he was received was large and luxurious, with an Olympic-size pool and various kinds of sports facilities. On the way they had to change cars three times for reasons of security, but they were not stopped at the many police checkpoints because of the heavy, pounding rain. Other checkpoints, the driver told him, were part of the Extraditables' security service. They drove for more than three hours, though the probability is that he was taken to one of Pablo Escobar's residences in Medellín, and the driver made a good number of detours so the father would think they were far from La Loma.

He said he was met in the garden by some twenty men carrying weapons, and that he chastised them for their sinful lives and their reluctance to surrender. Pablo Escobar was waiting for him on the terrace. He was dressed in a casual white cotton outfit and had a long black beard. The fear confessed to by the father from the time of his arrival at La Loma, and then during the uncertainty of the drive, vanished when he saw him.

"Pablo," he said, "I've come so we can straighten this out."

Escobar responded with similar cordiality and with great respect. They sat in two of the armchairs covered in flowered cretonne in the living room, facing each other, their spirits ready for the kind of long talk old friends have. The father drank a whiskey that helped to calm him, while Escobar sipped at fruit juice as if he had all the time in the world. But the expected duration of the visit shrank to forty-five minutes because of the father's natural impatience and Escobar's speaking style, as concise and to the point as in his letters.

Concerned about the priest's lapses in memory, Villamizar had told him to take notes on their conversation. He did, but went even further, it seems. Citing his poor memory as the reason, he asked Escobar to write down his essential conditions, and when they were written he had him modify or cross them out, saying they were impossible to meet. This was how Escobar minimized the obsessive subject of removing the police he had accused of atrocities, and concentrated instead on security in the prison where he would be confined.

The priest recounted that he had asked Escobar if he was responsible for the assassinations of four presidential candidates. His oblique response was that he had not committed all the crimes attributed to him. He assured the father he had not been able to stop the killing of Professor Low Mutra on April 30 on a street in Bogotá, because the order had been given a long time before and there was no way to change it. As for the release of Maruja and Pacho, he avoided saying anything that might implicate him as the responsible party, but did say that the Extraditables kept them in normal conditions and in good health, and that they would be released as soon as terms for the surrender had been arranged. Regarding Pacho in particular, he said with utmost seriousness: "He's happy with his captivity." Finally, he acknowledged President Gaviria's good faith, and expressed his willingness to reach an agreement. That paper, written on at times by the father, and for the most part corrected and clarified in Escobar's own hand, was the first formal proposal for his surrender.

The father had stood to take his leave when one of his contact lenses fell out. He tried to put it back in, Escobar helped him, they asked for assistance from his staff, all to no avail. The father was desperate. "It's no use," he said. "The only one who can do it is Paulina." To his surprise, Escobar knew who she was and where she was at that moment.

"Don't worry, Father," he said. "If you like we can bring her here."

But the father had an unbearable desire to go home, and he preferred to leave not wearing his lenses. Before they said goodbye, Escobar asked him to bless a little gold medal he wore around his neck. The priest did so in the garden, besieged by the bodyguards.

"Father," they said, "you can't leave without giving us your blessing."

They kneeled. Don Fabio Ochoa had said that the mediation of Father García Herrero would be decisive for the surrender of Escobar's men. Escobar must have agreed, and perhaps that was why he kneeled with them, to set a good example. The priest blessed them all and also admonished them to return to a lawful life and help to establish peace.

It took just six hours. He returned to La Loma at about eight-thirty, under brilliant stars, and leaped from the car like a fifteen-year-old schoolboy.

"Take it easy, my boy," he said to Villamizar, "no problems here, I had them all on their knees."

It was not easy to calm him down. He was in an alarming state of excitement, and no palliative, and none of the Ochoa sisters' tranquilizing infusions, had any effect. It was still raining, but he wanted to fly back to Bogotá right away, announce the news, talk to the president, conclude the agreement without further delay, and proclaim peace. They managed to get him to sleep for a few hours, but in the middle of the night he was walking around the darkened house, talking to himself, reciting his inspired prayers, until sleep got the better of him at dawn.

When they reached Bogotá at eleven o'clock on the morning of May 16, the news was thundering across the radio. Villamizar met his son Andrés at the airport and embraced him with emotion. "Don't worry, son," he said. "Your mother will be out in three days." Rafael Pardo was less easy to convince when Villamizar called.

"I'm truly happy, Alberto," he said. "But don't hope for too much."

For the first time since the abduction, Villamizar went to a party given by friends, and no one could understand why he was so elated over something that was, after all, no more than a vague promise, like so many others made by Pablo Escobar. By this time Father García Herreros had been interviewed by all the news media—audio, visual, and print—in the country. He asked people to be tolerant with Escobar. "If we don't defraud him, he will become the great architect of peace," he said. And added, without citing Rousseau: "Deep down all men are good, although some circumstances can make them evil." And surrounded by a tangled mass of microphones, he said with no reservation:

"Escobar is a good man."

El Tiempo reported on Friday, May 17, that the father was the bearer of a private letter that he would give to President Gaviria on the following Monday. In reality, these were the notes he and Escobar had written together during their interview. On Sunday, the Extraditables issued a communiqué that almost went unnoticed in the clamor of news: "We have ordered the release of Francisco Santos and Maruja Pachón." They did not say when. The radio, however, took it as a fait accompli and crowds of excited reporters began to stand guard at the captives' houses.

It was over: Villamizar received a message from Escobar in which he said he would not release Maruja Pachón and Francisco Santos that day but the next—Monday, May 20—at seven in the evening. But on Tuesday, at nine in the morning, Villamizar would have to go back to Medellín for Escobar's surrender.

11

MARUJA HEARD the Extraditables' communiqué at seven o'clock on the evening of Sunday, May 19. It did not mention a time or a date for their release, and considering how the Extraditables operated, it could happen either in five minutes or two months later. The majordomo and his wife burst into the room, ready for a party.

"It's over!" they shouted. "We have to celebrate."

Maruja had a hard time convincing them to wait for a direct official order from one of Pablo Escobar's emissaries. The news did not surprise her, for in the past few weeks there had been unmistakable signs that things were going better than she had supposed when they made the disheartening promise to carpet the room. More and more friends and popular actors had appeared on recent broadcasts of "Colombia Wants Them Back." Her optimism renewed, Maruja followed the soap operas with so much attention that she thought she could find coded messages even in the glycerine tears of impossible loves. The news from Father García Herreros, which grew more spectacular every day, made it clear that the unbelievable was going to happen.

Maruja wanted to put on the clothes she had been wearing

when she arrived, foreseeing a sudden release that would have her appearing in front of the cameras dressed in a captive's melancholy sweatsuit. But the lack of new developments on the radio, and the disappointment of the majordomo who had expected the official order before he went to bed, put her on guard against playing the fool, if only to herself. She took a large dose of sleeping pills and did not wake until the following day, Monday, with the frightening impression that she did not know who she was, or where.

VILLAMIZAR HAD NOT been troubled by any doubts, for the communiqué from Escobar was unequivocal. He passed it on to the reporters, but they ignored it. At about nine, a radio station announced with great fanfare that Señora Maruja Pachón de Villamizar had just been released in the Salitre district. The reporters left in a stampede, but Villamizar did not move.

"They would never let her go in an isolated place like that, where anything could happen to her," he said. "It'll be tomorrow, for sure, and in a place that's safe."

A reporter barred his way with a microphone.

"What's surprising," he said, "is the confidence you have in those people."

"It's his word of honor," said Villamizar.

The reporters he knew best stayed in the hallways of the apartment—and some were at the bar—until Villamizar asked them to leave so he could lock up for the night. Others camped in vans and cars outside the building, and spent the night there.

On Monday Villamizar woke to the six o'clock news, as he always did, and stayed in bed until eleven. He tried to use the phone as little as possible, but there were constant calls from reporters and friends. The news of the day continued to be the wait for the hostages.

FATHER GARCÍA HERREROS had visited Mariavé on Thursday to tell her in confidence that her husband would be released the following Sunday. It has not been possible to learn how he obtained the news seventy-two hours before the first communiqué from the Extraditables, but the Santos family accepted it as fact. To celebrate they took a picture of Hernando with Mariavé and the children and published it on Saturday in *El Tiempo*, hoping that Pacho would understand it as a personal message. He did: As soon as he opened the paper in his captive's cell, Pacho had a clear intuition that his father's efforts had come to a successful conclusion. He spent an uneasy day waiting for the miracle, slipping innocent-seeming ploys into his conversation with the guards to see if he could catch them in an indiscretion, but he learned nothing. Radio and television, which had reported nothing else for several weeks, did not mention it at all that Saturday.

Sunday began the same way. It seemed to Pacho that the guards were tense and uneasy in the morning, but as the day wore on they made a gradual return to their Sunday routine: a special lunch of pizza, movies and taped television programs, some cards, some soccer. Then, when they least expected it, the newscast "Criptón" opened with the lead story: The Extraditables had announced the release of the last two hostages. Pacho jumped up with a triumphant shout and threw his arms around the guard on duty. "I thought I'd have a heart attack," he has said. But the guard responded with skeptical stoicism.

"Let's wait till we get confirmation," he said.

They made a rapid survey of other news programs on radio and television, and found the communiqué on all of them. One was transmitting from the editorial room at *El Tiempo*, and after eight months Pacho began to feel again the solid ground of a free life: the rather desolate atmosphere of the Sunday shift, the usual faces in their glass cubicles, his own work site. Following another repetition of the announcement of their imminent release, the television program's special correspondent waved the microphone and—like an ice cream cone—put it up to the mouth of a sports editor and asked:

"What do you think of the news?"

Pacho could not control the reflexive response of a chief editor.

"What a moronic question!" he said. "Was he expecting them to say I should be held for another month?"

As always, the radio news was less rigorous but more emotional. Many reporters were concentrating on Hernando Santos's house, broadcasting statements from every person who crossed their path. This increased Pacho's nervous tension, for it did not seem unreasonable to think he might be released that same night. "This was the start of the longest twenty-six hours of my life," he has said. "Each second was like an hour."

The press was everywhere. Television cameras moved back and forth from Pacho's house to his father's, both of which had been overflowing since Sunday night with relatives, friends, curious onlookers, and journalists from all over the world. Mariavé and Hernando Santos cannot remember how many times they went from one house to the other, following each unforeseen turn in the news, until Pacho was no longer certain which house was which on television. The worst thing was that at each one the same questions were asked over and over again, and the trip between the houses became intolerable. There was so much confusion that Hernando Santos could not get through the mob crowding around his own house, and had to slip in through the garage.

The off-duty guards came in to congratulate Pacho. They were so happy at the news that he forgot they were his jailers, and it turned into a party of *compadres* who were all the same age. At that moment he realized that his goal of rehabilitating his guards would be frustrated by his release. They were boys from the Antioquian countryside who had emigrated to Medellín, lost their way in the slums, and killed and were killed with no scruples. As a rule they came from broken homes where the father was a negative figure and the mother a very strong one. They were used to working for very high pay and had no sense of money.

When at last he fell asleep, Pacho had a horrifying dream that he was free and happy but suddenly opened his eyes and saw the ceiling unchanged. He spent the rest of the night tormented by the mad rooster—madder and closer than ever—and not knowing for certain where reality lay.

At six in the morning on Monday, the radio confirmed the news with no indication of the hour of their possible release. After countless repetitions of the original bulletin, it was announced that Father García Herreros would hold a press conference at noon following a meeting with President Gaviria: "Oh God," Pacho said to himself. "Don't let this man who has done so much for us screw it up at the last minute." At one in the afternoon they told him he would be freed, but he was not told anything else until after five, when one of the masked bosses said in an unemotional way that—in line with Escobar's feeling for publicity—Maruja would be released in time for the seven o'clock news, and he in time for the newscasts at nine-thirty.

MARUJA'S MORNING had been more pleasant. A low-ranking boss came into the room at about nine and said she would be released that afternoon. He also told her some of the details of Father García Herreros's efforts, perhaps by way of apology for an injustice he had committed on a recent visit when Maruja asked if her fate was in the hands of Father García Herreros. He had answered with a touch of mockery:

"Don't worry, you're much safer than that."

Maruja realized he had misinterpreted her question, and she was quick to clarify that she always had great respect for the father. It is true that at first she had ignored his television sermons, which at times were confusing and impenetrable, but after the first message to Escobar she understood that he was involved in her life, and she watched him night after night, paying very close attention. She had followed the steps he had taken, his visits to Medellín, the progress of his conversations with Escobar, and had no doubt he was on the right path. The boss's sarcasm, however, caused her to wonder if the father had less credit with the Extraditables than might be supposed from his public statements to journalists. The confirmation that she would soon be freed through his efforts made her feel happier.

After a brief conversation regarding the impact their release would have on the country, she asked about the ring that had been taken from her in the first house on the night of her abduction.

"Not to worry," he said. "All your things are safe."

"But I am worried," she said, "because it wasn't taken here but in that first house, and we never saw the man again. It wasn't you, was it?"

"Not me," he said. "But I already told you to take it easy, your things are safe. I've seen them."

The majordomo's wife offered to buy Maruja anything she needed. Maruja asked for mascara, lipstick, eyebrow pencil, and a pair of stockings to replace the ones that had been torn on the night she was kidnapped. Later the majordomo came in, troubled by the lack of new information regarding her release, afraid there had been a last-minute change in plans, as so often happened. Maruja, however, was calm. She showered, and dressed in the same clothing she had worn on the night of her abduction, except for the cream-colored jacket, which she would put on when she went out.

For the entire day the radio stations kept interest alive with speculations on the waiting hostages, interviews with their families, unconfirmed rumors that were canceled out the next minute by even more sensational ones. But nothing definite. Maruja listened to the voices of her children and friends with an anticipatory jubilation threatened by uncertainty. Again she saw her redecorated house, her husband conversing easily with a crowd of journalists who were growing tired of waiting. She had time to study the decorative details that had bothered her so much the first time, and her frame of mind improved. The guards took a break from their frenetic cleaning to watch and listen to the newscasts, and they tried to keep her spirits up but had less and less success as the afternoon wore on.

PRESIDENT GAVIRIA woke without the help of an alarm clock at five on the morning of his forty-first Monday in office. He got up without turning on the light so as not to disturb Ana Milena—who sometimes went to bed later than he did—and when he had shaved, showered, and dressed for the office, he sat in a folding chair that he kept outside the bedroom, in a cold, gloomy hallway, in order to hear the news without waking anyone. He listened to the radio newscasts on a pocket-size transistor that he held up to his ear and played at very low volume. He glanced through the papers, from the headlines to the advertisements, and tore out items to be dealt with later with his secretaries, advisers, and ministers. On one occasion he had found an article on something that was supposed to be taken care of and was not, and sent it to the appropriate minister with a single question scrawled in the margin: "When the hell is the ministry going to resolve this mess?" The solution was instantaneous.

The only news that day was the imminent release of the hostages, and that included his meeting with Father García Herreros to hear his report on the interview with Escobar. The president reorganized his day so that he would be available at a moment's notice. He canceled some meetings that could be postponed, and adjusted other. His first was with the presidential advisers, which he opened with his schoolboy's comment:

"Okay, let's finish this assignment."

Several of the advisers had just returned from Caracas, where they had talked on Friday with the reticent General Maza Márquez. In the course of the conversation the press adviser, Mauricio Vargas, had expressed his concern that no one, inside or outside the government, had a clear idea of where Pablo Escobar was really heading. Maza was sure he would not surrender because he trusted nothing but a pardon from the Constituent Assembly. Vargas replied with a question: What good would a pardon do for a man sentenced to death by his own enemies and by the Cali cartel? "It might help him, but it's not exactly a complete solution," he concluded. Escobar was in urgent need of a secure prison for himself and his people under the protection of the state.

The advisers raised the issue because of the fear that Father García Herreros would come to the twelve o'clock meeting with an unacceptable, eleventh-hour demand, without which Escobar would not surrender and not release the journalists. For the government, it would be an almost irreparable fiasco. Gabriel Silva, the adviser on foreign affairs, made two self-protective recommendations: first, that the president not attend the meeting alone, and second, that he issue as complete a communiqué as possible as soon as the meeting was over in order to forestall speculation. Rafael Pardo, who had flown to New York the day before, agreed by telephone.

The president received Father García Herreros at a special noon meeting. On one side were the priest, two clerics from his community, and Alberto Villamizar with his son Andrés; on the other, the president with his private secretary, Miguel Silva, and Mauricio Vargas. The presidential palace information services took photos and videos to give to the press if things went well. If not, at least the evidence of their failure would not be left up to the media.

The father, very conscious of the significance of the moment, told the president the details of his meeting with Escobar. He had no doubt at all that Escobar was going to turn himself in and free the hostages, and he backed up his words with the notes the two of them had written. For reasons of security that Escobar himself had outlined, his only condition was that the prison be the one in Envigado, not Itagüí.

The president read the notes and returned them to the father. He was struck by the fact that Escobar did not promise to release the prisoners but agreed only to raise the issue with the Extraditables. Villamizar explained that this was one of Escobar's many precautions: He had never admitted to holding the hostages so it could not be used as evidence against him.

The father asked what he should do if Escobar asked him to be present at his surrender. The president agreed that he should go. When the father raised doubts concerning the safety of the operation, the president replied that no one could provide better guarantees than Escobar for the safety of his own operation. Finally, the president indicated to the father—whose companions seconded the idea—that it was important to keep public statements to a minimum in order to avoid the damage that an inopportune word might create. The father agreed and even made a veiled final offer: "I've wanted to be of service in this, and I am at your disposal if you need me for anything else, like making peace with the other priest." It was clear to everyone that he was referring to the Spanish priest, Manuel Pérez, commander of the National Army of Liberation. The meeting took twenty minutes, and there was no official communiqué. Faithful to his promise, Father García Herreros displayed exemplary restraint in his statements to the press.

MARUJA WATCHED his news conference and learned nothing new. The television newscasts again showed reporters waiting at the houses of the hostages, which may well have been the same images shown the day before. Maruja also repeated the previous day's routine minute by minute, and had more than enough time to watch the afternoon soap operas. Damaris, energized by the official announcement, had granted her the privilege of choosing the menu for lunch, like condemned prisoners on the eve of their execution. Maruja said, with no touch of irony, that anything would be fine except lentils. But time grew short, Damaris could not go shopping, and there were only lentils with lentils for their farewell lunch.

For his part, Pacho put on the clothes he had been wearing the day of the kidnapping—these were too tight, since a sedentary life and bad food had made him put on weight—and sat down to listen to the news and smoke one cigarette after the other. He heard all kinds of stories about his release. He heard the corrections, the outright lies of his colleagues made reckless by the tension of waiting. He heard that he had been incognito in a restaurant, but the man eating there turned out to be one of his brothers.

He reread the editorials, the commentaries, the reports he had written on current events so he would not forget his trade, thinking he might publish them as a document of his captivity when he was freed. There were more than a hundred of them. He read one to his guards that had been written in December, when the traditional political class began its rantings against the legitimacy of the Constituent Assembly. Pacho lashed out at them with an energy and independence that were undoubtedly the product of his thinking in captivity: "We all know how you get votes in Colombia, and how countless parliamentarians won their elections," he said in an editorial note. He said that buying votes was rampant throughout the country, especially along the coast, that raffling off home appliances in exchange for electoral favors was the order of the day, and that many elected officials paid for their election through other kinds of political corruption, like charging fees over and above their public salaries and parliamentary compensation. And this was why, he said, the same people were always elected, and they, "faced with the possibility of losing their privileges, are now in an uproar." And he concluded with criticism that included himself: "The impartiality of the media—including *El Tiempo*—which was making progress after a long, hard struggle, has vanished."

The most surprising of his notes, however, was the one he wrote on the reactions of the political class when the M-19 won more than 10 percent of the vote for the Constituent Assembly. "The political aggression against the M-19," he wrote, "the strictures (or rather, discrimination) against it in the media, show how far we are from tolerance and how far we still have to go in modernizing what matters most: our minds." He said that the political class had celebrated electoral participation by the former guerrillas only to seem democratic, but when the votes amounted to more than 10 percent they turned to denunciations. And he concluded in the style of his grandfather, Enrique Santos Montejo ("Calibán"), the most widely read columnist in the history of Colombian journalism: "A very specific and traditional sector of Colombians killed the tiger and were frightened by its skin." Nothing could have been more surprising in someone who since elementary school had stood out as a precocious example of the romantic Right.

He tore up all his notes except for three that he decided to keep, for reasons he has not been able to explain. He also kept the rough drafts of the messages to his family and the president, and of his will. He would have liked to take the chain they had used to confine him to the bed, hoping that the artist Bernardo Salcedo could make a sculpture with it, but he was not allowed to keep it in case there were incriminating prints on it.

Maruja, however, did not want any memento of that hideous past, which she intended to erase from her life. But at about six that evening, when the door began to open from the outside, she realized how much those six months of bitterness were going to affect her. Since the death of Marina and the departure of Beatriz, this had been the hour of liberations or executions: the same in both cases. With her heart in her mouth she waited for the sinister ritual sentence: "We're going, get ready." It was the "Doctor," accompanied by the second-in-command who had been there the night before. They both seemed rushed.

"Now, now!" the "Doctor" urged Maruja. "Move it!"

She had imagined the moment so often that she felt overwhelmed by a strange need to gain some time, and she asked about her ring.

"I sent it with your sister-in-law," said the low-ranking boss.

"That's not true," Maruja replied with absolute calm. "You told me you had seen it after that."

More than the ring, what she wanted then was to embarrass him in front of his superior. But the "Doctor" pretended not to notice because of the pressure of time. The majordomo and his wife brought Maruja the bag that held her personal effects and the gifts that various guards had given her during her captivity: Christmas cards, the sweatsuit, the towel, magazines, a book or two. The gentle boys who had guarded her in the final days had nothing to give but medals and pictures of saints, and they asked her to pray for them, not to forget them, to do something to get them out of their bad life.

"Anything you want," said Maruja. "If you ever need me, get in touch with me and I'll help you."

The "Doctor" could do no less: "What can I give you to remember me by?" he said, rooting through his pockets. He took out a 9mm shell and handed it to Maruja.

"Here," he said, not really joking. "The bullet we didn't shoot you with."

It was not easy to free Maruja from the embraces of the majordomo and Damaris, who raised her mask as high as her nose to kiss her and ask that she not forget her. Maruja felt a sincere emotion. This was, after all, the end of the longest, most awful time of her life, and its happiest moment.

They covered her head with a hood that must have been the dirtiest, most foul-smelling one they could find. They put it on with the eye holes at the back of her head, and she could not avoid recalling that this was how they put the hood on Marina when they killed her. She was led, shuffling her feet in the darkness, to a car as comfortable as the one used for the abduction, and they sat her in the same spot, in the same position, and with the same precautions: her head resting on a man's knees so she could not be seen from the outside. They warned her that there were several police checkpoints, and if they were stopped Maruja had to take off the hood and behave herself.

AT ONE THAT AFTERNOON, Villamizar had eaten lunch with his son Andrés. At two-thirty he lay down for a nap, and made up for lost sleep until five-thirty. At six he had just come out of the shower, and was dressing to wait for his wife, when the telephone rang. He picked up the extension on the night table and said no more than "Hello?" An anonymous voice interrupted: "She'll arrive a few minutes after seven. They're leaving now." He hung up. The announcement was unexpected and Villamizar was grateful for it. He called the porter to make sure his car was in the garden, and the driver ready.

He put on a dark suit and a light tie with a diamond pattern to welcome his wife. He was thinner than ever, for he had lost nine pounds in six months. At seven he went to the living room to talk to the journalists while Maruja was arriving. Four of her children were there, and Andrés, their son. Only Nicolás, the musician in the family, was missing, and he would arrive from New York in a few hours. Villamizar sat in the chair closest to the phone.

BY THIS TIME Maruja was five minutes away from her release. In contrast to the night of the abduction, the drive to freedom was rapid and uneventful. At first they had taken an unpaved road, making the kinds of turns not recommended for a luxury car. Maruja could tell from the conversation that in addition to the man beside her, another was sitting next to the driver. She did not think that any of them was the "Doctor." After fifteen minutes they had her lie on the floor and stopped for about five minutes, but she did not know why. They came out onto a large, noisy avenue filled with heavy seven o'clock traffic, then turned with no difficulties onto another avenue. After no more than forty-five minutes altogether, they came to a sudden stop. The man next to the driver gave Maruja a frantic order:

"Now, get out, move."

The man sitting beside her tried to force her out of the car. Maruja struggled.

"I can't see," she shouted.

She tried to take off the hood but a brutal hand stopped her. "Wait five minutes before you take it off," he shouted. He shoved her out of the car. Maruja felt the vertigo of empty space, and terror, and thought they had thrown her over a cliff. Solid ground let her breathe again. While she waited for the car to drive away, she sensed she was on a street with little traffic. With great care she raised the hood, saw the houses among the trees with lights in the windows, and then she knew the truth of being free. It was 7:29, and 193 days had passed since the night she had been abducted.

A solitary automobile came down the avenue, made a U-turn, and stopped across the street, just opposite Maruja. Like Beatriz before her, she thought it could not be a coincidence. That car had to have been sent by the kidnappers to make sure her release was completed. Maruja went up to the driver's window.

"Please," she said, "I'm Maruja Pachón. They just let me go."

She only wanted someone to help her find a taxi. But the man let out a yell. Minutes earlier, listening to news on the radio about their imminent release, he had wondered: "Suppose I run into

Francisco Santos and he's looking for a ride?" Maruja longed to see her family, but she let him take her to the nearest house to use the telephone.

The woman in the house and her children all cried out and embraced her when they recognized her. Maruja felt numb, and everything that happened around her seemed like one more deception arranged by her kidnappers. The man who had taken her to the house was named Manuel Caro, and he was the son-in-law of the owner, Augusto Borrero, whose wife, a former activist in the New Liberalism Party, had worked with Maruja in Luis Carlos Galán's electoral campaign. But Maruja was seeing life from the outside, as if she were watching a movie screen. She asked for *aguardiente*—she never knew why—and drank it in one swallow. Then she telephoned her house, but had trouble remembering the number and misdialed twice. A woman answered right away: "Who is it?" Maruja recognized the voice and said, without melodrama:

"Alexandra, darling."

Alexandra shouted:

"Mamá! Where are you?"

Alberto Villamizar had jumped up from his chair when the phone rang but Alexandra, who was passing by, picked it up first. Maruja had begun to give her the address, but Alexandra did not have paper or pencil nearby. Villamizar took the receiver and greeted Maruja with stunning casualness:

"What do you say, baby. How are you?"

Maruja answered in the same tone:

"Fine, sweetheart, no problems."

He did have paper and pencil ready. He wrote down the address as Maruja gave it to him, but felt that something was not clear and asked to speak to somebody in the family. Borrero's wife gave him the missing details.

"Thanks very much," said Villamizar. "It's not far. I'm leaving now."

He forgot to hang up: The iron self-control he had maintained during the long months of tension suddenly melted away. He ran down the stairs two at a time and dashed across the lobby, followed by an avalanche of reporters armed to the teeth with their battle gear. Others, moving in the opposite direction, almost trampled him in the doorway.

"Maruja's free," he shouted. "Let's go."

He got into the car and slammed the door so hard he startled the dozing driver. "Let's go pick up the señora," Villamizar said. He gave him the address: Diagonal 107, No. 27-73. "It's a white house on the parallel road west of the highway," he said. But he said it so fast the driver became confused and started off in the wrong direction. Villamizar corrected him with a sharpness that was foreign to his character.

"Watch what you're doing," he shouted, "we have to be there in five minutes! If we get lost I'll cut off your balls!"

The driver, who had suffered the awful dramas of the abduction along with him, did not turn a hair. Villamizar caught his breath and directed him along the shortest, easiest roads, for he had visualized the route as he was given directions on the phone to be certain he would not get lost. It was the worst time for traffic, but not the worst day.

Andrés had pulled out behind his father, along with his cousin Gabriel, following the caravan of reporters who cut a path through traffic with fake ambulance sirens. Even though he was an expert driver, he became stuck in traffic, and could not move. Villamizar, on the other hand, arrived in the record time of fifteen minutes. He did not have to look for the house because some of the reporters who had been in his apartment were already arguing with the owner to let them in. Villamizar made his way through the noisy crowd. He did not have time to greet anyone, because the owner's wife recognized him and pointed to the stairs.

"This way," she said.

Maruja was in the main bedroom, where they had taken her to

freshen up while she waited for her husband. When she went in she had come face-to-face with a grotesque stranger: her reflection in the mirror. She looked bloated and flabby from nephritis, her eyelids swollen, her skin pasty and dry after six months of darkness.

Villamizar raced up the stairs, opened the first door he came to, and found himself in the children's room filled with dolls and bicycles. Then he opened the door facing him, and saw Maruja sitting on the bed in the checked jacket she had worn when she left the house on the day of her abduction, and freshly made up for him. "He came in like thunder," Maruja has said. She threw her arms around his neck, and their embrace was intense, long, and silent. The clamor of the reporters, who had overcome the owner's resistance and stormed into the house, broke the spell. Maruja gave a start. Villamizar smiled in amusement.

"Your colleagues," he said.

Maruja felt consternation. "I spent six months without looking in a mirror," she said. She smiled at her reflection, and it was not her. She stood erect, fluffed the hair pulled back at the nape of her neck, did what she could to make the woman in the mirror resemble the image of herself she had six months earlier. She failed.

"I look awful," she said, and showed her husband her swollen, misshapen fingers. "I didn't realize because they took my ring."

"You look perfect," Villamizar said.

He put his arm around her shoulder and walked her to the living room.

The reporters attacked with cameras, lights, and microphones. Maruja was dazzled. "Take it easy, guys," she said. "It'll be easier to talk in the apartment." Those were her first words.

THE SEVEN O'CLOCK news said nothing, but President Gaviria learned minutes later when he checked the radio that Maruja Pachón had been freed. He drove to her house with Mauricio

Vargas, but earlier they had left an official announcement of the release of Francisco Santos, which they expected at any moment. Mauricio Vargas had read it into the journalists' tape recorders on the condition they not broadcast it until they received official notification.

At this time Maruja was on her way home. A short while before she arrived, a rumor began to circulate that Pacho Santos had been freed, and the reporters unleashed the dog of the official announcement, which rushed out, barking with jubilation, over every station.

The president and Mauricio Vargas heard it in the car and celebrated the idea of having prerecorded it. But five minutes later the report was retracted.

"Mauricio," exclaimed Gaviria, "what a disaster!"

All they could do, however, was hope that events would occur as announced. In the meantime, since the overflowing crowd made it impossible for them to stay in Villamizar's apartment, they went up one floor to the apartment of Aseneth Velásquez to wait for Pacho's true release after his three false ones.

PACHO SANTOS HAD heard the announcement of Maruja's release, the premature announcement of his own, and the government's blunder. At that moment the man who had spoken to him in the morning came into his room, and led him by the arm, without a blindfold, down to the first floor. He saw that the house was empty, and one of his guards, convulsing with laughter, informed him they had moved out the furniture in a truck to avoid paying the last month's rent. They all said goodbye with huge hugs, and thanked Pacho for everything he had taught them. Pacho's reply was sincere:

"I learned a lot from you too."

In the garage they gave him a book to hold up to his face, as if he were reading, and intoned the warnings. If they ran into the police he had to jump out of the car so they could get away. And most important of all: He must not say he had been in Bogotá, but somewhere three hours away along a terrible highway. They had a gruesome reason: His captors knew Pacho was astute enough to have formed an idea of where the house was located, and he could not reveal it because the guards had lived openly in the neighborhood, taking no precautions at all, during the long days of his captivity.

"If you tell," the man in charge of his release concluded, "we'll have to kill all the neighbors to keep them from identifying us later on."

Across from the police kiosk at the intersection of Avenida Boyacá and Calle 80, the car stalled. They tried to start it again two, three, four times, but it did not turn over until the fifth attempt. They were all in a cold sweat. They drove two more blocks, took away the book, and let Pacho out on the corner with three 2,000-peso bills for the taxi. He took the first one that passed, and its young, amiable driver refused to charge him, and with blasts of the horn and joyful shouts cut a path through the mob waiting outside Pacho's house. The yellow journalists were disappointed: They had been expecting an emaciated, defeated man after 244 days of captivity, and instead they saw a Pancho Santos rejuvenated in spirit and body, and fatter, more reckless, more in love with life than ever. "They returned him exactly the same," declared his cousin Enrique Santos Calderón. Another cousin, infected by the family's jubilant mood, said: "He needed another six months."

BY NOW MARUJA was in her house. She had come home with Alberto, pursued by the mobile units that drove alongside them, preceded them, transmitting directly through all the snarled traffic. The drivers who were following the news on the radio recognized them as they passed and leaned on their horns in greeting, until the ovation spread all along the route.

Andrés Villamizar had tried to go back home when he lost sight of his father, but his driving was so merciless that the engine shook loose and a rod broke. He left his automobile in the care of the police at the nearest kiosk, and stopped the first car that passed: a dark-gray BMW driven by a sympathetic executive who had been listening to the news. Andrés told him who he was and why he needed help, and asked him to get as close to his house as he could.

"Get in," said the man, "but I warn you, if you're lying I'll make things hard for you."

At the corner of Carrera Séptima and Calle 80, he happened to see a friend driving an old Renault. Andrés continued on with her, but the car ran out of steam on the Circunvalar hill. Andrés squeezed into the last white Jeep from the National Radio Network (RCN).

The hill leading to the house was blocked by cars and a crowd of neighbors who had poured into the street. Maruja and Villamizar decided to leave the car and walk the last hundred meters, and without noticing it they got out at the same spot where she had been abducted. The first face Maruja recognized in the excited crowd was María del Rosario Ortiz, the originator and director of "Colombia Wants Them Back," which for the first time since its creation did not broadcast that night for lack of a subject. Then she saw Andrés, who had jumped out of the Jeep and was trying to get to his house just as a tall, determined police officer ordered the street closed. Andrés, in a moment of pure inspiration, looked him in the eye and said in a firm voice:

"I'm Andrés."

The officer knew nothing about him but let him pass. Maruja recognized him while he was running toward her and they embraced to the sound of applause. Patrol cars had to open a path for them. Maruja, Alberto, and Andrés began to climb the hill with full hearts, and were overcome by emotion. For the first time they burst into the tears that all three had wanted to hold back. And who could blame them: As far as the eye could see, a second crowd of good neighbors had hung flags from the windows of the tallest buildings and, with a springtime of white handkerchiefs and an immense ovation, saluted the jubilant adventure of her return home.

EPILOGUE

AT NINE the next morning, as planned, Villamizar landed in Medellín with less than an hour's sleep. The night had been a boisterous celebration of resurrection. At four in the morning, when they were finally alone in the apartment, Maruja and he were so elated by the day's events that they stayed in the living room until dawn exchanging belated news. At the La Loma hacienda he was welcomed with the usual banquet, but this time baptized with the champagne of liberation. It was a brief respite, however, because now the one in a hurry was Pablo Escobar, hiding somewhere in the world without the protection of the hostages. His new emissary was very tall and loquacious, a pure blond with a long golden mustache who was called the Monkey and had full authority to negotiate the surrender.

By order of President César Gaviria, the entire legal debate with Escobar's lawyers had been carried out through Dr. Carlos Eduardo Mejía, who reported to the justice minister. For the physical surrender, Mejía would represent Rafael Pardo for the government's side, and the other side would be represented by Jorge Luis Ochoa, the Monkey, and Escobar himself from the shadows.

Villamizar continued to be an active intermediary with the government, and Father García Herreros, who was a moral guarantor for Escobar, would remain available in the event of a major crisis.

Escobar's haste in having Villamizar come to Medellín the day after Maruja's release gave the impression that his surrender would be immediate, but it was soon evident that for him there were still a few diversionary tactics remaining. Everyone's greatest concern, Villamizar more than anyone, was that nothing happen to Escobar before he turned himself in. They had reason to worry: Villamizar knew that Escobar, or his survivors, would take it out of his hide if they even suspected him of not keeping his word. Escobar himself broke the ice when he telephoned him at La Loma and said without any preamble:

"Dr. Villa, are you happy?"

Villamizar had never seen or heard him, and he was struck by the absolute serenity of the voice that had no trace of his mythical aura. "I thank you for coming," Escobar continued without waiting for a reply, his earthly state revealed by his harsh shantytown diction. "You're a man of your word and I knew you wouldn't fail me." And then he came to the point:

"Let's start to arrange how I'll turn myself in."

In reality, Escobar already knew how he was going to turn himself in, but perhaps he wanted to review it again with a man in whom he had placed all his confidence. His lawyers and the director of Criminal Investigation, at times face-to-face and at times through the regional director, and always in coordination with the justice minister, had discussed every last detail of the surrender. When the legal questions stemming from each of their distinct interpretations of the presidential decrees had been clarified, the issues had been reduced to three: the prison, the staffing of the prison, and the role of the police and the army.

The prison—in the former Rehabilitation Center for Drug Addicts in Envigado—was almost finished. Villamizar and the Monkey visited it at Escobar's request on the day following the release of Maruja and Pacho Santos. Piles of rubble in the corners and the devastating effects of that year's heavy rains gave it a somewhat depressing appearance. The technical problems of security had been resolved. There was a double fence, 2.8 meters high, with fifteen rows of five-thousand-volt electrified barbed wire and seven watch towers, in addition to the two that guarded the entrance. These two installations would be further reinforced, as much to keep Escobar from escaping as to prevent anyone from killing him.

The only point that Villamizar found to criticize was an Italian-tiled bathroom in the room intended for Escobar, and he recommended changing it—and it was changed—to more sober decoration. The conclusion of his report was even more sober: "It seemed to me a very prisonlike prison." In fact, the folkloric splendor that would eventually shock the nation and compromise the government's prestige came later, from the inside, with an inconceivable program of bribery and intimidation.

Escobar asked Villamizar for a clean telephone number in Bogotá on which they could discuss the details of his physical surrender, and Villamizar gave him the number of his upstairs neighbor, Aseneth Velásquez. He thought no phone could be safer than hers, called at all hours of the day and night by writers and artists lunatic enough to unhinge the strongest-minded. The formula was simple and innocuous: An anonymous voice would call Villamizar's house and say, "In fifteen minutes, Doctor." Villamizar would go upstairs to Aseneth's apartment and Pablo Escobar himself would call a quarter of an hour later. On one occasion he was delayed in the elevator and Aseneth answered the phone. A raw Medellinese voice asked for Dr. Villamizar.

"He doesn't live here," said Aseneth.

"Don't worry about that," said the voice with amusement. "He's on his way up."

The person speaking was Pablo Escobar, live and direct, but Aseneth will know that only if she happens to read this book, for on that day Villamizar tried to tell her out of basic loyalty, and she—who is no fool—covered her ears.

"I don't want to know anything about anything," she said. "Do whatever you want in my house but don't tell me about it."

By this time Villamizar was traveling to Medellín several times a week. From the Hotel Intercontinental he would call María Lía, and she would send a car to take him to La Loma. On one of his early trips Maruja had gone with him to thank the Ochoas for their help. At lunch the question of her emerald and diamond ring came up, for it had not been returned to her on the night she was released. Villamizar had also mentioned it to the Ochoas, and they had sent a message to Escobar, but he did not reply. The Monkey, who was present, suggested giving her a new one, but Villamizar explained that Maruja wanted the ring for sentimental reasons, not for its monetary value. The Monkey promised to take the problem to Escobar.

Escobar's first call to Aseneth's house had to do with a "God's Minute" on which Father García Herreros accused him of being an unrepentant pornographer, and warned him to return to God's path. No one could understand his about-face. Escobar thought that if the priest had turned against him it must have been for a very significant reason, and he made his surrender conditional on an immediate public explanation. The worst thing for him was that his men had agreed to turn themselves in because of the faith they had in the father's word. Villamizar brought him to La Loma, and there the father made all kinds of explanations to Escobar by telephone. According to these, when the program was recorded an editing error made him say what in fact he had never said. Escobar taped the conversation, played it for his troops, and averted a crisis.

But there was still more. The government insisted on combined army and national guard patrols for the exterior of the prison, on cutting down the adjoining woods to make a firing range, and on its right to have the guards selected from a list compiled by a tripartite commission representing the central government, the municipality of Envigado, and the Prosecutor General's Office, since the prison was both municipal and national. Escobar opposed having guards close by because his enemies could murder him in the prison. He opposed combined patrols because—his lawyers claimed—no military forces were permitted inside a jail, according to the Law on Prisons. He opposed cutting down the nearby forest because it would permit helicopter landings and because he assumed a firing range was an area where prisoners would be the targets, until he was convinced that in military terms, a firing range is nothing more than a field with good visibility. And that, in fact, was the great advantage of the Rehabilitation Center—for the government and for the prisoners—because from anywhere in the building one had a clear view of the valley and the mountains, allowing more than enough time to respond to an attack. Then, at the last minute, the national director of Criminal Investigation wanted to build a fortified wall around the prison in addition to the barbed-wire fence. Escobar was furious.

On Thursday, May 30, *El Espectador* published a report—attributed to very reliable official sources—on the terms for surrender allegedly set by Escobar at a meeting between his lawyers and government spokesmen. The most sensational of these—according to the article—was the exile of General Maza Márquez and the dismissals of General Miguel Gómez Padilla, commander of the National Police, and General Octavio Vargas Silva, commander of the Police Office of Judicial Investigation (DIJIN).

PRESIDENT GAVIRIA met with General Maza Márquez in his office to clarify the origin of the report, which persons connected to the government had attributed to him. The interview lasted for half an hour, and knowing both men, it is impossible to imagine which of the two was more impassive. The general, in his soft, slow baritone, gave a detailed account of his inquiries into the case. The president listened in absolute silence. Twenty minutes later they said goodbye. The next day, the general sent the president an official six-page letter that repeated in minute detail what he had said, and documented their conversation.

According to his investigations—the letter said—the source of the report was Martha Nieves Ochoa, who had given it days before as an exclusive to the legal reporters at *El Tiempo*—the only ones who had it—and they could not understand how it had been published first in *El Espectador*. The general stated that he was a fervent supporter of Pablo Escobar's surrender. He reiterated his loyalty to his principles, obligations, and duties, and concluded: "For reasons known to you, Mr. President, many persons and entities are intent upon destabilizing my career, perhaps with the aim of placing me in a situation of risk that will allow them to carry out their plans against me."

Martha Nieves Ochoa denied being the source of the article, and did not speak of the matter again. Three months later, however—when Escobar was already in prison—Fabio Villegas, the secretary general to the president, asked General Maza to his office on behalf of the president, invited him into the Blue Room and, walking from one end to the other as if he were out for a Sunday stroll, communicated the president's decision to have him retire. Maza left convinced that this was evidence of an agreement with Escobar that the government had denied. In his words, "I was negotiated."

In any case, before this occurred, Escobar had let Maza know that the war between them had ended, that he had forgotten everything and was serious about his surrender: He was stopping the attacks, disbanding his men, and turning in his dynamite. As proof he sent him a list of hiding places for seven hundred kilos of explosives. Later, from prison, he would continue to disclose to the brigade in Medellín a series of caches totaling two tons. But Maza never trusted him.

Impatient over the delay in his surrender, the government appointed a man from Boyacá—Luis Jorge Pataquiva Silva—as director of the prison instead of an Antioquian, as well as twenty national guards from various departments, none from Antioquia. "In any event," said Villamizar, "if they want to bribe someone it makes no difference if he's from Antioquia or somewhere else." Escobar, weary of all the twisting and turning, barely discussed it. In the end it was agreed that the army and not the police would guard the entrance, and that exceptional measures would be taken to ease Escobar's fear that his food in prison might be poisoned.

The National Board of Prisons, on the other hand, adopted the same regulations regarding visits that applied to the Ochoa brothers in the maximum security block of Itagüí prison. The time for waking up was seven in the morning; the time for being confined and placed under lock and key in one's cell was eight in the evening. Escobar and his prison mates could have women visitors every Sunday, from eight in the morning until two in the afternoon; men could visit on Saturdays, and minors on the first and third Sunday of every month.

In the middle of the night on June 9, troops from the battalion of military police in Medellín relieved the cavalry unit that was guarding the sector, began to assemble an impressive security array, cleared the surrounding mountains of people who did not live in the area, and assumed total control of earth and heaven. There were no more excuses. Villamizar let Escobar know—with utmost sincerity—that he was grateful to him for Maruja's release, but was not prepared to take any more risks just so he could keep putting off his surrender. And he sent him a serious message: "From now on I'm not responsible." Escobar made his decision in two days, with one final condition: that the prosecutor general also be present at the surrender.

An unexpected problem could have caused a new delay: Escobar did not have an official identification document that would prove he was in fact the man giving himself up. One of his lawyers raised the issue with the government and requested official citizenship papers for him, not taking into account that Escobar, hunted by every armed force in the country, would have to go in person to the appropriate office of the Civil Registry. The emergency solution was that he would identify himself with his fingerprints and an old identification card he had once used and had notarized, declaring at the same time that he could not produce the card because it had been lost.

THE MONKEY woke Villamizar when he phoned at midnight on June 18 to tell him to go upstairs to take an urgent call. It was very late, but Aseneth's apartment resembled a happy inferno, with the accordion of Egidio Cuadrado and his *vallenatos* combo. Villamizar had to elbow his way through a frenetic jungle of elite cultural gossip. Aseneth, in typical fashion, blocked his path.

"I know now who's calling you," she said. "Be careful, because one false step and they'll have your balls."

She let him into her bedroom just as the phone rang. In the uproar that filled the house, Villamizar could barely make out what was most essential:

"Ready: Come to Medellín first thing tomorrow."

RAFAEL PARDO arranged for a Civil Aeronautics plane to be available at seven o'clock for the official committee that would witness the surrender. Villamizar, fearful of leaks, was at Father García Herreros's house by five. He found him in the oratory, the inevitable poncho over his cassock, just as he finished saying mass.

"Well, Father, let's go," he said. "We're flying to Medellín because Escobar's ready to surrender."

Traveling in the plane with them were Fernando García Herreros, one of the father's nephews who acted as his occasional assistant; Jaime Vázquez, from the Council on Public Information; Dr. Carlos Gustavo Arrieta, the prosecutor general for the republic; and Dr. Jaime Córdoba Triviño, the special prosecutor for human rights. At Olaya Herrera airport, in the center of Medellín, María Lía and Martha Nieves Ochoa were waiting for them.

The official committee was taken to the capitol building of the department of Antioquia. Villamizar and the father went to María Lía's apartment to have breakfast while last-minute arrangements were made for the surrender. There he learned that Escobar was already on his way, traveling by car and on foot to avoid the frequent police checkpoints. He was an expert in those evasive strategies.

Once again the father's nerves were on edge. One of his contact lenses fell out, he stepped on it, and was so exasperated that Martha Nieves had to take him to San Ignacio Opticians, where they solved his problem with a pair of normal glasses. The city teemed with rigorous checkpoints, and they were stopped at almost all of them, not to be searched but so the men could thank the good father for everything he was doing for Medellín. In that city where everything was possible, the best-kept secret in the world was already public knowledge.

The Monk came to María Lía's apartment at two-thirty, dressed for a day in the country with a light jacket and soft-soled shoes.

"Ready," he said to Villamizar. "Let's go to the capitol building. You take your car and I'll take mine."

He drove off alone. María Lía drove Villamizar, Father García Herreros, and Martha Nieves in her car. The two men got out at the capitol building. The women waited outside. The Monkey, no longer a cold, efficient technician, was trying to hide inside his own skin. He put on dark glasses and a golfer's hat, and kept in the background, behind Villamizar. Someone who saw him walking in with the priest rushed to telephone Rafael Pardo to say that Escobar—very blond, very tall and elegant—had just surrendered at the capitol building.

As they were preparing to leave, the Monkey received a call on his two-way radio informing him that a plane was heading for the airspace over the city. It was a military ambulance carrying several soldiers wounded in a clash with guerrillas in Urabá. It was getting late and the authorities were troubled, because the helicopters could not fly as dusk was falling, and delaying the surrender until the next day would be calamitous. Villamizar called Rafael Pardo, who rerouted the flight and repeated his categorical order that the sky be kept clear. As he waited for this to be settled, he wrote in his personal diary: "Not even birds will fly over Medellín today."

The first helicopter—a six-passenger Bell 206—took off from the roof of the capitol building a little after three, with the prosecutor general and Jaime Vázquez, Fernando García Herreros, and Luis Alirio Calle, a radio journalist whose enormous popularity was one more guarantee for Pablo Escobar's peace of mind. A security official would show the pilot the direct route to the prison.

The second helicopter—a twelve-passenger Bell 412—took off ten minutes later, when the Monkey received the order on his two-way radio. Villamizar flew with him and the father. As soon as they had taken off, they heard a report on the radio that the government's position had suffered a defeat in the Constituent Assembly, where non-extradition of nationals had just been approved by a vote of fifty-one to thirteen, with five abstentions, in a preliminary ballot that would be ratified later. Though there were no indications it had been planned, it was almost childish not to think Escobar had known ahead of time and had waited for that precise moment to surrender.

The pilots followed the Monkey's directions to the site where they would pick up Pablo Escobar and take him to prison. It was a very short flight, and at so low an altitude the directions seemed the kind you would give in a car: Take Eighth, keep going, turn right, more, a little more, to the park, that's it. Behind a grove of trees there suddenly appeared a splendid mansion surrounded by the bright colors of tropical flowers, with a soccer field as smooth as an enormous billiard table in the middle of El Poblado's traffic.

"Put it down over there," the Monkey said, pointing. "Don't turn off the engine."

Villamizar did not realize until they were right over the house that at least thirty armed men were waiting all around the field. When the helicopter landed on the grass, some fifteen bodyguards moved away from the group and walked uneasily to the helicopter in a circle around a man who was in no way inconspicuous. He had hair down to his shoulders, a very thick, rough-looking black beard that reached to his chest, and skin browned and weathered by a desert sun. He was thick-set, wore tennis shoes and a light-blue cotton jacket, had an easy walk and a chilling calm. Villamizar knew who he was at first sight only because he was different from all the other men he had ever seen in his life.

After saying goodbye to the nearest bodyguards with a series of powerful, rapid embraces, Escobar indicated to two of them that they should climb in the other side of the helicopter. They were Mugre and Otto, two of the men closest to him. Then he climbed in, paying no attention to the blades turning at half-speed. The first man he greeted before he sat down was Villamizar. He extended his warm, well-manicured hand and asked with no change in his voice:

"How are you, Dr. Villamizar?'

"How's it going, Pablo?" he replied.

Then Escobar turned to Father García Herreros with an amiable smile and thanked him for everything. He sat next to his two bodyguards, and only then did he seem to realize that the Monkey was there. Perhaps he had expected him only to give directions to Villamizar without getting into the helicopter.

"And you," Escobar said, "in the middle of this right to the end."

Nobody could tell if he was praising or berating him, but his tone was cordial. The Monkey, as confused as everyone else, shook his head and smiled.

"Ah, Chief!"

Then, in a kind of revelation, it occurred to Villamizar that Escobar was a much more dangerous man than anyone supposed, because there was something supernatural in his serenity and self-possession. The Monkey tried to close the door on his side but did not know how and the co-pilot had to do it. In the emotion of the moment, no one had thought to give any orders. The pilot, tense at the controls, asked a question:

"Do we take off now?"

Then Escobar let slip the only sign of his repressed anxiety.

He gave a quick order: "What do you think? Move it! Move it!"

When the helicopter lifted off from the grass, he asked Villamizar: "Everything's fine, isn't it, Doctor?" Villamizar, not turning around to look at him, answered with all his heart: "Everything's perfect." And that was all, because the flight was over. The helicopter flew the remaining distance almost grazing the trees, and came down on the prison soccer field—rock-strewn, its goalposts broken—next to the first helicopter, which had arrived a quarter of an hour earlier. The trip from the residence had taken less than fifteen minutes.

The next two minutes, however, were the most dramatic of all. Escobar tried to get out first, as soon as the door was opened, and found himself surrounded by the prison guards: some fifty tense, fairly bewildered men in blue uniforms who were aiming their weapons at him. Escobar gave a start, lost his control for a moment, and in a voice heavy with fearsome authority he roared:

"Lower your weapons, damn it!"

By the time the head of the guards gave the same order, Escobar's command had already been obeyed. Escobar and his companions walked the two hundred meters to the house where the prison officials, the members of the official delegation, and the first group of Escobar's men, who had come overland to surrender with him, were all waiting. Also present were Escobar's wife and his mother, who was very pale and on the verge of tears. As he passed he gave her an affectionate little pat on the shoulder and said: "Take it easy, Ma." The director of the prison came out to meet him, his hand extended.

"Señor Escobar," he introduced himself. "I'm Luis Jorge Pataquiva."

Escobar shook his hand. Then he raised his left pant leg and took out the pistol he was carrying in an ankle holster. It was a magnificent weapon: a Sig Sauer 9mm with a gold monogram inlaid on the mother-of-pearl handle. Escobar did not remove the clip but took out the bullets one by one and tossed them to the ground.

It was a somewhat theatrical gesture that seemed rehearsed, and it had its intended effect as a show of confidence in the warden whose appointment had caused so much concern. The following day it was reported that when he turned in his pistol Escobar had said to Pataquiva: "For peace in Colombia." No witness remembers this, least of all Villamizar, who was still dazzled by the beauty of the weapon.

Escobar greeted everyone. The special prosecutor held on to his hand as he said: "I am here, Señor Escobar, to make certain your rights are respected." Escobar thanked him with special deference. Then he took Villamizar's arm.

"Let's go, Doctor," he said. "You and I have a lot to talk about."

He led him to the end of the outside gallery, and they chatted there for about ten minutes, leaning against the railing, their backs to everyone. Escobar began by thanking him in formal terms. Then, with his awesome calm, he expressed regret for the suffering he had caused Villamizar and his family, but asked him to understand that the war had been very hard on both sides. Villamizar did not miss this opportunity to solve three great mysteries in his life: why they had killed Luis Carlos Galán, why Escobar had tried to kill him, and why he had abducted Maruja and Beatriz.

Escobar denied all responsibility for the first crime. "The fact is that everybody wanted to kill Dr. Galán," he said. He admitted being present at the discussions when the attack was decided, but denied taking part or having anything to do with what happened. "A lot of people were involved in that," he said. "I didn't even like the idea because I knew what would happen if they killed him, but once the decision was made I couldn't oppose it. Please tell doña Gloria that for me."

As for the second, he was very explicit: A group of friends in congress had convinced him that Villamizar was uncontrollable and stubborn and had to be stopped somehow before he succeeded in having extradition approved. "Besides," he said, "in that war we were fighting, just a rumor could get you killed. But now that I know you, Dr. Villamizar, thank God nothing happened to you."

As for Maruja's abduction, his explanation was simplistic. "I was kidnapping people to get something and I didn't get it, nobody was talking to me, nobody was paying attention, so I went after doña Maruja to see if that would work." He had no other reasons, but did drift into a long commentary about how he had gotten to know Villamizar over the course of the negotiations until he became convinced he was a serious, brave man whose word was as good as gold, and for that he pledged his eternal gratitude. "I know you and I can't be friends," he said. But Villamizar could be sure that nothing would happen to him or anybody in his family again.

"Who knows how long I'll be here," he said, "but I still have a lot of friends, so if any of you feels unsafe, if anybody tries to give you a hard time, you let me know and that'll be the end of it. You met your obligations to me, and I thank you and will do the same for you. You have my word of honor."

Before they said goodbye, Escobar asked Villamizar, as a final favor, to try to calm his mother and wife, who were both on the verge of hysteria. Villamizar did, without much hope of success, since both were convinced that the entire ceremony was nothing but a sinister trick on the part of the government to murder Escobar in prison. Finally Villamizar went into the director's office and dialed 284 33 00, the number of the presidential palace, which he knew by heart, and asked them to find Rafael Pardo no matter where he might be.

He was in the office of Mauricio Vargas, the press adviser, who answered the phone and passed Pardo the receiver without saying a word. Pardo recognized the grave, quiet voice, but this time it had a glowing aura.

"Dr. Pardo," said Villamizar, "I'm here with Escobar in prison."

Pardo—perhaps for the first time in his life—heard the news without passing it through the filter of doubt.

"How wonderful!" he said.

He made a rapid remark that Mauricio Vargas did not even try to interpret, hung up the phone, and walked into the president's office without knocking. Vargas, who is a born reporter twenty-four hours a day, suspected that Pardo's hurry, and the amount of time he spent in the office, meant that something important had happened. His nervous excitement could not tolerate a wait of more than five minutes. He went into the president's office without being announced, and found him laughing out loud at something Pardo had just said. Then he heard the news. Mauricio thought with pleasure about the army of journalists who would burst into his office any minute now, and he looked at his watch. It was 4:30 in the afternoon. Two months later, Rafael Pardo would be the first civilian named defense minister after fifty years of military ministers.

PABLO EMILIO ESCOBAR GAVIRIA had turned forty-one in December. According to the medical examination required when he entered prison, his state of health was that of "a young man in normal physical and mental condition." The only unusual observation was congestion in the nasal mucous membranes and something that looked like a plastic surgery scar on his nose, but he said he had been injured as a boy during a soccer game.

The document of voluntary surrender was signed by the national and regional directors of Criminal Investigation, and the special prosecutor for human rights. Escobar endorsed his signature with his thumbprint and the number of his lost identification card: 8.345.766, Envigado. The secretary, Carlos Alberto Bravo, added at the bottom of the document: "Having affixed his signature to this document, Señor Pablo Emilio Escobar requested that Dr. Alberto Villamizar Cárdenas also affix his signature to same, said signature appearing below." Villamizar signed, though he was never told in what capacity.

When this process had been completed, Pablo Escobar took his leave of everyone and walked into the cell where he would live as involved as ever in his business affairs, and also have the power of the state protecting his domestic tranquillity and security. Starting the next day, however, the very prisonlike prison described by Villamizar began to be transformed into a five-star hacienda with all kinds of luxuries, sports installations, and facilities for parties and pleasures, built with first-class materials brought in gradually in the false bottom of a supply van. When the government learned about the scandal 299 days later, it decided to transfer Escobar to another prison with no prior announcement. Just as incredible as the government's needing a year to find out what was going on was the fact that Escobar bribed a sergeant and two terrified soldiers with a plate of food and escaped on foot with his bodyguards through the nearby woods, under the noses of the functionaries and troops responsible for the transfer.

It was his death sentence. According to his subsequent statement, the government's action had been so strange and precipitous that he did not think they were really going to transfer him but kill him or turn him over to the United States. When he realized the enormity of his error, he undertook two parallel campaigns to have the government repeat the favor of imprisoning him: the greatest terrorist bombing offensive in the history of the country, and his offer to surrender without conditions of any kind. The government never acknowledged his proposals, the country did not succumb to the terror of the car bombs, and the police offensive reached unsustainable proportions.

The world had changed for Escobar. Those who could have helped him save his life again had no desire or reason to. Father García Herreros died of kidney failure on November 24, 1992, and Paulina—with no job and no savings—retired so far into a peaceful autumn with her children and good memories that today no one at "God's Word" even mentions her. Alberto Villamizar, named ambassador to Holland, received several messages from Escobar, but it was too late now for everything. His immense fortune, estimated at 3 billion dollars, was for the most part drained by the cost of the war or spent disbanding the cartel. His family found no place in the world where they could sleep without nightmares. Having become the biggest prey in our history, Escobar could not stay more than six hours in one spot, and in his crazed flight he left behind him a trail of dead innocents, and his own bodyguards murdered, captured, or gone over to the forces of his enemies. His security services, and even his own almost animal instinct for survival, lost the sharp edge of former days.

On December 2, 1993—one day after his forty-fourth birthday—he could not resist the temptation of talking on the phone with his son Juan Pablo who, with his mother and younger sister, had just returned to Bogotá following Germany's refusal to admit them. Juan Pablo, who was now more alert than his father, warned him after two minutes not to talk anymore because the police would trace the call. Escobar—whose devotion to his family was proverbial—ignored him. By this time the trace had established the exact phone in the Los Olivos district in Medellín that he was using. At 3:15 in the afternoon, an inconspicuous group of twenty-three special plainclothes police cordoned off the area, took over the house, and began to force the door to the second floor. Escobar heard them. "I'm hanging up," he said to his son on the telephone, "because something funny's going on here." Those were his last words.

VILLAMIZAR SPENT the night of the surrender in the noisiest, most dangerous clubs in the city, drinking man-size glasses of *aguardiente* with Escobar's bodyguards. The Monkey, drunk as a lord, told anyone who would listen that Dr. Villamizar was the only person the Chief had ever apologized to. At two in the morning he stood up and with no preliminaries said goodbye with a wave of his hand.

"So long, Dr. Villamizar," he said. "I have to disappear now, and we may never see each other again. It was a pleasure knowing you."

Villamizar, besotted with drink, was dropped off at La Loma at dawn. In the afternoon, the only topic of conversation on the plane to Bogotá was Pablo Escobar's surrender. Villamizar was one of the best-known men in the country that day, but no one recognized him in the crowded airports. The newspapers had indicated his presence at the prison but had published no photographs, and the real extent of his decisive participation in the entire capitulation process seemed destined for the shadows of secret glories.

Back home that afternoon, he realized that daily life was returning to normal. Andrés was studying in his room. Maruja was waging a difficult, silent war against her phantoms in order to become herself again. The Tang Dynasty horse was back in its usual place, between her prized mementos of Indonesia and her antiquities from half the world, rearing its front legs on the sacred table where she wanted it to be, in the corner where she dreamed of seeing it during the interminable nights of her captivity. She had returned to her offices at FOCINE in the same car—the bullet scars on the windows erased—from which she had been abducted, with a new, grateful driver in the dead chauffeur's seat. In less than two years she would be named education minister.

Villamizar, with no job and no desire to have one, with the bad taste of politics in his mouth, chose to rest for a time in his own way, making small household repairs, taking his leisure sip by sip with old drinking companions, doing the shopping himself so that he and his friends could enjoy the pleasures of the local cuisine. It was the perfect frame of mind for reading in the afternoon and growing a beard. One Sunday at lunch, when the mists of memory had already begun to rarefy the past, someone knocked at the door. They thought Andrés had forgotten his keys again. The servants had the day off, and Villamizar opened the door. A young man in a sports jacket handed him a small package wrapped in gift paper and tied with a gold ribbon, and then disappeared down the stairs without saying a word or giving him time to ask any questions. Villamizar thought it might be a bomb. In an instant he was shuddering with the nausea of the abduction, but he untied the bow and unwrapped the package with his fingertips, away from the dining room where Maruja was waiting for him. It was a case made of imitation leather, and inside the case, nestled in satin, was the ring they had taken from Maruja on the night she was abducted. One diamond chip was missing, but it was the same ring.

Maruja was stunned. She put it on, and realized she was recovering her health faster than she had imagined because now it fit her finger.

"How incredible!" she said with a hopeful sigh. "Somebody ought to write a book."

GABRIEL GARCÍA MÁRQUEZ

MEMORIES OF MY MELANCHOLY WHORES

'A Velvety pleasure to read. Márquez has composed, with his usual sensual gravity and Olympian humour, a love letter to the dying light.' John Updike

'The year I turned ninety, I wanted to give myself a gift of a night of wild love with an adolescent virgin…'

He has never married, never loved and never gone to bed with a woman he didn't pay. But on finding a young girl naked and asleep on the brothel owner's bed, a passion is ignited in his heart – and he feels, for the first time, the urgent pangs of love.

Each night, exhausted by her factory work, 'Delgadina' sleeps peacefully whilst he watches her quietly. During these solitary early hours, his love for her deepens and he finds himself reflecting on his newly found passion and the loveless life he has led. By day, his columns in the local newspaper are read avidly by those who recognise in his outpourings the enlivening and transformative power of love.

'Márquez describes this amorous, sometimes disturbing journey with the grace and vigour of a master storyteller' *Daily Mail*

'There is not one stale sentence, redundant word or unfinished thought' *The Times*

VOYAGE
AU CENTRE
DE LA TERRE

JULES VERNE

VOYAGE AU CENTRE

DE

LA TERRE

VIGNETTES PAR RIOU

BIBLIOTHÈQUE

D'ÉDUCATION ET DE RÉCREATION

J. HETZEL, EDITEUR

18, RUE JACOB, PARIS

I

LE 24 mai 1863, un dimanche, mon oncle, le
professeur Lidenbrock, revint précipitamment
vers sa petite maison située au numéro 19 de
Königstrasse, l'une des plus anciennes rues du
vieux quartier de Hambourg.

La bonne Marthe dut se croire fort en retard, car le dîner commençait à peine à chanter sur le fourneau de la cuisine.

« Bon, me dis-je, s'il a faim, mon oncle, qui est le plus impatient des hommes, va pousser des cris de détresse.

— Déjà M. Lidenbrock ! s'écria la bonne Marthe stupéfaite, en entrebâillant la porte de la salle à manger.

— Oui, Marthe ; mais le dîner a le droit de ne point être cuit, car il n'est pas deux heures. La demie vient à peine de sonner à Saint-Michel.

— Alors pourquoi M. Lidenbrock rentre-t-il ?

— Il nous le dira vraisemblablement.

— Le voilà ! je me sauve, monsieur Axel, vous lui ferez entendre raison. »

Et la bonne Marthe regagna son laboratoire culinaire.

Je restai seul. Mais de faire entendre raison au plus irascible des professeurs, c'est ce que mon caractère un peu indécis ne me permettait pas. Aussi je me préparais à regagner prudemment ma petite chambre du haut, quand la porte de la rue cria sur ses gonds ; de grands pieds firent craquer l'escalier de bois, et le maître de la maison, traversant la salle à manger, se précipita aussitôt dans son cabinet de travail.

Mais, pendant ce rapide passage, il avait jeté dans un coin sa canne à tête de casse-noisette, sur la table son large chapeau à poils rebroussés, et à son neveu ces paroles retentissantes :

« Axel, suis-moi ! »

Je n'avais pas eu le temps de bouger que le professeur me criait déjà avec un vif accent d'impatience :

« Eh bien ! tu n'es pas encore ici ? »

Je m'élançai dans le cabinet de mon redoutable maître.

Otto Lidenbrock n'était pas un méchant homme, j'en conviens volontiers ; mais, à moins de changements improbables, il mourra dans la peau d'un terrible original.

Il était professeur au Johannæum, et faisait un cours de minéralogie pendant lequel il se mettait régulièrement en colère une fois ou deux. Non point qu'il se préoccupât d'avoir des élèves assidus à ses leçons, ni du degré d'attention qu'ils lui accordaient, ni du succès qu'ils pouvaient obtenir par la suite ; ces détails ne l'inquiétaient guère. Il professait « subjectivement », suivant une expression de la philosophie allemande, pour lui et non pour les autres. C'était un savant égoïste, un puits de science dont la poulie grinçait quand on en voulait tirer quelque chose : en un mot, un avare.

Il y a quelques professeurs de ce genre en Allemagne.

Mon oncle, malheureusement, ne jouissait pas d'une extrême facilité de prononciation, sinon dans l'intimité, au moins quand il parlait en public, et c'est un défaut regrettable chez un orateur. En effet, dans ses démonstrations au Johannæum,

souvent le professeur s'arrêtait court; il luttait
contre un mot récalcitrant qui ne voulait pas glisser entre ses lèvres, un de ces mots qui résistent,
se gonflent et finissent par sortir sous la forme
peu scientifique d'un juron. De là, grande colère.

Or, il y a en minéralogie bien des dénominations
semi-grecques, semi-latines, difficiles à prononcer,
de ces rudes appellations qui écorcheraient les
lèvres d'un poète. Je ne veux pas dire du mal de
cette science. Loin de moi. Mais lorsqu'on se
trouve en présence des cristallisations rhomboé-
driques, des résines rétinasphaltes, des ghélénites,
des fangasites, des molybdates de plomb, des
tungstates de manganèse et des titaniates de zir-
cone, il est permis à la langue la plus adroite de
fourcher.

Donc, dans la ville, on connaissait cette par-
donnable infirmité de mon oncle, et on en abusait,
et on l'attendait aux passages dangereux, et il se
mettait en fureur, et l'on riait, ce qui n'est pas de
bon goût, même pour des Allemands. Et s'il y
avait toujours grande affluence d'auditeurs aux
cours de Lidenbrock, combien les suivaient assidû-
ment qui venaient surtout pour se dérider aux
belles colères du professeur!

Quoi qu'il en soit, mon oncle, je ne saurais
trop le dire, était un véritable savant. Bien qu'il
cassât parfois ses échantillons à les essayer trop
brusquement, il joignait au génie du géologue l'œil
du minéralogiste. Avec son marteau, sa pointe
d'acier, son aiguille aimantée, son chalumeau et

son flacon d'acide nitrique, c'était un homme très fort. A la cassure, à l'aspect, à la dureté, à la fusibilité, au son, à l'odeur, au goût d'un minéral quelconque, il le classait sans hésiter parmi les six cents espèces que la science compte aujourd'hui.

Aussi le nom de Lidenbrock retentissait avec honneur dans les gymnases et les associations nationales. MM. Humphry Davy, de Humboldt, les capitaines Franklin et Sabine, ne manquèrent pas de lui rendre visite à leur passage à Hambourg. MM. Becquerel, Ebelmen, Brewster, Dumas, Milne-Edwards, Sainte-Claire-Deville, aimaient à le consulter sur des questions les plus palpitantes de la chimie. Cette science lui devait d'assez belles découvertes, et, en 1853, il avait paru à Leipzig un *Traité de Cristallographie transcendante*, par le professeur Otto Lidenbrock, grand in-folio avec planches, qui cependant ne fit pas ses frais.

Ajoutez à cela que mon oncle était conservateur du musée minéralogique de M. Struve, ambassadeur de Russie, précieuse collection d'une renommée européenne.

Voilà donc le personnage qui m'interpellait avec tant d'impatience. Représentez-vous un homme grand, maigre, d'une santé de fer, et d'un blond juvénile qui lui ôtait dix bonnes années de sa cinquantaine. Ses gros yeux roulaient sans cesse derrière des lunettes considérables; son nez, long et mince, ressemblait à une lame affilée; les méchants prétendaient même qu'il était aimanté et qu'il attirait la limaille de fer. Pure calomnie :

Otto Lidenbrock était un homme grand, maigre (p. 5).

il n'attirait que le tabac, mais en grande abondance, pour ne point mentir.

Quand j'aurai ajouté que mon oncle faisait des enjambées mathématiques d'une demi-toise, et si je dis qu'en marchant il tenait ses poings solidement fermés, signe d'un tempérament impétueux, on le connaîtra assez pour ne pas se montrer friand de sa compagnie.

Il demeurait dans sa petite maison de König-strasse, une habitation moitié bois, moitié brique, à pignon dentelé; elle donnait sur l'un de ces canaux sinueux qui se croisent au milieu du plus ancien quartier de Hambourg que l'incendie de 1842 a heureusement respecté.

La vieille maison penchait un peu, il est vrai, et tendait le ventre aux passants; elle portait son toit incliné sur l'oreille, comme la casquette d'un étudiant de la Tugendbund; l'aplomb de ses lignes laissait à désirer; mais, en somme, elle se tenait bien, grâce à un vieil orme vigoureusement encastré dans la façade, qui poussait au printemps ses bourgeons en fleur à travers les vitraux des fenêtres.

Mon oncle ne laissait pas d'être riche pour un professeur allemand. La maison lui appartenait en toute propriété, contenant et contenu. Le contenu, c'était sa filleule Graüben, jeune Virlandaise de dix-sept ans, la bonne Marthe et moi. En ma double qualité de neveu et d'orphelin, je devins son aide-préparateur dans ses expériences.

J'avouerai que je mordis avec appétit aux

Il demeurait dans sa petite maison de Königstrasse (p. 7).

sciences géologiques; j'avais du sang de minéralogiste dans les veines, et je ne m'ennuyais jamais
en compagnie de mes précieux cailloux.

En somme, on pouvait vivre heureux dans cette
maisonnette de Königstrasse, malgré les impatiences de son propriétaire, car, tout en s'y prenant
d'une façon un peu brutale, celui-ci ne m'en
aimait pas moins. Mais cet homme-là ne savait
pas attendre, et il était plus pressé que nature.

Quand, en avril, il avait planté dans les pots de
faïence de son salon des pieds de réséda ou de
volubilis, chaque matin il allait régulièrement
les tirer par les feuilles afin de hâter leur croissance.

Avec un pareil original, il n'y avait qu'à obéir.
Je me précipitai donc dans son cabinet.

II

CE cabinet était un véritable musée. Tous les
échantillons du règne minéral s'y trouvaient
étiquetés avec l'ordre le plus parfait, suivant les
trois grandes divisions des minéraux inflammables, métalliques et lithoïdes.

Comme je les connaissais, ces bibelots de la
science minéralogique! Que de fois, au lieu de
muser avec les garçons de mon âge, je m'étais plu
à épousseter ces graphites, ces anthracites, ces
houilles, ces lignites, ces tourbes! Et les bitumes, les

résines, les sels organiques qu'il fallait préserver
du moindre atome de poussière! Et ces métaux,
depuis le fer jusqu'à l'or, dont la valeur relative
disparaissait devant l'égalité absolue des spécimens scientifiques! Et toutes ces pierres qui
eussent suffi à reconstruire la maison de Könïg-
strasse, même avec une belle chambre de plus,
dont je me serais si bien arrangé!

Mais, en entrant dans le cabinet, je ne songeais
guère à ces merveilles. Mon oncle seul occupait
ma pensée. Il était enfoui dans son large fauteuil
garni de velours d'Utrecht, et tenait entre les mains
un livre qu'il considérait avec la plus profonde
admiration.

« Quel livre! quel livre! » s'écriait-il.

Cette exclamation me rappela que le professeur
Lidenbrock était aussi bibliomane à ses moments
perdus; mais un bouquin n'avait de prix à ses
yeux qu'à la condition d'être introuvable, ou tout
au moins illisible.

« Eh bien! me dit-il, tu ne vois donc pas? Mais
c'est un trésor inestimable que j'ai rencontré ce
matin en furetant dans la boutique du juif Hevelius.

— Magnifique! » répondis-je avec un enthousiasme de commande.

En effet, à quoi bon ce fracas pour un vieil
in-quarto dont le dos et les plats semblaient faits
d'un veau grossier, un bouquin jaunâtre auquel
pendait un signet décoloré?

Cependant les interjections admiratives du
professeur ne discontinuaient pas.

« Vois, disait-il, en se faisant à lui-même demandes et réponses; est-ce assez beau? Oui, c'est admirable! Et quelle reliure! Ce livre s'ouvre-t-il facilement? Oui, car il reste ouvert à n'importe quelle page! Mais se ferme-t-il bien? Oui, car la couverture et les feuilles forment un tout bien uni, sans se séparer ni bâiller en aucun endroit! Et ce dos qui n'offre pas une seule brisure après sept cents ans d'existence! Ah! voilà une reliure dont Bozerian, Closs ou Purgold eussent été fiers! »

En parlant ainsi, mon oncle ouvrait et fermait successivement le vieux bouquin. Je ne pouvais faire moins que de l'interroger sur son contenu, bien que cela ne m'intéressât aucunement.

« Et quel est donc le titre de ce merveilleux volume? demandai-je avec un empressement trop enthousiaste pour n'être pas feint.

— Cet ouvrage! répondit mon oncle en s'animant, c'est l'*Heims-Kringla* de Snorre Turleson, le fameux auteur islandais du XIIe siècle! C'est la Chronique des princes norvégiens qui régnèrent en Islande!

— Vraiment! m'écriai-je de mon mieux, et sans doute c'est une traduction en langue allemande?

— Bon! riposta vivement le professeur, une traduction! Et qu'en ferais-je de ta traduction? Qui se soucie de ta traduction? Ceci est l'ouvrage original en langue islandaise, ce magnifique idiome, riche et simple à la fois, qui autorise les

combinaisons grammaticales les plus variées et de nombreuses modifications de mots!

— Comme l'allemand, insinuai-je avec assez de bonheur.

— Oui, répondit mon oncle en haussant les épaules, sans compter que la langue islandaise admet les trois genres comme le grec et décline les noms propres comme le latin!

— Ah! fis-je un peu ébranlé dans mon indifférence, et les caractères de ce livre sont-ils beaux?

— Des caractères! Qui te parle de caractères, malheureux Axel? Il s'agit bien de caractères! Ah! tu prends cela pour un imprimé? Mais, ignorant, c'est un manuscrit, et un manuscrit runique!...

— Runique?

— Oui! Vas-tu me demander maintenant de t'expliquer ce mot?

— Je m'en garderai bien », répliquai-je avec l'accent d'un homme blessé dans son amour-propre.

Mais mon oncle continua de plus belle et m'instruisit, malgré moi, de choses que je ne tenais guère à savoir.

« Les runes, reprit-il, étaient des caractères d'écriture usités autrefois en Islande, et, suivant la tradition, ils furent inventés par Odin lui-même! Mais regarde donc, admire donc, impie, ces types qui sont sortis de l'imagination d'un dieu! »

Ma foi, faute de réplique, j'allais me prosterner,

genre de réponse qui doit plaire aux dieux comme
aux rois, car elle a l'avantage de ne jamais les
embarrasser, quand un incident vint détourner le
cours de la conversation.

Ce fut l'apparition d'un parchemin crasseux
qui glissa du bouquin et tomba à terre.

Mon oncle se précipita sur ce brimborion avec
une avidité facile à comprendre. Un vieux document, enfermé depuis un temps immémorial dans
un vieux livre, ne pouvait manquer d'avoir un
haut prix à ses yeux.

« Qu'est-ce que cela ? » s'écria-t-il.

Et, en même temps, il déployait soigneusement
sur sa table un morceau de parchemin long de
cinq pouces, large de trois, et sur lequel s'allongeaient, en lignes transversales, des caractères de
grimoire.

En voici le fac-similé exact. Je tiens à faire connaître ces signes bizarres, car ils amenèrent le professeur Lidenbrock et son neveu à entreprendre
la plus étrange expédition du XIXᵉ siècle :

Le professeur considéra pendant quelques

instants cette série de caractères; puis il dit en
relevant ses lunettes :

« C'est du runique; ces types sont absolument
identiques à ceux du manuscrit de Snorre Turleson! Mais... qu'est-ce que cela peut signifier? »

Comme le runique me paraissait être une
invention de savants pour mystifier le pauvre
monde, je ne fus pas fâché de voir que mon oncle
n'y comprenait rien. Du moins cela me sembla
ainsi au mouvement de ses doigts qui commençaient à s'agiter terriblement.

« C'est pourtant du vieil islandais! » murmurait-il
entre ses dents.

Et le professeur Lidenbrock devait bien s'y
connaître, car il passait pour être un véritable
polyglotte. Non pas qu'il parlât couramment les
deux mille langues et les quatre mille idiomes
employés à la surface du globe, mais enfin il en
savait sa bonne part.

Il allait donc, en présence de cette difficulté,
se livrer à toute l'impétuosité de son caractère,
et je prévoyais une scène violente, quand deux
heures sonnèrent au petit cartel de la cheminée.

Aussitôt la bonne Marthe ouvrit la porte du cabinet en disant :

« La soupe est servie.

— Au diable la soupe, s'écria mon oncle, et celle
qui l'a faite, et ceux qui la mangeront! »

Marthe s'enfuit. Je volai sur ses pas, et, sans
savoir comment, je me trouvai assis à ma place
habituelle dans la salle à manger.

J'attendis quelques instants. Le professeur ne vint pas. C'était la première fois, à ma connaissance, qu'il manquait à la solennité du dîner. Et quel dîner, cependant! Une soupe au persil, une omelette au jambon relevée d'oseille à la muscade, une longe de veau à la compote de prunes, et, pour dessert, des crevettes au sucre, le tout arrosé d'un joli vin de la Moselle..

Voilà ce qu'un vieux papier allait coûter à mon oncle. Ma foi, en qualité de neveu dévoué, je me crus obligé de manger pour lui, en même temps que pour moi. Ce que je fis en conscience.

« Je n'ai jamais vu chose pareille! disait la bonne Marthe. M. Lidenbrock qui n'est pas à table!

— C'est à ne pas le croire.

— Cela présage quelque événement grave! » reprenait la vieille servante, hochant la tête.

Dans mon opinion, cela ne présageait rien, sinon une scène épouvantable quand mon oncle trouverait son dîner dévoré.

J'en étais à ma dernière crevette, lorsqu'une voix retentissante m'arracha aux voluptés du dessert. Je ne fis qu'un bond de la salle dans le cabinet.

III

« C'est évidemment du runique, disait le professeur en fronçant le sourcil. Mais il y a un secret, et je le découvrirai, sinon... »

Un geste violent acheva sa pensée.

« Mets-toi là, ajouta-t-il en m'indiquant la table du poing, et écris. »

En un instant je fus prêt.

« Maintenant, je vais te dicter chaque lettre de notre alphabet qui correspond à l'un de ces caractères islandais. Nous verrons ce que cela donnera. Mais, par saint Michel ! garde-toi bien de te tromper ! »

La dictée commença. Je m'appliquai de mon mieux. Chaque lettre fut appelée l'une après l'autre, et forma l'incompréhensible succession des mots suivants :

m.rnlls	esreuel	seecJde
sgtssmf	unteief	niedrke
kt,samn	atrateS	Saodrrn
emtnaeI	nuaect	rrilSa
Atvaar	.nscrc	ieaabs
ccdrmi	eeutul	frantu
dt,iac	oseibo	KediiY

Quand ce travail fut terminé, mon oncle prit vivement la feuille sur laquelle je venais d'écrire, et il l'examina longtemps avec attention.

« Qu'est-ce que cela veut dire ? » répétait-il machinalement.

Sur l'honneur, je n'aurais pu le lui apprendre. D'ailleurs il ne m'interrogea pas, et il continua de se parler à lui-même :

« C'est ce que nous appelons un cryptogramme, disait-il, dans lequel le sens est caché sous des

lettres brouillées à dessein, et qui convenablement disposées formeraient une phrase intelligible. Quand je pense qu'il y a là peut-être l'explication ou l'indication d'une grande découverte! »

Pour mon compte, je pensais qu'il n'y avait absolument rien, mais je gardai prudemment mon opinion.

Le professeur prit alors le livre et le parchemin, et les compara tous les deux.

« Ces deux écritures ne sont pas de la même main, dit-il; le cryptogramme est postérieur au livre, et j'en vois tout d'abord une preuve irréfragable. En effet, la première lettre est une double M qu'on chercherait vainement dans le livre de Turleson, car elle ne fut ajoutée à l'alphabet islandais qu'au XIVe siècle. Ainsi donc, il y a au moins deux cents ans entre le manuscrit et le document. »

Cela, j'en conviens, me parut assez logique.

« Je suis donc conduit à penser, reprit mon oncle, que l'un des possesseurs de ce livre aura tracé ces caractères mystérieux. Mais qui diable était ce possesseur? N'aurait-il point mis son nom en quelque endroit de ce manuscrit? »

Mon oncle releva ses lunettes, prit une forte loupe, et passa soigneusement en revue les premières pages du livre. Au verso de la seconde, celle du faux titre, il découvrit une sorte de macule, qui faisait à l'œil l'effet d'une tache d'encre. Cependant, en y regardant de près, on distinguait quelques caractères à demi effacés. Mon oncle

comprit que là était le point intéressant ; il s'acharna
donc sur la macule et, sa grosse loupe aidant, il
finit par reconnaître les signes que voici, caractères runiques qu'il lut sans hésiter :

ᛑᛆᛘᚾ ᛤᛏᛦᛐᚾᛐᛐᛐᚴ

« Arne Saknussemm ! s'écria-t-il d'un ton triomphant, mais c'est un nom cela, et un nom islandais
encore, celui d'un savant du XVIe siècle, d'un
alchimiste célèbre ! »

Je regardai mon oncle avec une certaine admiration.

« Ces alchimistes, reprit-il, Avicenne, Bacon,
Lulle, Paracelse, étaient les véritables, les seuls
savants de leur époque. Ils ont fait des découvertes dont nous avons le droit d'être étonnés.
Pourquoi ce Saknussemm n'aurait-il pas enfoui
sous cet incompréhensible cryptogramme quelque
surprenante invention ? Cela doit être ainsi. Cela
est. »

L'imagination du professeur s'enflammait à
cette hypothèse.

« Sans doute, osai-je répondre, mais quel
intérêt pouvait avoir ce savant à cacher ainsi
quelque merveilleuse découverte ?

— Pourquoi ? pourquoi ? Eh ! le sais-je ? Galilée
n'en a-t-il pas agi ainsi pour Saturne ? D'ailleurs,
nous verrons bien : j'aurai le secret de ce document, et je ne prendrai ni nourriture ni sommeil
avant de l'avoir deviné. »

« Oh ! » pensai-je.

« Ni toi non plus, Axel », reprit-il.

« Diable ! me dis-je, il est heureux que j'aie dîné pour deux ! »

« Et d'abord, fit mon oncle, il faut trouver la langue de ce « chiffre ». Cela ne doit pas être difficile. »

A ces mots, je relevai vivement la tête. Mon oncle reprit son soliloque :

« Rien n'est plus aisé. Il y a dans ce document cent trente-deux lettres qui donnent soixante-dix-neuf consonnes contre cinquante-trois voyelles. Or, c'est à peu près suivant cette proportion que sont formés les mots des langues méridionales, tandis que les idiomes du nord sont infiniment plus riches en consonnes. Il s'agit donc d'une langue du midi. »

Ces conclusions étaient fort justes.

« Mais quelle est cette langue ? »

C'est là que j'attendais mon savant, chez lequel cependant je découvrais un profond analyste.

« Ce Saknussemm, reprit-il, était un homme instruit ; or, dès qu'il n'écrivait pas dans sa langue maternelle, il devait choisir de préférence la langue courante entre les esprits cultivés du xvie siècle, je veux dire le latin. Si je me trompe, je pourrai essayer de l'espagnol, du français, de l'italien, du grec, de l'hébreu. Mais les savants du xvie siècle écrivaient généralement en latin. J'ai donc le droit de dire *a priori :* ceci est du latin. »

Je sautai sur ma chaise. Mes souvenirs de lati-

niste se révoltaient contre la prétention que cette suite de mots baroques pût appartenir à la douce langue de Virgile.

« Oui ! du latin, reprit mon oncle, mais du latin brouillé. »

« A la bonne heure ! pensai-je. Si tu le débrouilles, tu seras fin, mon oncle. »

« Examinons bien, dit-il en reprenant la feuille sur laquelle j'avais écrit. Voilà une série de cent trente-deux lettres qui se présentent sous un désordre apparent. Il y a des mots où les consonnes se rencontrent seules comme le premier « m.rnlls », d'autres où les voyelles, au contraire, abondent, le cinquième, par exemple, « unteief », ou l'avant-dernier, « oseibo ». Or, cette disposition n'a évidemment pas été combinée : elle est donnée *mathématiquement* par la raison inconnue qui a présidé à la succession de ces lettres. Il me paraît certain que la phrase primitive a été écrite régulièrement, puis retournée suivant une loi qu'il faut découvrir. Celui qui posséderait la clef de ce « chiffre » le lirait couramment. Mais quelle est cette clef ? Axel, as-tu cette clef ? »

A cette question je ne répondis rien, et pour cause. Mes regards s'étaient arrêtés sur un charmant portrait suspendu au mur, le portrait de Graüben. La pupille de mon oncle se trouvait alors à Altona, chez une de ses parentes, et son absence me rendait fort triste, car, je puis l'avouer maintenant, la jolie Virlandaise et le neveu du professeur s'aimaient avec toute la patience et

toute la tranquillité allemandes. Nous nous étions
fiancés à l'insu de mon oncle, trop géologue pour
comprendre de pareils sentiments. Graüben était
une charmante jeune fille blonde aux yeux bleus,
d'un caractère un peu grave, d'un esprit un peu
sérieux; mais elle ne m'en aimait pas moins.
Pour mon compte, je l'adorais, si toutefois ce
verbe existe dans la langue tudesque! L'image de
ma petite Virlandaise me rejeta donc, en un instant,
du monde des réalités dans celui des chimères,
dans celui des souvenirs.

Je revis la fidèle compagne de mes travaux et
de mes plaisirs. Elle m'aidait à ranger chaque jour
les précieuses pierres de mon oncle; elle les éti-
quetait avec moi. C'était une très forte miné-ra-
logiste que Mlle Graüben! Elle en eût remontré
à plus d'un savant. Elle aimait à approfondir les
questions ardues de la science. Que de douces
heures nous avions passées à étudier ensemble!
et combien j'enviai souvent le sort de ces pierres
insensibles qu'elle maniait de ses charmantes
mains!

Puis, l'instant de la récréation venu, nous sor-
tions tous les deux, nous prenions par les allées
touffues de l'Alster, et nous nous rendions de
compagnie au vieux moulin goudronné qui fait si
bon effet à l'extrémité du lac; chemin faisant, on
causait en se tenant par la main. Je lui racontais
des choses dont elle riait de son mieux. On arrivait
ainsi jusqu'au bord de l'Elbe, et, après avoir dit
bonsoir aux cygnes qui nagent parmi les grands

Graüben était une charmante jeune fille blonde (p. 21).

nénuphars blancs, nous revenions au quai par la barque à vapeur.

Or, j'en étais là de mon rêve, quand mon oncle, frappant la table du poing, me ramena violemment à la réalité.

« Voyons, dit-il, la première idée qui doit se présenter à l'esprit pour brouiller les lettres d'une phrase, c'est, il me semble, d'écrire les mots verticalement au lieu de les tracer horizontalement. »

« Tiens ! » pensai-je.

« Il faut voir ce que cela produit. Axel, jette une phrase quelconque sur ce bout de papier; mais, au lieu de disposer les lettres à la suite les unes des autres, mets-les successivement par colonnes verticales, de manière à les grouper en nombre de cinq ou six. »

Je compris ce dont il s'agissait, et immédiatement j'écrivis de haut en bas :

$$
\begin{array}{ccccc}
J & m & n & e & G & e \\
e & e & , & t & r & n \\
t' & b & m & i & a & ! \\
a & i & a & t & ü \\
i & e & p & e & b
\end{array}
$$

« Bon, dit le professeur sans avoir lu. Maintenant, dispose ces mots sur une ligne horizontale. »

J'obéis, et j'obtins la phrase suivante :

JmneGe ee,trn t'bmia! aiatü iepeb

« Parfait ! fit mon oncle en m'arrachant le papier des mains, voilà qui a déjà la physionomie du

vieux document : les voyelles sont groupées ainsi que les consonnes dans le même désordre ; il y a même des majuscules au milieu des mots, ainsi que des virgules, tout comme dans le parchemin de Saknussemm ! »

Je ne pus m'empêcher de trouver ces remarques fort ingénieuses.

« Or, reprit mon oncle en s'adressant directement à moi, pour lire la phrase que tu viens d'écrire, et que je ne connais pas, il me suffira de prendre successivement la première lettre de chaque mot, puis la seconde, puis la troisième, ainsi de suite. »

Et mon oncle, à son grand étonnement, et surtout au mien, lut :

Je t'aime bien, ma petite Graüben !

« Hein ! » fit le professeur.

Oui, sans m'en douter, en amoureux maladroit, j'avais tracé cette phrase compromettante !

« Ah ! tu aimes Graüben ? reprit mon oncle d'un véritable ton de tuteur.

— Oui... Non... balbutiai-je.

— Ah ! tu aimes Graüben ! reprit-il machinalement. Eh bien, appliquons mon procédé au document en question ! »

Mon oncle, retombé dans son absorbante contemplation, oubliait déjà mes imprudentes paroles. Je dis imprudentes, car la tête du savant ne pouvait comprendre les choses du cœur. Mais, heureusement, la grande affaire du document l'emporta.

Au moment de faire son expérience capitale, les yeux du professeur Lidenbrock lancèrent des éclairs à travers ses lunettes. Ses doigts tremblèrent, lorsqu'il reprit le vieux parchemin. Il était sérieusement ému. Enfin il toussa fortement, et d'une voix grave, appelant successivement la première lettre, puis la seconde de chaque mot, il me dicta la série suivante :

> *messunkaSenrA.icefdoK.segnittamurtn*
> *ecertserrette,rotaivsadua,ednecsedsadne*
> *lacartniiiluJsiratracSarbmutabiledmek*
> *meretarcsilucoYsleffenSnI*

En finissant, je l'avouerai, j'étais émotionné ; ces lettres, nommées une à une, ne m'avaient présenté aucun sens à l'esprit ; j'attendais donc que le professeur laissât se dérouler pompeusement entre ses lèvres une phrase d'une magnifique latinité.

Mais, qui aurait pu le prévoir ! un violent coup de poing ébranla la table. L'encre rejaillit, la plume me sauta des mains.

« Ce n'est pas cela ! s'écria mon oncle, cela n'a pas le sens commun ! »

Puis, traversant le cabinet comme un boulet, descendant l'escalier comme une avalanche, il se précipita dans Königstrasse, et s'enfuit à toutes jambes.

La vieille servante retourna dans sa cuisine
en gémissant (p. 27).

IV

« Il est parti ? s'écria Marthe en accourant au bruit de la porte de la rue qui, violemment refermée, venait d'ébranler la maison tout entière.

— Oui ! répondis-je, complètement parti !

— Eh bien ! et son dîner ? fit la vieille servante.

— Il ne dînera pas !

— Et son souper ?

— Il ne soupera pas !

— Comment ? dit Marthe en joignant les mains.

— Non, bonne Marthe, il ne mangera plus, ni personne dans la maison ! Mon oncle Lidenbrock nous met tous à la diète jusqu'au moment où il aura déchiffré un vieux grimoire qui est absolument indéchiffrable !

— Jésus ! nous n'avons donc plus qu'à mourir de faim ! »

Je n'osai pas avouer qu'avec un homme aussi absolu que mon oncle, c'était un sort inévitable.

La vieille servante, sérieusement alarmée, retourna dans sa cuisine en gémissant.

Quand je fus seul, l'idée me vint d'aller tout conter à Graüben. Mais comment quitter la maison ? Le professeur pouvait rentrer d'un instant à l'autre. Et s'il m'appelait ? Et s'il voulait recommencer ce travail logogryphique, qu'on eût vainement proposé au vieil Œdipe ! Et si

je ne répondais pas à son appel, qu'adviendrait-il ?

Le plus sage était de rester. Justement, un minéralogiste de Besançon venait de nous adresser une collection de géodes siliceuses qu'il fallait classer. Je me mis au travail. Je triai, j'étiquetai, je disposai dans leur vitrine toutes ces pierres creuses au-dedans desquelles s'agitaient de petits cristaux.

Mais cette occupation ne m'absorbait pas. L'affaire du vieux document ne laissait point de me préoccuper étrangement. Ma tête bouillonnait, et je me sentais pris d'une vague inquiétude. J'avais le pressentiment d'une catastrophe prochaine.

Au bout d'une heure, mes géodes étaient étagées avec ordre. Je me laissai aller alors dans le grand fauteuil d'Utrecht, les bras ballants et la tête renversée. J'allumai ma pipe à long tuyau courbe, dont le fourneau sculpté représentait une naïade nonchalamment étendue; puis je m'amusai à suivre les progrès de la carbonisation, qui de ma naïade faisait peu à peu une négresse accomplie. De temps en temps j'écoutais si quelque pas retentissait dans l'escalier. Mais non. Où pouvait être mon oncle en ce moment ? Je me le figurais courant sous les beaux arbres de la route d'Altona, gesticulant, tirant au mur avec sa canne, d'un bras violent battant les herbes, décapitant les chardons et troublant dans leur repos les cigognes solitaires.

Rentrerait-il triomphant ou découragé ? Qui aurait raison l'un de l'autre, du secret ou de lui ?

Je m'interrogeais ainsi, et, machinalement, je pris entre mes doigts la feuille de papier sur laquelle s'allongeait l'incompréhensible série de lettres tracées par moi. Je me répétais :

« Qu'est-ce que cela signifie ? »

Je cherchai à grouper ces lettres de manière à former des mots. Impossible! Qu'on les réunît par deux, trois, ou cinq, ou six, cela ne donnait absolument rien d'intelligible. Il y avait bien les quatorzième, quinzième et seizième lettres qui faisaient le mot anglais « ice ». La quatre-vingt-quatrième, la quatre-vingt-cinquième et la quatre-vingt-sixième formaient le mot « sir ». Enfin, dans le corps du document, et à la troisième ligne, je remarquai aussi les mots latins « rota », « mutabile », « ira », « nec », « atra ».

« Diable, pensai-je, ces derniers mots sembleraient donner raison à mon oncle sur la langue du document! Et même, à la quatrième ligne, j'aperçois encore le mot « luco » qui se traduit par « bois sacré ». Il est vrai qu'à la troisième ligne, on lit le mot « tabiled » de tournure parfaitement hébraïque, et à la dernière les vocables « mer, », « arc », « mère », qui sont purement français. »

Il y avait là de quoi perdre la tête! Quatre idiomes différents dans cette phrase absurde! Quel rapport pouvait-il exister entre les mots « glace, monsieur, colère, cruel, bois sacré, changeant, mère, arc ou mer ? » Le premier et le dernier seuls se rapprochaient facilement : rien

d'étonnant que, dans un document écrit en Islande, il fût question d'une « mer de glace ». Mais de là à comprendre le reste du cryptogramme, c'était autre chose.

Je me débattais donc contre une insoluble difficulté ; mon cerveau s'échauffait, mes yeux clignaient sur la feuille de papier ; les cent trente-deux lettres semblaient voltiger autour de moi, comme ces larmes d'argent qui glissent dans l'air autour de notre tête, lorsque le sang s'y est violemment porté.

J'étais en proie à une sorte d'hallucination ; j'étouffais ; il me fallait de l'air. Machinalement, je m'éventai avec la feuille de papier, dont le verso et le recto se présentèrent successivement à mes regards.

Quelle fut ma surprise, quand dans l'une de ces voltes rapides, au moment où le verso se tournait vers moi, je crus voir apparaître des mots parfaitement lisibles, des mots latins, entre autres « craterêm » et « terrestre » !

Soudain une lueur se fit dans mon esprit ; ces seuls indices me firent entrevoir la vérité ; j'avais découvert la loi du chiffre. Pour comprendre ce document, il n'était pas même nécessaire de le lire à travers la feuille retournée ! Non. Tel il était, tel il m'avait été dicté, tel il pouvait être épelé couramment. Toutes les ingénieuses combinaisons du professeur se réalisaient. Il avait eu raison pour la disposition des lettres, raison pour la langue du document ! Il s'en était fallu

de « rien » qu'il pût lire d'un bout à l'autre cette phrase latine, et ce « rien », le hasard venait de me le donner !

On comprend si je fus ému ! Mes yeux se troublèrent. Je ne pouvais m'en servir. J'avais étalé la feuille de papier sur la table. Il me suffisait d'y jeter un regard pour devenir possesseur du secret.

Enfin je parvins à calmer mon agitation. Je m'imposai la loi de faire deux fois le tour de la chambre pour apaiser mes nerfs, et je revins m'engouffrer dans le vaste fauteuil.

« Lisons », m'écriai-je, après avoir refait dans mes poumons une ample provision d'air.

Je me penchai sur la table ; je posai mon doigt successivement sur chaque lettre, et, sans m'arrêter, sans hésiter un instant, je prononçai à haute voix la phrase entière.

Mais quelle stupéfaction, quelle terreur m'envahit ! Je restai d'abord comme frappé d'un coup subit. Quoi ! ce que je venais d'apprendre s'était accompli ! Un homme avait eu assez d'audace pour pénétrer !...

« Ah ! m'écriai-je en bondissant, mais non ! mais non ! mon oncle ne le saura pas ! Il ne manquerait plus qu'il vînt à connaître un semblable voyage ! Il voudrait en goûter aussi ! Rien ne pourrait l'arrêter ! Un géologue si déterminé ! Il partirait quand même, malgré tout, en dépit de tout ! et il m'emmènerait avec lui, et nous n'en reviendrions pas ! Jamais ! jamais ! »

J'étais dans une surexcitation difficile à peindre.

« Non ! non ! ce ne sera pas, dis-je avec énergie, et puisque je peux empêcher qu'une pareille idée vienne à l'esprit de mon tyran, je le ferai. A tourner et retourner ce document, il pourrait par hasard·en découvrir la clef ! Détruisons-le. »

Il y avait un reste de feu dans la cheminée. Je saisis non seulement la feuille de papier, mais le parchemin de Saknussemm ; d'une main fébrile j'allais précipiter le tout sur les charbons et anéantir ce dangereux secret, quand la porte du cabinet s'ouvrit. Mon oncle parut.

V

Je n'eus que le temps de replacer sur la table le malencontreux document.

Le professeur Lidenbrock paraissait profondément absorbé. Sa pensée dominante ne lui laissait pas un instant de répit ; il avait évidemment scruté, analysé l'affaire, mis en œuvre toutes les ressources de son imagination pendant sa promenade, et il revenait appliquer quelque combinaison nouvelle.

En effet, il s'assit dans son fauteuil, et, la plume à la main, il commença à établir des formules qui ressemblaient à un calcul algébrique.

Je suivais du regard sa main frémissante ; je

ne perdais pas un seul de ses mouvements. Quelque résultat inespéré allait-il donc inopinément se produire ? Je tremblais, et sans raison, puisque la vraie combinaison, la « seule », étant déjà trouvée, toute autre recherche devenait forcément vaine.

Pendant trois longues heures, mon oncle travailla sans parler, sans lever la tête, effaçant, reprenant, raturant, recommençant mille fois.

Je savais bien que, s'il parvenait à arranger ces lettres suivant toutes les positions relatives qu'elles pouvaient occuper, la phrase se trouverait faite. Mais je savais aussi que vingt lettres seulement peuvent former deux quintillions, quatre cent trente-deux quatrillions, neuf cent deux trillions, huit milliards, cent soixante-seize millions, six cent quarante mille combinaisons. Or; il y avait cent trente-deux lettres dans la phrase, et ces cent trente-deux lettres donnaient un nombre de phrases différentes composé de cent trente-trois chiffres au moins, nombre presque impossible à énumérer et qui échappe à toute appréciation.

J'étais rassuré sur ce moyen héroïque de résoudre le problème.

Cependant le temps s'écoulait ; la nuit se fit ; les bruits de la rue s'apaisèrent ; mon oncle, toujours courbé sur sa tâche, ne vit rien, pas même la bonne Marthe qui entrouvrit la porte ; il n'entendit rien, pas même la voix de cette digne servante, disant :

« Monsieur soupera-t-il ce soir ? »

Aussi Marthe dut-elle s'en aller sans réponse. Pour moi, après avoir résisté pendant quelque temps, je fus pris d'un invincible sommeil, et je m'endormis sur un bout du canapé, tandis que mon oncle Lidenbrock calculait et raturait toujours.

Quand je me réveillai, le lendemain, l'infatigable piocheur était encore au travail. Ses yeux rouges, son teint blafard, ses cheveux entremêlés sous sa main fiévreuse, ses pommettes empourprées indiquaient assez sa lutte terrible avec l'impossible, et dans quelles fatigues de l'esprit, dans quelle contention du cerveau les heures durent s'écouler pour lui.

Vraiment, il me fit pitié. Malgré les reproches que je croyais être en droit de lui faire, une certaine émotion me gagnait. Le pauvre homme était tellement possédé de son idée, qu'il oubliait de se mettre en colère. Toutes ses forces vives se concentraient en un seul point, et, comme elles ne s'échappaient pas par leur exutoire ordinaire, on pouvait craindre que leur tension ne le fît éclater d'un instant à l'autre.

Je pouvais d'un geste desserrer cet étau de fer qui lui serrait le crâne, d'un mot seulement ! et je n'en fis rien.

Cependant j'avais bon cœur. Pourquoi restai-je muet en pareille circonstance ? Dans l'intérêt même de mon oncle.

« Non, non, répétai-je, non, je ne parlerai pas ! Il voudrait y aller, je le connais ; rien ne saurait l'arrêter. C'est une imagination volcanique,

et, pour faire ce que d'autres géologues n'ont point fait, il risquerait sa vie. Je me tairai; je garderai ce secret dont le hasard m'a rendu maître! Le découvrir, ce serait tuer le professeur Lidenbrock! Qu'il le devine, s'il le peut. Je ne veux pas me reprocher un jour de l'avoir conduit à sa perte! »

Ceci résolu, je me croisai les bras, et j'attendis. Mais j'avais compté sans un incident qui se produisit à quelques heures de là.

Lorsque la bonne Marthe voulut sortir de la maison pour se rendre au marché, elle trouva la porte close. La grosse clef manquait à la serrure. Qui l'avait ôtée? Mon oncle évidemment, quand il rentra la veille après son excursion précipitée.

Était-ce à dessein? Était-ce par mégarde? Voulait-il nous soumettre aux rigueurs de la faim? Cela m'eût paru un peu fort. Quoi! Marthe et moi, nous serions victimes d'une situation qui ne nous regardait pas le moins du monde? Sans doute, et je me souvins d'un précédent de nature à nous effrayer. En effet, il y a quelques années, à une époque où mon oncle travaillait à sa grande classification minéralogique, il demeura quarante-huit heures sans manger, et toute sa maison dut se conformer à cette diète scientifique. Pour mon compte, j'y gagnai des crampes d'estomac fort peu récréatives chez un garçon d'un naturel assez vorace.

Or, il me parut que le déjeuner allait faire défaut comme le souper de la veille. Cependant je résolus

Je me croisai les bras et j'attendis (p. 35).

d'être héroïque et de ne pas céder devant les exigences de la faim. Marthe prenait cela très au sérieux et se désolait, la bonne femme. Quant à moi, l'impossibilité de quitter la maison me préoccupait davantage et pour cause. On me comprend bien.

Mon oncle travaillait toujours ; son imagination se perdait dans le monde des combinaisons ; il vivait loin de la terre, et véritablement en dehors des besoins terrestres.

Vers midi, la faim m'aiguillonna sérieusement. Marthe, très innocemment, avait dévoré la veille les provisions du garde-manger ; il ne restait plus rien à la maison. Cependant je tins bon. J'y mettais une sorte de point d'honneur.

Deux heures sonnèrent. Cela devenait ridicule, intolérable même. J'ouvrais des yeux démesurés. Je commençai à me dire que j'exagérais l'importance du document ; que mon oncle n'y ajouterait pas foi ; qu'il verrait là une simple mystification ; qu'au pis aller on le retiendrait malgré lui, s'il voulait tenter l'aventure ; qu'enfin il pouvait découvrir lui-même la clef du « chiffre », et que j'en serais alors pour mes frais d'abstinence.

Ces raisons me parurent excellentes, que j'eusse rejetées la veille avec indignation ; je trouvai même parfaitement absurde d'avoir attendu si longtemps, et mon parti fut pris de tout dire.

Je cherchais donc une entrée en matière, pas trop brusque, quand le professeur se leva, mit son chapeau et se prépara à sortir.

Quoi! quitter la maison, et nous enfermer encore! Jamais.

« Mon oncle! » dis-je.

Il ne parut pas m'entendre.

« Mon oncle Lidenbrock? répétai-je en élevant la voix.

— Hein? fit-il comme un homme subitement réveillé.

— Eh bien! cette clef?

— Quelle clef? La clef de la porte?

— Mais non, m'écriai-je, la clef du document! »

Le professeur me regarda par-dessus ses lunettes; il remarqua sans doute quelque chose d'insolite dans ma physionomie, car il me saisit vivement le bras, et, sans pouvoir parler, il m'interrogea du regard. Cependant, jamais demande ne fut formulée d'une façon plus nette.

Je remuai la tête de haut en bas.

Il secoua la sienne avec une sorte de pitié, comme s'il avait affaire à un fou.

Je fis un geste plus affirmatif.

Ses yeux brillèrent d'un vif éclat; sa main devint menaçante.

Cette conversation muette dans ces circonstances eût intéressé le spectateur le plus indifférent. Et vraiment j'en arrivais à ne plus oser parler, tant je craignais que mon oncle ne m'étouffât dans les premiers embrassements de sa joie. Mais il devint si pressant qu'il fallut répondre.

« Oui, cette clef!... le hasard!...

— Que dis-tu? s'écria-t-il avec une indescriptible émotion.

— Tenez, dis-je en lui présentant la feuille de papier sur laquelle j'avais écrit, lisez.

— Mais cela ne signifie rien! répondit-il en froissant la feuille.

— Rien, en commençant à lire par le commencement, mais par la fin... »

Je n'avais pas achevé ma phrase que le professeur poussait un cri, mieux qu'un cri, un véritable rugissement! Une révélation venait de se faire dans son esprit. Il était transfiguré.

« Ah! ingénieux Saknussemm! s'écria-t-il, tu avais donc d'abord écrit ta phrase à l'envers? »

Et se précipitant sur la feuille de papier, l'œil trouble, la voix émue, il lut le document tout entier, en remontant de la dernière lettre à la première.

Il était conçu en ces termes :

> *In Sneffels Yoculis craterem kem delibat*
> *umbra Scartaris Julii intra calendas descende,*
> *audas viator, et terrestre centrum attinges.*
> *Kod feci. Arne Saknussemm.*

Ce qui, de ce mauvais latin, peut être traduit ainsi :

> *Descends dans le cratère du Yocul de*
> *Sneffels que l'ombre du Scartaris vient*
> *caresser avant les calendes de Juillet,*
> *voyageur audacieux, et tu parviendras*
> *au centre de la Terre. Ce que j'ai fait.*
> *Arne Saknussemm.*

Mon oncle, à cette lecture, bondit comme s'il eût inopinément touché une bouteille de Leyde. Il était magnifique d'audace, de joie et de conviction. Il allait et venait; il prenait sa tête à deux mains; il déplaçait les sièges; il empilait ses livres; il jonglait, c'est à ne pas le croire, avec ses précieuses géodes; il lançait un coup de poing par-ci, une tape par-là. Enfin ses nerfs se calmèrent et, comme un homme épuisé par une trop grande dépense de fluide, il retomba dans son fauteuil.

« Quelle heure est-il donc? demanda-t-il après quelques instants de silence.

— Trois heures, répondis-je.

— Tiens! mon dîner a passé vite. Je meurs de faim. A table. Puis ensuite...

— Ensuite?

— Tu feras ma malle.

— Hein! m'écriai-je.

— Et la tienne!» répondit l'impitoyable professeur en entrant dans la salle à manger.

VI

A CES paroles un frisson me passa par tout le corps. Cependant je me contins. Je résolus même de faire bonne figure. Des arguments scientifiques pouvaient seuls arrêter le professeur Lidenbrock. Or, il y en avait, et de bons, contre la possibilité

d'un pareil voyage. Aller au centre de la terre!
Quelle folie! Je réservai ma dialectique pour le
moment opportun, et je m'occupai du repas.

Inutile de rapporter les imprécations de mon
oncle devant la table desservie. Tout s'expliqua.
La liberté fut rendue à la bonne Marthe. Elle
courut au marché et fit si bien, qu'une heure
après, ma faim était calmée, et je revenais au
sentiment de la situation.

Pendant le repas, mon oncle fut presque gai;
il lui échappait de ces plaisanteries de savant
qui ne sont jamais bien dangereuses. Après le
dessert, il me fit signe de le suivre dans son cabinet.

J'obéis. Il s'assit à un bout de sa table de travail,
moi à l'autre.

« Axel, dit-il d'une voix assez douce, tu es
un garçon très ingénieux; tu m'as rendu là un
fier service, quand, de guerre lasse, j'allais abandonner cette combinaison. Où me serais-je égaré ?
Nul ne peut le savoir! Je n'oublierai jamais cela,
mon garçon, et de la gloire que nous allons acquérir
tu auras ta part. »

« Allons! pensai-je, il est de bonne humeur;
le moment est venu de discuter cette gloire. »

« Avant tout, reprit mon oncle, je te recommande
le secret le plus absolu, tu m'entends ? Je ne
manque pas d'envieux dans le monde des savants,
et beaucoup voudraient entreprendre ce voyage,
qui ne s'en douteront qu'à notre retour.

— Croyez-vous, dis-je, que le nombre de ces
audacieux fût si grand?

— Certes! qui hésiterait à conquérir une telle renommée? Si ce document était connu, une armée entière de géologues se précipiterait sur les traces d'Arne Saknussemm!

— Voilà ce dont je ne suis pas persuadé, mon oncle, car rien ne prouve l'authenticité de ce document.

— Comment! Et le livre dans lequel nous l'avons découvert!

— Bon! j'accorde que ce Saknussemm ait écrit ces lignes, mais s'ensuit-il qu'il ait réellement accompli ce voyage, et ce vieux parchemin ne peut-il renfermer une mystification? »

Ce dernier mot, un peu hasardé, je regrettai presque de l'avoir prononcé. Le professeur fronça son épais sourcil, et je craignais d'avoir compromis les suites de cette conversation. Heureusement il n'en fut rien. Mon sévère interlocuteur ébaucha une sorte de sourire sur ses lèvres, et répondit :

« C'est ce que nous verrons.

— Ah! fis-je un peu vexé; mais permettez-moi d'épuiser la série des objections relatives à ce document.

— Parle, mon garçon, ne te gêne pas. Je te laisse toute liberté d'exprimer ton opinion. Tu n'es plus mon neveu, mais mon collègue. Ainsi, va.

— Eh bien, je vous demanderai d'abord ce que sont ce Yocul, ce Sneffels et ce Scartaris, dont je n'ai jamais entendu parler?

— Rien n'est plus facile. J'ai précisément

reçu, il y a quelque temps, une carte de mon ami Augustus Peterman de Leipzig; elle ne pouvait arriver plus à propos. Prends le troisième atlas dans la seconde travée de la grande bibliothèque, série Z, planche 4.»

Je me levai, et, grâce à ces indications précises, je trouvai rapidement l'atlas demandé. Mon oncle l'ouvrit et dit :

« Voici une des meilleures cartes de l'Islande, celle de Handerson, et je crois qu'elle va nous donner la solution de toutes tes difficultés. »

Je me penchai sur la carte.

« Vois cette île composée de volcans, dit le professeur, et remarque qu'ils portent tous le nom de Yokul. Ce mot veut dire « glacier » en islandais, et, sous la latitude élevée de l'Islande, la plupart des éruptions se font jour à travers les couches de glace. De là cette dénomination de Yokul appliquée à tous les monts ignivomes de l'île.

— Bien, répondis-je; mais qu'est-ce que le Sneffels ? »

J'espérais qu'à cette demande il n'y aurait pas de réponse. Je me trompais. Mon oncle reprit :

« Suis-moi sur la côte occidentale de l'Islande. Aperçois-tu Reykjawik, sa capitale ? Oui. Bien. Remonte les fjörds innombrables de ces rivages rongés par la mer, et arrête-toi un peu au-dessous du soixante-cinquième degré de latitude. Que vois-tu là ?

Je me penchai sur la carte (p. 43).

— Une sorte de presqu'île semblable à un os décharné, que termine une énorme rotule.

— La comparaison est juste, mon garçon; maintenant, n'aperçois-tu rien sur cette rotule?

— Si, un mont qui semble avoir poussé en mer.

— Bon! c'est le Sneffels.

— Le Sneffels?

— Lui-même, une montagne haute de cinq mille pieds, l'une des plus remarquables de l'île, et à coup sûr la plus célèbre du monde entier, si son cratère aboutit au centre du globe.

— Mais c'est impossible! m'écriai-je, haussant les épaules et révolté contre une pareille supposition.

— Impossible! répondit le professeur Lidenbrock d'un ton sévère. Et pourquoi cela?

— Parce que ce cratère est évidemment obstrué par les laves, les roches brûlantes, et qu'alors...

— Et si c'est un cratère éteint?

— Éteint?

— Oui. Le nombre des volcans en activité à la surface du globe n'est actuellement que de trois cents environ; mais il existe une bien plus grande quantité de volcans éteints. Or, le Sneffels compte parmi ces derniers, et, depuis les temps historiques, il n'a eu qu'une seule éruption, celle de 1219; à partir de cette époque, ses rumeurs se sont apaisées peu à peu, et il n'est plus au nombre des volcans actifs. »

A ces affirmations positives je n'avais absolument rien à répondre; je me rejetai donc sur les

autres obscurités que renfermait le document.

« Que signifie ce mot Scartaris, demandai-je, et que viennent faire là les calendes de juillet ? »

Mon oncle prit quelques moments de réflexion. J'eus un instant d'espoir, mais un seul, car bientôt il me répondit en ces termes :

« Ce que tu appelles obscurité est pour moi lumière. Cela prouve les soins ingénieux avec lesquels Saknussemm a voulu préciser sa découverte. Le Sneffels est formé de plusieurs cratères ; il y avait donc nécessité d'indiquer celui d'entre eux qui mène au centre du globe. Qu'a fait le savant Islandais ? Il a remarqué qu'aux approches des calendes de juillet, c'est-à-dire vers les derniers jours du mois de juin, un des pics de la montagne, le Scartaris, projetait son ombre jusqu'à l'ouverture du cratère en question, et il a consigné le fait dans son document. Pouvait-il imaginer une indication plus exacte, et, une fois arrivés au sommet du Sneffels, nous sera-t-il possible d'hésiter sur le chemin à prendre ? »

Décidément mon oncle avait réponse à tout. Je vis bien qu'il était inattaquable sur les mots du vieux parchemin. Je cessai donc de le presser à ce sujet, et, comme il fallait le convaincre avant tout, je passai aux objections scientifiques, bien autrement graves, à mon avis.

« Allons, dis-je, je suis forcé d'en convenir, la phrase de Saknussemm est claire et ne peut laisser aucun doute à l'esprit. J'accorde même que le document a un air de parfaite authenticité.

Ce savant est allé au fond du Sneffels; il a vu l'ombre du Scartaris caresser les bords du cratère avant les calendes de juillet; il a même entendu raconter dans les récits légendaires de son temps que ce cratère aboutissait au centre de la terre; mais quant à y être parvenu lui-même, quant à avoir fait le voyage et à en être revenu, s'il l'a entrepris, non, cent fois non!

— Et la raison? dit mon oncle d'un ton singulièrement moqueur.

— C'est que toutes les théories de la science démontrent qu'une pareille entreprise est impraticable!

— Toutes les théories disent cela? répondit le professeur en prenant un air bonhomme. Ah! les vilaines théories! Comme elles vont nous gêner, ces pauvres théories! »

Je vis qu'il se moquait de moi, mais je continuai néanmoins :

« Oui! il est parfaitement reconnu que la chaleur augmente environ d'un degré par soixante-dix pieds de profondeur au-dessous de la surface du globe; or, en admettant cette proportionnalité constante, le rayon terrestre étant de quinze cents lieues, il existe au centre une température qui dépasse deux cent mille degrés. Les matières de l'intérieur de la terre se trouvent donc à l'état de gaz incandescent, car les métaux, l'or, le platine, les roches les plus dures, ne résistent pas à une pareille chaleur. J'ai donc le droit de demander s'il est possible de pénétrer dans un semblable milieu!

— Ainsi, Axel, c'est la chaleur qui t'embarrasse ?

— Sans doute. Si nous arrivions à une profondeur de dix lieues seulement, nous serions parvenus à la limite de l'écorce terrestre, car déjà la température est supérieure à treize cents degrés.

— Et tu as peur d'entrer en fusion ?

— Je vous laisse la question à décider, répondis-je avec humeur.

— Voici ce que je décide, répliqua le professeur Lidenbrock en prenant ses grands airs : c'est que ni toi ni personne ne sait d'une façon certaine ce qui se passe à l'intérieur du globe, attendu qu'on connaît à peine la douze-millième partie de son rayon ; c'est que la science est éminemment perfectible, et que chaque théorie est incessamment détruite par une théorie nouvelle. N'a-t-on pas cru jusqu'à Fourier que la température des espaces planétaires allait toujours diminuant, et ne sait-on pas aujourd'hui que les plus grands froids des régions éthérées ne dépassent pas quarante ou cinquante degrés au-dessous de zéro ? Pourquoi n'en serait-il pas ainsi de la chaleur interne ? Pourquoi, à une certaine profondeur, n'atteindrait-elle pas une limite infranchissable, au lieu de s'élever jusqu'au degré de fusion des minéraux les plus réfractaires ? »

Mon oncle plaçant la question sur le terrain des hypothèses, je n'eus rien à répondre.

« Eh bien, je te dirai que de véritables savants, Poisson entre autres, ont prouvé que, si une cha-

leur de deux cent mille degrés existait à l'intérieur
du globe, les gaz incandescents provenant des
matières fondues acquerraient une élasticité telle
que l'écorce terrestre ne pourrait y résister et
éclaterait comme les parois d'une chaudière
sous l'effort de la vapeur.

— C'est l'avis de Poisson, mon oncle, voilà tout.

— D'accord, mais c'est aussi l'avis d'autres
géologues distingués, que l'intérieur du globe
n'est formé ni de gaz, ni d'eau, ni des plus lourdes
pierres que nous connaissions, car, dans ce cas,
la terre aurait un poids deux fois moindre.

— Oh! avec les chiffres on prouve tout ce
qu'on veut!

— Et avec les faits, mon garçon, en est-il de
même? N'est-il pas constant que le nombre des
volcans a considérablement diminué depuis les
premiers jours du monde? et, si chaleur centrale
il y a, ne peut-on en conclure qu'elle tend à
s'affaiblir?

— Mon oncle, si vous entrez dans le champ
des suppositions, je n'ai plus à discuter.

— Et moi j'ai à dire qu'à mon opinion se joi-
gnent les opinions de gens fort compétents.
Te souviens-tu d'une visite que me fit le célèbre
chimiste anglais Humphry Davy en 1825?

— Aucunement, car je ne suis venu au monde
que dix-neuf ans après.

— Eh bien, Humphry Davy vint me voir à son
passage à Hambourg. Nous discutâmes longtemps,
entre autres questions, l'hypothèse de la liquidité

du noyau intérieur de la terre. Nous étions tous deux d'accord que cette liquidité ne pouvait exister, par une raison à laquelle la science n'a jamais trouvé de réponse.

— Et laquelle? dis-je un peu étonné.

— C'est que cette masse liquide serait sujette, comme l'Océan, à l'attraction de la lune, et conséquemment, deux fois par jour, il se produirait des marées intérieures qui, soulevant l'écorce terrestre, donneraient lieu à des tremblements de terre périodiques!

— Mais il est pourtant évident que la surface du globe a été soumise à la combustion, et il est permis de supposer que la croûte extérieure s'est refroidie d'abord, tandis que la chaleur se réfugiait au centre.

— Erreur, répondit mon oncle; la terre a été échauffée par la combustion de sa surface, non autrement. Sa surface était composée d'une grande quantité de métaux, tels que le potassium, le sodium, qui ont la propriété de s'enflammer au seul contact de l'air et de l'eau; ces métaux prirent feu quand les vapeurs atmosphériques se précipitèrent en pluie sur le sol; et peu à peu, lorsque les eaux pénétrèrent dans les fissures de l'écorce terrestre, elles déterminèrent de nouveaux incendies avec explosions et éruptions. De là les volcans si nombreux aux premiers jours du monde.

— Mais voilà une ingénieuse hypothèse! m'écriai-je un peu malgré moi.

— Et qu'Humphry Davy me rendit sensible,

ici même, par une expérience bien simple. Il composa une boule métallique faite principalement des métaux dont je viens de parler, et qui figurait parfaitement notre globe ; lorsqu'on faisait tomber une fine rosée à sa surface, celle-ci se boursouflait, s'oxydait et formait une petite montagne ; un cratère s'ouvrait à son sommet ; l'éruption avait lieu et communiquait à toute la boule une chaleur telle qu'il devenait impossible de la tenir à la main. »

Vraiment, je commençais à être ébranlé par les arguments du professeur ; il les faisait valoir, d'ailleurs, avec sa passion et son enthousiasme habituels.

« Tu le vois, Axel, ajouta-t-il, l'état du noyau central a soulevé des hypothèses diverses entre les géologues ; rien de moins prouvé que ce fait d'une chaleur interne ; suivant moi, elle n'existe pas, elle ne saurait exister ; nous le verrons, d'ailleurs, et, comme Arne Saknussemm, nous saurons à quoi nous en tenir sur cette grande question.

— Eh bien oui ! répondis-je, me sentant gagner à cet enthousiasme, oui, nous le verrons, si on y voit, toutefois.

— Et pourquoi pas ? Ne pouvons-nous compter sur des phénomènes électriques pour nous éclairer, et même sur l'atmosphère, que sa pression peut rendre lumineuse en s'approchant du centre ?

— Oui, dis-je, oui ! cela est possible, après tout.

— Cela est certain, répondit triomphalement

Je gagnai donc les bords de l'Elbe (p. 53).

mon oncle; mais silence, entends-tu? silence sur tout ceci, et que personne n'ait l'idée de découvrir avant nous le centre de la terre. »

VII

Ainsi se termina cette mémorable séance. Cet entretien me donna la fièvre. Je sortis du cabinet de mon oncle comme étourdi, et il n'y avait pas assez d'air dans les rues de Hambourg pour me remettre. Je gagnai donc les bords de l'Elbe, du côté du bac à vapeur qui met la ville en communication avec le chemin de fer de Harbourg.

Étais-je convaincu de ce que je venais d'apprendre? N'avais-je pas subi la domination du professeur Lidenbrock? Devais-je prendre au sérieux sa résolution d'aller au centre du massif terrestre? Venais-je d'entendre les spéculations insensées d'un fou ou les déductions scientifiques d'un grand génie? En tout cela, où s'arrêtait la vérité, où commençait l'erreur?

Je flottais entre mille hypothèses contradictoires, sans pouvoir m'accrocher à aucune.

Cependant je me rappelais avoir été convaincu, quoique mon enthousiasme commençât à se modérer; mais j'aurais voulu partir immédiatement et ne pas prendre le temps de la réflexion. Oui,

le courage ne m'eût pas manqué pour boucler
ma valise en ce moment.

Il faut pourtant l'avouer, une heure après
cette surexcitation tomba; mes nerfs se déten-
dirent, et des profonds abîmes de la terre je
remontai à sa surface.

« C'est absurde! m'écriai-je; cela n'a pas le sens
commun! Ce n'est pas une proposition sérieuse
à faire à un garçon sensé. Rien de tout cela n'existe.
J'ai mal dormi, j'ai fait un mauvais rêve. »

Cependant j'avais suivi les bords de l'Elbe
et tourné la ville. Après avoir remonté le port
j'étais arrivé à la route d'Altona. Un pressentiment
me conduisait, pressentiment justifié, car j'aperçus
bientôt ma petite Graüben qui, de son pied leste,
revenait bravement à Hambourg.

« Graüben! » lui criai-je de loin.

La jeune fille s'arrêta, un peu troublée, j'imagine,
de s'entendre appeler ainsi sur une grande route.
En dix pas je fus près d'elle.

« Axel! fit-elle surprise. Ah! tu es venu à ma
rencontre! C'est bien cela, monsieur. »

Mais, me regardant, Graüben ne put se méprendre à mon air inquiet, bouleversé.

« Qu'as-tu donc? dit-elle en me tendant la
main.

— Ce que j'ai, Graüben! » m'écriai-je.

En deux secondes et en trois phrases ma jolie
Virlandaise était au courant de la situation. Pendant quelques instants elle garda le silence. Son
cœur palpitait-il à l'égal du mien? Je l'ignore,

mais sa main ne tremblait pas dans la mienne. Nous fîmes une centaine de pas sans parler.

« Axel ! me dit-elle enfin.

— Ma chère Graüben !

— Ce sera là un beau voyage. »

Je bondis à ces mots.

« Oui, Axel, un voyage digne du neveu d'un savant. Il est bien qu'un homme se soit distingué par quelque grande entreprise !

— Quoi ! Graüben, tu ne me détournes pas de tenter une pareille expédition ?

— Non, cher Axel, et ton oncle et toi, je vous accompagnerais volontiers, si une pauvre fille ne devait être un embarras pour vous.

— Dis-tu vrai ?

— Je dis vrai. »

Ah ! femmes, jeunes filles, cœurs féminins toujours incompréhensibles ! Quand vous n'êtes pas les plus timides des êtres, vous en êtes les plus braves ! La raison n'a que faire auprès de vous. Quoi ! cette enfant m'encourageait à prendre part à cette expédition ! elle n'eût pas craint de tenter l'aventure ! Elle m'y poussait, moi qu'elle aimait cependant !

J'étais déconcerté, et, pourquoi ne pas le dire, honteux.

« Graüben, repris-je, nous verrons si demain tu parleras de cette manière.

— Demain, cher Axel, je parlerai comme aujourd'hui. »

Graüben et moi, nous tenant par la main, mais

Je trouvai mon oncle criant et s'agitant (p. 57).

gardant un profond silence, nous continuâmes notre chemin. J'étais brisé par les émotions de la journée.

« Après tout, pensai-je, les calendes de juillet sont encore loin, et, d'ici là, bien des événements se passeront qui guériront mon oncle de sa manie de voyager sous terre. »

La nuit était venue quand nous arrivâmes à la maison de Königstrasse. Je m'attendais à trouver la demeure tranquille, mon oncle couché suivant son habitude, et la bonne Marthe donnant à la salle à manger le dernier coup de plumeau du soir.

Mais j'avais compté sans l'impatience du professeur. Je le trouvai criant, s'agitant au milieu d'une troupe de porteurs qui déchargeaient certaines marchandises dans l'allée; la vieille servante ne savait où donner de la tête.

« Mais viens donc, Axel; hâte-toi donc, malheureux! s'écria mon oncle du plus loin qu'il m'aperçut. Et ta malle qui n'est pas faite, et mes papiers qui ne sont pas en ordre, et mon sac de voyage dont je ne trouve pas la clef, et mes guêtres qui n'arrivent pas! »

Je demeurai stupéfait. La voix me manquait. C'est à peine si mes lèvres purent articuler ces mots :

« Nous partons donc ?

— Oui, malheureux garçon, qui vas te promener au lieu d'être là!

— Nous partons ? répétai-je d'une voix affaiblie.

— Oui, après-demain matin, à la première heure. »

Je ne pus en entendre davantage, et je m'enfuis dans ma petite chambre.

Il n'y avait plus à en douter. Mon oncle venait d'employer son après-midi à se procurer une partie des objets et ustensiles nécessaires à son voyage ; l'allée était encombrée d'échelles de corde, de cordes à nœuds, de torches, de gourdes, de crampons de fer, de pics, de bâtons ferrés, de pioches, de quoi charger dix hommes au moins.

Je passai une nuit affreuse. Le lendemain, je m'entendis appeler de bonne heure. J'étais décidé à ne pas ouvrir ma porte. Mais le moyen de résister à la douce voix qui prononçait ces mots : « Mon cher Axel » ?

Je sortis de ma chambre. Je pensai que mon air défait, ma pâleur, mes yeux rougis par l'insomnie, allaient produire leur effet sur Graüben et changer ses idées.

« Ah ! mon cher Axel, me dit-elle, je vois que tu te portes mieux et que la nuit t'a calmé.

— Calmé ! » m'écriai-je.

Je me précipitai vers mon miroir. Eh bien ! j'avais moins mauvaise mine que je ne le supposais. C'était à n'y pas croire.

« Axel, me dit Graüben, j'ai longtemps causé avec mon tuteur. C'est un hardi savant, un homme de grand courage, et tu te souviendras que son sang coule dans tes veines. Il m'a raconté ses projets, ses espérances, pourquoi et comment il espère

atteindre son but. Il y parviendra, je n'en doute pas. Ah! cher Axel, c'est beau de se dévouer ainsi à la science! Quelle gloire attend M. Lidenbrock et rejaillira sur son compagnon! Au retour, Axel, tu seras un homme, son égal, libre de parler, libre d'agir, libre enfin de... »

La jeune fille, rougissante, n'acheva pas. Ses paroles me ranimaient. Cependant je ne voulais pas croire encore à notre départ. J'entraînai Graüben vers le cabinet du professeur.

« Mon oncle, dis-je, il est donc bien décidé que nous partons?

— Comment! tu en doutes?

— Non, dis-je afin de ne pas le contrarier. Seulement je vous demanderai ce qui nous presse.

— Mais le temps! le temps qui fuit avec une vitesse irréparable!

— Cependant nous ne sommes qu'au 26 mai, et jusqu'à la fin de juin...

— Eh! crois-tu donc, ignorant, qu'on se rende si facilement en Islande? Si tu ne m'avais pas quitté comme un fou, je t'aurais emmené au Bureau-office de Copenhague, chez Liffender et Co. Là, tu aurais vu que de Copenhague à Reykjawik il n'y a qu'un service, le 22 de chaque mois.

— Eh bien?

— Eh bien! si nous attendions au 22 juin, nous arriverions trop tard pour voir l'ombre du Scartaris caresser le cratère du Sneffels! Il faut donc gagner Copenhague au plus vite pour y chercher un moyen de transport. Va faire ta malle! »

Il n'y avait pas un mot à répondre. Je remontai dans ma chambre. Graüben me suivit. Ce fut elle qui se chargea de mettre en ordre, dans une petite valise, les objets nécessaires à mon voyage. Elle n'était pas plus émue que s'il se fût agi d'une promenade à Lubeck ou à Heligoland. Ses petites mains allaient et venaient sans précipitation. Elle causait avec calme. Elle me donnait les raisons les plus sensées en faveur de notre expédition. Elle m'enchantait, et je me sentais une grosse colère contre elle. Quelquefois je voulais m'emporter, mais elle n'y prenait garde et continuait méthodiquement sa tranquille besogne.

Enfin la dernière courroie de la valise fut bouclée. Je descendis au rez-de-chaussée.

Pendant cette journée, les fournisseurs d'instruments de physique, d'armes, d'appareils électriques, s'étaient multipliés. La bonne Marthe en perdait la tête.

« Est-ce que monsieur est fou ? » me dit-elle.

Je fis un signe affirmatif.

« Et il vous emmène avec lui ? »

Même affirmation.

« Où cela ? » dit-elle.

J'indiquai du doigt le centre de la terre.

« A la cave ? s'écria la vieille servante.

— Non, dis-je enfin, plus bas ! »

Le soir arriva. Je n'avais plus conscience du temps écoulé.

« A demain matin, dit mon oncle, nous partons à six heures précises. »

A dix heures je tombai sur mon lit comme une masse inerte.

Pendant la nuit mes terreurs me reprirent. Je la passai à rêver de gouffres! J'étais en proie au délire. Je me sentais étreint par la main vigoureuse du professeur, entraîné, abîmé, enlisé! Je tombais au fond d'insondables précipices avec cette vitesse croissante des corps abandonnés dans l'espace. Ma vie n'était plus qu'une chute interminable.

Je me réveillai à cinq heures, brisé de fatigue et d'émotion. Je descendis à la salle à manger. Mon oncle était à table. Il dévorait. Je le regardai avec un sentiment d'horreur. Mais Graüben était là. Je ne dis rien. Je ne pus manger.

A cinq heures et demie, un roulement se fit entendre dans la rue. Une large voiture arrivait pour nous conduire au chemin de fer d'Altona. Elle fut bientôt encombrée des colis de mon oncle.

« Et ta malle? me dit-il.

— Elle est prête, répondis-je en défaillant.

— Dépêche-toi donc de la descendre, ou tu vas nous faire manquer le train! »

Lutter contre ma destinée me parut alors impossible. Je remontai dans ma chambre, et, laissant glisser ma valise sur les marches de l'escalier, je m'élançai à sa suite.

En ce moment mon oncle remettait solennellement entre les mains de Graüben « les rênes » de sa maison. Ma jolie Virlandaise conservait

Marthe et la jeune fille nous adressèrent un dernier adieu (p. 63).

son calme habituel. Elle embrassa son tuteur, mais elle ne put retenir une larme en effleurant ma joue de ses douces lèvres.

« Graüben ! m'écriai-je.

— Va, mon cher Axel, va, me dit-elle, tu quittes ta fiancée, mais tu trouveras ta femme au retour. »

Je serrai Graüben dans mes bras, et je pris place dans la voiture. Marthe et la jeune fille, du seuil de la porte, nous adressèrent un dernier adieu. Puis les deux chevaux, excités par le sifflement de leur conducteur, s'élancèrent au galop sur la route d'Altona.

VIII

Altona, véritable banlieue de Hambourg, est tête de ligne du chemin de fer de Kiel, qui devait nous conduire au rivage des Belt. En moins de vingt minutes, nous entrions sur le territoire du Holstein.

A six heures et demie la voiture s'arrêta devant la gare ; les nombreux colis de mon oncle, ses volumineux articles de voyage furent déchargés, transportés, pesés, étiquetés, rechargés dans le wagon de bagages, et à sept heures nous étions assis l'un vis-à-vis de l'autre dans le même compartiment. La vapeur siffla, la locomotive se mit en mouvement. Nous étions partis.

Étais-je résigné? Pas encore. Cependant l'air frais du matin, les détails de la route rapidement renouvelés par la vitesse du train me distrayaient de ma grande préoccupation.

Quant à la pensée du professeur, elle devançait évidemment ce convoi trop lent au gré de son impatience. Nous étions seuls dans le wagon, mais sans parler. Mon oncle revisitait ses poches et son sac de voyage avec une minutieuse attention. Je vis bien que rien ne lui manquait des pièces nécessaires à l'exécution de ses projets.

Entre autres, une feuille de papier, pliée avec soin, portait l'en-tête de la chancellerie danoise, avec la signature de M. Christiensen, consul à Hambourg et l'ami du professeur. Cela devait nous donner toute facilité d'obtenir à Copenhague des recommandations pour le gouverneur de l'Islande.

J'aperçus aussi le fameux document précieusement enfoui dans la plus secrète poche du portefeuille. Je le maudis du fond du cœur, et je me remis à examiner le pays. C'était une vaste suite de plaines peu curieuses, monotones, limoneuses et assez fécondes : une campagne très favorable à l'établissement d'un railway et propice à ces lignes droites si chères aux compagnies de chemin de fer.

Mais cette monotonie n'eut pas le temps de me fatiguer, car, trois heures après notre départ, le train s'arrêtait à Kiel, à deux pas de la mer.

Nos bagages étant enregistrés pour Copenhague,

il n'y eut pas à s'en occuper. Cependant le professeur les suivit d'un œil inquiet pendant leur transport au bateau à vapeur. Là ils disparurent à fond de cale.

Mon oncle, dans sa précipitation, avait si bien calculé les heures de correspondance du chemin de fer et du bateau, qu'il nous restait une journée entière à perdre. Le steamer l'*Ellenora* ne partait pas avant la nuit. De là une fièvre de neuf heures, pendant laquelle l'irascible voyageur envoya à tous les diables l'administration des bateaux et des railways et les gouvernements qui toléraient de pareils abus. Je dus faire chorus avec lui, quand il entreprit le capitaine de l'*Ellenora* à ce sujet. Il voulait l'obliger à chauffer sans perdre un instant. L'autre l'envoya promener.

A Kiel, comme ailleurs, il faut bien qu'une journée se passe. A force de nous promener sur les rivages verdoyants de la baie au fond de laquelle s'élève la petite ville, de parcourir les bois touffus qui lui donnent l'apparence d'un nid dans un faisceau de branches, d'admirer les villas pourvues chacune de leur petite maison de bains froids, enfin de courir et de maugréer, nous atteignîmes dix heures du soir.

Les tourbillons de la fumée de l'*Ellenora* se développaient dans le ciel; le pont tremblotait sous les frissonnements de la chaudière; nous étions à bord et propriétaires de deux couchettes étagées dans l'unique chambre du bateau.

A dix heures un quart les amarres furent lar-

guées, et le steamer fila rapidement sur les sombres
eaux du Grand-Belt.

La nuit était noire ; il y avait belle brise et forte
mer ; quelques feux de la côte apparurent dans les
ténèbres ; plus tard, je ne sais où, un phare à éclats
étincela au-dessus des flots ; ce fut tout ce qui
resta dans mon souvenir de cette première traversée.

A sept heures du matin nous débarquions à
Korsör, petite ville située sur la côte occidentale
du Seeland. Là, nous sautions du bateau dans un
nouveau chemin de fer, qui nous emportait à
travers un pays non moins plat que les campagnes
du Holstein.

C'était encore trois heures de voyage avant
d'atteindre la capitale du Danemark. Mon oncle
n'avait pas fermé l'œil de la nuit. Dans son impatience, je crois qu'il poussait le wagon avec ses
pieds.

Enfin il aperçut une échappée de mer.

« Le Sund ! » s'écria-t-il.

Il y avait sur notre gauche une vaste construction qui ressemblait à un hôpital.

« C'est une maison de fous », dit un de nos
compagnons de voyage.

« Bon, pensai-je, voilà un établissement où
nous devrions finir nos jours ! Et, si grand qu'il
fût, cet hôpital serait encore trop petit pour
contenir toute la folie du professeur Lidenbrock ! »

Enfin, à dix heures du matin, nous prenions
pied à Copenhague ; les bagages furent chargés

sur une voiture et conduits avec nous à l'hôtel du Phœnix dans Bred-Gale. Ce fut l'affaire d'une demi-heure, car la gare est située en dehors de la ville. Puis mon oncle, faisant une toilette sommaire, m'entraîna à sa suite. Le portier de l'hôtel parlait l'allemand et l'anglais ; mais le professeur, en sa qualité de polyglotte, l'interrogea en bon danois, et ce fut en bon danois que ce personnage lui indiqua la situation du Muséum des Antiquités du Nord.

Le directeur de ce curieux établissement, où sont entassées des merveilles qui permettraient de reconstruire l'histoire du pays avec ses vieilles armes de pierre, ses hanaps et ses bijoux, était un savant, l'ami du consul de Hambourg, M. le professeur Thomson.

Mon oncle avait pour lui une chaude lettre de recommandation. En général, un savant en reçoit assez mal un autre. Mais ici ce fut tout autrement. M. Thomson, en homme serviable, fit un cordial accueil au professeur Lidenbrock et même à son neveu. Dire que son secret fut gardé vis-à-vis de l'excellent directeur du Muséum, c'est à peine nécessaire. Nous voulions tout bonnement visiter l'Islande en amateurs désintéressés.

M. Thomson se mit entièrement à notre disposition, et nous courûmes les quais afin de chercher un navire en partance.

J'espérais que les moyens de transport manqueraient absolument ; mais il n'en fut rien. Une petite goélette danoise, la *Valkyrie,* devait mettre

à la voile le 2 juin pour Reykjawik. Le capitaine,
M. Bjarne, se trouvait à bord. Son futur passager,
dans sa joie, lui serra les mains à les briser. Ce
brave homme fut un peu étonné d'une pareille
étreinte. Il trouvait tout simple d'aller en Islande,
puisque c'était son métier. Mon oncle trouvait
cela sublime. Le digne capitaine profita de cet
enthousiasme pour nous faire payer double le
passage sur son bâtiment. Mais nous n'y regardions pas de si près.

« Soyez à bord mardi, à sept heures du matin »,
dit M. Bjarne après avoir empoché un nombre
respectable de species-dollars.

Nous remerciâmes alors M. Thomson de ses
bons soins, et nous revînmes à l'hôtel du Phœnix.

« Cela va bien ! cela va très bien ! répétait mon
oncle. Quel heureux hasard d'avoir trouvé ce
bâtiment prêt à partir ! Maintenant déjeunons,
et allons visiter la ville. »

Nous nous rendîmes à Kongens-Nye-Torw,
place irrégulière où se trouve un poste avec deux
innocents canons braqués qui ne font peur à
personne. Tout près, au nº 5, il y avait une « res-
tauration » française, tenue par un cuisinier nommé
Vincent ; nous y déjeunâmes suffisamment pour
le prix modéré de quatre marks chacun [1].

Puis je pris un plaisir d'enfant à parcourir la
ville ; mon oncle se laissait promener ; d'ailleurs il
ne vit rien, ni l'insignifiant palais du roi, ni le joli

_____

1. 2 francs 75 centimes environ. *Note de l'auteur.*

pont du XVIIe siècle, qui enjambe le canal devant le Muséum, ni cet immense cénotaphe de Torwaldsen, orné de peintures murales horribles et qui contient à l'intérieur les œuvres de ce statuaire, ni, dans un assez beau parc, le château bonbonnière de Rosenborg, ni l'admirable édifice renaissance de la Bourse, ni son clocher fait avec les queues entrelacées de quatre dragons de bronze, ni les grands moulins des remparts, dont les vastes ailes s'enflaient comme les voiles d'un vaisseau au vent de la mer.

Quelles délicieuses promenades nous eussions faites, ma jolie Virlandaise et moi, du côté du port où les deux-ponts et les frégates dormaient paisiblement sous leur toiture rouge, sur les bords verdoyants du détroit, à travers ces ombrages touffus au sein desquels se cache la citadelle, dont les canons allongent leur gueule noirâtre entre les branches des sureaux et des saules!

Mais, hélas! elle était loin, ma pauvre Graüben, et pouvais-je espérer de la revoir jamais?

Cependant, si mon oncle ne remarqua rien de ces sites enchanteurs, il fut vivement frappé par la vue d'un certain clocher situé dans l'île d'Amak, qui forme le quartier sud-ouest de Copenhague.

Je reçus l'ordre de diriger nos pas de ce côté; je montai dans une petite embarcation à vapeur qui faisait le service des canaux, et, en quelques instants, elle accosta le quai de Dock-Yard.

Après avoir traversé quelques rues étroites où des galériens, vêtus de pantalons mi-partie jaunes

et gris, travaillaient sous le bâton des argousins, nous arrivâmes devant Vor-Frelsers-Kirk. Cette église n'offrait rien de remarquable. Mais voici pourquoi son clocher assez élevé avait attiré l'attention du professeur : à partir de la plate-forme, un escalier extérieur circulait autour de sa flèche, et ses spirales se déroulaient en plein ciel.

« Montons, dit mon oncle.

— Mais, le vertige ? répliquai-je.

— Raison de plus, il faut s'y habituer.

— Cependant...

— Viens, te dis-je, ne perdons pas de temps. »

Il fallut obéir. Un gardien, qui demeurait de l'autre côté de la rue, nous remit une clef, et l'ascension commença.

Mon oncle me précédait d'un pas alerte. Je le suivais non sans terreur, car la tête me tournait avec une déplorable facilité. Je n'avais ni l'aplomb des aigles ni l'insensibilité de leurs nerfs.

Tant que nous fûmes emprisonnés dans la vis intérieure, tout alla bien ; mais après cent cinquante marches l'air vint me frapper au visage, nous étions parvenus à la plate-forme du clocher. Là commençait l'escalier aérien, gardé par une frêle rampe, et dont les marches, de plus en plus étroites, semblaient monter vers l'infini.

« Je ne pourrai jamais ! m'écriai-je.

— Serais-tu poltron, par hasard ? Monte ! » répondit impitoyablement le professeur.

Force fut de le suivre en me cramponnant. Le

Le clocher de Frelsers-Kirk (p. 70).

grand air m'étourdissait; je sentais le clocher osciller sous les rafales; mes jambes se dérobaient; je grimpai bientôt sur les genoux, puis sur le ventre; je fermais les yeux; j'éprouvais le mal de l'espace.

Enfin, mon oncle me tirant par le collet, j'arrivai près de la boule.

« Regarde, me dit-il, et regarde bien! il faut prendre *des leçons d'abîme!* »

J'ouvris les yeux. J'aperçus les maisons aplaties et comme écrasées par une chute, au milieu du brouillard des fumées. Au-dessus de ma tête passaient des nuages échevelés, et, par un renversement d'optique, ils me paraissaient immobiles, tandis que le clocher, la boule, moi, nous étions entraînés avec une fantastique vitesse. Au loin, d'un côté s'étendait la campagne verdoyante, de l'autre étincelait la mer sous un faisceau de rayons. Le Sund se déroulait à la pointe d'Elseneur, avec quelques voiles blanches, véritables ailes de goéland, et dans la brume de l'est ondulaient les côtes à peine estompées de la Suède. Toute cette immensité tourbillonnait à mes regards.

Néanmoins il fallut me lever, me tenir droit, regarder. Ma première leçon de vertige dura une heure. Quand enfin il me fut permis de redescendre et de toucher du pied le pavé solide des rues, j'étais courbaturé.

« Nous recommencerons demain », dit mon professeur.

Et en effet, pendant cinq jours, je repris cet

exercice vertigineux, et, bon gré mal gré, je fis des progrès sensibles dans l'art « des hautes contemplations ».

IX

LE jour du départ arriva. La veille, le complaisant M. Thomson nous avait apporté des lettres de recommandations pressantes pour le comte Trampe, gouverneur de l'Islande, M. Pictursson, le coadjuteur de l'évêque, et M. Finsen, maire de Reykjawik. En retour, mon oncle lui octroya les plus chaleureuses poignées de main.

Le 2, à six heures du matin, nos précieux bagages étaient rendus à bord de la *Valkyrie*. Le capitaine nous conduisit à des cabines assez étroites et disposées sous une espèce de rouffle.

« Avons-nous bon vent ? demanda mon oncle.

— Excellent, répondit le capitaine Bjarne ; un vent de sud-est. Nous allons sortir du Sund grand largue et toutes voiles dehors. »

Quelques instants plus tard, la goélette, sous sa misaine, sa brigantine, son hunier et son perroquet, appareilla et donna à pleine toile dans le détroit. Une heure après, la capitale du Danemark semblait s'enfoncer dans les flots éloignés et la *Valkyrie* rasait la côte d'Elseneur. Dans la disposition nerveuse où je me trouvais, je m'attendais

à voir l'ombre d'Hamlet errant sur la terrasse légendaire.

« Sublime insensé! disais-je, tu nous approuverais sans doute! Tu nous suivrais peut-être pour venir au centre du globe chercher une solution à ton doute éternel! »

Mais rien ne parut sur les antiques murailles. Le château est, d'ailleurs, beaucoup plus jeune que l'héroïque prince de Danemark. Il sert maintenant de loge somptueuse au portier de ce détroit du Sund, où passent chaque année quinze mille navires de toutes les nations.

Le château de Krongborg disparut bientôt dans la brume, ainsi que la tour d'Helsinborg, élevée sur la rive suédoise, et la goélette s'inclina légèrement sous les brises du Cattégat.

La *Valkyrie* était fine voilière, mais avec un navire à voiles on ne sait jamais trop sur quoi compter. Elle transportait à Reykjawik du charbon, des ustensiles de ménage, de la poterie, des vêtements de laine et une cargaison de blé. Cinq hommes d'équipage, tous Danois, suffisaient à la manœuvrer.

« Quelle sera la durée de la traversée ? demanda mon oncle au capitaine.

— Une dizaine de jours, répondit ce dernier, si nous ne rencontrons pas trop de grains de nord-ouest par le travers des Feroë.

— Mais enfin, vous n'êtes pas sujet à éprouver des retards considérables ?

— Non, monsieur Lidenbrock; soyez tranquille, nous arriverons. »

Vers le soir la goélette doubla le cap Skagen à la pointe nord du Danemark, traversa pendant la nuit le Skager-Rak, rangea l'extrémité de la Norvège par le travers du cap Lindness et donna dans la mer du Nord.

Deux jours après, nous avions connaissance des côtes d'Écosse à la hauteur de Peterheade, et la *Valkyrie* se dirigea vers les Feroë en passant entre les Orcades et les Seethland.

Bientôt notre goélette fut battue par les vagues de l'Atlantique; elle dut louvoyer contre le vent du nord et n'atteignit pas sans peine les Feroë. Le 8, le capitaine reconnut Myganness, la plus orientale de ces îles, et, à partir de ce moment, il marcha droit au cap Portland, situé sur la côte méridionale de l'Islande.

La traversée n'offrit aucun incident remarquable. Je supportai assez bien les épreuves de la mer ; mon oncle, à son grand dépit, et à sa honte plus grande encore, ne cessa pas d'être malade.

Il ne put donc entreprendre le capitaine Bjarne sur la question du Sneffels, sur les moyens de communication, sur les facilités de transport ; il dut remettre ces explications à son arrivée et passa tout son temps étendu dans sa cabine, dont les cloisons craquaient par les grands coups de tangage. Il faut l'avouer, il méritait un peu son sort.

Le 11, nous relevâmes le cap Portland. Le temps, clair alors, permit d'apercevoir le Myrdals Yokul, qui le domine. Le cap se compose d'un gros morne,

à pentes roides, et planté tout seul sur la plage.

La *Valkyrie* se tint à une distance raisonnable
des côtes, en les prolongeant vers l'ouest, au
milieu de nombreux troupeaux de baleines et de
requins. Bientôt apparut un immense rocher
percé à jour, au travers duquel la mer écumeuse
donnait avec furie. Les îlots de Westman semblèrent
sortir de l'Océan, comme une semée de rocs sur
la plaine liquide. A partir de ce moment, la goélette prit du champ pour tourner à bonne distance
le cap Reykjaness, qui forme l'angle occidental de
l'Islande.

La mer, très forte, empêchait mon oncle de monter sur le pont pour admirer ces côtes déchiquetées
et battues par les vents du sud-ouest.

Quarante-huit heures après, en sortant d'une
tempête qui força la goélette de fuir à sec de toile,
on releva dans l'est la balise de la pointe Skagen,
dont les roches dangereuses se prolongent à une
grande distance sous les flots. Un pilote islandais
vint à bord, et, trois heures plus tard, la *Valkyrie*
mouillait devant Reykjawik dans la baie de Faxa.

Le professeur sortit enfin de sa cabine, un
peu pâle, un peu défait, mais toujours enthousiaste, et avec un regard de satisfaction dans les
yeux.

La population de la ville, singulièrement inté-
ressée par l'arrivée d'un navire dans lequel chacun
a quelque chose à prendre, se groupait sur le quai.

Mon oncle avait hâte d'abandonner sa prison
flottante, pour ne pas dire son hôpital. Mais avant

Vue de Reykjawik (p. 76).

de quitter le pont de la goélette, il m'entraîna à l'avant, et là, du doigt, il me montra, à la partie septentrionale de la baie, une haute montagne à deux pointes, un double cône couvert de neiges éternelles.

« Le Sneffels ! s'écria-t-il, le Sneffels ! »

Puis, après m'avoir recommandé du geste un silence absolu, il descendit dans le canot qui l'attendait. Je le suivis, et bientôt nous foulions du pied le sol de l'Islande.

Tout d'abord apparut un homme de bonne figure et revêtu d'un costume de général. Ce n'était cependant qu'un simple magistrat, le gouverneur de l'île, M. le baron Trampe en personne. Le professeur reconnut à qui il avait affaire. Il remit au gouverneur ses lettres de Copenhague, et il s'établit en danois une courte conversation à laquelle je demeurai absolument étranger, et pour cause. Mais de ce premier entretien il résulta ceci, que le baron Trampe se mettait entièrement à la disposition du professeur Lidenbrock.

Mon oncle reçut un accueil fort aimable du maire, M. Finsen, non moins militaire par le costume que le gouverneur, mais aussi pacifique par tempérament et par état.

Quant au coadjuteur, M. Picturssson, il faisait actuellement une tournée épiscopale dans le bailliage du Nord ; nous devions renoncer provisoirement à lui être présentés. Mais un charmant homme, et dont le concours nous devint fort précieux, ce fut M. Fridriksson, professeur de

sciences naturelles à l'école de Reykjawik. Ce savant modeste ne parlait que l'islandais et le latin ; il vint m'offrir ses services dans la langue d'Horace, et je sentis que nous étions faits pour nous comprendre. Ce fut, en effet, le seul personnage avec lequel je pus m'entretenir pendant mon séjour en Islande.

Sur trois chambres dont se composait sa maison, cet excellent homme en mit deux à notre disposition, et bientôt nous y fûmes installés avec nos bagages, dont la quantité étonna un peu les habitants de Reykjawik.

« Eh bien, Axel, me dit mon oncle, cela va, et le plus difficile est fait.

— Comment, le plus difficile ? m'écriai-je.

— Sans doute, nous n'avons plus qu'à descendre !

— Si vous le prenez ainsi, vous avez raison ; mais enfin, après avoir descendu, il faudra remonter, j'imagine ?

— Oh ! cela ne m'inquiète guère ! Voyons ! il n'y a pas de temps à perdre. Je vais me rendre à la bibliothèque. Peut-être s'y trouve-t-il quelque manuscrit de Saknussemm, et je serais bien aise de le consulter.

— Alors, pendant ce temps, je vais visiter la ville. Est-ce que vous n'en ferez pas autant ?

— Oh ! cela m'intéresse médiocrement. Ce qui est curieux dans cette terre d'Islande n'est pas dessus, mais dessous. »

Je sortis, et j'errai au hasard.

S'égarer dans les deux rues de Reykjawik n'eût pas été chose facile. Je ne fus donc pas obligé de demander mon chemin, ce qui, dans la langue des gestes, expose à beaucoup de mécomptes.

La ville s'allonge sur un sol assez bas et marécageux, entre deux collines. Une immense coulée de laves la couvre d'un côté et descend en rampes assez douces vers la mer. De l'autre s'étend cette vaste baie de Faxa, bornée au nord par l'énorme glacier du Sneffels, et dans laquelle la *Valkyrie* se trouvait seule à l'ancre en ce moment. Ordinairement, les garde-pêche anglais et français s'y tiennent mouillés au large ; mais ils étaient alors en service sur les côtes orientales de l'île.

La plus longue des deux rues de Reykjawik est parallèle au rivage ; là demeurent les marchands et les négociants, dans des cabanes de bois faites de poutres rouges horizontalement disposées ; l'autre rue, située plus à l'ouest, court vers un petit lac, entre les maisons de l'évêque et des autres personnages étrangers au commerce.

J'eus bientôt arpenté ces voies mornes et tristes ; j'entrevoyais parfois un bout de gazon décoloré, comme un vieux tapis de laine râpé par l'usage, ou bien quelque apparence de verger, dont les rares légumes, pommes de terre, choux et laitues, eussent figuré à l'aise sur une table lilliputienne ; quelques giroflées maladives essayaient aussi de prendre un petit air de soleil.

Vers le milieu de la rue non commerçante, je trouvai le cimetière public enclos d'un mur en

Une rue de Reykjawik (p. 80).

terre, et dans lequel la place ne manquait pas. Puis, en quelques enjambées, j'arrivai à la maison du gouverneur, une masure comparée à l'hôtel de ville de Hambourg, un palais auprès des huttes de la population islandaise.

Entre le petit lac et la ville s'élevait l'église, bâtie dans le goût protestant et construite en pierres calcinées dont les volcans font eux-mêmes les frais d'extraction; par les grands vents d'ouest, son toit de tuiles rouges devait évidemment se disperser dans les airs, au grand dommage des fidèles.

Sur une éminence voisine, j'aperçus l'École nationale, où, comme je l'appris plus tard de notre hôte, on professait l'hébreu, l'anglais, le français et le danois, quatre langues dont, à ma honte, je ne connaissais pas le premier mot. J'aurais été le dernier des quarante élèves que comptait ce petit collège, et indigne de coucher avec eux dans ces armoires à deux compartiments où de plus délicats étoufferaient dès la première nuit.

En trois heures j'eus visité non seulement la ville, mais ses environs. L'aspect général en était singulièrement triste. Pas d'arbres, pas de végétation, pour ainsi dire. Partout les arêtes vives des roches volcaniques. Les huttes des Islandais sont faites de terre et de tourbe, et leurs murs inclinés en dedans. Elles ressemblent à des toits posés sur le sol. Seulement ces toits sont des prairies relativement fécondes. Grâce à la chaleur de l'habitation, l'herbe y pousse avec assez de perfection, et on la fauche soigneusement à

l'époque de la fenaison, sans quoi les animaux domestiques viendraient paître sur ces demeures verdoyantes.

Pendant mon excursion, je rencontrai peu d'habitants. En revenant à la rue commerçante, je vis la plus grande partie de la population occupée à sécher, saler et charger des morues, principal article d'exportation. Les hommes paraissaient robustes, mais lourds, des espèces d'Allemands blonds à l'œil pensif, qui se sentent un peu en dehors de l'humanité, pauvres exilés relégués sur cette terre de glace, dont la nature aurait bien dû faire des Esquimaux, puisqu'elle les condamnait à vivre sur la limite du cercle polaire! J'essayais en vain de surprendre un sourire sur leur visage; ils riaient quelquefois par une sorte de contraction involontaire des muscles, mais ne souriaient jamais.

Leur costume consistait en une grossière vareuse de laine noire, connue dans les pays scandinaves sous le nom de « vadmel », un chapeau à vastes bords, un pantalon à liséré rouge et un morceau de cuir replié en manière de chaussure.

Les femmes, à figure triste et résignée, d'un type assez agréable, mais sans expression, étaient vêtues d'un corsage et d'une jupe de « vadmel » sombre : filles, elles portaient sur leurs cheveux tressés en guirlandes un petit bonnet de tricot brun; mariées, elles entouraient leur tête d'un mouchoir de couleur, surmonté d'un cimier de toile blanche.

Après une bonne promenade, lorsque je rentrai dans la maison de M. Fridriksson, mon oncle s'y trouvait déjà en compagnie de son hôte.

X

Le dîner était prêt; il fut dévoré avec avidité par le professeur Lidenbrock, dont la diète forcée du bord avait changé l'estomac en un gouffre profond. Ce repas, plus danois qu'islandais, n'eut rien de remarquable en lui-même; mais notre hôte, plus islandais que danois, me rappela les héros de l'antique hospitalité. Il me parut évident que nous étions chez lui plus que lui-même.

La conversation se fit en langue indigène, que mon oncle entremêlait d'allemand et M. Fridriksson de latin, afin que je pusse la comprendre. Elle roula sur des questions scientifiques, comme il convient à des savants; mais le professeur Lidenbrock se tint sur la plus excessive réserve, et ses yeux me recommandaient, à chaque phrase, un silence absolu touchant nos projets à venir.

Tout d'abord, M. Fridriksson s'enquit auprès de mon oncle du résultat de ses recherches à la bibliothèque.

« Votre bibliothèque! s'écria ce dernier, elle ne se compose que de livres dépareillés sur des rayons presque déserts.

— Comment! répondit M. Fridriksson, nous possédons huit mille volumes, dont beaucoup sont précieux et rares, des ouvrages en vieille langue scandinave, et toutes les nouveautés dont Copenhague nous approvisionne chaque année.

— Où prenez-vous ces huit mille volumes? Pour mon compte...

— Oh! monsieur Lidenbrock, ils courent le pays. On a le goût de l'étude dans notre vieille île de glace! Pas un fermier, pas un pêcheur qui ne sache lire et qui ne lise. Nous pensons que des livres, au lieu de moisir derrière une grille de fer, loin des regards curieux, sont destinés à s'user sous les yeux des lecteurs. Aussi ces volumes passent-ils de main en main, feuilletés, lus et relus, et souvent ils ne reviennent à leur rayon qu'après un an ou deux d'absence.

— En attendant, répondit mon oncle avec un certain dépit, les étrangers...

— Que voulez-vous! les étrangers ont chez eux leurs bibliothèques, et, avant tout, il faut que nos paysans s'instruisent. Je vous le répète, l'amour de l'étude est dans le sang islandais. Aussi, en 1816, nous avons fondé une Société littéraire qui va bien; des savants étrangers s'honorent d'en faire partie; elle publie des livres destinés à l'éducation de nos compatriotes et rend de véritables services au pays. Si vous voulez être un de nos membres correspondants, monsieur Lidenbrock, vous nous ferez le plus grand plaisir. »

Mon oncle, qui appartenait déjà à une centaine

de sociétés scientifiques, accepta avec une bonne
grâce dont fut touché M. Fridriksson.

« Maintenant, reprit celui-ci, veuillez m'indiquer
les livres que vous espériez trouver à notre bibliothèque, et je pourrai peut-être vous renseigner à
leur égard. »

Je regardai mon oncle. Il hésita à répondre.
Cela touchait directement à ses projets. Cependant,
après avoir réfléchi, il se décida à parler.

« Monsieur Fridriksson, dit-il, je voulais savoir
si, parmi les ouvrages anciens, vous possédiez
ceux d'Arne Saknussemm ?

— Arne Saknussemm ! répondit le professeur
de Reykjawik. Vous voulez parler de ce savant
du XVIe siècle, à la fois grand naturaliste, grand
alchimiste et grand voyageur ?

— Précisément.

— Une des gloires de la littérature et de la
science islandaises ?

— Comme vous dites.

— Un homme illustre entre tous ?

— Je vous l'accorde.

— Et dont l'audace égalait le génie ?

— Je vois que vous le connaissez bien. »

Mon oncle nageait dans la joie à entendre parler
ainsi de son héros. Il dévorait des yeux M. Fridriksson.

« Eh bien ! demanda-t-il, ses ouvrages ?

— Ah ! ses ouvrages, nous ne les avons pas.

— Quoi ! en Islande ?

— Ils n'existent ni en Islande ni ailleurs.

— Et pourquoi?

— Parce que Arne Saknussemm fut persécuté pour cause d'hérésie, et qu'en 1573 ses ouvrages furent brûlés à Copenhague par la main du bourreau.

— Très bien! Parfait! s'écria mon oncle, au grand scandale du professeur de sciences naturelles.

— Hein? fit ce dernier.

— Oui! tout s'explique, tout s'enchaîne, tout est clair, et je comprends pourquoi Saknussemm, mis à l'index et forcé de cacher les découvertes de son génie, a dû enfouir dans un incompréhensible cryptogramme le secret...

— Quel secret? demanda vivement M. Fridriksson.

— Un secret qui... dont..., répondit mon oncle en balbutiant.

— Est-ce que vous auriez quelque document particulier? reprit notre hôte.

— Non... Je faisais une pure supposition.

— Bien, répondit M. Fridriksson, qui eut la bonté de ne pas insister en voyant le trouble de son interlocuteur. J'espère, ajouta-t-il, que vous ne quitterez pas notre île sans avoir puisé à ses richesses minéralogiques?

— Certes, répondit mon oncle; mais j'arrive un peu tard; des savants ont déjà passé par ici?

— Oui, monsieur Lidenbrock; les travaux de MM. Olafsen et Povelsen exécutés par ordre du roi, les études de Troïl, la mission scientifique

de MM. Gaimard et Robert, à bord de la corvette française *La Recherche* [1], et dernièrement, les observations de savants embarqués sur la frégate *La Reine-Hortense* ont puissamment contribué à la reconnaissance de l'Islande. Mais, croyez-moi, il y a encore à faire.

— Vous pensez? demanda mon oncle d'un air bonhomme, en essayant de modérer l'éclair de ses yeux.

— Oui. Que de montagnes, de glaciers, de volcans à étudier, qui sont peu connus! Et tenez, sans aller plus loin, voyez ce mont qui s'élève à l'horizon. C'est le Sneffels.

— Ah! fit mon oncle, le Sneffels.

— Oui, l'un des volcans les plus curieux et dont on visite rarement le cratère.

— Éteint?

— Oh! éteint depuis cinq cents ans.

— Eh bien! répondit mon oncle, qui se croisait frénétiquement les jambes pour ne pas sauter en l'air, j'ai envie de commencer mes études géologiques par ce Seffel... Fessel... comment dites-vous?

— Sneffels », reprit l'excellent M. Fridriksson.

Cette partie de la conversation avait eu lieu en latin; j'avais tout compris, et je gardais à peine mon sérieux à voir mon oncle contenir sa satisfaction qui débordait de toutes parts; il essayait

1. *La Recherche* fut envoyée en 1835 par l'amiral Duperré pour retrouver les traces d'une expédition perdue, celle de M. de Blosseville et de *la Lilloise*, dont on n'a jamais eu de nouvelles.

de prendre un petit air innocent qui ressemblait
à la grimace d'un vieux diable.

« Oui, fit-il, vos paroles me décident! Nous
essaierons de gravir ce Sneffels, peut-être même
d'étudier son cratère!

— Je regrette bien, répondit M. Fridriksson,
que mes occupations ne me permettent pas de
m'absenter ; je vous aurais accompagné avec plaisir
et profit.

— Oh! non, oh! non, répondit vivement mon
oncle ; nous ne voulons déranger personne, monsieur Fridriksson ; je vous remercie de tout
mon cœur. La présence d'un savant tel que
vous eût été très utile, mais les devoirs de votre
profession... »

J'aime à penser que notre hôte, dans l'innocence
de son âme islandaise, ne comprit pas les grosses
malices de mon oncle.

« Je vous approuve fort, monsieur Lidenbrock,
dit-il, de commencer par ce volcan. Vous ferez
là une ample moisson d'observations curieuses.
Mais, dites-moi, comment comptez-vous gagner
la presqu'île du Sneffels?

— Par mer, en traversant la baie. C'est la route
la plus rapide.

— Sans doute ; mais elle est impossible à
prendre.

— Pourquoi?

— Parce que nous n'avons pas un seul canot à
Reykjawik.

— Diable!

— Il faudra aller par terre, en suivant la côte. Ce sera plus long, mais plus intéressant.

— Bon. Je verrai à me procurer un guide.

— J'en ai précisément un à vous offrir.

— Un homme sûr, intelligent?

— Oui, un habitant de la presqu'île. C'est un chasseur d'eider, fort habile, et dont vous serez content. Il parle parfaitement le danois.

— Et quand pourrai-je le voir?

— Demain, si cela vous plaît.

— Pourquoi pas aujourd'hui?

— C'est qu'il n'arrive que demain.

— A demain donc », répondit mon oncle avec un soupir.

Cette importante conversation se termina quelques instants plus tard par de chaleureux remerciements du professeur allemand au professeur islandais. Pendant ce dîner, mon oncle venait d'apprendre des choses importantes, entre autres l'histoire de Saknussemm, la raison de son document mystérieux, comme quoi son hôte ne l'accompagnerait pas dans son expédition, et que dès le lendemain un guide serait à ses ordres.

XI

LE soir, je fis une courte promenade sur les rivages de Reykjawik, et je revins de bonne heure me cou-

cher dans mon lit de grosses planches, où je dormis d'un profond sommeil.

Quand je me réveillai, j'entendis mon oncle parler abondamment dans la salle voisine. Je me levai aussitôt et je me hâtai d'aller le rejoindre.

Il causait en danois avec un homme de haute taille, vigoureusement découplé. Ce grand gaillard devait être d'une force peu commune. Ses yeux, percés dans une tête très grosse et assez naïve, me parurent intelligents. Ils étaient d'un bleu rêveur. De longs cheveux, qui eussent passé pour roux, même en Angleterre, tombaient sur ses athlétiques épaules. Cet indigène avait les mouvements souples, mais il remuait peu les bras, en homme qui ignorait ou dédaignait la langue des gestes. Tout en lui révélait un tempérament d'un calme parfait, non pas indolent, mais tranquille. On sentait qu'il ne demandait rien à personne, qu'il travaillait à sa convenance, et que, dans ce monde, sa philosophie ne pouvait être ni étonnée ni troublée.

Je surpris les nuances de ce caractère, à la manière dont l'Islandais écouta le verbiage passionné de son interlocuteur. Il demeurait les bras croisés, immobile au milieu des gestes multipliés de mon oncle ; pour nier, sa tête tournait de gauche à droite ; elle s'inclinait pour affirmer, et cela si peu, que ses longs cheveux bougeaient à peine. C'était l'économie du mouvement poussée jusqu'à l'avarice.

Certes, à voir cet homme, je n'aurais jamais

deviné sa profession de chasseur ; celui-là ne devait pas effrayer le gibier, à coup sûr, mais comment pouvait-il l'atteindre ?

Tout s'expliqua quand M. Fridriksson m'apprit que ce tranquille personnage n'était qu'un « chasseur d'eider », oiseau dont le duvet constitue la plus grande richesse de l'île. En effet, ce duvet s'appelle l'édredon, et il ne faut pas une grande dépense de mouvement pour le recueillir.

Aux premiers jours de l'été, la femelle de l'eider, sorte de joli canard, va bâtir son nid parmi les rochers des fjörds [1] dont la côte est toute frangée. Ce nid bâti, elle le tapisse avec de fines plumes qu'elle s'arrache du ventre. Aussitôt le chasseur, ou mieux le négociant, arrive, prend le nid, et la femelle de recommencer son travail. Cela dure ainsi tant qu'il lui reste quelque duvet. Quand elle s'est entièrement dépouillée, c'est au mâle de se plumer à son tour. Seulement, comme la dépouille dure et grossière de ce dernier n'a aucune valeur commerciale, le chasseur ne prend pas la peine de lui voler le lit de sa couvée ; le nid s'achève donc ; la femelle pond ses œufs ; les petits éclosent, et, l'année suivante, la récolte de l'édredon recommence.

Or, comme l'eider ne choisit pas les rocs escarpés pour y bâtir son nid, mais plutôt ces roches faciles et horizontales qui vont se perdre en mer, le chasseur islandais pouvait exercer son métier

---

1. Nom donné aux golfes étroits dans les pays scandinaves.

sans grande agitation. C'était un fermier qui n'avait ni à semer ni à couper sa moisson, mais à la récolter seulement.

Ce personnage grave, flegmatique et silencieux, se nommait Hans Bjelke; il venait à la recommandation de M. Fridriksson. C'était notre futur guide. Ses manières contrastaient singulièrement avec celles de mon oncle.

Cependant ils s'entendirent facilement. Ni l'un ni l'autre ne regardaient au prix; l'un prêt à accepter ce qu'on lui offrait, l'autre prêt à donner ce qui lui serait demandé. Jamais marché ne fut plus facile à conclure.

Or, des conventions il résulta que Hans s'engageait à nous conduire au village de Stapi, situé sur la côte méridionale de la presqu'île du Sneffels, au pied même du volcan. Il fallait compter par terre vingt-deux milles environ, voyage à faire en deux jours, suivant l'opinion de mon oncle.

Mais quand il apprit qu'il s'agissait de milles danois de vingt-quatre mille pieds, il dut rabattre de son calcul et compter, vu l'insuffisance des chemins, sur sept ou huit jours de marche.

Quatre chevaux devaient être mis à sa disposition, deux pour le porter, lui et moi, deux autres destinés à nos bagages. Hans, suivant son habitude, irait à pied. Il connaissait parfaitement cette partie de la côte, et il promit de prendre par le plus court.

Son engagement avec mon oncle n'expirait pas à notre arrivée à Stapi; il demeurait à son service

Hans, personnage grave, flegmatique et silencieux (p. 93).

pendant tout le temps nécessaire à ses excursions scientifiques, au prix de trois rixdales par semaine [1]. Seulement, il fut expressément convenu que cette somme serait comptée au guide chaque samedi soir, condition *sine qua non* de son engagement.

Le départ fut fixé au 16 juin. Mon oncle voulut remettre au chasseur les arrhes du marché, mais celui-ci refusa d'un mot.

« Efter, fit-il.

— Après », me dit le professeur pour mon édification.

Hans, le traité conclu, se retira tout d'une pièce.

« Un fameux homme, s'écria mon oncle, mais il ne s'attend guère au merveilleux rôle que l'avenir lui réserve de jouer.

— Il nous accompagne donc jusqu'au...

— Oui, Axel, jusqu'au centre de la terre. »

Quarante-huit heures restaient encore à passer ; à mon grand regret, je dus les employer à nos préparatifs ; toute notre intelligence fut employée à disposer chaque objet de la façon la plus avantageuse, les instruments d'un côté, les armes d'un autre, les outils dans ce paquet, les vivres dans celui-là. En tout quatre groupes.

Les instruments comprenaient :

1° Un thermomètre centigrade de Eigel, gradué jusqu'à cent cinquante degrés, ce qui me parais-

1. 16 francs 98 centimes.

sait trop ou pas assez. Trop, si la chaleur ambiante devait monter là, auquel cas nous aurions cuit. Pas assez, s'il s'agissait de mesurer la température de sources ou toute autre matière en fusion;

2° Un manomètre à air comprimé, disposé de manière à indiquer des pressions supérieures à celles de l'atmosphère au niveau de l'Océan. En effet, le baromètre ordinaire n'eût pas suffi, la pression atmosphérique devant augmenter proportionnellement à notre descente au-dessous de la surface de la terre;

3° Un chronomètre de Boissonnas jeune de Genève, parfaitement réglé au méridien de Hambourg;

4° Deux boussoles d'inclinaison et de déclinaison;

5° Une lunette de nuit;

6° Deux appareils de Ruhmkorff, qui, au moyen d'un courant électrique, donnaient une lumière très portative, sûre et peu encombrante [1].

Les armes consistaient en deux carabines de Purdley More et Co., et de deux revolvers Colt. Pourquoi des armes? Nous n'avions ni sauvages

---

1. L'appareil de M. Ruhmkorff consiste en une pile de Bunzen, mise en activité au moyen du bichromate de potasse, qui ne donne aucune odeur; une bobine d'induction met l'électricité produite par la pile en communication avec une lanterne d'une disposition particulière; dans cette lanterne se trouve un serpentin de verre où le vide a été fait, et dans lequel reste seulement un résidu de gaz carbonique ou d'azote. Quand l'appareil fonctionne, ce gaz devient lumineux en produisant une lumière blanchâtre et continue. La pile et la bobine sont placées dans un sac de cuir que le voyageur porte en bandoulière. La lanterne,

ni bêtes féroces à redouter, je suppose. Mais mon oncle paraissait tenir à son arsenal comme à ses instruments, surtout à une notable quantité de fulmicoton inaltérable à l'humidité, et dont la force expansive est très supérieure à celle de la poudre ordinaire.

Les outils comprenaient deux pics, deux pioches, une échelle de soie, trois bâtons ferrés, une hache, un marteau, une douzaine de coins et pitons de fer, et de longues cordes à nœuds. Cela ne laissait pas de faire un fort colis, car l'échelle mesurait trois cents pieds de longueur.

Enfin il y avait des provisions ; le paquet n'était pas gros, mais rassurant, car je savais qu'en viande concentrée et en biscuits secs il contenait pour six mois de vivres. Le genièvre en formait toute la partie liquide, et l'eau manquait totalement ; mais nous avions des gourdes, et mon oncle comptait sur les sources pour les remplir ; les objections que j'avais pu faire sur leur qualité, leur température et même leur absence, étaient restées sans succès.

Pour compléter la nomenclature exacte de nos articles de voyage, je noterai une pharmacie porta-

---

placée extérieurement, éclaire très suffisamment dans les profondes obscurités ; elle permet de s'aventurer, sans craindre aucune explosion, au milieu des gaz les plus inflammables, et ne s'éteint pas même au sein des plus profonds cours d'eau. M. Ruhmkorff est un savant et habile physicien. Sa grande découverte, c'est sa bobine d'induction qui permet de produire de l'électricité à haute tension. Il vient d'obtenir, en 1864, le prix quinquennal de 50 000 fr. que la France réservait à la plus ingénieuse application de l'électricité.

tive contenant des ciseaux à lames mousses, des attelles pour fracture, une pièce de ruban en fil écru, des bandes et compresses, du sparadrap, une palette pour saignée, toutes choses effrayantes ; de plus, une série de flacons contenant de la dextrine, de l'alcool vulnéraire, de l'acétate de plomb liquide, de l'éther, du vinaigre et de l'ammoniaque, toutes drogues d'un emploi peu rassurant ; enfin les matières nécessaires aux appareils de Ruhmkorff.

Mon oncle n'avait eu garde d'oublier la provision de tabac, de poudre de chasse et d'amadou, non plus qu'une ceinture de cuir qu'il portait autour des reins et où se trouvait une suffisante quantité de monnaie d'or, d'argent et de papier. De bonnes chaussures, rendues imperméables par un enduit de goudron et de gomme élastique, se trouvaient au nombre de six paires dans le groupe des outils.

« Ainsi vêtus, chaussés, équipés, il n'y a aucune raison pour ne pas aller loin », me dit mon oncle.

La journée du 14 fut employée tout entière à disposer ces différents objets. Le soir, nous dînâmes chez le baron Trampe, en compagnie du maire de Reykjawik et du docteur Hyaltalin, le grand médecin du pays. M. Fridriksson n'était pas au nombre des convives ; j'appris plus tard que le gouverneur et lui se trouvaient en désaccord sur une question d'administration et ne se voyaient pas. Je n'eus donc pas l'occasion de comprendre un mot de ce qui se dit pendant ce dîner semi-

officiel. Je remarquai seulement que mon oncle
parla tout le temps.

Le lendemain 15, les préparatifs furent achevés.
Notre hôte fit un sensible plaisir au professeur
en lui remettant une carte de l'Islande, incom-
parablement plus parfaite que celle d'Handerson,
la carte de M. Olaf Nikolas Olsen, réduite au
1/480 000, et publiée par la Société littéraire
islandaise, d'après les travaux géodésiques de
M. Scheel Frisac, et le levé topographique de
M. Bjorn Gumlaugsonn. C'était un précieux
document pour un minéralogiste.

La dernière soirée se passa dans une intime
causerie avec M. Fridriksson, pour lequel je me
sentais pris d'une vive sympathie ; puis, à la
conversation, succéda un sommeil assez agité, de
ma part du moins.

A cinq heures du matin, le hennissement de
quatre chevaux qui piaffaient sous ma fenêtre
me réveilla. Je m'habillai à la hâte, et je descendis
dans la rue. Là, Hans achevait de charger nos
bagages sans se remuer, pour ainsi dire. Cependant il opérait avec une adresse peu commune.
Mon oncle faisait plus de bruit que de besogne,
et le guide paraissait se soucier fort peu de ses
recommandations.

Tout fut terminé à six heures. M. Fridriksson
nous serra les mains. Mon oncle le remercia en
islandais de sa bienveillante hospitalité, et avec
beaucoup de cœur. Quant à moi, j'ébauchai dans
mon meilleur latin quelque salut cordial ; puis

nous nous mîmes en selle, et M. Fridriksson me
lança avec son dernier adieu ce vers que Virgile
semblait avoir fait pour nous, voyageurs incertains
de la route :

Et quacumque viam dederit fortuna sequamur.

XII

Nous étions partis par un temps couvert, mais
fixe. Pas de fatigantes chaleurs à redouter, ni
pluies désastreuses. Un temps de touristes.

Le plaisir de courir à cheval à travers un pays
inconnu me rendait de facile composition sur le
début de l'entreprise. J'étais tout entier au bon-
heur de l'excursionniste, fait de désirs et de
liberté. Je commençais à prendre mon parti de
l'affaire.

« D'ailleurs, me disais-je, qu'est-ce que je risque ?
de voyager au milieu du pays le plus curieux !
de gravir une montagne fort remarquable ! au
pis aller, de descendre au fond d'un cratère
éteint ! Il est bien évident que ce Saknussemm n'a
pas fait autre chose. Quant à l'existence d'une
galerie qui aboutisse au centre du globe, pure
imagination ! pure impossibilité ! Donc, ce qu'il
y a de bon à prendre de cette expédition, prenons-
le, et sans marchander. »

Ce raisonnement à peine achevé, nous avions quitté Reykjawik.

Hans marchait en tête, d'un pas rapide, égal, continu. Les deux chevaux chargés de nos bagages le suivaient, sans qu'il fût nécessaire de les diriger. Mon oncle et moi, nous venions ensuite, et vraiment sans faire trop mauvaise figure sur nos bêtes petites, mais vigoureuses.

L'Islande est une des plus grandes îles de l'Europe. Elle mesure quatorze cents milles de surface, et ne compte que soixante mille habitants. Les géographes l'ont divisée en quatre quartiers, et nous avions à traverser presque obliquement celui qui porte le nom de Pays du quart du Sud-Ouest, « Sudvestr Fjordùngr ».

Hans, en laissant Reykjawik, avait immédiatement suivi les bords de la mer. Nous traversions de maigres pâturages qui se donnaient bien du mal pour être verts ; le jaune réussissait mieux. Les sommets rugueux des masses trachytiques s'estompaient à l'horizon dans les brumes de l'est ; par moments, quelques plaques de neige, concentrant la lumière diffuse, resplendissaient sur le versant des cimes éloignées ; certains pics, plus hardiment dressés, trouaient les nuages gris et réapparaissaient au-dessus des vapeurs mouvantes, semblables à des écueils émergés en plein ciel.

Souvent ces chaînes de rocs arides faisaient une pointe vers la mer et mordaient sur le pâturage ; mais il restait toujours une place suffisante pour

passer. Nos chevaux, d'ailleurs, choisissaient d'instinct les endroits propices sans jamais ralentir leur marche. Mon oncle n'avait pas même la consolation d'exciter sa monture de la voix ou du fouet; il ne lui était pas permis d'être impatient. Je ne pouvais m'empêcher de sourire en le voyant si grand sur son petit cheval, et, comme ses longues jambes rasaient le sol, il ressemblait à un Centaure à six pieds.

« Bonne bête! bonne bête! disait-il. Tu verras, Axel, que pas un animal ne l'emporte en intelligence sur le cheval islandais. Neiges, tempêtes, chemins impraticables, rochers, glaciers, rien ne l'arrête. Il est brave, il est sobre, il est sûr. Jamais un faux pas, jamais une réaction. Qu'il se présente quelque rivière, quelque fjörd à traverser, et il s'en présentera, tu le verras sans hésiter se jeter à l'eau comme un amphibie, et gagner le bord opposé! Mais ne le brusquons pas, laissons-le agir, et nous ferons, l'un portant l'autre, nos dix lieues par jour.

— Nous, sans doute, répondis-je, mais le guide?

— Oh! il ne m'inquiète guère. Ces gens-là, cela marche sans s'en apercevoir. Celui-ci se remue si peu qu'il ne doit pas se fatiguer. D'ailleurs, au besoin, je lui céderai ma monture. Les crampes me prendraient bientôt, si je ne me donnais pas quelque mouvement. Les bras vont bien, mais il faut songer aux jambes. »

Cependant nous avancions d'un pas rapide.

Mon oncle ressemblait à un Centaure à six pieds (p. 102).

Le pays était déjà à peu près désert. Çà et là une ferme isolée, quelque boër [1] solitaire, bâti de bois, de terre, de morceaux de lave, apparaissait comme un mendiant au bord d'un chemin creux. Ces huttes délabrées avaient l'air d'implorer la charité des passants, et, pour un peu, on leur eût fait l'aumône. Dans ce pays, les routes, les sentiers même manquaient absolument, et la végétation, si lente qu'elle fût, avait vite fait d'effacer le pas des rares voyageurs.

Pourtant, cette partie de la province, située à deux pas de sa capitale, comptait parmi les portions habitées et cultivées de l'Islande. Qu'étaient alors les contrées plus désertes que ce désert ? Un demi-mille franchi, nous n'avions encore rencontré ni un fermier sur la porte de sa chaumière, ni un berger sauvage paissant un troupeau moins sauvage que lui ; seulement quelques vaches et des moutons abandonnés à eux-mêmes. Que seraient donc les régions convulsionnées, boule-versées par les phénomènes éruptifs, nées des explosions volcaniques et des commotions souter-raines ?

Nous étions destinés à les connaître plus tard ; mais, en consultant la carte d'Olsen, je vis qu'on les évitait en longeant la sinueuse lisière du rivage. En effet, le grand mouvement plutonique s'est concentré surtout à l'intérieur de l'île ; là les couches horizontales de roches superposées,

1. Maison du paysan islandais.

appelées trapps en langue scandinave, les bandes trachytiques, les éruptions de basalte, de tufs, de tous les conglomérats volcaniques, les coulées de lave et de porphyre en fusion, ont fait un pays d'une surnaturelle horreur. Je ne me doutais guère alors du spectacle qui nous attendait à la presqu'île du Sneffels, où ces dégâts d'une nature fougueuse forment un formidable chaos.

Deux heures après avoir quitté Reykjawik, nous arrivions au bourg de Gufunes, appelé « Aoal-kirkja » ou Église principale. Il n'offrait rien de remarquable. Quelques maisons seulement. A peine de quoi faire un hameau de l'Allemagne.

Hans s'y arrêta une demi-heure ; il partagea notre frugal déjeuner, répondit par oui ou par non aux questions de mon oncle sur la nature de la route, et lorsqu'on lui demanda en quel endroit il comptait passer la nuit :

« Gardär », dit-il seulement.

Je consultai la carte pour savoir ce qu'était Gardär. Je vis une bourgade de ce nom sur les bords du Hvalfjörd, à quatre milles de Reykjawik. Je la montrai à mon oncle.

« Quatre milles seulement ! dit-il. Quatre milles sur vingt-deux ! Voilà une jolie promenade. »

Il voulut faire une observation au guide, qui, sans lui répondre, reprit la tête des chevaux et se remit en marche.

Trois heures plus tard, toujours en foulant le gazon décoloré des pâturages, il fallut contourner le Kollafjörd, détour plus facile et moins long

qu'une traversée de ce golfe. Bientôt nous entrions dans un « pingstaœr », lieu de juridiction communale, nommé Ejulberg, et dont le clocher eût sonné midi, si les églises islandaises avaient été assez riches pour posséder une horloge ; mais elles ressemblent fort à leurs paroissiens, qui n'ont pas de montres, et qui s'en passent.

Là, les chevaux furent rafraîchis ; puis, prenant par un rivage resserré entre une chaîne de collines et la mer, ils nous portèrent d'une traite à l'« aoalkirkja » de Brantär, et un mille plus loin à Saurböer « Annexia », église annexe, située sur la rive méridionale du Hvalfjörd.

Il était alors quatre heures du soir ; nous avions franchi quatre milles [1].

Le fjörd était large en cet endroit d'un demi-mille au moins ; les vagues déferlaient avec bruit sur les rocs aigus ; ce golfe s'évasait entre des murailles de rochers, sorte d'escarpe à pic haute de trois mille pieds et remarquable par ses couches brunes que séparaient des lits de tuf d'une nuance rougeâtre. Quelle que fût l'intelligence de nos chevaux, je n'augurais pas bien de la traversée d'un véritable bras de mer opérée sur le dos d'un quadrupède.

« S'ils sont intelligents, dis-je, ils n'essaieront point de passer. En tout cas, je me charge d'être intelligent pour eux. »

Mais mon oncle ne voulait pas attendre. Il

1. Huit lieues.

piqua des deux vers le rivage. Sa monture vint
flairer la dernière ondulation des vagues et
s'arrêta. Mon oncle, qui avait son instinct à lui,
la pressa davantage. Nouveau refus de l'animal,
qui secoua la tête. Alors jurons et coups de fouet,
mais ruades de la bête, qui commença à désar-
çonner son cavalier. Enfin le petit cheval, ployant
ses jarrets, se retira des jambes du professeur et
le laissa tout droit planté sur deux pierres du
rivage, comme le colosse de Rhodes.

« Ah! maudit animal! s'écria le cavalier, subitement transformé en piéton, et honteux comme
un officier de cavalerie qui passerait fantassin.

— Färja, fit le guide en lui touchant l'épaule.

— Quoi! un bac?

— Der, répondit Hans en montrant un bateau.

— Oui, m'écriai-je, il y a un bac.

— Il fallait donc le dire! Eh bien, en route!

— Tidvatten, reprit le guide.

— Que dit-il?

— Il dit marée, répondit mon oncle en me tra-
duisant le mot danois.

— Sans doute, il faut attendre la marée?

— Förbida? demanda mon oncle.

— Ja », répondit Hans.

Mon oncle frappa du pied, tandis que les
chevaux se dirigeaient vers le bac.

Je compris parfaitement la nécessité d'attendre
un certain instant de la marée pour entreprendre
la traversée du fjörd, celui où la mer, arrivée à
sa plus grande hauteur, est étale. Alors le flux

Sa monture vint flairer la dernière ondulation des vagues (p. 107).

et le reflux n'ont aucune action sensible, et le
bac ne risque pas d'être entraîné, soit au fond du
golfe, soit en plein Océan.

L'instant favorable n'arriva qu'à six heures du
soir ; mon oncle, moi, le guide, deux passeurs et
les quatre chevaux, nous avions pris place dans
une sorte de barque plate assez fragile. Habitué
que j'étais aux bacs à vapeur de l'Elbe, je trouvai
les rames des bateliers un triste engin mécanique.
Il fallut plus d'une heure pour traverser le fjörd ;
mais enfin le passage se fit sans accident.

Une demi-heure après, nous atteignions l'« aoal-
kirkja » de Gardär.

XIII

Il aurait dû faire nuit, mais sous le soixante-
cinquième parallèle, la clarté nocturne des régions
polaires ne devait pas m'étonner ; en Islande,
pendant les mois de juin et juillet, le soleil ne se
couche pas.

Néanmoins la température s'était abaissée.
J'avais froid, et surtout faim. Bienvenu fut le
« boer » qui s'ouvrit hospitalièrement pour nous
recevoir.

C'était la maison d'un paysan, mais, en fait
d'hospitalité, elle valait celle d'un roi. A notre
arrivée, le maître vint nous tendre la main, et,

sans plus de cérémonie, il nous fit signe de le suivre.

Le suivre en effet, car l'accompagner eût été impossible. Un passage long, étroit, obscur, donnait accès dans cette habitation construite en poutres à peine équarries et permettait d'arriver à chacune des chambres; celles-ci étaient au nombre de quatre : la cuisine, l'atelier de tissage, la « badstofa », chambre à coucher de la famille, et, la meilleure entre toutes, la chambre des étrangers. Mon oncle, à la taille duquel on n'avait pas songé en bâtissant la maison, ne manqua pas de donner trois ou quatre fois de la tête contre les saillies du plafond.

On nous introduisit dans notre chambre, sorte de grande salle avec un sol de terre battue et éclairée d'une fenêtre dont les vitres étaient faites de membranes de mouton assez peu transparentes. La literie se composait de fourrage sec jeté dans deux cadres de bois peints en rouge et ornés de sentences islandaises. Je ne m'attendais pas à ce confortable; seulement il régnait dans cette maison une forte odeur de poisson sec, de viande macérée et de lait aigre dont mon odorat se trouvait assez mal.

Lorsque nous eûmes mis de côté notre harnachement de voyageurs, la voix de l'hôte se fit entendre, qui nous conviait à passer dans la cuisine, seule pièce où l'on fît du feu, même par les plus grands froids.

Mon oncle se hâta d'obéir à cette amicale injonction. Je le suivis.

La cheminée de la cuisine était d'un modèle antique; au milieu de la chambre, une pierre pour tout foyer; au toit, un trou par lequel s'échappait la fumée. Cette cuisine servait aussi de salle à manger.

A notre entrée, l'hôte, comme s'il ne vous avait pas encore vus, nous salua du mot « sællvertu », qui signifie « soyez heureux », et il vint nous baiser sur la joue.

Sa femme, après lui, prononça les mêmes paroles, accompagnées du même cérémonial; puis les deux époux, plaçant la main droite sur leur cœur, s'inclinèrent profondément.

Je me hâte de dire que l'Islandaise était mère de dix-neuf enfants, tous, grands et petits, grouillant pêle-mêle au milieu des volutes de fumée dont le foyer remplissait la chambre. A chaque instant j'apercevais une petite tête blonde et un peu mélancolique sortir de ce brouillard. On eût dit une guirlande d'anges insuffisamment débarbouillés.

Mon oncle et moi, nous fîmes très bon accueil à cette « couvée »; bientôt il y eut trois ou quatre de ces marmots sur nos épaules, autant sur nos genoux et le reste entre nos jambes. Ceux qui parlaient répétaient « sællvertu » dans tous les tons imaginables. Ceux qui ne parlaient pas n'en criaient que mieux.

Ce concert fut interrompu par l'annonce du repas. En ce moment rentra le chasseur, qui venait de pourvoir à la nourriture des chevaux, c'est-à-

dire qu'il les avait économiquement lâchés à travers champs; les pauvres bêtes devaient se contenter de brouter la mousse rare des rochers, quelques fucus peu nourrissants, et le lendemain elles ne manqueraient pas de venir d'elles-mêmes reprendre le travail de la veille.

« Sællvertu », fit Hans.

Puis tranquillement, automatiquement, sans qu'un baiser fût plus accentué que l'autre, il embrassa l'hôte, l'hôtesse et leurs dix-neuf enfants.

La cérémonie terminée, on se mit à table, au nombre de vingt-quatre, et par conséquent les uns sur les autres, dans le véritable sens de l'expression. Les plus favorisés n'avaient que deux marmots sur les genoux.

Cependant le silence se fit dans ce petit monde à l'arrivée de la soupe, et la taciturnité naturelle, même aux gamins islandais, reprit son empire. L'hôte nous servit une soupe au lichen et point désagréable, puis une énorme portion de poisson sec nageant dans du beurre aigri depuis vingt ans, et par conséquent bien préférable au beurre frais, d'après les idées gastronomiques de l'Islande. Il y avait avec cela du « skyr », sorte de lait caillé, accompagné de biscuit et relevé par du jus de baies de genièvre; enfin, pour boisson, du petit-lait mêlé d'eau, nommé « blanda » dans le pays. Si cette singulière nourriture était bonne ou non, c'est ce dont je ne pus juger. J'avais faim, et, au dessert, j'avalai jusqu'à la dernière bouchée une épaisse bouillie de sarrasin.

Le repas terminé, les enfants disparurent; les grandes personnes entourèrent le foyer où brûlaient de la tourbe, des bruyères, du fumier de vache et des os de poissons desséchés. Puis, après cette « prise de chaleur », les divers groupes regagnèrent leurs chambres respectives. L'hôtesse offrit de nous retirer, suivant la coutume, nos bas et nos pantalons; mais, sur un refus des plus gracieux de notre part, elle n'insista pas, et je pus enfin me blottir dans ma couche de fourrage.

Le lendemain, à cinq heures, nous faisions nos adieux au paysan islandais; mon oncle eut beaucoup de peine à lui faire accepter une rémunération convenable, et Hans donna le signal du départ.

A cent pas de Gardär, le terrain commença à changer d'aspect; le sol devint marécageux et moins favorable à la marche. Sur la droite, la série des montagnes se prolongeait indéfiniment comme un immense système de fortifications naturelles, dont nous suivions la contrescarpe; souvent des ruisseaux se présentaient à franchir qu'il fallait nécessairement passer à gué et sans trop mouiller les bagages.

Le désert se faisait de plus en plus profond; quelquefois, cependant, une ombre humaine semblait fuir au loin; si les détours de la route nous rapprochaient inopinément de l'un de ces spectres, j'éprouvais un dégoût soudain à la vue d'une tête gonflée, à peau luisante, dépourvue de cheveux, et de plaies repoussantes que trahissaient les déchirures de misérables haillons.

La malheureuse créature ne venait pas tendre sa main déformée; elle se sauvait, au contraire, mais pas si vite que Hans ne l'eût saluée du « sællvertu » habituel.

« Spetelsk, disait-il.

— Un lépreux! » répétait mon oncle.

Et ce mot seul produisait son effet répulsif. Cette horrible affection de la lèpre est assez commune en Islande; elle n'est pas contagieuse, mais héréditaire; aussi le mariage est-il interdit à ces misérables.

Ces apparitions n'étaient pas de nature à égayer le paysage qui devenait profondément triste; les dernières touffes d'herbes venaient mourir sous nos pieds. Pas un arbre, si ce n'est quelques bouquets de bouleaux nains semblables à des broussailles. Pas un animal, sinon quelques chevaux, de ceux que leur maître ne pouvait nourrir, et qui erraient sur les mornes plaines. Parfois un faucon planait dans les nuages gris et s'enfuyait à tire-d'aile vers les contrées du sud; je me laissais aller à la mélancolie de cette nature sauvage, et mes souvenirs me ramenaient à mon pays natal.

Il fallut bientôt traverser plusieurs petits fjörds sans importance, et enfin un véritable golfe; la marée, étale alors, nous permit de passer sans attendre et de gagner le hameau d'Alftanes, situé un mille au-delà.

Le soir, après avoir coupé à gué deux rivières riches en truites et en brochets, l'Alfa et l'Heta, nous fûmes obligés de passer la nuit dans une

« Un lépreux », répétait mon oncle (p. 114).

masure abandonnée, digne d'être hantée par tous les lutins de la mythologie scandinave; à coup sûr le génie du froid y avait élu domicile, et il fit des siennes pendant toute la nuit.

La journée suivante ne présenta aucun incident particulier. Toujours même sol marécageux, même uniformité, même physionomie triste. Le soir, nous avions franchi la moitié de la distance à parcourir, et nous couchions à « l'annexia » de Krösolbt.

Le 19 juin, pendant un mille environ, un terrain de lave s'étendit sous nos pieds; cette disposition du sol est appelée « hraun » dans le pays; la lave ridée à la surface affectait des formes de câbles tantôt allongés, tantôt roulés sur eux-mêmes; une immense coulée descendait des montagnes voisines, volcans actuellement éteints, mais dont ces débris attestaient la violence passée. Cependant quelques fumées de sources chaudes rampaient çà et là.

Le temps nous manquait pour observer ces phénomènes; il fallait marcher. Bientôt le sol marécageux reparut sous le pied de nos montures; de petits lacs l'entrecoupaient. Notre direction était alors à l'ouest; nous avions en effet tourné la grande baie de Faxa, et la double cime blanche du Sneffels se dressait dans les nuages à moins de cinq milles.

Les chevaux marchaient bien; les difficultés du sol ne les arrêtaient pas; pour mon compte, je commençais à être très fatigué; mon oncle demeurait ferme et droit comme au premier jour;

je ne pouvais m'empêcher de l'admirer à l'égal
du chasseur, qui regardait cette expédition comme
une simple promenade.

Le samedi 20 juin, à six heures du soir, nous
atteignions Büdir, bourgade située sur le bord de
la mer, et le guide réclamait sa paie convenue.
Mon oncle régla avec lui. Ce fut la famille même
de Hans, c'est-à-dire ses oncles et cousins ger-
mains, qui nous offrit l'hospitalité; nous fûmes bien
reçus, et sans abuser des bontés de ces braves gens,
je me serais volontiers refait chez eux des fatigues
du voyage. Mais mon oncle, qui n'avait rien à
refaire, ne l'entendait pas ainsi, et le lendemain
il fallut enfourcher de nouveau nos bonnes bêtes.

Le sol se ressentait du voisinage de la montagne
dont les racines de granit sortaient de terre, comme
celles d'un vieux chêne. Nous contournions
l'immense base du volcan. Le professeur ne le
perdait pas des yeux; il gesticulait, il semblait le
prendre au défi et dire : « Voilà donc le géant que
je vais dompter ! » Enfin, après quatre heures
de marche, les chevaux s'arrêtèrent d'eux-mêmes
à la porte du presbytère de Stapi.

XIV

Stapi est une bourgade formée d'une trentaine
de huttes, et bâtie en pleine lave sous les rayons du

soleil réfléchis par le volcan. Elle s'étend au fond
d'un petit fjörd encaissé dans une muraille basaltique du plus étrange effet.

On sait que le basalte est une roche brune
d'origine ignée. Elle affecte des formes régulières
qui surprennent par leur disposition. Ici la nature
procède géométriquement et travaille à la manière
humaine, comme si elle eût manié l'équerre, le
compas et le fil à plomb. Si partout ailleurs elle
fait de l'art avec ses grandes masses jetées sans
ordre, ses cônes à peine ébauchés, ses pyramides
imparfaites, avec la bizarre succession de ses lignes,
ici, voulant donner l'exemple de la régularité, et
précédant les architectes des premiers âges, elle
a créé un ordre sévère, que ni les splendeurs de
Babylone ni les merveilles de la Grèce n'ont jamais
dépassé.

J'avais bien entendu parler de la Chaussée des
Géants en Irlande, et de la Grotte de Fingal dans
l'une des Hébrides, mais le spectacle d'une substruction basaltique ne s'était pas encore offert à
mes regards.

Or, à Stapi, ce phénomène apparaissait dans
toute sa beauté.

La muraille du fjörd, comme toute la côte de la
presqu'île, se composait d'une suite de colonnes
verticales, hautes de trente pieds. Ces fûts droits
et d'une proportion pure supportaient une archi-
volte, faite de colonnes horizontales dont le
surplombement formait demi-voûte au-dessus
de la mer. A de certains intervalles, et sous cet

Le fjörd de Stapi encaissé dans une muraille basaltique (p. 117).

impluvium naturel, l'œil surprenait des ouvertures ogivales d'un dessin admirable, à travers lesquelles les flots du large venaient se précipiter en écumant. Quelques tronçons de basalte, arrachés par les fureurs de l'Océan, s'allongeaient sur le sol comme les débris d'un temple antique, ruines éternellement jeunes, sur lesquelles passaient les siècles sans les entamer.

Telle était la dernière étape de notre voyage terrestre. Hans nous y avait conduits avec intelligence, et je me rassurais un peu en songeant qu'il devait nous accompagner encore.

En arrivant à la porte de la maison du recteur, simple cabane basse, ni plus belle, ni plus confortable que ses voisines, je vis un homme en train de ferrer un cheval, le marteau à la main, et le tablier de cuir aux reins.

« Sællvertu, lui dit le chasseur.

— « God dag », répondit le maréchal ferrant en parfait danois.

— « Kyrkoherde », fit Hans en se retournant vers mon oncle.

— Le recteur ! répéta ce dernier. Il paraît, Axel, que ce brave homme est le recteur. »

Pendant ce temps, le guide mettait le « kyrkoherde » au courant de la situation ; celui-ci, suspendant son travail, poussa une sorte de cri en usage sans doute entre chevaux et maquignons, et aussitôt une grande mégère sortit de la cabane. Si elle ne mesurait pas six pieds de haut, il ne s'en fallait guère.

Je craignais qu'elle ne vînt offrir aux voyageurs le baiser islandais; mais il n'en fut rien, et même elle mit assez peu de bonne grâce à nous introduire dans sa maison.

La chambre des étrangers me parut être la plus mauvaise du presbytère, étroite, sale et infecte. Il fallut s'en contenter. Le recteur ne semblait pas pratiquer l'hospitalité antique. Loin de là. Avant la fin du jour, je vis que nous avions affaire à un forgeron, à un pêcheur, à un chasseur, à un charpentier, et pas du tout à un ministre du Seigneur. Nous étions en semaine, il est vrai. Peut-être se rattrapait-il le dimanche.

Je ne veux pas dire du mal de ces pauvres prêtres qui, après tout, sont fort misérables; ils reçoivent du gouvernement danois un traitement ridicule et perçoivent le quart de la dîme de leur paroisse, ce qui ne fait pas une somme de soixante marks courants [1]. De là, nécessité de travailler pour vivre; mais à pêcher, à chasser, à ferrer des chevaux, on finit par prendre les manières, le ton et les mœurs des chasseurs, des pêcheurs et autres gens un peu rudes; le soir même, je m'aperçus que notre hôte ne comptait pas la sobriété au nombre de ses vertus.

Mon oncle comprit vite à quel genre d'homme il avait affaire; au lieu d'un brave et digne savant, il trouvait un paysan lourd et grossier. Il résolut donc de commencer au plus tôt sa grande expédition et de quitter cette cure peu hospitalière. Il ne regar-

1. Monnaie de Hambourg, 90 francs environ.

dait pas à ses fatigues et résolut d'aller passer quelques jours dans la montagne.

Les préparatifs de départ furent donc faits dès le lendemain de notre arrivée à Stapi. Hans loua les services de trois Islandais pour remplacer les chevaux dans le transport des bagages; mais, une fois arrivés au fond du cratère, ces indigènes devaient rebrousser chemin et nous abandonner à nous-mêmes. Ce point fut parfaitement arrêté.

A cette occasion, mon oncle dut apprendre au chasseur que son intention était de poursuivre la reconnaissance du volcan jusqu'à ses dernières limites.

Hans se contenta d'incliner la tête. Aller là ou ailleurs, s'enfoncer dans les entrailles de son île ou la parcourir, il n'y voyait aucune différence. Quant à moi, distrait jusqu'alors par les incidents du voyage, j'avais un peu oublié l'avenir, mais maintenant je sentais l'émotion me reprendre de plus belle. Qu'y faire? Si j'avais pu tenter de résister au professeur Lidenbrock, c'était à Hambourg et non au pied du Sneffels.

Une idée, entre toutes, me tracassait fort, idée effrayante et faite pour ébranler des nerfs moins sensibles que les miens.

« Voyons, me disais-je, nous allons gravir le Sneffels. Bien. Nous allons visiter son cratère. Bon. D'autres l'ont fait qui n'en sont pas morts. Mais ce n'est pas tout. S'il se présente un chemin pour descendre dans les entrailles du sol, si ce malencontreux Saknussemm a dit vrai, nous allons

nous perdre au milieu des galeries souterraines du volcan. Or, rien n'affirme que le Sneffels soit éteint ! Qui prouve qu'une éruption ne se prépare pas ? De ce que le monstre dort depuis 1229, s'ensuit-il qu'il ne puisse se réveiller ? Et s'il se réveille, qu'est-ce que nous deviendrons ? »

Cela demandait la peine d'y réfléchir, et j'y réfléchissais. Je ne pouvais dormir sans rêver d'éruption. Or, le rôle de scorie me paraissait assez brutal à jouer.

Enfin je n'y tins plus ; je résolus de soumettre le cas à mon oncle le plus adroitement possible, et sous forme d'une hypothèse parfaitement irréalisable.

J'allai le trouver. Je lui fis part de mes craintes, et je me reculai pour le laisser éclater à son aise.

« J'y pensais », répondit-il simplement.

Que signifiaient ces paroles ? Allait-il donc entendre la voix de la raison ? Songeait-il à suspendre ses projets ? C'était trop beau pour être possible.

Après quelques instants de silence, pendant lesquels je n'osais l'interroger, il reprit en disant :

« J'y pensais. Depuis notre arrivée à Stapi, je me suis préoccupé de la grave question que tu viens de me soumettre, car il ne faut pas agir en imprudents.

— Non, répondis-je avec force.

— Il y a six cents ans que le Sneffels est muet, mais il peut parler. Or, les éruptions sont toujours précédées de phénomènes parfaitement connus.

J'ai donc interrogé les habitants du pays, j'ai étudié le sol, et je puis te le dire, Axel, il n'y aura pas d'éruption. »

A cette affirmation je restai stupéfait, et je ne pus répliquer.

« Tu doutes de mes paroles ? dit mon oncle, eh bien ! suis-moi. »

J'obéis machinalement. En sortant du presbytère, le professeur prit un chemin direct qui, par une ouverture de la muraille basaltique, s'éloignait de la mer. Bientôt nous étions en rase campagne, si l'on peut donner ce nom à un amoncellement immense de déjections volcaniques. Le pays paraissait comme écrasé sous une pluie de pierres énormes, de trapp, de basalte, de granit et de toutes les roches pyroxéniques.

Je voyais çà et là des fumerolles monter dans les airs ; ces vapeurs blanches, nommées « reykir » en langue islandaise, venaient des sources thermales, et elles indiquaient, par leur violence, l'activité volcanique du sol. Cela me paraissait justifier mes craintes. Aussi je tombai de mon haut quand mon oncle me dit :

« Tu vois toutes ces fumées, Axel ; eh bien, elles prouvent que nous n'avons rien à redouter des fureurs du volcan !

— Par exemple ! m'écriai-je.

— Retiens bien ceci, reprit le professeur : aux approches d'une éruption, ces fumerolles redoublent d'activité pour disparaître complètement pendant la durée du phénomène, car les

Je voyais çà et là des fumerolles monter dans les airs (p. 124).

fluides élastiques, n'ayant plus la tension nécessaire, prennent le chemin des cratères au lieu de
s'échapper à travers les fissures du globe. Si donc
ces vapeurs se maintiennent dans leur état habituel,
si leur énergie ne s'accroît pas, si tu ajoutes à cette
observation que le vent, la pluie ne sont pas rempla-
cés par un air lourd et calme, tu peux affirmer
qu'il n'y aura pas d'éruption prochaine.

— Mais...

— Assez. Quand la science a prononcé, il n'y a
plus qu'à se taire. »

Je revins à la cure l'oreille basse. Mon oncle
m'avait battu avec des arguments scientifiques.
Cependant j'avais encore un espoir, c'est qu'une
fois arrivés au fond du cratère, il serait impossible,
faute de galerie, de descendre plus profondément,
et cela en dépit de tous les Saknussemm du monde.

Je passai la nuit suivante en plein cauchemar au
milieu d'un volcan et des profondeurs de la terre,
je me sentis lancé dans les espaces planétaires sous
la forme de roche éruptive.

Le lendemain, 23 juin, Hans nous attendait
avec ses compagnons chargés des vivres, des outils
et des instruments. Deux bâtons ferrés, deux fusils,
deux cartouchières, étaient réservés à mon oncle
et à moi. Hans, en homme de précaution, avait
ajouté à nos bagages une outre pleine qui, jointe
à nos gourdes, nous assurait de l'eau pour huit
jours.

Il était neuf heures du matin. Le recteur et sa
haute mégère attendaient devant leur porte.

Ils voulaient sans doute nous adresser l'adieu suprême de l'hôte au voyageur. Mais cet adieu prit la forme inattendue d'une note formidable, où l'on comptait jusqu'à l'air de la maison pastorale, air infect, j'ose le dire. Ce digne couple nous rançonnait comme un aubergiste suisse et portait à un beau prix son hospitalité surfaite.

Mon oncle paya sans marchander. Un homme qui partait pour le centre de la terre ne regardait pas à quelques rixdales.

Ce point réglé, Hans donna le signal du départ, et quelques instants après nous avions quitté Stapi.

XV

Le Sneffels est haut de cinq mille pieds. Il termine, par son double cône, une bande trachytique qui se détache du système orographique de l'île. De notre point de départ on ne pouvait voir ses deux pics se profiler sur le fond grisâtre du ciel. J'apercevais seulement une énorme calotte de neige abaissée sur le front du géant.

Nous marchions en file, précédés du chasseur; celui-ci remontait d'étroits sentiers où deux personnes n'auraient pu aller de front. Toute conversation devenait donc à peu près impossible.

Au-delà de la muraille basaltique du fjörd de Stapi se présenta d'abord un sol de tourbe herbacée

et fibreuse, résidu de l'antique végétation des marécages de la presqu'île; la masse de ce combustible encore inexploité suffirait à chauffer pendant un siècle toute la population de l'Islande; cette vaste tourbière, mesurée du fond de certains ravins, avait souvent soixante-dix pieds de haut et présentait des couches successives de détritus carbonisés, séparées par des feuillets de tuf ponceux.

En véritable neveu du professeur Lidenbrock et malgré mes préoccupations, j'observais avec intérêt les curiosités minéralogiques étalées dans ce vaste cabinet d'histoire naturelle; en même temps je refaisais dans mon esprit toute l'histoire géologique de l'Islande.

Cette île, si curieuse, est évidemment sortie du fond des eaux à une époque relativement moderne. Peut-être même s'élève-t-elle encore par un mouvement insensible. S'il en est ainsi, on ne peut attribuer son origine qu'à l'action des feux souterrains. Donc, dans ce cas, la théorie de Humphry Davy, le document de Saknussemm, les prétentions de mon oncle, tout s'en allait en fumée. Cette hypothèse me conduisit à examiner attentivement la nature du sol, et je me rendis bientôt compte de la succession des phénomènes qui présidèrent à sa formation.

L'Islande, absolument privée de terrain sédimentaire, se compose uniquement de tuf volcanique, c'est-à-dire d'un agglomérat de pierres et de roches d'une texture poreuse. Avant l'existence des volcans, elle était faite d'un massif trappéen,

lentement soulevé au-dessus des flots par la poussée des forces centrales. Les feux intérieurs n'avaient pas encore fait irruption au-dehors.

Mais, plus tard, une large fente se creusa diagonalement du sud-ouest au nord-est de l'île, par laquelle s'épancha peu à peu toute la pâte trachytique. Le phénomène s'accomplissait alors sans violence; l'issue était énorme, et les matières fondues, rejetées des entrailles du globe, s'étendirent tranquillement en vastes nappes ou en masses mamelonnées. A cette époque apparurent les feldspaths, les syénites et les porphyres.

Mais, grâce à cet épanchement, l'épaisseur de l'île s'accrut considérablement, et, par suite, sa force de résistance. On conçoit quelle quantité de fluides élastiques s'emmagasina dans son sein, lorsqu'elle n'offrit plus aucune issue, après le refroidissement de la croûte trachytique. Il arriva donc un moment où la puissance mécanique de ces gaz fut telle qu'ils soulevèrent la lourde écorce et se creusèrent de hautes cheminées. De là le volcan fait du soulèvement de la croûte, puis le cratère subitement troué au sommet du volcan.

Alors aux phénomènes éruptifs succédèrent les phénomènes volcaniques. Par les ouvertures nouvellement formées s'échappèrent d'abord les déjections basaltiques, dont la plaine que nous traversions en ce moment offrait à nos regards les plus merveilleux spécimens. Nous marchions sur ces roches pesantes d'un gris foncé que le refroidissement avait moulées en prismes à base hexagone.

Au loin se voyaient un grand nombre de cônes aplatis, qui furent jadis autant de bouches igni-vomes.

Puis, l'éruption basaltique épuisée, le volcan, dont la force s'accrut de celle des cratères éteints, donna passage aux laves et à ces tufs de cendres et de scories dont j'apercevais les longues coulées éparpillées sur ses flancs comme une chevelure opulente.

Telle fut la succession des phénomènes qui constituèrent l'Islande; tous provenaient de l'action des feux intérieurs, et supposer que la masse interne ne demeurait pas dans un état permanent d'incandescente liquidité, c'était folie. Folie surtout de prétendre atteindre le centre du globe!

Je me rassurais donc sur l'issue de notre entreprise, tout en marchant à l'assaut du Sneffels.

La route devenait de plus en plus difficile; le sol montait; les éclats de roches s'ébranlaient, et il fallait la plus scrupuleuse attention pour éviter des chutes dangereuses.

Hans s'avançait tranquillement comme sur un terrain uni; parfois il disparaissait derrière les grands blocs, et nous le perdions de vue momentanément; alors un sifflement aigu, échappé de ses lèvres, indiquait la direction à suivre. Souvent aussi il s'arrêtait, ramassait quelques débris de rocs, les disposait d'une façon reconnaissable et formait ainsi des amers destinés à indiquer la route du retour. Précaution bonne en soi, mais que les événements futurs rendirent inutile.

Nous nous prêtions un mutuel secours à l'aide
de nos bâtons (p. 132).

Trois fatigantes heures de marche nous avaient
amenés seulement à la base de la montagne. Là,
Hans fit signe de s'arrêter, et un déjeuner sommaire fut partagé entre tous. Mon oncle mangeait
les morceaux doubles pour aller plus vite. Seulement, cette halte de réfection étant aussi une halte
de repos, il dut attendre le bon plaisir du guide, qui
donna le signal du départ une heure après. Les
trois Islandais, aussi taciturnes que leur camarade
le chasseur, ne prononcèrent pas un seul mot et
mangèrent sobrement.

Nous commencions maintenant à gravir les
pentes du Sneffels. Son neigeux sommet, par une
illusion d'optique fréquente dans les montagnes,
me paraissait fort rapproché, et cependant, que
de longues heures avant de l'atteindre! Quelle
fatigue surtout! Les pierres qu'aucun ciment de
terre, aucune herbe ne liaient entre elles, s'ébou-
laient sous nos pieds et allaient se perdre dans la
plaine avec la rapidité d'une avalanche.

En de certains endroits, les flancs du mont
faisaient avec l'horizon un angle de trente-six
degrés au moins; il était impossible de les gravir, et
ces raidillons pierreux devaient être tournés non
sans difficulté. Nous nous prêtions alors un mutuel
secours à l'aide de nos bâtons.

Je dois dire que mon oncle se tenait près de moi
le plus possible; il ne me perdait pas de vue, et,
en mainte occasion, son bras me fournit un solide
appui. Pour son compte, il avait sans doute le
sentiment inné de l'équilibre, car il ne bronchait

pas. Les Islandais, quoique chargés, grimpaient avec une agilité de montagnards.

A voir la hauteur de la cime du Sneffels, il me semblait impossible qu'on pût l'atteindre de ce côté, si l'angle d'inclinaison des pentes ne se fermait pas. Heureusement, après une heure de fatigues et de tours de force, au milieu du vaste tapis de neige développé sur la croupe du volcan, une sorte d'escalier se présenta inopinément, qui simplifia notre ascension. Il était formé par l'un de ces torrents de pierres rejetées par les éruptions, et dont le nom islandais est « stinâ ». Si ce torrent n'eût pas été arrêté dans sa chute par la disposition des flancs de la montagne, il serait allé se précipiter dans la mer et former des îles nouvelles.

Tel il était, tel il nous servit fort. La roideur des pentes s'accroissait, mais ces marches de pierre permettaient de les gravir aisément, et si rapidement même, qu'étant resté un moment en arrière pendant que mes compagnons continuaient leur ascension, je les aperçus déjà réduits, par l'éloignement, à une apparence microscopique.

A sept heures du soir, nous avions monté les deux mille marches de l'escalier, et nous dominions une extumescence de la montagne, sorte d'assise sur laquelle s'appuyait le cône proprement dit du cratère.

La mer s'étendait à une profondeur de trois mille deux cents pieds. Nous avions dépassé la limite des neiges perpétuelles, assez peu élevées en Islande par suite de l'humidité constante du climat.

Il faisait un froid violent. Le vent soufflait avec force. J'étais épuisé. Le professeur vit bien que mes jambes me refusaient tout service, et, malgré son impatience, il se décida à s'arrêter. Il fit donc signe au chasseur, qui secoua la tête en disant :

« Ofvanför.

— Il paraît qu'il faut aller plus haut », dit mon oncle.

Puis il demanda à Hans le motif de sa réponse.

« Mistour, répondit le guide.

— « Ja, mistour », répéta l'un des Islandais d'un ton assez effrayé.

— Que signifie ce mot ? demandai-je avec inquiétude.

— Vois », dit mon oncle.

Je portai mes regards vers la plaine. Une immense colonne de pierre ponce pulvérisée, de sable et de poussière s'élevait en tournoyant comme une trombe ; le vent la rabattait sur le flanc du Sneffels, auquel nous étions accrochés ; ce rideau opaque étendu devant le soleil produisait une grande ombre jetée sur la montagne. Si cette trombe s'inclinait, elle devait inévitablement nous enlacer dans ses tourbillons. Ce phénomène, assez fréquent lorsque le vent souffle des glaciers, prend le nom de « mistour » en langue islandaise.

« Hastigt, hastigt », s'écria notre guide.

Sans savoir le danois, je compris qu'il nous fallait suivre Hans au plus vite. Celui-ci commença à tourner le cône du cratère, mais en biaisant, de manière à faciliter la marche. Bientôt la trombe

Bientôt la trombe s'abattit sur la montagne (p. 134).

s'abattit sur la montagne, qui tressaillit à son choc; les pierres saisies dans les remous du vent volèrent en pluie comme dans une éruption. Nous étions, heureusement, sur le versant opposé et à l'abri de tout danger. Sans la précaution du guide, nos corps déchiquetés, réduits en poussière, fussent retombés au loin comme le produit de quelque météore inconnu.

Cependant Hans ne jugea pas prudent de passer la nuit sur les flancs du cône. Nous continuâmes notre ascension en zigzag; les quinze cents pieds qui restaient à franchir prirent près de cinq heures; les détours, les biais et contremarches mesuraient trois lieues au moins. Je n'en pouvais plus; je succombais au froid et à la faim. L'air, un peu raréfié, ne suffisait pas au jeu de mes poumons.

Enfin, à onze heures du soir, en pleine obscurité, le sommet du Sneffels fut atteint, et, avant d'aller m'abriter à l'intérieur du cratère, j'eus le temps d'apercevoir « le soleil de minuit » au plus bas de sa carrière, projetant ses pâles rayons sur l'île endormie à mes pieds.

XVI

Le souper fut rapidement dévoré et la petite troupe se casa de son mieux. La couche était dure, l'abri peu solide, la situation fort pénible, à cinq

mille pieds au-dessus du niveau de la mer. Cependant mon sommeil fut particulièrement paisible pendant cette nuit, l'une des meilleures que j'eusse passées depuis longtemps. Je ne rêvai même pas.

Le lendemain, on se réveilla à demi gelé par un air très vif, aux rayons d'un beau soleil. Je quittai ma couche de granit et j'allai jouir du magnifique spectacle qui se développait à mes regards.

J'occupais le sommet de l'un des deux pics du Sneffels, celui du sud. De là, ma vue s'étendait sur la plus grande partie de l'île. L'optique, commune à toutes les grandes hauteurs, en relevait les rivages, tandis que les parties centrales paraissaient s'enfoncer. On eût dit qu'une de ces cartes en relief d'Helbesmer s'étalait sous mes pieds. Je voyais les vallées profondes se croiser en tous sens, les précipices se creuser comme des puits, les lacs se changer en étangs, les rivières se faire ruisseaux. Sur ma droite se succédaient les glaciers sans nombre et les pics multipliés, dont quelques-uns s'empanachaient de fumées légères. Les ondulations de ces montagnes infinies, que leurs couches de neige semblaient rendre écumantes, rappelaient à mon souvenir la surface d'une mer agitée. Si je me retournais vers l'ouest, l'Océan s'y développait dans sa majestueuse étendue, comme une continuation de ces sommets moutonneux. Où finissait la terre, où commençaient les flots, mon œil le distinguait à peine.

Je me plongeais ainsi dans cette prestigieuse extase que donnent les hautes cimes, et cette fois

sans vertige, car je m'accoutumais enfin à ces
sublimes contemplations. Mes regards éblouis se
baignaient dans la transparente irradiation des
rayons solaires. J'oubliais qui j'étais, où j'étais, pour
vivre de la vie des elfes ou des sylphes, imaginaires
habitants de la mythologie scandinave. Je m'enivrais
de la volupté des hauteurs, sans songer aux abîmes
dans lesquels ma destinée allait me plonger avant
peu. Mais je fus ramené au sentiment de la réalité
par l'arrivée du professeur et de Hans, qui me
rejoignirent au sommet du pic.

Mon oncle, se tournant vers l'ouest, m'indiqua
de la main une légère vapeur, une brume, une
apparence de terre qui dominait la ligne des flots.

« Le Groënland, dit-il.

— Le Groënland ? m'écriai-je.

— Oui, nous n'en sommes pas à trente-cinq
lieues, et pendant les dégels les ours blancs arrivent
jusqu'à l'Islande, portés sur les glaçons du nord.
Mais cela importe peu. Nous sommes au sommet du
Sneffels, et voici deux pics, l'un au sud, l'autre
au nord. Hans va nous dire de quel nom les Islandais appellent celui qui nous porte en ce moment. »

La demande formulée, le chasseur répondit :
« Scartaris. »

Mon oncle me jeta un coup d'œil triomphant.
« Au cratère ! » dit-il.

Le cratère du Sneffels représentait un cône
renversé dont l'orifice pouvait avoir une demi-
lieue de diamètre. Sa profondeur, je l'estimais à
deux mille pieds environ. Que l'on juge de l'état

d'un pareil récipient, lorsqu'il s'emplissait de tonnerres et de flammes. Le fond de l'entonnoir ne devait pas mesurer plus de cinq cents pieds de tour, de telle sorte que ses pentes assez douces permettaient d'arriver facilement à sa partie inférieure. Involontairement je comparais ce cratère à un énorme tromblon évasé, et la comparaison m'épouvantait.

« Descendre dans un tromblon, pensai-je, quand il est peut-être chargé et qu'il peut partir au moindre choc, c'est œuvre de fous. »

Mais je n'avais pas à reculer. Hans, d'un air indifférent, reprit la tête de la troupe. Je le suivis sans mot dire.

Afin de faciliter la descente, Hans décrivait à l'intérieur du cône des ellipses très allongées. Il fallait marcher au milieu des roches éruptives, dont quelques-unes, ébranlées dans leurs alvéoles, se précipitaient en rebondissant jusqu'au fond de l'abîme. Leur chute déterminait des répercussions d'échos d'une étrange sonorité.

Certaines parties du cône formaient des glaciers intérieurs. Hans ne s'avançait alors qu'avec une extrême précaution, sondant le sol de son bâton ferré pour y découvrir les crevasses. A de certains passages douteux, il devint nécessaire de nous lier par une longue corde, afin que celui auquel le pied viendrait à manquer inopinément se trouvât soutenu par ses compagnons. Cette solidarité était chose prudente, mais elle n'excluait pas tout danger.

Cependant, et malgré les difficultés de la descente sur des pentes que le guide ne connaissait pas, la route se fit sans accident, sauf la chute d'un ballot de cordes qui s'échappa des mains d'un Islandais et alla par le plus court jusqu'au fond de l'abîme.

A midi nous étions arrivés. Je relevai la tête, et j'aperçus l'orifice supérieur du cône, dans lequel s'encadrait un morceau de ciel d'une circonférence singulièrement réduite, mais presque parfaite. Sur un point seulement se détachait le pic du Scartaris, qui s'enfonçait dans l'immensité.

Au fond du cratère s'ouvraient trois cheminées par lesquelles, au temps des éruptions du Sneffels, le foyer central chassait ses laves et ses vapeurs. Chacune de ces cheminées avait environ cent pieds de diamètre. Elles étaient là béantes sous nos pas. Je n'eus pas le courage d'y plonger mes regards. Le professeur Lidenbrock, lui, avait fait un examen rapide de leur disposition; il était haletant; il courait de l'une à l'autre, gesticulant et lançant des paroles incompréhensibles. Hans et ses compagnons, assis sur des morceaux de lave, le regardaient faire; ils le prenaient évidemment pour un fou.

Tout à coup mon oncle poussa un cri. Je crus qu'il venait de perdre pied et de tomber dans l'un des trois gouffres. Mais non. Je l'aperçus, les bras étendus, les jambes écartées, debout devant un roc de granit posé au centre du cratère, comme un énorme piédestal fait pour la statue d'un Pluton.

Il était dans la pose d'un homme stupéfait, mais dont la stupéfaction fit bientôt place à une joie insensée.

« Axel, Axel! s'écria-t-il, viens! viens! »

J'accourus. Ni Hans ni les Islandais ne bougèrent.

« Regarde », me dit le professeur.

Et, partageant sa stupéfaction, sinon sa joie, je lus sur la face occidentale du bloc, en caractères runiques à demi rongés par le temps, ce nom mille fois maudit :

ᛁᛆᚾᚵ ᛋᛁᛁᚳᚾᛌᛋᛋᛏᚷ

« Arne Saknussemm! s'écria mon oncle, doute-ras-tu encore? »

Je ne répondis pas, et je revins consterné à mon banc de lave. L'évidence m'écrasait.

Combien de temps demeurai-je ainsi plongé dans mes réflexions, je l'ignore. Tout ce que je sais, c'est qu'en relevant la tête je vis mon oncle et Hans seuls au fond du cratère. Les Islandais avaient été congédiés, et maintenant ils redescendaient les pentes extérieures du Sneffels pour regagner Stapi.

Hans dormait tranquillement au pied d'un roc, dans une coulée de lave où il s'était fait un lit improvisé; mon oncle tournait au fond du cratère, comme une bête sauvage dans la fosse d'un trappeur. Je n'eus ni l'envie ni la force de me lever, et prenant exemple sur le guide, je me laissai aller à un douloureux assoupissement, croyant

« Regarde ! » me dit le professeur (p. 141).

entendre des bruits ou sentir des frissonnements
dans les flancs de la montagne.

Ainsi se passa cette première nuit au fond du
cratère.

Le lendemain, un ciel gris, nuageux, lourd,
s'abaissa sur le sommet du cône. Je ne m'en aperçus
pas tant à l'obscurité du gouffre qu'à la colère
dont mon oncle fut pris.

J'en compris la raison, et un reste d'espoir me
revint au cœur. Voici pourquoi.

Des trois routes ouvertes sous nos pas une seule
avait été suivie par Saknussemm. Au dire du savant
islandais, on devait la reconnaître à cette particularité signalée dans le cryptogramme, que l'ombre du
Scartaris venait en caresser les bords pendant
les derniers jours du mois de juin.

On pouvait en effet considérer ce pic aigu comme
le style d'un immense cadran solaire, dont l'ombre
à un jour donné marquait le chemin du centre
du globe.

Or, si le soleil venait à manquer, pas d'ombre.
Conséquemment, pas d'indication. Nous étions au
25 juin. Que le ciel demeurât couvert pendant
six jours, et il faudrait remettre l'observation à
une autre année.

Je renonce à peindre l'impuissante colère du
professeur Lidenbrock. La journée se passa, et
aucune ombre ne vint s'allonger sur le fond du
cratère. Hans ne bougea pas de sa place; il devait
pourtant se demander ce que nous attendions,
s'il se demandait quelque chose! Mon oncle ne

m'adressa pas une seule fois la parole. Ses regards, invariablement tournés vers le ciel, se perdaient dans sa teinte grise et brumeuse.

Le 26, rien encore. Une pluie mêlée de neige tomba pendant toute la journée. Hans construisit une hutte avec des morceaux de lave. Je pris un certain plaisir à suivre de l'œil les milliers de cascades improvisées sur les flancs du cône, et dont chaque pierre accroissait l'assourdissant murmure.

Mon oncle ne se contenait plus. Il y avait de quoi irriter un homme plus patient, car c'était véritablement échouer au port.

Mais aux grandes douleurs, le Ciel mêle incessamment les grandes joies, et il réservait au professeur Lidenbrock une satisfaction égale à ses désespérants ennuis.

Le lendemain le ciel fut encore couvert; mais le dimanche, 28 juin, l'antépénultième jour du mois, avec le changement de lune vint le changement de temps. Le soleil versa ses rayons à flots dans le cratère. Chaque monticule, chaque roc, chaque pierre, chaque aspérité eut part à son lumineux effluve et projeta instantanément son ombre sur le sol. Entre toutes, celle du Scartaris se dessina comme une vive arête et se mit à tourner insensiblement avec l'astre radieux.

Mon oncle tournait avec elle.

A midi, dans sa période la plus courte, elle vint lécher doucement le bord de la cheminée centrale.

« C'est là! s'écria le professeur, c'est là! Au centre du globe! » ajouta-t-il en danois.

Je regardai Hans.

« Forüt! fit tranquillement le guide.

— En avant! » répondit mon oncle.

Il était une heure et treize minutes du soir.

XVII

LE véritable voyage commençait. Jusqu'alors les fatigues l'avaient emporté sur les difficultés; maintenant celles-ci allaient véritablement naître sous nos pas.

Je n'avais point encore plongé mon regard dans ce puits insondable où j'allais m'engouffrer. Le moment était venu. Je pouvais encore ou prendre mon parti de l'entreprise ou refuser de la tenter. Mais j'eus honte de reculer devant le chasseur. Hans acceptait si tranquillement l'aventure, avec une telle indifférence, une si parfaite insouciance de tout danger, que je rougis à l'idée d'être moins brave que lui. Seul, j'aurais entamé la série des grands arguments; mais en présence du guide je me tus; un de mes souvenirs s'envola vers ma jolie Virlandaise, et je m'approchai de la cheminée centrale.

J'ai dit qu'elle mesurait cent pieds de diamètre, ou trois cents pieds de tour. Je me penchai au-dessus d'un roc qui surplombait, et je regardai. Mes cheveux se hérissèrent. Le sentiment du vide

s'empara de mon être. Je sentis le centre de gravité
se déplacer en moi et le vertige monter à ma tête
comme une ivresse. Rien de plus capiteux que cette
attraction de l'abîme. J'allais tomber. Une main
me retint. Celle de Hans. Décidément je n'avais
pas pris assez de « leçons de gouffre » à la Frelsers-
Kirk de Copenhague.

Cependant, si peu que j'eusse hasardé mes
regards dans ce puits, je m'étais rendu compte
de sa conformation. Ses parois, presque à pic,
présentaient de nombreuses saillies qui devaient
faciliter la descente. Mais si l'escalier ne manquait
pas, la rampe faisait défaut. Une corde attachée à
l'orifice aurait suffi pour nous soutenir, mais
comment la détacher, lorsqu'on serait parvenu à
son extrémité inférieure ?

Mon oncle employa un moyen fort simple pour
obvier à cette difficulté. Il déroula une corde
de la grosseur du pouce et longue de quatre cents
pieds; il en laissa filer d'abord la moitié, puis il
l'enroula autour d'un bloc de lave qui faisait
saillie et rejeta l'autre moitié dans la cheminée.
Chacun de nous pouvait alors descendre en réunis-
sant dans sa main les deux moitiés de la corde qui
ne pouvait se défiler; une fois descendus de deux
cents pieds, rien ne nous serait plus aisé que de
la ramener en lâchant un bout et en halant sur
l'autre. Puis on recommencerait cet exercice
ad infinitum.

« Maintenant, dit mon oncle, après avoir achevé
ces préparatifs, occupons-nous des bagages;

ils vont être divisés en trois paquets, et chacun de nous en attachera un sur son dos; j'entends parler seulement des objets fragiles. »

L'audacieux professeur ne nous comprenait évidemment pas dans cette dernière catégorie.

« Hans, reprit-il, va se charger des outils et d'une partie des vivres; toi, Axel, d'un second tiers des vivres et des armes; moi, du reste des vivres et des instruments délicats.

— Mais, dis-je, et les vêtements, et cette masse de cordes et d'échelles, qui se chargera de les descendre?

— Ils descendront tout seuls.

— Comment cela? demandai-je.

— Tu vas le voir. »

Mon oncle employait volontiers les grands moyens et sans hésiter. Sur son ordre, Hans réunit en un seul colis les objets non fragiles, et ce paquet, solidement cordé, fut tout bonnement précipité dans le gouffre.

J'entendis ce mugissement sonore produit par le déplacement des couches d'air. Mon oncle, penché sur l'abîme, suivait d'un œil satisfait la descente de ses bagages, et ne se releva qu'après les avoir perdus de vue.

« Bon, fit-il. A nous maintenant. »

Je demande à tout homme de bonne foi s'il était possible d'entendre sans frissonner de telles paroles!

Le professeur attacha sur son dos le paquet des instruments; Hans prit celui des outils, moi celui

des armes. La descente commença dans l'ordre suivant : Hans, mon oncle et moi. Elle se fit dans un profond silence, troublé seulement par la chute des débris de roc qui se précipitaient dans l'abîme.

Je me laissai couler, pour ainsi dire, serrant frénétiquement la double corde d'une main, de l'autre m'arc-boutant au moyen de mon bâton ferré. Une idée unique me dominait : je craignais que le point d'appui ne vînt à manquer. Cette corde me paraissait bien fragile pour supporter le poids de trois personnes. Je m'en servais le moins possible, opérant des miracles d'équilibre sur les saillies de lave que mon pied cherchait à saisir comme une main.

Lorsqu'une de ces marches glissantes venait à s'ébranler sous les pas de Hans, il disait de sa voix tranquille :

« Gif akt !

— Attention ! » répétait mon oncle.

Après une demi-heure, nous étions arrivés sur la surface d'un roc fortement engagé dans la paroi de la cheminée.

Hans tira la corde par l'un de ses bouts ; l'autre s'éleva dans l'air ; après avoir dépassé le rocher supérieur, il retomba en raclant les morceaux de pierre et de lave, sorte de pluie, ou mieux, de grêle fort dangereuse.

En me penchant au-dessus de notre étroit plateau, je remarquai que le fond du trou était encore invisible.

La manœuvre de la corde recommença, et, une

La descente commença (p. 148).

demi-heure après, nous avions gagné une nouvelle profondeur de deux cents pieds.

Je ne sais si le plus enragé géologue eût essayé d'étudier, pendant cette descente, la nature des terrains qui l'environnaient. Pour mon compte, je ne m'en·inquiétai guère; qu'ils fussent pliocènes, miocènes, éocènes, crétacés, jurassiques, triasiques, perniens, carbonifères, dévoniens, siluriens ou primitifs, cela me préoccupa peu. Mais le professeur, sans doute, fit ses observations ou prit ses notes, car, à l'une des haltes, il me dit :

« Plus je vais, plus j'ai confiance. La disposition de ces terrains volcaniques donne absolument raison à la théorie de Davy. Nous sommes en plein sol primordial, sol dans lequel s'est produite l'opération chimique des métaux enflammés au contact de l'air et de l'eau. Je repousse absolument le système d'une chaleur centrale. D'ailleurs, nous verrons bien. »

Toujours la même conclusion. On comprend que je ne m'amusai pas à discuter. Mon silence fut pris pour un assentiment, et la descente recommença.

Au bout de trois heures, je n'entrevoyais pas encore le fond de la cheminée. Lorsque je relevais la tête, j'apercevais son orifice qui décroissait sensiblement. Ses parois, par suite de leur légère inclinaison, tendaient à se rapprocher. L'obscurité se faisait peu à peu.

Cependant nous descendions toujours; il me semblait que les pierres détachées des parois s'engloutissaient avec une répercussion plus mate

et qu'elles devaient rencontrer promptement le fond de l'abîme.

Comme j'avais eu soin de noter exactement nos manœuvres de corde, je pus me rendre un compte exact de la profondeur atteinte et du temps écoulé.

Nous avions alors répété quatorze fois cette manœuvre qui durait une demi-heure. C'était donc sept heures, plus quatorze quarts d'heure de repos ou trois heures et demie. En tout, dix heures et demie. Nous étions partis à une heure, il devait être onze heures en ce moment.

Quant à la profondeur à laquelle nous étions parvenus, ces quatorze manœuvres d'une corde de deux cents pieds donnaient deux mille huit cents pieds.

En ce moment la voix de Hans se fit entendre :

« Halt ! » dit-il.

Je m'arrêtai court au moment où j'allais heurter de mes pieds la tête de mon oncle.

« Nous sommes arrivés, dit celui-ci.

— Où ? demandai-je en me laissant glisser près de lui.

— Au fond de la cheminée perpendiculaire.

— Il n'y a donc pas d'autre issue ?

— Si, une sorte de couloir que j'entrevois et qui oblique vers la droite. Nous verrons cela demain. Soupons d'abord, nous dormirons après. »

L'obscurité n'était pas encore complète. On ouvrit le sac aux provisions, on mangea et chacun se coucha de son mieux sur un lit de pierres et de débris de lave.

Et quand, étendu sur le dos, j'ouvris les yeux, j'aperçus un point brillant à l'extrémité de ce tube long de trois mille pieds, qui se transformait en une gigantesque lunette.

C'était une étoile dépouillée de toute scintillation, et qui, d'après mes calculs, devait être β de la Petite Ourse.

Puis je m'endormis d'un profond sommeil.

XVIII

A HUIT heures du matin, un rayon du jour vint nous réveiller. Les mille facettes de la lave des parois le recueillaient à son passage et l'éparpillaient comme une pluie d'étincelles.

Cette lueur était assez forte pour permettre de distinguer les objets environnants.

« Eh bien, Axel, qu'en dis-tu ? s'écria mon oncle en se frottant les mains. As-tu jamais passé une nuit plus paisible dans notre maison de Königstrasse ? Plus de bruit de charrettes, plus de cris de marchands, plus de vociférations de bateliers !

— Sans doute, nous sommes fort tranquilles au fond de ce puits, mais ce calme même a quelque chose d'effrayant.

— Allons donc, s'écria mon oncle, si tu t'effraies déjà, que sera-ce plus tard ? Nous ne sommes pas

encore entrés d'un pouce dans les entrailles de la terre !

— Que voulez-vous dire ?

— Je veux dire que nous avons atteint seulement le sol de l'île ! Ce long tube vertical, qui aboutit au cratère du Sneffels, s'arrête à peu près au niveau de la mer.

— En êtes-vous certain ?

— Très certain. Consulte le baromètre. »

En effet, le mercure, après avoir peu à peu remonté dans l'instrument à mesure que notre descente s'effectuait, s'était arrêté à vingt-neuf pouces.

« Tu le vois, reprit le professeur, nous n'avons encore que la pression d'une atmosphère, et il me tarde que le manomètre vienne remplacer ce baromètre. »

Cet instrument allait, en effet, devenir inutile, du moment que le poids de l'air dépasserait sa pression calculée au niveau de l'Océan.

« Mais, dis-je, n'est-il pas à craindre que cette pression toujours croissante ne soit très pénible ?

— Non. Nous descendrons lentement, et nos poumons s'habitueront à respirer une atmosphère plus comprimée. Les aéronautes finissent par manquer d'air en s'élevant dans les couches supérieures, et nous, nous en aurons trop peut-être. Mais j'aime mieux cela. Ne perdons pas un instant. Où est le paquet qui nous a précédés dans l'intérieur de la montagne ? »

Je me souvins alors que nous l'avions vainement

cherché la veille au soir. Mon oncle interrogea Hans, qui, après avoir regardé attentivement avec ses yeux de chasseur, répondit :

« Der huppe ! »

— Là-haut. »

En effet, ce paquet était accroché à une saillie de roc, à une centaine de pieds au-dessus de notre tête. Aussitôt l'agile Islandais grimpa comme un chat, et, en quelques minutes, le paquet nous rejoignit.

« Maintenant, dit mon oncle, déjeunons, mais déjeunons comme des gens qui peuvent avoir une longue course à faire. »

Le biscuit et la viande sèche furent arrosés de quelques gorgées d'eau mêlée de genièvre.

Le déjeuner terminé, mon oncle tira de sa poche un carnet destiné aux observations ; il prit successivement ses divers instruments et nota les données suivantes :

Lundi 1er juillet

Chronomètre : 8 h 17 m du matin.
Baromètre : 29 p. 7 l.
Thermomètre : 6º.
Direction : E.-S.-E.

Cette dernière observation s'appliquait à la galerie obscure et fut indiquée par la boussole.

« Maintenant, Axel, s'écria le professeur d'une voix enthousiaste, nous allons nous enfoncer

véritablement dans les entrailles du globe. Voici
donc le moment précis auquel notre voyage
commence. »

Cela dit, mon oncle prit d'une main l'appareil
de Ruhmkorff suspendu à son cou ; de l'autre,
il mit en communication le courant électrique
avec le serpentin de la lanterne, et une assez
vive lumière dissipa les ténèbres de la galerie.

Hans portait le second appareil, qui fut également
mis en activité. Cette ingénieuse application
de l'électricité nous permettait d'aller longtemps en créant un jour artificiel, même au milieu
des gaz les plus inflammables.

« En route ! » fit mon oncle.

Chacun reprit son ballot. Hans se chargea de
pousser devant lui le paquet des cordages et des
habits, et, moi troisième, nous entrâmes dans la
galerie.

Au moment de m'engouffrer dans ce couloir
obscur, je relevai la tête, et j'aperçus une dernière fois, par le champ de l'immense tube, ce
ciel de l'Islande « que je ne devais plus revoir ».

La lave, à la dernière éruption de 1229, s'était
frayé un passage à travers ce tunnel. Elle tapis-
sait l'intérieur d'un enduit épais et brillant ; la
lumière électrique s'y réfléchissait en centuplant
son intensité.

Toute la difficulté de la route consistait à ne pas
glisser trop rapidement sur une pente inclinée
à quarante-cinq degrés environ ; heureusement certaines érosions, quelques boursouflures tenaient

lieu de marches, et nous n'avions qu'à descendre en laissant filer nos bagages retenus par une longue corde.

Mais ce qui se faisait marche sous nos pieds devenait stalactite sur les autres parois. La lave, poreuse en de certains endroits, présentait de petites ampoules arrondies : des cristaux de quartz opaque, ornés de limpides gouttes de verre et suspendus à la voûte comme des lustres, semblaient s'allumer à notre passage. On eût dit que les génies du gouffre illuminaient leur palais pour recevoir les hôtes de la terre.

« C'est magnifique! m'écriai-je involontairement. Quel spectacle, mon oncle! Admirez-vous ces nuances de la lave qui vont du rouge brun au jaune éclatant par dégradations insensibles? Et ces cristaux qui nous apparaissent comme des globes lumineux?

— Ah! tu y viens, Axel! répondit mon oncle. Ah! tu trouves cela splendide, mon garçon! Tu en verras bien d'autres, je l'espère. Marchons! marchons! »

Il aurait dit plus justement « glissons, » car nous nous laissions aller sans fatigue sur des pentes inclinées. C'était le *facilis descensus Averni* de Virgile. La boussole, que je consultais fréquemment, indiquait la direction du sud-est avec une imperturbable rigueur. Cette coulée de lave n'obliquait ni d'un côté ni de l'autre. Elle avait l'inflexibilité de la ligne droite.

Cependant la chaleur n'augmentait pas d'une

façon sensible. Ce qui donnait raison aux théories de Davy, et plus d'une fois je consultai le thermomètre avec étonnement. Deux heures après le départ, il ne marquait encore que 10°, c'est-à-dire un accroissement de 4°. Cela m'autorisait à penser que notre descente était plus horizontale que verticale. Quant à connaître exactement la profondeur atteinte, rien de plus facile. Le professeur mesurait exactement les angles de déviation et d'inclinaison de la route, mais il gardait pour lui le résultat de ses observations.

Le soir, vers huit heures, il donna le signal d'arrêt. Hans aussitôt s'assit. Les lampes furent accrochées à une saillie de lave. Nous étions dans une sorte de caverne où l'air ne manquait pas. Au contraire. Certains souffles arrivaient jusqu'à nous. Quelle cause les produisait? A quelle agitation atmosphérique attribuer leur origine? C'est une question que je ne cherchai pas à résoudre en ce moment. La faim et la fatigue me rendaient incapable de raisonner. Une descente de sept heures consécutives ne se fait pas sans une grande dépense de forces. J'étais épuisé. Le mot « halte » me fit donc plaisir à entendre. Hans étala quelques provisions sur un bloc de lave, et chacun mangea avec appétit. Cependant une chose m'inquiétait; notre réserve d'eau était à demi consommée. Mon oncle comptait la refaire aux sources souterraines, mais jusqu'alors celles-ci manquaient absolument. Je ne pus m'empêcher d'attirer son attention sur ce sujet.

Les lampes furent accrochées à une saillie de lave (p. 157).

« Cette absence de sources te surprend ? dit-il.

— Sans doute, et même elle m'inquiète. Nous n'avons plus d'eau que pour cinq jours.

— Sois tranquille, Axel, je te réponds que nous trouverons de l'eau, et plus que nous n'en voudrons.

— Quand cela ?

— Quand nous aurons quitté cette enveloppe de lave. Comment veux-tu que des sources jaillissent à travers ces parois ?

— Mais peut-être cette coulée se prolonge-t-elle à de grandes profondeurs. Il me semble que nous n'avons pas encore fait beaucoup de chemin verticalement.

— Qui te fait supposer cela ?

— C'est que, si nous étions très avancés dans l'intérieur de l'écorce terrestre, la chaleur serait plus forte.

— D'après ton système, répondit mon oncle. Qu'indique le thermomètre ?

— Quinze degrés à peine, ce qui ne fait qu'un accroissement de neuf degrés depuis notre départ.

— Eh bien, conclus.

— Voici ma conclusion. D'après les observations les plus exactes, l'augmentation de la température à l'intérieur du globe est d'un degré par cent pieds. Mais certaines conditions de localité peuvent modifier ce chiffre. Ainsi, à Yakoust en Sibérie, on a remarqué que l'accroissement d'un degré avait lieu par trente-six pieds. Cette différence dépend évidemment de la conductibilité des

roches. J'ajouterai aussi que, dans le voisinage d'un volcan éteint, et à travers le gneiss, on a remarqué que l'élévation de la température était d'un degré seulement pour cent vingt-cinq pieds. Prenons donc cette dernière hypothèse, qui est la plus favorable, et calculons.

— Calcule, mon garçon.

— Rien n'est plus facile, dis-je en disposant des chiffres sur mon carnet. Neuf fois cent vingt-cinq pieds donnent onze cent vingt-cinq pieds de profondeur.

— Rien de plus exact.

— Eh bien ?

— Eh bien, d'après mes observations, nous sommes arrivés à dix mille pieds au-dessous du niveau de la mer.

— Est-il possible ?

— Oui, ou les chiffres ne sont plus les chiffres ! »

Les calculs du professeur étaient exacts. Nous avions déjà dépassé de six mille pieds les plus grandes profondeurs atteintes par l'homme, telles que les mines de Kitz-Bahl dans le Tyrol, et celles de Wuttemberg en Bohême.

La température, qui aurait dû être de quatre-vingt-un degrés en cet endroit, était de quinze à peine. Cela donnait singulièrement à réfléchir.

Le lendemain mardi, 30 juin, à six heures, la descente fut reprise.

Nous suivions toujours la galerie de lave, véritable rampe naturelle, douce comme ces plans inclinés qui remplacent encore l'escalier dans les vieilles maisons. Ce fut ainsi jusqu'à midi dix-sept minutes, instant précis où nous rejoignîmes Hans, qui venait de s'arrêter.

« Ah! s'écria mon oncle, nous sommes parvenus à l'extrémité de la cheminée. »

Je regardai autour de moi. Nous étions au centre d'un carrefour, auquel deux routes venaient aboutir, toutes deux sombres et étroites. Laquelle convenait-il de prendre? Il y avait là une difficulté.

Cependant mon oncle ne voulut paraître hésiter ni devant moi ni devant le guide; il désigna le tunnel de l'est, et bientôt nous y étions enfoncés tous les trois.

D'ailleurs, toute hésitation devant ce double chemin se serait prolongée indéfiniment, car nul indice ne pouvait déterminer le choix de l'un ou de l'autre; il fallait s'en remettre absolument au hasard.

La pente de cette nouvelle galerie était peu sensible, et sa section fort inégale. Parfois une succession d'arceaux se déroulait devant nos pas comme les contre-nefs d'une cathédrale gothique.

Parfois une succession d'arceaux se déroulait
devant nous (p. 161).

Les artistes du Moyen Age auraient pu étudier là toutes les formes de cette architecture religieuse qui a l'ogive pour générateur. Un mille plus loin, notre tête se courbait sous les cintres surbaissés du style roman, et de gros piliers engagés dans le massif pliaient sous la retombée des voûtes. A de certains endroits, cette disposition faisait place à de basses substructions qui ressemblaient aux ouvrages des castors, et nous nous glissions en rampant à travers d'étroits boyaux.

La chaleur se maintenait à un degré supportable. Involontairement je songeais à son intensité, quand les laves vomies par le Sneffels se précipitaient par cette route si tranquille aujourd'hui. Je m'imaginais les torrents de feu brisés aux angles de la galerie et l'accumulation des vapeurs surchauffées dans cet étroit milieu !

« Pourvu, pensai-je, que le vieux volcan ne vienne pas à se reprendre d'une fantaisie tardive ! »

Ces réflexions, je ne les communiquai point à l'oncle Lidenbrock ; il ne les eût pas comprises. Son unique pensée était d'aller en avant. Il marchait, il glissait, il dégringolait même, avec une conviction qu'après tout il valait mieux admirer.

A six heures du soir, après une promenade peu fatigante, nous avions gagné deux lieues dans le sud, mais à peine un quart de mille en profondeur.

Mon oncle donna le signal du repos. On mangea sans trop causer, et l'on s'endormit sans trop réfléchir.

Nos dispositions pour la nuit étaient fort simples ; une couverture de voyage, dans laquelle on se roulait, composait toute la literie. Nous n'avions à redouter ni froid, ni visite importune. Les voyageurs qui s'enfoncent au milieu des déserts de l'Afrique, au sein des forêts du nouveau monde, sont forcés de veiller les uns sur les autres pendant les heures du sommeil. Mais ici, solitude absolue et sécurité complète. Sauvages ou bêtes féroces, aucune de ces races malfaisantes n'était à craindre.

On se réveilla le lendemain frais et dispos. La route fut reprise. Nous suivions un chemin de lave comme la veille. Impossible de reconnaître la nature des terrains qu'il traversait. Le tunnel, au lieu de s'enfoncer dans les entrailles du globe, tendait à devenir absolument horizontal. Je crus remarquer même qu'il remontait vers la surface de la terre. Cette disposition devint si manifeste vers dix heures du matin, et par suite si fatigante, que je fus forcé de modérer notre marche.

« Eh bien, Axel, dit impatiemment le professeur.

— Eh bien, je n'en peux plus, répondis-je.

— Quoi ! après trois heures de promenade sur une route si facile !

— Facile, je ne dis pas non, mais fatigante à coup sûr.

— Comment ! quand nous n'avons qu'à descendre !

— A monter, ne vous en déplaise !

— A monter ! fit mon oncle en haussant les épaules.

— Sans doute: Depuis une demi-heure, les pentes se sont modifiées, et à les suivre ainsi, nous reviendrons certainement à la terre d'Islande. »

Le professeur remua la tête en homme qui ne veut pas être convaincu. J'essayai de reprendre la conversation. Il ne me répondit pas et donna le signal du départ. Je vis bien que son silence n'était que de la mauvaise humeur concentrée.

Cependant j'avais repris mon fardeau avec courage, et je suivais rapidement Hans, que précédait mon oncle. Je tenais à ne pas être distancé. Ma grande préoccupation était de ne point perdre mes compagnons de vue. Je frémissais à la pensée de m'égarer dans les profondeurs de ce labyrinthe.

D'ailleurs, si la route ascendante devenait plus pénible, je m'en consolais en songeant qu'elle me rapprochait de la surface de la terre. C'était un espoir. Chaque pas le confirmait, et je me réjouissais à cette idée de revoir ma petite Graüben.

A midi un changement d'aspect se produisit dans les parois de la galerie. Je m'en aperçus à l'affaiblissement de la lumière électrique réfléchie par les murailles. Au revêtement de lave succédait la roche vive. Le massif se composait de couches inclinées et souvent disposées verticalement. Nous étions en pleine époque de transition, en pleine période silurienne [1].

---

1. Ainsi nommée parce que les terrains de cette période sont fort étendus en Angleterre, dans les contrées habitées autrefois par la peuplade celtique des Silaures.

« C'est évident, m'écriai-je, les sédiments des eaux ont formé, à la seconde époque de la terre, ces schistes, ces calcaires et ces grès! Nous tournons le dos au massif granitique! Nous ressemblons à des gens de Hambourg, qui prendraient le chemin de Hanovre pour aller à Lubeck. »

J'aurais dû garder pour moi mes observations. Mais mon tempérament de géologue l'emporta sur la prudence, et l'oncle Lidenbrock entendit mes exclamations.

« Qu'as-tu donc? dit-il.

— Voyez! répondis-je en lui montrant la succession variée des grès, des calcaires et les premiers indices des terrains ardoisés.

— Eh bien?

— Nous voici arrivés à cette période pendant laquelle ont apparu les premières plantes et les premiers animaux!

— Ah! tu penses?

— Mais regardez, examinez, observez! »

Je forçai le professeur à promener sa lampe sur les parois de la galerie. Je m'attendais à quelque exclamation de sa part. Mais il ne dit pas un mot, et continua sa route.

M'avait-il compris ou non? Ne voulait-il pas convenir, par amour-propre d'oncle et de savant, qu'il s'était trompé en choisissant le tunnel de l'est, ou tenait-il à reconnaître ce passage jusqu'à son extrémité? Il était évident que nous avions quitté la route des laves, et que ce chemin ne pouvait conduire au foyer du Sneffels.

Cependant je me demandai si je n'accordais pas une trop grande importance à cette modification des terrains. Ne me trompais-je pas moi-même ? Traversions-nous réellement ces couches de roches superposées au massif granitique ?

« Si j'ai raison, pensai-je, je dois trouver quelque débris de plante primitive, et il faudra bien se rendre à l'évidence. Cherchons. »

Je n'avais pas fait cent pas que des preuves incontestables s'offrirent à mes yeux. Cela devait être, car, à l'époque silurienne, les mers renfermaient plus de quinze cents espèces végétales ou animales. Mes pieds, habitués au sol dur des laves, foulèrent tout à coup une poussière faite de débris de plantes et de coquilles. Sur les parois se voyaient distinctement des empreintes de fucus et de lycopodes. Le professeur Lidenbrock ne pouvait s'y tromper ; mais il fermait les yeux, j'imagine, et continuait son chemin d'un pas invariable.

C'était un entêtement poussé hors de toutes limites. Je n'y tins plus. Je ramassai une coquille parfaitement conservée, qui avait appartenu à un animal à peu près semblable au cloporte actuel ; puis, je rejoignis mon oncle et je lui dis :

« Voyez !

— Eh bien, répondit-il tranquillement, c'est la coquille d'un crustacé de l'ordre disparu des trilobites. Pas autre chose.

— Mais n'en concluez-vous pas ?...

— Ce que tu conclus toi-même ? Si. Parfaite-

ment. Nous avons abandonné la couche de granit et la route des laves.. Il est possible que je me sois trompé ; mais je ne serai certain de mon erreur qu'au moment où j'aurai atteint l'extrémité de cette galerie.

— Vous avez raison d'agir ainsi, mon oncle, et je vous approuverais, si nous n'avions à craindre un danger de plus en plus menaçant.

— Et lequel ?

— Le manque d'eau.

— Eh bien ! nous nous rationnerons, Axel. »

XX

EN effet, il fallut se rationner. Notre provision ne pouvait durer plus de trois jours. C'est ce que je reconnus le soir au moment du souper. Et, fâcheuse expectative, nous avions peu d'espoir de rencontrer quelque source vive dans ces terrains de l'époque de transition.

Pendant toute la journée du lendemain, la galerie déroula devant nos pas ses interminables arceaux. Nous marchions presque sans mot dire. Le mutisme de Hans nous gagnait.

La route ne montait pas, du moins d'une façon sensible. Parfois même elle semblait s'incliner. Mais cette tendance, peu marquée d'ailleurs, ne devait pas rassurer le professeur, car la nature

des couches ne se modifiait pas, et la période de transition s'affirmait davantage.

La lumière électrique faisait splendidement étinceler les schistes, le calcaire et les vieux grès rouges des parois. On aurait pu se croire dans une tranchée ouverte au milieu du Devonshire, qui donna son nom à ce genre de terrains. Des spécimens de marbres magnifiques revêtaient les murailles, les uns d'un gris agate avec des veines blanches capricieusement accusées, les autres de couleur incarnat ou d'un jaune taché de plaques rouges; plus loin, des échantillons de griottes à couleurs sombres, dans lesquels le calcaire se relevait en nuances vives.

La plupart de ces marbres offraient des empreintes d'animaux primitifs. Depuis la veille, la création avait fait un progrès évident. Au lieu des trilobites rudimentaires, j'apercevais des débris d'un ordre plus parfait; entre autres, des poissons Ganoïdes et ces Sauropteris dans lesquels l'œil du paléontologiste a su découvrir les premières formes du reptile. Les mers dévoniennes étaient habitées par un grand nombre d'animaux de cette espèce, et elles les déposèrent par milliers sur les roches de nouvelle formation.

Il devenait évident que nous remontions l'échelle de la vie animale dont l'homme occupe le sommet. Mais le professeur Lidenbrock ne paraissait pas y prendre garde.

Il attendait deux choses : ou qu'un puits vertical vînt à s'ouvrir sous ses pieds et lui permettre de

reprendre sa descente, ou qu'un obstacle l'empê-
chât de continuer cette route. Mais le soir arriva
sans que cette espérance se fût réalisée.

Le vendredi, après une nuit pendant laquelle
je commençai à ressentir les tourments de la soif,
notre petite troupe s'enfonça de nouveau dans
les détours de la galerie.

Après dix heures de marche, je remarquai que
la réverbération de nos lampes sur les parois
diminuait singulièrement. Le marbre, le schiste,
le calcaire, le grès des murailles, faisaient place
à un revêtement sombre et sans éclat. A un moment
où le tunnel devenait fort étroit, je m'appuyai
sur sa paroi de gauche.

Quand je retirai ma main, elle était entièrement
noire. Je regardai de plus près. Nous étions
en pleine houillère.

« Une mine de charbon! m'écriai-je.

— Une mine sans mineurs, répondit mon oncle.

— Eh! qui sait?

— Moi, je sais, répliqua le professeur d'un ton
bref, et je suis certain que cette galerie percée
à travers ces couches de houille n'a pas été faite
de la main des hommes. Mais que ce soit ou non
l'ouvrage de la nature cela m'importe peu. L'heure
du souper est venue. Soupons. »

Hans prépara quelques aliments. Je mangeai
à peine, et je bus les quelques gouttes d'eau
qui formaient ma ration. La gourde du guide à
demi pleine, voilà tout ce qui restait pour désal-
térer trois hommes.

« Une mine de charbon ! » m'écriai-je (p. 171).

Après leur repas, mes deux compagnons s'étendirent sur leurs couvertures et trouvèrent dans le sommeil un remède à leurs fatigues. Pour moi, je ne pus dormir, et je comptai les heures jusqu'au matin.

Le samedi, à six heures, on repartit. Vingt minutes plus tard, nous arrivions à une vaste excavation ; je reconnus alors que la main de l'homme ne pouvait pas avoir creusé cette houillère ; les voûtes en eussent été étançonnées, et véritablement elles ne se tenaient que par un miracle d'équilibre.

Cette espèce de caverne comptait cent pieds de largeur sur cent cinquante de hauteur. Le terrain avait été violemment écarté par une commotion souterraine. Le massif terrestre, cédant à quelque puissante poussée, s'était disloqué, laissant ce large vide où des habitants de la terre pénétraient pour la première fois.

Toute l'histoire de la période houillère était écrite sur ces sombres parois, et un géologue en pouvait suivre facilement les phases diverses. Les lits de charbon étaient séparés par des strates de grès ou d'argile compacts, et comme écrasés par les couches supérieures.

A cet âge du monde qui précéda l'époque secondaire, la terre se recouvrit d'immenses végétations dues à la double action d'une chaleur tropicale et d'une humidité persistante. Une atmosphère de vapeurs enveloppait le globe de toutes parts, lui dérobant encore les rayons du soleil.

De là cette conclusion que les hautes températures ne provenaient pas de ce foyer nouveau. Peut-être même l'astre du jour n'était-il pas prêt à jouer son rôle éclatant. Les « climats » n'existaient pas encore, et une chaleur torride se répandait à la surface entière du globe, égale à l'équateur et aux pôles. D'où venait-elle ? de l'intérieur du globe.

En dépit des théories du professeur Lidenbrock, un feu violent couvait dans les entrailles du sphéroïde ; son action se faisait sentir jusqu'aux dernières couches de l'écorce terrestre ; les plantes, privées des bienfaisants effluves du soleil, ne donnaient ni fleurs ni parfums, mais leurs racines puisaient une vie forte dans les terrains brûlants des premiers jours.

Il y avait peu d'arbres, des plantes herbacées seulement, d'immenses gazons, des fougères, des lycopodes, des sigillaires, des astérophyllites, familles rares dont les espèces se comptaient alors par milliers.

Or, c'est précisément à cette exubérante végétation que la houille doit son origine. L'écorce encore élastique du globe obéissait aux mouvements de la masse liquide qu'elle recouvrait. De là des fissures, des affaissements nombreux. Les plantes, entraînées sous les eaux, formèrent peu à peu des amas considérables.

Alors intervint l'action de la chimie naturelle ; au fond des mers, les masses végétales se firent tourbe d'abord ; puis, grâce à l'influence des gaz,

et sous le feu de la fermentation, elles subirent une minéralisation complète.

Ainsi se formèrent ces immenses couches de charbon qu'une consommation excessive doit, pourtant, épuiser en moins de trois siècles, si les peuples industriels n'y prennent garde.

Ces réflexions me venaient à l'esprit pendant que je considérais les richesses houillères accumulées dans cette portion du massif terrestre. Celles-ci, sans doute, ne seront jamais mises à découvert. L'exploitation de ces mines reculées demanderait des sacrifices trop considérables. A quoi bon, d'ailleurs, quand la houille est encore répandue pour ainsi dire à la surface de la terre dans un grand nombre de contrées? Aussi, telles je voyais ces couches intactes, telles elles seraient lorsque sonnerait la dernière heure du monde.

Cependant nous marchions, et seul de mes compagnons j'oubliais la longueur de la route pour me perdre au milieu de considérations géologiques. La température restait sensiblement ce qu'elle était pendant notre passage au milieu des laves et des schistes. Seulement, mon odorat était affecté par une odeur très prononcée de protocarbure d'hydrogène. Je reconnus immédiatement dans cette galerie la présence d'une notable quantité de ce fluide dangereux auquel les mineurs ont donné le nom de grisou, et dont l'explosion a si souvent causé d'épouvantables catastrophes.

Heureusement, nous étions éclairés par les ingénieux appareils de Ruhmkorff. Si, par malheur,

nous avions imprudemment exploré cette galerie la torche à la main, une explosion terrible eût fini le voyage en supprimant les voyageurs.

Cette excursion dans la houillère dura jusqu'au soir. Mon oncle contenait à peine l'impatience que lui causait l'horizontalité de la route. Les ténèbres, toujours profondes à vingt pas, empêchaient d'estimer la longueur de la galerie, et je commençais à la croire interminable, quand soudain, à six heures, un mur se présenta inopinément à nous. A droite, à gauche, en haut, en bas, il n'y avait aucun passage. Nous étions arrivés au fond d'une impasse.

« Eh bien, tant mieux! s'écria mon oncle, je sais au moins à quoi m'en tenir. Nous ne sommes pas sur la route de Saknussemm, et il ne reste plus qu'à revenir en arrière. Prenons une nuit de repos, et avant trois jours, nous aurons regagné le point où les deux galeries se bifurquent.

— Oui, dis-je, si nous en avons la force!

— Et pourquoi non?

— Parce que, demain, l'eau manquera tout à fait.

— Et le courage manquera-t-il aussi? » dit le professeur en me regardant d'un œil sévère.

Je n'osai lui répondre.

Le lendemain, le départ eut lieu de grand matin. Il fallait se hâter. Nous étions à cinq jours de marche du carrefour.

Je ne m'appesantirai pas sur les souffrances de notre retour. Mon oncle les supporta avec la colère d'un homme qui ne se sent pas le plus fort ; Hans avec la résignation de sa nature pacifique ; moi, je l'avoue, me plaignant et me désespérant ; je ne pouvais avoir de cœur contre cette mauvaise fortune.

Ainsi que je l'avais prévu, l'eau fit tout à fait défaut à la fin du premier jour de marche. Notre provision liquide se réduisit alors à du genièvre, mais cette infernale liqueur brûlait le gosier, et je ne pouvais même en supporter la vue. Je trouvais la température étouffante. La fatigue me paralysait. Plus d'une fois, je faillis tomber sans mouvement. On faisait halte alors ; mon oncle ou l'Islandais me réconfortaient de leur mieux. Mais je voyais déjà que le premier réagissait péniblement contre l'extrême fatigue et les tortures nées de la privation d'eau.

Enfin, le mardi 7 juillet, en nous traînant sur les genoux, sur les mains, nous arrivâmes à demi morts au point de jonction des deux galeries. Là je demeurai comme une masse inerte, étendu sur le sol de lave. Il était dix heures du matin.

Hans et mon oncle, accotés à la paroi, essayèrent de grignoter quelques morceaux de biscuit. De longs gémissements s'échappaient de mes lèvres tuméfiées. Je tombai dans un profond assoupissement.

Au bout de quelque temps, mon oncle s'approcha de moi et me souleva entre ses bras :

« Pauvre enfant! » murmura-t-il avec un véritable accent de pitié.

Je fus touché de ces paroles, n'étant pas habitué aux tendresses du farouche professeur. Je saisis ses mains frémissantes dans les miennes. Il se laissa faire en me regardant. Ses yeux étaient humides.

Je le vis alors prendre la gourde suspendue à son côté. A ma grande stupéfaction, il l'approcha de mes lèvres :

« Bois », fit-il.

Avais-je bien entendu? Mon oncle était-il fou? Je le regardais d'un air hébété. Je ne voulais pas le comprendre.

« Bois », reprit-il.

Et relevant sa gourde, il la vida tout entière entre mes lèvres.

Oh! jouissance infinie! Une gorgée d'eau vint humecter ma bouche en feu, une seule, mais elle suffit à rappeler en moi la vie qui s'échappait.

Je remerciai mon oncle en joignant les mains.

« Oui, fit-il, une gorgée d'eau! la dernière! entends-tu bien? la dernière! Je l'avais précieusement gardée au fond de ma gourde. Vingt

Et relevant sa gourde, il la vida tout entière
entre mes lèvres (p. 177).

fois, cent fois, j'ai dû résister à mon effrayant désir de la boire! Mais non, Axel, je la réservais pour toi.

— Mon oncle! murmurai-je pendant que de grosses larmes mouillaient mes yeux.

— Oui, pauvre enfant, je savais qu'à ton arrivée à ce carrefour, tu tomberais à demi mort, et j'ai conservé mes dernières gouttes d'eau pour te ranimer.

— Merci! merci!» m'écriai-je.

Si peu que ma soif fût apaisée, j'avais cependant retrouvé quelque force. Les muscles de mon gosier, contractés jusqu'alors, se détendaient, et l'inflammation de mes lèvres s'était adoucie. Je pouvais parler.

« Voyons, dis-je, nous n'avons maintenant qu'un parti à prendre; l'eau nous manque; il faut revenir sur nos pas ».

Pendant que je parlais ainsi, mon oncle évitait de me regarder; il baissait la tête; ses yeux fuyaient les miens.

« Il faut revenir, m'écriai-je, et reprendre le chemin du Sneffels. Que Dieu nous donne la force de remonter jusqu'au sommet du cratère!

— Revenir! fit mon oncle, comme s'il répondait plutôt à lui qu'à moi-même.

— Oui, revenir, et sans perdre un instant. »

Il y eut ici un moment de silence assez long.

« Ainsi donc, Axel, reprit le professeur d'un ton bizarre, ces quelques gouttes d'eau ne t'ont pas rendu le courage et l'énergie?

— Le courage !

— Je te vois abattu comme avant, et faisant encore entendre des paroles de désespoir ! »

A quel homme avais-je affaire et quels projets son esprit audacieux formait-il encore ?

« Quoi ! vous ne voulez pas ?...

— Renoncer à cette expédition, au moment où tout annonce qu'elle peut réussir ! Jamais !

— Alors il faut se résigner à périr ?

— Non, Axel, non ! pars. Je ne veux pas ta mort ! Que Hans t'accompagne. Laisse-moi seul !

— Vous abandonner !

— Laisse-moi, te dis-je ! J'ai commencé ce voyage ; je l'accomplirai jusqu'au bout, ou je n'en reviendrai pas. Va-t'en, Axel, va-t'en ! »

Mon oncle parlait avec une extrême surexcitation. Sa voix, un instant attendrie, redevenait dure, menaçante. Il luttait avec une sombre énergie contre l'impossible ! Je ne voulais pas l'abandonner au fond de cet abîme, et, d'un autre côté, l'instinct de la conservation me poussait à le fuir.

Le guide suivait cette scène avec son indifférence accoutumée. Il comprenait cependant ce qui se passait entre ses deux compagnons. Nos gestes indiquaient assez la voie différente où chacun de nous essayait d'entraîner l'autre ; mais Hans semblait s'intéresser peu à la question dans laquelle son existence se trouvait en jeu, prêt à partir si l'on donnait le signal du départ, prêt à rester à la moindre volonté de son maître.

Que ne pouvais-je en cet instant me faire enten-dre de lui! Mes paroles, mes gémissements, mon accent auraient eu raison de cette froide nature. Ces dangers que le guide ne paraissait pas soup-çonner, je les lui eusse fait comprendre et toucher du doigt. A nous deux nous aurions peut-être convaincu l'entêté professeur: Au besoin, nous l'aurions contraint à regagner les hauteurs du Sneffels!

Je m'approchai de Hans. Je mis ma main sur la sienne. Il ne bougea pas. Je lui montrai la route du cratère. Il demeura immobile. Ma figure haletante disait toutes mes souffrances. L'Islandais remua doucement la tête, et désignant tranquil-lement mon oncle :

« Master, fit-il.

— Le maître! m'écriai-je, insensé! non, il n'est pas le maître de ta vie! il faut fuir! il faut l'en-traîner! m'entends-tu? me comprends-tu? »

J'avais saisi Hans par le bras. Je voulais l'obli-ger à se lever. Je luttais avec lui. Mon oncle intervint.

« Du calme, Axel, dit-il. Tu n'obtiendras rien de cet impassible serviteur. Ainsi, écoute ce que j'ai à te proposer. »

Je me croisai les bras, en regardant mon oncle bien en face.

« Le manque d'eau, dit-il, met seul obstacle à l'accomplissement de mes projets. Dans cette galerie de l'est, faite de laves, de schistes, de houilles, nous n'avons pas rencontré une seule

molécule liquide. Il est possible que nous soyons plus heureux en suivant le tunnel de l'ouest. »

Je secouai la tête avec un air de profonde incrédulité.

« Écoute-moi jusqu'au bout, reprit le professeur en forçant la voix. Pendant que tu gisais ici sans mouvement, j'ai été reconnaître la conformation de cette galerie. Elle s'enfonce directement dans les entrailles du globe, et, en peu d'heures, elle nous conduira au massif granitique. Là, nous devons rencontrer des sources abondantes. La nature de la roche le veut ainsi, et l'instinct est d'accord avec la logique pour appuyer ma conviction. Or, voici ce que j'ai à te proposer. Quand Colomb a demandé trois jours à ses équipages pour trouver les terres nouvelles, ses équipages, malades, épouvantés, ont cependant fait droit à sa demande, et il a découvert le nouveau monde. Moi, le Colomb de ces régions souterraines, je ne te demande qu'un jour encore. Si, ce temps écoulé, je n'ai pas rencontré l'eau qui nous manque, je te le jure, nous reviendrons à la surface de la terre. »

En dépit de mon irritation, je fus ému de ces paroles et de la violence que se faisait mon oncle pour tenir un pareil langage.

« Eh bien ! m'écriai-je, qu'il soit fait comme vous le désirez, et que Dieu récompense votre énergie surhumaine. Vous n'avez plus que quelques heures à tenter le sort. En route ! »

Lᴀ descente recommença cette fois par la nouvelle galerie. Hans marchait en avant, selon son habitude. Nous n'avions pas fait cent pas, que le professeur, promenant sa lampe le long des murailles, s'écriait :

« Voilà les terrains primitifs ! nous sommes dans la bonne voie, marchons ! marchons ! »

Lorsque la terre se refroidit peu à peu aux premiers jours du monde, la diminution de son volume produisit dans l'écorce des dislocations, des ruptures, des retraits, des fendilles. Le couloir actuel était une fissure de ce genre, par laquelle s'épanchait autrefois le granit éruptif. Ses mille détours formaient un inextricable labyrinthe à travers le sol primordial.

A mesure que nous descendions, la succession des couches composant le terrain primitif apparaissait avec plus de netteté. La science géologique considère ce terrain primitif comme la base de l'écorce minérale, et elle a reconnu qu'il se compose de trois couches différentes, les schistes, les gneiss, les micaschistes, reposant sur cette roche inébranlable qu'on appelle le granit.

Or, jamais minéralogistes ne s'étaient rencontrés dans des circonstances aussi merveilleuses pour étudier la nature sur place. Ce que la sonde, machine inintelligente et brutale, ne pouvait

rapporter à la surface du globe de sa texture interne, nous allions l'étudier de nos yeux, le toucher de nos mains.

A travers l'étage des schistes, colorés de belles nuances vertes, serpentaient des filons métalliques de cuivre, de manganèse avec quelques traces de platine et d'or. Je songeais à ces richesses enfouies dans les entrailles du globe et dont l'avide humanité n'aura jamais la jouissance! Ces trésors, les bouleversements des premiers jours les ont enterrés à de telles profondeurs, que ni la pioche, ni le pic ne sauront les arracher à leur tombeau.

Aux schistes succédèrent les gneiss, d'une structure stratiforme, remarquables par la régularité et le parallélisme de leurs feuillets, puis les mica-schistes disposés en grandes lamelles rehaussées à l'œil par les scintillations du mica blanc.

La lumière des appareils, répercutée par les petites facettes de la masse rocheuse, croisait ses jets de feu sous tous les angles, et je m'imaginais voyager à travers un diamant creux, dans lequel les rayons se brisaient en mille éblouissements.

Vers six heures, cette fête de la lumière vint à diminuer sensiblement, presque à cesser ; les parois prirent une teinte cristallisée, mais sombre ; le mica se mélangea plus intimement au feldspath et au quartz, pour former la roche par excellence, la pierre dure entre toutes, celle qui supporte, sans en être écrasée, les quatre étages de terrains du globe. Nous étions murés dans l'immense prison de granit.

Je m'imaginais voyager à travers un diamant (p. 185).

Il était huit heures du soir. L'eau manquait toujours. Je souffrais horriblement. Mon oncle marchait en avant. Il ne voulait pas s'arrêter. Il tendait l'oreille pour surprendre les murmures de quelque source. Mais rien !

Cependant mes jambes refusaient de me porter. Je résistais à mes tortures pour ne pas obliger mon oncle à faire halte. C'eût été pour lui le coup du désespoir, car la journée finissait, la dernière qui lui appartînt.

Enfin mes forces m'abandonnèrent. Je poussai un cri et je tombai.

« A moi ! je meurs ! »

Mon oncle revint sur ses pas. Il me considéra en croisant ses bras ; puis ces paroles sourdes sortirent de ses lèvres :

« Tout est fini ! »

Un effrayant geste de colère frappa une dernière fois mes regards, et je fermai les yeux.

Lorsque je les rouvris, j'aperçus mes deux compagnons immobiles et roulés dans leur couverture. Dormaient-ils ? Pour mon compte, je ne pouvais trouver un instant de sommeil. Je souffrais trop, et surtout de la pensée que mon mal devait être sans remède. Les dernières paroles de mon oncle retentissaient dans mon oreille. « Tout était fini ! » car dans un pareil état de faiblesse, il ne fallait même plus songer à regagner la surface du globe.

Il y avait une lieue et demie d'écorce terrestre ! Il me semblait que cette masse pesait de tout son

poids sur mes épaules. Je me sentais écrasé, et je m'épuisais en efforts violents pour me retourner sur ma couche de granit.

Quelques heures se passèrent. Un silence profond régnait autour de nous, un silence de tombeau. Rien n'arrivait à travers ces murailles dont la plus mince mesurait cinq milles d'épaisseur.

Cependant, au milieu de mon assoupissement, je crus entendre un bruit. L'obscurité se faisait dans le tunnel. Je regardai plus attentivement, et il me sembla voir l'Islandais qui disparaissait, la lampe à la main.

Pourquoi ce départ? Hans nous abandonnait-il? Mon oncle dormait. Je voulus crier. Ma voix ne put trouver passage entre mes lèvres desséchées. L'obscurité était devenue profonde, et les derniers bruits venaient de s'éteindre.

« Hans nous abandonne! m'écriai-je. Hans! Hans! »

Ces mots, je les criais en moi-même. Ils n'allaient pas plus loin. Cependant, après le premier instant de terreur, j'eus honte de mes soupçons contre un homme dont la conduite n'avait rien eu jusque-là de suspect. Son départ ne pouvait être une fuite. Au lieu de remonter la galerie il la descendait. De mauvais desseins l'eussent entraîné en haut, non en bas. Ce raisonnement me calma un peu, et je revins à un autre ordre d'idées. Hans, cet homme paisible, un motif grave avait pu seul l'arracher à son repos. Allait-il donc à la découverte? Avait-il entendu pendant la nuit

silencieuse quelque murmure dont la perception
n'était pas arrivée jusqu'à moi ?

XXIII

PENDANT une heure, j'imaginai dans mon cerveau
en délire toutes les raisons qui avaient pu faire
agir le tranquille chasseur. Les idées les plus absur-
des s'enchevêtrèrent dans ma tête. Je crus que
j'allais devenir fou !

Mais enfin un bruit de pas se produisit dans les
profondeurs du gouffre. Hans remontait. La
lumière incertaine commençait à glisser sur les
parois, puis elle déboucha par l'orifice du couloir.
Hans parut.

Il s'approcha de mon oncle, lui mit la main sur
l'épaule et l'éveilla doucement. Mon oncle se
leva.

« Qu'est-ce donc ? fit-il.

— « Vatten », répondit le chasseur.

Il faut croire que, sous l'inspiration des violentes douleurs, chacun devient polyglotte. Je
ne savais pas un seul mot de danois, et cependant
je compris d'instinct le mot de notre guide.

« De l'eau ! de l'eau ! m'écriai-je, battant des
mains, gesticulant comme un insensé.

— De l'eau ! répétait mon oncle. « Hvar ? »
demanda-t-il à l'Islandais.

— « Nedat », répondit Hans.

Où ? En bas ! Je comprenais tout. J'avais saisi les mains du chasseur, et je les pressais, tandis qu'il me regardait avec calme.

Les préparatifs du départ ne furent pas longs, et bientôt nous cheminions dans un couloir dont la pente atteignait deux pieds par toise.

Une heure plus tard, nous avions fait mille toises environ et descendu deux mille pieds.

En ce moment, j'entendis distinctement un son inaccoutumé courir dans les flancs de la muraille granitique, une sorte de mugissement sourd, comme un tonnerre éloigné. Pendant cette première demi-heure de marche, ne rencontrant point la source annoncée, je sentais les angoisses me reprendre ; mais alors mon oncle m'apprit l'origine des bruits qui se produisaient.

« Hans ne s'est pas trompé, dit-il, ce que tu entends là, c'est le mugissement d'un torrent.

— Un torrent ? m'écriai-je.

— Il n'y a pas à en douter. Un fleuve souterrain circule autour de nous ! »

Nous hâtâmes le pas, surexcités par l'espérance. Je ne sentais plus ma fatigue. Ce bruit d'une eau murmurante me rafraîchissait déjà. Il augmentait sensiblement. Le torrent, après s'être longtemps soutenu au-dessus de notre tête, courait maintenant dans la paroi de gauche, mugissant et bondissant. Je passais fréquemment ma main sur le roc, espérant y trouver des traces de suintement ou d'humidité. Mais en vain.

Une demi-heure s'écoula encore. Une demi-lieue fut encore franchie.

Il devint alors évident que le chasseur, pendant son absence, n'avait pu prolonger ses recherches au-delà. Guidé par un instinct particulier aux montagnards, aux hydroscopes, il « sentit » ce torrent à travers le roc, mais certainement il n'avait point vu le précieux liquide ; il ne s'y était pas désaltéré.

Bientôt même il fut constant que, si notre marche continuait, nous nous éloignerions du courant dont le murmure tendait à diminuer.

On rebroussa chemin. Hans s'arrêta à l'endroit précis où le torrent semblait être le plus rapproché.

Je m'assis près de la muraille, tandis que les eaux couraient à deux pieds de moi avec une violence extrême. Mais un mur de granit nous en séparait encore.

Sans réfléchir, sans me demander si quelque moyen n'existait pas de se procurer cette eau, je me laissai aller à un premier moment de désespoir.

Hans me regarda, et je crus voir un sourire apparaître sur ses lèvres.

Il se leva et prit la lampe. Je le suivis. Il se dirigea vers la muraille. Je le regardai faire. Il colla son oreille sur la pierre sèche, et la promena lentement en écoutant avec grand soin. Je compris qu'il cherchait le point précis où le torrent se faisait entendre plus bruyamment. Ce point, il le rencontra dans la paroi latérale de gauche, à trois pieds au-dessus du sol.

Combien j'étais ému! Je n'osais deviner ce que voulait faire le chasseur! Mais il fallut bien le comprendre et l'applaudir, et le presser de mes caresses, quand je le vis saisir son pic pour attaquer la roche elle-même.

« Sauvés! m'écriai-je.

— Oui, répétait mon oncle avec frénésie, Hans a raison! Ah! le brave chasseur! Nous n'aurions pas trouvé cela! »

Je le crois bien! Un pareil moyen, quelque simple qu'il fût, ne nous serait pas venu à l'esprit. Rien de plus dangereux que de donner un coup de pioche dans cette charpente du globe. Et si quelque éboulement allait se produire qui nous écraserait! Et si le torrent, se faisant jour à travers le roc, allait nous envahir! Ces dangers n'avaient rien de chimérique; mais alors les craintes d'éboulement ou d'inondation ne pouvaient nous arrêter, et notre soif était si intense que pour l'apaiser nous eussions creusé au lit même de l'Océan.

Hans se mit à ce travail, que ni mon oncle ni moi nous n'eussions accompli. L'impatience emportant notre main, la roche eût volé en éclats sous ses coups précipités. Le guide, au contraire, calme et modéré, usa peu à peu le rocher par une série de petits coups répétés, creusant une ouverture large de six pouces. J'entendais le bruit du torrent s'accroître, et je croyais déjà sentir l'eau bienfaisante rejaillir sur mes lèvres.

Bientôt le pic s'enfonça de deux pieds dans la muraille de granit. Le travail durait depuis plus

d'une heure. Je me tordais d'impatience! Mon
oncle voulait employer les grands moyens. J'eus
de la peine à l'arrêter, et déjà il saisissait son
pic, quand soudain un sifflement se fit entendre.
Un jet d'eau s'élança de la muraille et vint se briser
sur la paroi opposée.

Hans, à demi renversé par le choc, ne put retenir
un cri de douleur. Je le compris lorsque, plongeant
mes mains dans le jet liquide, je poussai à mon
tour une violente exclamation. La source était
bouillante.

« De l'eau à cent degrés! m'écriai-je.

— Eh bien, elle refroidira », répondit mon oncle.

Le couloir s'emplissait de vapeurs, tandis qu'un
ruisseau se formait et allait se perdre dans les
sinuosités souterraines; bientôt nous y puisions
notre première gorgée.

Ah! quelle jouissance! Quelle incomparable
volupté! Qu'était cette eau? D'où venait-elle?
Peu importait. C'était de l'eau, et, quoique chaude
encore, elle ramenait au cœur la vie prête à s'échapper. Je buvais sans m'arrêter, sans goûter même.

Ce ne fut qu'après une minute de délectation
que je m'écriai :

« Mais c'est de l'eau ferrugineuse!

— Excellente pour l'estomac, répliqua mon
oncle, et d'une haute minéralisation! Voilà un
voyage qui vaudra celui de Spa ou de Tœplitz!

— Ah! que c'est bon!

— Je le crois bien, une eau puisée à deux lieues
sous terre! Elle a un goût d'encre qui n'a rien de

Un jet d'eau s'élança de la muraille (p. 192).

désagréable. Une fameuse ressource que Hans nous a procurée là! Aussi je propose de donner son nom à ce ruisseau salutaire.

— Bien! » m'écriai-je.

Et le nom de « Hans-bach » fut aussitôt adopté.

Hans n'en fut pas plus fier. Après s'être modérément rafraîchi, il s'accota dans un coin avec son calme accoutumé.

« Maintenant, dis-je, il ne faudrait pas laisser perdre cette eau.

— A quoi bon? répondit mon oncle, je soupçonne la source d'être intarissable.

— Qu'importe! remplissons l'outre et les gourdes, puis nous essaierons de boucher l'ouverture. »

Mon conseil fut suivi. Hans, au moyen d'éclats de granit et d'étoupe, essaya d'obstruer l'entaille faite à la paroi. Ce ne fut pas chose facile. On se brûlait les mains sans y parvenir; la pression était trop considérable, et nos efforts demeurèrent infructueux.

« Il est évident, dis-je, que les nappes supérieures de ce cours d'eau sont situées à une grande hauteur, à en juger par la force du jet.

— Cela n'est pas douteux, répliqua mon oncle; il y a là mille atmosphères de pression, si cette colonne d'eau a trente-deux mille pieds de hauteur. Mais il me vient une idée.

— Laquelle?

— Pourquoi nous entêter à boucher cette ouverture?

— Mais, parce que... »

J'aurais été embarrassé de trouver une raison.

« Quand nos gourdes seront vides, sommes-nous assurés de pouvoir les remplir ?

— Non, évidemment.

— Eh bien, laissons couler cette eau ! Elle descendra naturellement et guidera ceux qu'elle rafraîchira en route !

— Voilà qui est bien imaginé ! m'écriai-je, et avec ce ruisseau pour compagnon, il n'y a plus aucune raison pour ne pas réussir dans nos projets.

— Ah ! tu y viens, mon garçon, dit le professeur en riant.

— Je fais mieux que d'y venir, j'y suis.

— Un instant ! Commençons par prendre quelques heures de repos. »

J'oubliais vraiment qu'il fît nuit. Le chronomètre se chargea de me l'apprendre. Bientôt chacun de nous, suffisamment restauré et rafraîchi, s'endormit d'un profond sommeil.

XXIV

LE lendemain, nous avions déjà oublié nos douleurs passées. Je m'étonnai tout d'abord de n'avoir plus soif, et j'en demandai la raison. Le ruisseau qui coulait à mes pieds en murmurant se chargea de me répondre.

On déjeuna et l'on but de cette excellente eau ferrugineuse. Je me sentais tout ragaillardi et décidé à aller loin. Pourquoi un homme convaincu comme mon oncle ne réussirait-il pas, avec un guide industrieux comme Hans, et un neveu « déterminé » comme moi ? Voilà les belles idées qui se glissaient dans mon cerveau ! On m'eût proposé de remonter à la cime du Sneffels, que j'aurais refusé avec indignation.

Mais il n'était heureusement question que de descendre.

« Partons ! » m'écriai-je, éveillant par mes accents enthousiastes les vieux échos du globe.

La marche fut reprise le jeudi à huit heures du matin. Le couloir de granit, se contournant en sinueux détours, présentait des coudes inattendus, et affectait l'imbroglio d'un labyrinthe ; mais, en somme, sa direction principale était toujours le sud-est. Mon oncle ne cessait de consulter avec le plus grand soin sa boussole, pour se rendre compte du chemin parcouru.

La galerie s'enfonçait presque horizontalement, avec deux pouces de pente par toise, tout au plus. Le ruisseau coulait sans précipitation en murmurant sous nos pieds. Je le comparais à quelque génie familier qui nous guidait à travers la terre, et de la main je caressais la tiède naïade dont les chants accompagnaient nos pas. Ma bonne humeur prenait volontiers une tournure mythologique.

Quant à mon oncle, il pestait contre l'horizontalité de la route, lui, « l'homme des verticales ».

Son chemin s'allongeait indéfiniment, et au lieu de glisser le long du rayon terrestre, suivant son expression, il s'en allait par l'hypoténuse. Mais nous n'avions pas le choix, et tant que l'on gagnait vers le centre, si peu que ce fût, il ne fallait pas se plaindre.

D'ailleurs, de temps en temps, les pentes s'abaissaient; la naïade se mettait à dégringoler en mugissant, et nous descendions plus profondément avec elle.

En somme, ce jour-là et le lendemain, on fit beaucoup de chemin horizontal, et relativement peu de chemin vertical.

Le vendredi soir, 10 juillet, d'après l'estime, nous devions être à trente lieues au sud-est de Reykjawik et à une profondeur de deux lieues et demie.

Sous nos pieds s'ouvrit alors un puits assez effrayant. Mon oncle ne put s'empêcher de battre des mains en calculant la roideur de ses pentes.

« Voilà qui nous mènera loin, s'écria-t-il, et facilement, car les saillies du roc font un véritable escalier ! »

Les cordes furent disposées par Hans de manière à prévenir tout accident. La descente commença. Je n'ose l'appeler périlleuse, car j'étais déjà familiarisé avec ce genre d'exercice.

Ce puits était une fente étroite pratiquée dans le massif, du genre de celles qu'on appelle «faille». La contraction de la charpente terrestre, à l'époque de son refroidissement, l'avait évidemment

produite. Si elle servit autrefois de passage aux matières éruptives vomies par le Sneffels, je ne m'expliquais pas comment celles-ci n'y laissèrent aucune trace. Nous descendions une sorte de vis tournante qu'on eût crue faite de la main des hommes.

De quart d'heure en quart d'heure, il fallait s'arrêter pour prendre un repos nécessaire et rendre à nos jarrets leur élasticité. On s'asseyait alors sur quelque saillie, les jambes pendantes, on causait en mangeant, et l'on se désaltérait au ruisseau.

Il va sans dire que, dans cette faille, le Hans-bach s'était fait cascade au détriment de son volume; mais il suffisait et au-delà à étancher notre soif; d'ailleurs, avec les déclivités moins accusées, il ne pouvait manquer de reprendre son cours paisible. En ce moment, il me rappelait mon digne oncle, ses impatiences et ses colères, tandis que, par les pentes adoucies, c'était le calme du chasseur islandais.

Le 11 et le 12 juillet, nous suivîmes les spirales de cette faille, pénétrant encore de deux lieues dans l'écorce terrestre, ce qui faisait près de cinq lieues au-dessous du niveau de la mer. Mais, le 13, vers midi, la faille prit, dans la direction du sud-est, une inclinaison beaucoup plus douce, environ de quarante-cinq degrés.

Le chemin devint alors aisé et d'une parfaite monotonie. Il était difficile qu'il en fût autrement. Le voyage ne pouvait être varié par les incidents du paysage.

Nous descendions une sorte de vis tournante (p. 198).

Enfin, le mercredi 15, nous étions à sept lieues sous terre et à cinquante lieues environ du Sneffels. Bien que nous fussions un peu fatigués, nos santés se maintenaient dans un état rassurant, et la pharmacie de voyage était encore intacte.

Mon oncle notait heure par heure les indications de la boussole, du chronomètre, du manomètre et du thermomètre, celles-là mêmes qu'il a publiées dans le récit scientifique de son voyage. Il pouvait donc se rendre facilement compte de sa situation. Lorsqu'il m'apprit que nous étions à une distance horizontale de cinquante lieues, je ne pus retenir une exclamation.

« Qu'as-tu donc? demanda-t-il.

— Rien, seulement je fais une réflexion.

— Laquelle, mon garçon?

— C'est que, si vos calculs sont exacts, nous ne sommes plus sous l'Islande.

— Crois-tu?

— Il est facile de nous en assurer. »

Je pris mes mesures au compas sur la carte.

« Je ne me trompais pas, dis-je. Nous avons dépassé le cap Portland, et ces cinquante lieues dans le sud-est nous mettent en pleine mer.

— Sous la pleine mer, répliqua mon oncle en se frottant les mains.

— Ainsi, m'écriai-je, l'Océan s'étend au-dessus de notre tête!

— Bah! Axel, rien de plus naturel! N'y a-t-il pas à Newcastle des mines de charbon qui s'avancent au loin sous les flots? »

Le professeur pouvait trouver cette situation fort simple, mais la pensée de me promener sous la masse des eaux ne laissa pas de me préoccuper. Et cependant, que les plaines et les montagnes de l'Islande fussent suspendues sur notre tête, ou les flots de l'Atlantique, cela différait peu, en somme, du moment que la charpente granitique était solide. Du reste, je m'habituai promptement à cette idée, car le couloir, tantôt droit, tantôt sinueux, capricieux dans ses pentes comme dans ses détours, mais toujours courant au sud-est, et toujours s'enfonçant davantage, nous conduisit rapidement à de grandes profondeurs.

Quatre jours plus tard, le samedi 18 juillet, le soir, nous arrivâmes à une espèce de grotte assez vaste ; mon oncle remit à Hans ses trois rixdales hebdomadaires, et il fut décidé que le lendemain serait un jour de repos.

XXV

Je me réveillai donc, le dimanche matin, sans cette préoccupation habituelle d'un départ immédiat. Et, quoique ce fût au plus profond des abîmes, cela ne laissait pas d'être agréable. D'ailleurs, nous étions faits à cette existence de troglodytes. Je ne pensais guère au soleil, aux étoiles, à la lune, aux arbres, aux maisons, aux villes, à toutes ces

superfluités terrestres dont l'être sublunaire s'est fait une nécessité. En notre qualité de fossiles, nous faisions fi de ces inutiles merveilles.

La grotte formait une vaste salle. Sur son sol granitique coulait doucement le ruisseau fidèle. A une pareille distance de sa source, son eau n'avait plus que la température ambiante et se laissait boire sans difficulté.

Après le déjeuner, le professeur voulut consacrer quelques heures à mettre en ordre ses notes quotidiennes.

« D'abord, dit-il, je vais faire des calculs, afin de relever exactement notre situation ; je veux pouvoir, au retour, tracer une carte de notre voyage, une sorte de section verticale du globe, qui donnera le profil de l'expédition.

— Ce sera fort curieux, mon oncle ; mais vos observations auront-elles un degré suffisant de précision ?

— Oui. J'ai noté avec soin les angles et les pentes. Je suis sûr de ne point me tromper. Voyons d'abord où nous sommes. Prends la boussole et observe la direction qu'elle indique. »

Je regardai l'instrument, et, après un examen attentif, je répondis :

« Est-quart-sud-est.

— Bien ! fit le professeur, notant l'observation et établissant quelques calculs rapides. J'en conclus que nous avons fait quatre-vingt-cinq lieues depuis notre point de départ.

— Ainsi nous voyageons sous l'Atlantique ?

— Parfaitement.

— Et dans ce moment une tempête s'y déchaîne peut-être, et des navires sont secoués sur notre tête par les flots et l'ouragan ?

— Cela se peut.

— Et les baleines viennent frapper de leur queue les murailles de notre prison ?

— Sois tranquille, Axel, elles ne parviendront pas à l'ébranler. Mais revenons à nos calculs. Nous sommes dans le sud-est, à quatre-vingt-cinq lieues de la base du Sneffels, et, d'après mes notes précédentes, j'estime à seize lieues la profondeur atteinte.

— Seize lieues ! m'écriai-je.

— Sans doute.

— Mais c'est l'extrême limite assignée par la science à l'épaisseur de l'écorce terrestre.

— Je ne dis pas non.

— Et ici, suivant la loi de l'accroissement de la température, une chaleur de quinze cents degrés devrait exister.

— « Devrait », mon garçon.

— Et tout ce granit ne pourrait se maintenir à l'état solide et serait en pleine fusion.

— Tu vois qu'il n'en est rien et que les faits, suivant leur habitude, viennent démentir les théories.

— Je suis forcé d'en convenir, mais enfin cela m'étonne.

— Qu'indique le thermomètre ?

— Vingt-sept degrés six dixièmes.

— Il s'en manque donc de quatorze cent soixante-quatorze degrés quatre dixièmes que les savants n'aient raison. Donc l'accroissement proportionnel de la température est une erreur. Donc Humphry Davy ne se trompait pas. Donc je n'ai pas eu tort de l'écouter. Qu'as-tu à répondre ?

— Rien. »

A la vérité, j'aurais eu beaucoup de choses à dire. Je n'admettais la théorie de Davy en aucune façon, je tenais toujours pour la chaleur centrale, bien que je n'en ressentisse point les effets. J'aimais mieux admettre, en vérité, que cette cheminée d'un volcan éteint, recouverte par les laves d'un enduit réfractaire, ne permettait pas à la température de se propager à travers ses parois.

Mais, sans m'arrêter à chercher des arguments nouveaux, je me bornai à prendre la situation telle qu'elle était.

« Mon oncle, repris-je, je tiens pour exacts tous vos calculs, mais permettez-moi d'en tirer une conséquence rigoureuse.

— Va, mon garçon, à ton aise.

— Au point où nous sommes, sous la latitude de l'Islande, le rayon terrestre est de quinze cent quatre-vingt-trois lieues à peu près ?

— Quinze cent quatre-vingt-trois lieues et un tiers.

— Mettons seize cents lieues en chiffres ronds. Sur un voyage de seize cents lieues, nous en avons fait douze ?

— Comme tu dis.

— Et cela au prix de quatre-vingt-cinq lieues de diagonale?

— Parfaitement.

— En vingt jours environ?

— En vingt jours.

— Or, seize lieues font le centième du rayon terrestre. A continuer ainsi, nous mettrons donc deux mille jours, ou près de cinq ans et demi à descendre! »

Le professeur ne répondit pas.

« Sans compter que, si une verticale de seize lieues s'achète par une horizontale de quatre-vingts, cela fera huit mille lieues dans le sud-est, et il y aura longtemps que nous serons sortis par un point de la circonférence avant d'en atteindre le centre!

— Au diable tes calculs! répliqua mon oncle avec un mouvement de colère. Au diable tes hypothèses! Sur quoi reposent-elles? Qui te dit que ce couloir ne va pas directement à notre but? D'ailleurs j'ai pour moi un précédent. Ce que je fais là, un autre l'a fait, et où il a réussi je réussirai à mon tour.

— Je l'espère; mais, enfin, il m'est bien permis...

— Il t'est permis de te taire, Axel, quand tu voudras déraisonner de la sorte. »

Je vis bien que le terrible professeur menaçait de reparaître sous la peau de l'oncle, et je me tins pour averti.

« Maintenant, reprit-il, consulte le manomètre. Qu'indique-t-il?

— Une pression considérable.

— Bien. Tu vois qu'en descendant doucement, en nous habituant peu à peu à la densité de cette atmosphère, nous n'en souffrons aucunement.

— Aucunement, sauf quelques douleurs d'oreilles.

— Ce n'est rien, et tu feras disparaître ce malaise en mettant l'air extérieur en communication rapide avec l'air contenu dans tes poumons.

— Parfaitement, répondis-je, bien décidé à ne plus contrarier mon oncle. Il y a même un plaisir véritable à se sentir plongé dans cette atmosphère plus dense. Avez-vous remarqué avec quelle intensité le son s'y propage?

— Sans doute. Un sourd finirait par y entendre à merveille.

— Mais cette densité augmentera sans aucun doute?

— Oui, suivant une loi assez peu déterminée. Il est vrai que l'intensité de la pesanteur diminuera à mesure que nous descendrons. Tu sais que c'est à la surface même de la terre que son action se fait le plus vivement sentir, et qu'au centre du globe les objets ne pèsent plus.

— Je le sais; mais, dites-moi, cet air ne finira-t-il pas par acquérir la densité de l'eau?

— Sans doute, sous une pression de sept cent dix atmosphères.

— Et plus bas?

— Plus bas, cette densité s'accroîtra encore.

— Comment descendrons-nous alors ?

— Eh bien, nous mettrons des cailloux dans nos poches.

— Ma foi, mon oncle, vous avez réponse à tout. »

Je n'osai pas aller plus avant dans le champ des hypothèses, car je me serais encore heurté à quelque impossibilité qui eût fait bondir le professeur.

Il était évident, cependant, que l'air, sous une pression qui pouvait atteindre des milliers d'atmosphères, finirait par passer à l'état solide, et alors, en admettant que nos corps eussent résisté, il faudrait s'arrêter, en dépit de tous les raisonnements du monde.

Mais je ne fis pas valoir cet argument. Mon oncle m'aurait encore riposté son éternel Saknussemm, précédent sans valeur, car, en tenant pour avéré le voyage du savant Islandais, il y avait une chose bien simple à répondre :

Au XVIᵉ siècle, ni le baromètre ni le manomètre n'étaient inventés ; comment donc Saknussemm avait-il pu déterminer son arrivée au centre du globe ?

Mais je gardai cette objection pour moi, et j'attendis les événements.

Le reste de la journée se passa en calculs et en conversation. Je fus toujours de l'avis du professeur Lidenbrock, et j'enviai la parfaite indifférence de Hans, qui, sans tant chercher les effets et les causes, s'en allait aveuglément où le menait la destinée.

Il faut l'avouer, les choses jusqu'ici se passaient bien, et j'aurais eu mauvaise grâce à me plaindre. Si la « moyenne » des difficultés ne s'accroissait pas, nous ne pouvions manquer d'atteindre notre but. Et quelle gloire alors! J'en étais arrivé à faire de ces raisonnements à la Lidenbrock. Sérieusement. Cela tenait-il au milieu étrange dans lequel je vivais? Peut-être.

Pendant quelques jours, des pentes plus rapides, quelques-unes même d'une effrayante verticalité, nous engagèrent profondément dans le massif interne. Par certaines journées, on gagnait une lieue et demie à deux lieues vers le centre. Descentes périlleuses, pendant lesquelles l'adresse de Hans et son merveilleux sang-froid nous furent très utiles. Cet impassible Islandais se dévouait avec un incompréhensible sans-façon, et, grâce à lui, plus d'un mauvais pas fut franchi dont nous ne serions pas sortis seuls.

Par exemple, son mutisme s'augmentait de jour en jour. Je crois même qu'il nous gagnait. Les objets extérieurs ont une action réelle sur le cerveau. Qui s'enferme entre quatre murs finit par perdre la faculté d'associer les idées et les mots. Que de prisonniers cellulaires devenus imbéciles, sinon fous, par le défaut d'exercice des facultés pensantes!

Descente verticale (p. 208).

Pendant les deux semaines qui suivirent notre dernière conversation, il ne se produisit aucun incident digne d'être rapporté. Je ne retrouve dans ma mémoire, et pour cause, qu'un seul événement d'une extrême gravité. Il m'eût été difficile d'en oublier le moindre détail.

Le 7 août, nos descentes successives nous avaient amenés à une profondeur de trente lieues, c'est-à-dire qu'il y avait sur notre tête trente lieues de rocs, d'océan, de continents et de villes. Nous devions être alors à deux cents lieues de l'Islande.

Ce jour-là, le tunnel suivait un plan peu incliné.

Je marchais en avant. Mon oncle portait l'un des deux appareils de Ruhmkorff, et moi l'autre. J'examinais les couches de granit.

Tout à coup, me retournant, je m'aperçus que j'étais seul.

« Bon, pensais-je, j'ai marché trop vite, ou bien Hans et mon oncle se sont arrêtés en route. Allons, il faut les rejoindre. Heureusement le chemin ne monte pas sensiblement. »

Je revins sur mes pas. Je marchai pendant un quart d'heure. Je regardai. Personne. J'appelai. Point de réponse. Ma voix se perdit au milieu des caverneux échos qu'elle éveilla soudain.

Je commençai à me sentir inquiet. Un frisson me parcourut tout le corps.

« Un peu de calme, dis-je à haute voix. Je suis sûr de retrouver mes compagnons. Il n'y a pas deux routes ! Or, j'étais en avant, retournons en arrière. »

Je remontai pendant une demi-heure. J'écoutai

si quelque appel ne m'était pas adressé, et, dans cette atmosphère si dense, il pouvait m'arriver de loin. Un silence extraordinaire régnait dans l'immense galerie.

Je m'arrêtai. Je ne pouvais croire à mon isolement. Je voulais bien être égaré, non perdu. Égaré, on se retrouve.

« Voyons, répétai-je, puisqu'il n'y a qu'une route, puisqu'ils la suivent, je dois les rejoindre. Il suffira de remonter encore. A moins que, ne me voyant pas, et oubliant que je les devançais, ils n'aient eu la pensée de revenir en arrière. Eh bien ! même dans ce cas, en me hâtant, je les retrouverai. C'est évident ! »

Je répétai ces derniers mots comme un homme qui n'est pas convaincu. D'ailleurs, pour associer ces idées si simples et les réunir sous forme de raisonnement, je dus employer un temps fort long.

Un doute me prit alors. Étais-je bien en avant ? Certes, Hans me suivait, précédant mon oncle. Il s'était même arrêté pendant quelques instants pour rattacher ses bagages sur son épaule. Ce détail me revenait à l'esprit. C'est à ce moment même que j'avais dû continuer ma route.

« D'ailleurs, pensai-je, j'ai un moyen sûr de ne pas m'égarer, un fil pour me guider dans ce labyrinthe, et qui ne saurait casser, mon fidèle ruisseau. Je n'ai qu'à remonter son cours, et je retrouverai forcément les traces de mes compagnons. »

Ce raisonnement me ranima, et je résolus de me

remettre en marche sans perdre un instant.

Combien je bénis alors la prévoyance de mon oncle, lorsqu'il empêcha le chasseur de boucher l'entaille faite à la paroi de granit ! Ainsi cette bienfaisante source, après nous avoir désaltérés pendant la route, allait me guider à travers les sinuosités de l'écorce terrestre.

Avant de remonter, je pensai qu'une ablution me ferait quelque bien.

Je me baissai donc pour plonger mon front dans l'eau du Hans-bach !

Que l'on juge de ma stupéfaction !

Je foulais un granit sec et raboteux ! Le ruisseau ne coulait plus à mes pieds !

XXVII

Je ne puis peindre mon désespoir. Nul mot de la langue humaine ne rendrait mes sentiments. J'étais enterré vif, avec la perspective de mourir dans les tortures de la faim et de la soif.

Machinalement je promenai mes mains brûlantes sur le sol. Que ce roc me sembla desséché !

Mais comment avais-je abandonné le cours du ruisseau ? Car, enfin, il n'était plus là ! Je compris alors la raison de ce silence étrange, quand j'écoutai pour la dernière fois si quelque appel de mes compagnons ne parviendrait pas à mon oreille.

Ainsi, au moment où mon premier pas s'engagea dans la route imprudente, je ne remarquai point cette absence du ruisseau. Il est évident qu'à ce moment une bifurcation de la galerie s'ouvrit devant moi, tandis que le Hans-bach, obéissant aux caprices d'une autre pente, s'en allait avec mes compagnons vers des profondeurs inconnues!

Comment revenir? De traces, il n'y en avait pas. Mon pied ne laissait aucune empreinte sur ce granit. Je me brisais la tête à chercher la solution de cet insoluble problème. Ma situation se résumait en un seul mot: perdu!

Oui! perdu à une profondeur qui me semblait incommensurable! Ces trente lieues d'écorce terrestre pesaient sur mes épaules d'un poids épouvantable. Je me sentais écrasé.

J'essayai de ramener mes idées aux choses de la terre. C'est à peine si je pus y parvenir. Hambourg, la maison de Königstrasse, ma pauvre Graüben, tout ce monde sous lequel je m'égarais passa rapidement devant mon souvenir effaré. Je revis dans une vive hallucination les incidents du voyage, la traversée, l'Islande, M. Fridriksson, le Sneffels! Je me dis que si, dans ma position, je conservais encore l'ombre d'une espérance, ce serait signe de folie, et qu'il valait mieux désespérer!

En effet, quelle puissance humaine pouvait me ramener à la surface du globe et disjoindre ces voûtes énormes qui s'arc-boutaient au-dessus de ma tête? Qui pouvait me remettre sur la route du retour et me réunir à mes compagnons?

« Oh ! mon oncle ! » m'écriai-je avec l'accent du désespoir.

Ce fut le seul mot de reproche qui me vint aux lèvres, car je compris ce que le malheureux homme devait souffrir en me cherchant à son tour.

Quand je me vis ainsi en dehors de tout secours humain, incapable de rien tenter pour mon salut, je songeai aux secours du Ciel. Les souvenirs de mon enfance, ceux de ma mère que je n'avais connue qu'au temps des baisers, revinrent à ma mémoire. Je recourus à la prière, quelque peu de droits que j'eusse d'être entendu du Dieu auquel je m'adressais si tard, et je l'implorai avec ferveur.

Ce retour vers la Providence me rendit un peu de calme, et je pus concentrer sur ma situation toutes les forces de mon intelligence.

J'avais pour trois jours de vivres, et ma gourde était pleine. Cependant je ne pouvais rester seul plus longtemps. Mais fallait-il monter ou descendre ?

Monter évidemment ! monter toujours !

Je devais arriver au point où j'avais abandonné la source, à la funeste bifurcation. Là, une fois le ruisseau sous les pieds, je pourrais toujours regagner le sommet du Sneffels.

Comment n'y avais-je pas songé plus tôt ! Il y avait évidemment là une chance de salut. Le plus pressé était donc de retrouver le cours du Hansbach.

Je me levai et, m'appuyant sur mon bâton ferré, je remontai la galerie. La pente en était assez roide.

Je songeai aux secours du Ciel (p. 214).

Je marchais avec espoir et sans embarras, comme un homme qui n'a pas le choix du chemin à suivre.

Pendant une demi-heure, aucun obstacle n'arrêta mes pas. J'essayais de reconnaître ma route à la forme du tunnel, à la saillie de certaines roches, à la disposition des anfractuosités. Mais aucun signe particulier ne frappait mon esprit, et je reconnus bientôt que cette galerie ne pouvait me ramener à la bifurcation. Elle était sans issue. Je me heurtai contre un mur impénétrable, et je tombai sur le roc.

De quelle épouvante, de quel désespoir je fus saisi alors, je ne saurais le dire. Je demeurai anéanti. Ma dernière espérance venait de se briser contre cette muraille de granit.

Perdu dans ce labyrinthe dont les sinuosités se croisaient en tous sens, je n'avais plus à tenter une fuite impossible. Il fallait mourir de la plus effroyable des morts! Et, chose étrange, il me vint à la pensée que, si mon corps fossilisé se retrouvait un jour, sa rencontre à trente lieues dans les entrailles de la terre soulèverait de graves questions scientifiques!

Je voulus parler à voix haute, mais de rauques accents passèrent seuls entre mes lèvres desséchées. Je haletais.

Au milieu de ces angoisses, une nouvelle terreur vint s'emparer de mon esprit. Ma lampe s'était faussée en tombant. Je n'avais aucun moyen de la réparer. Sa lumière pâlissait et allait me manquer!

Je regardai le courant lumineux s'amoindrir dans le serpentin de l'appareil. Une procession d'ombres mouvantes se déroula sur les parois assombries. Je n'osais plus abaisser ma paupière, craignant de perdre le moindre atome de cette clarté fugitive ! A chaque instant il me semblait qu'elle allait s'évanouir et que « le noir » m'envahissait.

Enfin une dernière lueur trembla dans la lampe. Je la suivis, je l'aspirai du regard, je concentrai sur elle toute la puissance de mes yeux, comme sur la dernière sensation de lumière qu'il leur fût donné d'éprouver, et je demeurai plongé dans les ténèbres immenses.

Quel cri terrible m'échappa ! Sur terre, au milieu des plus profondes nuits, la lumière n'abandonne jamais entièrement ses droits ! Elle est diffuse, elle est subtile, mais, si peu qu'il en reste, la rétine de l'œil finit par la percevoir ! Ici, rien. L'ombre absolue faisait de moi un aveugle dans toute l'acception du mot.

Alors ma tête se perdit. Je me relevai les bras en avant, essayant les tâtonnements les plus douloureux. Je me pris à fuir, précipitant mes pas au hasard dans cet inextricable labyrinthe, descendant toujours, courant à travers la croûte terrestre, comme un habitant des failles souterraines, appelant, criant, hurlant, bientôt meurtri aux saillies des rocs, tombant et me relevant ensanglanté, cherchant à boire ce sang qui m'inondait le visage, et attendant toujours que quelque muraille vînt offrir à ma tête un obstacle pour s'y briser !

Où me conduisit cette course insensée? Je
l'ignorerai toujours. Après plusieurs heures, sans
doute à bout de forces, je tombai comme une
masse inerte le long de la paroi, et je perdis tout
sentiment d'existence!

XXVIII

Quand je revins à la vie, mon visage était mouillé,
mais mouillé de larmes. Combien dura cet état
d'insensibilité, je ne saurais le dire. Je n'avais plus
aucun moyen de me rendre compte du temps.
Jamais solitude ne fut semblable à la mienne,
jamais abandon si complet!

Après ma chute, j'avais perdu beaucoup de sang.
Je m'en sentais inondé! Ah! combien je regrettai
de n'être pas mort « et que ce fût encore à faire » !
Je ne voulais plus penser. Je chassai toute idée et,
vaincu par la douleur, je me roulai près de la paroi
opposée.

Déjà je sentais l'évanouissement me reprendre,
et, avec lui, l'anéantissement suprême, quand un
bruit violent vint frapper mon oreille. Il ressemblait au roulement prolongé du tonnerre, et
j'entendis les ondes sonores se perdre peu à peu
dans les lointaines profondeurs du gouffre.

D'où provenait ce bruit? De quelque phénomène
sans doute, qui s'accomplissait au sein du massif

terrestre! L'explosion d'un gaz, ou la chute de quelque puissante assise du globe!

J'écoutai encore. Je voulus savoir si ce bruit se renouvellerait. Un quart d'heure se passa. Le silence régnait dans la galerie. Je n'entendais même plus les battements de mon cœur.

Tout à coup mon oreille, appliquée par hasard sur la muraille, crut surprendre des paroles vagues, insaisissables, lointaines. Je tressaillis.

« C'est une hallucination! » pensai-je.

Mais non. En écoutant avec plus d'attention, j'entendis réellement un murmure de voix. Mais de comprendre ce qui se disait, c'est ce que ma faiblesse ne me permit pas. Cependant on parlait. J'en étais certain.

J'eus un instant la crainte que ces paroles ne fussent les miennes, rapportées par un écho. Peut-être avais-je crié à mon insu. Je fermai fortement les lèvres et j'appliquai de nouveau mon oreille à la paroi.

« Oui, certes, on parle! on parle! »

En me portant même à quelques pieds plus loin le long de la muraille, j'entendis distinctement. Je parvins à saisir des mots incertains, bizarres, incompréhensibles. Ils m'arrivaient comme s'ils eussent été prononcés à voix-basse, murmurés, pour ainsi dire. Le mot « forloräd » était plusieurs fois répété, avec un accent de douleur.

Que signifiait-il? Qui le prononçait? Mon oncle ou Hans, évidemment. Mais si je les entendais, ils pouvaient donc m'entendre.

« A moi! criai-je de toutes mes forces, à moi! »

J'écoutai, j'épiai dans l'ombre une réponse, un cri, un soupir. Rien ne se fit entendre. Quelques minutes se passèrent. Tout un monde d'idées avait éclos dans mon esprit. Je pensai que ma voix affaiblie ne pouvait arriver jusqu'à mes compagnons.

« Car ce sont eux, répétai-je. Quels autres hommes seraient enfouis à trente lieues sous terre ? »

Je me remis à écouter. En promenant mon oreille sur la paroi, je trouvai un point mathématique où les voix paraissaient atteindre leur maximum d'intensité. Le mot « forloräd » revint encore à mon oreille; puis ce roulement de tonnerre qui m'avait tiré de ma torpeur.

« Non, dis-je, non. Ce n'est point à travers le massif que ces voix se font entendre. La paroi est faite de granit, et elle ne permettrait pas à la plus forte détonation de la traverser! Ce bruit arrive par la galerie même! Il faut qu'il y ait là un effet d'acoustique tout particulier! »

J'écoutai de nouveau, et cette fois, oui! cette fois! j'entendis mon nom distinctement jeté à travers l'espace!

C'était mon oncle qui le prononçait! Il causait avec le guide, et le mot « forloräd » était un mot danois!

Alors je compris tout. Pour me faire entendre, il fallait précisément parler le long de cette muraille qui servirait à conduire ma voix comme le fil conduit l'électricité.

Mais je n'avais pas de temps à perdre. Que mes compagnons se fussent éloignés de quelques pas, et le phénomène d'acoustique eût été détruit. Je m'approchai donc de la muraille, et je prononçai ces mots, aussi distinctement que possible :

« Mon oncle Lidenbrock ! »

J'attendis dans la plus vive anxiété. Le son n'a pas une rapidité extrême. La densité des couches d'air n'accroît même pas sa vitesse ; elle n'augmente que son intensité. Quelques secondes, des siècles, se passèrent, et enfin ces paroles arrivèrent à mon oreille.

« Axel, Axel ! est-ce toi ? »

. . . .

« Oui ! oui ! » répondis-je.

. . . .

« Mon enfant, où es-tu ? »

. . . .

« Perdu, dans la plus profonde obscurité ! »

. . . .

« Mais ta lampe ? »

. . . .

« Éteinte. »

. . . .

« Et le ruisseau ? »

. . . .

« Disparu. »

. . . .

« Axel, mon pauvre Axel, reprends courage ! »

. . . .

.« Axel! Axel! est-ce toi? » (p. 221).

« Attendez un peu, je suis épuisé ! Je n'ai plus la force de répondre. Mais parlez-moi ! »

. . . .

« Courage, reprit mon oncle. Ne parle pas, écoute-moi. Nous t'avons cherché en remontant et en descendant la galerie. Impossible de te trouver. Ah ! je t'ai bien pleuré, mon enfant ! Enfin, te supposant toujours sur le chemin du Hans-bach, nous sommes redescendus en tirant des coups de fusil. Maintenant, si nos voix peuvent se réunir, pur effet d'acoustique ! nos mains ne peuvent se toucher ! Mais ne te désespère pas, Axel ! C'est déjà quelque chose de s'entendre ! »

. . . .

Pendant ce temps j'avais réfléchi. Un certain espoir, vague encore, me revenait au cœur. Tout d'abord, il y avait une chose qu'il m'importait de connaître. J'approchai donc mes lèvres de la muraille, et je dis :

« Mon oncle ? »

. . . .

« Mon enfant ? » me fut-il répondu après quelques instants.

« Il faut d'abord savoir quelle distance nous sépare. »

. . . .

« Cela est facile. »

. . . .

« Vous avez votre chronomètre ? »

. . . .

« Oui. »

. . . .

« Eh bien, prenez-le. Prononcez mon nom en notant exactement la seconde où vous parlerez. Je le répéterai dès qu'il me parviendra, et vous observerez également le moment précis auquel vous arrivera ma réponse. »

. . . .

« Bien, et la moitié du temps compris entre ma demande et ta réponse indiquera celui que ma voix emploie pour arriver jusqu'à toi. »

. . . .

« C'est cela, mon oncle. »

. . . .

« Es-tu prêt ? »

. . . .

« Oui. »

. . . .

« Eh bien, fais attention, je vais prononcer ton nom. »

. . . .

J'appliquai mon oreille sur la paroi et dès que le mot « Axel » me parvint, je répondis immédiatement « Axel », puis j'attendis.

. . . .

« Quarante secondes, dit alors mon oncle. Il s'est écoulé quarante secondes entre les deux mots ; le son met donc vingt secondes à monter. Or, à mille vingt pieds par seconde, cela fait vingt mille quatre cents pieds, ou une lieue et demie et un huitième. »

. . . .

« Une lieue et demie ! » murmurai-je.

. . . .

« Eh ! cela se franchit, Axel ! »

. . . .

« Mais faut-il monter ou descendre ? »

. . . .

« Descendre, et voici pourquoi. Nous sommes arrivés à un vaste espace, auquel aboutissent un grand nombre de galeries. Celle que tu as suivie ne peut manquer de t'y conduire, car il semble que toutes ces fentes, ces fractures du globe, rayonnent autour de l'immense caverne que nous occupons. Relève-toi donc et reprends ta route. Marche, traîne-toi, s'il le faut, glisse sur les pentes rapides, et tu trouveras nos bras pour te recevoir au bout du chemin. En route, mon enfant, en route ! »

. . . .

Ces paroles me ranimèrent.

« Adieu, mon oncle, m'écriai-je ; je pars. Nos voix ne pourront plus communiquer entre elles, du moment que j'aurai quitté cette place ! Adieu donc ! »

. . . .

« Au revoir, Axel ! au revoir ! »

. . . .

Tels furent les derniers mots que j'entendis.

Cette surprenante conversation faite au travers de la masse terrestre, échangée à plus d'une lieue de distance, se termina sur ces paroles d'espoir.

Je fis une prière de reconnaissance à Dieu, car il m'avait conduit parmi ces immensités sombres au seul point peut-être où la voix de mes compagnons pouvait me parvenir.

Cet effet d'acoustique très étonnant s'expliquait facilement par les seules lois physiques; il provenait de la forme du couloir et de la conductibilité de la roche. Il y a bien des exemples de cette propagation de sons non perceptibles aux espaces intermédiaires. Je me souviens qu'en maint endroit ce phénomène fut observé, entre autres, dans la galerie intérieure du dôme de Saint-Paul à Londres, et surtout au milieu de ces curieuses cavernes de Sicile, ces latomies situées près de Syracuse, dont la plus merveilleuse en ce genre est connue sous le nom d'Oreille de Denys.

Ces souvenirs me revinrent à l'esprit, et je vis clairement que, puisque la voix de mon oncle arrivait jusqu'à moi, aucun obstacle n'existait entre nous. En suivant le chemin du son, je devais logiquement arriver comme lui, si les forces ne me trahissaient pas.

Je me levai donc. Je me traînai plutôt que je ne marchai. La pente était assez rapide. Je me laissai glisser.

Bientôt la vitesse de ma descente s'accrut dans une effrayante proportion, et menaçait de ressembler à une chute. Je n'avais plus la force de m'arrêter.

Tout à coup le terrain manqua sous mes pieds. Je me sentis rouler en rebondissant sur les aspé-

rités d'une galerie verticale, un véritable puits.
Ma tête porta sur un roc aigu, et je perdis connaissance.

XXIX

Lorsque je revins à moi, j'étais dans une demi-
obscurité, étendu sur d'épaisses couvertures. Mon
oncle veillait, épiant sur mon visage un reste d'existence. A mon premier soupir, il me prit la main ; à
mon premier regard il poussa un cri de joie.

« Il vit ! il vit ! s'écria-t-il.

— Oui, répondis-je d'une voix faible.

— Mon enfant, dit mon oncle en me serrant sur
sa poitrine, te voilà sauvé ! »

Je fus vivement touché de l'accent dont furent
prononcées ces paroles, et plus encore des soins
qui les accompagnèrent. Mais il fallait de telles
épreuves pour provoquer chez le professeur un
pareil épanchement.

En ce moment Hans arriva. Il vit ma main dans
celle de mon oncle ; j'ose affirmer que ses yeux
exprimèrent un vif contentement.

« God dag, dit-il.

— Bonjour, Hans, bonjour, murmurai-je. Et
maintenant, mon oncle, apprenez-moi où nous
sommes en ce moment.

— Demain, Axel, demain ; aujourd'hui tu es

encore trop faible; j'ai entouré ta tête de compresses
qu'il ne faut pas déranger; dors donc, mon garçon,
et demain tu sauras tout.

— Mais au moins, repris-je, quelle heure, quel
jour est-il ?

— Onze heures du soir, c'est aujourd'hui
dimanche, 9 août, et je ne te permets plus de
m'interroger avant le 10 du présent mois. »

En vérité, j'étais bien faible, et mes yeux se fermèrent involontairement. Il me fallait une nuit de
repos; je me laissai donc assoupir sur cette pensée
que mon isolement avait duré quatre longs jours.

Le lendemain, à mon réveil, je regardai autour
de moi. Ma couchette, faite de toutes les couvertures de voyage, se trouvait installée dans une
grotte charmante, ornée de magnifiques stalag-
mites, et dont le sol était recouvert d'un sable fin.
Il y régnait une demi-obscurité. Aucune torche,
aucune lampe n'était allumée, et cependant, certaines clartés inexplicables venaient du dehors
en pénétrant par une étroite ouverture de la
grotte. J'entendais aussi un murmure vague et
indéfini, semblable au gémissement des flots qui
se brisent sur une grève, et parfois les sifflements
de la brise.

Je me demandai si j'étais bien éveillé, si je rêvais
encore, si mon cerveau, fêlé dans ma chute, ne
percevait pas des bruits purement imaginaires.
Cependant, ni mes yeux ni mes oreilles ne pouvaient se tromper à ce point.

« C'est un rayon du jour, pensai-je, qui se glisse

Ma couchette se trouvait installée dans une grotte (p. 228).

par cette fente de rochers! Voilà bien le murmure des vagues! Voilà le sifflement de la brise! Est-ce que je me trompe, ou sommes-nous revenus à la surface de la terre? Mon oncle a-t-il donc renoncé à son expédition, ou l'aurait-il heureusement terminée? »

Je me posais ces insolubles questions, quand le professeur entra.

« Bonjour, Axel! fit-il joyeusement. Je gagerais volontiers que tu te portes bien!

— Mais oui, dis-je en me redressant sur les couvertures.

— Cela devait être, car tu as tranquillement dormi. Hans et moi, nous t'avons veillé tour à tour, et nous avons vu ta guérison faire des progrès sensibles.

— En effet, je me sens ragaillardi, et la preuve, c'est que je ferai honneur au déjeuner que vous voudrez bien me servir!

— Tu mangeras, mon garçon! La fièvre t'a quitté. Hans a frotté tes plaies avec je ne sais quel onguent dont les Islandais ont le secret, et elles se sont cicatrisées à merveille. C'est un fier homme que notre chasseur! »

Tout en parlant, mon oncle apprêtait quelques aliments que je dévorai, malgré ses recommandations. Pendant ce temps je l'accablai de questions auxquelles il s'empressa de répondre.

J'appris alors que ma chute providentielle m'avait précisément amené à l'extrémité d'une galerie presque perpendiculaire; comme j'étais

arrivé au milieu d'un torrent de pierres, dont la moins grosse eût suffi à m'écraser, il fallait en conclure qu'une partie du massif avait glissé avec moi. Cet effrayant véhicule me transporta ainsi jusque dans les bras de mon oncle, où je tombai sanglant, inanimé.

« Véritablement, me dit-il, il est étonnant que tu ne te sois pas tué mille fois. Mais, pour Dieu! ne nous séparons plus, car nous risquerions de ne jamais nous revoir. »

« Ne nous séparons plus! » Le voyage n'était donc pas fini? J'ouvris de grands yeux étonnés, ce qui provoqua immédiatement cette question :

« Qu'as-tu donc, Axel?

— Une demande à vous adresser. Vous dites que me voilà sain et sauf?

— Sans doute.

— J'ai tous mes membres intacts?

— Certainement.

— Et ma tête?

— Ta tête, sauf quelques contusions, est parfaitement à sa place sur tes épaules.

— Eh bien, j'ai peur que mon cerveau ne soit dérangé.

— Dérangé?

— Oui. Nous ne sommes pas revenus à la surface du globe?

— Non, certes!

— Alors il faut que je sois fou, car j'aperçois la lumière du jour, j'entends le bruit du vent qui souffle et de la mer qui se brise!

— Ah! n'est-ce que cela?

— M'expliquerez-vous?...

— Je ne t'expliquerai rien, car c'est inexplicable; mais tu verras et tu comprendras que la science géologique n'a pas encore dit son dernier mot.

— Sortons donc, m'écriai-je en me levant brusquement.

— Non, Axel, non! le grand air pourrait te faire du mal.

— Le grand air?

— Oui, le vent est assez violent. Je ne veux pas que tu t'exposes ainsi.

— Mais je vous assure que je me porte à merveille.

— Un peu de patience, mon garçon. Une rechute nous mettrait dans l'embarras, et il ne faut pas perdre de temps, car la traversée peut être longue.

— La traversée?

— Oui, repose-toi encore aujourd'hui, et nous nous embarquerons demain.

— Nous embarquer?»

Ce dernier mot me fit bondir.

Quoi! nous embarquer! Avions-nous donc un fleuve, un lac, une mer à notre disposition? Un bâtiment était-il mouillé dans quelque port intérieur?

Ma curiosité fut excitée au plus haut point. Mon oncle essaya vainement de me retenir. Quand il vit que mon impatience me ferait plus de mal que la satisfaction de mes désirs, il céda.

Je m'habillai rapidement. Par surcroît de précaution, je m'enveloppai de l'une des couvertures et je sortis de la grotte.

XXX

D'ABORD je ne vis rien. Mes yeux déshabitués de la lumière se fermèrent brusquement. Lorsque je pus les rouvrir, je demeurai encore plus stupéfait qu'émerveillé.

« La mer! m'écriai-je.

— Oui, répondit mon oncle, la mer Lidenbrock, et, j'aime à le croire, aucun navigateur ne me disputera l'honneur de l'avoir découverte et le droit de la nommer de mon nom! »

Une vaste nappe d'eau, le commencement d'un lac ou d'un océan, s'étendait au-delà des limites de la vue. Le rivage, largement échancré, offrait aux dernières ondulations des vagues un sable fin, doré, parsemé de ces petits coquillages où vécurent les premiers êtres de la création. Les flots s'y brisaient avec ce murmure sonore particulier aux milieux clos et immenses. Une légère écume s'envolait au souffle d'un vent modéré, et quelques embruns m'arrivaient au visage. Sur cette grève légèrement inclinée, à cent toises environ de la lisière des vagues, venaient mourir les contreforts de rochers énormes qui montaient en s'évasant à

Une vaste nappe d'eau s'étendait devant mes yeux (p. 233).

une incommensurable hauteur. Quelques-uns, déchirant le rivage de leur arête aiguë, formaient des caps et des promontoires rongés par la dent du ressac. Plus loin, l'œil suivait leur masse nettement profilée sur les fonds brumeux de l'horizon.

C'était un océan véritable, avec le contour capricieux des rivages terrestres, mais désert et d'un aspect effroyablement sauvage.

Si mes regards pouvaient se promener au loin sur cette mer, c'est qu'une lumière « spéciale » en éclairait les moindres détails. Non pas la lumière du soleil avec ses faisceaux éclatants et l'irradiation splendide de ses rayons, ni la lueur pâle et vague de l'astre des nuits, qui n'est qu'une réflexion sans chaleur. Non. Le pouvoir éclairant de cette lumière, sa diffusion tremblotante, sa blancheur claire et sèche, le peu d'élévation de sa température, son éclat supérieur en réalité à celui de la lune, accusaient évidemment une origine électrique. C'était comme une aurore boréale, un phénomène cosmique continu, qui remplissait cette caverne capable de contenir un océan.

La voûte suspendue au-dessus de ma tête, le ciel, si l'on veut, semblait fait de grands nuages, vapeurs mobiles et changeantes, qui, par l'effet de la condensation, devaient, à de certains jours, se résoudre en pluies torrentielles. J'aurais cru que, sous une pression aussi forte de l'atmosphère, l'évaporation de l'eau ne pouvait se produire, et cependant, par une raison physique qui m'échappait, il y avait de larges nuées étendues dans l'air.

Mais alors « il faisait beau ». Les nappes électriques produisaient d'étonnants jeux de lumière sur les nuages très élevés. Des ombres vives se dessinaient à leurs volutes inférieures, et souvent, entre deux couches disjointes, un rayon se glissait jusqu'à nous avec une remarquable intensité. Mais, en somme, ce n'était pas le soleil, puisque la chaleur manquait à sa lumière. L'effet en était triste, souverainement mélancolique. Au lieu d'un firmament brillant d'étoiles, je sentais par-dessus ces nuages une voûte de granit qui m'écrasait de tout son poids, et cet espace n'eût pas suffi, tout immense qu'il fût, à la promenade du moins ambitieux des satellites.

Je me souvins alors de cette théorie d'un capitaine anglais qui assimilait la terre à une vaste sphère creuse, à l'intérieur de laquelle l'air se maintenait lumineux par suite de sa pression, tandis que deux astres, Pluton et Proserpine, y traçaient leurs mystérieuses orbites. Aurait-il dit vrai ?

Nous étions réellement emprisonnés dans une énorme excavation. Sa largeur, on ne pouvait la juger, puisque le rivage allait s'élargissant à perte de vue, ni sa longueur, car le regard était bientôt arrêté par une ligne d'horizon un peu indécise. Quant à sa hauteur, elle devait dépasser plusieurs lieues. Où cette voûte s'appuyait sur ses contreforts de granit, l'œil ne pouvait l'apercevoir; mais il y avait un tel nuage suspendu dans l'atmosphère, dont l'élévation devait être estimée à deux mille

toises, altitude supérieure à celle des vapeurs terrestres, et due sans doute à la densité considérable
de l'air.

Le mot « caverne » ne rend évidemment pas ma
pensée pour peindre cet immense milieu. Mais
les mots de la langue humaine ne peuvent suffire à
qui se hasarde dans les abîmes du globe.

Je ne savais pas, d'ailleurs, par quel fait géologique expliquer l'existence d'une pareille excavation. Le refroidissement du globe avait-il donc pu
la produire ? Je connaissais bien, par les récits des
voyageurs, certaines cavernes célèbres, mais aucune
ne présentait de telles dimensions.

Si la grotte de Guachara, en Colombie, visitée
par M. de Humboldt, n'avait pas livré le secret de
sa profondeur au savant qui la reconnut sur un
espace de deux mille cinq cents pieds, elle ne s'étendait vraisemblablement pas beaucoup au-delà.
L'immense caverne du Mammouth, dans le Ken-
tucky, offrait bien des proportions gigantesques,
puisque sa voûte s'élevait à cinq cents pieds au-
dessus d'un lac insondable, et que des voyageurs la
parcoururent pendant plus de dix lieues sans rencontrer la fin. Mais qu'étaient ces cavités auprès
de celle que j'admirais alors, avec son ciel de
vapeurs, ses irradiations électriques et une vaste
mer renfermée dans ses flancs ? Mon imagination
se sentait impuissante devant cette immensité.

Toutes ces merveilles, je les contemplais en
silence. Les paroles me manquaient pour rendre
mes sensations. Je croyais assister, dans quelque

planète lointaine, Uranus ou Neptune, à des
phénomènes dont ma nature « terrestrielle » n'avait
pas conscience. A des sensations nouvelles, il
fallait des mots nouveaux, et mon imagination ne
me les fournissait pas. Je regardais, je pensais,
j'admirais avec une stupéfaction mêlée d'une
certaine quantité d'effroi.

L'imprévu de ce spectacle avait rappelé sur mon
visage les couleurs de la santé ; j'étais en train de me
traiter par l'étonnement et d'opérer ma guérison
au moyen de cette nouvelle thérapeutique ; d'ailleurs, la vivacité d'un air très dense me ranimait,
en fournissant plus d'oxygène à mes poumons.

On concevra sans peine qu'après un emprison-
nement de quarante-sept jours dans une étroite
galerie, c'était une jouissance infinie que d'aspirer
cette brise chargée d'humides émanations salines.

Aussi n'eus-je point à me repentir d'avoir quitté
ma grotte obscure. Mon oncle, déjà fait à ces
merveilles, ne s'étonnait plus.

« Te sens-tu la force de te promener un peu ? me
demanda-t-il.

— Oui, certes, répondis-je, et rien ne me sera
plus agréable.

— Eh bien, prends mon bras, Axel, et suivons les
sinuosités du rivage. »

J'acceptai avec empressement, et nous commen-
çâmes à côtoyer cet océan nouveau. Sur la gauche,
des rochers abrupts, grimpés les uns sur les autres,
formaient un entassement titanesque d'un prodigieux effet. Sur leurs flancs se déroulaient d'innom-

brables cascades, qui s'en allaient en nappes limpides et retentissantes. Quelques légères vapeurs,
sautant d'un roc à l'autre, marquaient la place des
sources chaudes, et des ruisseaux coulaient doucement vers le bassin commun, en cherchant dans
les pentes l'occasion de murmurer plus agréable-
ment.

Parmi ces ruisseaux je reconnus notre fidèle
compagnon de route, le Hans-bach, qui venait se
perdre tranquillement dans la mer, comme s'il
n'eût jamais fait autre chose depuis le commencement du monde.

« Il nous manquera désormais, dis-je avec un
soupir.

— Bah! répondit le professeur, lui ou un autre,
qu'importe. »

Je trouvai la réponse un peu ingrate.

Mais en ce moment mon attention fut attirée
par un spectacle inattendu. A cinq cents pas, au
détour d'un haut promontoire, une forêt haute,
touffue, épaisse, apparut à nos yeux. Elle était
faite d'arbres de moyenne grandeur, taillés en
parasols réguliers, à contours nets et géométriques;
les courants de l'atmosphère ne semblaient pas
avoir prise sur leur feuillage, et, au milieu des
souffles, ils demeuraient immobiles comme un
massif de cèdres pétrifiés.

Je hâtais le pas. Je ne pouvais mettre un nom à
ces essences singulières. Ne faisaient-elles point
partie des deux cent mille espèces végétales
connues jusqu'alors, et fallait-il leur accorder une

place spéciale dans la flore des végétations lacus-
tres? Non. Quand nous arrivâmes sous leur
ombrage, ma surprise ne fut plus que de l'admiration.

En effet, je me trouvais en présence de produits
de la terre, mais taillés sur un patron gigantesque. Mon oncle les appela immédiatement de
leur nom.

« Ce n'est qu'une forêt de champignons », dit-il.

Et il ne se trompait pas. Que l'on juge du développement acquis par ces plantes chères aux
milieux chauds et humides. Je savais que le « lyco-
perdon giganteum » atteint, suivant Bulliard, huit
à neuf pieds de circonférence; mais il s'agissait
ici de champignons blancs, hauts de trente à quarante pieds, avec une calotte d'un diamètre égal.
Ils étaient là par milliers. La lumière ne parvenait
pas à percer leur épais ombrage, et une obscurité
complète régnait sous ces dômes juxtaposés comme
les toits ronds d'une cité africaine.

Cependant je voulus pénétrer plus avant. Un
froid mortel descendait de ces voûtes charnues.
Pendant une demi-heure, nous errâmes dans ces
humides ténèbres, et ce fut avec un véritable
sentiment de bien-être que je retrouvai les bords
de la mer.

Mais la végétation de cette contrée souterraine
ne s'en tenait pas à ces champignons. Plus loin
s'élevaient par groupes un grand nombre d'autres
arbres au feuillage décoloré. Ils étaient faciles à
reconnaître; c'étaient les humbles arbustes de la

« Ce n'est qu'une forêt de champignons », dit-il (p. 240).

terre, avec des dimensions phénoménales, des lycopodes hauts de cent pieds, des sigillaires géantes, des fougères arborescentes, grandes comme les sapins des hautes latitudes, des lépido-dendrons à tiges cylindriques bifurquées, terminées par de longues feuilles et hérissées de poils rudes comme de monstrueuses plantes grasses.

« Étonnant, magnifique, splendide ! s'écria mon oncle. Voilà toute la flore de la seconde époque du monde, de l'époque de transition. Voilà ces humbles plantes de nos jardins qui se faisaient arbres aux premiers siècles du globe ! regarde, Axel, admire ! Jamais botaniste ne s'est trouvé à pareille fête !

— Vous avez raison, mon oncle. La Providence semble avoir voulu conserver dans cette serre immense ces plantes antédiluviennes que la saga-cité des savants a reconstruites avec tant de bon-heur.

— Tu dis bien, mon garçon, c'est une serre ; mais tu dirais mieux encore en ajoutant que c'est peut-être une ménagerie.

— Une ménagerie !

— Oui, sans doute. Vois cette poussière que nous foulons aux pieds, ces ossements épars sur le sol.

— Des ossements ! m'écriai-je. Oui, des osse-ments d'animaux antédiluviens ! »

Je m'étais précipité sur ces débris séculaires faits d'une substance minérale indestructible [1]. Je

---

1. Phosphate de chaux.

mettais sans hésiter un nom à ces os gigantesques qui ressemblaient à des troncs d'arbres desséchés.

« Voilà la mâchoire inférieure du mastodonte, disais-je ; voilà les molaires du dinotherium ; voilà un fémur qui ne peut avoir appartenu qu'au plus grand de ces animaux, au megatherium. Oui, c'est bien une ménagerie, car ces ossements n'ont certainement pas été transportés jusqu'ici par un cataclysme. Les animaux auxquels ils appartiennent ont vécu sur les rivages de cette mer souterraine, à l'ombre de ces plantes arborescentes. Tenez, j'aperçois des squelettes entiers. Et cependant...

— Cependant ? dit mon oncle.

— Je ne comprends pas la présence de pareils quadrupèdes dans cette caverne de granit.

— Pourquoi ?

— Parce que la vie animale n'a existé sur la terre qu'aux périodes secondaires, lorsque le terrain sédimentaire a été formé par les alluvions, et a remplacé les roches incandescentes de l'époque primitive.

— Eh bien ! Axel, il y a une réponse bien simple à faire à ton objection, c'est que ce terrain-ci est un terrain sédimentaire.

— Comment ! à une pareille profondeur au-dessous de la surface de la terre !

— Sans doute, et ce fait peut s'expliquer géologiquement. A une certaine époque, la terre n'était formée que d'une écorce élastique, soumise à des mouvements alternatifs de haut et de bas, en vertu

des lois de l'attraction. Il est probable que des affaissements du sol se sont produits, et qu'une partie des terrains sédimentaires a été entraînée au fond des gouffres subitement ouverts.

— Cela doit être. Mais, si des animaux antédiluviens ont vécu dans ces régions souterraines, qui nous dit que l'un de ces monstres n'erre pas encore au milieu de ces forêts sombres ou derrière ces rocs escarpés ? »

A cette idée j'interrogeai, non sans effroi, les divers points de l'horizon; mais aucun être vivant n'apparaissait sur ces rivages déserts.

J'étais un peu fatigué. J'allai m'asseoir alors à l'extrémité d'un promontoire au pied duquel les flots venaient se briser avec fracas. De là mon regard embrassait toute cette baie formée par une échancrure de la côte. Au fond, un petit port s'y trouvait ménagé entre les roches pyramidales. Ses eaux calmes dormaient à l'abri du vent. Un brick et deux ou trois goélettes auraient pu y mouiller à l'aise. Je m'attendais presque à voir quelque navire sortant toutes voiles dehors et prenant le large sous la brise du sud.

Mais cette illusion se dissipa rapidement. Nous étions bien les seules créatures vivantes de ce monde souterrain. Par certaines accalmies du vent, un silence plus profond que les silences du désert descendait sur les rocs arides et pesait à la surface de l'océan. Je cherchais alors à percer des brumes lointaines, à déchirer ce rideau jeté sur le fond mystérieux de l'horizon. Quelles de-

mandes se pressaient sur mes lèvres? Où finissait cette mer? Où conduisait-elle? Pourrions-nous jamais en reconnaître les rivages opposés?

Mon oncle n'en doutait pas, pour son compte. Moi, je le désirais et je le craignais à la fois.

Après une heure passée dans la contemplation de ce merveilleux spectacle, nous reprîmes le chemin de la grève pour regagner la grotte, et ce fut sous l'empire des plus étranges pensées que je m'endormis d'un profond sommeil.

XXXI

Le lendemain je me réveillai complètement guéri. Je pensai qu'un bain me serait très salutaire, et j'allai me plonger pendant quelques minutes dans les eaux de cette Méditerranée. Ce nom, à coup sûr, elle le méritait entre tous.

Je revins déjeuner avec un bel appétit. Hans s'entendait à cuisiner notre petit menu; il avait de l'eau et du feu à sa disposition, de sorte qu'il put varier un peu notre ordinaire. Au dessert, il nous servit quelques tasses de café, et jamais ce délicieux breuvage ne me parut plus agréable à déguster.

« Maintenant, dit mon oncle, voici l'heure de la marée, et il ne faut pas manquer l'occasion d'étudier ce phénomène.

— Comment, la marée! m'écriai-je.

J'allai me plonger dans les eaux de cette Méditerranée (p. 245).

— Sans doute.

— L'influence de la lune et du soleil se fait sentir jusqu'ici ?

— Pourquoi pas ? Les corps ne sont-ils pas soumis dans leur ensemble à l'attraction universelle ? Cette masse d'eau ne peut donc échapper à cette loi générale. Aussi, malgré la pression atmosphérique qui s'exerce à sa surface, tu vas la voir se soulever comme l'Atlantique lui-même. »

En ce moment nous foulions le sable du rivage, et les vagues gagnaient peu à peu la grève.

« Voilà bien le flot qui commence, m'écriai-je.

— Oui, Axel, et d'après ces relais d'écume, tu peux voir que la mer s'élève d'une dizaine de pieds environ.

— C'est merveilleux !

— Non, c'est naturel.

— Vous avez beau dire, mon oncle, tout cela me paraît extraordinaire, et c'est à peine si j'en crois mes yeux. Qui eût jamais imaginé dans cette écorce terrestre un océan véritable, avec ses flux et ses reflux, avec ses brises, avec ses tempêtes !

— Pourquoi pas ? Y a-t-il une raison physique qui s'y oppose ?

— Je n'en vois pas, du moment qu'il faut abandonner le système de la chaleur centrale.

— Donc, jusqu'ici la théorie de Davy se trouve justifiée ?

— Évidemment, et dès lors rien ne contredit l'existence de mers ou de contrées à l'intérieur du globe.

— Sans doute, mais inhabitées.

— Bon! pourquoi ces eaux ne donneraient-elles pas asile à quelques poissons d'une espèce inconnue?

— En tout cas, nous n'en avons pas aperçu un seul jusqu'ici.

— Eh bien, nous pouvons fabriquer des lignes et voir si l'hameçon aura autant de succès ici-bas que dans les océans sublunaires.

— Nous essaierons, Axel, car il faut pénétrer tous les secrets de ces régions nouvelles.

— Mais où sommes-nous? mon oncle, car je ne vous ai point encore posé cette question à laquelle vos instruments ont dû vous répondre.

— Horizontalement, à trois cent cinquante lieues de l'Islande.

— Tout autant?

— Je suis sûr de ne pas me tromper de cinq cents toises.

— Et la boussole indique toujours le sud-est?

— Oui, avec une déclinaison occidentale de dix-neuf degrés et quarante-deux minutes, comme sur terre, absolument. Pour son inclinaison, il se passe un fait curieux que j'ai observé avec le plus grand soin.

— Et lequel?

— C'est que l'aiguille, au lieu de s'incliner vers le pôle, comme elle le fait dans l'hémisphère boréal, se relève au contraire.

— Il faut donc en conclure que le point d'attraction magnétique se trouve compris entre la sur-

face du globe et l'endroit où nous sommes parvenus ?

— Précisément, et il est probable que, si nous arrivions vers les régions polaires, vers ce soixante-dixième degré où James Ross a découvert le pôle magnétique, nous verrions l'aiguille se dresser verticalement. Donc, ce mystérieux centre d'attraction ne se trouve pas situé à une grande profondeur.

— En effet, et voilà un fait que la science n'a pas soupçonné.

— La science, mon garçon, est faite d'erreurs, mais d'erreurs qu'il est bon de commettre, car elles mènent peu à peu à la vérité.

— Et à quelle profondeur sommes-nous ?

— A une profondeur de trente-cinq lieues.

— Ainsi, dis-je en considérant la carte, la partie montagneuse de l'Écosse est au-dessus de nous, et, là, les monts Grampians élèvent à une prodigieuse hauteur leur cime couverte de neige.

— Oui, répondit le professeur en riant. C'est un peu lourd à porter, mais la voûte est solide ; le grand architecte de l'univers l'a construite en bons matériaux, et jamais l'homme n'eût pu lui donner une pareille portée ! Que sont les arches des ponts et les arceaux des cathédrales auprès de cette nef d'un rayon de trois lieues, sous laquelle un océan et ses tempêtes peuvent se développer à leur aise ?

— Oh ! je ne crains pas que le ciel me tombe sur

la tête. Maintenant, mon oncle, quels sont vos projets? Ne comptez-vous pas retourner à la surface du globe?

— Retourner! Par exemple! Continuer notre voyage, au contraire, puisque tout a si bien marché jusqu'ici.

— Cependant je ne vois pas comment nous pénétrerons sous cette plaine liquide.

— Oh! je ne prétends point m'y précipiter la tête la première. Mais si les océans ne sont, à proprement parler, que des lacs, puisqu'ils sont entourés de terre, à plus forte raison cette mer intérieure se trouve-t-elle circonscrite par le massif granitique.

— Cela n'est pas douteux.

— Eh bien! sur les rivages opposés, je suis certain de trouver de nouvelles issues.

— Quelle longueur supposez-vous donc à cet océan?

— Trente ou quarante lieues.

— Ah! fis-je, tout en imaginant que cette estime pouvait bien être inexacte.

— Ainsi, nous n'avons pas de temps à perdre, et dès demain nous prendrons la mer. »

Involontairement je cherchai des yeux le navire qui devait nous transporter.

« Ah! dis-je, nous nous embarquerons. Bien! Et sur quel bâtiment prendrons-nous passage?

— Ce ne sera pas sur un bâtiment, mon garçon, mais sur un bon et solide radeau.

— Un radeau! m'écriai-je. Un radeau est aussi

impossible à construire qu'un navire, et je ne vois
pas...

— Tu ne vois pas, Axel, mais si tu écoutais, tu
pourrais entendre !

— Entendre ?

— Oui, certains coups de marteau qui t'appren-
draient que Hans est déjà à l'œuvre.

— Il construit un radeau ?

— Oui.

— Comment ! il a déjà fait tomber des arbres
sous sa hache ?

— Oh ! les arbres étaient tout abattus. Viens,
et tu le verras à l'ouvrage. »

Après un quart d'heure de marche, de l'autre
côté du promontoire qui formait le petit port
naturel, j'aperçus Hans au travail. Quelques pas
encore, et je fus près de lui. A ma grande surprise, un radeau à demi terminé s'étendait sur le
sable ; il était fait de poutres d'un bois particulier, et un grand nombre de madriers, de courbes,
de couples de toute espèce, jonchaient littéra-
lement le sol. Il y avait là de quoi construire une
marine entière.

« Mon oncle, m'écriai-je, quel est ce bois ?

— C'est du pin, du sapin, du bouleau, toutes
les espèces des conifères du Nord, minéralisées
sous l'action des eaux de la mer.

— Est-il possible ?

— C'est ce qu'on appelle du « surtarbrandur »
ou bois fossile.

— Mais alors, comme les lignites, il doit avoir

la dureté de la pierre, et il ne pourra flotter ?

— Quelquefois cela arrive ; il y a de ces bois qui sont devenus de véritables anthracites ; mais d'autres, tels que ceux-ci, n'ont encore subi qu'un commencement de transformation fossile. Regarde plutôt », ajouta mon oncle en jetant à la mer une de ces précieuses épaves.

Le morceau de bois, après avoir disparu, revint à la surface des flots et oscilla au gré de leurs ondulations.

« Es-tu convaincu ? dit mon oncle.

— Convaincu surtout que cela n'est pas croyable ! »

Le lendemain soir, grâce à l'habileté du guide, le radeau était terminé ; il avait dix pieds de long sur cinq de large ; les poutres de surtarbrandur, reliées entre elles par de fortes cordes, offraient une surface solide, et, une fois lancée, cette embarcation improvisée flotta tranquillement sur les eaux de la mer Lidenbrock.

XXXII

LE 13 août, on se réveilla de bon matin. Il s'agissait d'inaugurer un nouveau genre de locomotion rapide et peu fatigant.

Un mât fait de deux bâtons jumelés, une vergue formée d'un troisième, une voile empruntée à nos couvertures, composaient le gréement du radeau.

Les cordes ne manquaient pas. Le tout était solide.

A six heures, le professeur donna le signal d'embarquer. Les vivres, les bagages, les instruments, les armes et une notable quantité d'eau douce recueillie dans les rochers, se trouvaient en place.

Hans avait installé un gouvernail qui lui permettait de diriger son appareil flottant. Il se mit à la barre. Je détachai l'amarre qui nous retenait au rivage. La voile fut orientée, et nous débordâmes rapidement.

Au moment de quitter le petit port, mon oncle, qui tenait à sa nomenclature géographique, voulut lui donner un nom, le mien, entre autres.

« Ma foi, dis-je, j'en ai un autre à vous proposer.

— Lequel ?

— Le nom de Graüben. Port-Graüben, cela fera très bien sur la carte.

— Va pour Port-Graüben. »

Et voilà comment le souvenir de ma chère Virlandaise se rattacha à notre aventureuse expédition.

La brise soufflait du nord-est. Nous filions vent arrière avec une extrême rapidité. Les couches très denses de l'atmosphère avaient une poussée considérable et agissaient sur la voile comme un puissant ventilateur.

Au bout d'une heure, mon oncle avait pu estimer assez exactement notre vitesse.

« Si nous continuons à marcher ainsi, dit-il, nous ferons au moins trente lieues par vingt-

quatre heures, et nous ne tarderons pas à reconnaître les rivages opposés. »

Je ne répondis pas, et j'allai prendre place à l'avant du radeau. Déjà la côte septentrionale s'abaissait à l'horizon. Les deux bras du rivage s'ouvraient largement comme pour faciliter notre départ. Devant mes yeux s'étendait une mer immense. De grands nuages promenaient rapidement à sa surface leur ombre grisâtre, qui semblait peser sur cette eau morne. Les rayons argentés de la lumière électrique, réfléchis çà et là par quelque gouttelette, faisaient éclore des points lumineux dans les remous de l'embarcation. Bientôt toute terre fut perdue de vue, tout point de repère disparut, et, sans le sillage écumeux du radeau, j'aurais pu croire qu'il demeurait dans une parfaite immobilité.

Vers midi, des algues immenses vinrent onduler à la surface des flots. Je connaissais la puissance végétative de ces plantes, qui rampent à une profondeur de plus de douze mille pieds au fond des mers, se reproduisent sous des pressions de quatre cents atmosphères et forment souvent des bancs assez considérables pour entraver la marche des navires; mais jamais, je crois, algues ne furent plus gigantesques que celles de la mer Lidenbrock.

Notre radeau longea des fucus longs de trois et quatre mille pieds, immenses serpents qui se développaient hors de la portée de la vue; je m'amusais à suivre du regard leurs rubans infinis, croyant toujours en atteindre l'extrémité, et pen-

Des algues immenses vinrent onduler à la surface
des flots (p. 254).

dant des heures entières ma patience était trompée, sinon mon étonnement.

Quelle force naturelle pouvait produire de telles plantes, et quel devait être l'aspect de la terre aux premiers siècles de sa formation, quand, sous l'action de la chaleur et de l'humidité, le règne végétal se développait seul à sa surface !

Le soir arriva, et, ainsi que je l'avais remarqué la veille, l'état lumineux de l'air ne subit aucune diminution. C'était un phénomène constant sur la durée duquel on pouvait compter.

Après le souper, je m'étendis au pied du mât, et je ne tardai pas à m'endormir au milieu d'indolentes rêveries.

Hans, immobile au gouvernail, laissait courir le radeau, qui, d'ailleurs, poussé vent arrière, ne demandait même pas à être dirigé.

Depuis notre départ de Port-Graüben, le professeur Lidenbrock m'avait chargé de tenir le « journal de bord », de noter les moindres observations, de consigner les phénomènes intéressants, la direction du vent, la vitesse acquise, le chemin parcouru, en un mot, tous les incidents de cette étrange navigation.

Je me bornerai donc à reproduire ici ces notes quotidiennes, écrites pour ainsi dire sous la dictée des événements, afin de donner un récit plus exact de notre traversée.

Vendredi 14 août. — Brise égale du N.-O. Le radeau marche avec rapidité et en ligne droite.

La côte reste à trente lieues sous le vent. Rien à l'horizon. L'intensité de la lumière ne varie pas. Beau temps, c'est-à-dire que les nuages sont fort élevés, peu épais et baignés dans une atmosphère blanche, comme serait de l'argent en fusion. Thermomètre : + 32 °C.

A midi Hans prépare un hameçon à l'extrémité d'une corde. Il l'amorce avec un petit morceau de viande et le jette à la mer. Pendant deux heures il ne prend rien. Ces eaux sont donc inhabitées? Non. Une secousse se produit. Hans tire sa ligne et ramène un poisson qui se débat vigoureusement.

« Un poisson! s'écrie mon oncle.

— C'est un esturgeon! m'écriai-je à mon tour, un esturgeon de petite taille! »

Le professeur regarde attentivement l'animal et ne partage pas mon opinion. Ce poisson a la tête plate, arrondie et la partie antérieure du corps couverte de plaques osseuses; sa bouche est privée de dents; des nageoires pectorales assez développées sont ajustées à son corps dépourvu de queue. Cet animal appartient bien à un ordre où les naturalistes ont classé l'esturgeon, mais il en diffère par des côtés assez essentiels.

Mon oncle ne s'y trompe pas, car, après un assez court examen, il dit :

« Ce poisson appartient à une famille éteinte depuis des siècles et dont on retrouve seulement les traces fossiles dans le terrain dévonien.

— Comment! dis-je, nous aurions pu prendre

vivant un de ces habitants des mers primitives ?

— Oui, répond le professeur en continuant ses observations, et tu vois que ces poissons fossiles n'ont aucune identité avec les espèces actuelles. Or, tenir un de ces êtres vivant c'est un véritable bonheur de naturaliste.

— Mais à quelle famille appartient-il ?

— A l'ordre des Ganoïdes, famille des Céphalaspides, genre...

— Eh bien ?

— Genre des Pterychtis, j'en jurerais ! Mais celui-ci offre une particularité qui, dit-on, se rencontre chez les poissons des eaux souterraines.

— Laquelle ?

— Il est aveugle !

— Aveugle !

— Non seulement aveugle, mais l'organe de la vue lui manque absolument. »

Je regarde. Rien n'est plus vrai. Mais ce peut être un cas particulier. La ligne est donc amorcée de nouveau et rejetée à la mer. Cet océan, à coup sûr, est fort poissonneux, car, en deux heures, nous prenons une grande quantité de Pterychtis, ainsi que des poissons appartenant à une famille également éteinte, les Dipterides, mais dont mon oncle ne peut reconnaître le genre. Tous sont dépourvus de l'organe de la vue. Cette pêche inespérée renouvelle avantageusement nos provisions.

Ainsi donc, cela paraît constant, cette mer ne renferme que des espèces fossiles, dans les-

quelles les poissons comme les reptiles sont d'autant plus parfaits que leur création est plus ancienne.

Peut-être rencontrerons-nous quelques-uns de ces sauriens que la science a su refaire avec un bout d'ossement ou de cartilage?

Je prends la lunette et j'examine la mer. Elle est déserte. Sans doute nous sommes encore trop rapprochés des côtes.

Je regarde dans les airs. Pourquoi quelques-uns de ces oiseaux reconstruits par l'immortel Cuvier ne battraient-ils pas de leurs ailes ces lourdes couches atmosphériques? Les poissons leur fourniraient une suffisante nourriture. J'observe l'espace, mais les airs sont inhabités comme les rivages.

Cependant mon imagination m'emporte dans les merveilleuses hypothèses de la paléontologie. Je rêve tout éveillé. Je crois voir à la surface des eaux ces énormes Chersites, ces tortues antédiluviennes, semblables à des îlots flottants. Sur les grèves assombries passent les grands mammifères des premiers jours, le Leptotherium, trouvé dans les cavernes du Brésil, le Mericotherium, venu des régions glacées de la Sibérie. Plus loin, le pachyderme Lophiodon, ce tapir gigantesque, se cache derrière les rocs, prêt à disputer sa proie à l'Anoplotherium, animal étrange, qui tient du rhinocéros, du cheval, de l'hippopotame et du chameau, comme si le Créateur, trop pressé aux premières heures du monde,

Le rêve d'Axel (p. 259).

eût réuni plusieurs animaux en un seul. Le Mastodonte géant fait tournoyer sa trompe et broie
sous ses défenses les rochers du rivage, tandis
que le Mégatherium, arc-bouté sur ses énormes
pattes, fouille la terre en éveillant par ses rugis-
sements l'écho des granits sonores. Plus haut, le
Protopithèque, le premier singe apparu à la surface du globe, gravit les cimes ardues. Plus haut
encore, le Pterodactyle, à la main ailée, glisse
comme une large chauve-souris sur l'air comprimé.
Enfin, dans les dernières couches, des oiseaux
immenses, plus puissants que le casoar, plus
grands que l'autruche, déploient leurs vastes ailes
et vont donner de la tête contre la paroi de la
voûte granitique.

Tout ce monde fossile renaît dans mon imagination. Je me reporte aux époques bibliques de
la création, bien avant la naissance de l'homme,
lorsque la terre incomplète ne pouvait lui suffire
encore. Mon rêve alors devance l'apparition des
êtres animés. Les mammifères disparaissent, puis
les oiseaux, puis les reptiles de l'époque secondaire, et enfin les poissons, les crustacés, les
mollusques, les articulés. Les zoophytes de la
période de transition retournent au néant à leur
tour. Toute la vie de la terre se résume en moi,
et mon cœur est seul à battre dans ce monde
dépeuplé. Il n'y a plus de saisons; il n'y a plus
de climats; la chaleur propre du globe s'accroît
sans cesse et neutralise celle de l'astre radieux.
La végétation s'exagère. Je passe comme une

ombre au milieu des fougères arborescentes, foulant de mon pas incertain les marnes irisées et les grès bigarrés du sol; je m'appuie au tronc des conifères immenses; je me couche à l'ombre des Sphenophylles, des Asterophylles et des Lycopodes hauts de cent pieds.

Les siècles s'écoulent comme des jours! Je remonte la série des transformations terrestres. Les plantes disparaissent; les roches granitiques perdent leur pureté; l'état liquide va remplacer l'état solide sous l'action d'une chaleur plus intense; les eaux courent à la surface du globe; elles bouillonnent, elles se volatilisent; les vapeurs enveloppent la terre, qui peu à peu ne forme plus qu'une masse gazeuse, portée au rouge blanc, grosse comme le soleil et brillante comme lui!

Au centre de cette nébuleuse, quatorze cent mille fois plus considérable que ce globe qu'elle va former un jour, je suis entraîné dans les espaces planétaires! Mon corps se subtilise, se sublime à son tour et se mélange comme un atome impondérable à ces immenses vapeurs qui tracent dans l'infini leur orbite enflammée!

Quel rêve! Où m'emporte-t-il? Ma main fiévreuse en jette sur le papier les étranges détails! J'ai tout oublié, et le professeur, et le guide, et le radeau! Une hallucination s'est emparée de mon esprit...

« Qu'as-tu? » dit mon oncle.

Mes yeux tout ouverts se fixent sur lui sans le voir.

« Prends garde, Axel, tu vas tomber à la mer ! »

En même temps, je me sens saisir vigoureusement par la main de Hans. Sans lui, sous l'empire de mon rêve, je me précipitais dans les flots.

« Est-ce qu'il devient fou ? s'écrie le professeur.

— Qu'y a-t-il ? dis-je enfin, revenant à moi.

— Es-tu malade ?

— Non, j'ai eu un moment d'hallucination, mais il est passé. Tout va bien, d'ailleurs ?

— Oui ! bonne brise, belle mer ! nous filons rapidement, et si mon estime ne m'a pas trompé, nous ne pouvons tarder à atterrir. »

A ces paroles, je me lève, je consulte l'horizon ; mais la ligne d'eau se confond toujours avec la ligne des nuages.

XXXIII

Samedi 15 août. — La mer conserve sa monotone uniformité. Nulle terre n'est en vue. L'horizon paraît excessivement reculé.

J'ai la tête encore alourdie par la violence de mon rêve.

Mon oncle n'a pas rêvé, lui, mais il est de mauvaise humeur. Il parcourt tous les points de l'espace avec sa lunette et se croise les bras d'un air dépité.

Je remarque que le professeur Lidenbrock tend

à redevenir l'homme impatient du passé, et je consigne le fait sur mon journal. Il a fallu mes dangers et mes souffrances pour tirer de lui quelque étincelle d'humanité ; mais, depuis ma guérison, la nature a repris le dessus. Et cependant, pourquoi s'emporter ? Le voyage ne s'accomplit-il pas dans les circonstances les plus favorables ? Est-ce que le radeau ne file pas avec une merveilleuse rapidité ?

« Vous semblez inquiet, mon oncle ? dis-je, en le voyant souvent porter la lunette à ses yeux.

— Inquiet ? Non.

— Impatient, alors ?

— On le serait à moins !

— Cependant nous marchons avec une vitesse...

— Que m'importe ? Ce n'est pas la vitesse qui est trop petite, c'est la mer qui est trop grande ! »

Je me souviens alors que le professeur, avant notre départ, estimait à une trentaine de lieues la longueur de cet océan souterrain. Or, nous avons déjà parcouru un chemin trois fois plus long, et les rivages du sud n'apparaissent pas encore.

« Nous ne descendons pas ! reprend le professeur. Tout cela est du temps perdu, et, en somme, je ne suis pas venu si loin pour faire une partie de bateau sur un étang ! »

Il appelle cette traversée une partie de bateau, et cette mer un étang !

« Mais, dis-je, puisque nous avons suivi la route indiquée par Saknussemm...

— C'est la question. Avons-nous suivi cette route ? Saknussemm a-t-il rencontré cette étendue d'eau ? L'a-t-il traversée ? Ce ruisseau que nous avons pris pour guide ne nous a-t-il pas complètement égarés ?

— En tout cas, nous ne pouvons regretter d'être venus jusqu'ici. Ce spectacle est·magnifique, et...

— Il ne s'agit pas de voir. Je me suis proposé un but, et je veux l'atteindre ! Ainsi ne me parle pas d'admirer ! »

Je me le tiens pour dit, et je laisse le professeur se ronger les lèvres d'impatience. A six heures du soir, Hans réclame sa paie, et ses trois rixdales lui sont comptées.

Dimanche 16 août. — Rien de nouveau. Même temps. Le vent a une légère tendance à fraîchir. En me réveillant, mon premier soin est de constater l'intensité de la lumière. Je crains toujours que le phénomène électrique ne vienne à s'obscurcir, puis à s'éteindre. Il n'en est rien. L'ombre du radeau est nettement dessinée à la surface des flots.

Vraiment cette mer est infinie ! Elle doit avoir la largeur de la Méditerranée, ou même de l'Atlantique. Pourquoi pas ?

Mon oncle sonde à plusieurs reprises. Il attache un des plus lourds pics à l'extrémité d'une corde qu'il laisse filer de deux cents brasses. Pas de fond. Nous avons beaucoup de peine à ramener notre sonde.

Quand le pic est remonté à bord, Hans me fait

remarquer à sa surface des empreintes fortement
accusées. On dirait que ce morceau de fer a été
vigoureusement serré entre deux corps durs.

Je regarde le chasseur.

« Tänder ! » dit-il.

Je ne comprends pas. Je me tourne vers mon
oncle, qui est entièrement absorbé dans ses
réflexions. Je ne me soucie pas de le déranger. Je
reviens vers l'Islandais. Celui-ci, ouvrant et refer-
mant plusieurs fois la bouche, me fait comprendre
sa pensée.

« Des dents ! » dis-je avec stupéfaction en considérant plus attentivement la barre de fer.

Oui ! ce sont bien des dents dont l'empreinte
s'est incrustée dans le métal ! Les mâchoires qu'elles
garnissent doivent posséder une force prodigieuse !
Est-ce un monstre des espèces perdues qui s'agite
sous la couche profonde des eaux, plus vorace que
le squale, plus redoutable que la baleine ? Je ne
puis détacher mes regards de cette barre à demi
rongée ! Mon rêve de la nuit dernière va-t-il devenir une réalité ?

Ces pensées m'agitent pendant tout le jour, et
mon imagination se calme à peine dans un sommeil
de quelques heures.

Lundi 17 août. — Je cherche à me rappeler les
instincts particuliers à ces animaux antédiluviens
de l'époque secondaire, qui, succédant aux mollusques, aux crustacés et aux poissons, précédèrent
l'apparition des mammifères sur le globe. Le

monde appartenait alors aux reptiles. Ces monstres régnaient en maîtres dans les mers jurassiques[1]. La nature leur avait accordé la plus complète organisation. Quelle gigantesque structure ! quelle force prodigieuse ! Les sauriens actuels, alligators ou crocodiles, les plus gros et les plus redoutables, ne sont que des réductions affaiblies de leurs pères des premiers âges !

Je frissonne à l'évocation que je fais de ces monstres. Nul œil humain ne les a vus vivants. Ils apparurent sur la terre mille siècles avant l'homme, mais leurs ossements fossiles, retrouvés dans ce calcaire argileux que les Anglais nomment le lias, ont permis de les reconstruire anatomiquement et de connaître leur colossale conformation.

J'ai vu au Muséum de Hambourg le squelette de l'un de ces sauriens qui mesurait trente pieds de longueur. Suis-je donc destiné, moi, habitant de la terre, à me trouver face à face avec ces représentants d'une famille antédiluvienne ? Non ! c'est impossible. Cependant la marque des dents puissantes est gravée sur la barre de fer, et à leur empreinte, je reconnais qu'elles sont coniques comme celles du crocodile.

Mes yeux se fixent avec effroi sur la mer. Je crains de voir s'élancer l'un de ces habitants des cavernes sous-marines.

Je suppose que le professeur Lidenbrock par-

---

1. Mers de la période secondaire qui ont formé les terrains dont se composent les montagnes du Jura.

tage mes idées, sinon mes craintes, car, après avoir examiné le pic, il parcourt l'Océan du regard.

« Au diable, dis-je en moi-même, cette idée qu'il a eue de sonder ! Il a troublé quelque animal dans sa retraite, et si nous ne sommes pas attaqués en route !... »

Je jette un coup d'œil sur les armes, et je m'assure qu'elles sont en bon état. Mon oncle me voit faire et m'approuve du geste.

Déjà de larges agitations produites à la surface des flots indiquent le trouble des couches reculées. Le danger est proche. Il faut veiller.

Mardi 18 août. — Le soir arrive, ou plutôt le moment où le sommeil alourdit nos paupières, car la nuit manque à cet océan, et l'implacable lumière fatigue obstinément nos yeux, comme si nous naviguions sous le soleil des mers arctiques. Hans est à la barre. Pendant son quart je m'endors.

Deux heures après, une secousse épouvantable me réveille. Le radeau a été soulevé hors des flots avec une indescriptible puissance et rejeté à vingt toises de là.

« Qu'y a-t-il ? s'écrie mon oncle. Avons-nous touché ? »

Hans montre du doigt, à une distance de deux cents toises, une masse noirâtre qui s'élève et s'abaisse tour à tour. Je regarde et je m'écrie :

« C'est un marsouin colossal !

— Oui, réplique mon oncle, et voilà maintenant un lézard de mer d'une grosseur peu commune.

Le radeau a été soulevé hors des flots (p. 268).

— Et plus loin un crocodile monstrueux ! Voyez sa large mâchoire et les rangées de dents dont elle est armée. Ah ! il disparaît !

— Une baleine ! une baleine ! s'écrie alors le professeur. J'aperçois ses nageoires énormes ! Vois l'air et l'eau qu'elle chasse par ses évents ! »

En effet, deux colonnes liquides s'élèvent à une hauteur considérable au-dessus de la mer. Nous restons surpris, stupéfaits, épouvantés, en présence de ce troupeau de monstres marins. Ils ont des dimensions surnaturelles, et le moindre d'entre eux briserait le radeau d'un coup de dent. Hans veut mettre la barre au vent, afin de fuir ce voisinage dangereux ; mais il aperçoit sur l'autre bord d'autres ennemis non moins redoutables : une tortue large de quarante pieds, et un serpent long de trente, qui darde sa tête énorme au-dessus des flots.

Impossible de fuir. Ces reptiles s'approchent ; ils tournent autour du radeau avec une rapidité que des convois lancés à grande vitesse ne sauraient égaler ; ils tracent autour de lui des cercles concentriques. J'ai pris ma carabine. Mais quel effet peut produire une balle sur les écailles dont le corps de ces animaux est recouvert ?

Nous sommes muets d'effroi. Les voici qui s'approchent ! D'un côté le crocodile, de l'autre le serpent. Le reste du troupeau marin a disparu. Je vais faire feu. Hans m'arrête d'un signe. Les deux monstres passent à cinquante toises du radeau, se précipitent l'un sur l'autre, et leur fureur les empêche de nous apercevoir.

Le combat s'engage à cent toises du radeau. Nous voyons distinctement les deux monstres aux prises.

Mais il me semble que maintenant les autres animaux viennent prendre part à la lutte, le marsouin, la baleine, le lézard, la tortue. A chaque instant je les entrevois. Je les montre à l'Islandais. Celui-ci remue la tête négativement.

« Tva, dit-il.

— Quoi! deux? Il prétend que deux animaux seulement...

— Il a raison, s'écrie mon oncle, dont la lunette n'a pas quitté les yeux.

— Par exemple!

— Oui! le premier de ces monstres a le museau d'un marsouin, la tête d'un lézard, les dents d'un crocodile, et voilà ce qui nous a trompés. C'est le plus redoutable des reptiles antédiluviens, l'ichthyosaurus!

— Et l'autre?

— L'autre, c'est un serpent caché dans la carapace d'une tortue, le terrible ennemi du premier, le plesiosaurus! »

Hans a dit vrai. Deux monstres seulement troublent ainsi la surface de la mer, et j'ai devant les yeux deux reptiles des océans primitifs. J'aperçois l'œil sanglant de l'ichthyosaurus, gros comme la tête d'un homme. La nature l'a doué d'un appareil d'optique d'une extrême puissance et capable de résister à la pression des couches d'eau dans les profondeurs qu'il habite. On l'a justement

nommé la baleine des Sauriens, car il en a la rapidité et la taille. Celui-ci ne mesure pas moins de
cent pieds, et je peux juger de sa grandeur quand
il dresse au-dessus des flots les nageoires verticales
de sa queue. Sa mâchoire est énorme, et d'après
les naturalistes, elle ne compte pas moins de cent
quatre-vingt-deux dents.

Le plesiosaurus, serpent à tronc cylindrique, à
queue courte, a les pattes disposées en forme de
rame. Son corps est entièrement revêtu d'une
carapace, et son cou, flexible comme celui du
cygne, se dresse à trente pieds au-dessus des flots.

Ces animaux s'attaquent avec une indescriptible
furie. Ils soulèvent des montagnes liquides qui
refluent jusqu'au radeau. Vingt fois nous sommes
sur le point de chavirer. Des sifflements d'une
prodigieuse intensité se font entendre. Les deux
bêtes sont enlacées. Je ne puis les distinguer l'une
de l'autre. Il faut tout craindre de la rage du
vainqueur.

Une heure, deux heures se passent. La lutte
continue avec le même acharnement. Les combattants se rapprochent du radeau et s'en éloignent
tour à tour. Nous restons immobiles, prêts à faire
feu.

Soudain l'ichthyosaurus et le plesiosaurus disparaissent en creusant un véritable maelström au
sein des flots. Plusieurs minutes s'écoulent. Le
combat va-t-il se terminer dans les profondeurs
de la mer?

Tout à coup une tête énorme s'élance au-dehors,

Ces animaux s'attaquent avec fureur (p. 272).

la tête du plesiosaurus. Le monstre est blessé à mort. Je n'aperçois plus son immense carapace. Seulement son long cou se dresse, s'abat, se relève, se recourbe, cingle les flots comme un fouet gigantesque et se tord comme un ver coupé. L'eau rejaillit à une distance considérable. Elle nous aveugle. Mais bientôt l'agonie du reptile touche à sa fin, ses mouvements diminuent, ses contorsions s'apaisent, et ce long tronçon de serpent s'étend comme une masse inerte sur les flots calmés.

Quant à l'ichthyosaurus, a-t-il donc regagné sa caverne sous-marine, ou va-t-il reparaître à la surface de la mer ?

XXXIV

Mercredi 19 août. — Heureusement le vent, qui souffle avec force, nous a permis de fuir rapidement le théâtre de la lutte. Hans est toujours au gouvernail. Mon oncle, tiré de ses absorbantes idées par les incidents de ce combat, retombe dans son impatiente contemplation de la mer.

Le voyage reprend sa monotone uniformité, que je ne tiens pas à rompre au prix des dangers d'hier.

Jeudi 20 août. — Brise N.-N.-E. assez inégale. Température chaude. Nous marchons avec une vitesse de trois lieues et demie à l'heure.

Vers midi, un bruit très éloigné se fait entendre. Je consigne ici le fait sans pouvoir en donner l'explication. C'est un mugissement continu.

« Il y a au loin, dit le professeur, quelque rocher, ou quelque îlot sur lequel la mer se brise. »

Hans se hisse au sommet du mât, mais ne signale aucun écueil. L'océan est uni jusqu'à sa ligne d'horizon.

Trois heures se passent. Les mugissements semblent provenir d'une chute d'eau éloignée. Je le fais remarquer à mon oncle, qui secoue la tête. J'ai pourtant la conviction que je ne me trompe pas. Courons-nous donc à quelque cataracte qui nous précipitera dans l'abîme ? Que cette manière de descendre plaise au professeur, parce qu'elle se rapproche de la verticale, c'est possible, mais à moi...

En tout cas, il doit y avoir à quelques lieues au vent un phénomène bruyant, car maintenant les mugissements se font entendre avec une grande violence. Viennent-ils du ciel ou de l'Océan ?

Je porte mes regards vers les vapeurs suspendues dans l'atmosphère, et je cherche à sonder leur profondeur. Le ciel est tranquille. Les nuages, emportés au plus haut de la voûte, semblent immobiles et se perdent dans l'intense irradiation de la lumière. Il faut donc chercher ailleurs la cause de ce phénomène.

J'interroge alors l'horizon pur et dégagé de toute brume. Son aspect n'a pas changé. Mais si ce bruit vient d'une chute, d'une cataracte, si tout

cet océan se précipite dans un bassin inférieur, si ces mugissements sont produits par une masse d'eau qui tombe, le courant doit s'activer, et sa vitesse croissante peut me donner la mesure du péril dont nous sommes menacés. Je consulte le courant. Il est nul. Une bouteille vide que je jette à la mer reste sous le vent.

Vers quatre heures Hans se lève, se cramponne au mât et monte à son extrémité. De là son regard parcourt l'arc de cercle que l'océan décrit devant le radeau et s'arrête sur un point. Sa figure n'exprime aucune surprise, mais son œil est devenu fixe.

« Il a vu quelque chose, dit mon oncle.

— Je le crois. »

Hans redescend, puis il étend son bras vers le sud en disant :

« Der nere !

— Là-bas ? » répond mon oncle.

Et saisissant sa lunette, il regarde attentivement pendant une minute, qui me paraît un siècle.

« Oui, oui ! s'écrie-t-il.

— Que voyez-vous ?

— Une gerbe immense qui s'élève au-dessus des flots.

— Encore quelque animal marin ?

— Peut-être.

— Alors mettons le cap plus à l'ouest, car nous savons à quoi nous en tenir sur le danger de rencontrer ces monstres antédiluviens !

— Laissons aller », répond mon oncle.

Je me retourne vers Hans. Hans maintient sa barre avec une inflexible rigueur.

Cependant, si de la distance qui nous sépare de cet animal, distance qu'il faut estimer à douze lieues au moins, on peut apercevoir la colonne d'eau chassée par ses évents, il doit être d'une taille surnaturelle. Fuir serait se conformer aux lois de la plus vulgaire prudence. Mais nous ne sommes pas venus ici pour être prudents.

On va donc en avant. Plus nous approchons, plus la gerbe grandit. Quel monstre peut s'emplir d'une pareille quantité d'eau et l'expulser ainsi sans interruption ?

A huit heures du soir, nous ne sommes pas à deux lieues de lui. Son corps noirâtre, énorme, montueux, s'étend dans la mer comme un îlot. Est-ce illusion, est-ce effroi ? Sa longueur me paraît dépasser mille toises ! Quel est donc ce cétacé que n'ont prévu ni les Cuvier ni les Blumembach ? Il est immobile et comme endormi ; la mer semble ne pouvoir le soulever, et ce sont les vagues qui ondulent sur ses flancs. La colonne d'eau, projetée à une hauteur de cinq cents pieds, retombe en pluie avec un bruit assourdissant. Nous courons en insensés vers cette masse puissante que cent baleines ne nourriraient pas pour un jour.

La terreur me prend. Je ne veux pas aller plus loin ! Je couperai, s'il le faut, la drisse de la voile ! Je me révolte contre le professeur, qui ne me répond pas.

Tout à coup Hans se lève, et montrant du doigt le point menaçant :

« Holme ! dit-il.

— Une île ! s'écrie mon oncle.

— Une île ! dis-je à mon tour en haussant les épaules.

— Évidemment, répond le professeur en poussant un vaste éclat de rire.

— Mais cette colonne d'eau ?

— « Geyser », fait Hans.

— Eh ! sans doute, geyser ! riposte mon oncle, un geyser pareil à ceux de l'Islande [1] ! »

Je ne veux pas, d'abord, m'être trompé si grossièrement. Avoir pris un îlot pour un monstre marin ! Mais l'évidence se fait, et il faut enfin convenir de mon erreur. Il n'y a là qu'un phénomène naturel.

A mesure que nous approchons, les dimensions de la gerbe liquide deviennent grandioses. L'îlot représente à s'y méprendre un cétacé immense dont la tête domine les flots à une hauteur de dix toises. Le geyser, mot que les Islandais prononcent « geysir » et qui signifie « fureur », s'élève majestueusement à son extrémité. De sourdes détonations éclatent par instants, et l'énorme jet, pris de colères plus violentes, secoue son panache de vapeurs en bondissant jusqu'à la première couche de nuages. Il est seul. Ni fumerolles, ni sources chaudes ne l'entourent, et toute la puissance

---

1. Source jaillissante très célèbre située au pied de l'Hécla.

Le geyser s'élève majestueusement (p. 278).

volcanique se résume en lui. Les rayons de la lumière électrique viennent se mêler à cette gerbe éblouissante, dont chaque goutte se nuance de toutes les couleurs du prisme.

« Accostons », dit le professeur.

Mais il faut éviter avec soin cette trombe d'eau qui coulerait le radeau en un instant. Hans, manœuvrant adroitement, nous amène à l'extrémité de l'îlot.

Je saute sur le roc. Mon oncle me suit lestement, tandis que le chasseur demeure à son poste, comme un homme au-dessus de ces étonnements.

Nous marchons sur un granit mêlé de tuf siliceux; le sol frissonne sous nos pieds comme les flancs d'une chaudière où se tord de la vapeur surchauffée; il est brûlant. Nous arrivons en vue d'un petit bassin central d'où s'élève le geyser. Je plonge dans l'eau qui coule en bouillonnant un thermomètre à déversement, et il marque une chaleur de cent soixante-trois degrés.

Ainsi donc cette eau sort d'un foyer ardent. Cela contredit singulièrement les théories du professeur Lidenbrock. Je ne puis m'empêcher d'en faire la remarque.

« Eh bien, réplique-t-il, qu'est-ce que cela prouve contre ma doctrine?

— Rien », dis-je d'un ton sec, en voyant que je me heurte à un entêtement absolu.

Néanmoins je suis forcé d'avouer que nous sommes singulièrement favorisés jusqu'ici, et que, pour une raison qui m'échappe, ce voyage s'accom-

plit dans des conditions particulières de température ; mais il me paraît évident, certain, que nous
arriverons un jour ou l'autre à ces régions où la
chaleur centrale atteint les plus hautes limites
et dépasse toutes les graduations des thermomètres.

Nous verrons bien. C'est le mot du professeur,
qui, après avoir baptisé cet îlot volcanique du nom
de son neveu, donne le signal de l'embarquement.

Je reste pendant quelques minutes encore à
contempler le geyser. Je remarque que son jet
est irrégulier dans ses accès, qu'il diminue parfois
d'intensité, puis reprend avec une nouvelle
vigueur, ce que j'attribue aux variations de pression des vapeurs accumulées dans son réservoir.

Enfin nous partons en contournant les roches
très accores du sud. Hans a profité de cette halte
pour remettre le radeau en état.

Mais avant de déborder, je fais quelques observations pour calculer la distance parcourue, et je
les note sur mon journal. Nous avons franchi deux
cent soixante-dix lieues de mer depuis Port-
Graüben, et nous sommes à six cent vingt lieues
de l'Islande, sous l'Angleterre.

XXXV

Vendredi 21 août. — Le lendemain le magnifique
geyser a disparu. Le vent a fraîchi, et nous a rapi-

dement éloignés de l'îlot Axel. Les mugissements
se sont éteints peu à peu.

Le temps, s'il est permis de s'exprimer ainsi,
va changer avant peu. L'atmosphère se charge
de vapeurs qui emportent avec elles l'électricité
formée par l'évaporation des eaux salines; les
nuages s'abaissent sensiblement et prennent une
teinte uniformément olivâtre; les rayons électriques peuvent à peine percer cet opaque rideau
baissé sur le théâtre où va se jouer le drame des
tempêtes.

Je me sens particulièrement impressionné,
comme l'est sur terre toute créature à l'approche
d'un cataclysme. Les « cumulus [1] » entassés dans
le sud présentent un aspect sinistre; ils ont cette
apparence « impitoyable » que j'ai souvent remar-
quée au début des orages. L'air est lourd, la mer
est calme.

Au loin, les nuages ressemblent à de grosses
balles de coton amoncelées dans un pittoresque
désordre; peu à peu ils se gonflent et perdent
en nombre ce qu'ils gagnent en grandeur; leur
pesanteur est telle qu'ils ne peuvent se détacher
de l'horizon; mais, au souffle des courants élevés,
ils se fondent peu à peu, s'assombrissent et présentent bientôt une couche unique d'un aspect
redoutable; parfois une pelote de vapeurs, encore
éclairée, rebondit sur ce tapis grisâtre et va se
perdre bientôt dans la masse opaque.

---

1. Nuages de formes arrondies.

Évidemment l'atmosphère est saturée de fluide ; j'en suis tout imprégné ; mes cheveux se dressent sur ma tête comme aux abords d'une machine électrique. Il me semble que, si mes compagnons me touchaient en ce moment, ils recevraient une commotion violente.

A dix heures du matin, les symptômes de l'orage sont plus décisifs ; on dirait que le vent mollit pour mieux reprendre haleine ; la nue ressemble à une outre immense dans laquelle s'accumulent les ouragans.

Je ne veux pas croire aux menaces du ciel, et cependant je ne puis m'empêcher de dire :

« Voilà un mauvais temps qui se prépare. »

Le professeur ne répond pas. Il est d'une humeur massacrante, à voir l'océan se prolonger indéfiniment devant ses yeux. Il hausse les épaules à mes paroles.

« Nous aurons de l'orage, dis-je en étendant la main vers l'horizon. Ces nuages s'abaissent sur la mer comme pour l'écraser ! »

Silence général. Le vent se tait. La nature a l'air d'une morte et ne respire plus. Sur le mât, où je vois déjà poindre un léger feu Saint-Elme, la voile détendue tombe en plis lourds. Le radeau est immobile au milieu d'une mer épaisse, sans ondulations. Mais, si nous ne marchons plus, à quoi bon conserver cette toile, qui peut nous mettre en perdition au premier choc de la tempête ?

« Amenons-la, dis-je, abattons notre mât ! Cela sera prudent !

— Non, par le diable! s'écrie mon oncle, cent fois non! Que le vent nous saisisse! que l'orage nous emporte! mais que j'aperçoive enfin les rochers d'un rivage, quand notre radeau devrait s'y briser en mille pièces! »

Ces paroles ne sont pas achevées que l'horizon du sud change subitement d'aspect. Les vapeurs accumulées se résolvent en eau, et l'air, violemment appelé pour combler les vides produits par la condensation, se fait ouragan. Il vient des extrémités les plus reculées de la caverne. L'obscurité redouble. C'est à peine si je puis prendre quelques notes incomplètes.

Le radeau se soulève, il bondit. Mon oncle est jeté de son haut. Je me traîne jusqu'à lui. Il s'est fortement cramponné à un bout de câble et paraît considérer avec plaisir ce spectacle des éléments déchaînés.

Hans ne bouge pas. Ses longs cheveux, repoussés par l'ouragan et ramenés sur sa face immobile, lui donnent une étrange physionomie, car chacune de leurs extrémités est hérissée de petites aigrettes lumineuses. Son masque effrayant est celui d'un homme antédiluvien, contemporain des ichthyosaures et des megatheriums.

Cependant le mât résiste. La voile se tend comme une bulle prête à crever. Le radeau file avec un emportement que je ne puis estimer, mais moins vite encore que ces gouttes d'eau déplacées sous lui, dont la rapidité fait des lignes droites et nettes.

Les cheveux de Hans sont hérissés d'aigrettes lumineuses (p. 284).

« La voile! la voile! dis-je, en faisant signe de l'abaisser.

— Non! répond mon oncle.

— « Nej », fait Hans en remuant doucement la tête.

Cependant, la pluie forme une cataracte mugissante devant cet horizon vers lequel nous courons en insensés. Mais avant qu'elle n'arrive jusqu'à nous, le voile de nuage se déchire, la mer entre en ébullition et l'électricité, produite par une vaste action chimique qui s'opère dans les couches supérieures, est mise en jeu. Aux éclats du tonnerre se mêlent les jets étincelants de la foudre; des éclairs sans nombre s'entrecroisent au milieu des détonations; la masse des vapeurs devient incandescente; les grêlons qui frappent le métal de nos outils ou de nos armes se font lumineux; les vagues soulevées semblent être autant de mamelons ignivomes sous lesquels couve un feu intérieur, et dont chaque crête est empanachée d'une flamme.

Mes yeux sont éblouis par l'intensité de la lumière, mes oreilles brisées par le fracas de la foudre! Il faut me retenir au mât, qui plie comme un roseau sous la violence de l'ouragan!!!

. . . .

[Ici mes notes de voyage devinrent très incomplètes. Je n'ai plus retrouvé que quelques observations fugitives, prises machinalement pour ainsi dire. Mais dans leur brièveté, dans leur obscurité même, elles sont empreintes de l'émotion qui me

dominait, et mieux que ma mémoire, elles donnent le sentiment de la situation.]

. . . .

Dimanche 23 août. — Où sommes-nous ? Emportés avec une incommensurable rapidité.

La nuit a été épouvantable. L'orage ne se calme pas. Nous vivons dans un milieu de bruit, une détonation incessante. Nos oreilles saignent. On ne peut échanger une parole.

Les éclairs ne discontinuent pas. Je vois des zigzags rétrogrades qui, après un jet rapide, reviennent de bas en haut et vont frapper la voûte de granit. Si elle allait s'écrouler ! D'autres éclairs se bifurquent ou prennent la forme de globes de feu qui éclatent comme des bombes. Le bruit général ne paraît pas s'en accroître ; il a dépassé la limite d'intensité que peut percevoir l'oreille humaine, et, quand toutes les poudrières du monde viendraient à sauter ensemble, « nous ne saurions en entendre davantage ».

Il y a émission continue de lumière à la surface des nuages ; la matière électrique se dégage incessamment de leurs molécules ; évidemment les principes gazeux de l'air sont altérés ; des colonnes d'eau innombrables s'élancent dans l'atmosphère et retombent en écumant.

Où allons-nous ?... Mon oncle est couché tout de son long à l'extrémité du radeau.

La chaleur redouble. Je regarde le thermomètre ; il indique... [Le chiffre est effacé.]

Lundi 24 août. — Cela ne finira pas! Pourquoi l'état de cette atmosphère si dense, une fois modifié, ne serait-il pas définitif?

Nous sommes brisés de fatigue. Hans comme à l'ordinaire. Le radeau court invariablement vers le sud-est. Nous avons fait plus de deux cents lieues depuis l'îlot Axel.

A midi la violence de l'ouragan redouble. Il faut saisir solidement tous les objets composant la cargaison. Chacun de nous s'attache également. Les flots passent par-dessus notre tête.

Impossible de s'adresser une seule parole depuis trois jours. Nous ouvrons la bouche, nous remuons nos lèvres; il ne se produit aucun son appréciable. Même en se parlant à l'oreille on ne peut s'entendre.

Mon oncle s'est approché de moi. Il a articulé quelques paroles. Je crois qu'il m'a dit : « Nous sommes perdus. » Je n'en suis pas certain.

Je prends le parti de lui écrire ces mots : « Amenons notre voile. »

Il me fait signe qu'il y consent.

Sa tête n'a pas eu le temps de se relever de bas en haut qu'un disque de feu apparaît au bord du radeau. Le mât et la voile sont partis tout d'un bloc, et je les ai vus s'enlever à une prodigieuse hauteur, semblables au ptérodactyle, cet oiseau fantastique des premiers siècles.

Nous sommes glacés d'effroi. La boule mi-partie blanche, mi-partie azurée, de la grosseur d'une bombe de dix pouces, se promène lentement, en tournant avec une surprenante vitesse sous

La boule de feu se promena lentement (p. 288).

la lanière de l'ouragan. Elle vient ici, là, monte sur un des bâtis du radeau, saute sur le sac aux provisions, redescend légèrement, bondit, effleure la caisse à poudre. Horreur! Nous allons sauter! Non. Le disque éblouissant s'écarte; il s'approche de Hans, qui le regarde fixement; de mon oncle, qui se précipite à genoux pour l'éviter; de moi, pâle et frissonnant sous l'éclat de la lumière et de la chaleur; il pirouette près de mon pied, que j'essaie de retirer. Je ne puis y parvenir.

Une odeur de gaz nitreux remplit l'atmosphère; elle pénètre le gosier, les poumons. On étouffe.

Pourquoi ne puis-je retirer mon pied? Il est donc rivé au radeau! Ah! la chute de ce globe électrique a aimanté tout le fer du bord; les instruments, les outils, les armes s'agitent en se heurtant avec un cliquetis aigu; les clous de ma chaussure adhèrent violemment à une plaque de fer incrustée dans le bois. Je ne puis retirer mon pied!

Enfin, par un effort violent, je l'arrache au moment où la boule allait le saisir dans son mouvement giratoire et m'entraîner moi-même, si...

Ah! quelle lumière intense! le globe éclate! nous sommes couverts par des jets de flammes!

Puis tout s'éteint. J'ai eu le temps de voir mon oncle étendu sur le radeau, Hans toujours à sa barre et « crachant du feu » sous l'influence de l'électricité qui le pénètre!

Où allons-nous? où allons-nous?

. . . .

Mardi 25 août. — Je sors d'un évanouissement prolongé. L'orage continue ; les éclairs se déchaînent comme une couvée de serpents lâchée dans l'atmosphère.

Sommes-nous toujours sur la mer ? Oui, emportés avec une vitesse incalculable. Nous avons passé sous l'Angleterre, sous la Manche, sous la France, sous l'Europe entière, peut-être !

. . . .

Un bruit nouveau se fait entendre ! Évidemment, la mer qui se brise sur des rochers !... Mais alors...

. . . .

XXXVI

Ici se termine ce que j'ai appelé « le journal du bord », heureusement sauvé du naufrage. Je reprends mon récit comme devant.

Ce qui se passa au choc du radeau contre les écueils de la côte, je ne saurais le dire. Je me sentis précipité dans les flots, et si j'échappai à la mort, si mon corps ne fut pas déchiré sur les rocs aigus, c'est que le bras vigoureux de Hans me retira de l'abîme.

Le courageux Islandais me transporta hors de la portée des vagues sur un sable brûlant où je me trouvai côte à côte avec mon oncle.

Puis, il revint vers ces rochers auxquels se

heurtaient les lames furieuses, afin de sauver quelques épaves du naufrage. Je ne pouvais parler ; j'étais brisé d'émotions et de fatigues ; il me fallut une grande heure pour me remettre.

Cependant, une pluie diluvienne continuait à tomber, mais avec ce redoublement qui annonce la fin des orages. Quelques rocs superposés nous offrirent un abri contre les torrents du ciel. Hans prépara des aliments auxquels je ne pus toucher, et chacun de nous, épuisé par les veilles de trois nuits, tomba dans un douloureux sommeil.

Le lendemain, le temps était magnifique. Le ciel et la mer s'étaient apaisés d'un commun accord. Toute trace de tempête avait disparu. Ce furent les paroles joyeuses du professeur qui saluèrent mon réveil. Il était d'une gaieté terrible.

« Eh bien, mon garçon, s'écria-t-il, as-tu bien dormi ? »

N'eût-on pas dit que nous étions dans la maison de Königstrasse, que je descendais tranquillement pour déjeuner, que mon mariage avec la pauvre Graüben allait s'accomplir ce jour même ?

Hélas ! pour peu que la tempête eût jeté le radeau dans l'est, nous avions passé sous l'Allemagne, sous ma chère ville de Hambourg, sous cette rue où demeurait tout ce que j'aimais au monde. Alors quarante lieues m'en séparaient à peine ! Mais quarante lieues verticales d'un mur de granit, et, en réalité, plus de mille lieues à franchir !

Toutes ces douloureuses réflexions traversèrent

rapidement mon esprit avant que je ne répondisse
à la question de mon oncle.

« Ah ça! répéta-t-il, tu ne veux pas dire si tu as
bien dormi?

— Très bien, répondis-je; je suis encore brisé,
mais cela ne sera rien.

— Absolument rien, un peu de fatigue, et voilà
tout.

— Mais vous me paraissez bien gai ce matin,
mon oncle.

— Enchanté, mon garçon! enchanté! Nous
sommes arrivés!

— Au terme de notre expédition?

— Non, mais au bout de cette mer qui n'en
finissait pas. Nous allons reprendre maintenant
la voie de terre et nous enfoncer véritablement
dans les entrailles du globe.

— Mon oncle, permettez-moi de vous faire une
question.

— Je te le permets, Axel.

— Et le retour?

— Le retour! Ah! tu penses à revenir quand on
n'est pas même arrivé?

— Non, je veux seulement demander comment
il s'effectuera.

— De la manière la plus simple du monde. Une
fois arrivés au centre du sphéroïde, ou nous trouverons une route nouvelle pour remonter à sa
surface, ou nous reviendrons tout bourgeoisement
par le chemin déjà parcouru. J'aime à penser qu'il
ne se fermera pas derrière nous.

— Alors il faudra remettre le radeau en bon état.

— Nécessairement.

— Mais les provisions, en reste-t-il assez pour accomplir toutes ces grandes choses ?

— Oui, certes. Hans est un garçon habile, et je suis sûr qu'il a sauvé la plus grande partie de la cargaison. Allons nous en assurer, d'ailleurs. »

Nous quittâmes cette grotte ouverte à toutes les brises. J'avais un espoir qui était en même temps une crainte ; il me semblait impossible que le terrible abordage du radeau n'eût pas anéanti tout ce qu'il portait. Je me trompais. A mon arrivée sur le rivage, j'aperçus Hans au milieu d'une foule d'objets rangés avec ordre. Mon oncle lui serra la main avec un vif sentiment de reconnaissance. Cet homme, d'un dévouement surhumain dont on ne trouverait peut-être pas d'autre exemple, avait travaillé pendant que nous dormions et sauvé les objets les plus précieux au péril de sa vie.

Ce n'est pas que nous n'eussions fait des pertes assez sensibles ; nos armes, par exemple ; mais enfin on pouvait s'en passer. La provision de poudre était demeurée intacte, après avoir failli sauter pendant la tempête.

« Eh bien, s'écria le professeur, puisque les fusils manquent, nous en serons quittes pour ne pas chasser.

— Bon ; mais les instruments ?

— Voici le manomètre, le plus utile de tous, et pour lequel j'aurais donné les autres ! Avec

lui, je puis calculer la profondeur et savoir quand nous aurons atteint le centre. Sans lui, nous risquerions d'aller au-delà et de ressortir par les antipodes ! »

Cette gaieté était féroce.

« Mais la boussole ? demandai-je.

— La voici, sur ce rocher, en parfait état, ainsi que le chronomètre et les thermomètres. Ah ! le chasseur est un homme précieux ! »

Il fallait bien le reconnaître ; en fait d'instruments, rien ne manquait. Quant aux outils et aux engins, j'aperçus, épars sur le sable, échelles, cordes, pics, pioches, etc.

Cependant il y avait encore la question des vivres à élucider.

« Et les provisions ? dis-je.

— Voyons les provisions », répondit mon oncle.

Les caisses qui les contenaient étaient alignées sur la grève dans un parfait état de conservation ; la mer les avait respectées pour la plupart, et, somme toute, en biscuits, viande salée, genièvre et poissons secs, on pouvait compter encore sur quatre mois de vivres.

« Quatre mois ! s'écria le professeur. Nous avons le temps d'aller et de revenir, et, avec ce qui restera, je veux donner un grand dîner à tous mes collègues du Johannæum ! »

J'aurais dû être habitué, depuis longtemps, au tempérament de mon oncle, et pourtant cet homme-là m'étonnait toujours.

« Maintenant, dit-il, nous allons refaire notre

provision d'eau avec la pluie que l'orage a versée
dans tous ces bassins de granit; par conséquent,
nous n'avons pas à craindre d'être pris par la soif.
Quant au radeau, je vais recommander à Hans de
le réparer de son mieux, quoiqu'il ne doive plus
nous servir, j'imagine!

— Comment cela? m'écriai-je.

— Une idée à moi, mon garçon. Je crois que nous
ne sortirons pas par où nous sommes entrés. »

Je regardai le professeur avec une certaine
défiance. Je me demandai s'il n'était pas devenu
fou. Et cependant « il ne savait pas si bien dire ».

« Allons déjeuner », reprit-il.

Je le suivis sur un cap élevé, après qu'il eut donné
ses instructions au chasseur. Là, de la viande sèche,
du biscuit et du thé composèrent un repas excellent, et, je dois l'avouer, un des meilleurs que
j'eusse fait de ma vie. Le besoin, le grand air, le
calme après les agitations, tout contribuait à me
mettre en appétit.

Pendant le déjeuner, je posai à mon oncle la
question de savoir où nous étions en ce moment.

« Cela, dis-je, me paraît difficile à calculer.

— A calculer exactement, oui, répondit-il; c'est
même impossible, puisque, pendant ces trois jours
de tempête, je n'ai pu tenir note de la vitesse et de
la direction du radeau; mais cependant nous pouvons relever notre situation à l'estime.

— En effet, la dernière observation a été faite
à l'îlot du geyser...

— A l'îlot Axel, mon garçon. Ne décline pas cet

honneur d'avoir baptisé de ton nom la première île découverte au centre du massif terrestre.

— Soit! A l'îlot Axel, nous avions franchi environ deux cent soixante-dix lieues de mer, et nous nous trouvions à plus de six cents lieues de l'Islande.

— Bien! partons de ce point alors, et comptons quatre jours d'orage, pendant lesquels notre vitesse n'a pas dû être inférieure à quatre-vingts lieues par vingt-quatre heures.

— Je le crois. Ce serait donc trois cents lieues à ajouter.

— Oui, et la mer Lidenbrock aurait à peu près six cents lieues d'un rivage à l'autre! Sais-tu bien, Axel, qu'elle peut lutter de grandeur avec la Méditerranée?

— Oui, surtout si nous ne l'avons traversée que dans sa largeur!

— Ce qui est fort possible!

— Et, chose curieuse, ajoutai-je, si nos calculs sont exacts, nous avons maintenant cette Méditerranée sur notre tête.

— Vraiment!

— Vraiment, car nous sommes à neuf cents lieues de Reykjawik!

— Voilà un joli bout de chemin, mon garçon; mais que nous soyons plutôt sous la Méditerranée que sous la Turquie ou sous l'Atlantique, cela ne peut s'affirmer que si notre direction n'a pas dévié.

— Non, le vent paraissait constant; je pense

donc que ce rivage doit être situé au sud-est de Port-Graüben.

— Bon, il est facile de s'en assurer en consultant la boussole. Allons consulter la boussole ! »

Le professeur se dirigea vers le rocher sur lequel Hans avait déposé les instruments. Il était gai, allègre, il se frottait les mains, il prenait des poses ! Un vrai jeune homme ! Je le suivis, assez curieux de savoir si je ne me trompais pas dans mon estime.

Arrivé au rocher, mon oncle prit le compas, le posa horizontalement et observa l'aiguille, qui, après avoir oscillé, s'arrêta dans une position fixe sous l'influence magnétique.

Mon oncle regarda, puis il se frotta les yeux et regarda de nouveau. Enfin il se retourna de mon côté, stupéfait.

« Qu'y a-t-il ? » demandai-je.

Il me fit signe d'examiner l'instrument. Une exclamation de surprise m'échappa. La fleur de l'aiguille marquait le nord là où nous supposions le midi ! Elle se tournait vers la grève au lieu de montrer la pleine mer !

Je remuai la boussole, je l'examinai ; elle était en parfait état. Quelque position que l'on fît prendre à l'aiguille, celle-ci reprenait obstinément cette direction inattendue.

Ainsi donc, il ne fallait plus en douter, pendant la tempête, une saute de vent s'était produite dont nous ne nous étions pas aperçus, et avait ramené le radeau vers les rivages que mon oncle croyait laisser derrière lui.

Il me serait impossible de peindre la succession des sentiments qui agitèrent le professeur Lidenbrock, la stupéfaction, l'incrédulité et enfin la colère. Jamais je ne vis un homme si décontenancé d'abord, si irrité ensuite. Les fatigues de la traversée, les dangers courus, tout était à recommencer! Nous avions reculé au lieu de marcher en avant!

Mais mon oncle reprit rapidement le dessus.

« Ah! la fatalité me joue de pareils tours! s'écria-t-il. Les éléments conspirent contre moi! L'air, le feu et l'eau combinent leurs efforts pour s'opposer à mon passage! Eh bien! l'on saura ce que peut ma volonté. Je ne céderai pas, je ne reculerai pas d'une ligne, et nous verrons qui l'emportera de l'homme ou de la nature! »

Debout sur le rocher, irrité, menaçant, Otto Lidenbrock, pareil au farouche Ajax, semblait défier les dieux. Mais je jugeai à propos d'intervenir et de mettre un frein à cette fougue insensée.

« Écoutez-moi, lui dis-je d'un ton ferme. Il y a une limite à toute ambition ici-bas; il ne faut pas lutter contre l'impossible; nous sommes mal équipés pour un voyage sur mer; cinq cents lieues ne se font pas sur un mauvais assemblage de poutres avec une couverture pour voile, un bâton en guise de mât, et contre les vents déchaînés. Nous

ne pouvons gouverner, nous sommes le jouet des tempêtes, et c'est agir en fous que de tenter une seconde fois cette impossible traversée ! »

De ces raisons toutes irréfutables je pus dérouler la série pendant dix minutes sans être interrompu, mais cela vint uniquement de l'inattention du professeur, qui n'entendit pas un mot de mon argumentation.

« Au radeau ! » s'écria-t-il.

Telle fut sa réponse. J'eus beau faire, supplier, m'emporter, je me heurtai à une volonté plus dure que le granit.

Hans achevait en ce moment de réparer le radeau. On eût dit que cet être bizarre devinait les projets de mon oncle. Avec quelques morceaux de surtarbrandur il avait consolidé l'embarcation. Une voile s'y élevait déjà et le vent jouait dans ses plis flottants.

Le professeur dit quelques mots au guide, et aussitôt celui-ci d'embarquer les bagages et de tout disposer pour le départ. L'atmosphère était assez pure et le vent nord-ouest tenait bon.

Que pouvais-je faire ? Résister seul contre deux ? Impossible. Si encore Hans se fût joint à moi. Mais non ! Il semblait que l'Islandais eût mis de côté toute volonté personnelle et fait vœu d'abnégation. Je ne pouvais rien obtenir d'un serviteur aussi inféodé à son maître. Il fallait marcher en avant.

J'allai donc prendre sur le radeau ma place accoutumée, quand mon oncle m'arrêta de la main.

« Nous ne partirons que demain », dit-il.

Je fis le geste d'un homme résigné à tout.

« Je ne dois rien négliger, reprit-il, et puisque la fatalité m'a poussé sur cette partie de la côte, je ne la quitterai pas sans l'avoir reconnue. »

Cette remarque sera comprise, quand on saura que nous étions revenus aux rivages du nord, mais non pas à l'endroit même de notre premier départ. Port-Graüben devait être situé plus à l'ouest. Rien de plus raisonnable dès lors que d'examiner avec soin les environs de ce nouvel atterrissage.

« Allons à la découverte ! » dis-je.

Et, laissant Hans à ses occupations, nous voilà partis. L'espace compris entre les relais de la mer et le pied des contreforts était fort large. On pouvait marcher une demi-heure avant d'arriver à la paroi de rochers. Nos pieds écrasaient d'innombrables coquillages de toutes formes et de toutes grandeurs, où vécurent les animaux des premières époques. J'apercevais aussi d'énormes carapaces dont le diamètre dépassait souvent quinze pieds. Elles avaient appartenu à ces gigantesques glyptodons de la période pliocène dont la tortue moderne n'est plus qu'une petite réduction. En outre le sol était semé d'une grande quantité de débris pierreux, sortes de galets arrondis par la lame et rangés en lignes successives. Je fus donc conduit à faire cette remarque, que la mer devait autrefois occuper cet espace. Sur les rocs épars et maintenant hors de ses atteintes, les flots avaient laissé des traces évidentes de leur passage.

Ceci pouvait expliquer jusqu'à un certain point l'existence de cet océan, à quarante lieues au-dessous de la surface du globe. Mais, suivant moi, cette masse liquide devait se perdre peu à peu dans les entrailles de la terre, et elle provenait évidemment des eaux de l'Océan qui se firent jour à travers quelque fissure. Cependant, il fallait admettre que cette fissure était actuellement bouchée, car toute cette caverne, ou mieux, cet immense réservoir, se fût rempli dans un temps assez court. Peut-être même cette eau, ayant eu à lutter contre des feux souterrains, s'était-elle vaporisée en partie. De là l'explication des nuages suspendus sur notre tête et le dégagement de cette électricité qui créait des tempêtes à l'intérieur du massif terrestre.

Cette théorie des phénomènes dont nous avions été témoins me paraissait satisfaisante, car, pour grandes que soient les merveilles de la nature, elles sont toujours explicables par des raisons physiques.

Nous marchions donc sur une sorte de terrain sédimentaire, formé par les eaux comme tous les terrains de cette période, si largement distribués à la surface du globe. Le professeur examinait attentivement chaque interstice de roche. Qu'une ouverture existât, et il devenait important pour lui d'en sonder la profondeur.

Pendant un mille, nous avons côtoyé les rivages de la mer Lidenbrock, quand le sol changea subitement d'aspect. Il paraissait bouleversé,

convulsionné par un exhaussement violent des couches inférieures. En maint endroit, des enfoncements ou des soulèvements attestaient une dislocation puissante du massif terrestre.

Nous avancions difficilement sur ces cassures de granit, mélangées de silex, de quartz et de dépôts alluvionnaires, lorsqu'un champ, plus qu'un champ, une plaine d'ossements apparut à nos regards. On eût dit un cimetière immense, où les générations de vingt siècles confondaient leur éternelle poussière. De hautes extumescences de débris s'étageaient au loin. Elles ondulaient jusqu'aux limites de l'horizon et s'y perdaient dans une brume fondante. Là, sur trois milles carrés, peut-être, s'accumulait toute l'histoire de la vie animale, à peine écrite dans les terrains trop récents du monde habité.

Cependant, une impatiente curiosité nous entraînait. Nos pieds écrasaient avec un bruit sec les restes de ces animaux anté-historiques, et ces fossiles dont les muséums des grandes cités se disputent les rares et intéressants débris. L'existence de mille Cuvier n'aurait pas suffi à recomposer les squelettes des êtres organiques couchés dans ce magnifique ossuaire.

J'étais stupéfait. Mon oncle avait levé ses grands bras vers l'épaisse voûte qui nous servait de ciel. Sa bouche ouverte démesurément, ses yeux fulgurants sous la lentille de ses lunettes, sa tête remuant de haut en bas, de gauche à droite, toute sa posture enfin dénotait un étonnement sans borne. Il se

Une plaine d'ossements apparut à nos regards (p. 303).

trouvait devant une inappréciable collection de Leptotherium, de Mericotherium, de Lophodions, d'Anoplotherium, de Megatherium, de Mastodontes, de Protopithèques, de Ptérodactyles, de tous les monstres antédiluviens entassés pour sa satisfaction personnelle. Qu'on se figure un bibliomane passionné transporté tout à coup dans cette fameuse bibliothèque d'Alexandrie brûlée par Omar et qu'un miracle aurait fait renaître de ses cendres ! Tel était mon oncle le professeur Lidenbrock.

Mais ce fut un bien autre émerveillement, quand, courant à travers cette poussière organique, il saisit un crâne dénudé, et s'écria d'une voix frémissante :

« Axel ! Axel ! une tête humaine !

— Une tête humaine ! mon oncle, répondis-je, non moins stupéfait.

— Oui, neveu ! Ah ! M. Milne-Edwards ! Ah ! M. de Quatrefages ! que n'êtes-vous là où je suis moi, Otto Lidenbrock ! »

XXXVIII

Pour comprendre cette évocation faite par mon oncle à ces illustres savants français, il faut savoir qu'un fait d'une haute importance en paléontologie s'était produit quelque temps avant notre départ.

Le 28 mars 1863, des terrassiers fouillant sous la direction de M. Boucher de Perthes les carrières de Moulin-Quignon, près d'Abbeville, dans le département de la Somme, en France, trouvèrent une mâchoire humaine à quatorze pieds au-dessous de la superficie du sol. C'était le premier fossile de cette espèce ramené à la lumière du grand jour. Près de lui se rencontrèrent des haches de pierre et des silex taillés, colorés et revêtus par le temps d'une patine uniforme.

Le bruit de cette découverte fut grand, non seulement en France, mais en Angleterre et en Allemagne. Plusieurs savants de l'Institut français, entre autres MM. Milne-Edwards et de Quatre-fages, prirent l'affaire à cœur, démontrèrent l'incontestable authenticité de l'ossement en question, et se firent les plus ardents défenseurs de ce « procès de la mâchoire, » suivant l'expression anglaise.

Aux géologues du Royaume-Uni qui tinrent le fait pour certain, MM. Falconer, Busk, Carpenter, etc., se joignirent des savants de l'Allemagne, et parmi eux, au premier rang, le plus fougueux, le plus enthousiaste, mon oncle Lidenbrock.

L'authenticité d'un fossile humain de l'époque quaternaire semblait donc incontestablement démontrée et admise.

Ce système, il est vrai, avait eu un adversaire acharné dans M. Élie de Beaumont. Ce savant de si haute autorité soutenait que le terrain de Moulin-Quignon n'appartenait pas au « diluvium », mais

à une couche moins ancienne, et, d'accord en cela avec Cuvier, il n'admettait pas que l'espèce humaine eût été contemporaine des animaux de l'époque quaternaire. Mon oncle Lidenbrock, de concert avec la grande majorité des géologues, avait tenu bon, disputé, discuté, et M. Élie de Beaumont était resté à peu près seul de son parti.

Nous connaissions tous ces détails de l'affaire, mais nous ignorions que, depuis notre départ, la question avait fait des progrès nouveaux. D'autres mâchoires identiques, quoique appartenant à des individus de types divers et de nations différentes, furent trouvées dans les terres meubles et grises de certaines grottes, en France, en Suisse, en Belgique, ainsi que des armes, des ustensiles, des outils, des ossements d'enfants, d'adolescents, d'hommes, de vieillards. L'existence de l'homme quaternaire s'affirmait donc chaque jour davantage.

Et ce n'était pas tout. Des débris nouveaux exhumés du terrain tertiaire pliocène avaient permis à des savants plus audacieux encore d'assigner une plus haute antiquité à la race humaine. Ces débris, il est vrai, n'étaient point des ossements de l'homme, mais seulement des objets de son industrie, des tibias, des fémurs d'animaux fossiles, striés régulièrement, sculptés pour ainsi dire, et qui portaient la marque d'un travail humain.

Ainsi, d'un bond, l'homme remontait l'échelle des temps d'un grand nombre de siècles ; il précédait le

mastodonte ; il devenait le contemporain de l'« ele-
phas meridionalis » ; il avait cent mille ans d'existence, puisque c'est la date assignée par les géologues les plus renommés à la formation du terrain
pliocène !

Tel était alors l'état de la science paléontologique,
et ce que nous en connaissions suffisait à expliquer
notre attitude devant cet ossuaire de la mer
Lidenbrock. On comprendra donc les stupéfac-
tions et les joies de mon oncle, surtout quand, vingt
pas plus loin, il se trouva en présence, on peut dire
face à face, avec un des spécimens de l'homme
quaternaire.

C'était un corps humain absolument reconnaissable. Un sol d'une nature particulière, comme
celui du cimetière Saint-Michel, à Bordeaux,
l'avait-il ainsi conservé pendant des siècles ? je ne
saurais le dire. Mais ce cadavre, la peau tendue et
parcheminée, les membres encore moelleux —
à la vue du moins —, les dents intactes, la chevelure abondante, les ongles des mains et des orteils
d'une grandeur effrayante, se montrait à nos yeux
tel qu'il avait vécu.

J'étais muet devant cette apparition d'un autre
âge. Mon oncle, si loquace, si impétueusement
discoureur d'habitude, se taisait aussi. Nous avions
soulevé ce corps. Nous l'avions redressé. Il nous
regardait avec ses orbites caves. Nous palpions son
torse sonore.

Après quelques instants de silence, l'oncle fut
vaincu par le professeur Otto Lidenbrock, emporté

C'était un corps humain absolument reconnaissable (p. 308).

par son tempérament, oublia les circonstances de
notre voyage, le milieu où nous étions, l'immense
caverne qui nous contenait. Sans doute il se crut
au Johannæum, professant devant ses élèves, car
il prit un ton doctoral, et s'adressant à un auditoire
imaginaire :

« Messieurs, dit-il, j'ai l'honneur de vous présenter un homme de l'époque quaternaire. De
grands savants ont nié son existence, d'autres non
moins grands l'ont affirmée. Les saint Thomas de la
paléontologie, s'ils étaient là, le toucheraient du
doigt, et seraient bien forcés de reconnaître leur
erreur. Je sais bien que la science doit se mettre en
garde contre les découvertes de ce genre ! Je
n'ignore pas quelle exploitation des hommes fossiles ont fait les Barnum et autres charlatans de
même farine. Je connais l'histoire de la rotule
d'Ajax, du prétendu corps d'Oreste retrouvé par
les Spartiates, et du corps d'Astérius, long de dix
coudées, dont parle Pausanias. J'ai lu les rapports
sur le squelette de Trapani découvert au XIVe
siècle, et dans lequel on voulait reconnaître Poly-
phème, et l'histoire du géant déterré pendant le
XVIe siècle aux environs de Palerme. Vous n'ignorez
pas plus que moi, messieurs, l'analyse faite auprès
de Lucerne, en 1577, de ces grands ossements que
le célèbre médecin Félix Plater déclarait appartenir
à un géant de dix-neuf pieds ! J'ai dévoré les trai-
tés de Cassanion, et tous ces mémoires, brochures,
discours et contre-discours publiés à propos du
squelette du roi des Cimbres, Teutobochus, l'enva-

hisseur de la Gaule, exhumé d'une sablonnière du Dauphiné en 1613! Au XVIIIᵉ siècle, j'aurais combattu avec Pierre Campet l'existence des préadamites de Scheuchzer! J'ai eu entre les mains l'écrit nommé *Gigans...* »

Ici reparut l'infirmité naturelle de mon oncle, qui en public ne pouvait pas prononcer les mots difficiles.

« L'écrit nommé *Gigans...* » reprit-il.

Il ne pouvait aller plus loin.

« *Gigantéo...* »

Impossible! Le mot malencontreux ne voulait pas sortir! On aurait bien ri au Johannæum!

« *Gigantostéologie* », acheva de dire le professeur Lidenbrock entre deux jurons.

Puis, continuant de plus belle, et s'animant :

« Oui, messieurs, je sais toutes ces choses! Je sais aussi que Cuvier et Blumenbach ont reconnu dans ces ossements de simples os de mammouth et autres animaux de l'époque quaternaire. Mais ici le doute seul sera une injure à la science! Le cadavre est là! Vous pouvez le voir, le toucher. Ce n'est pas un squelette, c'est un corps intact, conservé dans un but uniquement anthropologique! »

Je voulus bien ne pas contredire cette assertion.

« Si je pouvais le laver dans une solution d'acide sulfurique, dit encore mon oncle, j'en ferais disparaître toutes les parties terreuses et ces coquillages resplendissants qui sont incrustés en lui. Mais le précieux dissolvant me manque. Cependant, tel

il est, tel ce corps nous racontera sa propre histoire. »

Ici, le professeur prit le cadavre fossile et le manœuvra avec la dextérité d'un montreur de curiosités.

« Vous le voyez, reprit-il, il n'a pas six pieds de long, et nous sommes loin des prétendus géants. Quant à la race à laquelle il appartient, elle est incontestablement caucasique. C'est la race blanche, c'est la nôtre ! Le crâne de ce fossile est régulièrement ovoïde, sans développement des pommettes, sans projection de la mâchoire. Il ne présente aucun caractère de ce prognathisme qui modifie l'angle facial [1]. Mesurez cet angle, il est presque de quatre-vingt-dix degrés. Mais j'irai plus loin encore dans le chemin des déductions, et j'oserai dire que cet échantillon humain appartient à la famille japétique, répandue depuis les Indes jusqu'aux limites de l'Europe occidentale. Ne souriez pas, messieurs ! »

Personne ne souriait, mais le professeur avait une telle habitude de voir les visages s'épanouir pendant ses savantes dissertations !

« Oui, reprit-il avec une animation nouvelle, c'est là un homme fossile, et contemporain des mastodontes dont les ossements emplissent cet amphi-

1. L'angle facial est formé par deux plans, l'un plus ou moins vertical qui est tangent au front et aux incisives, l'autre horizontal, qui passe par l'ouverture des conduits auditifs et l'épine nasale inférieure. On appelle *prognathisme*, en langue anthropologique, cette projection de la mâchoire qui modifie l'angle facial.

théâtre. Mais de vous dire par quelle route il est arrivé là, comment ces couches où il était enfoui ont glissé jusque dans cette énorme cavité du globe, c'est ce que je ne me permettrai pas. Sans doute, à l'époque quaternaire, des troubles considérables se manifestaient encore dans l'écorce terrestre; le refroidissement continu du globe produisait des cassures, des fentes, des failles, où dévalait vraisemblablement une partie du terrain supérieur. Je ne me prononce pas, mais enfin l'homme est là, entouré des ouvrages de sa main, de ces haches, de ces silex taillés qui ont constitué l'âge de pierre, et à moins qu'il n'y soit venu comme moi en touriste, en pionnier de la science, je ne puis mettre en doute l'authenticité de son antique origine. »

Le professeur se tut, et j'éclatai en applaudissements unanimes. D'ailleurs mon oncle avait raison, et de plus savants que son neveu eussent été fort empêchés de le combattre.

Autre indice. Ce corps fossilisé n'était pas le seul de l'immense ossuaire. D'autres corps se rencontraient à chaque pas que nous faisions dans cette poussière, et mon oncle pouvait choisir le plus merveilleux de ces échantillons pour convaincre les incrédules.

En vérité, c'était un étonnant spectacle que celui de ces générations d'hommes et d'animaux confondus dans ce cimetière. Mais une question grave se présentait, que nous n'osions résoudre. Ces êtres animés avaient-ils glissé par une convul-

sion du sol vers les rivages de la mer Lidenbrock,
alors qu'ils étaient déjà réduits en poussière? Ou
plutôt vécurent-ils ici, dans ce monde souterrain,
sous ce ciel factice, naissant et mourant comme les
habitants de la terre? Jusqu'ici, les monstres
marins, les poissons seuls, nous étaient apparus
vivants! Quelque homme de l'abîme errait-il encore
sur ces grèves désertes?

XXXIX

Pendant une demi-heure encore, nos pieds foulèrent ces couches d'ossements. Nous allions en
avant, poussés par une ardente curiosité. Quelles
autres merveilles renfermait cette caverne, quels
trésors pour la science? Mon regard s'attendait à
toutes les surprises, mon imagination à tous les
étonnements.

Les rivages de la mer avaient depuis longtemps
disparu derrière les collines de l'ossuaire. L'imprudent professeur, s'inquiétant peu de s'égarer,
m'entraînait au loin. Nous avancions silencieuse-
ment, baignés dans les ondes électriques. Par un
phénomène que je ne puis expliquer, et grâce à
sa diffusion, complète alors, la lumière éclairait
uniformément les diverses faces des objets. Son
foyer n'existait plus en un point déterminé de
l'espace et elle ne produisait aucun effet d'ombre.
On aurait pu se croire en plein midi et en plein été,

C'était la végétation de l'époque
tertiaire dans toute sa magnificence (p. 316).

au milieu des régions équatoriales, sous les rayons verticaux du soleil. Toute vapeur avait disparu. Les rochers, les montagnes lointaines, quelques masses confuses de forêts éloignées, prenaient un étrange aspect sous l'égale distribution du fluide lumineux. Nous ressemblions à ce fantastique personnage d'Hoffmann qui a perdu son ombre.

Après une marche d'un mille, apparut la lisière d'une forêt immense, mais non plus un de ces bois de champignons qui avoisinaient Port-Graüben.

C'était la végétation de l'époque tertiaire dans toute sa magnificence. De grands palmiers, d'espèces aujourd'hui disparues, de superbes palmacites, des pins, des ifs, des cyprès, des thuyas, représentaient la famille des conifères, et se reliaient entre eux par un réseau de lianes inextricables. Un tapis de mousses et d'hépathiques revêtait moelleusement le sol. Quelques ruisseaux murmuraient sous ces ombrages, peu dignes de ce nom, puisqu'ils ne produisaient pas d'ombre. Sur leurs bords croissaient des fougères arborescentes semblables à celles des serres chaudes du globe habité. Seulement, la couleur manquait à ces arbres, à ces arbustes, à ces plantes, privés de la vivifiante chaleur du soleil. Tout se confondait dans une teinte uniforme, brunâtre et comme passée. Les feuilles étaient dépourvues de leur verdeur, et les fleurs elles-mêmes, si nombreuses à cette époque tertiaire qui les vit naître, alors sans couleurs et sans parfums, semblaient faites d'un papier décoloré sous l'action de l'atmosphère.

Mon oncle Lidenbrock s'aventura sous ces gigantesques taillis. Je le suivis, non sans une certaine appréhension. Puisque la nature avait fait là les frais d'une alimentation végétale, pourquoi les redoutables mammifères ne s'y rencontreraient-ils pas ? J'apercevais dans ces larges clairières que laissaient les arbres abattus et rongés par le temps, des légumineuses, des acérines, des rubiacées, et mille arbrisseaux comestibles, chers aux ruminants de toutes les périodes. Puis apparaissaient, confondus et entremêlés, les arbres des contrées si différentes de la surface du globe, le chêne croissant près du palmier, l'eucalyptus australien s'appuyant au sapin de la Norvège, le bouleau du Nord confondant ses branches avec les branches du kauris zélandais. C'était à confondre la raison des classificateurs les plus ingénieux de la botanique terrestre.

Soudain, je m'arrêtai. De la main, je retins mon oncle.

Le lumière diffuse permettait d'apercevoir les moindres objets dans la profondeur des taillis. J'avais cru voir... Non ! réellement, de mes yeux, je voyais des formes immenses s'agiter sous les arbres ! En effet, c'étaient des animaux gigantesques, tout un troupeau de mastodontes, non plus fossiles, mais vivants, et semblables à ceux dont les restes furent découverts en 1801 dans les marais de l'Ohio ! J'apercevais ces grands éléphants dont les trompes grouillaient sous les arbres comme une légion de serpents. J'entendais le bruit de leurs longues

défenses dont l'ivoire taraudait les vieux troncs. Les branches craquaient, et les feuilles arrachées par masses considérables s'engouffraient dans la vaste gueule de ces monstres.

Ce rêve où j'avais vu renaître tout ce monde des temps anté-historiques, des époques ternaire et quaternaire, se réalisait donc enfin! Et nous étions là, seuls, dans les entrailles du globe, à la merci de ses farouches habitants!

Mon oncle regardait.

« Allons, dit-il tout d'un coup en me saisissant le bras, en avant, en avant!

— Non! m'écriai-je, non! Nous sommes sans armes! Que ferions-nous au milieu de ce troupeau de quadrupèdes géants? Venez, mon oncle, venez! Nulle créature humaine ne peut braver impunément la colère de ces monstres.

— Nulle créature humaine! répondit mon oncle, en baissant la voix. Tu te trompes, Axel! Regarde, regarde là-bas! Il me semble que j'aperçois un être vivant! un être semblable à nous! un homme! »

Je regardai, haussant les épaules, et décidé à pousser l'incrédulité jusqu'à ses dernières limites. Mais, quoique j'en eus, il fallut bien me rendre à l'évidence.

En effet, à moins d'un quart de mille, appuyé au tronc d'un kauris énorme, un être humain, un Protée de ces contrées souterraines, un nouveau fils de Neptune, gardait cet innombrable troupeau de mastodontes!

Un Protée de ces contrées souterraines (p. 318).

Immanis pecoris custos, immanior ipse !

Oui ! *immanior ipse !* Ce n'était plus l'être fossile dont nous avions relevé le cadavre dans l'ossuaire, c'était un géant, capable de commander à ces monstres. Sa taille dépassait douze pieds. Sa tête, grosse comme la tête d'un buffle, disparaissait dans les broussailles d'une chevelure inculte. On eût dit une véritable crinière, semblable à celle de l'éléphant des premiers âges. Il brandissait de la main une branche énorme, digne houlette de ce berger antédiluvien.

Nous étions restés immobiles, stupéfaits. Mais nous pouvions être aperçus. Il fallait fuir.

« Venez, venez », m'écriai-je, en entraînant mon oncle, qui pour la première fois se laissa faire !

Un quart d'heure plus tard, nous étions hors de la vue de ce redoutable ennemi.

Et maintenant que j'y songe tranquillement, maintenant que le calme s'est refait dans mon esprit, que des mois se sont écoulés depuis cette étrange et surnaturelle rencontre, que penser, que croire ? Non ! c'est impossible ! Nos sens ont été abusés, nos yeux n'ont pas vu ce qu'ils voyaient ! Nulle créature humaine n'existe dans ce monde subterrestre ! Nulle génération d'hommes n'habite ces cavernes inférieures du globe, sans se soucier des habitants de sa surface, sans communication avec eux ! C'est insensé, profondément insensé !

J'aime mieux admettre l'existence de quelque animal dont la structure se rapproche de la struc-

ture humaine, de quelque singe des premières
époques géologiques, de quelque protopithèque,
de quelque mésopithèque semblable à celui que
découvrit M. Lartet dans le gîte ossifère de Sansan!
Mais celui-ci dépassait par sa taille toutes les mesures
données par la paléontologie moderne! N'importe!
Un singe, oui, un singe, si invraisemblable qu'il
soit! Mais un homme, un homme vivant, et avec
lui toute une génération enfouie dans les entrailles
de la terre! Jamais!

Cependant, nous avions quitté la forêt claire et
lumineuse, muets d'étonnement, accablés sous une
stupéfaction qui touchait à l'abrutissement. Nous
courions malgré nous. C'était une vraie fuite,
semblable à ces entraînements effroyables que l'on
subit dans certains cauchemars. Instinctivement,
nous revenions vers la mer Lidenbrock, et je ne
sais dans quelles divagations mon esprit se fût
emporté, sans une préoccupation qui me ramena à
des observations plus pratiques.

Bien que je fusse certain de fouler un sol entièrement vierge de nos pas, j'apercevais souvent des
agrégations de rochers dont la forme rappelait
ceux de Port-Graüben. Cela confirmait, d'ailleurs,
l'indication de la boussole et notre retour involontaire au nord de la mer Lidenbrock. C'était
parfois à s'y méprendre. Des ruisseaux et des
cascades tombaient par centaines des saillies de
rocs. Je croyais revoir la couche de surtarbrandur,
notre fidèle Hans-bach et la grotte où j'étais revenu
à la vie. Puis, quelques pas plus loin, la disposition

des contreforts, l'apparition d'un ruisseau, le profil surprenant d'un rocher venait me rejeter dans le doute.

Je fis part à mon oncle de mon indécision. Il hésita comme moi. Il ne pouvait s'y reconnaître au milieu de ce panorama uniforme.

« Évidemment, lui dis-je, nous n'avons pas abordé à notre point de départ, mais la tempête nous a ramenés un peu au-dessous, et en suivant le rivage, nous retrouverons Port-Graüben.

— Dans ce cas, répondit mon oncle, il est inutile de continuer cette exploration, et le mieux est de retourner au radeau. Mais ne te trompes-tu pas, Axel ?

— Il est difficile de se prononcer, mon oncle, car tous ces rochers se ressemblent. Je crois pourtant reconnaître le promontoire au pied duquel Hans a construit l'embarcation. Nous devons être près du petit port, si même ce n'est pas ici, ajoutai-je, en examinant une crique que je crus reconnaître.

— Non, Axel, nous retrouverions au moins nos propres traces, et je ne vois rien...

— Mais je vois, moi, m'écriai-je, en m'élançant vers un objet qui brillait sur le sable.

— Qu'est-ce donc ?

— Ceci », répondis-je.

Et je montrai à mon oncle un poignard couvert de rouille, que je venais de ramasser.

« Tiens ! dit-il, tu avais donc emporté cette arme avec toi ?

— Moi ? Aucunement ! Mais vous...

— Non, pas que je sache, répondit le professeur. Je n'ai jamais eu cet objet en ma possession.

— Voilà qui est particulier !

— Mais non, c'est très simple, Axel. Les Islandais ont souvent des armes de cette espèce, et Hans, à qui celle-ci appartient, l'aura perdue... »

Je secouai la tête. Hans n'avait jamais eu ce poignard en sa possession.

« Est-ce donc l'arme de quelque guerrier anté-diluvien, m'écriai-je, d'un homme vivant, d'un contemporain de ce gigantesque berger ? Mais non ! Ce n'est pas un outil de l'âge de pierre ! Pas même de l'âge de bronze ! Cette lame est d'acier... »

Mon oncle m'arrêta net dans cette route où m'entraînait une divagation nouvelle, et de son ton froid il me dit :

« Calme-toi, Axel, et reviens à la raison. Ce poignard est une arme du xvie siècle, une véritable dague, de celles que les gentilshommes portaient à leur ceinture pour donner le coup de grâce. Elle est d'origine espagnole. Elle n'appartient ni à toi, ni à moi, ni au chasseur, ni même aux êtres humains qui vivent peut-être dans les entrailles du globe !

— Oserez-vous dire ?...

— Vois, elle ne s'est pas ébréchée ainsi à s'enfoncer dans la gorge des gens ; sa lame est couverte d'une couche de rouille qui ne date ni d'un jour, ni d'un an, ni d'un siècle ! »

Le professeur s'animait, suivant son habitude, en se laissant emporter par son imagination.

« Axel, reprit-il, nous sommes sur la voie de la
grande découverte! Cette lame est restée abandonnée sur le sable depuis cent, deux cents, trois
cents ans, et s'est ébréchée sur les rocs de cette
mer souterraine!

— Mais elle n'est pas venue seule, m'écriai-je;
elle n'a pas été se tordre d'elle-même! quelqu'un
nous a précédés!...

— Oui! un homme.

— Et cet homme?

— Cet homme a gravé son nom avec ce poignard! Cet homme a voulu encore une fois
marquer de sa main la route du centre! Cherchons,
cherchons! »

Et, prodigieusement intéressés, nous voilà
longeant la haute muraille, interrogeant les
moindres fissures qui pouvaient se changer en
galerie.

Nous arrivâmes ainsi à un endroit où le rivage se
resserrait. La mer venait presque baigner le pied
des contreforts, laissant un passage large d'une
toise au plus. Entre deux avancées de roc, on aper-
cevait l'entrée d'un tunnel obscur.

Là, sur une plaque de granit, apparaissaient deux
lettres mystérieuses à demi rongées, les deux
initiales du hardi et fantastique voyageur :

« A. S.! s'écria mon oncle. Arne Saknussemm!
Toujours Arne Saknussemm! »

Depuis le commencement du voyage, j'avais passé par bien des étonnements : je devais me croire à l'abri des surprises et blasé sur tout émerveillement. Cependant, à la vue de ces deux lettres gravées là depuis trois cents ans, je demeurai dans un ébahissement voisin de la stupidité. Non seulement la signature du savant alchimiste se lisait sur le roc, mais encore le stylet qui l'avait tracée était entre mes mains. A moins d'être d'une insigne mauvaise foi, je ne pouvais plus mettre en doute l'existence du voyageur et la réalité de son voyage.

Pendant que ces réflexions tourbillonnaient dans ma tête, le professeur Lidenbrock se laissait aller à un accès un peu dithyrambique à l'endroit d'Arne Saknussemm.

« Merveilleux génie! s'écriait-il, tu n'as rien oublié de ce qui devait ouvrir à d'autres mortels les routes de l'écorce terrestre, et tes semblables peuvent retrouver les traces que tes pieds ont laissées, il y a trois siècles, au fond de ces souterrains obscurs! A d'autres regards que les tiens, tu as réservé la contemplation de ces merveilles! Ton nom, gravé d'étapes en étapes, conduit droit à son but le voyageur assez audacieux pour te suivre, et, au centre même de notre planète, il se trouvera encore inscrit de ta propre main. Eh bien! moi aussi, j'irai signer de mon nom cette dernière page de granit! Mais que, dès maintenant, ce cap

vu par toi près de cette mer découverte par toi
soit à jamais appelé le cap Saknussemm ! »

Voilà ce que j'entendis, ou à peu près, et je me
sentis gagner par l'enthousiasme que respiraient
ces paroles. Un feu intérieur se ranima dans ma
poitrine ! J'oubliais tout, et les dangers du voyage,
et les périls du retour. Ce qu'un autre avait fait, je
voulais le faire aussi, et rien de ce qui était humain
ne me paraissait impossible !

« En avant, en avant ! » m'écriai-je.

Je m'élançais déjà vers la sombre galerie, quand
le professeur m'arrêta, et lui, l'homme des empor-
tements, il me conseilla la patience et le sang-froid.

« Retournons d'abord vers Hans, dit-il, et rame-
nons le radeau à cette place. »

J'obéis à cet ordre, non sans déplaisir, et je me
glissai rapidement au milieu des roches du rivage.

« Savez-vous, mon oncle, disais-je en marchant,
que nous avons été singulièrement servis par les
circonstances jusqu'ici !

— Ah ! tu trouves, Axel ?

— Sans doute, et il n'est pas jusqu'à la tempête
qui ne nous ait remis dans le droit chemin. Béni
soit l'orage ! Il nous a ramenés à cette côte d'où
le beau temps nous eût éloignés ! Supposez un
instant que nous eussions touché de notre proue
(la proue d'un radeau !) les rivages méridionaux
de la mer Lidenbrock, que serions-nous devenus ?
Le nom de Saknussemm n'aurait pas apparu à
nos yeux, et maintenant nous serions abandonnés
sur une plage sans issue.

— Oui, Axel, il y a quelque chose de providentiel à ce que, voguant vers le sud, nous soyons précisément revenus au nord et au cap Saknussemm. Je dois dire que c'est plus qu'étonnant, et il y a là un fait dont l'explication m'échappe absolument.

— Eh! qu'importe! il n'y a pas à expliquer les faits, mais à en profiter!

— Sans doute, mon garçon, mais...

— Mais nous allons reprendre la route du nord, passer sous les contrées septentrionales de l'Europe, la Suède, la Sibérie, que sais-je! au lieu de nous enfoncer sous les déserts de l'Afrique ou les flots de l'Océan, et je ne veux pas en savoir davantage!

— Oui, Axel, tu as raison, et tout est pour le mieux, puisque nous abandonnons cette mer horizontale qui ne pouvait mener à rien. Nous allons descendre, encore descendre, et toujours descendre! Sais-tu bien que, pour arriver au centre du globe, il n'y a plus que quinze cents lieues à franchir!

— Bah! m'écriai-je, ce n'est vraiment pas la peine d'en parler! En route! en route! »

Ces discours insensés duraient encore quand nous rejoignîmes le chasseur. Tout était préparé pour un départ immédiat. Pas un colis qui ne fût embarqué. Nous prîmes place sur le radeau, et la voile hissée, Hans se dirigea en suivant la côte vers le cap Saknussemm.

Le vent n'était pas favorable à un genre d'embar-

cation qui ne pouvait tenir le plus près. Aussi, en maint endroit, il fallut avancer à l'aide des bâtons ferrés. Souvent les rochers, allongés à fleur d'eau, nous forcèrent à faire des détours assez longs. Enfin, après trois heures de navigation, c'est-à-dire vers six heures du soir, on atteignait un endroit propice au débarquement.

Je sautai à terre, suivi de mon oncle et de l'Islandais. Cette traversée ne m'avait pas calmé. Au contraire. Je proposai même de brûler « nos vaisseaux », afin de nous couper toute retraite. Mais mon oncle s'y opposa. Je le trouvai singulièrement tiède.

« Au moins, dis-je, partons sans perdre un instant.

— Oui, mon garçon ; mais auparavant, examinons cette nouvelle galerie afin de savoir s'il faut préparer nos échelles. »

Mon oncle mit son appareil de Ruhmkorff en activité ; le radeau, attaché au rivage, fut laissé seul ; d'ailleurs, l'ouverture de la galerie n'était pas à vingt pas de là, et notre petite troupe, moi en tête, s'y rendit sans retard.

L'orifice, à peu près circulaire, présentait un diamètre de cinq pieds environ ; le sombre tunnel était taillé dans le roc vif et soigneusement alésé par les matières éruptives auxquelles il donnait autrefois passage ; sa partie inférieure effleurait le sol, de telle façon que l'on pût y pénétrer sans aucune difficulté.

Nous suivions un plan presque horizontal,

Au bout de six pas, notre marche fut interrompue (p. 330).

quand, au bout de six pas, notre marche fut interrompue par l'interposition d'un bloc énorme.

« Maudit roc! » m'écriai-je avec colère, en me
voyant subitement arrêté par un obstacle infranchissable.

Nous eûmes beau chercher à droite et à gauche,
en bas et en haut, il n'existait aucun passage,
aucune bifurcation. J'éprouvai un vif désappoin-
tement, et je ne voulais pas admettre la réalité
de l'obstacle. Je me baissai. Je regardai au-dessous
du bloc. Nul interstice. Au-dessus. Même barrière
de granit. Hans porta la lumière de la lampe sur
tous les points de la paroi; mais celle-ci n'offrait
aucune solution de continuité. Il fallait renoncer
à tout espoir de passer.

Je m'étais assis sur le sol; mon oncle arpentait
le couloir à grands pas.

« Mais alors Saknussemm? m'écriai-je.

— Oui, fit mon oncle, a-t-il donc été arrêté par
cette porte de pierre?

— Non! non! repris-je avec vivacité. Ce quartier
de roc, par suite d'une secousse quelconque, ou
l'un de ces phénomènes magnétiques qui agitent
l'écorce terrestre, a brusquement fermé ce passage.
Bien des années se sont écoulées entre le retour
de Saknussemm et la chute de ce bloc. N'est-il
pas évident que cette galerie a été autrefois le
chemin des laves, et qu'alors les matières éruptives y circulaient librement? Voyez, il y a des
fissures récentes qui sillonnent ce plafond de
granit; il est fait de morceaux rapportés, de

pierres énormes, comme si la main de quelque géant eût travaillé à cette substruction; mais, un jour, la poussée a été plus forte, et ce bloc, semblable à une clef de voûte qui manque, a glissé jusqu'au sol en obstruant tout passage. C'est un obstacle accidentel que Saknussemm n'a pas rencontré, et si nous ne le renversons pas, nous sommes indignes d'arriver au centre du monde! »

Voilà comment je parlais! L'âme du professeur avait passé tout entière en moi. Le génie des découvertes m'inspirait. J'oubliais le passé, je dédaignais l'avenir. Rien n'existait plus pour moi à la surface de ce sphéroïde au sein duquel je m'étais engouffré, ni les villes, ni les campagnes, ni Hambourg, ni Königstrasse, ni ma pauvre Graüben, qui devait me croire à jamais perdu dans les entrailles de la terre!

« Eh bien! reprit mon oncle, à coups de pioche, à coups de pic, faisons notre route! renversons ces murailles!

— C'est trop dur pour le pic, m'écriai-je.

— Alors la pioche!

— C'est trop long pour la pioche!

— Mais!...

— Eh bien! la poudre! la mine! minons, et faisons sauter l'obstacle!

— La poudre!

— Oui! il ne s'agit que d'un bout de roc à briser!

— Hans, à l'ouvrage! » s'écria mon oncle.

L'Islandais retourna au radeau, et revint bientôt avec un pic dont il se servit pour creuser un four-

neau de mine. Ce n'était pas un mince travail. Il
s'agissait de faire un trou assez considérable pour
contenir cinquante livres de fulmicoton, dont la
puissance expansive est quatre fois plus grande
que celle de la poudre à canon.

J'étais dans une prodigieuse surexcitation
d'esprit. Pendant que Hans travaillait, j'aidai
activement mon oncle à préparer une longue
mèche faite avec de la poudre mouillée et renfermée dans un boyau de toile.

« Nous passerons ! disais-je.

— Nous passerons », répétait mon oncle.

A minuit, notre travail de mineurs fut entièrement terminé ; la charge de fulmicoton se trouvait enfouie dans le fourneau, et la mèche, se
déroulant à travers la galerie, venait aboutir au-
dehors.

Une étincelle suffisait maintenant pour mettre
ce formidable engin en activité.

« A demain », dit le professeur.

Il fallut bien me résigner et attendre encore
pendant six grandes heures !

XLI

Le lendemain, jeudi, 27 août, fut une date célèbre
de ce voyage subterrestre. Elle ne me revient pas
à l'esprit sans que l'épouvante ne fasse encore

battre mon cœur. A partir de ce moment, notre raison, notre jugement, notre ingéniosité n'ont plus voix au chapitre, et nous allons devenir le jouet des phénomènes de la terre.

A six heures, nous étions sur pied. Le moment approchait de frayer par la poudre un passage à travers l'écorce de granit.

Je sollicitai l'honneur de mettre le feu à la mine. Cela fait, je devais rejoindre mes compagnons sur le radeau qui n'avait point été déchargé; puis nous prendrions du large, afin de parer aux dangers de l'explosion, dont les effets pouvaient ne pas se concentrer à l'intérieur du massif.

La mèche devait brûler pendant dix minutes, selon nos calculs, avant de porter le feu à la chambre des poudres. J'avais donc le temps nécessaire pour regagner le radeau.

Je me préparai à remplir mon rôle, non sans une certaine émotion.

Après un repas rapide, mon oncle et le chasseur s'embarquèrent, tandis que je restais sur le rivage. J'étais muni d'une lanterne allumée qui devait me servir à mettre le feu à la mèche.

« Va, mon garçon, me dit mon oncle, et reviens immédiatement nous rejoindre.

— Soyez tranquille, répondis-je, je ne m'amuserai point en route. »

Aussitôt je me dirigeai vers l'orifice de la galerie. J'ouvris ma lanterne, et je saisis l'extrémité de la mèche.

Le professeur tenait son chronomètre à la main.

« Es-tu prêt ? me cria-t-il.

— Je suis prêt.

— Eh bien ! feu, mon garçon ! »

Je plongeai rapidement dans la flamme la mèche, qui pétilla à son contact, et, tout courant, je revins au rivage.

« Embarque, fit mon oncle, et débordons. »

Hans, d'une vigoureuse poussée, nous rejeta en mer. Le radeau s'éloigna d'une vingtaine de toises.

C'était un moment palpitant. Le professeur suivait de l'œil l'aiguille du chronomètre.

« Encore cinq minutes, disait-il. Encore quatre ! Encore trois ! »

Mon pouls battait des demi-secondes.

« Encore deux ! Une !... Croulez, montagnes de granit ! »

Que se passa-t-il alors ? Le bruit de la détonation, je crois que je ne l'entendis pas. Mais la forme des rochers se modifia subitement à mes regards ; ils s'ouvrirent comme un rideau. J'aperçus un insondable abîme qui se creusait en plein rivage. La mer, prise de vertige, ne fut plus qu'une vague énorme, sur le dos de laquelle le radeau s'éleva perpendiculairement.

Nous fûmes renversés tous les trois. En moins d'une seconde, la lumière fit place à la plus profonde obscurité. Puis je sentis l'appui solide manquer, non à mes pieds, mais au radeau. Je crus qu'il coulait à pic. Il n'en était rien. J'aurais voulu adresser la parole à mon oncle ; mais le

« Croulez, montagnes de granit ! » (p. 334).

mugissement des eaux l'eût empêché de m'entendre.

Malgré les ténèbres, le bruit, la surprise, l'émotion, je compris ce qui venait de se passer.

Au-delà du roc qui venait de sauter, il existait
un abîme. L'explosion avait déterminé une sorte
de tremblement de terre dans ce sol coupé de
fissures, le gouffre s'était ouvert, et la mer, chan-
gée en torrent, nous y entraînait avec elle.

Je me sentis perdu.

Une heure, deux heures, que sais-je! se passèrent ainsi. Nous nous serrions les coudes, nous
nous tenions les mains afin de n'être pas précipités
hors du radeau. Des chocs d'une extrême violence
se produisaient, quand il heurtait la muraille.
Cependant ces heurts étaient rares, d'où je conclus
que la galerie s'élargissait considérablement.
C'était, à n'en pas douter, le chemin de Saknussemm; mais, au lieu de le descendre seuls, nous
avions, par notre imprudence, entraîné toute une
mer avec nous.

Ces idées, on le comprend, se présentèrent à
mon esprit sous une forme vague et obscure. Je
les associais difficilement pendant cette course
vertigineuse qui ressemblait à une chute. A en
juger par l'air qui me fouettait le visage, elle
devait surpasser celle des trains les plus rapides.
Allumer une torche dans ces conditions était donc
impossible, et notre dernier appareil électrique
avait été brisé au moment de l'explosion.

Je fus donc fort surpris de voir une lumière

briller tout à coup près de moi. La figure calme de Hans s'éclaira. L'adroit chasseur était parvenu à allumer la lanterne, et, bien que sa flamme vacillât à s'éteindre, elle jeta quelques lueurs dans l'épouvantable obscurité.

La galerie était large. J'avais eu raison de la juger telle. L'insuffisante lumière ne nous permettait pas d'apercevoir ses deux murailles à la fois. La pente des eaux qui nous emportaient dépassait celle des plus insurmontables rapides de l'Amérique. Leur surface semblait faite d'un faisceau de flèches liquides décochées avec une extrême puissance. Je ne puis rendre mon impression par une comparaison plus juste. Le radeau, pris par certains remous, filait parfois en tournoyant. Lorsqu'il s'approchait des parois de la galerie, j'y projetais la lumière de la lanterne, et je pouvais juger de sa vitesse à voir les saillies du roc se changer en traits continus, de telle sorte que nous étions enserrés dans un réseau de lignes mouvantes. J'estimai que notre vitesse devait atteindre trente lieues à l'heure.

Mon oncle et moi, nous regardions d'un œil hagard, accotés au tronçon du mât, qui, au moment de la catastrophe, s'était rompu net. Nous tournions le dos à l'air, afin de ne pas être étouffés par la rapidité d'un mouvement que nulle puissance humaine ne pouvait enrayer.

Cependant les heures s'écoulaient. La situation ne changeait pas, mais un incident vint la compliquer.

En cherchant à mettre un peu d'ordre dans la cargaison, je vis que la plus grande partie des objets embarqués avaient disparu au moment de l'explosion, lorsque la mer nous assaillit si violemment! Je voulus savoir exactement à quoi m'en tenir sur nos ressources, et, la lanterne à la main, je commençai mes recherches. De nos instruments, il ne restait plus que la boussole et le chronomètre. Les échelles et les cordes se réduisaient à un bout de câble enroulé autour du tronçon de mât. Pas une pioche, pas un pic, pas un marteau, et, malheur irréparable, nous n'avions de vivres que pour un jour!

Je fouillai les interstices du radeau, les moindres coins formés par les poutres et la jointure des planches! Rien! Nos provisions consistaient uniquement en un morceau de viande sèche et quelques biscuits.

Je regardais d'un air stupide! Je ne voulais pas comprendre! Et cependant de quel danger me préoccupais-je? Quand les vivres eussent été suffisants pour des mois, pour des années, comment sortir des abîmes où nous entraînait cet irrésistible torrent? A quoi bon craindre les tortures de la faim, quand la mort s'offrait déjà sous tant d'autres formes? Mourir d'inanition, est-ce que nous en aurions le temps?

Pourtant, par une inexplicable bizarrerie de l'imagination, j'oubliai le péril immédiat pour les menaces de l'avenir qui m'apparurent dans toute leur horreur. D'ailleurs, peut-être pourrions-

nous échapper aux fureurs du torrent et revenir à la surface du globe. Comment? Je l'ignore. Où? Qu'importe? Une chance sur mille est toujours une chance, tandis que la mort par la faim ne nous laissait d'espoir dans aucune proportion, si petite qu'elle fût.

La pensée me vint de tout dire à mon oncle, de lui montrer à quel dénuement nous étions réduits, et de faire l'exact calcul du temps qui nous restait à vivre. Mais j'eus le courage de me taire. Je voulais lui laisser tout son sang-froid.

En ce moment, la lumière de la lanterne baissa peu à peu et s'éteignit entièrement. La mèche avait brûlé jusqu'au bout. L'obscurité redevint absolue. Il ne fallait plus songer à dissiper ces impénétrables ténèbres. Il restait encore une torche, mais elle n'aurait pu se maintenir allumée. Alors, comme un enfant, je fermai les yeux pour ne pas voir toute cette obscurité.

Après un laps de temps assez long, la vitesse de notre course redoubla. Je m'en aperçus à la réverbération de l'air sur mon visage. La pente des eaux devenait excessive. Je crois véritablement que nous ne glissions plus. Nous tombions. J'avais en moi l'impression d'une chute presque verticale. La main de mon oncle et celle de Hans, cramponnées à mes bras, me retenaient avec vigueur.

Tout à coup, après un temps inappréciable, je ressentis comme un choc; le radeau n'avait pas heurté un corps dur, mais il s'était subitement

arrêté dans sa chute. Une trombe d'eau, une immense colonne liquide s'abattit à sa surface. Je fus suffoqué. Je me noyais...

Cependant cette inondation soudaine ne dura pas. En quelques secondes je me retrouvai à l'air libre que j'aspirai à pleins poumons. Mon oncle et Hans me serraient le bras à le briser, et le radeau nous portait encore tous les trois.

XLII

JE suppose qu'il devait être alors dix heures du soir. Le premier de mes sens qui fonctionna, après ce dernier assaut, fut le sens de l'ouïe. J'entendis presque aussitôt, car ce fut acte d'audition véritable, j'entendis le silence se faire dans la galerie et succéder à ces mugissements qui, depuis de longues heures, remplissaient mon oreille. Enfin ces paroles de mon oncle m'arrivèrent comme un murmure :

« Nous montons !

— Que voulez-vous dire ? m'écriai-je.

— Oui, nous montons ! nous montons ! »

J'étendis le bras ; je touchai la muraille ; ma main fut mise en sang. Nous remontions avec une extrême rapidité.

« La torche ! la torche ! » s'écria le professeur.

Hans, non sans difficultés, parvint à l'allumer,

et la flamme, se maintenant de bas en haut, malgré
le mouvement ascensionnel, jeta assez de clarté
pour éclairer toute la scène.

« C'est bien ce que je pensais, dit mon oncle.
Nous sommes dans un puits étroit, qui n'a pas
quatre toises de diamètre. L'eau, arrivée au fond
du gouffre, reprend son niveau et nous remonte
avec elle.

— Où ?

— Je l'ignore, mais il faut se tenir prêts à tout
événement. Nous montons avec une vitesse que
j'évalue à deux toises par seconde, soit cent vingt
toises par minute, ou plus de trois lieues et demie
à l'heure. De ce train-là, on fait du chemin.

— Oui, si rien ne nous arrête, si ce puits a une
issue ! Mais s'il est bouché, si l'air se comprime
peu à peu sous la pression de la colonne d'eau,
si nous allons être écrasés !

— Axel, répondit le professeur avec un grand
calme, la situation est presque désespérée, mais
il y a quelques chances de salut, et ce sont celles-là
que j'examine. Si à chaque instant nous pouvons
périr, à chaque instant aussi nous pouvons être
sauvés. Soyons donc en mesure de profiter des
moindres circonstances.

— Mais que faire ?

— Réparer nos forces en mangeant. »

A ces mots, je regardai mon oncle d'un œil
hagard. Ce que je n'avais pas voulu avouer, il
fallait enfin le dire :

« Manger ? répétai-je.

La torche jeta assez de clarté pour éclairer
toute la·scène (p. 341).

— Oui, sans retard. »

Le professeur ajouta quelques mots en danois. Hans secoua la tête.

« Quoi ! s'écria mon oncle, nos provisions sont perdues ?

— Oui, voilà ce qui reste de vivres ! un morceau de viande sèche pour nous trois ! »

Mon oncle me regardait sans vouloir comprendre mes paroles.

« Eh bien ! dis-je, croyez-vous encore que nous puissions être sauvés ? »

Ma demande n'obtint aucune réponse.

Une heure se passa. Je commençais à éprouver une faim violente. Mes compagnons souffraient aussi, et pas un de nous n'osait toucher à ce misérable reste d'aliments.

Cependant, nous montions toujours avec une extrême rapidité. Parfois l'air nous coupait la respiration comme aux aéronautes dont l'ascension est trop rapide. Mais si ceux-ci éprouvent un froid proportionnel à mesure qu'ils s'élèvent dans les couches atmosphériques, nous subissions un effet absolument contraire. La chaleur s'accroissait d'une inquiétante façon et devait certainement atteindre en ce moment quarante degrés.

Que signifiait un pareil changement ? Jusqu'alors les faits avaient donné raison aux théories de Davy et de Lidenbrock ; jusqu'alors des conditions particulières de roches réfractaires, d'électricité, de magnétisme avaient modifié les lois générales de la nature, en nous faisant une température modé-

rée, car la théorie du feu central restait, à mes yeux, la seule vraie, la seule explicable. Allions-nous revenir à un milieu où ces phénomènes s'accomplissaient dans toute leur rigueur et dans lequel la chaleur réduisait les roches à un complet état de fusion? Je le craignais, et je dis au professeur :

« Si nous ne sommes pas noyés ou brisés, si nous ne mourons pas de faim, il nous reste toujours la chance d'être brûlés vifs. »

Il se contenta de hausser les épaules et retomba dans ses réflexions.

Une heure s'écoula, et, sauf un léger accroissement dans la température, aucun incident ne modifia la situation. Enfin mon oncle rompit le silence.

« Voyons, dit-il, il faut prendre un parti.

— Prendre un parti? répliquai-je.

— Oui. Il faut réparer nos forces. Si nous essayons, en ménageant ce reste de nourriture, de prolonger notre existence de quelques heures, nous serons faibles jusqu'à la fin.

— Oui, jusqu'à la fin, qui ne se fera pas attendre.

— Eh bien! qu'une chance de salut se présente, qu'un moment d'action soit nécessaire, où trouverons-nous la force d'agir, si nous nous laissons affaiblir par l'inanition?

— Eh! mon oncle, ce morceau de viande dévoré, que nous restera-t-il?

— Rien, Axel, rien. Mais te nourrira-t-il davantage à le manger des yeux? Tu fais là les raison-

nements d'un homme sans volonté, d'un être sans énergie !

— Ne désespérez-vous donc pas ? m'écriai-je avec irritation.

— Non ! répliqua fermement le professeur.

— Quoi ! vous croyez encore à quelque chance de salut ?

— Oui ! certes, oui ! et tant que son cœur bat, tant que sa chair palpite, je n'admets pas qu'un être doué de volonté laisse en lui place au désespoir. »

Quelles paroles ! L'homme qui les prononçait en de pareilles circonstances était certainement d'une trempe peu commune.

« Enfin, dis-je, que prétendez-vous faire ?

— Manger ce qui reste de nourriture jusqu'à la dernière miette et réparer nos forces perdues. Ce repas sera notre dernier, soit ! mais au moins, au lieu d'être épuisés, nous serons redevenus des hommes.

— Eh bien ! dévorons ! » m'écriai-je.

Mon oncle prit le morceau de viande et les quelques biscuits échappés au naufrage ; il fit trois portions égales et les distribua. Cela donnait environ une livre d'aliment pour chacun. Le professeur mangea avidement, avec une sorte d'emportement fébrile ; moi, sans plaisir, malgré ma faim, presque avec dégoût ; Hans, tranquillement, modérément, mâchant sans bruit de petites bouchées, les savourant avec le calme d'un homme que les soucis de l'avenir ne pouvaient inquiéter. Il avait, en furetant

bien, retrouvé une gourde à demi pleine de genièvre ; il nous l'offrit, et cette bienfaisante liqueur eut le pouvoir de me ranimer un peu.

« Förtrafflig! dit Hans en buvant à son tour.

— Excellente! » riposta mon oncle.

J'avais repris quelque espoir. Mais notre dernier repas venait d'être achevé. Il était alors cinq heures du matin.

L'homme est ainsi fait, que sa santé est un effet purement négatif ; une fois le besoin de manger satisfait, on se figure difficilement les horreurs de la faim ; il faut les éprouver pour les comprendre. Aussi, au sortir d'un long jeûne, quelques bouchées de biscuit et de viande triomphèrent de nos douleurs passées.

Cependant, après ce repas, chacun se laissa aller à ses réflexions. A quoi songeait Hans, cet homme de l'extrême occident, que dominait la résignation fataliste des Orientaux ? Pour mon compte, mes pensées n'étaient faites que de souvenirs, et ceux-ci me ramenaient à la surface de ce globe que je n'aurais jamais dû quitter. La maison de König-strasse, ma pauvre Graüben, la bonne Marthe, passèrent comme des visions devant mes yeux, et, dans les grondements lugubres qui couraient à travers le massif, je croyais surprendre le bruit des cités de la terre.

Pour mon oncle, « toujours à son affaire », la torche à la main, il examinait avec attention la nature des terrains ; il cherchait à reconnaître sa situation par l'observation des couches superpo-

sées. Ce calcul, ou mieux cette estime, ne pouvait
être que fort approximative; mais un savant est
toujours un savant, quand il parvient à conserver
son sang-froid, et certes le professeur Lidenbrock
possédait cette qualité à un degré peu ordinaire.

Je l'entendais murmurer des mots de la science
géologique; je les comprenais, et je m'intéressais
malgré moi à cette étude suprême.

« Granit éruptif, disait-il. Nous sommes encore à
l'époque primitive; mais nous montons! nous
montons! Qui sait? »

Qui sait? Il espérait toujours. De sa main il
tâtait la paroi verticale, et, quelques instants plus
tard, il reprenait ainsi :

« Voilà les gneiss! voilà les micaschistes! Bon!
à bientôt les terrains de l'époque de transition,
et alors... »

Que voulait dire le professeur? Pouvait-il mesurer l'épaisseur de l'écorce terrestre suspendue
sur notre tête? Possédait-il un moyen quelconque
de faire ce calcul? Non. Le manomètre lui manquait, et nulle estime ne pouvait le suppléer.

Cependant la température s'accroissait dans une
forte proportion et je me sentais baigné au milieu
d'une atmosphère brûlante. Je ne pouvais la comparer qu'à la chaleur renvoyée par les fourneaux
d'une fonderie à l'heure des coulées. Peu à peu,
Hans, mon oncle et moi, nous avions dû quitter
nos vestes et nos gilets; le moindre vêtement
devenait une cause de malaise, pour ne pas dire
de souffrance.

Peu à peu, nous avions dû quitter nos vêtements (p. 347).

« Montons-nous donc vers un foyer incandescent? m'écriai-je, à un moment où la chaleur redoublait.

— Non, répondit mon oncle, c'est impossible! c'est impossible!

— Cependant, dis-je en tâtant la paroi, cette muraille est brûlante! »

Au moment où je prononçai ces paroles, ma main ayant effleuré l'eau, je dus la retirer au plus vite.

« L'eau est brûlante! » m'écriai-je.

Le professeur, cette fois, ne répondit que par un geste de colère.

Alors une invincible épouvante s'empara de mon cerveau et ne le quitta plus. J'avais le sentiment d'une catastrophe prochaine, et telle que la plus audacieuse imagination n'aurait pu la concevoir. Une idée, d'abord vague, incertaine, se changeait en certitude dans mon esprit. Je la repoussai, mais elle revint avec obstination. Je n'osais la formuler. Cependant quelques observations involontaires déterminèrent ma conviction. A la lueur douteuse de la torche, je remarquai des mouvements désordonnés dans les couches granitiques; un phénomène allait évidemment se produire, dans lequel l'électricité jouait un rôle; puis cette chaleur excessive, cette eau bouillante!... Je voulus observer la boussole.

Elle était affolée!

XLIII

Oui, affolée! L'aiguille sautait d'un pôle à l'autre avec de brusques secousses, parcourait tous les points du cadran, et tournait, comme si elle eût été prise de vertige.

Je savais bien que, d'après les théories les plus acceptées, l'écorce minérale du globe n'est jamais dans un état de repos absolu; les modifications amenées par la décomposition des matières internes, l'agitation provenant des grands courants liquides, l'action du magnétisme, tendent à l'ébranler incessamment, alors même que les êtres disséminés à sa surface ne soupçonnent pas son agitation. Ce phénomène ne m'aurait donc pas autrement effrayé, ou du moins, il n'eût pas fait naître dans mon esprit une idée terrible.

Mais d'autres faits, certains détails *sui generis*, ne purent me tromper plus longtemps. Les détonations se multipliaient avec une effrayante intensité. Je ne pouvais les comparer qu'au bruit que feraient un grand nombre de chariots entraînés rapidement sur le pavé. C'était un tonnerre continu.

Puis la boussole affolée, secouée par les phénomènes électriques, me confirmait dans mon opinion. L'écorce minérale menaçait de se rompre, les massifs granitiques de se rejoindre, la fissure de se combler, le vide de se remplir, et nous,

pauvres atomes, nous allions être écrasés dans cette formidable étreinte.

« Mon oncle, mon oncle! m'écriai-je, nous sommes perdus.

— Quelle est cette nouvelle terreur? me répondit-il avec un calme surprenant. Qu'as-tu donc?

— Ce que j'ai! Observez ces murailles qui s'agitent, ce massif qui se disloque, cette chaleur torride, cette eau qui bouillonne, ces vapeurs qui s'épaississent, cette aiguille folle, tous les indices d'un tremblement de terre! »

Mon oncle secoua doucement la tête.

« Un tremblement de terre? dit-il.

— Oui!

— Mon garçon, je crois que tu te trompes!

— Quoi! vous ne reconnaissez pas les symptômes?...

— D'un tremblement de terre? non! J'attends mieux que cela!

— Que voulez-vous dire?

— Une éruption, Axel.

— Une éruption! dis-je. Nous sommes dans la cheminée d'un volcan en activité!

— Je le pense, dit le professeur en souriant, et c'est ce qui peut nous arriver de plus heureux! »

De plus heureux! Mon oncle était-il devenu fou? Que signifiaient ces paroles? Pourquoi ce calme et ce sourire?

« Comment! m'écriai-je, nous sommes pris dans une éruption! la fatalité nous a jetés sur le chemin des laves incandescentes, des roches en

feu, des eaux bouillonnantes, de toutes les matières éruptives! nous allons être repoussés, expulsés, rejetés, vomis, expectorés dans les airs avec les quartiers de rocs, les pluies de cendres et de scories, dans un tourbillon de flammes, et c'est ce qui peut nous arriver de plus heureux!

— Oui, répondit le professeur en me regardant par-dessus ses lunettes, car c'est la seule chance que nous ayons de revenir à la surface de la terre! »

Je passe rapidement sur les mille idées qui se croisèrent dans mon cerveau. Mon oncle avait raison, absolument raison, et jamais il ne me parut ni plus audacieux ni plus convaincu qu'en ce moment où il attendait et supputait avec calme les chances d'une éruption.

Cependant nous montions toujours; la nuit se passa dans ce mouvement ascensionnel; les fracas environnants redoublaient; j'étais presque suffoqué, je croyais toucher à ma dernière heure, et, pourtant, l'imagination est si bizarre, que je me livrai à une recherche véritablement enfantine. Mais je subissais mes pensées, je ne les dominais pas!

Il était évident que nous étions rejetés par une poussée éruptive; sous le radeau, il y avait des eaux bouillonnantes, et sous ces eaux toute une pâte de lave, un agrégat de roches qui, au sommet du cratère, se disperseraient en tous sens. Nous étions donc dans la cheminée d'un volcan. Pas de doute à cet égard.

Mais cette fois, au lieu du Sneffels, volcan éteint,

il s'agissait d'un volcan en pleine activité. Je me demandai donc quelle pouvait être cette montagne et sur quelle partie du monde nous allions être expulsés.

Dans les régions septentrionales, cela ne faisait aucun doute. Avant ses affolements, la boussole n'avait jamais varié à cet égard. Depuis le cap Saknussemm, nous avions été entraînés directement au nord pendant des centaines de lieues. Or, étions-nous revenus sous l'Islande? Devions-nous être rejetés par le cratère de l'Hécla ou par ceux des sept autres monts ignivomes de l'île? Dans un rayon de cinq cents lieues, à l'ouest, je ne voyais sous ce parallèle que les volcans mal connus de la côte nord-ouest de l'Amérique. Dans l'est, un seul existait sous le quatre-vingtième degré de latitude, l'Esk, dans l'île de Jean Mayen, non loin du Spitzberg! Certes, les cratères ne manquaient pas, et ils se trouvaient assez spacieux pour vomir une armée tout entière! Mais lequel nous servirait d'issue, c'est ce que je cherchais à deviner.

Vers le matin, le mouvement d'ascension s'accéléra. Si la chaleur s'accrut, au lieu de diminuer, aux approches de la surface du globe, c'est qu'elle était toute locale et due à une influence volcanique. Notre genre de locomotion ne pouvait plus me laisser aucun doute dans l'esprit. Une force énorme, une force de plusieurs centaines d'atmosphères produite par les vapeurs accumulées dans le sein de la terre, nous poussait irrésistiblement. Mais

à quels dangers innombrables elle nous exposait!

Bientôt des reflets fauves pénétrèrent dans la galerie verticale qui s'élargissait; j'apercevais à droite et à gauche des couloirs profonds semblables à d'immenses tunnels d'où s'échappaient des vapeurs épaisses; des langues de flammes en léchaient les parois en pétillant.

« Voyez! voyez, mon oncle! m'écriai-je.

— Eh bien! ce sont des flammes sulfureuses. Rien de plus naturel dans une éruption.

— Mais si elles nous enveloppent?

— Elles ne nous envelopperont pas.

— Mais si nous étouffons?

— Nous n'étoufferons pas. La galerie s'élargit, et, s'il le faut, nous abandonnerons le radeau pour nous abriter dans quelque crevasse.

— Et l'eau! l'eau montante?

— Il n'y a plus d'eau, Axel, mais une sorte de pâte lavique qui nous soulève avec elle jusqu'à l'orifice du cratère. »

La colonne liquide avait effectivement disparu pour faire place à des matières éruptives assez denses, quoique bouillonnantes. La température devenait insoutenable, et un thermomètre exposé dans cette atmosphère eût marqué plus de soixante-dix degrés! La sueur m'inondait. Sans la rapidité de l'ascension, nous aurions été certainement étouffés.

Cependant le professeur ne donna pas suite à sa proposition d'abandonner le radeau, et il fit bien. Ces quelques poutres mal jointes offraient

une surface solide, un point d'appui qui nous eût manqué partout ailleurs.

Vers huit heures du matin, un nouvel incident se produisit pour la première fois. Le mouvement ascensionnel cessa tout à coup. Le radeau demeura absolument immobile.

« Qu'est-ce donc? demandai-je, ébranlé par cet arrêt subit comme par un choc.

— Une halte, répondit mon oncle.

— Est-ce l'éruption qui se calme?

— J'espère bien que non. »

Je me levai. J'essayai de voir autour de moi. Peut-être le radeau, arrêté par une saillie de roc, opposait-il une résistance momentanée à la masse éruptive. Dans ce cas, il fallait se hâter de le dégager au plus vite.

Il n'en était rien. La colonne de cendres, de scories et de débris pierreux avait elle-même cessé de monter.

« Est-ce que l'éruption s'arrêterait? m'écriai-je.

— Ah! fit mon oncle les dents serrées, tu le crains, mon garçon; mais rassure-toi, ce moment de calme ne saurait se prolonger; voilà déjà cinq minutes qu'il dure, et avant peu nous reprendrons notre ascension vers l'orifice du cratère. »

Le professeur, en parlant ainsi, ne cessait de consulter son chronomètre, et il devait avoir encore raison dans ses pronostics. Bientôt le radeau fut repris d'un mouvement rapide et désordonné qui dura deux minutes à peu près, et il s'arrêta de nouveau.

« Bon, fit mon oncle en observant l'heure, dans dix minutes il se remettra en route.

— Dix minutes ?

— Oui. Nous avons affaire à un volcan dont l'éruption est intermittente. Il nous laisse respirer avec lui. »

Rien n'était plus vrai. A la minute assignée, nous fûmes lancés de nouveau avec une extrême rapidité. Il fallait se cramponner aux poutres pour ne pas être rejeté hors du radeau. Puis la poussée s'arrêta.

Depuis, j'ai réfléchi à ce singulier phénomène sans en trouver une explication satisfaisante. Toutefois, il me paraît évident que nous n'occupions pas la cheminée principale du volcan, mais bien un conduit accessoire, où se faisait sentir un effet de contrecoup.

Combien de fois se reproduisit cette manœuvre, je ne saurais le dire. Tout ce que je puis affirmer, c'est qu'à chaque reprise du mouvement, nous étions lancés avec une force croissante et comme emportés par un véritable projectile. Pendant les instants de halte, on étouffait ; pendant les moments de projection, l'air brûlant me coupait la respiration. Je pensai un instant à cette volupté de me retrouver subitement dans les régions hyperboréennes par un froid de trente degrés au-dessous de zéro. Mon imagination surexcitée se promenait sur les plaines de neige des contrées arctiques, et j'aspirais au moment où je me roulerais sur les tapis glacés du pôle ! Peu à peu, d'ailleurs, ma tête,

Le radeau ondula sur des flots de laves (p. 358).

brisée par ces secousses réitérées, se perdit. Sans
les bras de Hans, plus d'une fois je me serais
brisé le crâne contre la paroi de granit.

Je n'ai donc conservé aucun souvenir précis
de ce qui se passa pendant les heures suivantes.
J'ai le sentiment confus de détonations continues,
de l'agitation du massif, d'un mouvement giratoire dont fut pris le radeau. Il ondula sur des
flots de laves, au milieu d'une pluie de cendres.
Les flammes ronflantes l'enveloppèrent. Un ouragan qu'on eût dit chassé d'un ventilateur immense
activait les feux souterrains. Une dernière fois,
la figure de Hans m'apparut dans un reflet
d'incendie, et je n'eus plus d'autre sentiment que
cette épouvante sinistre des condamnés attachés à
la bouche d'un canon, au moment où le coup
part et disperse leurs membres dans les airs.

XLIV

QUAND je rouvris les yeux, je me sentis serré à
la ceinture par la main vigoureuse du guide. De
l'autre main il soutenait mon oncle. Je n'étais
pas blessé grièvement, mais brisé plutôt par une
courbature générale. Je me vis couché sur le versant d'une montagne, à deux pas d'un gouffre
dans lequel le moindre mouvement m'eût précipité. Hans m'avait sauvé de la mort, pendant
que je roulais sur les flancs du cratère.

« Où sommes-nous ? » demanda mon oncle, qui me parut fort irrité d'être revenu sur terre.

Le chasseur leva les épaules en signe d'ignorance.

« En Islande, dis-je.

— « Nej », répondit Hans.

— Comment ! non ! s'écria le professeur.

— Hans se trompe », dis-je en me soulevant.

Après les surprises innombrables de ce voyage, une stupéfaction nous était encore réservée. Je m'attendais à voir un cône couvert de neiges éternelles, au milieu des arides déserts des régions septentrionales, sous les pâles rayons d'un ciel polaire, au-delà des latitudes les plus élevées ; et, contrairement à toutes ces prévisions, mon oncle, l'Islandais et moi, nous étions étendus à mi-flanc d'une montagne calcinée par les ardeurs du soleil qui nous dévorait de ses feux.

Je ne voulais pas en croire mes regards ; mais la réelle cuisson dont mon corps était l'objet ne permettait aucun doute. Nous étions sortis à demi nus du cratère, et l'astre radieux, auquel nous n'avions rien demandé depuis deux mois, se montrant à notre égard prodigue de lumière et de chaleur, nous versait à flots une splendide irradiation.

Quand mes yeux furent accoutumés à cet éclat dont ils avaient perdu l'habitude, je les employai à rectifier les erreurs de mon imagination. Pour le moins, je voulais être au Spitzberg, et je n'étais pas d'humeur à en démordre aisément.

Le professeur avait le premier pris la parole et dit :

« En effet, voilà qui ne ressemble pas à l'Islande.

— Mais l'île de Jean Mayen ? répondis-je.

— Pas davantage, mon garçon. Ceci n'est point un volcan du nord avec ses collines de granit et sa calotte de neige.

— Cependant...

— Regarde, Axel, regarde ! »

Au-dessus de notre tête, à cinq cents pieds au plus, s'ouvrait le cratère d'un volcan par lequel s'échappait, de quart d'heure en quart d'heure, avec une très forte détonation, une haute colonne de flammes, mêlée de pierres ponces, de cendres et de laves. Je sentais les convulsions de la montagne qui respirait à la façon des baleines, et rejetait de temps à autre le feu et l'air par ses énormes évents. Au-dessous et par une pente assez roide, les nappes de matières éruptives s'étendaient à une profondeur de sept à huit cents pieds, ce qui ne donnait pas au volcan une hauteur totale de trois cents toises. Sa base disparaissait dans une véritable corbeille d'arbres verts, parmi lesquels je distinguai des oliviers, des figuiers et des vignes chargées de grappes vermeilles.

Ce n'était point l'aspect des régions arctiques, il fallait bien en convenir.

Lorsque le regard franchissait cette verdoyante enceinte, il arrivait rapidement à se perdre dans les eaux d'une mer admirable ou d'un lac, qui faisait de cette terre enchantée une île large de quelques lieues à peine. Au levant, se voyait un

petit port, précédé de quelques maisons, et dans lequel des navires d'une forme particulière se balançaient aux ondulations des flots azurés. Au-delà, des groupes d'îlots sortaient de la plaine liquide, et si nombreux, qu'ils ressemblaient à une vaste fourmilière. Vers le couchant, des côtes éloignées s'arrondissaient à l'horizon; sur les unes se profilaient des montagnes bleues d'une harmonieuse conformation; sur les autres, plus lointaines, apparaissait un cône prodigieusement élevé, au sommet duquel s'agitait un panache de fumée. Dans le nord, une immense étendue d'eau étincelait sous les rayons solaires, laissant poindre çà et là l'extrémité d'une mâture ou la convexité d'une voile gonflée au vent.

L'imprévu d'un pareil spectacle en centuplait encore les merveilleuses beautés.

« Où sommes-nous? où sommes-nous? » répétais-je à mi-voix.

Hans fermait les yeux avec indifférence, et mon oncle regardait sans comprendre.

« Quelle que soit cette montagne, dit-il enfin, il y fait un peu chaud; les explosions ne discontinuent pas, et ce ne serait vraiment pas la peine d'être sortis d'une éruption pour recevoir un morceau de roc sur la tête. Descendons, et nous saurons à quoi nous en tenir. D'ailleurs, je meurs de faim et de soif. »

Décidément le professeur n'était point un esprit contemplatif. Pour mon compte, oubliant le besoin et les fatigues, je serais resté à cette place pendant

de longues heures encore, mais il fallut suivre mes compagnons.

Le talus du volcan offrait des pentes très roides; nous glissions dans de véritables fondrières de cendres, évitant les ruisseaux de lave qui s'allongeaient comme des serpents de feu. Tout en descendant, je causais avec volubilité, car mon imagination était trop remplie pour ne point s'en aller en paroles.

« Nous sommes en Asie, m'écriais-je, sur les côtes de l'Inde, dans les îles Malaises, en pleine Océanie! Nous avons traversé la moitié du globe pour aboutir aux antipodes de l'Europe.

— Mais la boussole? répondait mon oncle.

— Oui! la boussole! disais-je d'un air embarrassé. A l'en croire, nous avons toujours marché au nord.

— Elle a donc menti?

— Oh! menti!

— A moins que ceci ne soit le pôle nord!

— Le pôle! non; mais... »

Il y avait là un fait inexplicable. Je ne savais qu'imaginer.

Cependant nous nous rapprochions de cette verdure qui faisait plaisir à voir. La faim me tourmentait et la soif aussi. Heureusement, après deux heures de marche, une jolie campagne s'offrit à nos regards, entièrement couverte d'oliviers, de grenadiers et de vignes qui avaient l'air d'appartenir à tout le monde. D'ailleurs, dans notre dénuement, nous n'étions point gens à y regarder

de si près. Quelle jouissance ce fut de presser ces fruits savoureux sur nos lèvres et de mordre à pleines grappes dans ces vignes vermeilles! Non loin, dans l'herbe, à l'ombre délicieuse des arbres, je découvris une source d'eau fraîche, où notre figure et nos mains se plongèrent voluptueusement.

Pendant que chacun s'abandonnait ainsi à toutes les douceurs du repos, un enfant apparut entre deux touffes d'oliviers.

« Ah! m'écriai-je, un habitant de cette heureuse contrée! »

C'était une espèce de petit pauvre, très misérablement vêtu, assez souffreteux, et que notre aspect parut effrayer beaucoup; en effet, demi-nus, avec nos barbes incultes, nous avions fort mauvaise mine, et, à moins que ce pays ne fût un pays de voleurs, nous étions faits de manière à effrayer ses habitants.

Au moment où le gamin allait prendre la fuite, Hans courut après lui et le ramena, malgré ses cris et ses coups de pied.

Mon oncle commença par le rassurer de son mieux et lui dit en bon allemand :

« Quel est le nom de cette montagne, mon petit ami ? »

L'enfant ne répondit pas.

« Bon, dit mon oncle, nous ne sommes point en Allemagne. »

Et il refit la même demande en anglais.

L'enfant ne répondit pas davantage. J'étais très intrigué.

« Est-il donc muet ? » s'écria le professeur, qui, très fier de son polyglottisme, recommença la même question en français.

Même silence de l'enfant.

« Alors essayons de l'italien », reprit mon oncle, et il dit en cette langue :

« *Dove noi siamo ?*

— Oui ! où sommes-nous ? » répétai-je avec impatience.

L'enfant de ne point répondre.

« Ah çà ! parleras-tu ? s'écria mon oncle, que la colère commençait à gagner, et qui secoua l'enfant par les oreilles. *Come si noma questa isola ?*

— *Stromboli* », répondit le petit pâtre, qui s'échappa des mains de Hans et gagna la plaine à travers les oliviers.

Nous ne pensions guère à lui ! Le Stromboli ! Quel effet produisit sur mon imagination ce nom inattendu ! Nous étions en pleine Méditerranée, au milieu de l'archipel éolien de mythologique mémoire, dans l'ancienne Strongyle, où Éole tenait à la chaîne les vents et les tempêtes. Et ces montagnes bleues qui s'arrondissaient au levant, c'étaient les montagnes de la Calabre ! Et ce volcan dressé à l'horizon du sud, l'Etna, le farouche Etna lui-même.

« Stromboli ! Stromboli ! » répétai-je.

Mon oncle m'accompagnait de ses gestes et de ses paroles. Nous avions l'air de chanter un chœur !

Du sommet du Stromboli (p. 364).

Ah! quel voyage! quel merveilleux voyage! Entrés par un volcan, nous étions sortis par un autre, et cet autre était situé à plus de douze cents lieues du Sneffels, de cet aride pays de l'Islande jeté aux confins du monde! Les hasards de cette expédition nous avaient transportés au sein des plus harmonieuses contrées de la terre. Nous avions abandonné la région des neiges éternelles pour celles de la verdure infinie, et laissé au-dessus de nos têtes le brouillard grisâtre des zones glacées pour revenir au ciel azuré de la Sicile!

Après un délicieux repas composé de fruits et d'eau fraîche, nous nous remîmes en route pour gagner le port de Stromboli. Dire comment nous étions arrivés dans l'île ne nous parut pas prudent : l'esprit superstitieux des Italiens n'eût pas manqué de voir en nous des démons vomis du sein des enfers; il fallut donc se résigner à passer pour d'humbles naufragés. C'était moins glorieux, mais plus sûr.

Chemin faisant, j'entendais mon oncle murmurer :

« Mais la boussole! la boussole, qui marquait le nord! Comment expliquer ce fait?

— Ma foi! dis-je avec un grand air de dédain, il ne faut pas l'expliquer, c'est plus facile!

— Par exemple! un professeur au Johannæum qui ne trouverait pas la raison d'un phénomène cosmique, ce serait une honte! »

En parlant ainsi, mon oncle, demi-nu, sa bourse de cuir autour des reins et dressant ses lunettes

Mon oncle, demi-nu et dressant ses lunettes
sur son nez (p. 366).

sur son nez, redevint le terrible professeur de minéralogie.

Une heure après avoir quitté le bois d'oliviers,
nous arrivions au port de San-Vicenzo, où Hans
réclamait le prix de sa treizième semaine de
service, qui lui fut compté avec de chaleureuses
poignées de main.

En cet instant, s'il ne partagea pas notre émotion bien naturelle, il se laissa aller du moins à
un mouvement d'expansion extraordinaire.

Du bout de ses doigts il pressa légèrement nos
deux mains et se mit à sourire.

XLV

Voici la conclusion d'un récit auquel refuseront
d'ajouter foi les gens les plus habitués à ne s'étonner de rien. Mais je suis cuirassé d'avance contre
l'incrédulité humaine.

Nous fûmes reçus par les pêcheurs strombo-
liotes avec les égards dus à des naufragés. Ils nous
donnèrent des vêtements et des vivres. Après
quarante-huit heures d'attente, le 31 août, un petit
speronare nous conduisit à Messine, où quelques
jours de repos nous remirent de toutes nos fatigues.

Le vendredi 4 septembre, nous nous embarquions
à bord du *Volturne*, l'un des paquebots-poste des

messageries impériales de France, et, trois jours plus tard, nous prenions terre à Marseille, n'ayant plus qu'une seule préoccupation dans l'esprit, celle de notre maudite boussole. Ce fait inexplicable ne laissait pas de me tracasser très sérieusement. Le 9 septembre au soir, nous arrivions à Hambourg.

Quelle fut la stupéfaction de Marthe, quelle fut la joie de Graüben, je renonce à le décrire.

« Maintenant que tu es un héros, me dit ma chère fiancée, tu n'auras plus besoin de me quitter, Axel ! »

Je la regardai. Elle pleurait en souriant.

. Je laisse à penser si le retour du professeur Lidenbrock fit sensation à Hambourg. Grâce aux indiscrétions de Marthe, la nouvelle de son départ pour le centre de la terre s'était répandue dans le monde entier. On ne voulut pas y croire, et, en le revoyant, on n'y crut pas davantage.

Cependant la présence de Hans, et diverses informations venues d'Islande modifièrent peu à peu l'opinion publique.

Alors mon oncle devint un grand homme, et moi, le neveu d'un grand homme, ce qui est déjà quelque chose. Hambourg donna une fête en notre honneur. Une séance publique eut lieu au Johannæum, où le professeur fit le récit de son expédition et n'omit que les faits relatifs à la boussole. Le jour même, il déposa aux archives de la ville le document de Saknussemm, et il exprima son vif regret de ce que les circonstances, plus fortes que

sa volonté, ne lui eussent pas permis de suivre jusqu'au centre de la terre les traces du voyageur islandais. Il fut modeste dans sa gloire, et sa réputation s'en accrut.

Tant d'honneur devait nécessairement lui susciter des envieux. Il en eut, et comme ses théories, appuyées sur des faits certains, contredisaient les systèmes de la science sur la question du feu central, il soutint par la plume et par la parole de remarquables discussions avec les savants de tous pays.

Pour mon compte, je ne puis admettre sa théorie du refroidissement : en dépit de ce que j'ai vu, je crois et je croirai toujours à la chaleur centrale ; mais j'avoue que certaines circonstances encore mal définies peuvent modifier cette loi sous l'action de phénomènes naturels.

Au moment où ces questions étaient palpitantes, mon oncle éprouva un vrai chagrin. Hans, malgré ses instances, avait quitté Hambourg ; l'homme auquel nous devions tout ne voulut pas nous laisser lui payer notre dette. Il fut pris de la nostalgie de l'Islande.

« Farval », dit-il un jour, et sur ce simple mot d'adieu, il partit pour Reykjawik, où il arriva heureusement.

Nous étions singulièrement attachés à notre brave chasseur d'eider ; son absence ne le fera jamais oublier de ceux auxquels il a sauvé la vie, et certainement je ne mourrai pas sans l'avoir revu une dernière fois.

Pour conclure, je dois ajouter que ce *Voyage au centre de la terre* fit une énorme sensation dans le monde. Il fut imprimé et traduit dans toutes les langues ; les journaux les plus accrédités s'en arrachèrent les principaux épisodes, qui furent commentés, discutés, attaqués, soutenus avec une égale conviction dans le camp des croyants et des incrédules. Chose rare ! mon oncle jouissait de son vivant de toute la gloire qu'il avait acquise, et il n'y eut pas jusqu'à M. Barnum qui ne lui proposât de « l'exhiber » à un très haut prix dans les États de l'Union.

Mais un ennui, disons même un tourment, se glissait au milieu de cette gloire. Un fait demeurait inexplicable, celui de la boussole ; or pour un savant, pareil phénomène inexpliqué devient un supplice de l'intelligence. Eh bien ! le Ciel réservait à mon oncle d'être complètement heureux.

Un jour, en rangeant une collection de minéraux dans son cabinet, j'aperçus cette fameuse boussole et je me mis à l'observer.

Depuis six mois elle était là, dans son coin, sans se douter des tracas qu'elle causait.

Tout à coup, quelle fut ma stupéfaction ! Je poussai un cri. Le professeur accourut.

« Qu'est-ce donc ? demanda-t-il.

— Cette boussole !...

— Eh bien ?

— Mais son aiguille indique le sud et non le nord !

— Que dis-tu ?

— Voyez ! ses pôles sont changés.

— Changés! »

Mon oncle regarda, compara, et fit trembler la maison par un bond superbe.

Quelle lumière éclairait à la fois son esprit et le mien!

« Ainsi donc, s'écria-t-il, dès qu'il recouvra la parole, après notre arrivée au cap Saknussemm, l'aiguille de cette damnée boussole marquait le sud au lieu du nord?

— Évidemment.

— Notre erreur s'explique alors. Mais quel phénomène a pu produire ce renversement des pôles?

— Rien de plus simple.

— Explique-toi, mon garçon.

— Pendant l'orage, sur la mer Lidenbrock, cette boule de feu qui aimantait le fer du radeau avait tout simplement désorienté notre boussole!

— Ah! s'écria le professeur en éclatant de rire, c'était donc un tour de l'électricité? »

A partir de ce jour, mon oncle fut le plus heureux des savants, et moi le plus heureux des hommes, car ma jolie Virlandaise, abdiquant sa position de pupille, prit rang dans la maison de Königstrasse en la double qualité de nièce et d'épouse. Inutile d'ajouter que son oncle fut l'illustre professeur Otto Lidenbrock, membre correspondant de toutes les sociétés scientifiques, géographiques et minéralogiques des cinq parties du monde.

FIN

JULES VERNE
1828-1905

I

Jules Verne a écrit quatre-vingts romans (ou longues nouvelles), publié plusieurs grands ouvrages de vulgarisation comme *Géographie illustrée de la France et de ses colonies* (1868), *Histoire des grands voyages et des grands voyageurs* (1878), *Christophe Colomb* (1883) et fait représenter, seul ou en collaboration, une quinzaine de pièces de théâtre. Sa célébrité est centenaire puisqu'elle date des années 1863-1865 qui furent celles de la publication de : *Cinq semaines en ballon, Voyage au centre de la terre. De la terre à la lune*, ses trois premiers grands romans. Dans un siècle qui compte des génies comme Balzac, Dickens, Dumas père, Tolstoï, Dostoïevski, Tourguenief, Flaubert, Stendhal, George Éliot, Zola – pour ne citer que dix noms parmi ceux des grands maîtres de ce siècle du roman – il apparaît un peu en marge, comme un prodigieux artisan en matière de fictions, comme un enchanteur aux charmes inépuisables et, dans une certaine mesure, comme un voyant, capable d'imaginer, un demi-siècle (ou un siècle) avant leur naissance quelques-unes des plus étonnantes conquêtes de la science.

On a tout dit sur ce sujet et il est même arrivé qu'on mette du mystère là où il n'y en avait pas, qu'on auréole l'écrivain de pouvoirs surnaturels, qu'on en fasse un magicien. Il est plus véridique de le voir comme un homme de son temps, sensible à la richesse de découvertes scientifiques dont il s'informe avec un soin constant et scrupuleux; comme un travailleur infatigable, attelé quotidiennement pendant près d'un demi-siècle à *faire passer* dans le roman, en les prolongeant par une extrapolation foisonnante, les conquêtes et les découvertes des savants de son époque. Son extrapolation rejoint certes l'avenir, mais elle ne prévoit pas tous les cheminements de la science. Jules Verne est un poète du XIXᵉ siècle, non pas un ingénieur du XXᵉ. La radio, les rayons X, le cinéma, l'automobile, qu'il a vus naître, ne jouent pas dans son œuvre un rôle important. Et on peut remarquer, par exemple, que le moteur même du *Nautilus*, et le canon qui envoie des astronautes vers la lune, sont des machines de théâtre. Mais un de ses plus beaux romans, *les Cinq Cents Millions de la Begum*, évoque le premier satellite artificiel, et le *Nautilus* précède de dix ans les sous-marins de l'ingénieur Laubeuf...

Jules Verne ne fournit pas les moyens techniques qui permettraient la réalisa-

tion des engins modernes : il évoque l'existence et les pouvoirs de ceux-ci. Il n'est pas un surhomme – mais Edison lui-même, « vrai » savant, n'a pas prévu l'avenir de ses propres découvertes... Les bouleversements que peut apporter la science pure échappent à la prévision, et nos auteurs de science-fiction, en 1965, ne sont sans doute pas plus proches de l'an 2100 que Jules Verne n'était proche, en 1875 ou 1880, du monde d'aujourd'hui travaillé par la science nucléaire...

Il était quelqu'un d'autre : un créateur qui ne fait pas concurrence à la science mais en incarne la poésie puissante, parfois terrible, dans des mythes fascinants ; un créateur qui, aux écoutes d'un monde que les chemins de fer et les paquebots transforment, pressent des aventures où l'homme et la machine vont devenir un couple au destin fabuleux. Il est sur le seuil d'un monde.

D'un monde, non pas de l'univers dans sa totalité. Il n'est pas métaphysicien : ses astronautes n'emportent pas l'âme de Pascal dans leur voyage à travers le champ stellaire ; ni sociologue : c'est déraison que de chercher dans *Michel Strogoff* une analyse « cachée » des forces révolutionnaires russes au XIXᵉ siècle. Mais, conteur, romancier-dramaturge, créateur de fictions, il relaie et développe, avec une verve et une santé inépuisables, un génie qu'eut aussi le grand Dumas père. Celui-ci nourrissait son œuvre en la conduisant vers le passé ; Jules Verne vibre et crée à l'intersection du présent et de l'avenir.

II

Il naquit à Nantes le 8 février 1828. Son père, Pierre Verne, fils d'un magistrat de Provins, s'était rendu acquéreur en 1825 d'une étude d'avoué et avait épousé en 1827 Sophie Allotte de la Fuÿe, d'une famille nantaise aisée qui comptait des navigateurs et des armateurs. Jules Verne eut un frère : Paul (1829-1897) et trois sœurs : Anna, Mathilde et Marie. A six ans, il prend ses premières leçons de la veuve d'un capitaine au long cours et à huit entre avec son frère au petit séminaire de Saint-Donatien. En 1839, ayant acheté l'engagement d'un mousse, il s'embarque sur un long-courrier en partance pour les Indes. Rattrapé à Paimbœuf par son père il avoue être parti pour rapporter à sa cousine Caroline Tronson un collier de corail. Mais, rudement tancé, il promet : « Je ne voyagerai plus qu'en rêve. »

A la rentrée scolaire de 1844, il est inscrit au lycée de Nantes où il fera sa rhétorique et sa philosophie. Ses baccalauréats passés, et comme son père lui destine sa succession, il commence son droit. Sans cesser d'aimer Caroline, et tout en écrivant ses premières œuvres : des sonnets et une tragédie en vers ; un théâtre... de marionnettes refuse la tragédie, que le cercle de famille n'applaudit pas, et dont on ignore tout, même le titre.

Caroline se marie en 1847, au grand désespoir de Jules Verne. Il passe son premier examen de droit à Paris où il ne demeure que le temps nécessaire. L'année suivante, il compose une autre œuvre dramatique, assez libre celle-là, qu'on lit en petit comité au *Cercle de la Cagnotte*, à Nantes. Le théâtre l'attire et le théâtre c'est Paris. Il obtient de son père l'autorisation d'aller terminer ses études de droit dans la capitale où il débarque, pour la seconde fois, le 12 novembre 1848. Il n'a pas oublié les dédains de Caroline et écrit à un de ses amis, le musicien Aristide Hignard (qui sera son collaborateur au théâtre) : « ... je pars puisqu'on n'a pas voulu de moi, mais les uns et les autres verront de quel bois était fait ce pauvre jeune homme qu'on appelle Jules Verne ».

A Paris il s'installe, avec un autre jeune Nantais en cours d'études, Édouard Bonamy, dans une maison meublée, rue de l'Ancienne-Comédie. Avide de tout savoir, mais bridé par une pension calculée au plus près du strict nécessaire, il joue au naturel, avec Bona-

my, l'*Habit vert* de Musset et Augier : ne possédant à eux deux qu'une tenue de soirée complète, les deux étudiants vont dans le monde alternativement. Avide de tout lire, Jules Verne jeûnera trois jours pour s'acheter le théâtre de Shakespeare...

Il écrit, et naturellement pour le théâtre. Avec d'autant plus de confiance qu'il a fait la connaissance de Dumas[1] père et assisté, au Théâtre-Historique, dans la loge même de l'écrivain à l'une des premières représentations de *La Jeunesse des Mousquetaires* (21 février 1849).

En 1849 il mène de front trois sujets, dont deux semblent venir de Dumas lui-même : *La Conspiration des Poudres*, *Drame sous la Régence*, et une comédie en vers en un acte : *Les Pailles rompues*. C'est le troisième sujet qui plaît à Dumas : la pièce voit les feux de la rampe au Théâtre-Historique le 12 juin 1850. On la jouera douze fois — et elle sera présentée le 7 novembre au théâtre Graslin à Nantes. Succès d'estime que suit la composition de deux pièces : *Les Savants* et *Qui me rit* qui ne seront pas représentées. Mais le droit n'est pas oublié et Jules Verne passe sa thèse (1850). Selon le vœu de son père il devrait alors s'inscrire au barreau de Nantes ou prendre sa charge d'avoué. Fermement, l'écrivain refuse : la seule carrière qui lui convienne est celle des lettres.

Il ne quitte pas Paris et, pour boucler son budget, doit donner des leçons. Sans cesser d'écrire : en 1852 il publie dans *Le Musée des Familles* : *Les premiers navires de la marine mexicaine* et *Un Voyage en ballon* qui figurera plus tard dans le volume *Le Docteur Ox* sous le titre *Un drame dans les airs*, deux récits où déjà se devine le futur auteur des *Voyages extraordinaires*. La même année il devient secrétaire d'Edmond Seveste[2]

qui en 1851 a installé, dans les murs du *Théâtre-Historique*, l'*Opéra-National*, dénommé en avril 1852 et pour dix ans le *Théâtre-Lyrique*.

En avril 1852, Jules Verne publie dans *le Musée des Familles* sa première longue nouvelle : *Martin Paz*, récit historique où la rivalité ethnique des Espagnols, des Indiens et des métis au Pérou se mêle à une intrigue sentimentale. L'écrivain de vingt-quatre ans possède déjà cette ouverture historico-géographique qui fera de lui un des visionnaires de son époque.

Le 20 avril 1853, sur la scène – qu'il connaît bien maintenant – du Théâtre-Lyrique, Jules Verne voit représenter *Le Colin Maillard*, une opérette en un acte dont il a écrit le livret avec Michel Carré et dont son ami Aristide Hignard a composé la musique. Quarante représentations : c'est presque un succès – et la pièce est imprimée chez Michel-Lévy. L'année suivante, peu après la mort de Jules Seveste, il quitte le Théâtre-Lyrique et se met au travail, dans son petit logement du boulevard Bonne-Nouvelle ; il publie la première version de *Maître Zaccharius* (1854) puis *Un Hivernage dans les glaces* (1855) sans cesser d'écrire pour le théâtre. En 1856

---

1. Fondé par Dumas, inauguré le 20 février 1847, le Théâtre-Historique avait été construit sur le boulevard du Temple, à un emplacement qu'on peut aujourd'hui situer approximativement, place de la République, entre Les Magasins Réunis et le terre-plein qui leur fait face. Déclaré en faillite le 20 décembre 1850, il sera exploité sous le nom de Théâtre-Lyrique et détruit en 1863, un an après les autres théâtres du boulevard du Crime, en application des plans du préfet Haussmann.

2. Celui-ci mourut, en février 1852. Son frère cadet Jules lui succéda, mais mourut en 1854 du choléra apporté par les combattants de Crimée.

il fait la connaissance de celle qu'il épousera le 10 janvier 1857 : Honorine-Anne-Hébé Morel, née du Fraysne de Viane, veuve de vingt-six ans, mère de deux fillettes. Jules Verne, grâce aux relations de son beau-père à un apport de Pierre Verne (50 000 francs) entre à la Bourse de Paris comme associé de l'agent de change Eggly. Il s'installe alors boulevard Montmartre puis rue de Sèvres. L'œuvre de sa vie continue de se nourrir d'immenses lectures et aussi de ses premiers grands voyages (Angleterre et Écosse 1859, Norvège et Scandinavie 1861) sans qu'il renonce pour autant à l'expression dramatique : il donne en 1860, aux Bouffes-Parisiens, dirigés par Offenbach, une opérette mise en musique par Hignard : *M. de Chimpanzé*, et en 1861 au Vaudeville, une comédie écrite en collaboration avec Charles Wallut : *Onze jours de siège*. La même année, le 3 août 1861, naît Michel Verne, qui sera son unique enfant.

1862 : il présente à l'éditeur Hetzel *Cinq semaines en ballon* et signe un contrat qui l'engage pour les vingt années suivantes. Sa vraie carrière va commencer : le roman, qui paraît en décembre 1862, remporte un succès triomphal, en France d'abord puis dans le monde. Jules Verne peut abandonner la Bourse sans inquiétude. Hetzel lui demande en effet une collaboration régulière à un nouveau magazine, le *Magasin d'Éducation et de Récréation*. C'est dans les colonnes de ce journal, et dès le premier numéro (20 mars 1864), que paraîtront *Les Aventures du Capitaine Hatteras*, avant leur publication en volume. La même année verra la sortie en librairie de *Voyage au centre de la terre* que suivra en 1865 *De la terre à la lune* (avec ce sous-titre pour nous savoureux : *Trajet direct en 97 heures 20 minutes*).

C'est le grave *Journal des Débats* qui a publié en feuilleton *De la Terre à la Lune* puis *Autour de la lune* : le public de Jules Verne, dès l'origine de sa carrière, est double ; un public d'adolescents qui fait le succès du *Magasin d'Éducation et Récréation* ; un public d'adultes que le « jeu » scientifique de l'écrivain passionne. Le physicien et astronome Jules Janssen, le mathématicien Joseph Bertrand refont les calculs de Jules Verne — et vérifient, dit-on (il serait sans doute imprudent de ne pas placer ici un point d'interrogation), l'exactitude des courbes, paraboles et hyperboles qui définissent le trajet du boulet-wagon de *De la Terre à la Lune*. Et ceux d'entre les lecteurs du *Journal des Débats* que l'astronomie ne passionne pas sont sensibles à la verve d'un Jules Verne, qui met dans son roman beaucoup de la légèreté aimable d'un vaudevilliste boulevardier... Il n'est pas superflu de noter, à ce moment où s'ouvre pour l'écrivain sa carrière véritable, qu'elle l'éclaire alors d'une lumière de gaieté et de fantaisie proche de celle qui règne et régnera chez ses confrères des théâtres — les Labiche, Meilhac et Halévy, Gondinet et bien d'autres moins connus : Jules Verne, qu'on considère comme un auteur dramatique (homme de théâtre plutôt) ou comme romancier, appartient au Second Empire d'Offenbach autant qu'au XIXᵉ siècle de la science. Il est parisien (et même Parisien) et cosmopolite ; il se plaît dans son époque et avec ses amis, manifestant dans sa vie comme dans ses livres une cordialité généreuse, à peine ironique, qui est, pour le fond, celle-là même des hommes de lettres et de théâtre dont les livres et les répliques ont coloré une part du Second Empire. Et il n'est pas douteux que le succès de Jules Verne trouve sa source dans cette bonne humeur railleuse, cette allégresse surveillée autant que dans le foisonnement de son imagination. A dix-sept ans, on le lit et on l'aime comme un guide fraternel, explorateur de contrées inconnues ; on peut le retrouver plus tard sous les apparences, à peine désuètes, d'un camarade de cercle disert d'un conteur inlassable, à l'invention fertile, au jugement rapide, véridique, sagement ironique. Reconnaître ces deux Jules Verne, c'est comprendre une des raisons de sa durable présence. Son succès est populaire, dans ce sens qu'il se nourrit d'une approbation générale, voire d'une manière d'affection dont les racines sont profondes. On l'aime moins gravement que d'autres, sans doute : Balzac, Hugo, Tolstoï, Flaubert, Zola nous tiennent et nous gouvernent. Jules Verne est un compagnon

d'une autre race, et sa voix est moins haute mais elle est pleine et juste.

Et surtout, peut-être, elle s'installe dans une durée, dans un monde. Il y a en effet un monde de Jules Verne, extraordinaire et fraternel, ouvert sur l'imaginaire et d'une puissante ressemblance avec le réel. Ce monde il l'explore avec une rigueur inlassable dans la série des *Voyages extraordinaires* que nous venons de voir naître, et qui se poursuivra durant quarante années. Les jalons sont des titres connus : *Les Enfants du capitaine Grant* (1867) *Vingt mille lieues sous les mers* (1869), *Le Tour du monde en quatre-vingts jours* (1873), *L'Ile mystérieuse* (1874), *Michel Strogoff* (1876), *Les Indes Noires* (1877), *Un Capitaine de quinze ans* (1878), *Les Tribulations d'un Chinois en Chine* (1879), *Les Cinq Cents millions de la Bégum* (1879), *Le Rayon vert* (1882), *Kéraban le têtu* (1883), *L'Archipel en feu* (1884), *Mathias Sandorf* (1885), *Robur le Conquérant* (1886), *Deux ans de vacances* (1888), *Le Château des Carpathes* (1892), *L'Ile à hélice* (1895), *Face au drapeau* (1896), *Le superbe Orénoque* (1898), *Un drame en Livonie* (1904), *Maître du Monde* (1904).

On ne peut citer toutes les œuvres; mais le rapprochement de vingt d'entre elles suffit à évoquer les grands moments d'une réussite quasi continue que l'écrivain, on le sait, avait préparée (sinon prévue) de longue main. Cette préparation explique sinon la fécondité de Jules Verne, du moins une solidité que l'abondance menacera rarement : s'il n'a pas écrit seulement des romans de premier ordre, il n'a rien publié d'indifférent. Il avait une conscience artisanale (on en a la preuve, maintes fois répétée, dans ses lettres) et une dure exigence envers lui-même. Ses années de grande production sont, pour l'essentiel, organisées selon le travail en cours. Voyages, lectures, composition, se succèdent et surtout s'enchaînent.

En 1866, après ses premiers succès, il loua une maison au Crotoy, dans l'estuaire de la Somme, et bientôt acheta son premier bateau baptisé du prénom de son fils : le *Saint-Michel*. C'est une simple chaloupe de pêche, que quelques aménagements rendront propre à la navigation de plaisance; un lieu de travail aussi; un instrument de travail et de connaissance concrète : croisières sur la Manche, descente et remontée de Seine, c'est dans ces petits voyages que naissent peu à peu les voyages extraordinaires. Jules Verne ne se contente pas longtemps des fleuves et des côtes. En avril 1867, il part pour les États-Unis avec son frère Paul à bord du *Great-Eastern*, grand navire à roues construit pour la pose du câble téléphonique transocéanien. Et au retour il se plonge dans *Vingt mille lieues sous les mers* dont il écrit une grande partie à bord du *Saint-Michel*, qu'il nomme son « cabinet de travail flottant ».

En 1870-1871, Jules Verne est mobilisé comme garde-côte au Crotoy, ce qui ne l'empêche pas d'écrire : quand la maison Hetzel reprendra son activité, il aura quatre livres devant lui. En 1872 il s'installe à Amiens, ville natale et familiale de sa femme. Deux ans plus tard il achètera un hôtel particulier et un vrai yacht : le *Saint-Michel II*. *Le Tour du monde en quatre-vingts jours* qu'il a porté

à la scène avec la ... ... n frère Paul disparaîtra d'Ennery, remp... ... 02, il est atteint de la Porte-Saint-Mart... ... où il sera joué p... ... ... ne ... pleine, aucune place pour croisières, vie bourgeoise : c'est un l'ennui. C'est à peu près tout ce que je équilibre où le travail joue le premier demande », a-t-il écrit dans les années de rôle. gloire et de santé.

Le travail et l'argent : Jules Verne sait fort bien gérer le patrimoine littéraire que représentent ses romans – et leurs « suites ». La période de 1872 à 1886, disent ceux qui furent les témoins de sa vie, fût l'apogée de sa gloire et de sa fortune.

Au calendrier des romans et des pièces. (*Le Docteur Ox*, musique d'Offenbach sur un livret de Philippe Gille et Arnold Mortier, 1877; *Les Enfants du Capitaine Grant*, avec Adolphe d'Ennery, 1878; *Michel Strogoff*, id. 1880; *Voyage à travers l'impossible*, id. 1882; *Mathias Sandorf*, de William Busnach et Georges Maurens, 1887), il faut épingler quelques dates. Le grand bal travesti donné à Amiens en 1877 au cours duquel l'astronaute-photographe Nadar – vieil ami de Jules Verne et modèle de Michel Ardan, auquel il a donné par anagramme son nom – jaillit de l'obus de *De la Terre à la Lune*... L'achat d'un nouveau yacht, le *Saint-Michel III*... La rencontre en 1878 du jeune Aristide Briand, élève au lycée de Nantes[1], ses croisières en Norvège, Irlande, Écosse (1880), dans la mer du Nord et la Baltique (1881), en Méditerranée (1884). Son élection au Conseil Municipal d'Amiens sur une liste radicale que quelques biographes baptisent abusivement « ultra-rouge » (1889). Il a perdu son père en 1871, sa

En 1886-1887, après un drame dont on connaît peu de choses[3] et la vente de son yacht, il renonce à sa vie libre et voyageuse, et jette l'ancre à Amiens où il prend très au sérieux ses fonctions municipales. Le romancier et l'administrateur sont satisfaits l'un de l'autre. « Paris ne me reverra plus », écrit-il en 1892 à l'une de ses sœurs. 1884-1905 : les biographes de Jules Verne le montrent mélancolique, silencieux et citent ces lignes d'une lettre à son frère (1er août 1894) : « Toute gaieté m'est devenue insupportable, mon caractère est profondément altéré, et j'ai reçu des coups dont je ne me remettrai jamais. » Mais à cette citation on pourrait en opposer d'autres, sans ombres. Et il est aventureux, pour le moins, de colorer tragiquement les dernières années de Jules Verne. Il travailla jusqu'à ce qu'il ne puisse plus tenir une plume. « Quand je ne travaille pas, je ne me sens plus vivre », dit-il en présence de l'écrivain italien De Amicis. Et il travaille, se passionnant pour les *Aventures d'Arthur Gordon Pym* d'Edgar Poe, l'un des auteurs qu'il admire le plus, depuis cinquante ans. Et il écrit la suite des aventures du héros américain : *Le Sphinx des Glaces*. Il écrira encore dix livres, avant de mourir le 24 mars 1905, dans sa maison d'Amiens.

---

2. Il avait publié chez Hetzel un livre sur les croisières accomplies avec son frère à bord du *Saint-Michel III : De Rotterdam à Copenhague* (1881).

3. Il fut blessé de deux balles de revolver par un jeune homme qu'on a dit atteint de fièvre cérébrale (?).

---

1. Jules Verne a nommé Briant un des personnages de *Deux ans de vacances*. On a commenté cette ressemblance des noms. Cf. Marcel Moré : *Le très curieux Jules Verne*, Gallimard, 1960.

IMPRIMÉ EN FRANCE PAR BRODARD ET TAUPIN
58, rue Jean Bleuzen - Vanves - Usine de La Flèche.
LIBRAIRIE GÉNÉRALE FRANÇAISE - 14, rue de l'Ancienne-Comédie - Paris.

ISBN : 2 - 253 - 01254 - 8   30/2029/4

He just wanted a decent book to read ...

Not too much to ask, is it? It was in 1935 when Allen Lane, Managing Director of Bodley Head Publishers, stood on a platform at Exeter railway station looking for something good to read on his journey back to London. His choice was limited to popular magazines and poor-quality paperbacks – the same choice faced every day by the vast majority of readers, few of whom could afford hardbacks. Lane's disappointment and subsequent anger at the range of books generally available led him to found a company – and change the world.

'We believed in the existence in this country of a vast reading public for intelligent books at a low price, and staked everything on it'
Sir Allen Lane, 1902–1970, founder of Penguin Books

The quality paperback had arrived – and not just in bookshops. Lane was adamant that his Penguins should appear in chain stores and tobacconists, and should cost no more than a packet of cigarettes.

Reading habits (and cigarette prices) have changed since 1935, but Penguin still believes in publishing the best books for everybody to enjoy. We still believe that good design costs no more than bad design, and we still believe that quality books published passionately and responsibly make the world a better place.

So wherever you see the little bird – whether it's on a piece of prize-winning literary fiction or a celebrity autobiography, political tour de force or historical masterpiece, a serial-killer thriller, reference book, world classic or a piece of pure escapism – you can bet that it represents the very best that the genre has to offer.

Whatever you like to read – trust Penguin.

GABRIEL GARCÍA MÁRQUEZ

IN EVIL HOUR

'A masterly book' *Guardian*

'César Montero was dreaming about elephants. He'd seen them at the movies on Sunday ...'

Only moments later, César is led away by police as they clear the crowds away from the man he has just killed.

But César is not the only man to be riled by the rumours being spread in his Colombian hometown – under the cover of darkness, someone creeps through the streets sticking malicious posters to walls and doors. Each night the respectable townsfolk retire to their beds fearful that they will be the subject of the following morning's lampoons.

As paranoia seeps through the town and the delicate veil of tranquility begins to slip, can the perpetrator be uncovered before accusation and violence leave the inhabitants' sanity in tatters?

'*In Evil Hour* was the book which was to inspire my own career as a novelist. I owe my writing voice to that one book!' Jim Crace

'Belongs to the very best of Márquez's work ... Should on no account be missed' *Financial Times*

'A splendid achievement' *The Times*

GABRIEL GARCÍA MÁRQUEZ

THE STORY OF A SHIPWRECKED SAILOR

'A gripping tale of survival' *The Times*

'On February 22 we were told that we would be returning to Columbia ...'

In 1955, eight crew members of *Caldas*, a Colombian destroyer, were swept overboard. Velasco alone survived, drifting on a raft for ten days without food or water. Márquez retells the survivor's amazing tale of endurance, from his loneliness and thirst to his determination to survive.

The Story of a Shipwrecked Sailor was Márquez's first major, and controversial, work, published in a Colombian newspaper, *El Espectador*, in 1955 and then in book form in 1970.

'The story of Velasco on his raft, his battle with sharks over a succulent fish, his hallucinations, his capture of a seagull which he was unable to eat, his subsequent droll rescue, has all the grip of archetypal myth. Reads like an epic' *Independent*

GABRIEL GARCÍA MÁRQUEZ

CHRONICLE OF A DEATH FORETOLD

'My favourite book by one of the world's greatest authors. You're in the hands of a master' Mariella Frostrup

'On the day they were going to kill him, Santiago Nasar got up at five-thirty in the morning to wait for the boat the bishop was coming on …'

When newly-wed Angela Vicario and Bayardo San Román are left to their wedding night, Bayardo discovers that his new wife is no virgin. Disgusted, he returns Angela to her family home that very night, where her humiliated mother beats her savagely and her two brothers demand to know her violator, whom she names as Santiago Nasar.

As he wakes to thoughts of the previous night's revelry, Santiago is unaware of the slurs that have been cast against him. But with Angela's brothers set on avenging their family honour, soon the whole town knows who they plan to kill, where, when and why.

'A masterpiece' *Evening Standard*

'A work of high explosiveness – the proper stuff of Nobel prizes. An exceptional novel' *The Times*

'Brilliant writer, brilliant book' *Guardian*

GABRIEL GARCÍA MÁRQUEZ

LOVE IN THE TIME OF CHOLERA

'An amazing celebration of the many kinds of love between men and women'
The Times

'It was inevitable: the scent of bitter almonds always reminded him of the fate of unrequited love ...'

Fifty-one years, nine months and four days have passed since Fermina Daza rebuffed hopeless romantic Florentino Ariza's impassioned advances and married Dr. Juvenal Urbino instead. During that half century, Florentino has fallen into the arms of many delighted women, but has loved none but Fermina. Having sworn his eternal love to her, he lives for the day when he can court her again.

When Fermina's husband is killed trying to retrieve his pet parrot from a mango tree, Florentino seizes his chance to declare his enduring love. But can young love find new life in the twilight of their lives?

'A love story of astonishing power and delicious comedy' *Newsweek*

'A delight' Melvyn Bragg

GABRIEL GARCÍA MÁRQUEZ

ONE HUNDRED YEARS OF SOLITUDE

'The greatest novel in any language of the last 50 years. Marquez writes in this lyrical, magical language that no-one else can do' Salman Rushdie

'Many years later, as he faced the firing squad, Colonel Aureliano Buendía was to remember that distant afternoon when his father took him to discover ice ...'

Pipes and kettledrums herald the arrival of gypsies on their annual visit to Macondo, the newly founded village where José Arcadio Buendía and his strong-willed wife, Úrsula, have started their new life. As the mysterious Melquíades excites Aureliano Buendía's father with new inventions and tales of adventure, neither can know the significance of the indecipherable manuscript that the old gypsy passes into their hands.

Through plagues of insomnia, civil war, hauntings and vendettas, the many tribulations of the Buendía household push memories of the manuscript aside. Few remember its existence and only one will discover the hidden message that it holds...

'Should be required reading for the entire human race' *New York Times*

'No lover of fiction can fail to respond to the grace of Márquez's writing' *Sunday Telegraph*

'It's the most magical book I have ever read. I think Márquez has influenced the world' Carolina Herrera